CRIMINAL DISSENT

CRIMINAL DISSENT

PROSECUTIONS UNDER THE ALIEN AND SEDITION ACTS OF 1798

WENDELL BIRD

Harvard University Press

Cambridge, Massachusetts
London, England
2020

Second printing

Publication of this book has been supported through the generous provisions of the Maurice and Lula Bradley Smith Memorial Fund.

Library of Congress Cataloging-in-Publication Data

Names: Bird, Wendell R., author.
Title: Criminal dissent : prosecutions under the Alien and Sedition Acts of 1798 / Wendell Bird.
Description: Cambridge, Massachusetts : Harvard University Press, 2020. | Includes bibliographical references and index.
Identifiers: LCCN 2019028694 | ISBN 9780674976139 (hardcover)
Subjects: LCSH: Alien and Sedition laws, 1798. | Seditious libel—Law and legislation—United States—History—18th century. | Freedom of expression—United States—History—18th century. | United States—History—1797–1801.
Classification: LCC E327 .B57 2019 | DDC 973.4/4—dc23
LC record available at https://lccn.loc.gov/2019028694

For Julie,
with love

Contents

The Sedition Act Third Campaign: "The Reign of Witches" and the Election of 1800

The Alien Act: "Worthy of the 8th. or 9th. Century"

CRIMINAL DISSENT

Introduction

THE FEDERALIST PARTY—the party of George Washington, John Adams, and Alexander Hamilton—was never able to arrest its decline after the election of 1800, an election that began a quarter century of Republican Party rule nationally, under Thomas Jefferson, James Madison, and then James Monroe. That decline resulted in significant part from Federalist sponsorship and enforcement of the Alien and Sedition Acts of 1798.[1] Yet, contrary to all odds, the Federalists have enjoyed a comeback in the last quarter century in biographies, in some histories, and in keeping Hamilton on the currency. Do the Federalists deserve their newfound popularity?

The clashes of the Federalists and the Republicans over the Alien and Sedition Acts during 1798–1801—over freedoms of press and speech—were the first battles over the Bill of Rights. Did those clashes, so soon after the First Amendment was proposed in 1789 and ratified in 1791, show that its protections were only narrow and modest?

A complete account of the Alien and Sedition Acts has long been needed to assist consideration of these questions and understanding of that first battle over the Bill of Rights. This account includes over twice as many prosecutions and planned expulsions as previously recognized. It shows that Federalist use of the acts against the opposition party and Republican newspapers was far greater than has been appreciated.

The Federalists and the Stain of the Alien and Sedition Acts

The Federalists achieved much, without doubt. They built a new government upon the framework of the Constitution, in place of the failed government under the Articles of Confederation. They established the new government's financial system out of chaos, funding its debt and creating a national bank. They kept their promise to the antifederalists to support a Bill of Rights. They kept the new country out of declared war, first with Great Britain and then with France, and they protected the nation from entangling alliances. They created an army and navy, and exhibited federal strength in subduing the Whiskey Rebellion. These and other things brought a prosperous decade for most Americans.[2]

But the Federalists cannot be evaluated accurately without including in the balance the Alien and Sedition Acts. Those laws were introduced by Federalist legislators and passed with Federalist votes. The Alien Act gave the president virtually unlimited discretion to select and deport noncitizens. The Sedition Act made it a crime, in effect, to criticize the president, Congress, the federal government as a whole, or its measures, whether by press or speech. To most Federalists, the Sedition Act followed the common law and merely punished lying, and there was no constitutional right to lie. Many biographies of the leading Federalists, and some histories of Federalism, downplay or ignore the Federalists' role in supporting the Alien and Sedition Acts.[3]

Alexander Hamilton does not appear as illustrious as John Trumbull painted him, when his portrait includes his support of the Alien and Sedition Acts. His wing of the Federalist Party, which would come to be known as the High Federalists, sponsored those laws, though Hamilton did not participate in the legislative process beyond important written comments. He said that under the proposed Alien Act "the mass ought to be obliged to leave the Country" with "a few" exceptions, and that the draconian Senate draft of the Sedition Act only should be moderated so as not to "establish a tyranny."[4] A half year later, he branded the Virginia and Kentucky Resolutions a "conspiracy to overturn the government," and (as effective commander of the federal army) he said the federal government "must attack and arraign its enemies," by letting a force "be drawn towards Virginia" in order to "put Virginia to the Test of resistance."[5] A half year after that, besides asking his state to prosecute a critic for seditious libel, Hamilton lobbied to broaden the Sedition Act to criminalize criticism of "any Officer whatsoever," as well as to deport the "Renegade Aliens" who "conduct more than one of the most incendiary presses" (newspapers) in the country.[6] His willingness to use his army against disobedient states was real, as seen by his support of the army marching into Pennsylvania to suppress noncompliance with federal taxes during the Fries Rebellion and his advocacy of authorizing its use to annex Florida and to "liberate" South America from Spain.[7] Yet many of Hamilton's biographers give very brief treatment to his views and plans for the Alien and Sedition Acts or are entirely silent.[8] Some even portray him as an opponent.[9]

President George Washington, retiring a year before 1798, does not look as resplendent either, when he is seen as not just "first in war, first in peace, and first in the hearts of his countrymen," but also first in supporting the Alien and Sedition Acts. He had long objected to the concept of an opposition party and had long chafed at being "buffitted in the public prints by a set of infamous scribblers," even to the point of making that one of his reasons for not seeking reelection. Washington agreed with "a justification of the Sedition & Alien Laws" written by Judge Alexander Addison, sending it to John Marshall to read and then to forward to Justice Bushrod Washington. He dismissed the opposition's arguments against the laws as mere "unfounded and ill-favored forebodings."[10] The former president believed it was time "to resort to protecting Laws against aliens," who in "many instances are sent among us . . . for the *express purpose* of poisoning the minds of our people" and threatening the union. He similarly supported the Sedition Act and an ongoing prosecution of the leading opposition editor, writing to the law's chief enforcer that "the object of such Publications as the Aurora and other Papers of the same complexion" was "to destroy all confidence, that the People might . . . have in their government; thereby dissolving it."[11] As with Hamilton, many pro-Federalist biographers of Washington skip over his support of the Alien and Sedition Acts.[12]

President John Adams also falls under the shadow of the Alien and Sedition Acts. Though he did not call for them, he signed them into law. He then expressly authorized and encouraged four of the leading prosecutions. Adams said of William Duane, the editor of the nation's leading opposition newspaper, that if the United States attorney "does not think this paper libellous, he is not fit for his office; and if he does not prosecute it, he will not do his duty," and on top of that, the "matchless effrontery of this Duane merits the execution of the alien law" by deportation. The president had a "firm belief" that the Sedition Act "is warranted by the constitution," and called Timothy Pickering's published defense of it "excellent."[13] As for the Alien Act, Adams signed at least three orders for deportations under the Alien Act, revoked the exequaturs of four diplomats, and refused entry to a group of French citizens on the basis that "[w]e have had too many French philosophers already." After his presidency, Adams still defended the laws as "constitutional and salutary."[14] Biographers and historians often are silent on Adams's role and encouragement, or else they minimize them.[15]

The Republicans and Opposition to the Alien and Sedition Acts

In contrast with these powerful and influential Federalist leaders, nearly all the victims of the Alien and Sedition Acts were ordinary people: newspaper editors, other critics of the Federalist government, raisers of liberty poles, and the like. They suffered greatly: prison sentences and fines, and in some cases closures of newspapers, indefinite imprisonment because of inability to pay fines, forced sale of all their household property, and other privations. To them, the period of the Alien and Sedition Acts was this country's "reign of terror."[16] All but two of the people prosecuted were supporters of the opposition party.[17] The sufferings of these victims need to be considered in assessing the Federalists and their achievements.

Besides the imprisonments, fines, and closures, freedoms of press and speech were chilled by this Federalist legislation, and that also needs to be weighed in the balance. The Alien and Sedition Acts were aimed directly at the opposition newspapers and at the opposition party generally. Thomas Jefferson saw their implications as soon as they were introduced into Congress, differing sharply with the positive assessments by Hamilton, Washington, and Adams:

> Still it would place aliens not protected by treaties under absolute government. They have brought into the lower house a sedition bill, which among other enormities, undertakes to make printing certain matters criminal, tho' one of the amendments to the constitution has so expressly taken religion, printing presses &c. out of their coercion. Indeed this bill and the Alien bill both are so palpably in the teeth of the constitution as to shew they mean to pay no respect to it.[18]

The consequence for the Sedition Act's victims was not just chilling, but curtailment of freedoms of press and speech. Some leading Republican newspapers were closed permanently—John Daly Burk's *Time Piece,* Matthew Lyon's *Scourge of Aristocracy,* and William Durell's *Mount Pleasant Register.* Many others were closed down temporarily—Benjamin Franklin Bache's *Aurora,* Jacob Schneider's *Readinger Adler,* Charles Holt's *Bee,* and Anthony Haswell's *Vermont Gazette.* Others were intimidated to drop a strong Republican stance—particularly Thomas Adams's *Independent Chronicle* for the year after his death, or were forced to sell—Ann Greenleaf's *Argus* and her *Greenleaf's New York Journal.*

This was the controversy that quickly became the first national battle over the Bill of Rights.

The Prevailing Understanding of Freedoms of Press and Speech

A parallel and equally important question raised by the Alien and Sedition Acts is whether an expansive understanding of freedoms of press and speech only appeared in reaction to those laws, and not before. The dominant scholarly view is "that the revolutionary generation did not seek to wipe out the core idea of seditious libel, that the government may be criminally assaulted by mere words; . . . that the theory of freedom of political expression remained quite narrow until 1798, except for a few aberrant statements." In that view, the First Amendment's protections of press and speech "substantially embodied the Blackstonian definition and left the law of seditious libel in force," and "[n]o other definition of freedom of the press by anyone anywhere in America before 1798" existed.[19] That view has been expressed by a large number of scholars of the Federalist era,[20] as well as by a large number of scholars of the First Amendment.[21] It includes the claim that there was no other approach except the narrow one before 1798.[22] That view has been around for a long time, since the congressional debates in 1798 and the congressional report on the Alien and Sedition Acts in early 1799, which quoted Blackstone's "universally admitted definition of 'the liberty of the press'" and insisted that "liberty of the press has always been understood in this manner, and no other." There is no question that many Federalists held Sir William Blackstone's view, that "Liberty of the press . . . consists in laying no *previous* restraints upon publications, and not in freedom from censure for criminal matter when published" (seditious libel).[23] That was true of the several Federalist sponsors of the Alien and Sedition Acts, and of the five Supreme Court justices who presided over court proceedings under the Sedition Act. However, it was not true of all of the Federalists or all of the early Supreme Court justices,[24] and it certainly was not true of most Republicans.

By contrast, not one of the victims of prosecutions advocated that narrow Blackstonian view, even before there was any hint of a sedition law being enacted or of their being indicted. Instead, they uniformly had advocated a broad view and, once it was enacted, they uniformly saw the Sedition Act as directly contrary to the First Amendment. For example, in 1793–1794 Benjamin Franklin Bache asserted the right to print "discussions concerning public men or measures" grounded on "liberty of the Press," and (in a reprinted article) the right "to censure the most exalted Patrician" whose measures were "inimical to the public weal" as part of "freedom of enquiry through the medium of an unrestrained press."[25] Bache and other victims were not alone. A large number of people, during the quarter century preceding the First Amendment, expressed that expansive understanding of freedoms of press and speech, as I have discussed elsewhere.[26] That understanding did not first appear in 1798 but instead was widely expressed in America a generation earlier during the Stamp Act crisis of 1765 and became dominant after that in newspaper discussions and popular debates outside of colonial courtrooms.

The Histories of the Alien and Sedition Acts and Freedoms of Press and Speech

It has been over sixty years since the definitive book on the Alien and Sedition Acts of 1798 was written.[27] That book summarized the context of those laws, and the federal indictments under them (three indictments were and are generally recognized under common law and fourteen under the Sedition Act[28]), based mostly on newspaper accounts and some period correspondence. That leading book did not use the original federal court records as sources for its descriptions of more than two of the prosecutions, and it used very few of the original papers of the federal official supervising the prosecutions (Secretary of State Timothy Pickering).[29] The same was true of the other sixty-year-old study, and of the two recent books on the Alien and Sedition Acts, though they are fascinating to read and though the most recent one adds significantly to scholarship in the field.[30] Also, the sixty-year-old studies could not benefit from the more recent editions of the papers of Washington, Adams, Jefferson, Madison, Hamilton, and the early Supreme Court, which are extensively used here.

This book takes a different approach in recounting the history of the Alien and Sedition Acts. It is based on the original court records and prosecutor records, which provide much more, and much more accurate, information about the use of those laws against the political opposition. For example, those original records show that the first indictment and the first conviction under the Sedition Act was of Lespenard Colie in New Jersey, not Rep. Matthew Lyon. They resolve a debate about whether William Durell was prosecuted under the common law of seditious libel or the Sedition Act, documenting that he and also John Daly Burk and Dr. James Smith were initially prosecuted under common law but were reindicted under the Sedition Act. They show that there was not just one but two indictments of Matthew Lyon, and not the accepted two but four prosecutions of

William Duane, editor of the *Aurora,* under the Sedition Act. The original records show, contrary to the general belief that no defendant prevailed, that one was acquitted at trial (Dr. Samuel Shaw); they show that the indictment of Thomas Adams was drafted to include his brother Abijah Adams. They prove, contrary to the accepted story of no Federalists being prosecuted, that one Federalist editor was indicted, though not taken through trial (Alden Spooner), and that another Federalist was indicted and tried under the Sedition Act (Jedidiah Peck). Original records also show that a prosecution was planned against Aristides, and identify him (Dr. Samuel Brown), and they show ten other planned prosecutions.

That approach more than doubles the number of confirmed Sedition Act prosecutions and of confirmed contemplated prosecutions. The long-recognized total has been fourteen Sedition Act indictments and three common law indictments, in older[31] and newer studies.[32] That number is increased by fourteen further indictments for seditious press and speech in violation of the second section of the Sedition Act, eleven more indictments for seditious combinations and seditious counseling in violation of the first section of the Sedition Act (involving eighty-three defendants), and eleven authorized and contemplated prosecutions. Many of the added cases demonstrate an unrecognized second campaign of prosecutions in early 1799, after the first campaign in the latter half of 1798; the remainder are previously unacknowledged defendants in a third campaign in the latter half of 1799 and the first half of 1800.

The increased number of confirmed Sedition Act prosecutions—from fourteen to fifty-one confirmed cases that were filed or authorized—shows far more serious and more determined Federalist efforts to criminalize dissent and to suppress the opposition press and party than has been recognized, tilting the scales significantly in weighing the Federalist Party's legacy. When viewed not by numbers of cases but by numbers of defendants, the impact on individual freedoms is even more dramatic. The number of defendants increases from 14 to 126, in addition to those under common law, consisting of the following. Prosecutions of opposition newspaper editors increase from eight to fourteen editors, plus five more authorized or attempted prosecutions, in addition to those under common law. Cases against opposition politicians increase from two to three, in addition to at least one contemplated prosecution. Filed plus authorized prosecutions of other ordinary people increase from four to twenty people, in addition to the eleven indictments of eighty-three people under the first section of the Sedition Act. These are summarized in the table at the end of the text.

That approach also doubles the number of planned Alien Act cases, though it remains true that none was brought to conclusion. It identifies the mysterious subjects of the second and third deportation orders, and it adds a number of targets of contemplated expulsions.

The known and the previously unknown victims of prosecutions, nearly all ordinary people, are important in their own right. Consequently, brief biographies are given for each, based on a variety of original sources about both the previously unknown victims and the previously recognized ones (only six of whom are in standard biographical encyclopedias or are the subjects of published biographies).

Other additions to the history of the Alien and Sedition Acts are that some prominent Federalists found those laws unconstitutional—contrary to the unchallenged claim that "not a single Federalist questioned the constitutionality of the Sedition Law"; and that half the states supported or did not oppose the Virginia and Kentucky Resolutions, including the Tennessee and Georgia Resolutions—contrary to the unquestioned assertion that the "mad and rebellious resolves of . . . Virginia and Kentucky, which were transmitted to all the other Legislatures in the Union[,] have been rejected by all."[33]

This book also emphasizes the defendants' statements, years before their prosecutions, about the expansiveness of freedoms of press and speech, and in some cases about the error of the Blackstonian view that their judges later adopted. Those statements show that long before 1798 there flourished a broad understanding of freedoms of press and speech, and a widespread rejection of the narrow Blackstonian understanding, in stark contrast to the claims that a broad understanding first appeared in reaction to the Alien and Sedition Acts. For example, Thomas Adams published an essay by Confederationist in late 1787 in his *Independent Chronicle,* during the debates on the proposed federal Constitution and on the demands for a bill of rights, which discussed how the crime of seditious libel would be affected by a protection for "liberty of the press" that "ought to be made in a BILL OF RIGHTS." The writer said that with such a protection, "let the *attorney-general,* of the United States, *file an information* against me for a *libel;* I will carry that declaration in my hand, as my shield and my constitutional defence."[34] For another example, Anthony Haswell published an essay by Cincinnatus (Arthur Lee) the same year in his *Vermont Gazette,* which demanded a bill of rights and then discussed how that constitutional protection would prevent liberty of the press from being "pulled down" by seditious libel prosecutions, such as those of Zenger in New York and Woodfall in England, and would prevent the press from being "restrained" by prosecution "for a libel."[35] He had published a similar essay by Lucius in 1785.

Why are the Alien and Sedition Acts important? The conflict over the Alien and Sedition Acts, as the first battle over the Bill of Rights, was the foundational debate on the breadth of freedoms of press and speech. It was also the decisive debate on the legitimacy of political dissent—whether it would be criminal—and of an opposition party. The conflict provoked the Virginia and Kentucky Resolutions, and the Tennessee and Georgia Resolutions, and provoked development of constitutional thought on point by Madison and others. The debates and prosecutions greatly influenced the election of 1800, and in and after that election the Alien and Sedition Acts were major causes of the decline and death of the Federalist Party. That election marked the country's first transfer of power between parties, and the beginning of a quarter century of Republican dominance. A number of outstanding chapter-length studies of the Alien and Sedition Acts have described those aftershocks.[36]

Virtually the same debate continues today. Immigration remains one of the most heated issues in American and European politics. Freedoms of press and speech face challenges worldwide, as most developed nations outside the United States continue to criminalize what amounts to seditious libel, while many developing nations suppress any political opposition. Inside the United States the scope of those freedoms faces its own challenges, such as restrictions on offensive speech or press. The history of the Alien and Sedition Acts shows the consequences of restricting the press and speech of the political opposition—mortal wounds to the Federalist Party in the elections it sought to influence and in its historical reputation ever since.

CHAPTER ONE

Federalist and Republican Views of Government

George Washington's administration enjoyed many successes and few failures. The first president would easily have been reelected had he chosen in 1796 to seek a third term. President John Adams's administration enjoyed one major success—peace abroad—but it split the party and was overshadowed by a number of failures. The second president was not reelected in 1800. A large part of the reason was the foremost of those failures, the Alien and Sedition Acts of 1798, which Adams signed into law and enforced. Those acts provoked the first battles over the Bill of Rights, the decisive battle over the legality of an opposition party, and the beginning of the end of the Federalist Party.

The Federalist era started well with the ratification of the Constitution, the unanimous election of George Washington as the first president, the adoption of the Bill of Rights, and the illusory expectation that political parties were a thing of the past. However, divisions were quick to appear, particularly over Alexander Hamilton's financial plan during 1790–1791,[1] over the French Revolution and its large ripple effects,[2] and over the Jay Treaty with Great Britain as it was ratified in 1795 and discussed long after.[3] Washington's neutrality policy helped keep the new American nation out of Europe's wars, and the Jay Treaty averted war with Britain, but as British attacks on American ships decreased, French attacks increased. Washington remained widely popular but lost his immunity from criticism as he condemned Democratic–Republican Societies, led an overwhelming military

FIGURE 1.1. John Adams. Portrait by John Trumbull (1793). Courtesy National Portrait Gallery, Smithsonian Institution.

response to the Whiskey Rebellion in western Pennsylvania, and signed the Jay Treaty.[4] As Washington left office, the deterioration of relations with France reached the point of a war at sea—the Quasi-War.[5]

By the time John Adams took office in March 1797, the Federalists and the Republicans had come to hold opposing views on a number of fundamental issues. The spirit of the times can be seen in the description of those polarized views by Thomas Cooper, a committed Republican and soon a Sedition Act defendant. Cooper's description of Federalist beliefs is useful, despite his personal bias:

> Those who think the power of the Executive ought rather to be encreased than diminished—who are fearful lest liberty should run into licentiousness, and would rather abridge than extend the rights of the people—who doubt about the practical expediency of a Republican Government, and begin to think a limited monarchy more tolerable than was heretofore supposed—who would strengthen the General [Government] at the expence of the State Governments, and stretch the meaning of the Federal Constitution to extend the powers of the President and Congress—who laugh at the efficiency of a militia—who are advocates for a standing army and a permanent navy as absolutely necessary,

> not only to repel aggressions from abroad, but to quell insurrections at home—who think the Commerce of the Country of sufficient importance to be protected at the expence of a foreign war supported by taxes paid by the Farmer, on whom alone all taxes fall—who make (the executive officers of Government . . .) synonimous with the constitution, and condemn as enemies of the one, all who may disapprove of the measures of the other—who think it dangerous to investigate the characters and opinions of the public servants unless under the strong controul of sedition laws—who regard aliens, particularly republican aliens, with distrust, and are apprehensive that the best constitution in the world is in perpetual danger from a handful of foreigners who come hither purposely to adopt it—such persons for the most part call themselves FEDERALISTS. Grades of difference they may be, but such are the leading features of the party so called.[6]

Foreign policy views of most Federalists could be added to this summary: their sympathy for Britain and wish for close ties with it, and their fear of intrigue and of attack by France. That led to their being disparaged as Tories or the British Party by Republicans.[7] One version of that sympathy was displayed by Adams, who called the English constitution "the most stupendous fabric of human invention," while warning of "the foul abominations of the French revolution."[8]

Cooper's description of Republicans showed many of their stark divergences from Federalists:

> Others there are, who are cautious of entrusting or extending power unless evidently necessary to the happiness of the people—who are jealous of reposing unlimited confidence in persons of superior station—who think the public character of every public man a fair object of discussion, of praise or of censure—that restraint upon investigation like the late sedition laws, imply a dread of it— . . . that a sincere friend to the Constitution and the Country, may sometimes disapprove the opinions and measures of the officers of Government—that the Commercial is not of equal importance with the Agricultural interest of America, that temporary depredations upon our vessels of trade by either of the contending powers, is not a sufficient reason for plunging us into the evils of a foreign war, the domestic dangers of a standing army, the temptation to contest which a navy will induce, or the expence of any of them at a period of acknowledged poverty—who regard an alien flying from the Tyranny of Europe as a friend, and rejoice in the accession of wealth and industry, from whatever quarter it may come—who believe the best way to make a man a good citizen, is to give him a stake and interest in the Country—who love the principles of our own Constitutions and rejoice at the downfal[l] of political Superstition in Europe—who glory in the appellation of REPUBLICANS.[9]

Foreign policy views of most Republicans could be added: their sympathy and support for France and their mistrust of Great Britain. That led to their being pilloried as Jacobins or the French Party by Federalists.

Federalists and Republicans and an Opposition

These descriptions pointed to three differences between Federalists and Republicans that, more than others, led to most Federalists supporting the Alien and Sedition Acts in 1798, and to most Republicans opposing those laws: views of deference, dissent, and freedoms of press and speech.

Most Federalists and Republicans differed in their views of a deferential political system, in contrast to a more democratic political system. In Cooper's words, the first group "doubt about the practical expediency of a Republican Government," while the latter group "are jealous of reposing unlimited confidence in persons of superior station." Thus, High Federalist George Cabot sought rule by "the wisest and best citizens," and feared "an inundation of democratic evil," by which government would be "trampled under the feet of barbarous democrats." Fisher Ames, too, hoped the government would be administered by "the only classes proper to make the selection from," and he cast a wary eye at "the error into which the multitude is prone to fall," such as "false notions of liberty" and fanaticism.[10] James McHenry, as he left his position as secretary of war, sneered at people of "inferior abilities, and men without the opportunity to be rightly informed or penetration to know when they are so." Oliver Wolcott, Jr., the secretary of the treasury, smirked with other Federalists at the "ancient usage of the aristocrats to pay respect to the sovereign people, by obsequious attentions whenever their suffrages have been requested," "soliciting the favour of individuals, with whom they associate on no other occasion," when "men of the first consideration condescend to collect dissolute and ignorant mobs of hundreds of individuals, to whom they make long speeches."[11] Such Federalists would stand for election but found it improper to campaign or solicit votes. Republican newspapers poked ridicule at Federalist conceits as the "*Better Sort*" who protected civilization against the "*swinish multitude*."[12]

The American Revolution had weakened many of the foundations of that hierarchical structure, in a number of ways beyond replacing monarchy with republican government.[13] The patriots embraced radical Whig ideology along with classical republicanism, and both philosophies were notably unfriendly to unfettered powers, limitations of individual rights, and demands for passive obedience to rulers.[14] Also, the Revolution brought a "revolution in rights," which included discussions in speeches and newspapers, state declarations of rights, development of natural rights theory, and broader rights in practice.[15] Moreover, the most influential loyalists were forced to emigrate and, in place of their positions, new state offices were created. A number of newly prosperous contenders for political office and leadership arose, enriched from military supply contracts, confiscated property sales, privateering, or speculation in government obligations.[16] Further, the American Revolution included a social transformation from the colonial order to a republican order, as Edward Countryman noted, which continued long afterward, though it failed to convey its benefits to many Americans—enslaved people, women, Native Americans, and others.[17] Most Federalists seemed to be less aware than most Republicans of the social changes prompted by the Revolution, at least until the electoral college divulged the results of the presidential election of 1800.

Most Federalists and Republicans also differed in their view of the permissibility of dissent in opposition to the administration.[18] A hierarchical view of government led to a Federalist expectation of deference, not criticism, toward the "leading men" in office. Federalists *were* the administration, filling nearly all political offices in the new federal government, and they readily characterized disparagement of any official as disparagement of the government. In Cooper's words, Federalists "condemn as enemies of the one [the government], all who may disapprove of the measures of the other [the executive officers]," while Republicans believe "that a sincere friend to the Constitution and the Country, may sometimes disapprove the opinions and measures of the officers of Government." From a Federalist standpoint, it was easy to view criticism as criminal defamation or sedition, the product of illegitimate factions and parties.

The danger of factions and political parties was a point of agreement when the Constitution was ratified. Factions and parties served private interests, while enlightened officials should serve the national interest; and factions and parties were accompanied by corruption as English parties showed. The key point on which Federalists and Republicans differed was which one of them was a faction or an incipient party. A dozen essays in *The Federalist* had denounced factions and parties. Washington's Farewell Address had warned of "the baneful effects of the spirit of party" and faction. Adams's inaugural speech condemned "the danger to our liberties" from parties determining elections or administrations. Consequently, people referred to their own side as the "Federalist interest" or the "Republican interest" in the early 1790s—not as parties—while they reprehended the other side as a faction or party.[19]

A related fundamental difference between most Federalists and most Republicans, at least once most Federalists shifted as the Alien and Sedition Acts were passed in mid-1798, was their views of freedom of speech and press, particularly about officials and government. As Cooper put it in 1799, Federalists "think it dangerous to investigate the characters and opinions of the public servants unless under the strong controul of sedition laws," while Republicans "think the public character of every public man a fair object of discussion, of praise or of censure," and believe "that restraint upon investigation like the late sedition laws, imply a dread" of investigation. Denying the legitimacy of an opposition, most Federalists viewed speech and press critical of the Federalist administration and its officials as sedition. Thus, President John Adams, in some replies to supportive addresses in 1798, upbraided the opposition as "a spirit of party, which scruples not to go all lengths of profligacy, falsehood, and malignity, in defaming our government," and was exultant that "domestic treachery" supporting France had been exposed and that "government have awed into silence the clamors of faction, and palsied the thousand tongues of calumny." He called on all citizens "to crush every attempt at disorganization, disunion, and anarchy," and reprehended "any who still plead the cause of France," who "ought to be esteemed our greatest enemies."[20]

That narrow view limited freedoms of press and speech in many ways. Beginning in 1798, many of the early Supreme Court justices, adopting that narrow definition of freedoms of press and speech, concluded that the Sedition Act did not violate those freedoms because it was a permissible subsequent punishment rather than a prohibited prior restraint.[21] Many Federalists joined Supreme Court Justice Samuel Chase in insisting that the only time for citizens' speech and press was during an election, after which the minority must surrender its judgment and let private opinion give way to the election results. In a prepared charge for a grand jury, he stressed the "duty" of submission, so that the minority must "surrender up their Judgement and will to the Decision of a *majority,*" and that "*Private* opinion must give way to *public* Judgement." Chase said it made no difference if the law enacted by Congress was unconstitutional; "he must be a vain, conceited individual who can think himself as capable to Judge of what is necessary for the support of Government as those whom the *nation* has chosen, & entrusted for that very purpose." Until an unconstitutional law was repealed, "it is the *Duty* of every Citizen to submit to it; and to give up his private Sentiments to the *public Will.*" Thus, criticism of government or its officers was seditious (the justice was discussing the Sedition Act): "The *false patriot* is the man, who . . . *wilfully misrepresents* his Government, and the conduct of its Officers; or, without *Just* cause, creates distrust and suspicion of *the Legislature,* or of *the Executive,* or of the *principal* Officers of Government; and *openly* opposes, or *secretly* foments and encourages *opposition* to the execution of the Laws." Under that charge and later the same day, the grand jury indicted Thomas Cooper for violating the Sedition Act, and a week later he was found guilty of disparaging the president, leading to a sentence of six months in prison and a fine of $400.[22] Another early Supreme Court justice, William Paterson, agreed that most people should "mind their business; instead of becoming newsmongers, and pestering themselves and others about political affairs, of which they know little or nothing." Justice James Iredell, also looking for a way to justify the Sedition Act, took the position that the First Amendment allowed infringements, just not abridgments, of freedoms of press and speech. He argued that the prohibition against any law "*abridging* the freedom of speech, or of the press" does not prohibit but "only limit[s] the exercise of the power. . . . Congress may make a law *respecting* the press, provided the law be such as not to *abridge its freedom.*"[23]

If opposition to government was illicit, at least beyond a point, then punishing it seemed to follow, whether the punishment was aimed at actions or at words. The stakes were high—preventing destruction of the government. Thus, Adams, in another of his public responses to addresses, warned that "hostility against the government" would leave it "ripe for a military despotism under the domination of a foreign power." Noah Webster argued that when "the Jacobin prints" allege "delinquencies of public officers," they threaten the overthrow of the government, because "no government can be durable and quiet under the licentiousness of the press that now disgraces our country. Jacobinism will prevail, unless more pains are taken to keep public opinion correct." Fisher Ames apparently was ready for the army to be the vehicle for keeping public opinion correct, identifying "Jefferson and Co., at the head of a stronger faction than any government can struggle with long, or prevail against at last, unless by military force."[24]

The weapons of choice for punishing opposition press and speech were the crimes of seditious libel and seditious words.[25] Sir William Blackstone described those crimes as part of English common law, and contended that they were not contrary to "liberty of the press" or "liberty of private sentiment" (speech) because those liberties were very narrow. He asserted that liberty of press only meant liberty from prior restraints, while allowing subsequent punishment "for criminal matter when published," and that liberty of speech only meant liberty to hold private sentiments, while allowing punishment of the "making public, of bad sentiments" as a crime.[26] Those justifying prosecution of seditious libel and seditious words not only claimed to follow the common law, but also claimed to protect the reputation, character, and honor of public officials, which the era's code of honor exalted as the loftiest of a person's property.[27] Few Federalists embraced Blackstone's approach before 1798, but many could not resist it during 1798–1801 as a ready justification for their political choice to suppress opposition press and speech by the Sedition Act. Most Republicans, bewildered, responded that the words of the First Amendment could not be clearer in prohibiting any law "abridging the freedom of speech, or of the press," and in thereby rejecting Blackstone's approach that allowed all forms of subsequent punishments of press or speech.[28]

Federalists and the Opposition Newspapers

Because opposition to the administration at first could not take the form of an acknowledged political party, it took the primary form of opposition newspapers.[29] The political value of newspapers had been proved in the colonial crisis before the Revolutionary War,[30] and had grown afterwards as they accounted for the preponderance of American printing and reading.[31] That is why newspaper editors were the primary targets of the Alien and Sedition Acts.

As antagonism developed between supporters and opponents of Hamilton's economic plan of 1790–1791, each group saw the need for a reliable newspaper in the seat of government, which had recently moved from New York to Philadelphia. Hamilton assisted John Fenno in sustaining the *Gazette of the United States,* awarding lucrative Treasury Department printing and personally lending him $200 during the winter of 1790–1791. Fenno reciprocated by pledging that the newspaper would be "entirely devoted to the support of the Constitution, & the Administration."[32] In the meantime, Jefferson assisted Philip Freneau in 1791 to establish the *National Gazette,* indirectly negotiating the editor's relocation to Philadelphia, employing him as a salaried State Department translator with only part-time duties, and awarding the department's printing business to his press.[33]

Hamilton quickly smelled a rat and, in July 1791, published the statement that the "Editor of the 'National Gazette' receives a salary from government," questioning whether it was for translation or for publications "to vilify . . . the administration . . . to oppose the measures of government." Three days later, he identified the rodent as Jefferson.[34] Jefferson too smelled a rat and protested to President Washington that the "late charges against me in Fenno's gazette" left no "doubt of their author." Hamilton soon created the appearance of a groundswell of attacks on Jefferson, popping up as "T.L." and "An American," then as "Fact," "Catullus," and "Plain Honest Man," in articles published in Fenno's paper.[35] When notified by Fenno in late 1793 of his inability to continue his *Gazette* without "a considerable loan" of $2,000, Hamilton immediately undertook to raise $1,000 in Philadelphia and two days later asked a Federalist senator to raise the balance in New York, emphasizing to others that "it is of consequence to the Foederal cause that he should be enabled to prosecute a paper."[36] As partisan division grew, the 1790s witnessed a "shift toward a more abrasive and personal style of political journalism," which Washington described as "stuffing their papers with *scurrility* & malignant declamation."[37] Part of that scurrility, Freneau's criticism of Washington, led to the president's insistence that Jefferson end Freneau's employment and official printing assignments. Without those, Freneau was forced to close the *National Gazette* in October 1793.

The Philadelphia *Aurora,* edited by Benjamin Franklin Bache (grandson of Benjamin Franklin), quickly took its place as the leading Republican newspaper, and other Republican newspapers were established or expanded.[38] Many were edited by immigrants, and the Alien Act was "aimed especially at the numerous refugees who had become newspaper editors and pamphleteers."[39] The most influential Republican papers became targets of prosecutions under the Sedition Act, after its passage in 1798, fulfilling Jefferson's prediction, when the Sedition Act was pending in Congress, that "the object of that is the suppression of the whig presses."[40]

Opposition Federalists and an Opposition Cabinet

President John Adams soon had not just Republicans and opposition newspapers to deal with, but an opposition wing of the Federalists. He later wrote that "the British faction was determined to have a war with France, and Alexander Hamilton at the head of the army," accurately identifying the most divisive issue as his renewed efforts at peace with France beginning in February 1799; those efforts were fractious even though they ultimately succeeded in averting full war.[41] That Federalist wing, led by Hamilton, came to be called the High Federalists, and became more and more at odds with the Adams Federalists.[42] The other wing, led by the president, was often given more colorful names, such as the "Adamites" or "Cunning half Jacobins" (by Wolcott), and "half-way Jacobin[s]" or "half federalists" (by Benjamin Goodhue and George Cabot).[43]

The same Federalists who most loudly denied the legitimacy of an opposing party generally were part of an opposing wing within Federalism. The three most important members of the Adams cabinet gave their loyalty to what became the High Federalist wing.

John Adams made one of his worst mistakes the moment his presidency began, when he decided to retain George Washington's cabinet rather than replacing all or most with new appointees who could be trusted. That holdover cabinet consisted of Secretary of State Timothy Pickering, Secretary of the Treasury Oliver Wolcott, Jr., and Secretary of War James McHenry, along with the part-time Attorney General Charles Lee.

Timothy Pickering (1745–1829), after participating in the Revolutionary War and breaking with George Washington at its end, moved from his native Massachusetts to Philadelphia, where he was unsuccessful in western land investments and in commerce. He moved to Pennsylvania's back counties and again failed financially. He was saved from ruin by federal offices in the Washington administration, in 1790 as representative to the Seneca Indians, the next year as postmaster general, in early 1795 as secretary of war, and later that year as secretary of state. Continuing as secretary of state when Adams took office, Pickering missed no opportunity to wage war against the president's peace initiatives, until he was finally terminated in May 1800. After opposing the president's reelection and wreaking further financial failure, Pickering was bailed out by relatives and friends who paid his debts, bought him a farm, and arranged his appointment to a Senate seat in 1803. In the Senate and then the House, Pickering was best known for involvement in several secessionist efforts culminating in the Hartford Convention, and for implacable support of Britain including even its attacks on American ships and its burning of the capitol during the War of 1812.[44] Adams later described him as "a man in a mask," concealing his "subterranean intrigues," "bitter and malignant, ignorant and jesuitical." Pickering's biographer saw him in much the same light, as "righteous, strident, and intolerant," "ambitious to be at the center of affairs," but "us[ing] power unwisely" and becoming unhinged over criticism.[45] Pickering showed all those characteristics as he directed enforcement of the Alien and Sedition Acts. Republicans found it unsurprising that he had been born in Salem, Massachusetts a half century after its witch trials.

Oliver Wolcott, Jr. (1760–1833), the son of a Connecticut governor who signed the Declaration of Independence, studied law and then became his state's comptroller in 1788. The next year, he was appointed auditor in the new federal Department of the Treasury, and then in 1791 he became its comptroller. When Hamilton left the Washington administration in January 1795, Wolcott became secretary of the treasury. When he was carried over by the Adams administration, Wolcott joined McHenry in remaining intensely loyal to Hamilton. Wolcott was not terminated when his colleagues left the cabinet, but waited to resign until November 1800 when his efforts failed to replace Adams with Charles Cotesworth Pinckney as the Federalist presidential candidate; his resignation took effect at the end of December. A decade later, Wolcott backed James Madison's handling of the War of 1812, became governor of Connecticut, and ran as a Republican for most of his ten terms.[46]

James McHenry (1753–1816) studied medicine and then participated in the Revolutionary War as a surgeon, before becoming assistant secretary to Washington and aide-de-camp to Lafayette. He attended part of the Constitutional Convention and was a signer of the Constitution. McHenry became secretary of war in February 1796, and when the military was expanded in 1798–1799, he relied heavily but secretly on Hamilton. Adams finally forced McHenry's resignation in May 1800, and that ended McHenry's public service.[47] During the military buildup, Hamilton quickly concluded that "McHenry, is wholly insufficient for his place, with the additional misfortune of not having himself the least suspicion of the fact!" Wolcott agreed about McHenry's "utter unfitness," as did Washington. But nothing was done until his resignation was compelled.[48]

The cabinet was expanded by the creation of a Department of Navy, and Benjamin Stoddert (1751–1813) was nominated to head it in May 1798.[49] Stoddert generally supported the president.

It is hard to say whether the holdover cabinet that Adams inherited, and chose to keep, was more mediocre or more disloyal. Its three major members excelled in both areas.

The inherited cabinet was undeniably second-rate. Washington had begun his presidency with the two brightest stars he could have chosen, Thomas Jefferson as secretary of state and Alexander Hamilton as secretary of the treasury, along with a trusted and successful general, Henry Knox, as secretary of war, and a former governor of Washington's home state, Edmund Randolph, as attorney general. When Jefferson and then Hamilton resigned, Washington could not have found equally talented successors, but he was unable to secure first-rank replacements at all. When selected, Pickering was his seventh choice as secretary of state, McHenry was his fourth choice as secretary of war, and Wolcott was elevated from a much lesser position as comptroller of the treasury.[50]

The inherited cabinet was also disloyal, that is to Adams throughout his presidency, even as Pickering, Wolcott, and McHenry were intensely loyal to Hamilton. The lone cabinet exception, after his new department was created, was the new secretary of the navy, Benjamin Stoddert,[51] until Adams finally terminated Pickering and pressed McHenry to resign. The very cabinet that led and strongly supported the prosecutions of Republicans for words critical of the president and the administration increasingly spoke disparagingly and acted obstructively toward that president. McHenry, for example, peppered his leaks to Hamilton of the president's cabinet communications with "Return the papers immediately" or "Burn this letter."[52] Adams was forced to preside over a silent war with most of his cabinet, as well as over a half-war with France.

The Quasi-War with France

The French Revolution had ignited European wars, which the United States tried to avoid by President George Washington's neutrality policy. The Jay Treaty had averted war with Great Britain and preserved trade with it, but seemed to France to violate the 1778 Franco-American Treaty and to abandon neutrality. With ratification of the Jay Treaty in 1795 came a reduction in British attacks and an increase in French attacks. France's defeat of Austria in April 1797 left Great Britain in a life-or-death struggle on land and sea with France and its Spanish ally. That struggle brought renewed French attacks on American ships that, because they never produced a formal declaration of war, were called the Half-War or the Quasi-War of 1797–1800.[53] In the four years before the peace convention was agreed to in September 1800, Michael Palmer has calculated that "French seizures, captures, detentions, condemnations, and confiscations of American ships, cargoes, and crews involved 2,309 vessels."[54]

Weeks after taking office in March 1797, Adams learned that France had refused to receive the new United States minister plenipotentiary, Charles Cotesworth Pinckney, which effectively severed diplomatic relations.[55] Adams called a special session of Congress for May 1797. In his speech to Congress, the new president announced "a fresh attempt at negotiation," while objecting that the French leader's speech "evinces a disposition to separate the people of the United States from the government," and "thus to produce divisions fatal to our peace." Adams also called for "effectual measures of defence" and recommended adding a "moderate naval force," arming merchant vessels, fortifying seaports, adding to the artillery and cavalry, forming "a provisional army," and organizing the militia.[56] Republicans called it a "war speech," and France treated it as insolent.[57] High Federalists were disappointed that Adams did not call for a declaration of war, then and after, and they could never muster the necessary votes in Congress.

Two weeks later, Adams nominated three envoys: Francis Dana, the Massachusetts chief justice, John Marshall, a Virginia Federalist, along with Pinckney, who France had rejected. When Dana declined for reasons of health, Adams nominated Elbridge Gerry, a Massachusetts moderate. French attacks on American shipping continued, and in late June 1797, Adams sent a report to Congress detailing them.[58] In the meantime, Congress approved some of the defense measures that Adams had recommended, but Republicans blocked most because of their opposition to a permanent military establishment.

The international situation was alarming. America's minister to The Hague warned that "an invasion" of Britain was expected, and it might "set in motion the revolutionary wheel in Engd."[59] France had already tried to land 6,000 troops in Ireland in December 1796, and landed a smaller force in Wales in February 1797, both without success. The following September, France's Coup of 18 Fructidor occurred, and the next day the triumvirate cracked down on political enemies, required aliens to leave, banned religion, arrested many editors and writers, and shut down at least twenty-nine newspapers.[60] Worried, Adams wrote to the secretary of treasury that the "French directory, I take it for granted, must have war," though, writing to the secretary of state, he hoped Charles Maurice de Talleyrand-Périgord (France's Minister for Foreign Affairs) "could not be for war." When Congress reconvened in November 1797, Adams reiterated the need for defense measures.[61]

As 1798 dawned, Adams asked his cabinet for advice about action if the new envoys were refused, including whether there should be "an immediate declaration of war"? America's ambassador to Britain, Rufus King, asked Secretary of State Timothy Pickering, "is it not indeed war"? King was commenting on a French decree, then under consideration and soon approved, that authorized seizure of neutral ships "loaded, in whole or in part, with English merchandise." The British quickly responded with an order in council imposing their own restrictions on neutral shipping.[62]

On March 4, 1798, Adams received dispatches from the envoys, and the next morning forwarded the lone uncoded one to Congress. That message, after describing the French decree, said there was "no hope of our being officially received by this Government, or that the objects of our mission will be in any way accomplished." Two weeks later, after the other messages were deciphered, the president wrote to Congress that they gave "no ground of expectation that the objects of their mission can be accomplished." He reiterated the need for measures to protect ships and sailors, to defend the coast, and to replenish arsenals, and he lifted the ban on arming merchant vessels.[63] Republicans in the House made the mistake of assuming that Adams was covering something up, and demanded the full dispatches, which he gladly sent on April 3 and which Congress ordered to be published and made public.[64] The Republicans found that their demand had helped the Federalist cause immeasurably.

The envoys' dispatches revealed what became known as the XYZ Affair. Associates of Talleyrand, identified as "X," "Y," and "Z," demanded bribes of £50,000 (about $250,000) and a loan to France of 32,000,000 Dutch Florins (about $6.4 million), before officials of France would receive and negotiate with Pinckney, Marshall, and Gerry. The American envoys ended discussions, with Pinckney erupting "No! No! Not a sixpence!"[65] Federalist toasts soon changed the phrase to "millions for defense, but not a penny for tribute." Marshall sailed back to America, and Pinckney left France as well after taking his daughter to the south to nurse her health. Over their objections, Gerry stayed in Paris but said he would act only as a private citizen, in order to prevent war. Pickering, like other High Federalists, found Gerry's conduct an act of "wrongheadedness, . . . folly, meanness and treachery," and said if the French "would then guillotine Mr. Gerry they would do a favor to this Country."[66]

Almost as damaging as the demand for a bribe was Monsieur Y's statement that there was a French party in America that obeyed instructions from Paris:

> you ought to know that the diplomatic skill of France, and the means she possesses in your country, are sufficient to enable her, with the French party in America, to throw the blame which will attend the rupture of the negotiations on the federalists, as you term yourselves, but on the British party, as France terms you; and you may assure yourselves this will be done.[67]

Adams immediately put that disclosure to use in May 1798: "The agents of a foreign Nation, have had too much color, for boasting . . . of having a party in this Country, devoted to their Interest." Elsewhere, he rejoiced that "the views of domestic treachery are now fully disclosed." In the same month, Hamilton seemed to rely on that and similar statements, as he warned that "the powerful faction which has for years opposed the Government is determined to go every length with France," including "to *new model* our constitution under the *influence* or *coertion* of France—to form with her a perpetual alliance *offensive* and *defensive,*" and in substance "to make this Country a province of France."[68] Other Federalists joined them in relying on Y's statement in the following two months to support the Alien and Sedition Acts.[69]

The result of the XYZ Affair was a national wave of patriotic hysteria. "A spirit of warm and high resentment against the rulers of France has suddenly burst forth in every part of the United States, and addresses from all bodies and descriptions of men are pouring like a torrent upon the President and both Houses of Congress," federal judge Robert Troup reported. "Every day brings us new and decisive proofs of the growing unanimity throughout the whole extent of our territory. Addresses to the President are constantly coming in—meetings are holding, and the people are resolving with heart and hand to support the government in all such measures as the public councils shall devise."[70] John Adams responded to each laudatory address. Sometimes his responses were moderate, treating "the opposition to the federal government" as merely "a difference of sentiment on public measures, not an alienation of affection to their country." Sometimes his responses were bellicose, assuming war would follow, such as his assurance the day he signed the Sedition Act that "you shall see no more delusive negotiations," and that "there is no alternative between war and submission to the executive of France."[71] Adams, not accustomed to adulation, was as surprised as everyone else that "since man was created and government was formed no public officer has stood higher in the confidence and affection of his countrymen than our present President now does." Even the highest of the High Federalists, George Cabot of Massachusetts, approved of the president's responses, noting that "all men, whose opinions I know, are unbounded in their applause of the manly, just, spirited, and instructive sentiments expressed by the President in his answers to the addresses."[72] Still a half year later, in November, "the President, Pinckney and Marshall are the most popular characters now in the country," except Washington. Poems lauded Adams: "Loud cheer the steady Statesman, Chief Ruler of our choice, In him ourselves we honour—shout with united voice, Health to firm, virtuous ADAMS." Ominously, another High Federalist, Sen. William Bingham of Pennsylvania, wrote that "[b]y the Addresses from all Quarters of the Union you will observe that the People are ripe for the Support of the most decisive Measures of the Government."[73]

John Marshall was the first of the envoys to return, and his appearance in Philadelphia on June 19 was described by a disheartened Jefferson as surrounded by "the utmost eclat." "The Secretary of state & many carriages, with all the city cavalry went to Frankfort to met him, and on his arrival here in the evening the bells rung until late in the night, & immense crowds were collected to see & make part of the shew, which was circuitously paraded through the streets." Jefferson and other committed Republicans fretted that "the madness of our government" was closing "whatever chance was left us, of escaping war, after the publication of the dispatches, the President's answers to the addresses pouring in on him," and other events.[74]

And war did seem inevitable, for a time. Adams had polled his cabinet again, in mid-March 1798, whether he should ask Congress for "an immediate declaration of war?" Congress finally authorized measures for war preparation. Pickering, the secretary of state, believed that France was stirring up a slave insurrection in the southern states and planning an invasion from a Caribbean island.[75] Hamilton feared "the possible overthrow of England" and, in that case, feared "the certainty of invasion" of the United States. He told Washington he saw "great probability that we may have to enter into a very serious struggle with France."[76] A French invasion of Ireland was being prepared, the American ambassador in London believed, and there were "French preparations to invade England or Ireland," Fisher Ames wrote.[77] Even Madison understood that "it was expected that the unrelenting temper of France would bring on a war," until new events intimated otherwise. By early June, Pickering believed war "so imminent even now, that the army ought forthwith to be raised." Rufus King agreed that France would declare war soon.[78]

That was welcome news to the High Federalists and other overheated partisans, who salivated for a declaration of war, though the issue "divide[d] the sentiments of the friends to our independence."[79] The more they failed to assemble the votes in Congress for war, the more they faulted the president for not calling for a declaration of war. By contrast, the prospect of war was most unwelcome news to Republicans, for as Jefferson recognized, if "war is forced on [us], the tory interest continues dominant." He hoped that "the war-party" would not outvote "the peace party."[80]

Congress was caught up in the wave of patriotic and war hysteria, from March through July 1798, in the session that gave birth to the Alien and Sedition Acts. It passed about thirty-five statutes dealing with external defense, the most important of which were the following: The first group dealt mostly with France's target, American ships, by establishing a navy, obtaining twelve warships, adding funds for port and harbor fortifications, buying or building galleys, and authorizing publicly-funded warships.[81] The next group of laws addressed land forces, creating a "Provisional Army" and authorizing volunteer corps, acquiring arms for state militia, and creating a marine corps.[82] Other laws suspended commerce with France, authorized merchant ships to defend themselves, and declared treaties with France void; soon after that, Adams revoked the exequaturs of all French diplomats in the United States.[83] Additional laws raised the funds for the new military establishment—the first direct tax on houses, lands, and slaves, a valuation act to implement it, and authority for the executive branch to borrow money.[84] Because the Provisional Army would only come into existence in the event of a declaration of war or actual or imminent invasion, and would only last seven months until Congress convened, another law created the "Additional Army" of 12,000 men plus some dragoons, who would be enlisted for the duration of the existing hostilities.[85] This defense legislation, directed against external foes, was closely related to the final group of laws, which was mostly directed against internal enemies.[86] That final group of four laws restricted naturalization, dealt with alien enemies, and included the Alien and Sedition Acts.[87]

Federalist Francophobia had deepened as a result of receiving the envoys' lengthy memorial to Talleyrand protesting their treatment,[88] and the envoys' memoranda on meetings with Talleyrand where he repeated the demand for a loan to help finance French wars.[89] It did not help matters that France reacted to passage of earlier defense legislation with an embargo against American ships entering French ports, on July 9, though it soon had to lift the embargo and its January decree after its fleet was virtually destroyed in the Battle of the Nile on August 1.[90]

Implementing America's defense measures was much slower than passing them. That was nowhere more true than establishing the army. Delay characterized every stage: selecting the generals, commissioning the officers, and enlisting the troops. Adams waited a month after signing the Provisional Army law, which authorized selection of a lieutenant general and commander-in-chief, before nominating George Washington to that position, on July 2, 1798.[91] He waited another two weeks to name the other generals, and for three months failed to commission them, because he insisted on making Gen. Alexander Hamilton the lowest in rank of the three major generals while his cabinet behind the scenes, Washington, and others insisted on making Hamilton the highest of the three.[92] A month after Adams finally backed down, Washington and the three major generals met to discuss organization of the army, but it was three months after the squabble about the generals ended before the first lower officers were notified of appointment, in January 1799, and it was months more before they were commissioned. No officers had been appointed in four states even by May 1799.[93] The primary reason for the delay in appointments was that the search was not just for qualified officers but for committed Federalists. Thus, Secretary of War McHenry's lists rejected candidates for being "anti-federal" or being "anti-governmental and of French principles," and Gen. Washington excluded "any who are known enemies to their own government." The same was true of volunteer companies. McHenry wrote that it was "important not to accept of Companies composed of disaffected persons."[94] Recruiting did not start until April 1799, nine months after the Additional Army was authorized, and never signed up more than three-fifths of the 12,000 men.[95] In effect, enlisting the soldiers for the Additional Army only began halfway between the dates of its congressional creation and its congressional suspension, and it never succeeded. "The delay in raising the army . . . has been shameful and almost unpardonable," Theodore Sedgwick lamented.[96]

If escalation of the Quasi-War was imminent, why was delay the outstanding feature of the defense measures? Adams never saw the need for a large expensive army, particularly one headed by Hamilton, and hindered the army's formation and Hamilton's elevation wherever possible. Cabot was right that the president's "old jealousy of Hamilton" extended to "raising an army." Adams instead believed in a navy: "Floating batteries and wooden walls have been my favorite system of warfare and defence." As war hysteria died away, the president quickly came to the conclusion that there was "no more prospect of seeing a French army here, than there is in heaven."[97] As for Hamilton (and the cabinet), his concern for every detail of recruiting, uniforms, weapons, manuals, supplies, barracks, etc., particularly after the threat of French invasion was no longer imminent, implied strongly that he was not planning primarily for a French attack but for a standing army with other uses. His proposal had been for a "regular Force of 20,000 men" and a Provisional Army of 30,000, and he had been disappointed to get only half of the first and none of the second except in case of a declaration of war or an invasion.[98] The obsessive concern for Federalist purity of the officers, more than for immediate readiness and even after the French threat abated, also implied strongly that Hamilton and many other Federalists saw use of the army against internal foes as more likely than against French invaders.

The New Diplomatic Mission

Adams gave the customary speech at the opening of Congress in early December 1798. Contrary to his cabinet's advice, he stated that the United States was willing to discuss peace with France, after receiving suitable assurances. "It is peace that we have uniformly and perseveringly cultivated; and harmony between us and France may be restored at her option." The required assurances were of France's willingness to receive another minister, and a "sincere disposition on the part of France to desist from hostility, to make reparation for the injuries heretofore inflicted on our commerce, and to do justice in future." In any event, defense measures would continue.[99]

But the defense measures were no longer against any real prospect of a French invasion; they were to strengthen America's hand in future negotiations with France, and in dealing with internal enemies. Adams remained quite certain that a French army would not appear on the shores or in heaven. Washington agreed that "late occurrences have rendered the prospect of invasion by France, less probable or more remote." Even Hamilton conceded privately that "[g]ood policy does not appear to me to require extensive appropriations for fortifications at the *present juncture.*"[100]

Adams sent a nomination of a minister plenipotentiary to the Senate in mid-February 1799. When the Senate rejected a single minister, he sent the nominations of Chief Justice Oliver Ellsworth, William Vans Murray, and Patrick Henry (and when the latter declined, William R. Davie), and the Senate confirmed them.[101] Their departures were delayed until Talleyrand's assurances arrived, and then by High Federalist opposition and by news of the coup d'état of June 18, 1799 that restructured the Directory. The envoys finally sailed in November, and during their voyage another coup occurred on November 9 when Napoleon overturned the Directory.[102]

The cabinet took immediate action to combat the grave threat of peace. When Adams announced the new peace mission to France, Pickering was quick to tell Washington that the cabinet members "were all thunderstruck when we heard of it," and that the mission was "considered as dishonourable and disastrous" by the "friends of his country." He informed Hamilton that we have "all been shocked and grieved at the nomination of a minister to negociate with France," a "degrading and mischievous measure" which was "against our unanimous opinions." He told Cabot that all "friends of his country are mortified and disgusted." Yet the peace mission was not really a surprise, because the December message to Congress had invited French overtures, and January instructions to Pickering and the rest of the cabinet had asked for the draft of a treaty.[103] When Adams found it time to send the envoys, in October 1799, Pickering again expressed his condemnation to various Federalists, telling Washington that "the most enlightened citizens and truest friends of our country . . . [a]ll deprecate the French mission," and stating to William Loughton Smith that "it is reprobated by every man whose opinion" he respected. Wolcott joined Pickering and "deprecate[d] this measure in respect to our foreign relations," and also because "the Federal party will be paralyzed."[104]

Despite High Federalist opposition, the new diplomatic mission succeeded in its main task of ending the Quasi-War by negotiating the Convention of Môrtefontaine in late 1800. Like the Jay Treaty, it failed to attain many of the mission's objectives, but it brought peace.[105] A disappointed Wolcott said he could only account for it on the assumption that "Ellsworth's mind has been enfeebled by sickness," and concluded that "the mission has proved as unfortunate as we considered it." Adams saw things differently, of course, and later called the renewed peace mission to France "the most brilliant feather in my cap."[106] And it was.

Adams and the Federalists lost the election of 1800 to Jefferson and the Republicans. One of the causes was widespread rejection of the Alien and Sedition Acts and their enforcement. Another of the most significant causes was the split of the Federalists between High Federalists and Adams Federalists. That split is also significant for another reason: the High Federalists criticized Adams at least as censoriously as Republicans ever had, and their immunity from even a threat of prosecution trumpeted that the Sedition Act was designed only for Republican critics.

Examples abound of High Federalists reviling the president. When Pickering and McHenry left the cabinet in spring of 1800, Pickering immediately told Hamilton he had "been contemplating the importance of a bold & frank exposure of A.," and would be happy "to furnish some facts." Wolcott encouraged Hamilton's attack on Adams, saying it was "a duty, to make known those defects & errors which disqualify Mr. Adams." Wolcott urged McHenry to join him in doing his part to "secure General Pinckney's election" in place of Adams.[107] Wolcott certainly did his own part in traducing the president, even while remaining as secretary of the treasury until December 31. He wrote to Cabot that "we shall never find ourselves in the straight road of federalism while Mr. Adams is president," ridiculing Federalist newspapers for "nonsensical paragraphs, attributing wisdom and firmness to the President." He wrote to Fisher Ames that "Mr. Adams ought not to be supported" for various reasons, such as that Adams "subverted the power and influence of the federalists," had a "temper of his mind" that was "revolutionary, violent, and vindictive," and effused pride and selfishness. Wolcott stated that he "believed it to be incompatible with honour and a suitable respect to my own character to serve under Mr. Adams"—but only stated that after he collected his salary for serving under Adams another six months while attacking Adams behind his back.[108]

High Federalist criticisms were scorching. Pickering castigated "the President's unbounded vanity, ambition, selfishness, revenge and a heart cankered with envy." Hamilton said that Adams "is more mad than I ever thought him" and "as wicked as he is mad."[109] Wolcott noted that "the people believe that their President is Crazy," and gave his own opinion that "no administration of the government of President Adams could be successful" because his "prejudices are too violent, and his resentments of men of influence are too keen." McHenry concurred that at times Adams "would speak in such a manner . . . as to persuade one that he was actually insane."[110] Other examples are given near the end of Chapter 13. Adams responded to fire with fire. In his showdown with McHenry where the president asked for his resignation, Adams stated that "Hamilton is an intriguant—the greatest intriguant in the World—a man devoid of every moral principle—a Bastard, and as much a foreigner as Gallatin." Elsewhere, Adams topped even that by periodically calling Hamilton "a bastard brat of a Scotch pedlar."[111]

Even then, the damage was not fully done. The two terminated cabinet members, and Wolcott (while still in office), encouraged and helped Hamilton as he wrote his attack on Adams. Hamilton acknowledged that some of the "most delicate of the facts stated, I hold from the three Ministers."[112]

Hamilton's pamphlet, at first privately circulated in September 1800 and then publicly printed in late October 1800, said that Adams had "great and intrinsic defects in his character, which unfit him for the office of Chief Magistrate," and listed a number of them, though Hamilton's surprise ending tepidly supported reelection.[113] The pamphlet and its proponents ended whatever chance Adams had of winning the presidency in the election of 1800, though Adams's own impolitic actions and characteristics may have ended that chance already. McHenry agreed with Hamilton's pamphlet, writing just after it reached the public that Adams showed "utter unfitness . . . to fill the office of President," because "[w]hether he is sportful, playful, witty, kind, cold, drunk, sober, angry, easy, stiff, jealous, careless, cautious, confident, close, open, it is almost always in the *wrong place* or to the *wrong persons.*"[114]

CHAPTER TWO

Passing Laws against Internal Enemies

As the 1790s progressed, the divisions between Federalists and Republicans widened. Each charged that the other was seeking to overthrow the Constitution and government under it—deviously rendering the federal government ineffectual or illicitly expanding it—and that the other was in league with a foreign power—France or Britain. Even wider chasms appeared between the partisan newspapers. Both sides saw enemies abounding. By 1798, maritime attacks and threats from France seemed to be escalating from a half-war to a full war, and invasion looked likely enough to require expensive defense measures and new taxes. In that year of deep suspicion toward the opposition and of war hysteria, the Alien and Sedition Acts were born.

Even in 1792, Alexander Hamilton was "unequivocally convinced" that "*Mr. Madison cooperating with Mr. Jefferson is at the head of a faction decidedly hostile to me and my administration, and actuated by views in my judgment subversive of the principles of good government and dangerous to the union, peace and happiness of the Country.*"[1] Hamilton came to that conclusion after James Madison, a coauthor of *The Federalist,* seemed to abandon his support for a stronger national government and opposed most of the secretary of the treasury's financial plan. Hamilton and Thomas Jefferson watched each other assist the establishment of partisan newspapers, which soon were practicing the scurrility characteristic of the decade.

Both Federalists and Republicans could and did see events during the 1790s as mounting proof that the opposing group sought to thwart the Constitution's plan of government and liberties, and to aid a hostile and dangerous foreign power. They began reprobating their opponents with names to reflect those sins—Jacobins and Monarchists, disorganizers and trimmers, opponents and friends of government. They became more adamant in their support of Britain or France when war was declared in 1793 between those foreign powers after the first stages of the French Revolution, and Federalists and Republicans generally gave opposite reactions toward the French minister's activities and the administration's neutrality policy. Their mutual suspicions grew. Federalists suspected that Republicans plotted overthrow of the Constitution through Democratic–Republican Societies, and were behind the Whiskey Rebellion against an excise tax, all the while hoping to sponsor a French Revolution in America. Republicans suspected that their opponents usurped powers for the federal government that the Constitution did not give, and sought to bring monarchical features into the government, while wishing to enter an alliance with Britain against France. The debates over the Jay Treaty in 1795 and 1796 deepened divisions. Republicans believed that the treaty favored the northerly Federalist states over the southerly Republican states, and tied the United States to Britain, while violating the Franco–American Treaty of 1778 that had been critical to winning the Revolutionary War. Federalists saw Republican opposition to their measures as evidence of disloyal faction, and a calculated effort to break down allegiance to the national government, if not a secret Republican allegiance to France.[2] By April 1797, John Quincy Adams, ambassador to the Netherlands, reported to his father that the Directory was "determined upon a war with the government of the United States," and that it expected "to derive support from a part of the American people" when the French army arrived, enabling them to form a new "southern republic . . . in alliance with France."[3]

Internal Foes

By early 1798, many leading Federalists had come to the belief that domestic Jacobins (Republicans) indeed would support French invaders and might launch a revolution even before that. In April, Hamilton wrote that "there is in this Country a decided *French Faction*," and added self-servingly that there is "no other foreign faction." Washington was alarmed at reports that "letters have been intercepted from some M——rs of C—g—ss" to the Directory of France "of a treasonable nature." In May, Hamilton warned

Washington that, even facing the probability of "a very serious struggle with France," the "powerful faction which has for years opposed the Government is determined to go every length with France," including modifying the Constitution "under the *influence* or *coertion* of France," and forming "with her a perpetual alliance *offensive* and *defensive*."[4] Meanwhile, the minister to Britain, Rufus King, feared France could employ "the means among ourselves upon which she relies to effect her purposes."[5] Others warned that internal attacks were imminent. The Illuminati from the continent had come to America to overthrow its government, just as it had come to France and purportedly provoked the French Revolution, Rev. Jedidiah Morse preached in Boston, in May 1798 (citing *Proofs of a Conspiracy,* which had been published in America recently).[6] The French might land 10,000 "blacks and people of color" in South Carolina or Virginia and incite a slave insurrection as they attacked, Gen. Henry Knox cautioned President John Adams the next month. Dr. George Logan's mission to France was to bring back soldiers to incite that insurrection, Federalist editor William Cobbett informed Secretary of State Timothy Pickering.[7] Hamilton warned others that "the French Faction in America," or "as many of them as may dare[,] will join the standard of France" if it invaded the country.[8] Accusations worsened as the Quasi-War expanded. What "the faction" in Virginia wanted was "[n]othing short of DISUNION, and the heads of JOHN ADAMS, and ALEXANDER HAMILTON; & some few others perhaps," a Federalist in that state said. Joel Barlow's address could be used by Pickering "in proving the connection between our Patriots and the Directory," former Sen. George Cabot of Massachusetts informed the secretary of state.[9] Even a leading eulogy upon George Washington's death could not stand silent on the threat that factions were "ready to be the allies of France, and to aid her in the work of destruction" and subversion, seeking "to revolutionize the American government." The leading Federalist newspaper, the *Gazette of the United States,* regularly rang the alarm about "a faction, . . . dangerous from its activity and wickedness," that had a prime object to "render our country subservient, if not tributary, to *France,*" and other Federalist papers characterized Republicans as a "nest of traitors, or a set of revolters to France."[10]

On the other side, many leading Republicans had come to the belief that Federalists were plotting antirepublican changes to the Constitution and seeking an alliance with Britain. In a letter that ruefully became public, Jefferson wrote in 1796 that "an Anglican, monarchical and aristocratical party has sprung up, whose avowed object is to draw over us the substance as they have already done the forms of the British government"; he added that George Washington was one of the Federalist "apostates who have gone over to these heresies." James Madison, the next year, denounced "the Monarchichal party" whose "progressive apostacy from the principles of our Revolution & Government" continued and whose "tide of evil is nearly at its flood."[11] In early 1798, Madison cautioned that Federalists, particularly Adams, were secret monarchists who sought to involve America "in a war on the side of England" and to "warp[] the public mind towards Monarchy." Speaking of Adams, he added that "abolition of Royalty was it seems not one of his Revolutionary principles."[12]

It was a short step for Federalists and Republicans to see their Jacobinical or monarchical counterparts as seditious enemies. A few months before the Alien and Sedition Acts passed, Secretary of State Timothy Pickering, who would head their enforcement, wrote to Hamilton about "our internal enemies" and specifically listed Vice President Thomas Jefferson and Benjamin Franklin Bache, editor of the leading Republican newspaper, the *Aurora.* Just before the Sedition Act was signed into law, former Rep. Fisher Ames advised Pickering that "[i]nternal foes can do us twice as much harm as they could in open war," which he hoped would be declared.[13] Retired Sen. George Cabot also worried about "internal foes" and also identified Jefferson as one of them.[14] Attorney General Charles Lee, in a legal opinion for the president, said the greatest "danger may be apprehended from internal enemies and the French faction." Lt. Gen. George Washington, the newly commissioned head of the army, feared the "inemical party" was stronger than was believed, and identified it with the "French Party in the United States" which he had no doubt was "a well organized body." Federalist newspapers called the "friends of Jefferson—the enemies of the United States."[15]

Those internal enemies threatened not only to support French invaders, but to launch insurrection against the federal government in the meantime, as leading Federalists saw things. Rufus King was gravely concerned that France "will endeavour to overthrow us by the Divisions among ourselves which she will excite"—a critical element of sedition. Former Sen. Tristram Dalton alerted Adams that "our external and internal Enemies" sought "to divide our Counsels & People," after "Traitors . . . misled them in their opinions of the Inhabitants of these States."[16] The field commander of the army, Gen. Alexander Hamilton, opposed any reduction in its size, because "with a view to the possibility of internal disorders alone, the force authorised is not too considerable," even though he conceded that the current risk of French invasion no longer required extensive spending for fortifications. (By disorders he meant opposition to the Alien and Sedition Acts and to the new direct tax and valuation law.) Hamilton believed that one wing of the Republican Party sought "overthrow of the Government by stripping it of its due energies," and the other wing sought to overthrow the government by "a Revolution after the manner of Buonaparte."[17] "Federalists in private asserted repeatedly: the need for an army to 'save us from internal opposition,'" as Richard Kohn noted in *Eagle and Sword.*[18]

Federalist reactions to the Virginia and Kentucky Resolutions, in late 1798, provide examples of their widespread belief that Republicans were seditious. Hamilton immediately concluded that "the proceedings of Virginia and Kentucke" were "evidence . . . of a regular conspiracy to overturn the government," and probably of an intent "to encourage a hostile foreign power to decline accommodation and proceed in hostility." His suggestion was "to subdue a *refractory* & powerful *state,*" by letting part of the army "be drawn towards Virginia for which there is an obvious pretext," and then to "put Virginia to the Test of resistance," as we will see. Secretary of War James McHenry agreed that the country was "threatened . . . from within by a party" that favored France and censured the government, and that Republicans had not just differences of opinion but "party animosity, which, . . . approximates to insurrection and revolt."[19] Secretary of State Timothy Pickering joined Hamilton in seeing the Virginia and Kentucky Resolutions as "hostile to the General Government," "outrageous attempts to break the union," and "mad and rebellious resolves." Other High Federalists, such as Sen. Theodore Sedgwick of Massachusetts, viewed the Virginia and Kentucky Resolutions as "little short of a declaration of war."[20]

There were other suspected enemies as well, besides Republicans, as many Federalists saw things, and all the other suspects were aliens. The particularly objectionable aliens were the French, the foreign-born newspaper editors, other immigrant radicals, and the Irish. "French Spies then swarmed in our Cities and in the Country," Adams later recalled, and some were "intollerably, turbulent, impudent and seditious." Nearly as alarming, "*aliens* in the interest of foreign nations, are taking a lead in our politics," Noah Webster complained to Pickering three days after the Sedition Act was signed, referring to leading Republican newspaper editors.[21] Among what some called "hordes of foreigners," immigrant radicals were particularly feared by Federalists. Almost as objectionable were the "hordes of wild Irishmen" immigrating to America, as Rep. Harrison Gray Otis called them; Secretary of State Timothy Pickering too was horrified by the "United Irish Desperadoes."[22]

A strong desire to suppress these enemies—citizen and noncitizen—was a major reason why most High Federalists wanted to declare war against France, even when a French invasion looked quite unlikely. Attorney General Charles Lee wrote to the president that it would be impossible "to restrain the French agents and French partizans and the French generally in our country, from seditious and evil doings," not to mention "internal enemies," "unless the two nations be declared in a state of war." Cabot wrote to Secretary of Treasury Oliver Wolcott, Jr. that "war, open and declared, . . . would also extinguish the hopes of internal foes," because "traitors and sedition-mongers who are now protected and tolerated, would then be easily restrained."[23] Sedgwick railed that declaring war "should have superseded the necessity of alien & sedition laws—without them we might have hanged traitors and exported frenchmen."[24] And only a declaration of war would bring the Alien Enemies Act into effect, unless there were an invasion.

Without a belief in the legitimacy of an opposition, Federalists and Republicans tended to attribute their opponents' positions to insidious motives and seditious conspiracies. That underlay Federalists calling their opponents Jacobins, and Republicans calling their opponents Tories. That caused Federalists to characterize Logan's private peace mission to France "as a secret mission from the Jacobins here to sollicit an army from France, instruct them as to their landing &c.," and to describe the receipt and publication by Benjamin Franklin Bache of French minister Talleyrand's letter as "a traiterous correspondence between the Jacobins here and the French Directory."[25] Republicans similarly demonized the other side.

Such fears were not entirely without basis. The new government was fragile and untested, and in classical theory a republic could only survive in a much smaller area. The French Revolution, and the wars that it ignited with Britain and its allies, caused both sides to threaten American shipping. France invaded other countries as far away as Egypt, and for a time appeared to pose danger to America's mainland. Both Britain and France had colonies that bordered America, as did Spain, and those foreign powers acted as a magnet for frontier conspiracies like the Blount conspiracy.[26] Many Americans did, in fact, encourage one or the other combatant—most Federalists favored Britain, whose trade generated most of the federal government's revenue; and most Republicans favored France, whose assistance had been crucial in the Revolutionary War.[27]

The Federalist-led Congress searched for means to protect the country against the surge of noncitizens, and against suspect Republicans, opposition newspapers, and other internal enemies. It found a ready model in Great Britain's proclamation restricting aliens and in its two sedition laws of 1795—the Treasonable and Seditious Practices Act and the Seditious Meetings and Assemblies Act.[28] Concern about "the dangers with which we are threatened from internal enemies," as Federalist Rep. John W. Kittera of Pennsylvania said, brought hope that the alien friends "bill would not only pass, but that it would be followed by a strong sedition bill."[29] His wish came to pass.

Passage of the Alien Acts

Congress passed, and President John Adams signed, the Alien and Sedition Acts in June and July 1798. Signing those laws became the largest mistake of the Adams administration, one that generated ever-increasing political opposition and marked his administration with an indelible historical blot. It was a larger mistake than retaining a disloyal cabinet, incurring Hamilton's ire over the rank of the generals and other things, or splitting the Federalists with an abruptly announced new mission to France, because none of that involved violating the Constitution and infringing individual rights.

The Alien and Sedition Acts—the Alien Friends Act (June 25, 1798) and the Sedition Act (July 14, 1798)[30]—were accompanied by two other laws. The Naturalization Act (June 18, 1798) and the Alien Enemies Act (July 6, 1798) showed the climate of opinion about immigration, and the ardent desire of most Federalists to restrict citizenship and alien activities.[31]

The Naturalization Act almost tripled the years of residency required for citizenship, from five years to fourteen years. It also added a requirement that white noncitizens register their arrival to the United States within forty-eight hours and receive a certificate from specified officials (or if already in the United States, within six months), or else they could be brought into court, fined, and required to provide a surety bond. And the law federalized naturalization, ending the joint authority states had exercised over granting citizenship. The Naturalization Act was obviously designed, as Federalist Rep. Samuel Sitgreaves blithely admitted, to reduce the number of new Republican voters and officeholders "by extending the time of residence of aliens so far, as to prevent them from ever becoming citizens," and so they "would be effectually excluded from holding offices in the Government."[32] The fourteen-year period exploited the exclusionary potential of onerous requirements for citizenship.[33] The original proposal on April 17, 1798, by Connecticut Rep. Joshua Coit, was "to suspend" naturalization or else to amend it, and some fellow Federalists proposed to disqualify foreign-born individuals forever from voting or holding office.[34] Rep. Robert Goodloe Harper went further, saying "it was high time we should recover from the mistake . . . of admitting foreigners to citizenship," and proposing to "prevent[] any person becoming entitled to the rights of a citizen of the United States, except by birth." William Smith Shaw, the president's nephew, was one of the Federalists who "believe[d] the grand cause of all our present difficulties may be traced to this source—to so many *hordes of Foreigners* imigrating to America," and he hoped to follow the English approach of making aliens not "capable of receiving any office whatever."[35] Disqualification of immigrants from voting and officeholding was rejected, but Federalist sponsors had little good to say about the foreign-born. Rep. Samuel Sewall "saw no good . . . to be derived to the country from admitting these [Irish] persons to citizenship, but much danger," and Rep. James A. Bayard "believed there were as many Jacobins and vagabonds come into the United States during the last two years" as in any normal ten year period. Republicans debated with fervor, but ultimately lost their challenges to the fourteen-year residency requirement by a single vote, in both the House and the Senate.[36] The 1798 law, with the most lengthy residency requirement in United States history, was finally repealed after Jefferson became president, restoring the five-year residence requirement and loosening the registration requirement.[37]

The Alien Enemies Act authorized the president to provide for arresting, restraining, or removing natives and citizens of a hostile nation, which had declared war, or threatened or perpetrated an "invasion or predatory incursion." Excepted were those who had become naturalized citizens of the United States. The law also authorized federal and state courts to hold hearings on complaints and to impose sentences.[38] Legislation for alien enemies split off from early versions of the Naturalization Act in May 1798, and then sat in committee for most of June, as legislation was passed for alien friends.[39] Because the Alien Enemies Act was only effective during wartime, the bill passed both houses of Congress with bipartisan votes. A version of the Alien Enemies Act remains on the books currently.[40]

Jefferson immediately saw what was going on with these laws regulating aliens and other internal enemies. He wrote to Madison that

> one of the war-party, in a fit of unguarded passion declared some time ago they would pass a citizen bill, an alien bill, & a sedition bill. [A]ccordingly some days ago Coit laid a motion on the table of the H. of R. for modifying the citizen law. . . . Hillhouse laid on the table of the Senate a motion for giving power to send away suspected aliens. [T]his is understood to be meant for Volney & Collot, but it will not stop there. . . . [T]here is now only wanting, to accomplish the whole declaration beforementioned, a sedition bill which we shall certainly soon see proposed. [T]he object of that is the suppression of the whig presses. . . . [T]he war-hawks talk of Septemberizing, Deportation, and the examples for quelling sedition set by the French Executive.[41]

Soon the "citizen bill" and two alien laws were in place, as Jefferson expected.

The Alien Friends Act was proposed and passed because Federalists sought power to restrain or remove any aliens, in peace as well as in war, not just those that were natives or citizens of a country at war, who could be dealt with by an Alien Enemies Act. The supporters sought to reach not only French Jacobins but also noncitizen newspaper editors, other radicals, Irish immigrants, and other "hordes of immigrants," with or without war.

The Alien Friends Act, from its first draft to its final text, was so broad that it authorized deportation of any of these target noncitizens, and of any noncitizen at all, without any declaration of war and without any evidence. As Jefferson's letter to Madison indicated, a motion by Sen. James Hillhouse of Connecticut started the legislative process, on April 25, 1798 (six days after the House passed a resolution to consider what became the alien enemies bill). Hillhouse's motion was approved and a committee was appointed the next day, consisting only of Federalists.[42] Its first draft of the alien friends bill, on May 4, like the final law, gave the president discretionary power to deport "all such aliens as he shall judge dangerous to the *peace* and *safety* of the United States." After printing that draft, the Republican *Aurora* ridiculed its creators as "the *wisest* and *most enlightened* Senate in the world."[43] That first draft was even more harsh than the final law in four provisions that were later dropped: requiring all aliens to carry permits; criminalizing "any seditious writing, printing or speaking" or any action to "intermeddle with or disturb the government"; criminalizing anyone harboring, entertaining, or concealing any alien; and punishing overstays of permits or unauthorized returns with life imprisonment at hard labor or life banishment. The Senate passed a toned-down bill on June 8, by a party-line vote of 16 to 7, and sent it to the House.[44]

There, Rep. Albert Gallatin of Pennsylvania led the Republican opposition. He argued against the alien friends bill on four primary grounds: the Constitution did not grant any federal power over aliens but left that as a power retained by the states; the bill left aliens "subject to the arbitrary control of one man only," the president; it violated the Constitution's restriction on regulating the migration of persons before 1808; and it deprived noncitizens of jury trial and other Sixth Amendment rights in ordering deportation, imprisonment, and fines.[45] Comparing the alien enemies bill that was pending, Gallatin observed that "it seems as if gentlemen were more desirous of guarding against alien friends than alien enemies." Rep. Harrison Gray Otis and Rep. Robert Goodloe Harper, the House co-sponsors and leaders of the Federalist defense of the bill, responded that federal power to provide for the common defense warranted the bill, that the migration clause applied to slaves and not to aliens, and that noncitizens only were present at the nation's sufferance and did not have constitutional rights.[46] Gallatin mocked the Federalists by noting that each speech claimed that a different constitutional provision authorized the legislation on alien friends—the commerce power, the tax power, the preamble, self-preservation, the war power, and so on.[47] After two full days of debate, and spurred along by the release of the XYZ Affair correspondence and the return of the first of the envoys, John Marshall, the House passed the bill by a partisan 46–40 vote.[48]

The final Alien Friends Act, which the president signed on June 25, 1798, was indeed more punitive toward alien friends than the Alien Enemies Act was toward alien enemies, and gave the president even more discretion. Its first section empowered the president to deport any aliens essentially at his whim, if either "he shall judge [them] dangerous to the peace and safety of the United States, or shall have reasonable grounds to suspect [they] are concerned in any treasonable or secret machinations against the government." If such a deportation order was issued, the aliens could apply for licenses, which the president discretionarily "may grant" if they "prove[d] to the satisfaction of the president . . . that no injury or danger" would result, and the licenses could be limited to "such time as he shall judge proper" and to "such place as he may designate." If the aliens did not comply with the deportation order and did not obtain licenses, the federal courts could convict the aliens and imprison them for up to three years. The second section authorized the president to do still more at his discretion, deporting any alien held in prison "whenever he may deem it necessary for the public safety," and arresting and speeding the deportation of any alien who had been ordered to depart "when, in the opinion of the President, the public safety requires" a speedy removal. Further, if a deported alien returned, he or she could be convicted by the federal courts and "imprisoned so long as, in the opinion of the President, the public safety may require."[49] Under other sections, captains of arriving ships were required to submit reports of all aliens aboard their vessels, so that the secretary of state could keep a registry; and expelled aliens could take their property or leave it safe from confiscation. The only provision that reflected Republican success limited the law to two years.[50]

Virtually every provision of the Alien Friends Act gave unlimited power to the president or to the courts. The central provision empowered the president to deport any aliens if "he shall judge [them] dangerous to the peace and safety of the United States," or if he had reasonable ground "to suspect" they were involved in "secret machinations against the government." The *Aurora* ridiculed the latter ground as being "*suspected* of being *suspicious.*"[51] The accused aliens had no opportunity to oppose deportation or offer evidence before deportation was ordered, and after that the president could deny or grant licenses without reason or explanation; there was no hearing or trial, jury, or appeal to courts. The only point at which aliens could be heard in court was if they failed to leave or returned, and in that case the courts could rubber stamp convictions and impose prison sentences for violating deportation orders or for returning, merely upon evidence that the aliens overstayed or returned.

The reactions of Republicans and Federalists were typified by Thomas Jefferson and Alexander Hamilton, each writing on June 7 after the penultimate reading of the Senate bill. Jefferson lamented that the alien friends bill "would place aliens . . . under absolute government" because of the arbitrary powers given to the president, and that the sedition "bill and the Alien bill both are so palpably in the teeth of the constitution as to shew they mean to pay no respect to it." Hamilton, by contrast, sounded jubilant. "If an alien Bill passes," the policy should be that

> the mass ought to be obliged to leave the Country—the provisions in our Treaties in favour of Merchants ought to be observed & there ought to be *guarded* exceptions of characters whose situations would expose them too much if sent away & whose demeanour among us has been unexceptionable. There are a few such. Let us not be cruel or violent.[52]

Hamilton's words are quoted in full, because often his last sentence is cited without the context that "the mass" should be deported and only merchants and "a few" asylum seekers should be kept. His words were not idle observations—he was writing to the official who would head enforcement of the Alien Friends Act, Secretary of State Pickering. Abigail Adams, whose spouse would sign the law six days later, wished that Congress would quit "dilly dallying about passing a Bill enabling the President to seize suspisious persons."[53]

Jefferson's epithet was the most devastating: it was "an Alien bill worthy of the 8th. or 9th. century." Madison's was a strong second place: it was "a monster that must for ever disgrace its parents."[54]

Passage of the Sedition Act

The Naturalization Act, Alien Enemies Act, and Alien Friends Act dealt with internal enemies who were aliens, but did not reach internal enemies who were citizens. The Sedition Act dealt with citizens as well. It made it a crime to "write, print, utter or publish" any seditious libel or seditious speech "against the government of the United States, or either house of Congress . . . or the President." The Sedition Act defined *sedition* as printing (seditious libel) or speech (seditious words) with intent to do any of seven things: "defame the said government, . . . Congress . . . , or the President, or to bring them . . . into contempt or disrepute, or to excite against them the hatred of the good people of the United States, or to stir up sedition . . . , or to excite any unlawful combinations therein, for opposing or resisting any law . . . or any act of the President . . . , or to resist, oppose, or defeat any such law or act, or to aid, encourage or abet any hostile designs of any foreign nation."[55]

The focus of the Sedition Act was restricting political speech—opinion about government, its officials, and its measures—as that language made clear. Further, the aim of the sponsors was restricting one side's political speech—in Jefferson's words, "the suppression of the whig presses" (the Republican newspapers). The same day, Abigail Adams said much the same, as she hoped Congress would "pass a sedition bill" so that it could be used against Republican editors (Bache of the *Aurora* and Thomas Adams of the *Independent Chronicle*): "not a paper from Bache press issues nor from Adams Chronical, but what might have been prossecuted as libels upon the President and Congress."[56] At the end of congressional debates on the sedition bill, Gallatin exclaimed, "do they not avow that the true object of the law is to enable one party to oppress the other; . . . to have the power to punish printers who may publish against them?" The primary purpose of the Sedition Act was nothing less than to "try to eliminate the opposition."[57]

Seditious libel and seditious words had long been crimes under English common law, and that criminal prohibition had focused on publications and speeches that were critical of the governmental administration or its officials.[58] In his commentaries on that common law, Sir William Blackstone had written that "seditious . . . libels are punished by the English [common] law," and that criminalizing "any dangerous or offensive writings . . . is necessary for the preservation of peace and good order, of government and religion."[59] Abigail Adams gave a similar rationale, when she wrote that seditious writing—"this continued abuse, deception, and falshood"—must be suppressed because it "tends to destroy that confidence & Harmony which is the Life Health & security of a Republick."[60] Blackstone claimed that criminally prosecuting seditious libel did not violate liberty of the press, under the ancient common law, because "liberty of the press . . . consists in laying no *previous* restraints upon publications, and not in freedom from censure for criminal matter when published." He made the same claim about criminally prosecuting seditious words, that it did not violate freedom of speech, under common law, because "liberty of private sentiment is still left; the disseminating, or making public, of bad sentiments, destructive of the ends of society, is the crime which society corrects."[61] But neither was an accurate description of the ancient common law; the formulation was

Blackstone's in 1769, and it did not appear in the common law until a court decision the next year.[62]

Federalists and Republicans agreed on one thing: that the "house is almost exactly divided," as Sen. Theodore Sedgwick said, with "52 determined and rancorous Jacobins, and 54 who profess attachment to the government."[63] As a result, Jefferson saw serious danger signs in late April 1798 when five prominent Republicans left the session, and warned that "in this state of things they [Federalists] will carry what they please," including not only an alien bill but "a sedition bill."[64]

The House of Representatives made the rumors come true when Federalist Rep. Samuel Sewall, an alien bill sponsor, proposed to draft a bill, on May 18, 1798, and then offered "A Bill for the Prevention and Restraint of Dangerous and Seditious Persons," on June 4.[65] Referred to as an omnibus alien and sedition bill, one of its sections addressed sedition of two types and made both federal crimes. The first was to "combine or conspire together, with intent, and for the purpose of opposing any measure of the government," operation of law, or officer, and the second was "by any writing, printing, or advised speaking, [to] threaten such officer . . . with any damage to his character, person or property," or to "counsel, advise, or attempt" any insurrection or riot.[66] The House debated Sewall's bill on June 16, focusing on its provisions regarding aliens, but it did not take final action on it that day. Curiously, Rep. John Allen of Connecticut, who became one of the sponsors of the Sedition Act, "defied any person to know what was intended" or meant by the provisions of this omnibus bill.[67] From the other side, Jefferson's comment was directed at this House omnibus bill and the Senate alien bill when he said the bills were "so palpably in the teeth of the constitution as to shew they mean to pay no respect to it." The Senate soon broke the issues of aliens and sedition into separate bills.[68]

The Senate addressed the issue of sedition when Sen. James Lloyd of Maryland offered "A Bill To Define More Particularly the Crime of Treason, and To Define and Punish the Crime of Sedition," on June 26, 1798.[69] Its opening section was directed at what Federalists abhorred most—the French party—and it grabbed everyone's attention by declaring the government and people of France "enemies to the United States" and by imposing the death penalty on Americans "who shall adhere to the aforesaid enemies . . . giving them aid and comfort." Its third and fourth sections adopted the sedition provision of Sewall's bill, and added criminalization of virtually any criticism of government: any "writing, printing, publishing or speaking" that attempted to "defame or weaken the government and laws" by "any seditious or inflammatory declarations" either that the government in enacting any law acted with "motives hostile to the constitution, or liberties," or "tending to justify the hostile conduct of the French government," or attempting "to defame the President . . . or any Court or Judge."[70] That new crime was breathtakingly far reaching and would encompass most Republican sentiments, printed or spoken. Alexander Hamilton, though an advocate of alien and sedition laws, wrote that some of Lloyd's provisions were "highly exceptionable" because they could "establish a tyranny" or engender civil war and could solidify the opposition. The bill was referred to a Senate committee with only Federalist members.[71] Lloyd's bill was made less extreme by Federalist-sponsored amendments, which removed the first section entirely and narrowed the second and third sections somewhat. Another amendment added punishments for violations—under the second section a fine up to $5,000 and imprisonment up to five years, and under the third section $2,000 and two years. A further amendment inserted an evidentiary provision for prosecutions of "any editor, printer or publisher of any public newspaper," which showed the main target of the sedition bill.[72]

The Senate approved the modified Lloyd bill by a vote of 18 to 6, ironically on July 4, 1798. That irony was not lost on Republicans such as Sen. Henry Tazewell of Virginia; he wrote to Jefferson that its passage was "an unauspicious event to have happened on the 4th of July."[73] As Lloyd's bill went to the House, it replaced Sewall's bill and attracted more extreme House sponsors.

The House began debates on the Senate sedition bill on July 5 and continued all day.[74] The most extreme House sponsor, Federalist Rep. Allen, gave the first and most important speech and made it abundantly clear that the main target of the sedition bill was Republican newspapers. "Let gentlemen look at certain papers printed in this city and elsewhere, and ask themselves whether an unwarrantable and dangerous combination does not exist to overturn and ruin the Government." He singled out the leading Republican newspapers in the two largest cities—the *Aurora* and the *Time Piece*—and quoted them as examples of sedition that needed to be quashed.[75] Allen regarded it as criminal sedition for the *Aurora* "to persuade the people that peace with France is in our power; nay, that she is sincerely desirous of it, on proper grounds, but that we reject her offers, and proceed to . . . war." He regarded it as a criminal *"combination against the Government"* to attempt "to persuade the people of certain facts," which he believed were unfounded, "that Mr. X has power to treat alone, or that the French Government is willing to treat with him on fair and honorable terms." He said the *Aurora* "furnish[ed] demonstrations without number." Allen clearly understood, and wished, the sedition bill to reach and suppress such disagreement with the administration, and he gave a number of other examples including the congressional speech of Rep. Edward Livingston against the alien friends bill and that representative's claim that "each man has the right of deciding for himself . . . that the law is unconstitutional," as well as publishing such congressional speeches.[76] Allen restated the purpose of the sedition bill—to deprive the Republicans of opposition newspapers:

> The Jacobins of our country, too, sir, are determined to preserve in their hands, the same weapon ["all the presses in the nation"]; it is our business to wrest it from them.[77]

Central to the House debates were freedoms of press and speech. Rep. Allen asked the Republicans "whether they seriously think the liberty of the press authorizes such publications?" and answered that "freedom of the press and opinions was never understood to give the right" of publishing sedition. The next most extreme sponsor, Rep. Robert Goodloe Harper of South Carolina, elaborated on why freedoms of press and speech were not violated by the sedition bill, advocating Blackstone's approach that "the true meaning" of those freedoms "is no more than that a man shall be at liberty to print what he pleases, provided he does not offend against the laws [by sedition], and not that no law shall be passed to regulate this liberty of the press."[78] Several other Federalists joined in endorsing Blackstone's approach.[79] To the contrary, the leading Republican opponents of the sedition bill, Rep. Edward Livingston of New York and Rep. Albert Gallatin of Pennsylvania, argued that the sedition bill was "an abridgment of the liberty of the press, which the Constitution has said shall not be abridged," rejecting Blackstone's approach.[80] The House continued debates on the bill on July 9 for most of the day, and on July 10 all day.[81] Several other Republicans supported Livingston's and Gallatin's position on the First Amendment, such as Rep. John Nicholas of Virginia, who added that the Amendment's meaning was that "the General Government has been forbidden to touch the press."[82]

Other arguments were raised as well.[83] Some Federalists, like Harper, "believed the common-law doctrine of libels [was] applicable to the Government of the United States."[84] Meanwhile, various Republicans, like Nicholas, contended that no constitutional provision or federal law adopted it, and, with Gallatin, added that "if the jurisdiction did exist, where was the necessity" of the Sedition Act?[85] Various Federalists, like Harper, denied that "liberty of the press include[d] sedition and licentiousness," while some Republicans, like Nicholas, asked "where they drew the line between the liberty and licentiousness" of the press?[86] Federalists generally believed that sedition would destroy a country, and government must protect itself against that, while most Republicans said that to "restrict the press, would be to destroy the elective principle, by taking away the information necessary to election" choices.[87] Federalists such as Otis defended the Sedition Act under a government's "right to preserve and defend itself," while Republicans such as Rep. Nathaniel Macon of North Carolina denied that the federal government had any enumerated power to pass a sedition law.[88] Rep. Samuel Dana of Connecticut and other Federalists argued that the First Amendment does not protect "the liberty of uttering malicious falsehood," while Livingston and other Republicans responded that the constitutional method of dealing with falsehood is more speech—"to disprove the fact" rather than "to prosecute the man who makes the charge."[89] Various Federalists believed that the sedition bill simply followed the common law, while Republicans either denied the existence of federal common law or found its narrow freedoms of press and speech overridden by the First Amendment. At the end of the day, the House passed the amended sedition bill by a close vote of 44 to 41, on July 10. The Senate agreed to its changes.[90]

President John Adams signed the Sedition Act on July 14. Adams later described the Sedition Act as something he did not ask for, which is technically correct. But Adams did nothing to discourage passage of the act, and instead immediately signed it into law and supported its enforcement against Republican newspaper editors. Before the Sedition Act was passed, the president's view of the political opposition was that "the degraded and the deluded characters may tremble, lest they should be condemned to . . . being conveyed in safety within the lines of an invading enemy." Three months after he signed the Sedition Act, Adams wrote to Pickering that the secretary of state's unqualified defense of the necessity and constitutionality of the law was "excellent," "concinnate and consummate."[91] A year later, the president was pressing for the Sedition Act's enforcement against opposition newspapers.

The final Sedition Act, which took effect on July 14, 1798, criminalized two things: opposing federal laws and criticizing the government, Congress, or president.[92] More specifically, its less used first section made it a crime to "unlawfully combine or conspire," with intent to do any of three things—"to oppose any measure . . . , to impede the operation of any law . . . , or to intimidate or prevent" any official from performing his duties—or with acts to "counsel, advise or attempt to procure any insurrection, riot, [or] unlawful assembly." The more used second section made it a crime to "write, print, utter or publish" (or to cause or assist that) "any false, scandalous and malicious writing or writings against the government . . . Congress . . . or the President," with intent to do any of seven things mentioned earlier: "to defame" them, "to bring them . . . into contempt or disrepute," "to excite against them . . . the hatred" of the people, "to stir up sedition," "to excite any unlawful combinations" for opposing any law or presidential act, "to resist, oppose, or defeat any such law or act," or "to aid, encourage or abet any hostile designs of any foreign nation."[93] The penalty for violating the first section remained a fine of up to $5,000 and imprisonment of a half year to five years, and for violating the second section remained a fine of up to $2,000 and imprisonment of up to two years. The Sedition Act would expire on the last full day of John Adams's term in office, in March 1801.

The Sedition Act ended with two provisions that modified common law. First, a defendant was allowed "to give in evidence in his defence, the truth of the matter . . . charged as a libel." That was contrary to the common law rule that truth was no defense and, incredibly, aggravated the crime.[94] However, the truth defense was of little help, because opinions could not be proved true, and facts could not be proved true either when judges required defendants to prove truth beyond a reasonable doubt.[95] Second, juries had the "right to determine the law and the fact," meaning that juries could enter a general verdict of guilt or innocence. That too was contrary to the common law rule that the jury only determined if the defendant wrote, spoke, or printed the challenged statement (and if contested, the jury also determined if innuendos in the statement meant what the prosecutor claimed they meant), while the judges determined if the statement was libelous, was made with criminal intent, and caused harm.[96] However, placing that authority in the jury's hands had little effect when Federalist marshals selected Federalist jurors and when Federalist judges conducted biased trials.[97] Because of these two new provisions, some scholars have called the Sedition Act "a significant liberalization of the common law."[98] However, the new provisions produced no discernible benefit for defendants; only one jury acquitted a defendant in a Sedition Act trial.

The partisan bias of the Sedition Act was exhibited not only by its criminalization of press and speech opposing institutions that the Federalists controlled (the government, presidency, and Congress), but by its lack of protection of the one high office that the Federalists did not control (the vice presidency). Most scholars have also found partisan bias in the expiration of the Sedition Act at the end of Adams's term in office. However, that argument based on the expiration date is greatly weakened by two facts. The expiration date in the final law was proposed by a member of Congress who voted against the Sedition Act (George Dent of Maryland), who was a moderate Federalist soon transitioning to the Republican Party.[99] His motion lengthened the two-year provision proposed by a Federalist sponsor, Robert Goodloe Harper, which in turn had lengthened the one-year term originally offered by Harper.[100] Also, a further extension of the expiration date was proposed and supported by most Federalists when the Sedition Act was about to expire.[101] The Federalist supporters clearly did not view the Sedition Act as a short-term palliative—they instead defended it energetically at every stage. They probably started with a short term and kept lengthening it when they found they had the votes, much as the Federalist supporters of the Alien Friends Act did.[102] As for Dent's motion, he may well have been trying to make the sedition bill unpalatable to other moderate Federalists, knowing as everyone did that the vote would be close. However, his reasoning and that of others voting on the expiration date was not recorded.

The constitutionality of the Sedition Act continued to be debated after Congress passed the law. During the years the Sedition Act was in force, the titans sparred as James Madison wrote Virginia's Report and John Marshall opposed him by writing Virginia's Minority Address, and as a dozen books or booklets argued the constitutional issues. In recent years, some scholars have defended the constitutionality of the Sedition Act and of criminalization of seditious libel,[103] though the majority have assailed the constitutionality of both under modern doctrines of the United States Supreme Court.[104] Some have argued that the original First Amendment protection for freedoms of speech and press was narrow because Congress approved the Sedition Act just nine years after it approved the Bill of Rights, but David A. Anderson demolished that argument by showing the minimal overlap between the members of Congress supporting both.[105]

It is often claimed that all Federalists supported, and all Republicans opposed, the Sedition Act.[106] While most of each party did, there were Federalist opponents, and their numbers grew over time. The most visible was John Marshall of Virginia, as a candidate for Congress, who secretly wrote the Minority Address defending the law's constitutionality, but publicly stated that he would "certainly have opposed" the Alien and Sedition Acts as "useless."[107] For that, "[o]ur good people all censure Mr. Marshall," Cabot told Pickering. The "Virginia Federalists are little better than half-way Jacobin," Benjamin Goodhue wrote to Pickering, and Pickering "regret[ted] his answers" but hoped they were merely "an 'electioneering trick.'"[108] The first lady wrote that "Marshall has sunk his Character very much," Fisher Ames said "his character is done with," and even two years later the new speaker of the house was castigating Marshall's "foolish declaration, relative to the alien & sedition laws" (Theodore Sedgwick). While "reprobating" Marshall's statement, High Federalists hypothesized that "[s]ome allowance too should be made for the influence of the Atmosphere of Virginia, which doubtless makes every one who breathes it visionary & . . . incredibly credulous."[109] Because of that abuse, and because Pickering prosecuted people for calling the laws unconstitutional, most other Federalist opponents of the Alien and Sedition Acts objected privately, not publicly.

"[T]hese two laws, especially the sedition bill, are view[ed] by a great many well meaning men, as unwarranted by the constitution," Marshall acknowledged.[110] The Federalist opponents who this author has discovered include vice presidential candidate Charles Cotesworth Pinckney (the envoy, and signer of the Constitution, who was later the Federalist presidential candidate in 1804 and 1808), Gov. Edward Rutledge of South Carolina, former Gov. Patrick Henry of Virginia, and former Secretary of State Edmund Randolph (also a former attorney general, who did not affiliate with the Republicans until 1798). In addition, various Federalists were "in the act of passing, or preparing to pass, from one party to another" in 1798, John Jay noted, and many of those opposed the Sedition Act. They included Dr. Benjamin Rush, future governor John Page of Virginia, and future senator John Armstrong of New York; some who had already become Republicans such as Gov. Thomas McKean of Pennsylvania and Chief Justice Edmund Pendleton of Virginia; some who made the transition and changed views of the Sedition Act after 1798 such as District Judge Cyrus Griffin and District Judge Gunning Bedford; and many in state legislatures such as Jedidiah Peck and Ambrose Spencer of New York.[111] As Congress voted to enact the Sedition Act in July 1798, five other Federalists voted against it.[112]

Annual efforts were made to repeal the Sedition Act, and each time additional Federalists voted against it, often as part of their transition between parties. There was a House vote to adopt a committee report defending the constitutionality of the Alien and Sedition Acts in February 1799, and three additional Federalists voted against it.[113] There was a Republican effort in the House to repeal the Sedition Act in January 1800, and seven more Federalists voted against it.[114] There was another House attempt to extend the Sedition Act and to repeal parts of it in January and February 1801, and five additional Federalists voted with the Republicans.[115] The total of Federalist defections in the House was six times the three-vote margin (44 to 41) by which the Sedition Act originally passed that chamber. Federalists, acknowledging the transitioning moderate Federalists, preferred to call them "apostates from us."[116]

One of the most remarkable things about the Sedition Act, and about the Alien Friends Act, is that they were not designed to take effect in time of war, as the Alien Enemies Act was, but instead they were designed to take effect in time of peace as well as war. Further, their expiration dates were not the end of hostilities, but specific dates.

Enforcement of the Alien and Sedition Acts

The original law that established the federal courts, the Judiciary Act of 1789, created the federal position of an attorney general but only gave the attorney general authority over federal Supreme Court cases. He "was not authorized to give instructions" to federal prosecutors in lower court cases, as the first attorney general complained. The attorney general was part-time and practiced law on the side.[117] The Judiciary Act also created the position of an "attorney for the United States in [each] district" (essentially each state) but did not give that attorney a salary, instead providing compensation by the fees that a court taxed. Consequently, the United States attorneys were also part-time, practicing law on the side, and they had limited incentive to initiate prosecutions unless instructed to do so.[118] In response to the silence of the Judiciary Act, the secretary of state assumed the responsibility to direct the United States attorneys, from 1789 onward throughout the 1790s. The president also occasionally gave instructions to them.[119]

Secretary of State Timothy Pickering was not just willing but zealous to direct the United States attorneys in enforcing the Alien and Sedition Acts, more so than in enforcing any other federal laws. He was in charge of enforcement, as we will see in most prosecutions, and he not only scrutinized Republican newspapers for sedition but kept a file of them.[120] Pickering periodically instructed the United States attorneys "to prosecute the publisher, for every libel upon the Government or its officers, which may appear" in particular newspapers.[121] It has been said that "his letters were not put in terms of orders,"[122] but they were received and followed as orders, and they only used terms like "request" as a matter of polite custom.

The United States Circuit Courts had exclusive jurisdiction over serious crimes, such as violations of the Alien and Sedition Acts, that were cognizable under federal authority.[123] When a prosecution was begun by a United States attorney, a federal judge would have the defendant arrested for trial, and would set bail in the form of a bond, so the defendant did not have to remain imprisoned until trial. The Circuit Courts held session twice a year, when a United States Supreme Court justice appeared in each state to sit with the local United States District Court judge, and it was in these Circuit Courts that Sedition Act trials occurred.[124]

FIGURE 2.1. Secretary of State Timothy Pickering. Engraving by T. B. Welsh after Gilbert Stuart. Library of Congress.

Pickering enthusiastically defended the constitutionality of the Alien and Sedition Acts. For example, he responded to a petition for their repeal by emphatically arguing in their support. He added that questioning the laws' constitutionality was itself seditious ("such declarations tend to excite disobedience to the laws, hatred to the government, insurrection, and revolt"), and returned the petition to its senders refusing to deliver it to the president.[125] His view was that of John Fenno, the editor of the leading Federalist newspaper: "It is *Patriotism* to write in favour of our government—it is Sedition to write against it."[126]

Pickering's enforcement efforts sought just what Jefferson had predicted: "the suppression of the whig presses." Most of the Sedition Act prosecutions that Pickering planned and ordered, and that Adams ordered or approved, were aimed squarely at the opposition press and at the opposition party—at press and speech that supporters of the Sedition Act sought to suppress. Those prosecutions occurred in three campaigns—in 1798 after passage of the act, in early 1799 to crush the Fries Rebellion, and in late 1799 through mid-1800 to help the Federalist Party win the 1800 elections.

Similarly, all of the planned Alien Act prosecutions were aimed at noncitizen newspaper editors and at noncitizen groups that typically supported the opposition party—French, Irish, radical, and other immigrants.

The dark cloud of the Alien and Sedition Acts had a silver lining, however, that Madison expressed to Jefferson as soon as such laws looked likely, in May 1798:

> It is to [be] hoped however that any arbitrary attacks on the freedom of the Press will . . . make them recoil on the wicked authors. No other check to desperate projects seems now to be left. The Sanguinary faction ought not however to adopt the spirit of Roburespierre without recollecting the shortness of his triumphs & the perpetuity of his infamy.[127]

His hope proved to be right.

THE SEDITION ACT FIRST CAMPAIGN (1798)

THE "SUPPRESSION OF THE WHIG PRESSES"

[O]ne of the war-party, in a fit of unguarded passion declared some time ago they would pass a citizen bill, an alien bill, & a sedition bill. . . . Hillhouse laid on the table of the Senate a motion for giving power to send away suspected aliens. [T]his is understood to be meant for Volney & Collot, but it will not stop there. . . . [T]here is now only wanting, to accomplish the whole declaration beforementioned, a sedition bill which we shall certainly soon see proposed. [T]he object of that is the suppression of the whig presses.

—*Thomas Jefferson to James Madison (April 26, 1798)*

CHAPTER THREE

Common Law Sedition Prosecutions

PROSECUTIONS OF THREE newspaper editors were started days before the Sedition Act became law on the fourteenth of July 1798, and as Jefferson predicted two months earlier, they were aimed at "suppression of the whig presses."[1] Those editors published the leading Republican newspapers in the two largest cities in the United States—Benjamin Franklin Bache's *Aurora Daily Advertiser* in Philadelphia and John Daly Burk's and James Smith's *Time Piece* in New York City. A prosecution of a fourth editor was started three days after the Sedition Act was signed into law—William Durell of the *Mt. Pleasant Register* in rural New York. They were prosecuted because they published articles critical of the president, Congress, or the federal government—in other words, articles offensive to the governing party and supportive of the opposition. The prosecutions were treated as so urgent that the arrest of Bache could not be delayed eighteen days, and the arrest of Burk and Smith could not be delayed eight days, until the Sedition Act could be passed and signed into law. Instructions to arrest Durell had been given sixteen days before the act became law, and he was arrested before a copy of the new law reached the United States attorney for New York, just three days after President John Adams signed the act. The only apparent reason for the urgency in these cases was an effort by Secretary of State Timothy Pickering and others to suppress influential Republican newspapers and their censure of the administration, as quickly as possible.

Because the Sedition Act was not yet in place, the cases against Bache, Burk, and Smith had to be brought under the common law (centuries of case law). Under English common law, seditious libel was a crime. As Matthew Bacon's treatise said, published words were an aggravated criminal libel if they defamed "Persons employed in a public Capacity, . . . as they tend to scandalize the Government, by reflecting on those who are intrusted with the Administration of public Affairs, which . . . have a direct Tendency to breed in the People a Dislike of their Governors, and incline them to Faction and Sedition." Criticism of government officials could not be tolerated; it threatened government itself.[2]

However, there were two complications. Many people, including Bache and Burk themselves, viewed the First Amendment's protections of freedoms of press and speech as inconsistent with continued use of the English common law of seditious libel and of seditious words.[3] Also, there was debate whether the federal government had any common law at all. The main arguments on the Federalist side soon became that Americans prized the common law, and that the framers of the Constitution had assumed the existence of federal common law crimes and consequently had only specified a few crimes such as treason. The main arguments on the Republican side soon became that the Constitution did not adopt England's common law, with its 160 capital offenses and its hundreds of other crimes, as part of the new nation's law, and that to adopt that common law as part of national law would transmute the federal courts from "the least dangerous branch" to enforcers of large criminal and civil codes never enacted by Congress. Both sides agreed that the states had adopted large parts of the common law that were not inconsistent with their constitutions and laws.

These issues were not entirely new, because there had been three earlier prosecutions by the federal government that arguably were of seditious libel. The reason it is only arguable that those were cases under a federal common law of seditious libel is that they involved offenses under the law of nations, which was both freestanding and described as part of the common law. Justice James Iredell charged a federal grand jury on April 7, 1795 that "offences of individuals against the law of nations" were the basis for prosecution of "violation of the privileges of an Ambassador, or other public Minister."[4] Iredell's grand jury responded, that same day, by indicting Thomas Greenleaf, editor of *Greenleaf's New-York Journal*, for an article defaming the British minister. Neither the indictment nor the attorney general's opinion (which had been sought before proceeding) in that case was clear about whether the alleged crime was under a federal common law of seditious libel or under the law of nations.[5] The same was true of the other two cases. The 1795 case was dropped, but two years later Greenleaf was indicted again for defaming the British consul general. This time he was convicted and fined $700.[6] Another 1797 case was brought against William Cobbett, editor of *Porcupine's Gazette,* for libeling the Spanish minister and the Spanish king.[7] The federal grand jury refused to indict him (returning the indictment marked "ignoramus"), in April 1798, though in an unrelated case Pennsylvania courts proved far less friendly to Cobbett.[8]

It is no coincidence that these pre-1798 prosecutions all involved defamation of foreign envoys. The dominant issue of the 1790s was the war between Britain and France, and their allies, which followed the French Revolution, and the ripple effects on American loyalties and commerce. American newspapers divided, as the emerging political parties did, between Anglophile Federalists and Francophile Republicans, and the more partisan newspapers had much to say about the warring nations, their leaders, and their diplomats. There may be a second major reason why these prosecutions all involved envoys—why there was not one federal prosecution for libeling American officials or the American government before 1798. That is that, while the law of nations was a generally accepted basis for prosecuting defamation of envoys, federal common law was not generally accepted as a ground for prosecuting crimes not prohibited by the Constitution or federal statutes.[9] Thus, there were no federal common law prosecutions for seditious libel for the vitriolic criticism of President George Washington and Alexander Hamilton that appeared during the 1790s in Republican newspapers such as the *Aurora.* That changed in 1798, as the three prosecutions of four newspaper editors—all Republicans—were attempted for violation of a federal common law crime of seditious libel.

Benjamin Franklin Bache and the Philadelphia *Aurora*

Benjamin Franklin Bache (1769–1798) was the grandson of Benjamin Franklin. He was one of the few well-educated and relatively affluent individuals who were prosecuted for seditious libel during the crisis years of 1798–1801.[10] When his grandfather traveled to France as an American commissioner during the American Revolution, Bache accompanied him for the entire nine years. The youth's Enlightenment education during those years began at a school near Paris, continued at another in Geneva, and proceeded with tutors, before he was trained as a printer. After returning to America, he attended and graduated from University of Pennsylvania. That education was important, because Franklin "was training his grandson in a trade he regarded not only as a public service, in that it educated citizens of the republic, but also as an influence on foreign relations" and domestic policy, as Bache's leading intellectual biographer, Jeffery Smith, observed.[11] His grandfather "had much at heart the success of his grandson," and "built and furnished a printing-house for him"—a state-of-the-art one. After Franklin's death, that became the site of a new newspaper. It also became the site of a new marriage, as Bache married Margaret Hartman Markoe. She was the daughter of a Danish immigrant to St. Croix, who owned a plantation there until his death, after which the daughter and mother had moved to Philadelphia.[12]

The Foremost Opposition Newspaper

Bache began his Philadelphia newspaper, originally called *The General Advertiser, and Political, Commercial, Agricultural and Literary Journal,* at the beginning of October 1790, when he was just twenty-one years old. His opening issue made the standard promise by such papers of impartiality.[13] The newspaper soon began to advocate Republican principles, though scholars disagree about whether the change occurred in a half year, as his leading general biographer James Tagg concluded, or in two to three years.[14] Thomas Jefferson took an interest in Bache, providing regular issues of a Leyden paper that offered alternate views to the London newspapers, whose news and essays were typically reprinted, and suggesting the need for a national "republican vehicle of news established between the seat of government and all it's parts."[15] Bache failed to adopt his suggestion, and Jefferson looked elsewhere for a national Republican newspaper, settling on Philip Freneau's *National Gazette.*

Bache sensed approaching opportunity as the *National Gazette* ailed, ultimately expiring in October 1793, and stepped up his Republican content. President George Washington soon fumed that "[t]he publications in Freneau's and Beach's Papers are outrages on common decency," while Vice President John Adams found "Baches Paper" to be "nearly as bad as Freneaux's" as both "maul the President."[16] Adams referred to a mocking advertisement in the *General Advertiser* for a poet laureate, addressed "To the Noblesse and Courtiers of the United States," which said that to qualify for the position "*monarchical prettinesses* must be highly extolled, such as levies, drawing rooms, stately nods instead of shaking hands, titles of office, seclusion from the people, &c." The advertisement sarcastically warned that "[i]t is founded in human nature that when [nonaristocratic] men are exalted above their fellows they should be seized with vertigo," and would "diminish that *reverence and submission,* which ought necessarily to be annexed to every important office" and which "ought to be *the Majesty of the Officers of Government.*"[17]

FIGURE 3.1. Benjamin Franklin Bache. Courtesy New-York Historical Society Museum and Library.

Bache's newspaper quickly became the foremost opposition newspaper nationally, and Bache soon became the semiofficial pamphlet printer of the emerging Republican Party, as well as an active political organizer.[18] In the midst of these changes, the newspaper was renamed in 1794 as the *Aurora General Advertiser,* because it would *"diffuse light"* and *"dispel the shades of ignorance."*[19] The *Aurora*'s primacy became clear in the most heated political fight during Washington's second administration, the dispute over the Jay Treaty with Britain, which was negotiated in 1794 but was not ratified until 1795. Though Washington and the Senate tried to keep its terms secret, to avoid a public firestorm, Bache printed an article summarizing its terms, and then produced a pamphlet with the treaty's full text.[20] The *Aurora* followed that with various series of articles by Valerius, Hancock, Belisarius, Atticus, and others condemning the treaty and rallying Republican opposition.[21]

After the Jay Treaty was ratified, Bache remained on high alert against Federalist transgressions, and particularly against the formerly sacrosanct George Washington.[22] In late 1795, the *Aurora* published Calm Observer's articles charging Washington with taking more than his authorized compensation as president.[23] Bache also reprinted a pamphlet of forged letters from the Revolutionary War that accused the general of insincere patriotism and secret British loyalty. Washington later protested that these "impudent forgeries of letters, carrying my signature, which Mr Bache has taken so much pains to impose on the public as genuine productions," show that Bache's "calumnies are to be exceeded only by his Impudence, and both stand unrivalled."[24] In mid-1796, essays in the *Aurora* critical of Washington and his administration led Jefferson to assure Washington that he was not the source. Washington lamented that such assaults "publish things that do not . . . exist" and "mutilate" things that do exist "to make them subserve the purposes which they have." Until the last year or two, the president had "had no conception that Parties Would, or even could go, the length I have been Witness to," including that efforts to prevent war had caused him to be "accused of being the enemy of one Nation, and subject to the influence of another." As a result, "every act of my Administration would be tortured, and the grossest, and most insidious misrepresentations of them be made . . . in such exag[g]erated, and indecent terms as could scarcely be applied to a Nero; a notorious defaulter; or even to a common pickpocket."[25] The worst was yet to come.

Thomas Paine's *Letter to George Washington,* published by Bache in December 1796, did portray the president as worse than Nero or a notorious defaulter, calling him "treacherous in private friendship . . . and a hypocrite in public life," and finding the decision difficult "whether you are an apostate or an impostor; whether you have abandoned good principles, or whether you ever had any?" Madison, on seeing the second of the three letters, told Jefferson that it showed Paine's "rancour against the President," a rancor which apparently arose because Washington had not pressed Robespierre to release Paine from French prison. Oliver Wolcott, Jr. and other Federalists saw Paine's booklet as "containing the most infamous calumnies" as well as embodying efforts of "France to destroy the publick confidence in the Friends of Govt."[26] Then Jasper Dwight's *Letter to George Washington . . . Containing Strictures on His Address,*" excoriating the president's Farewell Address, was published by Bache the same month. Written pseudonymously by William Duane, who in two years would become the *Aurora*'s editor, the booklet said the Farewell Address was greeted with exultation by "the avowed enemies of equal Liberty, the decided friends of monarchy, the open advocates of privileged and distinct classes," and especially the former tories. "Posterity will in vain search for the monuments of wisdom in your administration," it continued, listing instead numerous monuments of infamy such as the Hamilton financial system, the "British Treaty," Washington's attachment to the Revolution only from "disappointed ambition" in not getting a British army commission, and his posturing as the "great champion of American Freedom" while "enjoying the fruits of their labour" of "five hundred of the human species in slavery."[27]

Far from finished, Bache launched his greatest assault on Washington in 1797, in an anonymous booklet probably written by himself, entitled *Remarks Occasioned by the Late Conduct of Mr. Washington.*[28] In the preface, Bache identified his purpose as "to prove the want of claim in Mr. Washington either to the gratitude or confidence of his country." Most of the booklet reproached every action of Washington's military career and presidency, saying that he sought to establish a monarchy, was "dangerous in public affairs," and while pretending "to be of no party" found that "party support is his only resource." The rest of the booklet upbraided Washington's character, finding him "wanting in great qualities" and instead "avaricious" (while giving a "specious shew of disinterestedness"), passionate about "being noticed," weak in understanding, wanting in "elevation of mind," and governed by "certain characters" (Hamilton).[29] However, the impact of these attacks was more harmful to Bache than to Washington, as a family friend observed: Bache "is now considered in the most despicable light by the most respectable part of his fellow citizens, and by almost every one whom he might formerly have considered as his particular friends."[30] Perhaps Bache finally realized that, as he moved on to other targets.

Bache redirected some of his fire at the new president, John Adams, whose election the *Aurora* had actively opposed.[31] Soon, the first lady, Abigail

Adams, complained to her sister that "Ben Bache is as usual abusing the President," and a month later, that an immigrant writer who "fled from England for publishing libels" was "employ[e]d by the Jacobins here to excite a spirit of opposition to the Government" by writing for the *Aurora*. She wrote to her son that Bache continued in "his old way" by "a low malicious kind of abuse and scur[r]ility" against "the Character of Gentlemen."[32]

Bache seemed to be involved in most radical causes. He served as the publishing house for France's controversial ministers to the United States, and for propaganda from the French government, while spinning positively the Terror, coups, and shipping attacks. He published Thomas Paine's challenge to organized religion and biblical inspiration and served as "Paine's quasi-official publisher, distributor, and book-seller in America." Bache charged the British minister, Robert Liston, with being "a principal" in the conspiracy, when Sen. William Blount was charged with a scheme to sell Spanish Florida and Louisiana to Britain and was expelled from office. "British gold has been profusely scattered in this country, to effect a disunion with the French Republic, and to form a union with the Monarchy of England." Bache also charged Timothy Pickering with involvement. After James Monroe was recalled from his position as minister to France, Bache published his book upbraiding Washington and his foreign policy as anti-French.

Why the relentless attacks on Washington, more than on any other? Bache correctly perceived that Washington was the most important pillar of the Federalist Party, as well as an exponent of many things Bache regarded as antirepublican. From his youth, Bache had not held Washington in the awe most Americans felt, because Bache was far away in France throughout the American Revolution, and was instead awed by another renowned American whose name he bore. Immersed in attacks on Washington, Bache lost his sense of perspective to recognize when his campaign became counterproductive.

Earlier Prosecutions of Bache and Reynolds

Bache prodded Pickering again in January 1798, with the allegation that Pickering improperly charged for a free passport. An article in the *Aurora* described "a shameful breach of the laws" when a merchant met with what he thought was the secretary of state to get a passport, and upon asking what he owed, was told "*there is no particular sum charged,* it is left to people's own generosity." The merchant paid five dollars. Pickering indignantly wrote a response for publication in the *Aurora,* saying that "the charge is utterly *false,* and as *malicious* as it is *false,*" and he attached the merchant's affidavit saying that he mistakenly thought he was meeting with Pickering when it was actually a clerk. Pickering also indicated that he was considering a seditious libel prosecution, by noting that such a breach of the laws "would be criminal."[33] Despite Pickering's self-righteous denials, the truth was that two of his employees did receive payments for passports, as he admitted to George Washington the next day. Pickering reverted to bombast as he told another correspondent that he would "see in the Lying Chronicle [Boston's leading Republican newspaper] a libel on me from the Lying Aurora," whose slanders he had "for nearly two years submitted," and that the "Jacobinic scoundrels feasted on the imaginary discovery of guilt."[34]

Pickering was sufficiently provoked to say he would "consult two or three friends who are lawyers, on the nature of the libel, and if they pronounce the matter actionable, I shall prosecute the malicious author and publisher." He noted that the author "is doubtless a Dr. Reynolds," who "lately fled from justice in Ireland, but is now the intimate friend of Bache." In a postscript, Pickering said that "Bache, on demand for the author, has given up Dr. James Reynolds" (identified him as the author).[35]

Dr. James Reynolds was a physician who had become the chair of the Dublin region of the United Irishmen in 1793. The United Irishmen were a radical organization that sought to free Ireland from British rule, and after 1795 that invited France's support for an insurrection.[36] Quickly reported to the British government, Reynolds was arrested for high treason and imprisoned in Newgate for five months. He fled to the United States the next year, exchanging a picture of Thomas Paine in his cell for a hanged figure of King George III on his ship. In Philadelphia he again mixed medical practice with radical politics, and was a leader of the radical Irish. There was some truth in Abigail Adams's claim that he was "one of Baches slanderers," because Reynolds was a caustic writer for the *Aurora.* One of his recent essays had celebrated Washington's departure from the presidency, saying that "the name of Washington from this day ceases to give a currency to political iniquity; and to legalize corruption."[37] Reynolds also appeared as an activist for United Irishmen in the "seditious riot" at St. Mary's Church in February 1799, discussed in Chapter 10.

Pickering had the United States attorney for Pennsylvania, William Rawle, file "two cases against Bache and Reynolds" in February 1798.[38] Bache responded in amazement that Pickering acknowledged that wrongdoing had occurred in his department and yet treated the disclosure of that "truth" as a violation of law and as an "effusion of party spirit." Further, though the merchant was the person who first made the disclosure, Pickering showed "zeal in screening Mr. Wotherspoon from the charge of having propagated the report of improper practices committed in his office, and resting it on Doct. Reynolds" instead.[39]

Were these governmental seditious libel prosecutions of Bache and Reynolds, or were they just private libel cases? James Morton Smith assumed that the Bache suit was a "personal libel suit" (he was not aware of this Reynolds suit). But the cases were filed by the United States attorney for Pennsylvania, not by the two private attorneys who had reviewed the matter for Pickering. If they were personal libel suits, Pickering would have had to pay the legal fees, and he was notoriously cheap. (He once accepted a dinner invitation on the express condition that he would not be required to reciprocate.) He might justify having the government engage the United States attorney to prosecute common law seditious libel suits arising from criticism of a high federal official, under his view of federal common law crimes. The Reynolds suit continued to have William Rawle serve as legal counsel for the plaintiff even after Rawle ceased to be the United States attorney, though he might have begun a federal prosecution and then continued the case in private practice.[40] It is not clear-cut whether the cases were federal seditious libel prosecutions or private libel cases.

Bache did not endear himself to President John Adams any more than he did to Pickering. Paine's *Letter to George Washington,* which Bache had published, had condemned Adams's "treasonable" belief "that the Presidency should be made hereditary" and his actions as "sycophant of every thing in power," and had called him one of "the disguised traitors that call themselves federalists." Letters printed in the *Aurora* characterized Adams in many ways including "the querulous and cankered murmurs of blind, bald, crippled, toothless Adams."[41] Abigail Adams privately boiled over not only about that one, but about "this lying wretch of Baches" and the *Aurora*'s program "to calumniate the President, his family [and] his administration," and about "the grose lies daily published in the Aurora, Argus, & Chronicle." She complained that the *Aurora* would "render the Proclamation Ridiculous" that called for a fast day, as "the vile incend[i]aries keep up in Baches paper the most wicked and base, voilent & caluminiating abuse."[42] The first lady had long railed that "all the writers in that paper are said to be foreigners, many of them fugitives from the Halter in their own Country, incend[i]aries who kindle Flames where ever they go," who should be "consignd to the Element they delight in" (which was not heaven); and she looked forward to passage of a sedition law because "not a paper from Bache press issues" but "what might have been prossecuted as libels upon the President and Congress."[43] Much of the Federalist press matched her fervor, such as William Cobbett's description of "the notorious Jacobin":

"Bache, Editor of the *Aurora,* Printer to the French Directory, Distributor General of the principles of Insurrection, Anarchy and confusion; the greatest fool, and most stubborn sans culotte in the United States," with "understrappers in the different parts of the United States." Many of the Federalists in Congress agreed, condemning "a vile incendiary paper published in this city, which constantly teems with the most atrocious abuse of all the measures of the Government, and its administrators."[44]

Thomas Jefferson agreed with Abigail Adams on one thing, that as a sedition act was considered by Congress, "Bache is thought a main object of it." A major House sponsor of the Sedition Act, Rep. John Allen, brandished a copy of the *Aurora* while speaking in favor of the proposed law, and said Bache's paper was "the great engine of all these treasonable combinations" and "a genuine Jacobinic press."[45]

Arrest and Indictment

Bache had been attacked in Federalist newspapers, his house had been assaulted by mobs twice in May 1798, and he was physically attacked twice.[46] However, the most severe attack he suffered was an indictment for seditious libel at the end of June 1798.[47]

The *Aurora* published a long letter from Talleyrand, the French foreign minister, to the American envoys, expressing France's desire for peace and willingness to negotiate differences, along with a haughty defense of France's actions, on June 16. Bache's paper printed the letter before a copy had reached Congress from the Department of State (in each case after being translated). Pickering's reaction was typical of High Federalists: that department "was making a translation when Bache's paper came in. Talleyrand must therefore have transmitted it to one of his friends here for publication, lest, perhaps he imagined the President would not make it public." Pickering only had received it two days earlier, on June 14.[48] Two days after it appeared in the *Aurora,* as Congress received the Talleyrand letter from Pickering, Rep. George Thatcher told his House of Representatives colleagues that the letter "had already been printed in the French paper of this city [the *Aurora*], and he believed by order of the Executive Directory" of France. Rep. Robert Goodloe Harper, a House sponsor of the Alien and Sedition Acts, told his colleagues that the truth of Thatcher's positions "was too evident to be for a moment doubted," because it had long been clear "that France had her secret agents in this country, and that every means had been made use of to excite resistance to the measures of our Government, and to raise a spirit of faction in the country favorable to the views of France." Bache's publication of Talleyrand's address "was only one of the ramifications of the scheme," and Harper believed events "would lead to the discovery of a treasonable correspondence carried on by persons in this country with France, of the most criminal nature." Quoting Harper, Jefferson worried that Federalists set out "to implicate whom they pleased."[49]

The Federalists' outcry resulted from two ulterior concerns, beyond Bache receiving and publicizing the letter before it reached Congress. First, Talleyrand's letter deflated the High Federalist push for war with France by showing that France wanted to negotiate differences and was not threatening war. Second, Bache's apparent advance copy of the letter created an opportunity to imprison or discredit him as a French agent and to shut down the leading opposition paper.

Bache responded by demanding that Thatcher produce "the evidence which he pretends to be in possession of." Bache described congressional vapors under the heading "Tories in an Uproar," and noted that "if it had not been for this free press," the "people of America would not have known of Mr. Talleyrand's dispatch, until after they had been 'committed by a declaration of war.'"[50]

The tempest continued as Federalist papers and leaders each offered their own speculations about how Bache got Talleyrand's letter before Congress did. The *Gazette of the United States* said that "Mr. Keeder from Paris" brought "dispatches from the French directory to Benjamin Franklin Bache" under Talleyrand's seal, and delivered one to Bache.[51] Stephen Higginson soon informed Pickering, a friend, that William Lee brought packets "for the Leaders of our Jacobin faction," including "Jefferson, Munroe, Randolph, Genet, Baldwin, Burr, Bache, and several other members of Congress," totaling "15 or more," and urged the secretary of state "to intercept" them because they "may lead to detect Conspiracies."[52] Wolcott did intercept a number of packets, including the one for Bache, and a separate letter to Jefferson, the vice president.[53]

Federalist newspapers were as committed to a partisan viewpoint as the *Aurora*. The *Gazette* published a letter claiming that while "Monsieur Bache" denies correspondence with "his Master Talleyrand," his shameful abuse of the government showed that "he is a *French agent*"; "who can doubt of his being a secret agent of the French"?[54]

Bache gave his account of how he got Talleyrand's letter. In a sworn affidavit, he said that the Talleyrand letter was "delivered to him for publication by a gentleman of this city"—not by packet from Talleyrand—while a pamphlet written by Pinchon came in an envelope from the French Ministry of Foreign Affairs, where he worked, and was brought by William Lee and John Kidder as they sailed from France but had not yet reached Bache.[55] In "The Plot [U]nravelled," Bache characterized the attacks on the *Aurora* as a plot. He announced that he finally received the missing packet, which had been intercepted by the federal government—handwritten on its back was "Received, June 20, from William Lee, Oliv. Wolcott," and "Received in the mail from New York, June 22d, 1798, T. Pickering." The pamphlets were as far as they could be from sedition, only discussing British affairs and not saying anything about the United States at all.[56]

The remainder of that article and another became the basis of the criminal prosecution of Bache for seditious libel of government officials—Secretary of the Treasury Oliver Wolcott, Jr. and Secretary of State Timothy Pickering as well as President John Adams. Bache said that Wolcott went to New York "to view the suspected letters," and "to determine whether it was worth while to violate every principle of law and honour to get at their contents." (In fact, Federalist William Dunlap's diary confirms that Wolcott came to New York to investigate the "letters from Talleyrand . . . to Bache & others," and that William Lee offered him the letters.[57]) Bache accused Wolcott and Pickering of "detaining property not belonging to them," being "enemies of the best interests of his country," going "not only without law, but against the law," and taking it upon themselves "to violate and injure the rights and character of the Editor," all the while being "creatures of the executive, subject to his will and pleasure." Underlying all of this was a valid legal claim: "The letter directed to the Editor was his property: What right had Oliver Wolcott to receive it? and then to send it to a third person?"[58]

The next day, June 26, Bache was arrested at the order of Pickering.[59] He was taken to the chambers of Judge Richard Peters of the United States District Court in Philadelphia, to set a day for Bache to post a recognizance bond assuring that he would appear during the next United States Circuit Court. Court records of the United States Supreme Court show Bache's federal prosecution in the Circuit Court (where, twice a year, a Supreme Court justice would join the local District Court judge to hear cases), and they show his attorneys' attempt to block that prosecution by a motion filed in the Supreme Court.[60] However, the records of the lower courts do not fill in details about Bache's case for several reasons: they are incomplete, largely because the federal courts closed soon after in response to a yellow fever epidemic, and then Bache died of yellow fever before the next scheduled session of the Circuit Court.[61] Some details can be filled in from the extensive newspaper coverage of Bache's case, both in his own *Aurora* and in Federalist newspapers.[62]

The charge against Bache was "libelling the President & the Executive Government, in a manner tending to excite sedition and opposition to the laws, by sundry publication and re-publication." That seditious libel charge was made under common law; the final version of the sedition bill was not introduced until that same day, and it was not signed into law for nearly three weeks. Judge Peters released Bache on bond until a hearing three days later. Bache quickly published a statement that a federal prosecution could not occur under the common law for seditious libel "according to the recent opinion of Judge Chase," and that the editor trusted that "the ultimate decision will turn not on the right of jurisdiction, but on the Liberty of the Press." What Bache referred to, a recent opinion of Justice Samuel Chase of the United States Supreme Court (while sitting on a Circuit Court), stated that "the *United States,* as a Federal government, have no common law."[63] Unfortunately, the other judge sitting on the Circuit Court had disagreed, and that was Judge Peters.

Bache used the time until the hearing to tweak the noses of his opponents, and to print a pamphlet that began with the statement that "[a] free press is a most formidable engine to tyrants of every description," and contrasted that with the administration determining "to enlist this country on the side of despotism and then to pass alien, treason and sedition bills."[64]

At the hearing on June 29, Bache's attorneys argued *"that the Federal Courts had no common law jurisdiction in criminal cases,"* citing Justice Chase's opinion. Judge Peters said that he continued to disagree. The issue whether the court had jurisdiction over this common law prosecution for seditious libel would have to be resolved by a higher court, and Bache's counsel said they needed time to brief the issue and to seek state court remedies. Peters confirmed that if Bache agreed to a recognizance bond to ensure his attendance at the upcoming session, he "wa[i]ved no right of exception to the jurisdiction of the Federal Court." The judge then required "security in 2000 dollars himself, with two sureties in 1000 dollars each," for his appearance at the future session, in lieu of Bache being held in jail. The amount was quite high—the maximum fine for seditious libel would soon be $2,000 under the Sedition Act—but it was immediately paid. The *Gazette of the United States* sniped that the bail was paid by a tobacconist and a tavern-keeper, with a hatter standing by; "a *farrago* of such pure, genuine jacobinical, democratical spirits."[65]

In August, Bache's attorneys filed the promised motion in the United States Supreme Court for a writ of prohibition against consideration of the case by the Circuit Court in its October session in Philadelphia.[66] The basis presumably was lack of federal court jurisdiction over common law crimes.

The yellow fever epidemic in Philadelphia began in early August, and it was more serious than in recent years. Bache remained in town to keep the *Aurora* running, even as federal offices were moved and most residents who could fled. Bache did not survive to be vindicated in court, as he hoped; he died of yellow fever on September 10, 1798. His rival, John Fenno of the *Gazette of the United States,* died four days later, from the same cause. The Supreme Court's docket said that Bache's appeal was "Abated by Death of the defendant."[67]

Bache was gone, but the *Aurora* was not. Margaret Bache announced that it would continue, and confirmed that Bache's most qualified assistant, William Duane, would edit the paper. After nearly a two month gap, the *Aurora* resumed publication on the first of November 1798, and announced that it would follow Bache's dying wish, "that his paper should be continued with inflexible fidelity to the principles upon which it was founded."[68] To the chagrin of the Adams administration, his wish came true and the *Aurora* continued to be the leading Republican newspaper through the rest of the period of the Alien and Sedition Acts and into the nineteenth century. Jefferson, who never seems to have tried to discourage the *Aurora*'s vituperation, later noted that the paper "has unquestionably rendered incalculable services to republicanism thro' all it's struggles with the federalists." Fenno, whose Federalist paper mirrored the *Aurora*'s virulent personal attacks, had recently postulated that "[i]f Bache is ever exalted, it will be to the station of Prometheus, where the excruciating vulture of public scorn . . . will amply punish the disgrace and injuries heaped on his country, by the venality, perfidy and malice of a base and unnatural miscreant."[69] Each pointed to central characteristics of Bache. As a courageous editor, he and his *Aurora* were vital parts of the rise and success of an opposition party, providing news and opinion that was reprinted by Republican newspapers throughout the country and challenging nearly every action of the Federalist administrations. At the same time, Bache and his *Aurora* lowered the already low standards against personal attacks, which many Federalist papers matched, and calumniated the good as well as the bad of the Federalist Party.

Bache's Broad Understanding of Freedoms of Press and Speech

The prosecution focused Bache's mind on freedoms of press and speech, and on the threats posed by the pending sedition bill and the just enacted Alien Friends Act. The *Aurora* stepped up its coverage of those issues to a near-daily basis. The sedition bill violated the First Amendment prohibition on "*abridging the freedom of speech nor of the press.*"[70] The Alien Act's dangers were that "personal liberty is subject to the caprice of an individual," the president, and that a "system of espionage" would further infringe liberty.[71] Two days after the Sedition Act was signed into law, Bache addressed that act and his prosecution, and the rights of the people in a republican government, including their First Amendment rights in particular. Alluding to the Declaration of Independence, he wrote that "government is instituted for the benefit of the people," and it is "the sworn duty of the administration to protect" the rights of the people. Yet "[t]he efforts of the administration seem to protect themselves." "One of the first rights of a freeman is to speak or to publish his sentiments; if any government founded upon the will of the people passes any ordinance to abridge this right, it is as much a crime. . . ." The stream continued of articles disapproving of the Sedition Act.[72]

It is no surprise that everyone prosecuted for seditious libel advocated an expansive view of freedoms of press and speech after they were indicted. Did that broad view first appear in 1798, or had the newspaper editors and other defendants expressed it in prior years? For the first couple of years after founding the *General Advertiser,* Bache was as moderate in his comments on freedom of press and speech as he was on national politics generally. His announcement in the first issue extolled *"freedom of the press"* as *"the bulwark of liberty,"* and he periodically mentioned rationales for that freedom, such as that the press protects freedom by restraining arbitrary government and checking corrupt officials, and informs the public and its voting.[73] The *Aurora* intermittently addressed problematic aspects of seditious libel in those early years. "No man can tell what is and what is not a libel," or "how far the fair liberty of the press extends, and where the abuse of it begins." Further, treatment of true statements as criminal libels was absurd, and allowing conviction without proof of criminal intent was wrong.[74]

The *Aurora* began to proclaim a broader understanding of freedoms of press and speech as it began to advocate a radical viewpoint generally.[75] It started to emphasize that "[p]ublic men are all amenable to the tribunal of the press in a free state," through "public investigation of their conduct" and public reproach where deserved. It began to note that public officials were protected by the same laws as everyone else that prohibited defamation and authorized private libel actions, and to question "why screen them from censure" and prosecute as a crime the "censure [of] the misconduct of their Servants?" By late 1793–1794, Bache also became more explicit about "discussions concerning public men or measures" being grounded on "liberty of the Press," and (in a reprinted article) about the right "to censure the most exalted Patrician" whose measures were "inimical to the public weal" as part of "freedom of enquiry through the medium of an unrestrained press."[76] During the furor over Calm Observer's claims about Washington's compensation in late 1795, the *Aurora* printed a letter saying that Wolcott's threat to prosecute Bache for seditious libel amounted to "threatening the liberty of the press," and Bache equated the right to publish "strictures upon men high in office" with "a free press," which was the palladium of all rights. Other burdens such as a tax on newspapers similarly violated liberty of the press, though seditious libel was the most common threat.[77]

As a congressional committee proposed the first version of the sedition bill in early June 1798, Bache printed the First Amendment immediately before printing the bill, clearly implying that he found freedom of press and speech contradictory to the bill's criminalization of seditious libel. (The bill prohibited any alien or citizen "by any writing, printing, or advised speaking" threatening any "officer, or person in public trust, with any damage to his character, person, or property," among other things.) By mid-June, Bache became more explicit and warned that the bill would "propose to deprive us of the freedom of thinking, *speaking* and *writing,* and that for the sake of not checking the officers of government, in a career that threatens this country with ruin."[78]

Shortly before that in February 1798, Bache had condemned restrictions on newspaper reporting of congressional debates as an attempt "to muzzle the press." The restriction ordered by the speaker of the House, Jonathan Dayton, required newspapers to limit reporting of an altercation between Federalist Rep. Roger Griswold and Republican Rep. Matthew Lyon to the wording used in the House's journal (controlled by Federalists). When the speaker said newspaper reporting was a matter of mere privilege, which could be revoked, Bache insisted that it was "a right" when the chamber was not in closed session.[79] Because Bache refused to limit reporting to officially approved wording, he was barred from the House floor, where reporters could hear far better than in the public gallery, and he was relegated to the gallery for the rest of his career. In the same article, Bache charged Dayton with "conduct to prevent the freedom of speech" by working to suppress Democratic-Republican Societies and by failing to call for order and to protect Lyon when Griswold attacked him with a hickory cane. Four months later, Bache described his banishment from the House floor for "asserting the freedom of his press against the arbitrary mandate of the Speaker" as a tyrannic act "[t]o injure his press and to prevent a free and firm statement of the proceedings from meeting the public eye."[80]

In all this, Bache was advocating, at first in small strokes and then in large strokes, the position on freedoms of press and speech that the Republican Party asserted in late 1798: that those freedoms allowed censure of government, its measures, and its officials, and that they were not confined to narrow meanings such as merely prohibiting prior restraints, but were infringed by any sort of substantial restraint on the press or speech.

John Daly Burk and James Smith and the New York *Time Piece*

John Daly Burk (c.1776–1808), like Bache, was a radical, who with Dr. James Smith edited the most outspoken Republican newspaper in New York City during 1797–1798.[81] Burk had started college studies at University of Dublin, but had been expelled for "Atheism and Antechristianism" (a charge he disputed).[82] His arrival in the United States in the mid-1790s was heralded by a newspaper account that placed a target on his back:

> Papers by the Franklin Capt. McLellan, from Dublin, bring intelligence of a formidable and extensive conspiracy, to separate that country from England, and establish a republican form of government in conjunction with the French government. . . .
>
> Mr. John Burk, the chief of this conspiracy and the one who was to manage the attack in the capital, after many hair breadth escapes, during the space of four months, had the good fortune to get on board the Franklin, and in her arrived at this point.

That 1796 article went on to say he had attempted "Republicanising the University" of Dublin, and was expelled for "inculcating Deistical principles"; he "formed a chain of Democratical Societies" in Ireland, and "opened an intercourse with the government of France" (which was at war with Britain). He studied law but could not be licensed to practice "in consequence of his notoriety in politics."[83]

As extraordinary as that newspaper account sounded, it was substantially true, though Burk was barely twenty years of age when he arrived. Burk himself wrote, three years later, that he was charged with the crime of sedition, as "the reputed projector of this conspiracy," and was forced "instantly to leave Ireland."[84] Though some accounts say that all he did was join other students in undertaking to rescue an Irishman being marched to his death, newer studies find that Burk had been part of "a revolutionary cell within the United Irish movement," with Dr. James Reynolds, and had established secret societies that "plotted insurrection" against British rule.[85] Because of a spy in Burk's cell, some of its ten members were convicted and executed, and Burk, also charged with high treason, fled to America. His background did not go unnoticed; Abigail Adams referred to him as "a banished Irishman of Revolutionary principles," a year later.[86]

Soon after arriving in Boston, Burk established a newspaper, the *Polar Star* (probably named after the United Irishmen's *Northern Star*), which lasted a half year until early 1797. He wrote two plays, *Bunker-Hill,* which was highly successful when staged in 1797, and *Female Patriotism,* which was so spectacularly unsuccessful that it was cancelled after opening night in early 1798.[87] After the *Polar Star* failed and the successful play moved to New York City, Burk moved as well in mid-1797. He started writing two other plays and an epic poem, *The Columbiad,* that was so insufferable that it was never published, other than in excerpts in his newspaper that were brief enough not to be lethal to subscribers.[88]

Dr. James Smith (1738–1812), a physician, was with Bache one of the few affluent and well-educated defendants in seditious libel prosecutions during the crisis years of 1798–1801.[89] He graduated from the College of New Jersey (Princeton) in 1757, and completed his medical studies in Leyden in 1764. He was the "first professor of chemistry and materia medica at King's College" (later Columbia) from 1767–1770, before wandering abroad. Smith was described by former judge Robert Troup of the United States District Court, days after the 1798 prosecution was filed, as "an elderly man" formerly "connected with Ld. G. Gordon in his famous riots," and "a brother of the famous Wm. Smith, late Chief Justice of Canada" (of Quebec).[90]

That description is accurate. His brother indeed was William Smith, Jr., a loyalist during the American Revolution who resettled in Quebec and became its chief justice. Their father was William Smith, Sr., a wealthy lawyer and later New York justice, whose most famous case was defending John Peter Zenger against seditious libel charges (until being disbarred by the colonial court).[91] Dr. Smith was involved in the Gordon Riots in 1780 in England, during the Revolutionary War, as a letter shows that he wrote that year to John Jay, the American minister to Spain. In the letter, Smith claimed to be a spy for America, during his "long residence in England" carrying on "secret correspondence" to give "intelligence of the sailing and destination of their Fleets," endeavoring "to impede the progress of their arms by dividing the people from the Government," and causing "the flames of discontent to spread" with the war. An "Order of the privy council was issued to apprehend me as the Cataline of the conspiracy and secret Agent of Doctor Franklin to Burn the City," and Smith was taken into custody but then was temporarily released, enabling him to flee to Brussels and then to America.[92] In striking contrast, John Adams, an envoy to France, suspected that Smith was "a Spy both upon the Americans and the French," and added that Smith "gave Dr. Franklin a great deal of Vexation." As is apparent, Adams did not like Dr. Smith, calling his wife "a most perfect Antithesis to beauty in the face and to Elegance in Person"—and "infinitely too good for him." Smith later claimed to have written three pamphlets supporting America while in London.[93]

The Leading Opposition Newspaper in the Second Largest City

Burk began to edit an existing New York City newspaper, the *Time Piece,* in partnership with Dr. Smith, on April 11, 1798, and they became its owners by the June 15 issue (which added that it was printed for "the proprietors").[94] The paper had been founded by another ardent Republican, Philip Freneau, who earlier founded the *National Gazette.* Burk's and Smith's financial backer was a subject of curiosity, and former judge Robert Troup stated the most common assumption: Aaron "Burr is much suspected to be interested in the press. It is confidently said he was security for the purchase money of the press." The judge was likely right, because the previous owner Matthew L. Davis was a Burr protege, and Burk lacked funds for the purchase. A year earlier Burk had dedicated his successful play to Aaron Burr, and four days before Troup's letter one of the two sureties for Burk's bond was Burr, who Burk later described as "a friend & a father."[95]

Under Burk and Smith, the *Time Piece* was "by far the most radical newspaper in the city," and one of only two Republican newspapers there. Burk was much like Bache, a child of the enlightenment, who fulminated against aristocracy, believed the French Revolution to be an epochal advance, proclaimed "that the British treaty alone is the cause of all the evils we now suffer," and defended France when the XYZ Affair came to light.[96]

Soon, rumors swirled, which Burk tried to counter on June 27, that he had said "he wished this country invaded by France." Burk called it "so villainous a falsehood."[97] Then, Themistocles, in an article in the rival *Commercial Advertiser,* claimed to have heard Burk welcome the news "that the French had effected their landing in Ireland," and heard Burk add "that he would not give a damn for the Federal villains in this country—that he believed the French would come here, and he wished to God they would, when every scoundrel in favor of this government would be put to the guillotine." Themistocles then quoted a *Time Piece* editorial from six days before that called the president a "mock Monarch." The article was quickly reprinted by other New York papers, and was excerpted by the *Gazette of the United States* and the *Aurora* in Philadelphia, followed by reprints elsewhere.[98]

Burk responded with affidavits from himself and his printer conceding that he had hoped the news was true about the French liberating Ireland, but assuring that it was "the farthest from his thoughts" to hope that the French would invade America. Both affidavits added that if the news was true, "there would be no necessity to put in force the alien and seditious bill against him," because, as the employee said, with Ireland freed "he would go out of the country of his own accord." Burk understood that he was one of the targets of the Alien and Sedition Acts. A few days later, a different sworn statement was sent by a merchant, Stephen Wendover, to Timothy Pickering, saying that he heard Burk say what Themistocles reported—and that Burk was an alien.[99]

Burk seemed to confirm Themistocles's allegations by having the *Time Piece* report that "Citizen *John D. Burk*" chaired "a large and respectable meeting of United Irishmen" in New York City to commemorate the fourth of July. Burk listed toasts, among others, condemning the Alien Act (the Sedition Act had not yet been enacted), calling for a "*Fourth* and *Fourteenth* of July to Ireland" that "[w]e will die to atchieve," and praising the "American, French," and other republics. The article seemed to confirm the existence of an American organization of United Irishmen, and the toasts appeared to confirm Federalist fears that American members were ready to fight for foreign revolution and in support of French invaders. Burk continued to publish notices that seemed to show a domestic organization of United Irishmen, with himself in the thick of it, such as in the final issue of the *Time Piece* on August 30, 1798: "The United Irishmen of New-York, congratulate their Brethren in Philadelphia and Elsewhere; on the Irish Revolution."[100]

The same day that Burk tried to counter rumors about what he had said, on June 27, he published an essay on monarchs under the title "Extract from Junius' Letters" (though it was not actually one of Junius's letters from the early 1770s). The essay said that monarchs perpetrate crimes and are villains, and it was there that Burk called the president a "mock Monarch," who attempted "to extinguish the sentiment of liberty" and was "without patriotism," and who had a "court composed of tories and speculators," deserving "execration" as well as contempt.[101] On July 2 (the day before Themistocles appeared in the *Commercial Advertiser*), Burk printed a short commentary on Elbridge Gerry's letter to the president from France, where Gerry remained when the other two envoys returned after the XYZ Affair, and alleged that the copy that Adams forwarded to Congress was in part a forgery. In the same issue of the *Time Piece,* Burk reported "that T. Pickering and William Cobbett, have been closetted together for the purpose of organizing a system of *Espionage,*" and, tempting fate, Burk strongly implied that Pickering had poisoned a United Irishman named Mitchell.[102] Three days later, Rep. John Allen quoted the "mock Monarch" passage as the House of Representatives considered the sedition bill,[103] and the next day, it became part of the charges against Burk and Smith.

Arrest for a "Wicked, False and Malicious Libel"

Burk and Smith were arrested on July 6, 1798, and they were taken by the federal marshals to Judge John Sloss Hobart of the United States District Court.[104] The case was a single case prosecuting both of them. The arrest warrant was based on two affidavits. The affidavit of Joseph C. Cooper said that he bought the July 2 issue of the *Time Piece* at its office, and was sent a copy by James Smith, its proprietor along with John Burk. The affidavit of Stephen Wendover said that the Themistocles article appeared in the *Commercial Advertiser* and that he heard Burk make the statements Themistocles quoted. (Wendover evidently was that pseudonymous writer.)[105] The prosecution was based on three counts of seditious libel: "publishing a wicked, false and malicious libel upon the President," publishing "a wicked, false and malicious libel on Timothy Pickering Secretary of State," both "on the second day of July" in the *Time Piece,* and "uttering certain seditious expressions."[106]

The judge set bail at $4,000 each for Burk and Smith, to assure their appearance at the United States Circuit Court for trial in September. Each of them signed recognizance bonds for half that amount and sureties signed bonds for half. Burk's sureties were Col. Henry Rutgers along with Aaron Burr (leading Republicans) while Smith's were family members.[107] The United States attorney for New York, Richard Harison, probably had received informal instructions before the arrest on July 6, because only on July 7 did the secretary of state, Timothy Pickering, send formal instructions to him to prosecute Burk (without mention of Smith).

Pickering's instruction letter enclosed the July 2 issue of the *Time Piece,* with its "false & inflamatory charge" that the president had sent Congress a copy of Gerry's letter with "alterations in it to promote certain ends in this country." Pickering pointed Harison to Themistocles's article in the *Commercial Advertiser* about a "treasonable speech of Burke," and he instructed Harison to examine other issues of the *Time Piece* for "those of a similar seditious tendency." The secretary of state then told Harison to prosecute Burk for sedition, after which the editor would be "sent away" under the Alien Act. Pickering explained that the *Time Piece* was "a vehicle of the most profuse and attrocious slander, of the Government, & a ready instrument of sedition," and that its libels should be prosecuted if the United States attorney found them contrary to the law, even if "Burke should prove to be an Alien." After that, "[i]f Burke be an Alien, no man is a fitter object for the operation of the Alien Act."[108]

The pressure of the prosecution was too great for Burk's and Smith's partnership and for their newspaper. They fell out in mid-July, though there is probably not more than a grain of truth in a Federalist paper's colorful account. It recounted that Burk was about to include in the *Time Piece* another "most violent invective against the President," when Dr. Smith refused to see it printed, saying it went "too far and would even work a forfeiture of their recognizance" (they would each lose $2,000). Burk was said to have "called Smith a paltry old woman" and "a driveling old p—s Doctor," and Smith was said to have called him "a damn'd rascal, and an unprincipled *alien,*" before each began lobbing fistfuls of ink-covered type at each other.[109] Burk and Smith each claimed to be defamed but did not deny their falling out. Burk published a notice that the partnership was dissolved and subscription payments should be made to him, and Smith published a notice that the paper would not publish any libelous matter and that he would not be answerable for any debts Burk incurred for the paper.[110]

Smith's notice that the *Time Piece* would not publish any criticism of the administration is one of many examples of the chilling effect of a threatened prosecution against exercising freedoms of press and speech. That chilling effect soon became a freeze. The *Time Piece* closed its doors after its August 30, 1798 issue, with Burk publishing advertisements elsewhere urging Smith to come to the negotiating table and resume publication (and expressing his "resentment and indignation"), and Smith steadfastly refusing to run up more debts or risk more prosecutions.[111] The end of the newspaper probably made a settlement possible with the prosecutors, just as it did with Ann Greenleaf a year and a half later.

As the United States Circuit Court opened its session in New York on September 1, 1798, the yellow fever epidemic intervened in a different way from its intervention in Philadelphia, where Bache died. All twenty-four men who received summons to appear as grand jurors failed to show up, so the court could not indict Burk and Smith, and Justice William Paterson and Judge John Sloss Hobart quickly ended the session. Burk and Smith also failed to show up, as did William Durell, the editor of the Mount Pleasant *Register,* who faced similar charges.[112] The court's next session, in April 1799, could not proceed either, because no Supreme Court justice showed up. Burk and Smith were lucky that the April 1799 session fell through, because the justice assigned to it was Justice Samuel Chase, the most harsh enforcer of the Sedition Act, who was ill. The panel at the following session would be Paterson and Hobart again.[113] The clerk of court assured Pickering that the United States attorney's intention was "to have him [Burk] indicted, if possible, at the next Circuit Court, with a view to a prosecution in case he should hereafter appear within the United States."[114]

At the Circuit Court's following session, on September 4, 1799, Burk and Smith were indicted by the grand jury, almost certainly under the Sedition Act. The indictment was summarized in the court's minutes:

> An Indictment against the Defendants for having on the second day of July in the Twenty second year of the Independence of the United States at the City of New York in the New York District wickedly maliciously and unlawfully printed and published and caused and procured to be printed and published a certain false scandalous and malicious Libel of and concerning John Adams then and now President of the United States in a certain Newspaper called "The Time Piece" and also for having afterwards to wit, on the same second day of July in the same Twenty second year of the Independence of the said United States at the said City of New York in the said New York District wickedly maliciously and unlawfully printed and published and caused and procured to be printed and published in a certain other newspaper called "The Time Piece" a certain other false wicked scandalous and malicious libel of and concerning the said John Adams then and now President of the said United States.[115]

That first ground was the July 2 newspaper saying the Gerry letter sent to Congress was a forgery. It is likely that the second ground meant delivering on July 2 ("publish[ing]") a copy of the June 26 newspaper with the "mock Monarch" language ("a certain other newspaper"). Those were the topics of the two affidavits in the court file that supported the arrest warrant, and the person signing the affidavit about the "mock Monarch" statement had been summoned to the court that day to testify.[116]

All sources on the Sedition Act treat Burk's and Smith's case as only a common law prosecution, not one that ever became a Sedition Act prosecution, but none of those writings cites the court's minutes for September 1799. The minutes for September 4 show that, after a brief unrelated case, the grand jury handed down four indictments: *United States v. Ann Greenleaf, United States v. Jedediah Peck, United States v. William Durell,* and *United States v. James Smith and John D. Burk.* The first and second have always been understood to be under the Sedition Act, and the third and fourth were summarized in very similar language by the court's minutes (the actual indictment of Burk and Smith is not in the court record). Further, the original count for publishing "a wicked, false and malicious libel on Timothy Pickering Secretary of State" was dropped, because though that was a potential violation of the common law crime of seditious libel, it was not a violation of the Sedition Act. Thus, though Burk and Smith were originally arrested under the common law of seditious libel, they were later indicted under the Sedition Act. And if the objective of the case was "to try the force of government in protecting the character and conduct of its officers from the ribaldry and abuse uttered against them in certain papers," as Robert Troup wrote,[117] one would expect the indictment to be on the strongest basis for success, the Sedition Act rather than the common law.

Between the 1798 and 1799 sessions of the Circuit Court, a settlement for Burk was proposed by him to his surety and friend, Aaron Burr, which Burr then negotiated with the prosecutor. Burk's reason was that he was certain to lose the case "from the violence of party spirit and the mode of packing Juries," and even if he miraculously won, "as an alien I was still at the mercy of the President." Pickering got the president's approval, and then authorized the United States attorney "to let him off, on the condition . . . that he Burke forthwith quit the United States" in a specified ship, though they would "keep the prosecution . . . in a state to be resumed, in case he should violate the terms." Pickering was emphatic that "[s]uch a turbulent mischievous person ought not to remain on this side the Atlantic," and was worried that Burk would go to Spanish Florida or Louisiana.[118] Burk apparently agreed to sail to France, his purpose being to "work for another invasion of Ireland."[119] At that point, the case was dismissed (by filing a nolle prosequi). However, five months later, Pickering was alarmed to receive a letter from Burk saying he was traveling via Charleston to Spanish New Orleans. Pickering warned the governor of the neighboring Mississippi Territory to watch for this "turbulent, dangerous man" who had "published some villainous libels against the President," and to alert the Spanish authorities. Pickering also had a clerk arrange for copies of the indictment and the minutes to be sent to the governor of the Mississippi Territory, so that if Burk left New Orleans "he may be again arrested upon the indictment" before "his seditious inclinations may operate."[120] That is why, as the clerk of court told Pickering, a new indictment of Burk was arranged by the Circuit Court in September 1799.

After entering that settlement of his case, Burk went not to France or to Spanish territory but to Virginia, where he lived in hiding under an alias until the Alien Act expired at the end of the day on June 24, 1800 and until the Sedition Act expired on March 3, 1801 just before Jefferson took the presidential oath. Burk's explanation to Jefferson, in June 1801, was that he feared being seized and executed by Britain, claiming "an actual attempt to seize me" and "well founded apprehensions that I was watched by the Spies of the British minister."[121] Ironically, Burk's success in hiding in Virginia was probably because of Federalist newspapers, which had reported that "*Burke,* the United Irishman, has left the country," and that "the infamous Burke, who was expelled [from] the college of Dublin for blasphemy," was "hanged at Ennis" in Ireland.[122] After it was safe to leave hiding, Burk became the principal of a new college, a practicing attorney, and a citizen once the Naturalization Act was replaced in 1802. He gave Republican orations, wrote other plays and a lengthy *History of Virginia*, and gave a formal dinner when Aaron Burr came through Petersburg. Burk died in a duel in April 1808.[123]

Dr. Smith, by contrast, was not blessed with a settlement. He pled not guilty the day after he was indicted, and the next day was ordered to appear at the April 1800 session. In effect, he had to show up at each biannual session of the Circuit Court after September 1798 through April 1800, in order not to be jailed and not to have his recognizance bonds collected; but each time there was no trial.[124] It is hard to see the later delays as anything but an effort to coerce him not to resume the *Time Piece* or other Republican writing. Governmental intimidation is clear when two things are compared: the rush to arrest Burk and Smith, which could not wait eight days until the pending Sedition Act was passed, and the sluggishness in negotiating and enforcing Burk's settlement and in proceeding with Smith's trial. The major objective had been accomplished—shutting down the *Time Piece* and its editors.

That is exactly what one critic soon alleged. John Wood said that the "Time-Piece was, in consequence, dropped, and this being the point which Mr. Adams wished to accomplish, the trial of Dr. Smith was never brought forward." Adams, from retirement, complained that in 1800 Dr. Smith "furnished Mr. Wood in New York with a part of the Billingsgate which composed his History."[125]

Burk's Expansive Understanding of Freedoms of Press and Speech

Burk's and Smith's immediate response to their arrest on July 6, 1798 was to reprint the Declaration of Independence in the next issue of the *Time Piece* and then to reprint the Bill of Rights in the following issue, placing it immediately after a report on congressional debate on the sedition bill and immediately before a letter saying the sedition bill violated the First Amendment.[126] They reiterated in the next four issues that "extinguishment is now the order of the day" for "freedom, of speech, and liberty of the press," that (as a toast said) the Constitution needed protection "against unconstitutional laws . . . and the reign of terror," that (quoting the words of the First Amendment) freedoms of speech and press were endangered, and that the Sedition Act is "an unconstitutional law." They reprinted an *Aurora* comment that "Congress infracted the Constitution, by *abridging the freedom of speech and of the press,*" and they published poems against the Alien Act (one ended by urging noncitizens to embark to where "liberty is not a crime").[127]

They also argued that seditious libel was inconsistent with freedom of press, indirectly by saying in an editorial that there was only "partial liberty of the English press," and then directly in a lengthy excerpt from a book discussing "the absurdity of the theory" of seditious libel because "no punishment can justly be awarded against any writing or words derogatory to religion or political government." That excerpt reasoned that "that which will stand the test of examination, cannot need the support of penal statutes," and that the penal statutes were simply "a continual instrument of usurpation and injustice [by] the ruling party" in place of allowing truth to battle misrepresentation. "Libels against public establishments and measures . . . ought to pass unpunished," and the sole exception should be if their "avowed intention . . . is to lead to immediate violence."[128] In addition, throughout the two weeks after Burk and Smith were arrested, every issue contained an article or squib extolling freedoms of press and speech, and an excerpt from a leading Irish radical lawyer's "defence of the Liberty of the Press."[129]

It is unsurprising that the editors argued for an expansive understanding of freedoms of press and speech after being arrested, but it turns out that they, like Bache, also argued for that expansive view long before their prosecution. Burk in 1794, in his account of his college trial, proclaimed his "liberty of speech," paired that with "freedom of enquiry and discussion," and condemned their denial by "worthy children of the tenth century" practicing persecution. During his half year with the *Polar Star,* in 1796, Burk reprinted that freedom of speech passage and printed a critique of British Tories who could *"with coolness see [themselves] deprived of the liberty of speech,"* and equally could see freedom of press destroyed *"without exertion"* in its defense. A month later, Burk darkly predicted an approaching time when "liberty of the press is invaded" by oligarchs who "have in all ages been the mortal enemies of all literary freedom," and added that oligarchs did so by twisting any defense of liberty so it "is construed by these men into a libel."[130] As he and Dr. Smith assumed editorial control of the *Time Piece,* they placed a prominent statement at the top of the first page saying that the paper would be "wholly Republican" and would not support "a government of Terror, in efforts to suppress the liberty of speech and the press." The statement, which they reprinted in the next seven issues as well, claimed the liberty and duty to "hold up to public abhorrence those who attempt to violate it" (liberty of speech and the press).[131]

As the sedition bill was under consideration in June 1798, Burk said that its sponsor "wished to punish the people for *speaking* or *thinking*" and was "guilty of something like *treason*" against the Constitution. Burk attacked criminalizing seditious libel, objecting that to disagree with the chief magistrate "would be sedition," and asking "[i]s it Sedition to say the President is incorrect in a part of History?"[132] In early July as soon as he heard of Bache's arrest, before his own arrest, Burk printed a proposal to raise funds to assist him, calling Bache a "defender of the Liberty of the press." He asserted the "freedom of speech" to condemn "public mischief," and to have magistrates' "deeds openly examined, and publicly scanned." Burk and Smith kept up a constant drumbeat that unrestricted broad freedoms of press and speech are critical to liberty, in the weeks before their arrest,[133] and ended on the fourth of July with the famous opening of one of *Cato's Letters* on the natural right of freedom of speech (including freedom of press):

> Without freedom of thought, there can be no such thing as wisdom; and no such thing as public liberty, without freedom of speech; which is the right of every man, as far as by it he does not hurt and controul the right of another; and this is the only check which it ought to suffer, the only bounds which it ought to know.
>
> . . . . Whoever would overthrow the liberty of the nation, must begin by subduing the liberty of speech; a thing terrible to public traitors.[134]

William Durell and the *Mount Pleasant Register*

William Durell, editor of the *Mount Pleasant Register,* reprinted another newspaper's article on June 19, 1798, before the sedition bill was even introduced in Congress. Timothy Pickering issued instructions to prosecute him on June 28, two days after the bill was introduced. The arrest warrant was issued on July 17, three days after the Sedition Act was signed by the president, but almost certainly before a copy of the new law reached the United States attorney in New York.[135] With prosecutions against "two New York presses" as well as the *Aurora,* Republican newspapers warned of "The System of Terror."[136] Thus, Durell initially was prosecuted under the common law of seditious libel. Like Burk and Smith, Durell's prosecution, after beginning under the common law, was converted to a Sedition Act prosecution at the time Pickering reinvigorated old prosecutions and pressed for new ones, during the summer and fall of 1799.

Thus, three cases against four individuals were filed in federal courts under the common law of seditious libel—those of Benjamin Franklin Bache, John Daly Burk and Dr. James Smith, and William Durell. All but the last were begun days before the Sedition Act was enacted, and all but the first were later reindicted as prosecutions under the Sedition Act. All were specifically authorized by Timothy Pickering, the secretary of state in the Adams administration, and it does not appear to be coincidental that the first two cases were filed against the editors of the leading Republican newspapers in the nation's two largest cities. In a pattern that would be followed nearly everywhere, the prosecutions were only of Republican newspapers or speakers, and were pursued until the opposition paper or activity was closed down, or until the individual died, or otherwise until the government won at trial. In the years before, as well as during the prosecutions, these newspaper editors advocated an expansive view of freedoms of press and speech, and they understood those freedoms to protect criticism of public officials and of public measures. As the leading opposition newspapers were prosecuted, the editors immediately realized that a battle was underway over the First Amendment.

CHAPTER FOUR

Targeting Opposition Members of Congress

THE HOUSE OF Representatives was closely divided between the Federalists and the Republicans in 1798. The Republicans had been numerous enough to block most defense legislation during 1797. The future speaker of the house, in April 1798, said that the "house is almost exactly divided—there are 52 determined and rancorous Jacobins, and 54 who profess attachment to the government." In the next few months, the Alien Friends Act passed the House with a narrow 46–40 vote, and the Sedition Act was even closer with a 44–41 vote,[1] and that only because several Republicans left the capitol early.

Shoring up the Federalist majority by expelling two Republican members of the House was a tempting idea. Federalist Rep. John Allen struggled with that temptation when he said that "I believe there are men in this country, in this House, whose hatred and abhorrence of our Government leads them to prefer another" (France). Republican congressman Albert Gallatin, speaking against the sedition bill, warned that "the true object of the law is to enable one party to oppress the other."[2]

The first person brought to trial under the Sedition Act, in October 1798, was Republican Rep. Matthew Lyon of Vermont (though he was not the first person indicted under the law). An attempt to prosecute another member of Congress was made that same month, as Secretary of State Timothy Pickering gave instructions to prosecute Republican congressman John Clopton of Virginia. Even the Republican clergyman who carried a petition

FIGURE 4.1. Matthew Lyon. Courtesy Fleming Museum of Art, University of Vermont, gift of Mr. and Mrs. Robert R. Canfield.

from Vermont citizens to President John Adams, asking him to pardon and release Lyon, was arrested and imprisoned four months later, under the pretext of an old and uncollectable debt.

Rep. Matthew Lyon and Denigrating the President

Matthew Lyon (1749–1822), like John Daly Burk, Dr. James Reynolds, and William Duane, was one of what many Federalists reviled as the "wild Irish," and was a systematic challenger of the hierarchical society of eighteenth-century America. Lyon was well described by his leading biographer, Aleine Austin, as an "example of the self-made man who embraced the politics of democracy while challenging the control exercised by the social and economic elite."[3] He fled an apprenticeship under a printer in Ireland when he was fifteen years old, and he paid for his passage to America by becoming an indentured laborer for a period. His master exchanged his remaining indenture term for two stags.

Soon after his service ended, Lyon purchased property and moved to the Hampshire Grants, an area of clouded land titles that both New Hampshire and New York claimed and sold, even after the Privy Council upheld New York's colonial title. That brought a continuing risk that New York's "aristocrats" would enforce their claims, and continuing vigilance against that by the Green Mountain Boys. Lyon became a member and a colonel, and he participated in their victories at Fort Ticonderoga and Crown Point at the beginning of the Revolutionary War. He then enlisted in the Continental Army as a second lieutenant and was in service during the victory at Saratoga, resigning afterwards to become a colonel in the Vermont militia. He also participated in the new Vermont state government, and was not bashful about conflicts of interest in buying property confiscated from loyalists. He married the daughter of the first governor.[4]

Lyon was granted land and the right to establish the town of Fairhaven (sometimes called Fair Haven), on the west border of Vermont near New York, and he and his family relocated there in 1783. He built a tavern, lumber and paper mills, and ironworks.[5]

Lyon also established a Republican newspaper in 1793, named *Farmers' Library,* making his son James the editor.[6] His primary reason was to bolster his quest for a seat in the federal House of Representatives after unsuccessful efforts in 1791 and 1792. After failing again in the 1794 election, his quest finally succeeded in 1796, and he largely won by newspaper. Early on, Lyon was an outspoken Republican, seeking "to emancipate this country from the domination of a set of men," the "aristocracy" (meaning Federalists, especially those running Vermont), while championing the "RIGHTS of MAN."[7] During that time, he was also among the "strong supporters . . . if not active members" of the Democratic–Republican Societies, which arose to champion the French Revolution and democracy, before they withered away after criticism from President George Washington. The *Farmers' Library* newspaper gave extensive "coverage of the Vermont societies," and was the vehicle for notices of their meetings.[8] It also periodically printed articles by Lyon, which regularly condemned "aristocrats, who are every day strengthening the undue influence" of the Federalist majority, and that majority's efforts "to vie with European Courts in frivolous gaudy appearances," as well as taxes and debts, which in turn were "screwing the hard-earnings out of poor people's pockets" to pay "enormous salaries." The newspaper regularly supported the ultimate radical of the 1790s, Thomas Paine.[9]

In all of this, Lyon's press was the "most notorious" exception to "the general rule that printers in the mid-1790s Republican press . . . shied away from partisanship," as Jeffrey Pasley notes. That general rule resulted from a desire for revenue from advertisements and governmental printing. Lyon brought about another exception, as he became "the first former printer" to win a seat in Congress.[10]

Lyon suffered regular abuse starting as soon as he arrived in Washington to take his congressional seat. Peter Porcupine (editor William Cobbett) announced with fanfare,

> *TO-MORROW Morning at 11 o'clock, will be exposed to public view, The*
>
> LYON OF VERMONT!
>
> THIS singular animal is said to have been caught on the bog of Hibernia, and, when a whelp, transported to America; curiosity induced a New-Yorker to buy him, and moving into the country, afterwards exchanged him for a yoke of young bulls with a Vermontese. He was petted in the neighbourhood of governor Chittenden, and soon became so domesticated that a daughter of his excellency would stroke him and play with him as with a monkey.

Other articles referred to "Citizen Lyon" and, discussing his opposition stances, observed that "certain flies will at any time quit *a bed of roses* to alight on *an excrement.*"[11] Lyon's actions in Congress ensured that the abuse did not stay outside its walls. His first motion there was to remove the words "wisdom, dignity, and moderation" from the House's ritual response to the president's speech (the first one he ever heard), after John Adams opened Congress on May 23, 1797. Lyon quickly followed that with a motion to excuse the opposition from attending the ceremonial delivery of that formal response to the opening speech, because such pomp was "a boyish piece of business" and was "pageantry" that should be abolished.[12] He was all things that well-born Federalists despised: Irish, an indentured laborer, an ardent Republican, an opposition newspaper editor, and an iconoclast toward deferential social structure. In late January 1798, things went from bad to worse.

Lyon's fight in the House of Representatives with Roger Griswold, a Connecticut Federalist, changed him from the target of Federalist ridicule to the lasting target of Federalist wrath. As reported in Federalist newspapers, Lyon said that Connecticut Federalists did not represent "the wishes of their constituents," and that he had to fight them when they crossed the border into his own district, and could defeat them if he started a Republican newspaper in Connecticut. Griswold asked "whether he fought them with a wooden sword," and Lyon, snapping after months of mockery, responded by spitting at his face. What Griswold referred to was a Revolutionary War mutiny by Lyon's soldiers who moved their station to evade hostile Indians, contrary to their orders. For that, Lyon had been court-martialed and relieved of his command, and was compelled to carry a wooden sword—though the commanding general soon arranged his reengagement and later promoted Lyon.[13]

Immediately after the spitting incident, a motion to expel Lyon from Congress was made, and it was supported three days later by a Federalist-controlled committee. The House voted 52 to 44 to expel Lyon, but that fell short of the necessary two-thirds.[14] Three days after that vote failed to vindicate him, Griswold (in his own words) bought a hickory cane and "gave him the first blow—I call'd him a scoundrel & struck him with my cane, and pursued him with more than twenty blows on his head and back until he got possession of a pair of tongues" (fireplace tongs) to defend himself. A motion to expel both men was made, but with Griswold at risk, the Federalist committee report opposed expulsion, and the House followed its recommendation.[15] The debates on the issue consumed two weeks of the congressional session. Federalists focused on Lyon's improper fights with a social superior, violating the rules of honor that Joanne Freeman so well describes.[16] Pickering, the official who nine months later would authorize the Sedition Act prosecution of Lyon, condemned "the disgraceful act of Mr Lyon" in spitting at Griswold and then "having committed a new offence in striking Mr. Griswold" (apparently by Lyon wielding his head to attack Griswold's hickory cane). Abigail Adams decried "the Brutal conduct of that Wild Irishman Lyon" who "Spit in the face of a man whose shoes he was not worthy to clean." Fisher Ames was aghast at "this unspeakable brutality, committed on Griswold," apparently also seeing no brutality committed on Lyon.[17] Republicans, of course, saw it differently: "gladiator Griswold" made a surprise attack on "Lyon, an unarmed and aged man." Thomas Jefferson told James Madison why the issue was given so much legislative time: "to get rid of his vote was the most material object," since in the House "the majorities are of 1. 2. or 3. only." Lyon narrowed those majorities as he voted against the Alien and Sedition Acts.[18]

The Lyon-Griswold incident launched new waves of ridicule of the "spitting Irish Lyon" or "the Beast," and of his wooden sword:

> Not Hudibras's Steel so trusty
> Which lack of fighting had made rusty,
> Nor yet la Mancha's sword so bright,
> Kept by the watching, valourous Knight
> Forever ready for the fight;
> Nor any Sword e'er girded thigh on
> Can match this matchless Sword of Lyon.[19]

As Lyon sought reelection to Congress in the latter half of 1798, his leading Federalist opponent, who edited the *Rutland Herald*, refused to print Lyon's essays. Consequently, Lyon started a new Republican newspaper, *The Scourge of Aristocracy* (by "aristocracy" he still meant Federalists), again edited by his son James.[20] Its first issue, on October 1, 1798, came out four days before Lyon's arrest. It proclaimed that it would present "the Republican interest," and it printed the letter that Lyon's opponent would not print. The newspaper stated that Lyon's duty in Congress was not to support the administration blindly, but to support the Constitution and his constituents' interest.[21] That new paper was not the formal basis for his prosecution, but it did make it more urgent to stop Lyon. Lyon's electioneering speeches and writings, which criticized the president and the government while furthering Lyon's candidacy, became the basis for his prosecution.

Indictment and Arrest

Justice William Paterson opened the United States Circuit Court in Rutland, Vermont on October 3, 1798, joined by Judge Samuel Hitchcock (who had been Lyon's opponent in his congressional race two years earlier).[22] Paterson, before being appointed to the Supreme Court by President George Washington, had been a New Jersey senator and governor.[23] Following the normal procedure, the Supreme Court justice on the panel read a charge to the grand jury to instruct it about federal laws that it might have reason to enforce. The grand jury then would approve indictments prepared by the United States attorney (as the chief federal prosecutor in each state was then called), or would approve a presentment written (theoretically) by the grand jury itself. When grand juries approved indictments, they found them "a true bill"; when they rejected them, they wrote "not a true bill" or "ignoramus." Those approved proceeded to trial, unless there was a guilty plea, where a petit jury would hear the case and would receive instructions from the judges on the law and, commonly, on the facts as well.

Paterson's charge to the grand jury singled out "two species of offences, which, under the existing circumstances of the United States, merit your particular attention": forgery of notes of the Bank of the United States, and "seditious practices, and false, scandalous, and malicious writings, publications, and libels against the government of the United States." He added that the second offense had become "so frequent, dangerous, and alarming" that Congress passed the Sedition Act, which he read and then summarized. Paterson was pressing hard for an indictment under the Sedition Act, devoting the majority of his charge to it, in the nation's second charge to grand juries after passage of the Sedition Act. (The first was the day before in New Jersey by Justice William Cushing.) Paterson's next tack was to describe the inherent wickedness of violations. "The man, who is guilty of publishing false, defamatory, and malicious writings or libels against the government of his country, its measures, and its constituted authorities" must "stand self-condemned," for he "sins against light" and must know that he violates "clear and known duty." The consequences were grave, under what amounted to the British royal judges' view that seditious libel threatens to cause the collapse of government and society. "They destroy confidence, excite distrust, disseminate discord and the elements of disorganization, alienate the affections of the people from their government, disturb the peace of society, and endanger our political union and existence," so that "[n]o government, indeed, can long subsist." Paterson seemed to override the defense of truth that the Sedition Act provided, when he added that "nothing short of idiocy can operate as an excuse."[24] Instead of wicked questioning of rulers and laws, "[t]o support them is our primary duty," and "[o]bservance of the laws and obedience to legal authority are the great bulwark of public liberty." He ended the charge with a soliloquy against sedition. "Ah licentiousness! thou bane of republics, and more to be dreaded than hosts of external foes. The truth is, that libellous publications and seditious practices are inconsistent with genuine freedom, and subversive of good government," tending to anarchy and despotism.[25] Only one thing was missing in Paterson's charge—any mention of the First Amendment or any discussion of why "written or printed detraction" of the government, its measures, and its officials was not safeguarded by freedoms of press and speech.

The grand jury gave a formal reply to Justice Paterson's charge. It, like many other grand jury replies before other Sedition Act trials, supported the claim Lyon and many other defendants made, that the grand juries and trial juries, which were selected by Federalist marshals, were hand-picked from stalwart Federalists and were irretrievably biased. That reply, the day the grand jury indicted Lyon, expressed "their unanimous sentiments of gratitude and thanks for the solemn, momentous and invaluable charge delivered them by the Hon. Judge at the opening of this session." It agreed with what he "so powerfully expressed, that licentiousness more endangers the liberties and independence of a free Government than hosts of invading foes," and lamented "that our liberties, in some instances, are abused to licentiousness." As was common, the grand jury asked Paterson to provide his written charge to the press because it was sufficiently valuable to deserve publication.[26]

Matthew Lyon was indicted under the Sedition Act, on October 5, 1798.[27] The indictment charged three violations of the act: publishing in *Spooner's*

Vermont Journal a letter to voters critical of the president and the administration; reading during campaign speeches a letter from Paris written by Joel Barlow that was derogatory of the president and the Senate; and aiding and abetting Barlow's own seditious libel. (Barlow, to whom we will return later, was a poet and Republican fan of the French Revolution.) A complicating factor was that Lyon's letter in *Spooner's Vermont Journal* was written on June 28, before the Sedition Act was enacted, but was published after it, on July 31. Barlow's letter was similarly written before but read after.[28]

The language of Lyon's letter in *Spooner's Vermont Journal* that the indictment called seditious libel was a statement that President John Adams subordinated the public welfare to power and pomp, and fired or rejected qualified officials. Lyon made that statement in response to an earlier charge in that newspaper that he was disloyal in voting against Adams's defense legislation.[29] The core of his letter that was cited in the indictment said,

> As to the executive, when I shall see the efforts of that power bent on the promotion of the comfort, the happiness, and accommodation of the people, that executive shall have my zealous and uniform support; but whenever I shall, on the part of the Executive, see every consideration of the public welfare swallowed up in a continual grasp for power, in an unbounded thirst for ridiculous pomp, foolish adulation, or selfish av[a]rice; when I shall behold men of real merit daily turned out of office for no other cause but independency of sentiment; . . . I shall not be their humble advocate.[30]

The indictment charged that this was a "libel of and concerning the said John Adams President of the United States and the executive government of the United States," and it tracked the language of the Sedition Act.[31] That, and the rest of the indictment, showed how relatively mild criticism could be treated as criminal libel under the Sedition Act, and how opinion as well as fact could send someone to prison.

The part of the Barlow letter, written from Paris, that the indictment claimed was seditious libel was a description of the president's speech in November 1797 as a "bullying speech" and of the Senate's response as a "stupid answer of your Senate," along with its further characterization of the speech as qualified for "a mad-house" and of the response as servile.

> The speech of *John Adams,* at the opening of Congress in November, was waited for here with as much expectation as if peace or war depended upon it. It was hoped that after he had sent his commissioners, he would at least avoid the use of insulting language against the nation with whom he was pretending to treat. But when we found him [saying] . . . that they had turned pirates and plunderers, and it would [be] necessary to be perpetually armed against them, tho you were at peace. We wondered that the answer of both houses, had not been an order to send him to a mad-house. Instead of this, the

senate have echoed the speech with more servility than even George the third experienced from either house of parliament.[32]

The reason Barlow objected to Adams's speech and the Senate's response was weighty, that they risked kindling full-scale war with France. Barlow's letter also argued that the president "play[ed] the bully, by forcing a man back [Charles Cotesworth Pinckney], who had just been driven out of Paris," and feared that the envoys' dispatches would cause the president to make "another desperate leap into the regions of madness." The indictment alleged that this was a seditious libel toward Adams's speech, the Senate's answer, and the government generally.[33]

Jefferson's immediate analysis was that "[t]he words called seditious were only general censures of the proceedings of Congress & of the President."[34] When he wrote that, he had already drafted the Kentucky Resolutions, condemning the Alien and Sedition Acts as unconstitutional.

Scholars have made much of the language of Lyon's indictment—and of other Sedition Act indictments—that the accused was "a malicious and seditious person and of a depraved mind and wicked and diabolical disposition," who published or spoke "with force and arms."[35] In actuality, that was simply formbook wording for indictments for seditious libel, which was called "a mere form in informations" and indictments and which had long been used in English cases.[36] That language was used in most American indictments under the Sedition Act.

An arrest warrant was issued for Lyon later in the day after the grand jury approved the indictment, and he was brought to court the next day. He pleaded not guilty. Lyon and a friend each signed recognizance bonds for $1,000 to ensure his appearance in court for trial.[37]

The next day, summonses were served on several witnesses to compel their attendance at trial. Alden Spooner, the editor of *Spooner's Vermont Journal,* had printed Lyon's letter and was required to bring the original. His brother Judah Paddock Spooner, the printer for Lyon's publications, evidently had printed the Barlow letter in pamphlet form. Dr. Samuel Shaw apparently had funded or arranged the printing of the pamphlet. All three appeared at trial.[38]

The First Trial under the Sedition Act

The trial was held on October 8, 1798, from late morning to 8:00 that night.[39] It did not begin earlier in the morning because Lyon had not heard back over the weekend from the two lawyers he had contacted for representation, and so he asked for an hour's delay. He finally learned that they were unavailable, and then turned to Israel Smith, the state's chief justice, who was unwilling to represent him because there was no time for preparation, but who was willing to attend the trial and provide informal assistance. Justice Paterson offered to continue the trial until the May 1799 session, but Lyon, knowing that unresolved criminal charges would doom his reelection campaign, and that the May session would be in the Federalist stronghold of Windsor, "chose to come to trial" then and to represent himself.[40] Lyon did not help himself as his own lawyer—he did not call any witnesses or offer any exhibits. According to the Federalist newspaper, he "repeatedly observed that the jurors were packed, and brought from towns known to be inimical to him" when he ran for Congress, alluding to sharp geographical divisions in the state.[41] Paterson did nothing about Lyon's concern that Federalist marshals had hand-picked Federalist jurors, but did allow each side to exclude one juror when bias was shown.[42]

When Lyon offered the defense "that the sedition law was unconstitutional," that defense "was stricken off by the court," though Lyon was not stopped from raising that defense as he presented his case and as he argued to the jury. His main three points were that "the court had no jurisdiction" because an unconstitutional law was void, or at least that there was no jurisdiction over "writings composed before its passage"; that "the publication was innocent" of seditious intent; and that its "contents were true."[43] To show the truth of his claims that the president sought pomp and parade, Lyon asked Paterson if he had not seen such things when dining at the White House. Incredibly, Paterson answered and responded as a witness, denying that he had seen pomp but instead simplicity. However, he ceased to answer Lyon's questions once his answers would help Lyon instead of the prosecutor. Then, according to Lyon, when the United States attorney for Vermont, Charles Marsh, finished his closing argument, Paterson rose to instruct the jury and did not offer Lyon a chance to make his own closing argument, until Lyon asked "why I should not be heard" too.[44]

Justice Paterson's charge to the trial jury again foreclosed Lyon's main defense. "You have nothing whatever to do with the constitutionality or unconstitutionality of the sedition law," he said, because "until this law is declared null and void by a tribunal competent for the purpose, its validity cannot be disputed."[45] He did not illuminate how the Sedition Act could be declared null and void if no one was allowed to argue that. In charging the jury, Paterson told them how to convict Lyon, but not how to acquit him: "you will have to consider whether language such as that here complained of could have been uttered with any other intent than that of making odious or contemptible the President and government, and bringing them both into disrepute. If you find such is the case, the offence is made out, and you must render a verdict of guilty."[46] Further, that language did not permit political disagreement with the president and the administration, or at least anything but ineffective mild disagreement. Lyon's account recounted still more bias: Paterson "proceeded to dwell on the intention and wickedness of it, in the most elaborate manner; he descended to insinuate that the Barlow letter, as it was called, was a forgery; he said, let men of letters read that letter and compare it with Barlow's writings, and they would pronounce it none of his. He told the jury that my defence was merely an appeal to their feelings," and Paterson "supported the constitutionality" of the Sedition Act. Lyon's account is fairly credible, because it is consistent with Paterson's charge to the grand jury, which Lyon had not been present to hear (and which Paterson had declined to publish in the newspaper).[47]

Paterson said the jury had only two issues to determine: "Did Mr. Lyon publish the writing given in the indictment? Did he do so seditiously?" (by which he meant with seditious intent). His limitation of the jury to only those two issues contradicted the Sedition Act's provision that the jury had a right to determine "the law and the fact"—in other words to give a general verdict of "guilty" or "not guilty." Thus, Paterson, like the judges in nearly all the Sedition Act trials, overrode the two provisions of the Sedition Act that were supposed to liberalize the English common law of seditious libel, by omitting and contradicting the jury's right to enter a general verdict, and also by omitting the defendant's right to offer a defense of truth. Further, Paterson instructed the jury that both of the issues he listed must be resolved against Lyon, rendering him guilty. He said "[o]n the first point, the evidence is undisputed, and in fact, he himself concedes the fact of publication." According to Paterson's trial notes, on the second point, the seditious or criminal intent should be inferred from the act of publishing (printing or reading) seditious libel: "2. Whether the matters set forth as charges be criminal. . . . reading is a publication—Poison may be kept in a closet, but must not be administered as cordials—The malignity consists in the publication." Soon after, Paterson repeated that "[t]he guilt consists in the public'n."[48] The jury initially was unanimous but for one juror, and it deliberated for an hour that evening until that juror acquiesced. The jury then gave the verdict that Lyon was guilty.

Overall, Justice Paterson denied Lyon a fair trial in at least seven ways. He allowed a biased jury pool, ignoring objections. He rejected Lyon's central defense, that the Sedition Act violated the First Amendment. He testified and contradicted at least two of Lyon's other arguments. His jury instructions were biased, if they were anything like Wharton printed or Lyon recalled. Paterson limited the jury to two issues instead of what the Sedition Act allowed. He then told the jury that those two issues must be resolved against Lyon. He based a harsh sentence on a legislator's presumed knowledge of the evil of seditious libel. The *Scourge* quoted "a Southern paper" summing up Lyon's trial: he was convicted by "A *Judge* appointed by *John Adams,* an *Attorney* appointed by *John Adams,* a *Jury* summoned, selected by a *Marshal* appointed by *John Adams!!!!*"[49]

Stricter Sentencing and Mistreatment for a Member of Congress

Sentencing took place the day after the trial. Lyon pled financial distress, but was told that punishment must be strict because "as a member of the federal legislature, you must be well acquainted with the mischiefs which flow from an unlicensed abuse of government."[50] Lyon had been "convicted of writing, Printing, uttering & publishing certain false Scandalous & Seditious Libels, and of aiding abetting and assisting therein," in violation of the Sedition Act. Consequently, he was sentenced to imprisonment for four months, a fine of $1,000, and court costs of $60.96. Imprisonment would continue until the fine and costs were paid, along with the costs of commitment and the marshal's fees.[51] Lyon was surprised and shocked that the sentence included imprisonment, as a member of Congress and for words that were his communications to constituents and his appeals to voters in an election.

Lyon plaintively described his imprisonment in a letter from jail, which was published as a handbill, in the *Scourge,* and in most Republican newspapers.[52] When his sentence was announced, Lyon asked the marshal, Jabez Fitch, "if they would go with me to my lodgings" to "take care of my papers," and that was refused. The congressman was immediately taken to the prison in Vergennes, which his *Scourge* decried as a "little molehill of Aristocracy," forty-four miles away, instead of to the nearby prison in Rutland.[53] On the way, he was treated as a dangerous criminal, followed by two troopers with pistols, though he promised to go peacefully with the marshal. Arriving in Vergennes, the marshal insisted on the circuitous route through "almost the whole length of the little city" instead of the direct route, to exhibit him to the citizens and to the legislature, which was in session. Fitch told him that in prison he would not "have the use of pen, ink and paper," and at first enforced that order, then allowed pen and ink so long as Fitch "must see everything I sent out of the jail," and finally removed that affront. Lyon desperately needed paper and pen, because he had to carry on his reelection campaign from his jail cell—he was the first member of Congress to campaign from jail. Soon after, he learned that he won the primary election, but he did not quite receive a majority in a multicandidate field, so there would be a runoff in December. He used his imprisonment to full advantage, heading each letter and column with "In Gaol at Vergennes."

Lyon's shared cell, by his account, was "the common receptacle for horse-thieves, money-makers [defrauders], runaway negroes, or any kind of felons," groups that received anything but pleasant jail accommodations. The cell was about "sixteen feet long by twelve wide, with a necessary [toilet bucket] in one corner, which affords a stench about equal to the Philadelphia docks in the month of August." Light came only through a single window, "about twenty inches by sixteen," with iron bars. Cold came through too, because it had no glass, and there was no fireplace or stove.[54] After three weeks when he "suffered more with the cold than I had in twenty years," Lyon finally was provided glass in the open window, and after nearly another week, was allowed to buy a stove for heat. In the meantime, other prisoners cycled in and out of the room, such as one with "such a terrible dysentery as caused the room to smell worse than any hospital."[55]

Because Lyon was unable to pay his fine and costs, and faced the prospect of remaining in jail after his four-month sentence ended, efforts were made to raise the money in three ways. First, Lyon got authorization to hold a lottery, with the winner receiving some of his property. A year later, the newspaper editor (Anthony Haswell) who published advertisements for that lottery, with sympathetic language about Lyon's trial and imprisonment, was himself indicted under the Sedition Act. Second, Republican politicians contributed to a fund, and Sen. Stevens Thomson Mason of Virginia carried the cash to Vermont by a long horseback ride and made payment. Third, Vermont Republicans tried to raise the money, and thousands signed a petition to the president to remit the fine (which the president refused to receive).[56]

When Lyon was finally released on February 9, he had won his reelection effort, had won far more votes than in his previous victory, and had repainted his portrait with a martyr's halo. He stepped outside to be greeted by throngs of admirers, who accompanied him some distance.[57] Fearing a new arrest, Lyon announced that he was on his way to his seat in Congress, in order to come under the constitutional protection from arrest for members on the way to and from sessions. He wrote to his constituents that, though two judges and a jury found him guilty, "more than three thousand five hundred enlightened Freemen have declared him Not Guilty."[58]

The common statement is mistaken that Lyon was the "first victim" of the Alien and Sedition Acts. (Luther Baldwin, Brown Clark, and Lespenard Colie were the first arrested under those laws, two days earlier, and Colie was the first person sentenced under them.) But it is true that Lyon's was the first trial under the laws, or as a Republican newspaper in Connecticut more colorfully canonized him, Lyon was "the first martyr to the cause of liberty, under this law."[59] His was an arduous road to martyrdom, and he was an unlikely saint—he was coarse and self-promoting, his property came mostly from exploiting conflicts of interest, he had flirted with schemes to foment a Canadian rebellion against Britain and to foment a Vermont affiliation with Britain, and later he may have been involved in early phases of the Burr conspiracy.[60]

After the dust settled, Lyon proved right in fearing a new indictment, because he was reindicted a year after his first indictment (as we will see in Chapter 12), alongside the editor who published his lottery advertisement and the doctor who apparently funded or arranged printing the Barlow letter as a pamphlet. On his first day back in Congress in Philadelphia, Lyon confronted a new effort to unseat him, for having been "convicted of being a notorious and seditious person, and of a depraved mind, and wicked and diabolical disposition" (quoting the form language of his indictment), but it again failed. After the presidential election of 1800, as the House took its final vote on the Jefferson-Burr deadlock, Lyon cast Vermont's vote for Jefferson (after the state's other representative finally ceased tying the state's vote), becoming part of the decisive shift of four states to Jefferson.[61] Days before Jefferson took office, Lyon reminded him that those who participated in his prosecution—the marshal Fitch and the United States attorney Marsh—should not "be suffered to remain one day in office to disgrace the Administration." Though Jefferson did not replace Federalist officials who had fairly filled their offices, he quickly replaced Fitch and Marsh. The day Adams left office, Lyon fired off a public letter to "Citizen John Adams," tweaking him for "your mad zeal for monarchy and Britain, your love of pomp" and for most other "seditious libels" for which he had been prosecuted; it called Lyon's prosecution "the most base, cruel, assuming and faithless, that ever disgraced the councils of any nation."[62]

When his term in Congress ended in 1801, Lyon moved with several neighboring families to the friendlier environs of Kentucky, where he again created a new town, Eddyville. He was elected to Congress from his new Kentucky district in 1803, and repeated his earlier creation of several businesses. However, he lost his seat in the 1810 election, and a few years later he lost everything financially when his barge of beef and pork ran aground in the Mississippi River. Lyon's years ended with a minor appointment as factor of a small trading station with Native Americans, on the frontier in Arkansas, and with an effort to recover funds by petitioning Congress to repay his $1,000 fine and costs, in 1820.[63] Congress set no speed records and only refunded them in the 1840s.

This case is one of many examples of the Sedition Act being applied to Republican words but not to identical Federalist words. Matthew Lyon was prosecuted for repeating Joel Barlow's statement that Adams should have been sent "to a mad-house," but Secretary of Treasury Oliver Wolcott was not charged for writing that "the people believe that their President is Crazy." Former Secretary of War James McHenry was not prosecuted for writing of the "madness or folly, which he has displayed as President."[64]

This case is also one of many examples of the Sedition Act being used to prosecute speech as well as printing. The count about the Barlow letter alleged that Lyon read it in speeches. Other prosecutions of speech appear in later chapters: David Brown, Lespenard Colie, Luther Baldwin and Brown Clark, David Garvin, Jacob Greenawalt, Morris Llewellyn and friends (their speech was symbolic—a liberty pole), Langford Herring, Rev. Jacob Eyerman, and Dr. Samuel Shaw (in his case, facilitating or funding speech). Seditious words were as criminal as seditious printing under the Sedition Act.

A Broad Understanding of Freedoms of Press and Speech

In 1793 and 1794, closer to when the First Amendment was ratified than when the Sedition Act was passed, Lyon stressed the vital role in republican government of the people's right to scrutinize officials and to criticize them. The "Public are interested in the investigation of the virtues and vices of the person who comes forward for an important appointment," and "have a right to demand a scrutiny of his conduct." Another article said the people, associating in the controversial Democratic–Republican Societies, should "watch over the government," examine officials' conduct, "and after proper scrutiny, pronounce against those among their servants" who "neglect, or opperate against the interest of the community."[65] In an article on why legislators should not be lawyers, Lyon was well on the road to his later express rejection of the common law of seditious libel, as he listed as the third of twelve reasons that lawyers "revere the opinions of, and look up to, ancient British Judges . . . who have derived their greatness, and sucked their principles from the very poisonous breast of monarchy itself." On June 20, 1798, Lyon responded to rumors that a sedition bill might be introduced by saying that he would oppose it, "as it will tend to prevent due investigation" of misdeeds of governmental officials, and because a congressman had a right "to expose the truth in my usual way to my constituents."[66]

During the four months when Lyon was in jail, he carried on the fight through his newspaper, the *Scourge of Aristocracy*. The *Scourge* repeatedly condemned the Sedition Act as an "unconstitutional law," something "the Constitution forbid Congress to pass," and called the Alien and Sedition Acts "direct violations of the Constitution." It published Rep. Edward Livingston's speech against the Sedition Act, which said that the law was contrary "to the direct letter of the Constitution," quoting the First Amendment. The *Scourge* excerpted the address from Prince Edward County, Virginia, asserting that "the freedom of speech [was] criminated and restricted" by the Sedition Act.[67] The newspaper found the Alien Act equally unconstitutional.[68]

Further, the *Scourge* advocated a broad understanding of freedoms of press and speech. It reprinted resolutions from Fayette, Kentucky affirming "the privilege of speaking and publishing our sentiments, on all public questions" (and that "all laws made to impair or destroy it are void"). It published resolutions from Woodford, Kentucky positing that "to speak, write, and censure freely, are privileges of which a freeman cannot divest himself, much less be abridged in them by others," because "the freedom of speech, the liberty of the press, . . . are among the inseparable rights of Freemen"—unalienable rights. A vital part of those freedoms was the right to "examine into the conduct of" and to "censure those servants for the abuse of power"—to forbid or to punish that "is tyranny more insufferable than Asiatic."[69] It quoted Livingston rejecting criminalization of seditious libel: "when gentlemen speak of *slanders against the Government,* I know of no such thing"—"there ought to be no such power." And the *Scourge* quoted Tiberius to the same effect: "*in a free State, the thoughts and tongues of every man ought to be free,*" so that the emperor would not allow prosecution "when the Senate would have proceeded against some who had published libels against him." As soon as word reached Lyon in jail of the Virginia and Kentucky Resolutions, he endorsed them as the work of "Patriots of Virginia and Kentucky" to oppose "*Tyranny,* and *unconstitutional Laws.*"[70]

When Lyon wrote to John Adams as he left office, he reiterated many of the same themes. When Adams became president, "this country was happy in the freedom of speech and of the press," until the Constitution was "trampled on" by the Sedition Act and its prosecutions. The foundation of seditious libel law was "childish nonsense about dividing the people from the government," because the people were never divided from the government but only from "you and your executive officers" who were not themselves the government. "The judiciary" under Adams "made alarming encroachments on the rights of man" by "endeavouring to introduce the crude, cruel, undigested, inapt, and obsolete system of the common law into our national jurisprudence."[71]

Jefferson reacted to the Lyon prosecution by describing the chilling effect of the Sedition Act on freedoms of press and speech: "I know not which mortifies me most, that I should fear to write what I think, or my country bear such a state of things."[72]

Rev. John C. Ogden

John Cosens Ogden (1751–1800), who delivered the Vermont petition to pardon Lyon, evolved from calm younger years in New Jersey and graduation from Princeton to combative later years as his financial plight worsened. Unsuccessful and bitter at not being appointed to his father-in-law's lucrative post as collector of the largest port in Connecticut, he turned angrily on the dominant force in the state's politics and religion, the Congregational denomination and its members. Ogden was ordained as an Episcopal priest in 1788 and served that denomination's church in Portsmouth, New Hampshire, until his controversy with a Congregational minister led to his ouster in 1793. Eyeing the former Anglican properties in Vermont, he moved to a small town there and sought legislative support for claiming them. When that mission failed in 1795, Ogden left Vermont to become an itinerant Episcopal preacher, radiating from Troy, New York while leaving his wife and children with her mother in Connecticut.[73]

Ogden, thwarted at every turn by Congregationalists and Federalists (essentially the same in Connecticut at the time), became an outspoken pamphleteer against them and "a violent Democrat" around 1796.[74] He was consumed with righteous indignation against claims of such opponents as Rev. Jedidiah Morse and Rev. Timothy Dwight that "Jacobin societies acted in concert, and under the direction of the Illuminati in Europe" and the "Illuminated French Revolutionists," in a "'*great plan of a general overturning of religion and government.*'" In response, Ogden smote the Congregationalist and Federalist establishment by calling them "the New England Illuminati," terming their monthly meetings "the Calvinist Clubs," and charging them (as his subtitle said) with "Destroying the Religion and Government of the United States." His attack was adopted by some of the Republican press.[75] At the same time, Ogden launched a second holy war for a government job—a collectorship, a position as secretary to the envoys, or anything else that paid well.[76]

Ogden agreed to deliver the petition, which several thousand Vermont voters had signed, to President John Adams in Philadelphia.[77] He did so out of support both for Lyon and for himself, hoping to ask personally for a federal appointment. The petition besought the president to pardon Lyon,

FIGURE 4.2. Reverend John Cosens Ogden. Engraving by Charles Balthazar Julien Févret de Saint-Mémin (1798). Courtesy National Portrait Gallery, Smithsonian Institution.

so that the person western Vermonters elected to represent them in Congress could do so. It also called it "extremely dangerous for the partizans on one side to be set judicially to pronounce on the intentions of persons on the other" side, and found it unfair that nearly everyone on Lyon's grand jury and trial jury were political opponents. The petition appealed to the "good intentions, and good disposition of our President." When Ogden presented it to Adams on December 31, 1798, that good disposition was not very evident, as Adams asked if Lyon himself had petitioned and, on learning that he had not, declined to receive it. The president's reason was that "repentance ought to precede mercy" or (as it is variously reported) "penitence must precede pardon." Desecrating the holy quest for employment, Adams added that Ogden's "*interference on the part of col. Lyon will prevent your receiving any favors from me.*"[78]

In 1785, Ogden had borrowed money and signed a note to repay Oliver Wolcott, Jr. of Connecticut "Sixty pounds in Soldiers notes" the next year.[79] He was unable to pay it then or through the years.

As Ogden returned from Philadelphia to eastern New York in early 1799, he detoured into Connecticut to assist publication of his new book in Litchfield and to see his family in New Haven. Oliver Wolcott, Jr. was now secretary of the treasury, and his brother Frederick was a Litchfield attorney and the clerk of court. As soon as Ogden arrived in Litchfield, the brother filed suit for Oliver Wolcott, Jr. against Ogden to collect the 1785 debt. Not surprisingly, attorney Frederick Wolcott was able to get clerk of court Frederick Wolcott to issue an attachment and arrest warrant for Ogden immediately, on February 4, 1799. It required the sheriff or constable to attach $300 worth of property of Ogden or, if that was not possible, to "attach his body, & him" to appear in court the next month. Ogden was arrested by the sheriff the next day, who "committed him to the keeper of the gaol in Litchfield."[80] As Ogden put it, "Oliver Wolcott . . . has cast me into prison for a small sum due honestly to him." At the court appearance, Frederick Wolcott "recovered Judgment against John C. Ogden" for $187.50 (principal, interest, and costs of suit) in the Court of Common Pleas, on March 26, 1799, and the court order (signed by clerk Frederick Wolcott) required the sheriff and constables to keep Ogden in prison "until he pay unto the said Wolcott the full sums above-mentioned."[81] Ogden was not represented by any attorney.

Frederick Wolcott reported to his brother, before the March court session, that the "vile, lying rascal" had not yet taken "the *poor prisoner's oath*," but if he did the Wolcotts would have to "support him in Prison." By March 7, Ogden had done so, because he wrote that Oliver Wolcott had deposited $76 "to pension a poor parson, retained in prison by his suit."[82] He wrote pathetically about the privations of his various cells. Ogden asked influential people to encourage Oliver Wolcott to drop this "fruitless prosecution," since the minister could pay nothing.[83] Recognizing that Ogden indeed could not pay the debt, Frederick Wolcott got him to sign a new promissory note in exchange for release from jail, on June 10, 1799. Wolcott reported to his brother on this and said "there was no probability that you would recover any money of him." The new note was to force Ogden to stay out of the state under the continuing threat that "I will again attach & confine him."[84]

Newspapers across the country carried periodic articles about Ogden's prosecution. Federalist papers reported that "PARSON OGDEN, one of the *Editors* of the *Aurora,* is imprisoned in Litchfield for debt," canonizing him as one of "two martyrs to Jacobinism" and an "idle vicious spendthrift." (They baptized Ogden as an "Editor" based on anonymous articles he wrote for the *Aurora* describing Lyon's unfair trial and barbaric imprisonment, in which the cold wind "whistled" and Lyon's limbs were "benumbed.")[85] Soon, Federalist papers downgraded him to a "clerical lunatic, confined in Litchfield jail, for money squandered away." Republican papers were quick to say Ogden's arrest for debt was a pretext. "The respectable clergyman" who "interceded in behalf of col. Lyon, during his imprisonment, was on his return from Philadelphia arrested on the suite of Oliver Wolcott, esq. Secretary of the Treasury of the U. States (can we here say 'from no political motives?') and thrown into prison."[86]

Was this a de facto Sedition Act prosecution of Ogden? There is strong circumstantial evidence that it was, though no direct evidence. The prosecution was ordered by a cabinet member, Secretary of Treasury Oliver Wolcott. A half year earlier, he had assisted with the prosecution of another enemy, Benjamin Franklin Bache, as we saw in the preceding chapter. The timing was damning. No prosecution for the debt had been filed in the previous thirteen years, even though Ogden had visited Litchfield periodically during those years, including early 1798, and had visited New Haven as well, including 1797.[87] Then the prosecution was initiated immediately after Ogden returned through Connecticut, in February 1799, after presenting the Vermont petition to the president for a Sedition Act defendant, in December 1798. The only thing that was different in early February 1799, compared with the preceding thirteen years, was that Ogden had delivered the petition and had been added to Adams's mental list of seditious spokespeople ("Cooper, Matthew Lyon, Parson Ogden," along with Duane, Greenleaf, Paine, Callender, and others).[88] Wolcott certainly knew of the petition and its rejection. Further, the lawsuit was transparently futile. There was never any chance of the prosecution bringing about payment for the debt, as Frederick Wolcott acknowledged, and instead prosecution could only increase Oliver Wolcott's loss since he had to pay for jail lodging expenses. Moreover, there was a political reason for arresting Ogden on some other ground instead of under the Sedition Act, because a Sedition Act arrest for delivering a seditious petition inevitably would be attacked as a violation of the First Amendment freedom of petition (which was far more widely used in the 1790s than today). Republican newspapers certainly viewed Ogden's arrest for debt as tantamount to arrest under the Sedition Act.[89] Ogden himself saw the arrest as "revenge upon me for my errand to President Adams, with the petitions" for Lyon and also as a way to defeat his application for the collector position. Various scholars have viewed it as "requir[ing] little imagination, however, to conceive that Ogden's support of Lyon caused his arrest."[90] Thus, the plaintiff, the timing, the futility of the suit, the net cost of the suit, and the motive all indicate that Ogden was nominally prosecuted for a debt because that was an easier tactic than prosecuting him for sedition.

There is no surviving evidence that Secretary of State Timothy Pickering participated in this with Wolcott, a few buildings away, but he was aware of some of Ogden's activities. Pickering was notified by Col. Allan McLane, four days after Wolcott filed suit, that Ogden "paid our village a visit last week," leaving McLane "almost delirious at seeing our once happy Country disordered by such infamous instruments" who were "plotting against his Country." The elements of Ogden's plot that McLane mentioned were soliciting "on foot a subscription to support Holts Infamous paper of Connecticut" (later that year the subject of a Sedition Act prosecution), and writing an article "in our little Jacobin paper." McLane asked "what is to be done, is our President, and all the Executive Department, our members of Congress, and every officer of government, civil and military[,] to be callumnated Libelled and traduced, and no Remidy?" (McLane's delirium was so serious that his spelling grew worse with each line of his letter.) According to Ogden, Pickering and everyone in Philadelphia was aware of Ogden's departure to go to Litchfield, and "the post had time to bring letters and orders" there to have him arrested.[91]

Finally leaving after four months in jail, Ogden had his revenge on Connecticut by writing his "History of Ecclesiastical Oppressions" and having it published by James Lyon. Federalists had their own revenge on Ogden by "a party of soldiers, about twenty in number," who drove him out of town by forcing "me to attend them two miles and a half" in the country while "calling me, a Democrat an[d] Jacobin and a Frenchman," the day after he was released.[92] Ogden only lived another year and a quarter, leaving behind his spouse and three children.

Rep. John Clopton and Denouncing the President

The prosecution of Matthew Lyon was not the first, or the last, of an opposition member of Congress during the late 1790s. A grand jury in Virginia, chaired by a retired Federalist judge, approved a presentment against Rep. Samuel J. Cabell based on the words of his letters to constituents in 1797. Then in the same month when Lyon was prosecuted, Pickering took steps toward prosecution of another Republican, John Clopton, based on the words of his letters to voters.

The Prior Threat to Rep. Samuel J. Cabell

Cabell (1756–1818), a William and Mary graduate, Revolutionary War officer, and wealthy planter,[93] wrote a public letter to constituents that was critical of President Washington's foreign policy and of John Adams's recent election.[94] When the next federal Circuit Court opened, Supreme Court Justice James Iredell charged the grand jury that "able and disinterested men" should be elected, and that "any public officer, who has misbehaved, is liable to trial, punishment, and disgrace." He added characteristic Federalist reasoning that the people's role was to elect representatives, and then if a citizen "disapproves of any public authoritative decision" made by them the only recourse is "to submit to it with diffidence and respect," because dissent would cause "differences of opinion to corrode into enmity, jealousy to rankle into distrust, weak men to delude by their folly, abandoned men to disturb the order of society by their crimes," and ultimately a foreign nation to conquer the country. That same day, the grand jury issued a presentment of "the circular Letters of several members of the late Congress, and particularly Letters with the Signature of Samuel J: Cabell," which were "a real evil" because they endeavor "to disseminate unfounded calumnies against the happy Government of the United States, and thereby to separate the people therefrom." That presentment was the more ominous because the foreman of the grand jury was recently retired Supreme Court Justice John Blair.[95]

The presentment provoked a storm of Republican protest, including a blistering circular letter to the nation from Cabell, which expressed the broad view of freedoms of press and speech that nearly two years later was central to the Virginia and Kentucky Resolutions. Cabell objected that it was "a regular practice of the federal judges, to make political discourses to the grand jurors," and that the judges had "become a band of political preachers" who did "not complain of violations of any law" but instead "complain of opinions." They were "making use of their power and influence . . . to control the freedom of individual opinion," and causing the grand jury to arrogate "authority for censuring the independence of private opinion." Cabell then asserted the right of a member of Congress, at "a distance from my constituents," "to give them such information relative to their public concerns, as I possessed," and defiantly added that he would "continue to act the part of a watchful centinel," unintimidated by "a political charge from the bench" that did not address his arguments at all.[96]

Other Republicans expressed similar outrage that was also based on an expansive understanding of freedoms of press and speech, in mid-1797. Virginia Sen. Henry Tazewell wrote that a court and jury making themselves "a tribunal of political Censors" was "inimical to the freedom of opinion" and to "the liberties of their Country," and was an "attack on the freedom of political opinion." Thomas Jefferson wrote that "the charges of the federal judges" were inviting grand juries "to become inquisitors on the freedom of speech, of writing and of principle." Two months later, Jefferson underscored the chilling effect of the presentment on other members of Congress: "going in the public papers just at the moment when Congress was together," it "produced a great effect both on it's friends & foes in that body, very much to the disheartening & mortification of the latter."[97] Scaevola, in a brilliant essay, said that the "presentment is a violent attack upon the liberty of America" and an attempt "to annihilate the liberty of the press," because it endeavored to prescribe "the manner in which they shall discuss public measures." If the jury found Cabell's letter seditious, "they are unsupported by the laws of the United States." Scaevola added that if the grand jury followed the law, "they should have presented your charge," not Cabell's letter. Peregrine Fitzhugh, from Maryland, wrote that the aristocratic party was branding anyone "as an enemy to his Country who shall dare to speak or write with freedom on Men and measures," and was tearing the "Fabric which has been erected at so great an expence of blood and Treasure."[98] Marius joined in disagreeing that the law could forbid "certain opinions" such as those "disapprobative of the measures of government," saying that it instead must be "peculiarly careful . . . to preserve from the least degree of restraint, the freedom of opinion." He also denied that the English common law of seditious libel was in force, saying "a predilection for the English law" had led the writer astray and that "our freedom flows not from so impure a source."[99]

There were many contrary statements, of course, such as William R. Davie, soon-to-be governor of North Carolina, who reiterated the English common law rule that acts of private persons "which have a direct tendency to destroy or disturb the Peace, good Government, or happiness of the Community" are "proper objects for a Judge's charge," including "the disorganising effect of the correspondence of certain members of Congress."[100] Iredell himself denied that he provoked the grand jury's presentment, saying that he gave "the same charge" in Maryland two weeks earlier. However, he had then rewritten the charge he gave in Pennsylvania four weeks before that to aim it at Republican speech, and had had plenty of time to hear of Cabell's circular letter. Iredell also had confided to his wife that he approved of the presentment—it showed "a temper highly suitable to our present situation"—just after it was announced.[101] He did nothing to quash that presentment of Cabell and other members of Congress.

Jefferson, by contrast, did take action, drafting a petition urging the Virginia legislature to protest, such as by impeaching the grand jurors. He revised his petition to proclaim "the right of free correspondence between citizen and citizen" and to call it "a natural right of every individual citizen, not the gift of municipal law." Virginia's lower house passed that resolution, by a 92–53 margin, decrying the grand jury presentment as "a subjection of the natural right of speaking and writing freely," as well as of the right of political representation.[102]

Neither side took further action. The United States attorney did not indict Cabell or other members of Congress, and Virginia's upper house did not vote on the resolution.

Clopton's Expansive View of Freedoms of Press and Speech

John Clopton (1756–1816) was another of the voices condemning Iredell's charge and the grand jury's presentment, based on an expansive understanding of freedoms of press and speech. Clopton had graduated from the predecessor to University of Pennsylvania in 1776, and fought in the Revolutionary War and was wounded at the Battle of Brandywine. He owned a plantation and practiced law, and in 1795 he was elected to the House of Representatives, where he served four years and then from 1801 to 1816.[103] Clopton was a heated opponent of the Alien and Sedition Acts and an avid supporter of the Virginia and Kentucky Resolutions.[104] He was stunned to find himself a target for prosecution two weeks after Lyon was convicted under the Sedition Act, in October 1798.

Clopton immediately had seen that his circular letters, along with Cabell's, were referred to by the grand jury's presentment of "the circular Letters of several members of the late Congress" in May 1797. Responding defiantly, he sent another circular letter to his constituents expressing his indignation at the presentment as "an attack upon the common right of every individual to a *free exercise* of opinion." The presentment's function was to restrict information and to exclude "the people from knowledge of the measures of their government." Its result was "to weaken the responsibility of the public servants" and "to introduce *evils*" like those in "the darker ages of despotism." Clopton noted that the grand jury's limited job was to identify crimes, and he denounced "erecting themselves into a body of political censors" who arrogated authority over the legislative branch and said it "should be regulated" by "*their* political creed." The overall consequence was to threaten "violation of a sacred right" by encouraging "a dangerous encroachment on the liberty of opinion."[105] Clopton's 1797 reasoning, like Cabell's, presupposed a wide scope for freedoms of press and speech, and left little if any room for a federal crime of seditious libel.

Steps Toward Prosecuting Another Member of Congress

Clopton was opposed by John Marshall in the 1798 elections for Congress. Marshall gave two reasons for standing for the seat: a personal request by George Washington, and "a punishment for some unknown sins."[106]

"Buckskin," a Federalist, published a letter in a Richmond newspaper supporting Marshall and attacking Clopton's circular and private letters because they encouraged attachment to the French government and excited discontents with the American government. Buckskin added that Clopton had sent "some *private* letters—too violent even to be made *Circular*"—in which "he calls the President of the United States a traitor—says he is grasping at absolute power—that he has bribed a majority of the House of Representatives, &c." Buckskin said that one such letter was in the hands of "Mr. W. P. of Hanover." Clopton responded immediately, placing a denial in the next issue, and attaching a statement by William Pollard of Hanover that denied "knowledge of any letter" saying those things.[107]

Secretary of State Timothy Pickering, who directed enforcement of the Sedition Act, learned of the article and wrote to Marshall's brother-in-law, Edward Carrington, a strong Virginia Federalist, saying "I do think the printer ought to be examined with a view to the prosecution of the writer. Such infamous and mischievous [words?] ought not to pass unnoticed." Pickering also asked Carrington to get the letter from Pollard, unaware that Pollard had denied its existence. Carrington responded that, while Pollard had supported Clopton with a certificate, Buckskin had repelled "the effects of the certificate" by a second letter. Further, a gentleman was "ready to make oath to the truth of Buckskin's charge," and someone else had charged Clopton "on the same ground" in the newspaper.[108]

Pickering's letter was sent just two weeks after Lyon was convicted and sentenced, stating his plan and gathering necessary evidence to prosecute another Republican member of Congress under the Sedition Act.[109] Pickering proposed to bring criminal charges against the member of Congress shortly before election day.

That prosecution of Clopton did not go forward, however, because Marshall discouraged it, perhaps persuading Carrington to stay out of the discussion. Marshall told Pickering that the "jacobin presses" teem with attacks "leveld particularly at me," which would "soon recommence."[110] The Alien and Sedition Acts already were his greatest obstacle to winning his congressional race in Virginia, and he had already announced that he would not have voted for those laws because they were useless and divisive, though he did not question their constitutionality.[111] Marshall did not want the Alien and Sedition Acts to become the only issue in the election, by his opponent being prosecuted under them and perhaps writing election letters from jail as Lyon would. Marshall's call was a good one, because with the wind of the XYZ Affair in his sails, he narrowly defeated Clopton for the congressional seat.

It is breathtaking that one member of Congress could be prosecuted and imprisoned for his electioneering speech and newspaper letter, and that another was only spared prosecution and imprisonment for his private letter to constituents because his opponent found that inexpedient. Further, that occurred in a narrowly divided House of Representatives, where rendering one or two members unable to vote could change the result of close votes such as that on the Sedition Act itself. Prosecuting members of Congress threatened not only freedoms of press and speech, but the right of citizens to select representatives in Congress, to communicate with them, and to be represented by their votes. And that was precisely the purpose of the prosecution of Rep. Matthew Lyon and of the planned prosecution of Rep. John Clopton.

CHAPTER FIVE

Keeping the North Safe from Sedition

FOUR MONTHS AFTER sedition prosecutions of the editors of the leading Republican newspapers were begun in America's two largest cities, New York and Philadelphia, a Sedition Act prosecution was begun of the editor of the leading Republican paper in the third or fourth largest city, Boston. October 1798 witnessed the first of three major campaigns in Sedition Act prosecutions against opposition newspapers, opposition members of Congress, and opposition speech—the Vermont case against Rep. Matthew Lyon, the contemplated Virginia case against Rep. John Clopton, the Boston prosecution against editor Thomas Adams, other Massachusetts prosecutions and some New Jersey prosecutions. The two other Massachusetts prosecutions were brought when "sedition" reared its ugly head in an outspoken Federalist's town, Dedham, Massachusetts. The New Jersey cases were initiated even earlier in October 1798, against one man in New Jersey for consigning the president to perdition and against two men there for drunken comments critical of the president. Yet, even with that many pending prosecutions and the failed ones that the next chapter describes, the campaign in the latter half of 1798 paled by comparison to the second and third campaigns in early 1799 and in mid-1799 through mid-1800. All were led by Secretary of State Timothy Pickering.

The reason the 1798 campaign centered around October 1798 was that it and November 1798 were the months when most semiannual circuit court sessions were held, where indictments could be approved by federal grand juries. By contrast, the next spring's circuit court sessions saw fewer Sedition Act prosecutions of Republican newspapers because Timothy Pickering and John Adams were then distracted by the treason and sedition cases generated by the Fries Rebellion and by the president's announcement of a new diplomatic mission to France.

Thomas Adams and the *Independent Chronicle*

Thomas Adams (c. 1757–1799) was from an "humble background," his father being "clerk of the Faneuil Hall marketplace" in Boston.[1] Adams, after serving as a private in the Revolutionary War, began work as a printer in 1778. Six years later, Adams and a business partner bought an existing newspaper, Boston's *Independent Chronicle,* which had been a leading whig paper during the Revolution. Their purchase took effect at the beginning of 1784.[2] They immediately succeeded in becoming the official state printers, but that success rendered the newspaper "relatively nondescript" politically throughout the 1780s and until Republican content burst forth with polarization over the French Revolution. As a result, Thomas Adams lost government printing in 1796, and the *Chronicle* became an outspoken opposition newspaper.[3] In that change, Adams courageously chose "to privilege their political commitments over economic security, and even personal safety," so intertwined were his "professional and political identities," as Seth Cotlar observed. That elevation of printers to be "'principals' in the political life of the new republic" (even while their presses "claimed to be 'independent'") had peaked before and during the American Revolution, and again peaked during the Alien and Sedition Act crisis.[4]

The *Chronicle*'s evolution paralleled the emergence of an opposition party. Its shift was quite visible to John Adams in late 1793, when his wife commented to him that the *Chronicle* "has become as much of a party paper as Freneaus." Two years earlier the newspaper published a weekly excerpt from Thomas Paine's *Rights of Man.*[5] In 1793 it printed a defense of the French Revolution, and of the resulting "virtues and improvements" in France, and deplored the "disgusting scene" of "a group of Aristocratic Americans, Tories, &c. rejoicing" at disorder in France. In 1795 it reprehended the Jay Treaty.[6]

Under the editorship of Thomas Adams, the *Chronicle*'s influence grew to become "the chief medium in New England for the dissemination of [the Republican] political viewpoint," and its columns were "widely copied by printers of other newspapers in and out of New England," as John B. Hench, the leading biographer of Thomas Adams and the newspaper, noted. Adams was assisted by his older brother, Abijah Adams, a "far from prosperous" tailor, who was hired as the bookkeeper sometime after Thomas Adams's business partner died in 1790.[7]

President John Adams placed the *Chronicle* high on his list of hated newspapers, if Abigail Adams's comments to him were any indication. She fulminated, stung by the *Chronicle*'s exaggerations of the president's compensation, that it "has more low Billingsgate than even Bache," "has more of the true spirit of satan" than the *Aurora* by adding to it "the Lies, falshoods calumny and bitterness of his own," and like the *Aurora* carries "grose lies daily publishd." In April 1798, she lamented that "nothing will have an Effect" on the "wicked and base, voilent & caluminiating abuse" in opposition newspapers until "congress pass a sedition Bill," and that opportunities were being lost because "not a paper" from the *Chronicle* appears "but what might have been prossecuted as libels upon the President and Congress."[8] In May, she warned that if Bache "& his Agents Chronicle" were "not suppressed, we shall come to a civil war," and in July, the first lady hoped "a similar prossecution will take place in Boston if the Chronical" reprinted Burk's outrages. Federalist newspapers despised the *Chronicle* every bit as much. After the Sedition Act was signed in July 1798, the leading Federalist paper gloated that for "the Chronicle scribblers" and their falsehoods, "[t]heir evening has arrived.—the noxious quality of their poisons have expired."[9]

The *Chronicle* ensured that it would remain high on the president's list by regularly publishing articles challenging the constitutionality of the Alien and Sedition Acts, as we will see shortly. Thomas Adams was prosecuted under the Sedition Act "largely because of the paper's strong opposition to their enactment," Hench and others concluded.[10]

Arrest and Indictment

Justice William Paterson, following his circuit from Vermont, gave the grand jury in Boston the same charge that he had given Rep. Matthew Lyon's jury in Rutland.[11] A Federalist newspaper, the *Massachusetts Mercury,* described it as "an elegant display of Jurisprudential and Political Science," and said it was "received with general admiration," at least by Federalists. Sitting with Paterson on the bench was Judge John Lowell, the district court judge in Boston.[12]

Later that day, after Paterson's charge, the grand jury approved an indictment of Thomas Adams for three violations of the Sedition Act, on Saturday, October 20, 1798. The three violations were three articles printed in the *Independent Chronicle,* which were characterized as "intending to defame the Government of the said United States & both Houses of the Congress of the United States, and the President," to bring them "into contempt," to "stir up sedition" against them, and "to aid, encourage and abet the hostile designs of the republic of France against the said United States." By that indictment, Thomas Adams became "the first important editor to be indicted under the Sedition Act."[13] (William Durell's newspaper was much smaller and he had not yet been reindicted under the Sedition Act, and Rep. Matthew Lyon's newspaper was small.)

The first count was based on an article upbraiding the Adams administration for colluding with Britain and threatening American liberties. The majority of the indictment's extracts from the article will be quoted because they show how federal attorneys and judges, under the guise of explaining references ("innuendos"), often aggressively rewrote publications that they prosecuted and punished. Additions to the prosecuted articles were in parentheses, typically beginning with the word "meaning."

> At a time like the present, big with the fate of your dearest rights and privileges, it becomes all those who still dare to resist oppression from *whatever source* it may come, to exert themselves in defence of their invaded liberties (meaning that the liberties of the people are invaded by the Government of the United States)[.] A fellow citizen fully persuaded of this great truth, now addresses you.
>
> Americans, when you look around you, and behold yourselves on the brink of a War with France, the most powerful nation under Heaven, your liberties of speech and of the press infringed (meaning by the Government of the United States)[,] your houses and lands burdened with enormous taxes to support a *Standing* Army (meaning the army of the United States)[,] your best patriots calumniated by a subject of George the 3d, publishing a paper under the very nose if not sanction of your administration (meaning that the Government of the United States encouraged, supported or promoted a paper to be published by a British subject for the calumniation of the patriots)[,] are you not led to enquire, from whence come these things? Surely you are and with one voice exclaim[,] they originated in a Funding System (meaning the Act of Law of the United States . . .) and were perfected in a *British Treaty* (meaning the Treaty of Amity Commerce and Navigation).[14]

The article's reference to liberties of speech and press being infringed was a reference to the Alien and Sedition Acts; the indictment treated it as a crime to allege that those rights were infringed by a law. The article continued by urging citizens to "awake, unite, put confidence in each other, *form yourselves into societies*, establish committees of correspondence," and "give your votes to such men only who will support the Constitution"—all peaceful means—which the indictment quoted as if they were criminal and incendiary.

The second count was based on an article calling John Adams's answers to various citizen addresses "one of the greatest libels that was ever thrown by one nation on another," because those answers "propagate[d] the belief that the French government had asked bribes of the American commissioners." Instead, the article contended, X, Y, and Z were British and Dutch, and so were not officials for which France was responsible. (This was one of the wishful ways Republicans attempted to explain away the XYZ Affair, and to portray it as Federalist deceit.) The indictment treated that claim as a seditious libel on its face, along with the article's references to a presidential appointee receiving a sinecure and a prospective appointee being "one of the greatest brawlers of the faction" (Federalists).[15] The third count grew out of an article listing steps that "Tyrants" take. The indictment defined "Tyrants" or "they" as "meaning the Government of the United States," and treated calling the government's actions tyrannical as the crime of seditious libel. The steps tyrants took were those Republicans opposed: antagonizing countries favoring freedom while allying with countries exhibiting despotism; supporting venal newspapers; misleading the people by unauthorized dispatches ("meaning the dispatches from the late Envoys" on the XYZ Affair); adopting measures to "borrow money, raise a standing army, equip a navy, impose innumerable taxes," and harm commerce; and taking action to "impoverish the people so far as to *oblige them* to seek refuge" under the Tyrant.[16]

The indictment of Thomas Adams was a mess, the most disordered in any Sedition Act case. Count one gave the date of the first article as August 23 instead of September 24, and count three gave the date of the third article as September 24 instead of August 23 (which should have rendered the conviction under those counts void).[17] Cross-outs and interlineations were on most pages, and half of the wrong newspaper article was pasted in count one without being the basis of any further allegation. The reason for the mess was not that the alleged sedition had just occurred, because the three articles ranged from one to two months old. The likely reason is that Justice Paterson arrived with a copy of the Lyon indictment in hand and pressed for an immediate indictment of Adams, which was prepared so hurriedly that a clean copy could not be made.

This has led to confusion as some writings on the Sedition Act say that Thomas Adams's brother, Abijah, was also indicted in the federal prosecution. The indictment originally did list Abijah Adams in each of the three counts, but in each case his name was crossed out.[18] That excision was most likely done by the United States attorney at the time other excisions and interlineations were made, and not by the grand jury since it would not have had the legal knowledge to require those other revisions. The reason was most likely that the United States attorney learned that Abijah Adams was a mere bookkeeper for the *Chronicle,* who did not print or publish the articles and who might be acquitted by the jury if included.

An arrest warrant for Thomas Adams was issued the next Tuesday, October 23, and he was brought before the court that day. He pleaded not guilty, and his trial was set for early June 1799, when the Circuit Court would hold its next session in Boston.[19] Two days later, Adams published a brief notice that he had been arraigned for "libellous and seditious publications," and said that further comment "will be deferred till after the trial." In the next issue, he was not able to resist publishing a brief notice that his trial "for pretended Seditious publications" would not occur until June 1799. The following Monday, he appeared in court again with two sureties, to sign a recognizance bond in the amount of $2,000 by himself, with another $1,000 each by the sureties, to secure Adams's appearance at trial.[20] The required amount was high, in comparison to his maximum fine under the relevant provision of the Sedition Act, which was $2,000.

Thomas Adams had long been unwell; shortly before his arrest he had spent three months convalescing at Saratoga Springs in New York. Under the pressure of pending federal and state prosecutions, he sold the newspaper to his former partner, James White, effective the first of May 1799. Nine days later, Adams died.[21] Under White's direction the *Chronicle* "became a largely nonpartisan paper for more than a year"—the crucial year preceding the presidential contest of 1800. After that, White sold the *Chronicle* to Abijah Adams and Ebenezer Rhoades, who returned it to Republican principles.[22]

Abijah Adams's Trial

While Thomas Adams awaited his June 1799 trial in the federal prosecution under the Sedition Act, he and his brother Abijah (c. 1754–1816) were subjected to a state prosecution under the common law of seditious libel.[23] The case arose from two other articles that the *Chronicle* printed in February 1799, as the Massachusetts General Court (its legislature) debated its response to the Virginia and Kentucky Resolutions, which protested the Alien and Sedition Acts as unconstitutional. The Massachusetts response, among other things, denied that a state legislature could properly judge whether laws passed by Congress were unconstitutional under the federal Constitution. In response, the articles asserted that the legislators' resolution that a sovereign state *"shall have no right to decide on any invasion of his constitutional powers"* violated their oath of allegiance to Massachusetts, and that their failure to acknowledge such an invasion by the Alien and Sedition Acts "aimed a *death wound* to the Constitution of the United States," so that their names "will rot *above ground* and be unsavoury to the nostrils of every lover of Republican freedom" (part of the common law punishment for treason).[24] At its base, the prosecution of the Adams brothers was for attacking the constitutionality of the Alien and Sedition Acts and supporting the Virginia and Kentucky Resolutions.

The Adams brothers were indicted during state Chief Justice Francis Dana's circuit in Suffolk County (Boston) on February 19, 1799, after Dana used his grand jury charge (as a friendly source recounted it) to call "the attention of the Jury in a very pointed manner to the Chronicles, a number of which he held in his hand," and particularly to "a piece, which the Judge declared to be of a mischievous & *seditious* tendency, as it was clearly meant thereby to alienate the confidence of the good people of this State from their lawful Representatives & Government, by spreading false, scandalous & wicked slander against their characters." Dana added that subscribing to the *Chronicle* would assist "a traiterous enmity to the Government."[25] Abijah Adams was arrested a week later and posted bond, while Thomas Adams provided a certificate of two doctors confirming that arresting him and haling him to court would endanger his life because of his terminal illness.

The trial of Abijah Adams took place on the first three days of March 1799, and though it was under common law rather than the Sedition Act, it echoed prosecutions under that act. The prosecution, led by the commonwealth's attorney general, James Sullivan, argued that English common law, including the caselaw of seditious libel, had been adopted by Massachusetts. Further, he argued that freedom of press under the state constitution provided no defense, because it only meant freedom from prior restraints before publication, under that English common law. The prosecutor and the judges relied on Sir William Blackstone's narrow definition of liberty of press to that effect.[26]

Disputing that, the defense attorneys, led by George Blake, attempted to offer broad definitions of freedom of press from John Adams's writings and from the Massachusetts Declaration of Rights, which protected freedom of press in expansive language without any hint of Blackstone's restricted meaning; but the chief justice excluded that argument. The defense made three arguments: that under "the constitution and laws of Massachusetts no indictment was maintainable for a libel against the government," that each article was "not in itself libellous," and "that the mere Book-Keeper" was not guilty of seditious libel.[27] Most of the emphasis was on the first argument. The state constitution safeguarded freedom of press in unqualified terms, and that was said to override colonial adoption of the English common law of seditious libel, especially since the state's adoption of English common law was expressly limited to the parts not repugnant to the state constitution. Seditious libel itself was an illegitimate crime that had long been used as "an engine of state to prostrate" everything "opposed to the will of a monarch, however unjust or arbitrary." The definition of "liberty of the press" "could not be supposed to consist merely in its freedom from previous restraint," because that would leave it "altogether destitute of any real substantial quality of freedom," since something published could immediately be prosecuted. Liberty of the press especially protected commentary on "public men and public measures." The *Chronicle*'s summary and elaboration of these defense arguments, probably by George Blake, is one of the outstanding discussions of freedoms of press and speech, and of the dangers of doctrines of seditious libel, during the crisis years of 1798–1801.[28]

Nevertheless, the jury found Abijah Adams guilty of publishing seditious libel, on March 4. Later, after the chief justice delivered a diatribe on "the monstrous positions" of the Virginia Resolutions and the seditiousness of the *Chronicle* articles, he imposed a sentence of thirty days in prison, payment of court costs, and a good behavior bond of $500.[29] Local Republicans visited Abijah Adams in prison, including elderly Samuel Adams, and carried on a subscription to assist him financially.[30] The *Chronicle* announced the end of Abijah Adams's imprisonment, picking up on the chief justice's praise of the "precious birthright" of the common law, by saying the release was "after partaking of an *adequate proportion* of his *'birthright.'*" Adams himself called the "spirit of political persecution" little more than "a reign of terror."[31]

A Broad Understanding of Freedoms of Press and Speech and Concern about Seditious Libel

Thomas Adams published a barrage of articles condemning the Alien and Sedition Acts as unconstitutional, probably a larger and more regular number than any other Republican newspaper. When a sedition bill was first proposed in Congress, the *Chronicle* began its commentary by quoting the First Amendment and calling the "bill so diametrically opposed" to it that its supporters must be "actuated by motives hostile to the Constitution." The article noted that "[w]hat is meant by *defaming a Law* is beyond my comprehension," and it warned that soon to "laugh at the cut of a coat of a member of Congress" would be criminal. A brief article again quoted the First Amendment, and asked about the Senate sponsor of the sedition bill: "was Mr. Lloyd exempted from his oath" to support the Constitution?[32]

An article on the "Gag Bill" posited that freedom to "speak their sentiments" was part of being "freemen," and that no law can "intimidate them in expressing their opinions on publick men and publick measures." Bad measures that threatened liberties needed to be censured, and "[h]onest measures will appear more conspicuously so, by publick investigation." That was followed by a squib announcing a subscription to assist Bache as he defended "the Liberty of the Press."[33]

When word of the passage of the Sedition Act reached Boston, the *Chronicle* announced that "we are now 'abridged the freedom of the press,'" and showing the law's chilling effect, added that "we may be afraid to mention the *doings* of individuals in Congress, for fear it should be considered, 'as bringing them into contempt or disrepute' and injuring them in the minds of the people." The next issue placed at the top of the front page the heading "Sedition Bill," the words of the First Amendment, the text of the new law, and then the heading "Alien Bill," with its text. Later in that issue, a particularly passionate essay on the Sedition Act portrayed it as a servant of the antichrist ("she bears in her forehead the indelible marks of her parentage") committed to "open malignity" to the Constitution. After skipping one issue, an essay on "Freedom of Opinion and the Liberty of the Press" continued the apocalyptic language by expecting that "the flames of persecution" raged with peculiar violence "against the important obstacle to the brands of oppression *a free and Independent PRESS*"—the flames coming from "the fanatic rage of federalism"—after becoming "weary of the old expedients" of "public threats and private calumny." Instead a "system of terror" was enacted—the Sedition Act. That article, probably written by Thomas Adams, warned that the new system would "crush the free expression of public sentiment."[34] These and later articles stated, or assumed, that the Sedition Act violated constitutional freedoms of press or speech and viewed those freedoms as quite broad. That doubtless was why Hench concluded that they largely were the reason for the federal prosecution of Adams under the Sedition Act.

When the federal court indicted Thomas Adams, the barrage of articles on freedoms of press and speech immediately increased. The *Chronicle* carried three such articles in the issue following his indictment. One was resolutions from Mason County and surrounding counties in Virginia, which branded the Alien and Sedition Acts "as infractions of our Constitution," because "speaking and publishing our sentiments on all public questions" and "approving or censuring our public servants" is part of "freedom of the press and of speech" as well as "a natural right." Other articles announced that Rep. Matthew Lyon had been arrested and convicted, and that "*Timothy* [Pickering] justifies the sedition act, in his late insolent and officious answer to the Virginians" (the Prince Edward County petition).[35] The next issue, immediately after Thomas Adams's arrest, had another trio of articles. One, announcing that prosecution, pledged that the *Chronicle* "will always support the RIGHTS OF THE PEOPLE, and the LIBERTY OF THE PRESS." Another article reprinted resolutions from Bourbon County, Kentucky saying that the Sedition Act abridged the right "to print and publish our sentiments upon public characters and measures, which is guaranteed to us by our federal and state Constitutions," and "which no law can take away." Another resolution said the Alien Act "is inhuman, unjust, and unconstitutional," degrading to America "as a land of freedom, and as an asylum," and menacing by arming the president "with arbitrary, dangerous, and despotic powers." A third article published resolutions from Louisa County, Virginia asserting that the Sedition Act's operation was "greatly to impair the liberty of the press" under the Constitution, which included "a right to investigate the conduct of our governors." The next issue printed yet another trio of articles: resolutions from Powhatan County, Virginia condemning the Alien and Sedition Acts as "tyrannical and unconstitutional," a report on Lyon as "the first victim under the Sedition bill," and a letter to John Marshall challenging his conclusion that the laws were merely ill-advised and not unconstitutional.[36] And so the *Chronicle* continued.

Thomas Adams's broad understanding of freedoms of press and speech was not a 1798 epiphany; he had expressed similar views beginning with his first issue of the *Chronicle* in 1784. In their front-page announcement, the *Chronicle*'s new owners stated "our own sentiments, views and designs":

> In matters of politics, news-papers are centinels placed upon the out posts of the constitution, and should never be punished, but for sleeping or neglect of duty—
> They hold the rod and the wreath; may mark the wicked man. . . .
> They may stimulate a desire of learning—
> They may be made instrumental in disseminating principles of virtue and morality, a love of religion, and a spirit of liberty—[37]

Thus, Adams's and his partner's position appears to have been that prosecutions for seditious libel were illegitimate ("In matters of politics . . . should never be punished"), though they acknowledged that "news-papers may degenerate into instruments for promoting every thing base," which was properly remedied by punishment of private defamation. Similarly, an essay by Confederationist in late 1787, during the debates on the proposed federal Constitution and on calls for a bill of rights, discussed how the crime of seditious libel would be affected by a protection for "liberty of the press" that "ought to be made in a BILL OF RIGHTS." The writer said that with such a protection, "let the *attorney-general*, of the United States, *file an information* against me for a *libel;* I will carry that declaration in my hand, as my shield and my constitutional defence."[38] That was one of many appearances in the 1780s (and before) of a view finding seditious libel irreconcilable with liberties of press and speech—a view that Leonard Levy and others claim did not come into existence until 1798 and after.[39]

The *Chronicle* published periodic articles by correspondents reiterating its 1784 statement that a newspaper "may mark the wicked man," or may disapprove public officials and measures, as part of freedoms of press and speech. In 1793, an article affirmed the right "to consider the conduct of our PRESIDENT," and "the power of the President," without it being treated as an attack on the nearly sacrosanct George Washington or on the government. In 1795, another article contended that criticizing the administration was not criticizing the government or the Constitution—it denied that "the president is the constitution or the government, and an opposition to his measures is an opposition to the national compact."[40] Of course, the strong view of freedoms of press and speech was not the only view published by the *Chronicle* before its shift to greater partisanship in the early 1790s,[41] but it was the dominant view before and the only view from the early 1790s onward. Its roots in the *Chronicle* went back to the beginning of Thomas Adams's ownership in 1784, and it continued to his death.

Benjamin Fairbanks and the Liberty Pole

Benjamin Fairbanks (1745–1834) was a fifth-generation citizen of Massachusetts and "one of the richest farmers in Dedham," southwest of Boston. When word arrived of British soldiers advancing toward Lexington in 1775, Fairbanks marched as a minute man, as did his wife Mary's father, Capt. Daniel Draper. Fairbanks continued in the militia as a sergeant for at least part of the Revolutionary War, then he returned to farming.[42]

Revolutionary War Expression and "Sedition Poles"

Liberty poles appeared widely before and during the American Revolution to support the patriot side of the conflict, often with a written message on a board.[43] In the late 1790s, Republicans periodically raised liberty poles to claim the legacy of the Revolution and to show support for their side of the Republican–Federalist domestic conflicts and of the French–British

FIGURE 5.1. Raising the Liberty Pole. Engraving by John C. McRae (c. 1875). Library of Congress.

international conflict. They were shocked to hear Federalists call them "sedition poles" or "Jacobin poles." "What! is it to be deemed seditious and considered as an act of insurrection in our citizens to erect a Liberty Pole reared in commemoration of our dear-bought FREEDOM and INDEPENDENCE," which were raised when "we were in colonial subjection to Great-Britain, at the commencement of the revolution" and which the king "considered *rebellion*"?[44]

Dedham, Massachusetts was also, unfortunately for Benjamin Fairbanks, the home of Fisher Ames, an outspoken Federalist member of Congress until his 1797 retirement, and a self-appointed watchman against Jacobin advances after that. The town was closely divided between Federalists and Republicans. Ames had observed in July 1798 that "Jacobinism, in the vicinity of Boston, is not yet dead, it sleepeth," and he soon learned to his horror that Jacobinism awakeneth from its slumber.[45] Later in the year, he discovered that democrats "abound in Dedham," and he warned that the "devil of sedition is immortal, and we, the saints, have an endless struggle to maintain with him." In that struggle with the Jacobins, he believed that the "government must display its power *in terrorem.*" Though the crafty Jacobins may not always be visible, Ames reasoned that "they rest in their lurking-places," acting "like serpents in winter, the better to concoct their venom."[46]

A liberty pole was raised in Dedham on October 22, 1798, with Fairbanks's help, and it carried a placard that soon became the basis for two prosecutions under the Sedition Act:

> No Stamp-Act, no Sedition, no Alien Bills, no Land-Tax;
> downfall to the Tyrants of America,
> peace and retirement to the President,
> long live the Vice-President and the Minority;
> may moral virtue be the basis of civil government.[47]

That menace did not endanger the town long. The liberty pole was "cut down by some federal young men of Dedham," who assembled to oppose "the seditious," as Ames reported to Pickering, even before Judge John Lowell of the federal district court ordered the federal marshal to destroy it.[48]

Arrest and Conviction under the Sedition Act

Fairbanks was arrested on November 6, for assisting with the liberty pole and its message,[49] and was brought before the federal district court the next day. His bail was set at the high level of $2,000 from himself (his maximum fine under the Sedition Act) and $2,000 from sureties, to ensure his appearance at the next Circuit Court.[50] Federalist newspapers reported that Fairbanks was "a deluded ringleader, charged with being an accessory in erecting this rallying point of insurrection and civil war," the "Jacobin pole." Republican newspapers responded with incredulity: "who would have believed it, had it then been foretold, that the People of America, after having fought seven long years to obtain their Independence," would be "seized and dragged into confinement by their own government, for erecting a pole in remembrance of that very Independence?"[51]

Fairbanks was indicted for violating the Sedition Act, in early June 1799, as Justice Samuel Chase presided over the United States Circuit Court in Boston along with Judge Lowell.[52] Chase, before being appointed to the Supreme Court by President George Washington, had been a longstanding Maryland representative in Congress and an equally longstanding participant in financial scandals; later he was the first Supreme Court justice impeached (though not convicted).[53] The indictment charged Fairbanks with aiding and assisting the raising of the liberty pole with its message, and thereby undertaking "to defame the Government of the United States & the Congress & President of said United States & to bring them into dispute & excite against them the hatred of the good people of the United States & to stir up sedition."

Fairbanks initially pled not guilty, but changed that to guilty. As he changed his plea, he submitted a written statement to the court, which asserted that he had no idea "how heinous an offence it was" to raise the liberty pole and placard, and promised never again to fail to support the laws and the government. His groveling statement showed the in terrorem effect—not just a chilling effect—of the Sedition Act:

> *To the Honorable the Judges of the Circuit Court, Sitting at Boston, June Session, 1799.*
>
> IT is true that I was present when the liberty pole was set up; but it was not then known by me nor perhaps by the others concerned, how heinous an offence it was. I had been urged to attend, and had refused to do it, or to assist in making the pole. Afterwards I was so much misled as to attend. I am now fully sensible of my offence; and not wishing to aggravate it, but to make atonement as far as I can for it, I freely confess my fault, without putting the government to the trouble of a trial. I hope the honorable Court will take into consideration this circumstance, and every other in my case, to mitigate the penalties of the law. . . . I will try to conduct so in future, as to shew my sincerity and duty as a good citizen, in support of the laws and government of the United States.[54]

The penitent defendant had one ace up his sleeve.

When Fairbanks was sentenced, Fisher Ames appeared as a character witness for him (though declining to appear as his lawyer), and urged the court "to mitigate the severity of the sentence." His basis was that Fairbanks was "a man of integrity" with "a good estate," though he had "a warm and irritable temperament, too credulous and too sudden in his impressions." In an early form of the insanity defense, Ames stated that Fairbanks had been under "*delusion*" from the "artful and inflammatory sophistry" of David Brown, the defendant in a separate prosecution. Though Fairbanks "was criminal in the affair of the *Sedition Pole,*" he "freely confessed his fault" and promised to return to being a good citizen.[55] As the result of Fairbanks's letter and Ames's testimony, Justice Chase found "one object of punishment, *reformation,* to be already accomplished," and meted out one of the mildest sentences of any Sedition Act sentence: a $5 fine plus court costs, and six hours imprisonment.[56] With that, Chase's store of clemency was exhausted, as David Brown soon learned.

David Brown, "Apostle of Sedition"

David Brown (1747–1814), who spurred raising the Dedham liberty pole, was a shoemaker and carpenter from Connecticut and was described as a common laborer.[57] He was described in newspaper accounts as from Bethlehem, Connecticut and as a soldier in the Revolutionary War. In fact, he moved to Bethlehem from Torrington, three towns north, where he and his wife were members of the First Congregational Church beginning in 1761; the move was late in that decade. Brown's first deed buying land in Torrington said he was originally "of Windsor," Connecticut, four towns to the east. Windsor records show that Brown was born in 1747, and that his great-grandfather Peter Brown moved to Connecticut from Duxbury, Massachusetts in the mid-1600s.[58]

That "wandering apostle of sedition," as Fisher Ames described him, had devoted two years before his 1799 arrest and sentence to writing and speaking on politics. He was said to have claimed to have traveled to nineteen countries in Europe and to almost all the American states, including eighty towns in Massachusetts. His wife, Philena Garnsey Brown, apparently died in 1800 while Brown was still in prison for violating the Sedition Act.[59]

"Blowing the Trumpet of Sedition"

Dedham was under attack, Ames believed. Besides the liberty pole, it had been threatened by Brown's preaching of Republican politics. Fairbanks identified Brown as the person who deluded him and others. Fisher Ames identified Brown as not only the one that "got them ready to set up a liberty-pole" but also a Jacobin runner. "They [the Jacobins] have sent runners everywhere to blow the trumpet of sedition. One David Brown, a vagabond ragged fellow, has lurked about in Dedham, telling everybody the sins and enormities of the government." In his testimony at Fairbanks's sentencing, Ames joined in placing the blame for corrupting Fairbanks and others squarely on "that wandering apostle of sedition."[60]

Brown was certainly a radical, though not a violent one, as is evident in his writings that were the basis of his indictment for sedition.[61] His "Dissertation" outlined many of the concerns of the radical wing of the Republicans, and he believed they added up to looming tyranny. Brown's first concern was economic fraud, that the leaders (all Federalists) fraudulently grabbed all public benefits. He said that occurred by their buying up government obligations while knowing Hamilton's funding system would pass, by their vast purchases of western lands after authorizing their sale, and by their appointment or election to federal offices with a "pension list" of high salaries. As a result, "five hundred out of the Union of five million receive all the benefit of public property."[62]

Brown's second and third concerns were foreign policy and democracy. America violated its obligations to France and supported Britain. Further, the "devilish" Jay Treaty was so one-sided that it "might as well have signed that the British Parliament should set in Philadelphia and give laws." Contrary to democracy, the federal government taught "that a few men were cloth'd by God to govern in Church and State, and that the rest were made for the express purpose to see how miserable he could make them."[63]

Another essay by Brown began by excoriating the newly-imposed taxes, which it connected to the Jay Treaty. It then warned that a federal quest for war with France was a "pretext to enslave the farmers," as part of "an eternal struggle between the laboring part of the Community and those lazy rascals that have invented every means that the Devil has put into their heads to destroy the labouring part of the Community." Federal officials acted "more like the enthusiastic ravings of mad men than the servants of the people." The prosecutor's excerpts ended with the alarming warning that if the people "do not get a redress of their grievances by petitioning for it, they will finally break out like the burning mountain of Etna."[64] Though the court record does not mention it, it is possible (as Robert W. T. Martin has suggested) that Brown also read to crowds from an unpublished manuscript written by William Manning in 1798, entitled "The Key of Libberty."[65]

When Brown's writings in the indictment are assessed, they would appear to pose far more danger to English grammar than to the federal government. He was a radical, but in a great American tradition of freedom of thought, and nothing quoted by the indictment was a threat of causing violence. The examples in the indictment also show the unfairness of those who call him "semiilliterate."[66]

Arrest and Conviction

After Fairbanks was arrested and placed under bail in early November 1798, a warrant was prepared for Brown's arrest, and a search was made but he was not found. Four months later, Brown turned up in Andover, Massachusetts, and was hurriedly arrested by Essex County authorities on March 22, 1799. The county's complaint said Brown publicly read papers of "an Inflammatory and seditious nature against the government and laws of this Commonwealth."[67] The county court required a recognizance bond for his release of $2,000 (half from him and half from sureties), which Brown was unable to provide, so he was put in Salem's jail (107 years after most victims were jailed in Salem for the witch trials). The federal courts learned quickly of Brown's arrest, possibly from a newspaper article on the "Arrest of an Itinerant Jacobin," which mentioned a trove of manuscripts that Brown had when arrested, offering federal prosecutors a dream fishing expedition. A week later, the federal Circuit Court placed witnesses under bonds to assure their appearance at Brown's federal trial in June.[68]

The United States Circuit Court opened on Saturday, June 1, and Justice Chase gave his grand jury charge the following Monday. The grand jury indicted Brown that week.[69] The court issued an arrest warrant for Brown on Wednesday, addressed to the jailer for Essex County, and he released Brown to the federal court the next day. The indictment was read to Brown on Thursday, and when he pled not guilty, his trial was set for the following Saturday.[70]

The indictment charged Brown with violating the Sedition Act by three instances of defaming the government, Congress, and the President. The first was reading the quoted parts of his "Dissertation" to crowds and individuals, and the second was reading from his other essay. The third was the liberty pole and its message.[71]

Brown's plea of not guilty made a trial necessary, a daunting proceeding for a defendant in a Sedition Act criminal case without a lawyer. He changed the plea to guilty, probably after hearing of Chase's leniency toward Fairbanks, and gave a statement that was much toned down from Fairbanks's contrite statement. With the guilty plea on record, Justice Chase took the then unusual action of insisting that the prosecutor's witnesses still give their testimony against Brown, justifying it as necessary to determine Brown's degree of guilt. Luther Ellis testified that Brown held the ladder while the placard was nailed to the pole, and Amariah Chapin said that Brown paid him to paint its message. Joseph Kingsbury related that Brown discussed Thomas Paine's *Age of Reason* with his brother, and Horatio Townsend said Brown quoted from Joel Barlow. Chase told Brown that he needed "to evidence his sincerity and contrition by disclosing to the Government those who had prompted and aided him in his mischievous and dangerous pursuits." Brown declined, saying he would lose all his friends. The justice then lectured Brown on the "malignity and magnitude of his offences" and his "disorganizing doctrines, and impudent falsehoods; and the very alarming and dangerous excesses to which he attempted to incite the uninformed part of the community."[72]

Chase's reason for insisting that the witnesses testify was evidently to justify a harsh sentence, because he then sentenced Brown (who had asked "that his punishment may be wholly by *imprisonment* and not by *fine*") to a $400 fine, court costs, and eighteen months' imprisonment. The imprisonment would continue indefinitely until the fine and court costs were paid.[73]

The contrast in Chase's sentencing is stark between the "opulent" farmer, who Fisher Ames vouched for, and the "vagabond ragged fellow," as Ames called him, who could not afford payment of his fine in order to leave prison at the end of his term and could not even afford a copy of his court judgment in order to petition for relief. Most of the Sedition Act defendants were poor, other than Benjamin Franklin Bache and perhaps Dr. James Smith (and a few of the contemplated defendants); a typical newspaper editor typically operated at a deficit and had to close the paper after a few years. This meant that the majority of Sedition Act defendants could not afford legal representation, and stood alone in facing a biased judge, a well-trained United States attorney, and a prosperous panel of Federalist jurors. Their poverty also meant that months of imprisonment were economically disastrous and were unrelieved by the comforts that money could buy—better food, better quarters, more firewood.

One witness against Brown, Dr. Nathaniel Ames, ignored his summons, refusing to appear the day the other witnesses testified. He was missed but not forgotten. Four months later, he was surprised to be served a warrant from the federal court and was "carried without warning to Boston . . . , like a felon, for pretended contempt." Dr. Ames was fined eight dollars and taken to jail, where he was refused copies of the court papers. His view of attorneys and judges was not very complimentary; he wrote in his diary, "I was set among pickpocks at the Bar and was spunged of 8 dollars" more. Dr. Ames's view of his Federalist brother was not much better; he refused to attend Fisher Ames's interment because it was a Federalist "political funeral."[74]

Brown petitioned to President John Adams for release by habeas corpus in June 1800, with the pathetic note that he could not petition sooner because he could not pay to obtain a copy of the judgment.[75] He petitioned again in February 1801. He does not appear to have received any responses.

His case fell on more friendly ears as Thomas Jefferson became president in March 1801. Brown was released by the new president's pardon, issued eight days after taking office.[76] Brown had been given the longest prison sentence of any Sedition Act victim, and was in prison the longest of them all—over two years—consisting of two and a half months in county jail, his eighteen month sentence, and four more months because of inability to pay his fine or provide bond.

The sequel to the story is that the nefarious author of the message on Dedham's liberty pole, who the courts sought unsuccessfully, was finally identified in 1811. He was none other than Fisher Ames's brother, the Republican doctor.[77] That also explained why Dr. Ames was insistent on resisting the summons to testify in David Brown's trial.

Lespenard Colie, Damning the President

The first indictment and conviction under the Sedition Act was of Lespenard Colie of New Jersey; both occurred on October 3, 1798. Though Colie (c. 1770–1827) has been described as "a French migrant," his family had been in New Jersey for over a hundred years, and he was a member of the Presbyterian Church in Springfield, New Jersey. Fragmentary records show him as a teenager holding a farm job, where he was paid monthly and could "go home Saturday Nights & find your own Washing," and then show him as an adult selling boards and hay.[78] He and his wife Sarah lived in Springfield, ten miles west of Newark, where he paid taxes from 1795 to 1821, and where he advertised a house for sale in early 1798. Colie had been too young to serve in the Revolutionary War, but became part of the Essex County militia. He was described as "very poor," and ultimately that was the reason for his low fine.[79]

Colie was charged with saying "that if the French came he would join them & fight for a shilling a day, & would deliver up any that were inimical to them—& for D_____g the P________" (damning the president). His statement may have been made during the last week of June 1798, when newspapers reported that some Newark area citizens were "remanded before the Judge of the District Court of the United States" for "having spoken their sentiments on the subject of the President," or it may have been made at the same time as Luther Baldwin's and Brown Clark's jovial outbursts.[80] There is no compelling basis for assuming either date. On October 3, 1798, Colie was brought before the United States Circuit Court in Trenton and indicted by the grand jury for seditious words.[81] The presiding judge was Justice William Cushing of the United States Supreme Court, joined by Judge Robert Morris. Cushing had earlier been an associate justice and the chief justice of the Massachusetts Supreme Judicial Court.[82] His wife accompanied him on the circuit, and recorded what Colie was charged with exclaiming.

The term "seditious words" could refer to a common law crime or to a Sedition Act violation. Some Federalist newspapers said of Luther Baldwin and Brown Clark, who were indicted for the same offense the same day, that they were indicted under the common law and not under the Sedition Act.[83] If so, the same was probably true of Lespenard Colie. Which was it?

Justice Cushing charged the grand jury on October 2, 1798, and it then withdrew. The next morning, the grand jury handed down the three indictments for seditious words (the only indictments it handed down that session). In that grand jury charge, Cushing quoted and summarized the Sedition Act, before he quoted and summarized the Alien Enemies Act, and then defended its constitutionality.[84] Only the indictment of Luther Baldwin survives, and it could be read either way, as being for common law seditious libel or for a Sedition Act violation. The other two indictments would have been worded similarly, since they were written by the same United States attorney and were approved and handed down the same day. Republican newspapers were emphatic that the indictments were under the Sedition Act.[85] In the context of Cushing's grand jury charge under the Sedition Act, and his encouragement of indictments under it, the indictments almost certainly charged violations of the Sedition Act rather than of common law seditious libel.[86]

Cushing's grand jury charge began with the duty to "respect the support of GOVERNMENT," the "absolute importance" of "orderly government," and the virtues of President Adams including his "unshaken independent spirit of liberty, and eminent displays of genius in the most useful services to his country in the most critical crimes, for above 30 years." (The typesetting error of "crimes" rather than "times" could have, but did not, lead to its own Sedition Act case.) Cushing lamented the "unceasing torrent of calumnies" about officials that came from a faction and some presses, and asked "[h]ow is it possible for any free government to stand the shock of such perpetual, inveterate, malicious hostile attacks?" He acknowledged the citizens' "undoubted right to express their opinions upon public matters, in a decent manner," and he later explained that limitation, saying that liberty of the press does not include "a right to print and propagate scandalous and malicious falsehoods."[87] As he quoted the Sedition Act, Cushing said that "printing and publishing false, scandalous and malicious writings against the government, with intent to stir up sedition or insurrection—or resistance to the laws"—was "a dangerous offence in all societies" and could "overturn the freest government in the world." In defending the law's constitutionality, he said that "liberty of the press" allowed people "to publish any truths they please" and only prohibited "malicious lies and slander." Notably as he discussed liberty of the press, Cushing did not define it as only freedom from prior restraints, such as licensing requirements, or quote Blackstone's definition.[88]

Colie initially pleaded not guilty. After the indictments of Baldwin and Clark were announced, Colie changed his plea to guilty. Justice Cushing then sentenced him to a fine of $40 and court costs, but no prison time other than until he paid the fine and costs.[89] That was the third lightest sentence in any Sedition Act case (Jacob Greenawalt being the lightest, with no fine or imprisonment, and Langford Herring next, with only court costs), and one of the only five that did not impose a term of imprisonment (besides those, only Baldwin and Clark).

Colie's case showed that speech critical of the government and its officials would not be tolerated any more than captious press would be tolerated. It also showed that freedom of speech, as well as freedom of press, was restricted by the Sedition Act, just as Matthew Lyon's second count and David Brown's speeches had shown, and as was evident in the prosecutions of Luther Baldwin and Brown Clark, as well as of David Garvin, Jacob Greenawalt, Morris Llewellyn and friends, Langford Herring, Rev. Jacob Eyerman, and Dr. Samuel Shaw.

Luther Baldwin and Brown Clark, Wishing a Cannonball Would Hit POTUS

The second and third indictments under the Sedition Act were of Luther Baldwin and Brown Clark of New Jersey, also on October 3, 1798. These three indictments were less significant than the prosecutions of a member of Congress, Matthew Lyon, or of the editor of New England's leading newspaper, Thomas Adams, both later in October 1798. Instead, the Baldwin and Clark prosecutions involved drunken jest in wishing that one of the celebratory cannonballs would hit the president's posterior. The Baldwin and Clark cases have brought mirth to discussions of the Sedition Act, as historians have solemnly declared that the threat against POTUS (the posterior of the United States) was the "case in which the enforcement of the Sedition Law hit bottom." Period Republican newspapers were horrified that any Republican would be accused of "firing at such a disgusting target as the—of J.A."[90] The English crime of threatening the head of the king was being extended to threatening the posterior of the ruler!

Luther Baldwin (c. 1752–1804) and Brown Clark were obscure citizens of Newark, New Jersey.[91] Baldwin's paternal great-great-grandfather immigrated to Milford, Connecticut from England in 1639, where he and his children were members of the Congregational church. Baldwin's great-grandfather moved to Newark, New Jersey in 1666, where Baldwin's grandparents and parents later lived.[92] Baldwin was a "wagoner" during at least part of the Revolutionary War, and he paid taxes in Newark during 1779–1796.[93] He was described as a "waterman" in his indictment, and used his sloop for odd jobs such as buying and selling hay, repairing bridges when rivers were frozen (charging users a half toll), ferrying passengers across New York harbor, and selling lumber. He was evidently a Republican, because all his business advertisements were in an outspoken Republican newspaper. His death came in May 1804.[94]

Baldwin's role in the American Revolution became a matter of dispute in 1803, as Federalist papers tired of hearing pathetic stories about his sedition prosecution and went on the offensive. They claimed that Baldwin, after serving on the patriot side for a five-month term, decided the British prospects were better and became a loyalist, carrying on trade with the British, which led to his property being confiscated after he failed to appear at a New Jersey hearing. Republican newspapers responded that he did not desert, that his sale of poultry and eggs to the British in New York City was a cover for gaining and providing information to General Washington, and that the missed hearing meant nothing because his estate was not confiscated.[95] There were indeed New Jersey spy rings—particularly those led by John Honeyman and by John and Baker Hendricks—though no hard evidence has been found to place Baldwin in one of them. When the Hendricks brothers were arrested by patriot forces, George Washington gave orders to "put a stop to the prosecution," because "they were employed by Colo. Dayton last summer to procure intelligence of the movements of the Enemy," which was "indispensably necessary." And they had been allowed "to carry small quantities of provisions and to bring back a few Goods the better to cover their real designs." The Hendricks also operated a pair of whaleboats that were authorized as privateers and that required a crew. The truth appears to be the Republican account, because of the response to Baldwin's petition for compensation in 1790 for war service as a spy. The secretary of war's report found that his claim to have been "employed to obtain intelligence from the city of New-York" had been "established in an authentic manner."[96]

Drunken Banter about the President's Posterior

President John Adams, traveling from the nation's capital in Philadelphia to his home in Quincy, Massachusetts, reached Newark during the late afternoon of July 27, 1798. The "brigade horse, infantry, and grenadiers" assembled, along with the militia, "marched to the spot where the President landed, and escorted him to his lodgings." Meanwhile, the artillery company assembled on the Battery and fired "a federal salute," and other cannon were fired "from the Fort at Governor's Island, and from the British frigate Topaz" with nineteen guns; and "bells were rang."[97]

Baldwin, approaching a tavern, heard the cannon discharges honoring President John Adams, and exclaimed in a "loud voice" (according to the indictment) that the president "is a *damned rascal* and ought to have his *arse kicked.*" He then said, "I wish one of the charges would pass thro' his arse." The indictment said this was "to the great scandal and contempt of the President of the United States and government."[98] A later account, widely reprinted from Newark's Republican newspaper, plausibly gave the context of Baldwin's tipsiness and Brown Clark's minor role:

> Luther Baldwin happening to be coming towards John Burnet's dram-shop, a person that was there [Brown Clark] says to Luther, there goes the President, and they are firing at his a—: Luther, a little merry replies, that he did not care if they fired through his a—: Then exclaims the dram seller, that is sedition.

Unfortunately for the merry duo, the tavern owner, John Burnet, was a Federalist and was on the payroll as a salaried postmaster. He reported the incident to the United States attorney, and was required to post bond to assure his appearance as a witness against Baldwin at the upcoming session of the United States Circuit Court.[99]

The prosecution initially was evidently under the common law of seditious libel, like the prosecutions of Burk and Durell, until the indictments on October 3.

Baldwin's words kept evolving during his prosecution. Federalist newspapers, in delayed notices of his arrest, reported that he expressed "a wish that the President of the United States was dead." Republican accounts were that "*he did not care* if the persons who were firing some cannon as the President was passing through the town, were to fire through his body (loaded only with powder)."[100] The incident continues to evolve; some authors describe the case as "the jailing of a drunkard for refusing to stand as the president rode by."[101]

Arrests and Indictments

Baldwin's and Clark's separate indictments for seditious words were handed down from the grand jury after Lespenard Colie's, on October 3, 1798.[102] Unlike Colie, they were not in court that day and so they were arrested and placed under bonds to ensure their appearance at the next court session.[103] In that next session of the Circuit Court on April 2, 1799, both pleaded not guilty, and were required to enter new recognizance bonds for their appearance for trial at the October session—Baldwin for $500 and a surety for another $500, and Clark for $500 and two sureties for another $500. Witnesses were also bound over to appear, including John Burnet to testify against Baldwin.[104]

Both Baldwin and Clark changed their pleas to guilty in court on October 3, 1799, a year after their indictments. Baldwin was fined $150 plus court costs, and Clark was fined $50 plus costs, with both being kept in custody until those amounts were paid. The reason for the low fines is that they were "penitent" as "speakers of sedition," as Justice Bushrod Washington wrote.[105]

These cases were ludicrous, as the *Aurora* observed. It was "astonishing how men with common sense could be found to support such prosecutions or juries to recognize such absurd charges," other than to attack the opposition.[106] Inebriated men had been criminally charged with sedition for their merry banter about harmless blanks.

But these cases showed something far more serious, a political double standard. The local Republican paper protested: "Most of the Papers in the United States, which are violent in advocating the justice of the Sedition Bill, teem with the most virulent invectives against Thomas Jefferson: and yet such editors are unmolested. Why this partiality?" "[N]one of the Federal Grand Juries have ever presented a *'federal'* printer." Republican newspapers claimed that a leading Federalist member of Congress and sponsor of the Sedition Act, Robert Goodloe Harper, said essentially the same thing about the president that tipsy Luther Baldwin had said: "*I wish the horses may run away with him* (the President) *and break his neck,*" in reaction to Adams announcing new envoys to France. "But why is not this man, that wishes such terrible wishes about the President, arrested and punished?"[107]

Baldwin's and Clark's cases raised not just levity but also significant questions about freedoms of speech and press. One resulting essay on the Sedition Act, in Newark's Republican newspaper, noted that "all who can read, must know, that Congress is expressly forbidden by the constitution to form any law restricting the freedom of speech or the liberty of the press, and consequently, that they have no more right to enact that law, than the great Mogul would have, and it is no more obligatory on the citizens of the United States than an act of the British Parliament." Another essay said that Baldwin's "arrest proves how little confidence is to be reposed in the limitations of the law"—instead the Sedition Act showed "arbitrary power" as in "the days of Harry the Eighth."[108]

CHAPTER SIX

Failed Prosecutions

THE SEDITION ACT prosecutions just discussed were not the full scope of Secretary of State Timothy Pickering's plan for the first campaign to enforce the Sedition Act during the second half of 1798. There were a number of other targets eagerly aimed at by Pickering or by other zealous Federalist officials that did not work out. They included the only Republican in a high federal office, Thomas Jefferson; the noted poet and supporter of the French Revolution, Joel Barlow; the Republican editor of a Pennsylvania newspaper, John Israel; the writer of a "seditious" essay, Aristides; and an overlooked Georgian who damned the president, David Garvin.

Vice President Thomas Jefferson

The idea of surveillance of the vice president to find grounds to prosecute him under the Sedition Act is a startling thought, but so is the fact of investigating and arresting Matthew Lyon and contemplating an arrest of John Clopton and other Republican members of Congress. Pickering and many other Federalists planned to quash opposition speech and press wherever the legal case was strong enough for success in court.

The Vice President as an Internal Enemy

Pickering, three months before the Sedition Act passed, described Thomas Jefferson as one of "our internal enemies." Retired Sen. George Cabot similarly referred to Jefferson as one of the "internal foes." Sen. Theodore Sedgwick called Jefferson "the very life and soul of the opposition." As the XYZ papers were being considered by Congress, rumors flew that Jefferson had been "detected in a criminal correspondence with the French directory," even while older rumors survived of his "being involved in Blount's conspiracy."[1] Three months later, Rep. John Allen, in his key speech supporting the proposed sedition bill in Congress, after identifying the *Aurora* as "the great engine of all these treasonable combinations," condemned Jefferson as "walk[ing] the streets arm-in-arm" with its editor, Benjamin Franklin Bache (who was already being prosecuted for seditious libel), holding "midnight conference" with him, and being "nightly closeted with its editor." There was little doubt who Allen meant when he added that the *Aurora* contained "the opinions of certain great men," as it aimed "at the overthrow of this Government." Nor was there any doubt that Jefferson was the leader of the opposition, though he remained as veiled as possible; he was viewed as behind all Republican efforts. John Adams told Pickering that Dr. George Logan's unauthorized diplomatic mission was known only by "Mr. Jefferson, Mr. Genet, and Mr. Letombe," and asked whether it was constitutional for "a party of opposition to send embassies to foreign nations to obtain their interference in elections?"[2] After William Hindman was defeated for reelection to Congress, he said it was "the jacobinic jeffersonian Junto" who he hoped the Federalists would vanquish. Just after Adams yielded the presidency to Jefferson, he complained that it was the Republican editors and "their great patron and protector," Jefferson, who had defeated him.[3]

Federalist newspapers repeated Pickering's accusation. The leading one, the *Gazette of the United States,* called Jefferson one of the "*children of Sedition.*" A Boston paper, after claiming Jefferson directed Dr. Logan's diplomatic trip, hoped "[a] few more discharges from the artillery of the *Sedition Act* will compell the remaining garrisons of jacobinism to surrender prisoners" and pay fines. A Maine paper warned, "Let not the Jacobin think that a word will save or protect a man in the United States, though that word should be Republican, Vice president, or Jefferson."[4] To Jefferson they ascribed preternatural powers as the leader of the internal enemies. "The correspondent of *Mazzei,* is in the centre of the circle. His myrmidons, faithful to their duty, act as he directs, and bellow as he prescribes." According to a

Philadelphia paper, Jefferson was "the *Chief Juggler,*" who had "the entire management of the Jacobin puppets," and had divided them into "three Grand Departments," headed north to south by the Republican editors Thomas Cooper, William Duane, and James T. Callender, all "subject to the controul of the chief Juggler and his select council." In particular, the *Aurora* was "under the patronage of Mr. JEFFERSON!" and was "the general vehichle of all the falshood, and treason, of all the Jacobins in this country."[5]

The primary reason why Republicans, and Jefferson in particular, were viewed by most Federalists as internal enemies was that an opposition party was viewed as illegitimate and its disagreements with the ruling party were viewed as attacks on government. That was particularly true when the opposition party was favorable to a foreign country and a revolutionary one at that.

Initially, Jefferson had been a loyal cabinet member in the Washington administration, but he left at the end of 1793 after disagreements developed over Hamilton's financial plan, partisan newspapers, and other issues. After his departure, further disagreements arose over Washington's condemnation of Democratic-Republican Societies and support of the Jay Treaty, though Jefferson hastened to assure Washington that he had nothing to do with the *Aurora*'s attacks on the first president.[6] Their complete rupture came with the publication of Jefferson's letter to Philip Mazzei, which was translated and published in America in May 1797. That letter stated that "an Anglican, monarchical and aristocratical party has sprung up, whose avowed object is to draw over us the substance as they have already done the forms of the British government." It attacked George Washington and other Federalist "apostates who have gone over to these heresies, men who were Samsons in the field and Solomons in the council, but who have had their heads shorn by the harlot England." The *Gazette of the United States* and other Federalist newspapers immediately assailed Jefferson for accusing "the Federalists, including the venerable Washington and J. Adams, as being leagued in a wicked plot, to overturn this *good constitution,* and to establish a king, hereditary nobles, &c," and equally bombarded Jefferson's "faction in opposition to our government and its administration." As 1798 dawned, Federalist papers were still lambasting the "Jacobin faction" and "the Citizen Friend of Mazzei" who notified "the enemy that the government and people are at odds."[7]

Further, Federalists who charged Republicans with seditious acts excoriated Jefferson for directing them. He was said to be the "high officer in the Government, (infamous for his *foreign correspondence*)," who was "in daily and secret conference" with the "Gallic Editor of the Aurora." He was the issuer of introductory letters to Talleyrand and passports for Dr. Logan to make possible Logan's mission to France, which was "positive proof of a coalition between foreign enemies and domestic traitors." In Virginia Jefferson was "plotting some diabolical Plan against the Foederal Government," while also serving as "the Fountain of Mischief in this Country." He was rumored to be the author of the Virginia and Kentucky Resolutions. Jefferson's critics were not right in every allegation, but they were right that he was the head of the opposition.[8]

Investigation of Jefferson for Prosecution

Jefferson was a target of investigation. Pickering's fellow cabinet member, Secretary of the Treasury Oliver Wolcott, Jr., took the unusual step of traveling to New York City in June 1798 to investigate whether Bache—and Jefferson and other leading Republicans—had received advance copies from Talleyrand of diplomatic messages. Stephen Higginson told Wolcott, as he had told Pickering, that "the packets he received from Talleyrand" were addressed to "Jefferson, Monroe, Randolph, Baldwin, Genet, Bache," and others. Wolcott asked William Dunlap "repeatedly if there were any letters for Mr Jefferson," and intercepted and kept one of Jefferson's letters.[9]

When rumors about the authorship of the Virginia and Kentucky Resolutions swirled about, Jefferson was at his greatest risk, since Pickering regarded as seditious any statement that federal legislation or action was unconstitutional, and consequently denounced those resolutions as "hostile to the general government" and "outrageous attempts to break the union." Pickering was not alone; Theodore Sedgwick saw them as "a declaration of war," and George Cabot saw in them "the violent & seditious temper of Virginia."[10] As Adrienne Koch observed, "the second highest officer in the United States government might be charged with sedition if he overtly associated himself with a movement to declare two measures of the current Congress 'unconstitutional.'" Soon after, when participants in the Fries Rebellion were prosecuted during the first half of 1799, Fries referred to "great men" being involved, and President Adams told Wolcott that it is "of importance to discover, if possible, the *great men* alluded to by Fries" as being "at the bottom of this business." Throughout the period, Jefferson's mail was occasionally tampered with, such as two of his letters to James T. Callender that ended up in Pickering's files.[11]

Jefferson himself believed that he was at great risk of being prosecuted under the Sedition Act. Even before the act passed, he cautioned Madison to watch for "whether any of my letters are intercepted," and said he felt "inquietude for their safe conveyance." Three weeks later, one of his letters, which had been intercepted, was paraphrased in the leading Federalist newspaper. The *Aurora* soon warned of an overheard conversation that when "*the sedition bill is passed . . . we will begin first with* JEFFERSON *and* GALLATIN."[12] After the Sedition Act became law, Jefferson's worries about prosecution caused him to curtail all correspondence with Madison for long periods—from late June to late October 1798, when responses to the Alien and Sedition Acts were formulated and discussed, and from late November 1799 to early March 1800, when plans were laid against the wave of new prosecutions and for the upcoming elections. Jefferson also continued to be concerned about misuse of his correspondence to calumniate himself and the Republican cause. He trusted the "post offices with nothing confidential, persuaded that during the ensuing twelve-month they will lend their inquisitorial aid to furnish matter for new slanders." "Indeed the interception & publication of my letters exposes the republican cause as well as myself personally to so much obloquy."[13]

The Federalist administration applied a double standard, protecting the president but not the vice president in the text of the Sedition Act, and prosecuting even drunken jests about the president while assisting press attacks on the vice president. The *Aurora* and other Republican newspapers were quite aware of the double standard, noting that Federalist papers "teem with the most virulent invectives against Thomas Jefferson; and yet such editors are unmolested. Why this partiality?" Newark's *Centinel of Freedom* complained that Federalist printers "vilify none but Jefferson, Livingston, Gallatin and several other republicans of Congress." Jefferson was even more aware of his unfair treatment. He complained that he was the victim of "calumnies of every kind, from every department of government Executive, Legislative, & Judiciary, & from every minion of theirs holding office or seeking it." The obloquy peaked when he was a candidate for president in 1800, as he was widely denounced for his skeptical religious beliefs.[14] The willingness of most Federalists to oppose Jefferson by supporting Burr for the presidency, after Adams lost the election of 1800, is a good indication of the willingness of those Federalists to see Jefferson prosecuted.

Yet despite a strong desire to prosecute Jefferson and extensive investigation of his activities, no case was brought against him. Pickering failed to find sufficiently strong evidence to make conviction probable. Insufficient evidence instead would have made a martyr.

FIGURE 6.1. Joel Barlow. Drawing by John Vanderlyn (1798). Courtesy National Portrait Gallery, Smithsonian Institution, gift of Mr. and Mrs. Joel Barlow.

Joel Barlow and His Letter from Paris

Joel Barlow (1754–1812), a poet and American supporter of the French Revolution, wrote the controversial letter that Matthew Lyon read to audiences. Barlow grew up in Connecticut, where his parents were prosperous farmers, and attended the predecessor to Dartmouth College before graduating from Yale as a classmate of Oliver Wolcott, Jr. He served as a chaplain in the Revolutionary War, and wrote poetry with a mission of producing America's epic poem. In 1788 he began a fifteen year sojourn in Europe, initially representing an American company selling western land to Europeans, and after its collapse, running a successful shipping company in Hamburg. He then served as the American consul in Algiers, negotiating the freedom of enslaved American sailors, and negotiating treaties with the other Barbary countries, as his leading biographer, Richard Buel, describes.[15] Living many of those years in Paris, Barlow ardently supported the French Revolution and the beheading of Louis XVI, was granted French citizenship when George Washington was, and ran unsuccessfully to serve in the National Assembly. He was a radical, and a close friend of Thomas Paine and other radicals.[16] After returning to the United States in 1804 and continuing literary pursuits, he undertook one more diplomatic mission and died in 1812 after following the French army into and out of Russia to get Napoleon's signature on a treaty.

The Seditionist Who Was Aided and Abetted by Rep. Matthew Lyon

When Matthew Lyon was indicted and convicted of violating the Sedition Act, the third count was for aiding and abetting Joel Barlow's seditious libel in his letter from Paris. That letter was alleged to libel the president, the Senate, and the government by censuring Adams's "bullying speech" to Congress and the Senate's "stupid answer" (as discussed in Chapter 4), and more generally by expressing the Francophile view held by the Republicans in direct conflict with the Francophobe view embraced by the Federalists.[17] Lyon could only be guilty of aiding and abetting seditious libel if Barlow was himself chargeable with seditious libel for his letter.

Barlow's letter provided ample material for an indictment under the Sedition Act. Besides the portions quoted in Lyon's indictment, the letter called the Jay Treaty an "act of submission to the British Government" and of hostility to France, which was "thrust down the throats of the people of America." It said that the previous ambassador to France dealt with "the difficulties created by the madness of his predecessor" and "the continued folly of your Executive," Washington, who "was in the dotage of his natural life." Adams was "a reputed Royalist," who appointed three commissioners "to make the people of the United States believe that a negociation was offered" and who then picked people who would thwart success. Barlow was "in trembling expectation of seeing him give another desperate leap into the regions of madness."[18]

The Federalist press rendered a harsh verdict on Barlow's letter. The *Gazette of the United States* said it showed him to be "an absolute traitor to his country," while the *Connecticut Courant* said Lyon's disclosure of it was an example of "traitors to their country" encountering "a premature discovery of their treason." Baltimore's *Federal Gazette* reprinted an article on Barlow's "parricidal arm" as the "slanderer of Washington and Adams!," and the *New York Gazette* concluded that Barlow's letter "unquestionably was written in Talleyrand's bureau; while that arch apostate sat at the elbow of the duped American and dictated every word."[19] Others wrote of its "mixture of treachery to the author's own country, and a slavish devotedness to France, probably unrivalled in the black annals of treason," and of

Barlow's conversion to be "a jacobin, a democrat, a revolutionist, a French philosopher!" All these articles appeared in most Federalist papers. The *Spectator* reminded readers that a year after Louis XVI was beheaded, "*French* Barlow was making songs in favor of killing kings in mass," apparently referring to a song attributed to him beginning "God save the Guillotine" (to the tune of God Save the King) and featuring refrains such as

And when great George's poll,
Shall in the basket roll,
Let mercy then control,
The Guillotine. . . ."[20]

"The Tool of the Directory"

At the time of Lyon's trial, Pickering described to the president the Barlow letter and the author's criminality. Pickering wrote that Barlow was doomed to infamy by his letter, and placed a copy in his files to help bring that about.[21] Stephen Higginson wrote to Pickering that Barlow's letter was instigated by the Directory. George Cabot agreed that "citizen Barlow" was "the tool of the Directory." Robert Troup said that Barlow's letter "is an infamous libel on our government." Others kept Pickering informed on the poet.[22] Barlow was further doomed by his 1799 address to the American people, as Pickering eagerly sought a copy. After mid-1798, Pickering viewed Barlow as a criminal, and no longer saw him in the positive light that followed Barlow's success in negotiating with the Barbary pirates, when Pickering had written to Alexander Hamilton that Barlow "managed the negociations with Algiers with great ability" and might be considered as a possible member if a commission were sent to France.[23]

Barlow was not indicted, however. The reason was that he was out of the federal courts' jurisdiction, since he remained in France the entire time the Sedition Act was effective. Despite administration hostility, Barlow's later letter encouraging a new peace mission to France was read seriously by George Washington and forwarded to John Adams.[24] However, Adams stressed that "Barlows Letter, had I assure you very little Weight in determining me to this measure. . . . But in my opinion it is not often that We meet with a Composition which betrays so many and so unequivocal Symptoms of blackness of heart. The Wretch has destroyed his own Character. . . . Tom Paine is not a more worthless fellow." The president had already said that he "despise[d] the Letter as much as I have for some Years scorned the Man."[25] Adams certainly viewed Barlow as worthy of prosecution. But Pickering could never arrest Barlow because he remained in Europe.

John Israel and the *Herald of Liberty*

John Israel (c. 1777–1806), founder of two Republican newspapers in western Pennsylvania, grew up in Philadelphia where his father Israel Israel owned a tavern and was a Republican leader. The elder Israel was one of the two sureties for Bache when he was arrested for seditious libel. Carl E. Prince, in the leading biographical article on the younger Israel, noted that he "was generally thought of by the public as being Jewish," though he was nonpracticing and had Episcopalian maternal grandparents.[26] As a teenager, Israel joined a Democratic–Republican Society and was an apprentice to a printer (probably Bache). At age twenty-one, he moved across the state and founded a newspaper, *Herald of Liberty,* in Washington, Pennsylvania in early 1798.[27] Israel actively supported Republican candidates—particularly Albert Gallatin for Congress and Thomas McKean for governor—and served as "the Republican party's chief spokesman and manager in western Pennsylvania." He was rewarded by appointment to the paid part-time position of county recorder. Israel suffered a number of antisemitic verbal assaults in Pittsburgh's Federalist newspaper and by Federalist campaigners, but the assaults appear to have backfired.[28] Two years after establishing the *Herald of Liberty,* Israel confronted his assailants by founding the *Tree of Liberty* in Pittsburgh and moving there. His move and his new paper had "considerable pecuniary assistance" from the area's leading Republican, Hugh Henry Brackenridge, who built the printing office on his own property (Federalist opponents lampooned him as constructing a "*synagogue* on his own ground").[29] After Israel weathered a split in the Republican party in 1805, he sold the *Tree* at the end of the year. He died in 1806 from an infection following a small cut.[30]

Condemnation of the Sedition Act

Israel's *Herald of Liberty* was an "aggressively Republican" newspaper.[31] On its half-year anniversary, weeks after the Sedition Act was signed into law, Israel published an article defiantly describing the newspaper's viewpoint and responding to attacks on its editor.

> He has been termed a Jacobin; Disorganizer; and Enemy to the Country—in fact a Devil. If Jacobinism consists in a censure of such measures as are inimical to the interest of the People and the happiness of society—he is a Jacobin. If a Disorganizer be a person who always acts for the support of the laws after they have received the sanction of the constituted authorities; and who will always oppose the violation of the Constitution by any man or set of men—he is unquestionably a disorganizer.

The article then described the Federalist opponents as "an Anglo-monarchical party, who either by stopping or muzzling the press—or by calumniating men opposed to them in political opinions, hope to introduce principles subversive of our Constitution and liberties." Israel's second newspaper, the *Tree of Liberty*, was equally outspoken as a Republican paper. Federalist Sen. Uriah Tracy described it as "a red hot Democratic press and newspaper."[32]

That allusion to the Sedition Act as "stopping or muzzling the press" was typical of most issues of the *Herald*. Upon House passage, Israel commented that citizens "had better hold their tongues and make tooth picks of their pens." He quoted the First Amendment, and warned that pimps and spies would be "continually sneaking about" to report "any unguarded expression concerning public measures." Upon the Sedition Act becoming law, the *Herald* printed the First Amendment above the text of the statute. It also reprinted a defiant article from the *Independent Chronicle* saying that citizens should "speak their sentiments," because "[n]o laws can bind them *in opposition to the constitution*, nor terrors intimidate them in expressing their opinions." Citizens should give "manly censure on their servants" in government, and "none but the dishonest will ever attempt to arrest such animadversions."[33] Another essay in the *Herald* stated that "Sedition is a crime not known to the constitution of our country," and that only "a weak or unprincipled administration is obliged to resort to the most violent measures for its support, a restraint of the liberty of speech, and the press—an alien bill," and the like. The *Herald* published petitions against those laws, such as one from Madison County, Kentucky, protesting that "the Alien and Sedition bills, are infringements of the constitution and of natural right." At the same time, Israel's newspaper regularly reprinted articles on prosecutions under the Sedition Act, dripping with disapproval.[34]

Contemplation of Prosecution

Unfortunately for Israel, Federalist Judge Alexander Addison also lived in Washington, Pennsylvania. Addison, president of one circuit of the Pennsylvania county courts, wrote a long letter to Pickering, describing the sedition of the "Jacobin Printer here," and urging Pickering to have the United States attorney prosecute him. Addison enclosed a pamphlet that he had written defending the Alien and Sedition Acts, which he had turned into a charge given to the grand juries throughout his circuit of Pennsylvania courts.[35] Addison described "the predominancy of Jacobinism here" in the western half of the state, and lamented that "the people are taught and believe that Government is pursuing a systematic plan to deprive them of all their liberties," so that "all the friends of Government are hated and opposed as conspirators in this plot." He then got to the point of his letter:

> The cause of all this I believe is a Newspaper printed in this town by a son of Israel Israel. It spreads with great success and though constantly filled with falsehood is considered as the only vehicle of truth. It threatens the fall of the federal paper here (which is well conducted by a worthy and poor man) and the fall of federal principles.[36]

Addison had failed in causing John Israel to be prosecuted, which was why he was writing to Pickering. "I had once determined to bind him over to the federal court for publishing the Kentucky Resolutions," until he found that they already had been published by Philadelphia newspapers without consequence. Addison then had tried to have two different grand juries, "composed chiefly of men professors [adherents] of religion," to "have presented him for an impious mock prayer for the President on the Fast day," but they "refused to find the Bill."[37] That mock prayer of Adams began with a confession of his sins, which were "equal, if not superior to any other of the human race," and as numerous "as the sand on the sea shore." It listed examples, such as "political errors in my Defence of the Constitution, *alias* Panegyric on the British government," Adams's "pretended" admiration of "the cause in which we were engaged against Great Britain," and his endeavoring "to gull the people" and practicing "artifices" to "obtain the Presidential chair." It ended with a plea for "placing the crown upon the head of thy unworthy servant," or at least "upon the head of my son Quincey," and an admission that his proclamation for a day of prayer and fasting was actually "for a rallying point for the 'friends to law and order.'"[38]

Addison offered Pickering a second instance of sedition, besides Israel's mocking prayer: his printing of county resolutions calling the Alien and Sedition Acts unconstitutional:

> a seditious address to Mr. Gallatin pointedly censuring as unconstitutional and oppressive the Alien and Sedition Acts and if I remember also the Stamp Act. This address with Gallatin's answer (which gave not the least check to this libellous conduct) was triumphantly published in Israel's *Herald of Liberty* just before the election and contributed not a little to inflaming the passions of the people and promote[d] the unfavorable result for which the way was so well paved before.[39]

Thus, the offense of publishing sedition was made even more serious by seeking to influence an election! The resolutions that Addison mentioned were addressed by a citizen assembly to their representative in Congress, which did not strike Addison as making them legal. Those resolutions found "the 'Sedition Bill' to be *impolitic, unjust* and *unconstitutional*— . . .

unjust, because it will operate on the unwary, who have hitherto been accustomed freely to investigate public measures; and unconstitutional, because it goes to an abridgment of the liberty of speech and of the press—rights expressly guaranteed by the Constitution."[40] To Addison and to Pickering, such a statement violated the Sedition Act, and printing it did as well.

Addison ended the letter by urging that Pickering have the federal attorney prosecute Israel, using the deferential indirect language of the period. "Whether the deputy attornies of the United States ought to have express instructions" to present informations to the grand jury, or whether there ought to be "some other method adopted for counteracting detecting and suppressing of them," "it becomes not me to suggest."[41]

Pickering responded by saying that he would help in "dispersing your charge on the Liberty of Speech & of the Press." He did not discuss prosecution of John Israel, but there is no question that Israel should be prosecuted under Addison's analysis of the Sedition Act, and under Pickering's similar approach. Addison's view was that "when slanderous words are spoken of the constitution, or administration, or any of its acts or officers, they are ground for an indictment" for seditious libel." "No crime, therefore, is greater, than that slander, which diminishing the people's confidence in the government," undermines it.[42] In sum, "the liberty of the press is precisely as stated by Sir William Blackstone."[43]

It is clear that Addison was urging Pickering to initiate a federal prosecution of Israel under the Sedition Act. It is less clear whether the two grand jury refusals to indict—and a possible third—were all state court proceedings or whether one was a federal court proceeding. What they sought to indict—aspersing the president—was a federal rather than a state concern, and in other cases it was prosecuted by federal courts rather than state courts. No effort to indict Israel was made at the federal circuit court session scheduled for October 11, 1798, because it was cancelled due to the yellow fever epidemic.[44] But an effort might have been made at the circuit court session held on August 4 and 6–7, 1798, where the minutes state that court was held by Justice Samuel Chase and Judge Richard Peters but disclose nothing more.[45]

The war continued between Addison and Israel. Addison wrote to Israel's subscribers upbraiding the editor, censured them in court, and gave speeches against the *Herald*. After Israel's columns helped defeat James Ross for Pennsylvania's governorship, Ross and Addison sued him for defamation. Israel continued to fight back, Jeffrey Pasley suggests, because "here was living, breathing, ranting proof of all the Republicans' arguments against the present regime."[46] Israel immediately began managing and printing petitions urging the legislature to impeach Addison, saying he was "oppressive, tyrannical and partial in the administration of Justice, & guilty of great abuses." Israel's efforts were rewarded with success a few years later.[47]

The "Seditious" Essay of Aristides

William Rawle, the United States attorney for Pennsylvania, sent Timothy Pickering, a few streets away, a Kentucky newspaper containing a pseudonymous article by Aristides, along with a letter from "the gentleman who prosecutes for the United States under deputation from me." That was the normal way of seeking authorization for a Sedition Act prosecution. The letter Rawle enclosed was dated just after the Sedition Act passed in Congress, and it was from Parker Campbell in Washington County, Kentucky. It said that "a paper printed by Hunter & Beaumont in Washington Kentucky" contained a seditious article signed by Aristides, which was "more highly inflammatory . . . than any I have as yet seen." Campbell summarized the article as "an invitation to the Western Inhabitants in case of an open rupture with France, to separate from the east, and directly to oppose the measures of the Administration."[48] The newspaper published by Hunter and Beaumont was the *Washington Mirror,* a Republican paper.[49]

An earlier series of five essays by Aristides, on the same topic of irreconcilable differences between western and eastern regions, had appeared in September 1797 in another Kentucky newspaper, Lexington's *Kentucky Gazette.* Those essays argued that people in America's west "are so far removed from those foul nests of political iniquity, the large commercial cities on the Atlantic shore, that we can think and act like the free born sons of America ought to." By contrast, Federalists in the east had "uniformly and invariably adopted the British systems of government," including "imposts, duties and excise" that approach "fast to the hateful catalogue of our British model."[50] The 1797 essays by Aristides were almost certainly from the same author as the 1798 essay by Aristides that Pickering reviewed.

Those 1797 essays were reprinted in the District of Columbia's *Washington Gazette,* and they were read by Abigail Adams. She identified the "supposed Author" as "Doctor Brown, Brother of the senator of that name from Kentucky," who "has lately returnd from Edinburgh where he received a medical Education." The president's wife further described Dr. Brown, with obvious disapproval: he was "the founder of a Jacobinical club," where he appointed as the head "an Irishman and a Roman Catholic," and where "the rest of the club were composed Chiefly of Foreigeners of no Education." Brown then "removed to Kentucky." His essays amounted to seditious libel, Abigail Adams continued, saying their design was "to decry the Government of the united states, and to recommend one similar to the French constitution, with a directory."[51]

The Kentucky senator was John Brown, Jr., and he had two brothers who were physicians, William and Samuel. Samuel Brown (1769–1830) had studied medicine in Edinburgh, and was the likely author of the Aristides essay that Pickering saw, if the first lady was correct.[52]

Samuel Brown was the son of Rev. John Brown, a Scotch–Irish Presbyterian who immigrated to western Virginia and was the headmaster of the predecessor to Washington & Lee College. His mother, Margaret Preston, was also Scotch–Irish, the daughter of a cabinetmaker and land investor who came to America. The family's income was modest, but education was valued. Samuel Brown graduated from Dickinson College, before studying medicine at University of Edinburgh. Not meeting that university's requirement for three years of resident study, he received his medical degree from University of Aberdeen in 1794. He practiced medicine after that in Maryland, and after moving in 1797, in Lexington, Kentucky. Samuel Brown became a professor of medical subjects at Transylvania University from 1799–1806, and again from 1819–1825, and between those tenures moved to Mississippi, where he married Catherine Percy, and then to Alabama.[53]

Brown, like Dr. Nathaniel Ames and Dr. Samuel Shaw, held strong Republican political views. He wrote to Thomas Jefferson that "nothing which old Tories, Aristocrats & governmental Sycophants can say against you, will in any degree, diminish the confidence, which the good Citizens of this state repose in your abilities & patriotism. Never was a State more unanimous in execrating the measures supported by your Enemies." He enclosed resolutions approved by an assembly in Clark County, Kentucky, calling the Alien Friends Act "unconstitutional, impolitic, unjust and disgraceful," and condemning the Sedition Act as "the most abominable, that was ever attempted to be imposed upon a nation of free men." Brown hoped the Kentucky legislature would similarly "give such solemnity to the voice of the people, as will arrest the attention of our infatuated Rulers," anticipating the Kentucky Resolutions. He ended his letter by praising the French and the Irish.[54]

Pickering had in his hands on July 21, 1798 what he needed to prosecute Aristides, and he could identify him as easily as Abigail Adams did. Why did Pickering not prosecute Samuel Brown? The reason is the same as why he did not prosecute the Kentucky legislators and governor who approved the Kentucky Resolutions a few months later, even though Pickering and the president regarded those resolutions as violations of the Sedition Act. In each case, a prosecution would have to be brought in Kentucky, and victory would be unlikely there because opposition to the Alien and Sedition Acts was so widespread.

David Garvin, "Damning the President for an Old Fool"

David Garvin (c. 1773–c. 1817)[55] was an auctioneer (then called a vendue master) and miller in St. Mary's, a coastal town in Georgia just above the Florida border. He lived on the Georgia side in 1794, when he was listed as a taxpayer who did not own land, but he soon acquired a mill on the Florida side, on Martins Island.[56] In 1808, the American collector for St. Mary's led a break-in of his house in Spanish Florida to recover a "slave girl" he claimed to have bought from Garvin's creditors. Garvin was granted sixty acres in Spanish Florida in 1814, and unsuccessfully claimed 500 additional acres.[57] His case illustrates why only one other prosecution under the Sedition Act was attempted in the south.[58]

Arrest under the Sedition Act

Garvin's case so outraged Georgia's governor, a Republican, that he summarized it in his annual message to the legislature. Gov. James Jackson described the arrest by Capt. John F. Randolph and the state's prosecution of Randolph. He summarized the

> charge against an officer of the United States galley, for landing his men to take a citizen under the sedition act of the United States, as that officer is said to have declared, by order of the secretary of the navy department. Although I cannot believe the secretary ever issued such an order, and forbear to comment on the propriety of the law, I cannot help observing that an attempt of this nature, by a military or naval officer, in a place where the law is open, and the civil magistrate bound to take cognizance of offences against the union, is not only opposed to the constitution of the United States, but tends to foment jealousies ill suited to our present situation, when unanimity is so necessary; and whilst it impresses the idea of oppression, instead of that protection which I am certain the galley was intended for, operates to awaken apprehensions of an act, supposed by many not to be constitutional.[59]

The Sedition Act was the "act supposed by many not to be constitutional," as the governor's next sentence made evident. There, he stated that he was delivering the Kentucky Resolutions to the legislature, "on the subject of that act, and the alien law of the United States."

Jackson filled in more detail when he received a letter from the secretary of the navy, Benjamin Stoddert, who became aware of Jackson's objections when he saw "an extract of [the] address to the legislature," likely in the

Aurora.[60] Jackson responded that the "person injured" was "David Garwin" of St. Mary's, and that the "commander of a galley" was "Captn. Randolph," who "had justified himself as having received private orders" from Stoddert.[61] Jackson enclosed Garvin's affidavit and witness statements. The effort the governor put into gathering those documents showed the intensity of his objection.

Randolph, the new commander of one of the two federal galleys commissioned to protect the Georgia coast during the Quasi-War,[62] admitted that he attempted to arrest Garvin. Garvin responded with an affidavit signed by seven witnesses and sworn before a justice of the peace, which described the arrest:

> That they were present in the town of St. Mary's, on the 30th day of November 1798, and saw an armed force come from on board the Savannah Galley, then lying in the river opposite the town, and attempted to make a prisoner of David Garvin, a citizen of the said State—Captain John F. Randolph, ordered his Lieutenant, Shaw, who appeared intoxicated, to take the said Garvin, and carry him on board the said Galley, and confine him in irons—and if any resistance was made, to fire, run him threw, or bayonet him. The citizens then present, seeing the impropriety of Capt. Randolph's conduct, disarmed the party, and obliged them to go on board the said Galley.[63]

Randolph and Garvin described the incident and subsequent events in statements printed in a Savannah newspaper.

Suit and Countersuit

Garvin retaliated the next day, causing Randolph and his lieutenant to be arrested "with a States warrant, and carried before three Magistrates, who demanded his authority for his conduct." Randolph claimed that "he had private orders from the Secretary of the Navy, but shewed none." Instead, he assured the magistrates that he could prove Garvin to be "a seditious person." Garvin's charge was sent by one of the magistrates to Gov. Jackson, and was the charge referred to in his January message to the legislature.[64]

Randolph's statement charged that "Citizen Garvin," a member of "a French faction" who "boasted of his holding a commission under the French republic," frequently had "damned the President for an old fool." Garvin responded with a newspaper reply calling Randolph a "vain empty fool and a liar," and saying his "wife and children, you have neglected."[65]

A state prosecution of Randolph for riot ("an unlawful act of violence" by three people or more) resulted from Garvin's appearance before the three magistrates. In the Superior Court of Camden County, Georgia, the grand jury indicted Randolph in March 1799, and the judge "ordered that a bench warrant do issue" to require his appearance at the next session.[66] At that next session in October 1799, Randolph was found guilty, and was "fined in the sum of fifty dollars."[67]

In the meantime, a suit was filed against Garvin by Randolph in early December 1798, evidently for defamation. Garvin had not yet published his statement calling Randolph a "vain empty fool and liar," but probably had given more where that came from. The case languished and was finally dismissed.[68] No prosecution was ever brought in the United States Circuit Court, which met in Georgia in April and November 1799,[69] and anyone considering a prosecution would have noted the hostility of Georgia's governor, legislature,[70] and citizenry to the Sedition Act.

A mystery is why the otherwise fairly complete files of the federal war department do not contain Governor Jackson's reply and documents, Stoddert's letter to which Jackson responded, or Randolph's documents that he said he was sending "to the officers of government." By contrast, those files contain all the correspondence and documents about the objectionable Georgia conduct of Lt. Col. Henry Gaither, in the same time period.[71] The most notable clue is that the *Aurora* and most other Republican newspapers used the caption "Standing Army" for their reports of the Garvin case or commented that people must be "wilfully blind who cannot see what the federal administration want a standing army for."[72] Whig ideology and shared Federalist and Republican views associated a standing army with tyranny,[73] and Republicans repeatedly condemned Alexander Hamilton's army as exactly that sort of standing army. The federal government faced a public relations nightmare with Garvin's arrest, as it was in the midst of appointing officers for Hamilton's army and was about to begin enlisting soldiers. The most likely possibility, though impossible to prove, is that the documents relating to Garvin were too politically dangerous to retain in war department records.

Other Possible Contemplated Prosecutions

There are indications that four other prosecutions were contemplated under the Sedition Act during 1798, though they have not been confirmed in court or prosecutor records. They were of Gov. James Garrard of Kentucky, Dr. George Logan of Philadelphia, Charles Webber and Benjamin Brown of Vassalborough, Massachusetts, and the "Printer in Newburgh," New York. These warrant further research, particularly in their personal papers and in the United States attorneys' papers.

Gov. James Garrard (1749–1822) of Bourbon County, Kentucky grew up in Virginia, the son of a prosperous plantation owner and his improbably named wife, Mary Naughty. Garrard served in the Revolutionary War as a schooner captain and then a militia colonel, and afterward moved to the western country that became Kentucky. There, he ran a plantation and was involved in politics, and on the side, leaving his Huguenot ancestors' church, he pastored a Baptist church for a decade.[74] Garrard was elected as the new state's second governor, and was in office when the Kentucky Resolutions were adopted. He condemned the Alien and Sedition Acts in a fiery speech to the legislature, three days before the first chamber passed the Kentucky Resolutions. The speech warned that the Alien Act would bring oppression because banishment "depends upon the discretion, or, I may say, the caprice of an individual." The Sedition Act suppressed criticism of government "with penal terror," and "was rendered unconstitutional by that clause which forbids the enacting of any law abridging the freedom of speech or of the press." At the same time, Garrard urged the legislature to include a declaration of "your firm attachment to the Federal constitution," while "entering your protest against all unconstitutional laws."[75]

Pickering, always vigilant for sedition to prosecute, wrote just days after Philadelphia newspapers printed Garrard's speech that "[i]ncredible pains have been taken to misrepresent . . . the *Alien* and *Sedition* Laws," and that the Kentucky "Governor has made to the General Assembly a very impudent and inflammatory speech on the subject of those Laws." He found Garrard's sins compounded because he was supposed "to be a *new,* not a native Citizen" and "was a Baptist Preacher." The Federalist press was as rabid as Pickering for prosecution of Garrard—William Cobbett wrote that the governor's "most impudent speech" supported Cobbett's belief that France would aid "the Kentuckians in a revolt," and John Ward Fenno warned that Garrard's "attrocious strain of misrepresentation and falsehood" showed that he was "the first mover in this ambitious project" by which "[t]he revolt has at length been brot about in the state of Kentucky."[76] However, the difficulty of assembling a Federalist grand jury and trial jury and winning a verdict in Kentucky evidently tipped the balance in Garrard's case compared to Matthew Lyon's case.

Dr. George Logan (1753–1821) of Philadelphia was a medical doctor who only briefly practiced medicine, a gentleman farmer who undertook scientific agricultural experiments, and an exponent of Republican beliefs in and out of political office. His college studies were in England, and his medical studies were in Edinburgh. He was expelled by the Quakers for serving in the militia, but retained a passionate commitment to peacemaking.[77]

President John Adams, in his reply to the Senate's response to his speech in early December 1798, said "it deserved to be considered, whether that temerity and impertinence of individuals affecting to interfere in public affairs between France and the United States," which was intended to "separate them from their government," should be "inquired into and corrected." His reference was to Dr. Logan's private diplomatic mission to France, which had raised the outrage of the Federalist Party. Adams did not specify whether the inquiry and correction should be by legislation or a Sedition Act prosecution (since separating the people from their government was a form of sedition, and the Sedition Act prohibited exciting "the hatred of the good people of the United States" against the government or aiding or abetting "any hostile designs of any foreign nation against the United States"). The Senate responded by passing the Logan Act the next month.[78] No evidence has appeared of steps toward Sedition Act prosecution of Dr. Logan.

Charles Webber and Benjamin Brown of Vassalborough, then part of Massachusetts before Maine was granted statehood, were described in Federalist newspapers as the "ringleaders" of "a gang of Insurgents" who raised a *"Sedition Pole"* there, and "burnt the Alien and Sedition Laws," on November 15, 1798. Those newspapers went on to say that the "arm of government ought to punish these Jacobins immediately, to prevent the baneful consequences of civil commotion" and to deal with "an open insult to the Government" by raising such poles and burning the laws. In Republican newspapers, the "gang" grew to be "the loud huzzas of more than one hundred people," the "Sedition Pole" became a "LIBERTY POLE," and insurgency became "zeal that glows in their patriotic breasts."[79] Twelve days later, Federalist militia "demolished the disgraceful Signal of Opposition to the Federal Government erected by a small number of Jacobins," by "placing an ax at the root of the tree" so "that no more remembrance of so offensive an object might be seen." That Federalist report added that Charles Webber, the ringleader "stood trembling with fear," and that he "and a few other ignorant and misguided followers" were *"disorganizers and revilers of our virtuous administration."*[80]

The United States attorney, Daniel Davis of Portland,[81] immediately sent someone to investigate and, "if evidence should offer to warrant a prosecution, to cause the principal offenders to be arrested and bound over for trial," according to newspaper reports. Hearing of that, Webber and Brown "voluntarily came forward, subscribed the following declaration, and lodged it . . . for publication in the Newspapers," in exchange for the prosecution being dropped. Their declaration, like that of Benjamin Fairbanks, was exactly what it was captioned, an obsequious "recantation" of their prior speech and writing against the Alien and Sedition Acts:

RECANTATION.

[S]everal measures took place derogatory to the Government of the United States, and tending to bring the Authority and Laws of the same into contempt; such as erecting a Liberty Pole, and burning certain papers, called the Alien

> Act, and the Sedition Act. Convinced of the impropriety of those measures, and desirous to atone for the insult offered to the Government by them,
> We thus publicly declare our unfeigned sorrow for the part we took in those proceedings, and our determination for the future to respect the Constitution and Laws of the United States.
>
> CHARLES WEBBER,
> BENJAMIN BROWN . . .
> Dec. 6, 1798.[82]

The federal records of the United States Circuit Court and District Court do not mention the case, so the United States attorney upheld his end of the plea bargain, but that leaves the case uncorroborated.

The "Printer in Newburgh" was listed as arrested under the Sedition Act, in a list published by a Republican newspaper, the *Centinel of Freedom,* that was otherwise fully accurate. As of the date of the article, there was just one Republican newspaper in Newburgh, New York—the *Mirror.*[83]

No record of any prosecution has been found; all that has appeared is an account of a liberty pole that was raised by Republicans in Newburgh, and torn down by Federalists, just after the Sedition Act went into effect. Its message was

> 1776
> LIBERTY. JUSTICE.
> THE CONSTITUTION INVIOLATE.
> NO BRITISH ALLIANCE.
> NO SEDITION BILL.[84]

One other 1798 incident was mentioned by James Morton Smith as a possible arrest or attempted prosecution under the Sedition Act, though he noted that the newspaper article referred to "treasonable expressions." On further investigation, the arrest of James Bell, in Carlisle, Pennsylvania, turns out to be unrelated to the Sedition Act. Smith's newspaper article was dated July 30, 1798, but it reprinted an earlier newspaper of July 4. That initial report showed that the incident occurred before the Sedition Act was passed, and that it was action by state officials rather than federal officials. The charge was "Treasonable Expressions."[85] Federal court records do not mention Bell.

The year 1798 did not end with the Sedition Act prosecutions and plans discussed so far. It instead ended with the fireworks of the Kentucky and Virginia Resolutions.

CHAPTER SEVEN

The Virginia and Kentucky Resolutions

THE ALIEN and Sedition Acts converted Republican concerns about a consolidated government and its threat to liberties from an unsubstantiated fear to a manifest danger. The Virginia and Kentucky Resolutions provided a rallying point for Republicans and transformed them into a political party if they were not one already. The Virginia and Kentucky Resolutions in late 1798, followed by an additional Kentucky Resolution in late 1799 and Virginia's Report in early 1800, were the carefully planned Republican challenge to the Alien and Sedition Acts.

The resolutions are often dismissed in several ways that are worth reevaluating: that they were primarily statements of states' rights and not of First Amendment freedoms, that they were resoundingly rejected by all the other states, and that they challenged a law that merely restated what the common law already said. Dismissing the Virginia and Kentucky Resolutions in those ways ignores the centrality of their language about freedoms of press and speech, ignores the Tennessee and Georgia Resolutions and the actual split of the states, and ignores the serious implications of positing a federal common law.

The Kentucky Resolutions were secretly drafted by Thomas Jefferson in the weeks before October 4, 1798.[1] On that date, Wilson Cary Nicholas wrote that he had "put into the hands of Mr. John Breckinridge a copy of the resolutions that you sent me." Jefferson evidently had intended the resolutions for Virginia or North Carolina, and gave them to Nicholas, a

Virginia legislator. However, Nicholas noted that Kentucky's legislature met sooner and that a Kentucky legislator, Breckinridge, was soon traveling back from their region to his home state.[2] After revision, the Kentucky Resolutions were passed by the Kentucky legislature on November 10 and 13, 1798, with only three dissenting votes in the house and by unanimous vote in the senate. They were promptly approved by Gov. James Garrard.[3] The Kentucky Resolutions showed Jefferson to be even more "the very life and soul of the opposition" than Theodore Sedgwick had imagined.

The first of the nine resolutions stated the premise that the Constitution "delegated to [the federal] Government certain definite powers," and that "undelegated powers" are "void, and of no force." It posited that the Constitution is a compact of states, and that "each party has an equal right to judge for itself" whether federal action violates the Constitution. The second through sixth resolutions claimed that the Alien and Sedition Acts were unconstitutional on multiple grounds: that they created crimes outside the crimes the federal government had a delegated power to create, and that the Sedition Act was not authorized by any delegated power and violated the First Amendment prohibition of laws "abridging the freedom of speech, or of the press," while the Alien Act was not authorized by any delegated power and contravened the "migration or importation" clause (which had been opaquely written about the slave trade) and the Sixth Amendment (on rights in criminal trials). The seventh resolution condemned Federalist overreach that used the general welfare clause and the necessary and proper clause. The last two resolutions were the plan of action, calling for repeal of the Alien and Sedition Acts, and for other states to give "an expression of their sentiments on the acts" and their constitutionality, to declare them "void and of no force," and to request their repeal.[4]

Absent from the final version was Jefferson's draft language warning that a succession of such acts would "necessarily drive these states into revolution and blood," and calling for state nullification of unconstitutional federal laws. He had written that "where powers are assumed which have not been delegated a nullification of the act is the rightful remedy" by each state. Instead, the final Kentucky Resolutions used the refrain that "whensoever the General Government assumes undelegated powers, its acts are unauthoritative, void, and of no force."[5]

The Virginia Resolutions were secretly drafted by James Madison.[6] That followed Madison's private discussions with Jefferson and his receipt of a copy of the Kentucky Resolutions.[7] Madison's draft was delivered to the ubiquitous Wilson Cary Nicholas, who gave it to another Virginia legislator, John Taylor of Caroline. The Virginia Resolutions were passed by its

FIGURE 7.1. James Madison. Portrait by Gilbert Stuart (c. 1821). Courtesy National Gallery of Art, gift of Ailsa Mellon Bruce Fund.

legislature on December 21 and 24, 1798, by margins of 100–63 in the house of delegates and 14–3 in the state senate.[8]

The first four resolutions announced Virginia's premises: that it "will support the government of the United States in all measures" warranted by the Constitution, that it had the duty "to watch over and oppose every infraction of those principles," and most controversially, that the Constitution was a compact of states and that those states "are in duty bound, to interpose" themselves "in case of a deliberate, palpable and dangerous exercise of other powers not granted" the federal government, in order to protect state authority and citizen rights and liberties. Further, those powers not granted came instead from "forced constructions" of "general phrases" (the general welfare and necessary and proper clauses). The fifth and sixth resolutions denounced the Alien and Sedition Acts on several grounds: arrogating "a power no where delegated," violating the First Amendment, and contravening the express reservation made when Virginia ratified the Constitution, that freedom of press cannot be abridged or restrained. Those resolutions affirmed the central First Amendment "right of freely examining public characters and measures, and of free communication among the people thereon." The last two resolutions stated the plan of action: asking the other states to concur in declaring "that the acts aforesaid are unconstitutional" and in "maintaining unimpaired the authorities, rights, and liberties" of the states and people, along with transmitting copies of the resolutions to Virginia's members of Congress as instructions to seek their repeal.[9]

A month after the Virginia Resolutions, Virginia's legislature approved an Address to the People, as an explanation to constituents. It was not written or edited by Madison and consequently was not as powerful as the resolutions or even fully consistent with them.[10]

The Virginia and Kentucky Resolutions pursued parallel tracks, once Jefferson's draft language about bloodshed and about nullification was removed, though the Virginia Resolutions still were notably more moderate. Virginia's Resolutions were more vocal in pledging loyalty to the union and were vague about the status of unconstitutional laws, while the final Kentucky Resolutions remained more strident on those and other points. In responding to Madison's draft inviting other states to cooperate in maintaining state rights and individual liberties, Jefferson urged instead "an invitation: 'to concur with this commonwealth in declaring'" the acts "'null, void and of no force, or effect.'" Madison resisted that, and though others added that language, it was soon removed from the Virginia Resolutions. Other differences were in less controversial areas such as Virginia substituting separation of powers for Kentucky's reliance on Sixth Amendment rights.[11] Both resolutions reflected the longstanding alarm of their authors about "the progressive apostacy from the principles of our Revolution & Governments."[12]

Hostile Responses and Kentucky's and Virginia's Replies

The most significant opposition to the Virginia and Kentucky Resolutions came from Virginia's legislative minority, from eight state responses, a House of Representatives report, and many High Federalists. To these, Virginia and Kentucky replied.

The third of Virginia's House of Delegates that had opposed the resolutions published an Address of the Minority, which John Marshall drafted anonymously in January 1799.[13] In that address, the Alien Act was defended on the grounds that "dangerous aliens," which were all the law affected, could be dealt with under several general government powers: its exclusive authority over external concerns or nationwide concerns, its power to punish offenses against the law of nations, its power to protect against invasion (beyond just repelling invasion), its authority to prohibit migration after the constitutional suspension ended in 1808, and its authority to make laws necessary and proper to carry out its powers. The Sedition Act was defended as a restriction all countries found necessary, as essential to self-preservation ("continued calumnies against the government" will "produce in any society convulsions" that will injure or destroy it), and as authorized by the common law. The First Amendment was treated as an admission of federal power to regulate the press ("it would have been certainly unnecessary to have modified the legislative powers of Congress concerning the press, if the power itself does not exist"). That amendment was understood as not prohibiting regulation but only abridgment of the freedom of the press, and no abridgment resulted from the Sedition Act because it "does not punish any writing not before punishable" under the common law. Adopting Sir William Blackstone's narrow definition, freedom of press meant only "a liberty to publish, free from previous restraint," and not an impunity from subsequent punishment. Further, the minority address asserted, freedom of press had long been viewed as consistent with punishing seditious libel or other licentiousness.[14]

Eight states sent hostile responses, beginning in February and ending in October 1799. They were printed in 1799 and have been reprinted periodically.[15] The federal House of Representatives joined the attack, approving a report supporting the Alien and Sedition Acts by a narrow party-line vote of 52–48 in late February 1799.[16] The Alien Act, the report reasoned, was authorized by the constitutional requirement that the general government must protect each state, and by the necessary and proper clause. That act did not violate the Sixth Amendment assurance of jury trial in criminal prosecutions, because constitutional protections only applied to citizens, and because removal was not a criminal prosecution and did not require "dangerous aliens" to have committed any crime. The Sedition Act, the report continued, was necessary and proper for carrying into effect all constitutional provisions, "because the direct tendency of such [false, scandalous and malicious] writings is to obstruct the acts of government by exciting opposition to them, to endanger its existence by rendering it odious and contemptible in the eyes of the people, and to produce seditious combinations against the laws." The act did not violate the First Amendment, because (following Blackstone) "the liberty of the press consists not in a license for every man to publish what he pleases, without being liable to punishment if he should abuse this license," but "in a permission to publish without previous restraint." The report repeated that "liberty of the press has always been understood in this manner, and no other," following the "universally admitted definition of 'the liberty of the press'";

"a law to restrain its licentiousness" simply "cannot be considered as 'an abridgment' of its 'liberty.'" Further, liberty of the press never included "the publication of false, scandalous and malicious writings against the government," and that liberty was not abridged "by punishing him for doing that which he never had liberty to do." That led into a discussion of the common law crime of seditious libel, which the report said was enforceable by the federal government.[17]

Individual High Federalists gave their own typically vehement responses to Virginia and Kentucky. Alexander Hamilton, the effective commander of the federal army, called "the proceedings of Virginia and Kentucky" a "regular conspiracy to overturn the government," which was probably intended "to encourage a hostile foreign power" to attack; he proposed the military action toward Virginia that will be discussed later in Chapter 9.[18] Secretary of State Timothy Pickering, the director of enforcement of the Alien and Sedition Acts, was little short of explosive, writing to Col. David Humphreys that the Virginia and Kentucky Resolutions were "violent opposition" to those laws; to William Vans Murray that the resolutions were "hostile to the general government"; to Rufus King that they were "of the most inflammatory nature and hostile to the General Government," "outrageous attempts to break the union," and "mad and rebellious resolves"; and to Dr. Edward Stevens that the resolutions sought *"to sever the Union."*[19] Sen. Theodore Sedgwick of Massachusetts wrote that the Virginia Resolutions were "little short of a declaration of war," and former Sen. George Cabot called for "stern and sharp reproof given to the seditious Virginians."[20]

Republican Rejoinders

By August 1799, Jefferson believed it was time for Virginia and Kentucky to answer the opposing states and the congressional committee, to reiterate the protest against the "palpable violations of the constitutional compact" by the Alien and Sedition Acts, and to avoid any impression of acquiescence in adverse responses. He arranged a meeting in early September to discuss "a concert of action." Jefferson signaled the gravity of the meeting by writing to Madison that if "repetitions of these and other violations shall make it evident that the Federal government, disregarding the limitations of the federal compact, mean to exercise powers over us to which we have never assented," he was prepared to propose that in that case Virginia and Kentucky would "sever ourselves from that union we so much value, rather than give up the rights of self government which we have reserved."[21] Madison attended the meeting, and responses from both states followed.[22]

Kentucky passed an additional resolution in November 1799, in keeping with Jefferson's push for further action, though it was not drafted by the vice president.[23] The preamble characterized the Alien and Sedition Acts as "unconstitutional laws" and "alarming measures," and expressed disappointment that state responses had relied on "unfounded suggestions and uncandid insinuations . . . in place of fair reasoning." The resolution, after affirming Kentucky's unequivocal "attachment to the Union," protested that ruin would follow if "the general government be permitted to transgress the limits fixed by that compact, by a total disregard to the special delegations of power therein contained," and that despotism would result if "the general government is the exclusive judge of the extent of the powers delegated to it." Instead, each state, "being sovereign and independent, have the unquestionable right to judge of the infraction" of the Constitution. Consequently, Kentucky declared that "the said Alien and Sedition Laws are, in their opinion, palpable violations of the said Constitution," and "vitally wound the best rights of the citizen." Thus far, the 1799 resolution restated the points made in the 1798 resolutions in more moderate terms, but in one final assertion, the later resolution did what some opposing states had condemned, by replacing its "void, and of no force" language with nullification. Kentucky declared that "a nullification, by those sovereignties, of all unauthorized acts done under color of that instrument, is the rightful remedy."[24]

Virginia's Report was written by Madison as a more detailed response to the opposing states and to the Federalist committee, and it made a greater effort to employ moderate tones.[25] It was approved by the House of Delegates by a 60–40 vote on January 7, 1800, and by Virginia's Senate by a 15–6 vote during the week of January 12.[26] The Report quoted and commented on each of the eight original resolutions, in turn, and so began by reaffirming Virginia's commitment to the Constitution, the government, and the union, the enumeration of limited federal powers and state reservation of remaining powers, and the power and duty of states to interpose when the federal government exercised unauthorized powers that threatened rights and liberties. The bulk of the Report—almost two-thirds—discussed the fifth resolution on the Alien and Sedition Acts.[27]

The Alien Act was challenged on four grounds. The most important ones were that the act exercised a power that was not delegated to the federal government, and that it violated separation of powers by giving the president judicial powers to "judge dangerous" certain noncitizens and also legislative powers to define offenses such as suspicion of "secret machinations against the government." The Report denied that if alien friends were present by favor rather than right, they had no rights and could be expelled at will. It also denied that if the federal government had power to protect states against invasion, it had unlimited choice of means such as banishing alien friends.[28]

The Sedition Act was attacked by Virginia's Report as unconstitutional on three grounds. First, as with the Alien Act, the federal government had no delegated power to punish spoken and printed words as sedition. No federal power came from the Constitution's preamble, and there was no federal power for which the Sedition Act was necessary and proper to carry it into execution. No federal common law existed to provide federal power to criminalize sedition, because the Constitution did "not contain a sentence or syllable, that can be tortured" into incorporating a federal common law, and its careful system of delegated federal powers would be rendered meaningless by importing a vast common law with innumerable crimes and "incongruities, barbarisms, and bloody maxims." Further, the Tenth Amendment assured that the "powers not delegated to the United States," unless prohibited to the states, were "reserved to the States respectively, or to the people," and federal power from a federal common law "would be fatal" to most state power. Second, the First Amendment barred exactly that sort of abridgment of freedoms of speech and press—it denied to Congress "any power whatever on the subject." That amendment was added to assure that, though the Constitution did not delegate any power over the press, any assertion of power over the press was positively forbidden, including any claim of federal power to punish seditious libel or criticism of the government or its officials. That countered the argument in support of the Sedition Act that the First Amendment only barred abridgment, not regulation, of the press, because there was no delegated power of regulation.

Madison then heaped scorn on the argument made by defenders of the Sedition Act that freedom of press meant only the narrow common law definition:

> The freedom of the press under the common law, is, in the defences of the sedition act, made to consist in an exemption from all *previous* restraint on printed publications, by persons authorized to inspect and prohibit them. It appears to the committee, that this idea of the freedom of the press, can never be admitted to be the American idea of it: since a law inflicting penalties on printed publications, would have a similar effect with a law authorizing a previous restraint on them. It would seem a mockery to say, that no law should be passed, preventing publications from being made, but that laws might be passed for punishing them in case they should be made.

He explained that American jurisdictions "require a greater degree of freedom" to discuss government and its officials, because citizens elect executives and legislators here much more than occurs in Britain, and they require information and discussion about public officials and measures. Finally, every other right is guarded by the "right of freely examining public characters and measures" and of freely communicating about them.[29]

It was in Madison's discussion of seditious libel that he argued most brilliantly in the Report, flatly rejecting the criminality of seditious libel (the crime of criticizing the administration and its officials). Madison abandoned the common approach of directing attack at the framework within which the crime operated—inferring intent from publication, limiting jury issues, and so on—and went beyond that to contend that seditious libel was no legitimate crime at all. He wrote that criticism of the administration and its officials was not just permissible but justifiable and necessary for two reasons. First, public officials who have not "duly discharged [their] trust" actually "should be brought into contempt or disrepute, and incur the hatred of the people," and the only way to determine if they have duly discharged their trust is by "a free examination thereof, and a free communication among the people thereon." Rigid enforcement of seditious libel would unfairly shield officials even if "they should at any time deserve the contempt or hatred of the people." Second,

> Let it be recollected, lastly, that the right of electing the members of the government, constitutes more particularly the essence of a free and responsible government. The value and efficacy of this right, depends on the knowledge of the comparative merits and demerits of the candidates for public trust; and on the equal freedom, consequently, of examining and discussing these merits and demerits of the candidates respectively. . . . Should there happen . . . to be competitions between those who are, and those who are not, members of the government; what will be the situations of the competitors? Not equal; because the characters of the former will be covered by the "sedition act" from animadversions exposing them to disrepute among the people; whilst the latter may be exposed to the contempt and hatred of the people, without a violation of the act. What will be the situation of the people? Not free; because they will be compelled to make their election between competitors, whose pretensions they are not permitted by the act, equally to examine, to discuss, and to ascertain. And from both these situations, will not those in power derive an undue advantage.[30]

Throughout this discussion, Madison returned to a major rationale for broad freedoms of press and speech: the "information and communication among the people, which is indispensible to the just exercise of their electoral rights."

Characterization of the Virginia and Kentucky Resolutions and Report as Extreme?

How accurate were the Federalist congressional committee and the High Federalists in portraying the Virginia and Kentucky Resolutions as extreme? How accurate were Virginia's Report and the Republicans in attempting to portray the Virginia Resolutions as moderate? The answer depends on which of the many facets of the resolutions is in view.

One basis for characterizing the resolutions as extreme is the claim, made by Pickering and others, that it is seditious to express a challenge that an act of Congress is unconstitutional. That claim was indefensible, other than under the language of the Sedition Act itself prohibiting press and speech expressed with intent "to resist, oppose, or defeat any such [federal] law." Instead, English and American history was replete with examples of challenging laws as unconstitutional, ranging from Sir Edward Coke's denials that the monarch's creation of offenses was legal, to radical Whig criticisms of various governmental actions as violating the British constitution, to the colonists' protests against the Stamp Act and other prerevolutionary laws, to debates over Hamilton's financial proposals of 1790–1791, to recent denunciation of the Supreme Court's rejection of state sovereign immunity from suit in *Chisholm v. Georgia* in 1793.[31] Further, English and American history was replete with instances of the right of petitioning against unlawful legislation and actions, which was enshrined in each country's Bill of Rights. Douglas Bradburn is correct that the Virginia and Kentucky Resolutions were one more instance of "a broader movement of petitioning and remonstrance" from across the United States against and for the Alien and Sedition Acts.[32]

Another basis for characterizing the resolutions as extreme is the claim that state interposition to protect citizens' rights was a revolutionary and seditious doctrine. That claim ignored the long history of Americans "turn[ing] to their state legislatures to rally the opposition," and also ignored the constitutional principle of federalism and its corollary that there were separate federal powers and state powers.[33] Hamilton himself, in *The Federalist* eleven years before, had assured the public that

> the state Legislature, who will always be not only vigilant but suspicious and jealous guardians of the rights of the citizens, against incroachments from the Foederal government, will constantly have their attention awake to the conduct of the national rulers [and will] . . . sound the alarm to the people.

Nor did Hamilton see the states' role to be merely a passive watchman: their role would be "not only to be the VOICE but if necessary the ARM of their discontent."[34] Such a state role was so widely accepted that only the Massachusetts response expressly objected to interposition, and Virginia's Report only found defending it to require four paragraphs.

A further basis for characterizing the resolutions as extreme is the claim that forcible prevention of enforcement, secession, or sundering of the union was inherent in state interposition or nullification. That claim arises from an ambiguity in Madison's proposal for interposition and in Jefferson's for nullification:[35] did they mean simply a state's nonenforcement of the two laws, or a state's forcible prevention of federal enforcement of those laws, or (as Madison later claimed) most states' concurrence in objections to enforcement? If the meaning was nonenforcement without counterforce, Virginia's and Kentucky's proposals were not very different from the then-recent response of most states to the Supreme Court denial of their sovereign immunity in *Chisholm v. Georgia* in 1793. If the meaning was counterforce, Virginia only threatened that as a last resort after a series of violations of rights and after unsuccessful efforts at repeal or constitutional amendment. However, at that future point, Virginia's and Kentucky's remedies could lead to disunion, and their resolutions were cited for exactly that in the nullification controversy of 1832 and in the pre-Civil War years.[36] Madison foresaw that danger as he attempted to moderate interpretation of the resolutions in Virginia's Report, and as he later argued against nullification's proponents.[37] Similarly, Jefferson's language about nullification and about the Alien and Sedition Acts being not law but "altogether void and of no force" did not assume or require force, any more than did his later statement that the Sedition Act was "a nullity as absolute and as palpable as if Congress had ordered us to fall down and worship a golden image." Jefferson's view through most of this period appears to have been what he expressed to Edmund Pendleton in early 1799: "any thing like force would check the progress of public opinion & rally them round the errors of the government," because force "is not the kind of opposition the American people will admit"; so "keep away all shew of force and they will bear down the evil propensities of the government by the constitutional means of election & petition."[38] Whether Virginia or Kentucky actually contemplated the use of force in 1798–1800 is discussed in Chapter 9. What is unquestioned is that Virginia and Kentucky did not actually use force; instead, they passed resolutions, sought state concurrence, instructed their senators to seek repeal of the Alien and Sedition Acts, and in Virginia's case, provided attorneys when James Thomson Callender was prosecuted while the governor discouraged civil disobedience.

It is true that, in August 1799, Jefferson again recommended stronger language,[39] when he wrote to Madison that Republicans should be "determined, were we to be disappointed in this, to sever ourselves from that union we so much value, rather than give up the rights of self government." Madison must have successfully pressed him on that point in a meeting, because Jefferson soon stated that he receded from insisting on language to that effect, and acknowledged that "we should never think of separation but for repeated and enormous violations." Jefferson did not advocate counterforce, though he raised the possibility of separation from the union at a future date. Madison was more moderate, particularly in the Report of 1800. He stated that the declarations that the Alien and Sedition Acts were unconstitutional "are expressions of opinion, unaccompanied with any other effect." He listed "other means [that] might have been employed" by Virginia, and force was not among them.[40] "Although secession was openly discussed, neither Jefferson nor Madison was willing to advocate force to bring it about."[41]

What is the significance of the Virginia and Kentucky Resolutions? We have already noted that they were the most powerful and influential attack on the Alien and Sedition Acts. Their significance far exceeded that. They were a central part of the Republican strategy for the election of 1800 and a major element of the Republican victory.[42] They were an exposition of the Jeffersonian and the later-Madisonian view of the Constitution, of the Bill of Rights, of freedoms of press and speech in particular, and of federalism. They also articulated what became known as the "principles of 1798" featuring states' rights, which were later appropriated and misused by advocates of nullification, slavery, and segregation.[43]

States' Rights, Freedom of Speech and Press, or Both?

Academic discussions of the Virginia and Kentucky Resolutions often characterize them as primarily manifestos on states' rights, and as only secondarily statements of First Amendment rights and other civil rights. For example, Andrew Lenner said that "Republican charges that the Federalists were out to suppress free speech" were "disingenuous," and that "Republicans crafted their rhetoric to appeal to their states' right base as well as this emerging group of libertarians." David Jenkins wrote that "Republican opposition to the Sedition Act fundamentally relied upon the principles of federalism and the restriction of national power. The Kentucky and Virginia Resolutions best illustrate the Republicans' concerns for states' rights."[44] That argument is a longstanding one.[45] In addition, those who argue that the narrow Blackstone definition of freedom of press was exclusive or dominant when the First Amendment was ratified often claim that the Virginia and Kentucky Resolutions were "[f]ar from upholding freedom of the press," and instead primarily "argued on 'strict constructionist' grounds that the Sedition Act usurped a legislative power properly belonging to the states," to criminalize seditious libel.[46]

On the other hand, the approach taken in the leading article by Adrienne Koch and Harry Ammon, and by many other scholars, is that the resolutions "were intended *primarily* as a defense, practical and spirited, of civil liberties." The truth falls between these two approaches, particularly if the historically tainted term "states' rights" is replace by "federalism" or "constitutional federal and state powers."[47]

The Grounds in the Resolutions

The Virginia and Kentucky Resolutions based their arguments both on limited federal powers and on civil liberties (particularly First Amendment and Sixth Amendment rights). Thus, the Kentucky Resolutions began with delegated federal rights and reserved state rights, and were peppered with quotations of the Tenth Amendment (that undelegated powers are reserved to the states or the people). At the same time, most of the nine resolutions protested violations of the First Amendment by the Sedition Act, and of various constitutional provisions by the Alien Act. The Virginia Resolutions similarly emphasized both limited federal powers and civil liberties. The central resolutions condemned the Sedition Act as exercising "a power not delegated by the constitution" and "positively forbidden by one of the amendments" (the First Amendment), and decried the Alien Act with a similar combination of "power no where delegated" and "uniting legislative and judicial powers, to those of the executive." Similarly, Virginia's Report devoted roughly equal amounts of discussion to federalism and to First Amendment rights, "electoral rights," separation of powers, and the like.[48]

Neither state's resolutions defended state laws criminalizing seditious libel—though neither attacked them. Jefferson touched on the issue in an ambiguous and inconclusive manner. His draft of the Kentucky Resolutions said that "all lawful powers" respecting speech and press were reserved "to the states or the people," because of "their" (which?) retaining "the right of judging how far the licentiousness of speech and of the press may be abridged . . . , and how far those abuses which cannot be separated from their use should be tolerated."[49] The shorter Virginia Resolutions did not touch on the issue. However, Madison was clear in Virginia's Report. It attacked the rationales of the laws and court decisions that criminalized seditious libel and left no room for federal or state prosecution of seditious libel. Jefferson, too, certainly was genuinely concerned about any threat to freedoms of press and speech, writing in confidence to Elbridge Gerry, "did we ever expect to see the day when, breathing nothing but sentiments of love to our country & it's freedom & happiness, our correspondence must be as secret as if we were hatching it's destruction!"[50]

The Grounds in Contemporaneous Republican Discussions

Subsequent Republican discussions of the Sedition Act, during 1799–1800, generally emphasized First Amendment rights more than federal and state powers. Federalist defenses of the Sedition Act did the same. The Republican discussions, along with newspaper essays, are what some writers (quoted in the Introduction) described as expansive understandings of freedoms of press and speech that they assert only appeared in and after 1798, for example claiming that "the theory of freedom of political expression remained quite narrow until 1798, except for a few aberrant statements."[51]

Seven major Republican treatises in this period not only articulated, but emphasized, freedoms of press and speech in their attacks on the Alien and Sedition Acts and in their support of the Virginia and Kentucky Resolutions. The first ones came from the pens of three Georges: George Nicholas (the Kentucky brother of Wilson Cary Nicholas) in 1798, George Hay (a Virginia attorney who the next year would represent James T. Callender in his Sedition Act trial) in early January 1799, and George Blake (the Boston attorney who represented Abijah Adams at his trial) in essays in April and early May 1799.[52] Additional essays and treatises were published in 1799 by Thomas Cooper (a polymath, and briefly a rural Pennsylvania newspaper editor, soon to be a Sedition Act defendant), and St. George Tucker (the leading Virginia law professor, soon to produce the Republican edition of Blackstone). Other treatises came from Tunis Wortman (a New York lawyer) in 1800, and John Thomson (a Virginia lawyer) in 1801.[53] All of this efflorescence of Republican thought stressed freedoms of press and speech, defined broadly.[54]

There were, of course, Federalist treatises as well, which took a narrow approach to freedoms of press and speech, in defending the Alien and Sedition Acts. The leading ones were written by Attorney General Charles Lee, Henry Lee, Pennsylvania Judge Alexander Addison, and others.[55]

Though the Virginia and Kentucky Resolutions, and Virginia's Report, placed comparable emphasis on civil rights and federalism, the public discussion of the Alien and Sedition Acts grew in the direction of civil rights and away from states' rights. The claims that Republican opposition to the Sedition Act on First Amendment grounds was "disingenuous," or that it "fundamentally relied upon the principles of federalism," do not match the emphasis in the resolutions, Virginia's Report, or the treatises.

Rejection by All the Other States?

Scholarly discussions of the Virginia and Kentucky Resolutions usually describe them as rejected by all the other states, including the other southern states.[56] The leading book on the Federalist period said that "none of the other fourteen state legislatures so invited prove[d] willing to lend their concurrence to them. Ten emphatically rejected the Resolutions; the other four took no action at all." The leading article on the resolutions said that, "[w]ith no exceptions, the immediate comment was hostile." That characterization has been dominant for over two hundred years, since Pickering's many statements that the "mad and rebellious resolves of . . . Virginia and Kentucky, which were transmitted to all the other Legislatures in the Union[,] have been rejected by all." Those statements were endlessly repeated by Federalist newspapers.[57]

If the Virginia and Kentucky Resolutions were rejected by all the other states, the implication is that all the other states rejected their broad understanding of freedoms of press and speech, as well as their perception of the Constitution's balance between federal and state powers, as extreme views. Further implications are that the Alien and Sedition Acts were not widely seen as unconstitutional, and that Republican positions were not extensively supported.

However, if the Virginia and Kentucky Resolutions were only rejected by half the states, and were not rejected by the other half (by a mixture of support, divided legislatures, and nonopposition by tactical design), then those implications reverse. Virginia's and Kentucky's expansive positions on freedoms of press and speech would not have been widely repudiated, and their positions on federalism would not have been generally perceived as extreme. The Alien and Sedition Acts would have been more widely questioned, and Republican positions would have been more extensively supported. A Republican sweep of Congress and capture of the White House would not appear out of reach for 1800.

Two Approaches in the Opposing States' Responses

Eight states opposed the Virginia and Kentucky Resolutions (counting New York, though its legislative chambers could not agree on a common official response). They divided between two approaches. Seven states—Maryland, Delaware, Rhode Island, Massachusetts, New York, New Hampshire, and Vermont—based their opposition on the "opinion, that no state government, by a legislative act, is competent to declare an act of the federal government unconstitutional and void" (to use Maryland's language).[58]

Three of those states—Rhode Island, Massachusetts, and New Hampshire—also based their opposition on an additional ground, the "opinions" that the Alien and Sedition Acts "are within the powers delegated to Congress," which was obviously inconsistent with also saying that they "do not feel themselves authorized to consider and decide on the constitutionality of the Sedition and Alien laws" (to quote Rhode Island's language). An eighth state—Connecticut—based its opposition only on its belief that the Alien and Sedition Acts were constitutional.[59] The state legislatures approved these responses from January to June 1799, except that Vermont straggled in at the end of October.

Massachusetts, among the four states concluding that the Alien and Sedition Acts were constitutional, gave the only discussion of that conclusion, and also raised the only objection to interposition. It found the Alien Act constitutional on the grounds that noncitizens did not have constitutional rights beyond "temporary protection," and that removing "dangerous aliens" and, in fact, all aliens was allowed by the law of nations though there were no hostilities, and was necessary since "thousand of aliens . . . were ready to coöperate in any external attack" by France. Massachusetts found the Sedition Act constitutional because it did not abridge the "genuine liberty of speech and press," which was "liberty to utter and publish the truth" but not "licentiousness" that propagated falsehood. After that narrow Blackstone-like definition, the response paraphrased Blackstone's doublespeak: freedom of the press "is a security for the rational use, and not the abuse of the press; . . . this right is not infringed, but confirmed and established, by the late act of Congress." Also, the Sedition Act did what was necessary for self-preservation of the nation, which could not function "without the power to restrain seditious practices" and "to protect the officers thereof from abusive misrepresentations"; and the act simply codified, and ameliorated, the common law of seditious libel.[60]

The Tennessee and Georgia Resolutions

The other half of the states did not oppose the Virginia and Kentucky Resolutions, and like the states responding in opposition, they divided between two positions. Tennessee and Georgia passed resolutions supporting Virginia and Kentucky, while North Carolina and Pennsylvania were unable to get their legislative chambers to agree, and friendly South Carolina and closely-divided New Jersey did not take action for timing or tactical reasons. The nearly universal statements are mistaken that "[f]or Tennessee nothing can be said except that its legislature sent no reply to Virginia and Kentucky," that in Georgia there is "no mention of any action in the matter," and that "four Southern states took no action at all" to support the Virginia and Kentucky Resolutions.[61]

Instead, in Tennessee, Gov. John Sevier quickly transmitted the Kentucky Resolutions to the legislature, on December 7, 1798. The house saw the issue as so important that it proposed a joint session, and the senate, finding that unwieldy, instead proposed a "select committee of the two houses," which was formed.[62] That committee's report was delivered to the state senate on January 4, 1799, and the senate immediately "read and adopted" it and sent that over to the house. The same day, the house read and concurred with the committee report and then adopted the recommended resolution.[63] The next morning, the house and then the senate passed two additional resolutions, to communicate the first resolution to the state's congressional delegation so it could seek repeal, and to send a copy to Kentucky. The quick adoption of the Tennessee Resolutions was not surprising in a state that was "entirely devoid of a Federalist interest."[64]

The first of the Tennessee Resolutions, as the legislature adopted them on January 4, 1799, found the Alien and Sedition Acts "in several parts opposed to the constitution," and called for their repeal:

> Resolved, that it shall [be] and hereby is enjoined an instruction to the Senators and Representatives of the State of Tennessee in the Congress of the United States to use their best efforts in their respective powers, to procure at the present session of Congress, a repeal of an act of the Congress of the United States, entitled, "An act concerning aliens," passed on the twenty second day of June, in the year one thousand seven hundred & ninety eight, and also a repeal of one other act of the Congress of the United States, entitled, "An act, in addition to an act for the punishment of certain crimes against the United States["] [the Sedition Act], passed on the 14th day of July, in the year 1798, upon the ground that the said acts are in several parts opposed to the constitution, and are impolitic, oppressive, and unnecessary.[65]

The state house described the resolutions as being a response to "the resolutions of the State of Kentuckey," and the senate described them in similar terms. Tennessee's legislature adjourned the day it passed the additional resolutions, before the Virginia Resolutions arrived.[66]

The next month, Republican newspapers carried one-sentence reports that "the Alien and Sedition laws have met with the same fate in Tennessee, as in Virginia and Kentucky." Then in April 1799, Republican papers said that "the Legislature of Tennessee has adopted the Resolutions of the General Assembly of Kentucky, respecting certain late measures of the Federal Government."[67] Those published reports raise suspicions about the innocence of repeated Federalist statements that the Virginia and Kentucky Resolutions "have been rejected by all."

Similarly in Georgia, Gov. James Jackson transmitted the Kentucky Resolutions to the legislature in his opening message to the January 1799 session, along with his description of the attempted prosecution of David Garvin (described in Chapter 6) and his comment that the Sedition Act was "supposed by many not to be constitutional."[68] He transmitted the Virginia Resolutions when they arrived, later in January, and the Tennessee Resolutions when he received them the next month.[69] A legislative committee evidently did not complete its report before the legislature adjourned on February 16, and so its report was delivered in the next session in November 1799. That report, proposing a combined response to all the states whose resolutions and responses had been received, was approved by the state senate on November 22 (by a 16–4 vote) and by the house on December 4 (by 21–16).[70] However, the house immediately exhibited its discomfort with the wording, and it reconsidered and passed a modified version on December 5 that rejected two phrases. The senate approved the modified version that same day.[71]

The Georgia Resolution, in final form, responded to the communications from "other states on the subject of the alien and sedition laws," including those that had given their approval, with the following language:

> That to advise an approbation of those [alien and sedition] acts, as some states seem to have done, would be to speak a language foreign to their hearts; but the committee hope that they will be repealed without the interposition of the state legislature; they cannot, however, forbear expressing their sentiments on them, so far as to declare, that if the American government had no greater hold on the people's allegiance and fidelity, than those acts, it would not rest on that firm foundation which the committee hope and trust it does and ever will, on the affections of the citizens over whom it presides; rivitted by the acts of a wise and virtuous administration.[72]

Thus, Georgia did the principal thing that Virginia and Kentucky requested, in calling for repeal of the Alien and Sedition Acts, while refusing "approbation of those acts." Equally significant was the language that it rejected: it replaced "hope that they will be repealed without a necessity for the legislature of Georgia to enter into violent resolutions against them" with "hope that they will be repealed without the interposition of the state legislature." Georgia implied strongly that it would join with Virginia and Kentucky in interposition, and it removed language that could be construed as calling a stronger response "violent resolutions." The accuracy of that reading is supported by the other modification: Georgia rejected a then typical plaudit of the "administration which neither ought to court nor fear the liberty or licentiousness of the press, nor the praise, nor venom of the sycophant or malevolent."[73] There, it removed language that could be construed as praising the Adams administration and undercutting the need for repeal, which it had just called for, of the Alien and Sedition Acts.

Georgia's support of Virginia and Kentucky, like Tennessee's, was not a surprise. In both, the electoral vote for Jefferson was unanimous in 1796 and 1800. Both were "safe Republican states" and "indisputably Republican strongholds." Georgia's legislature was heavily Republican.[74] And Georgia's governor strongly supported the Virginia Resolutions, later writing to Virginia Gov. James Monroe that his state's response "meets with my entire approbation," including "its reasoning, its language, and the object it has in contemplation."[75]

Did the Tennessee and Georgia Resolutions amount to support of the Virginia and Kentucky Resolutions? They agreed with their sister states on the grand issue, repeal of the Alien and Sedition Acts.[76] They also did what Virginia and Kentucky asked. The Kentucky Resolutions ended by asking other states to "concur in declaring these acts void and of no force" and "in requesting their repeal." The Virginia Resolutions ended by urging the same two things—to "concur with this Commonwealth in declaring . . . that the acts aforesaid are unconstitutional," and to furnish a copy of the resolutions to the state's congressional delegation obviously to seek repeal—and a third thing, to "cooperat[e] with this State in maintaining unimpaired the authorities, rights, and liberties, reserved to the States respectively, or to the people." Virginia's Report repeated those calls to action.[77] Tennessee complied by saying that the Alien and Sedition Acts were "in several parts opposed to the Constitution" and urging repeal. Georgia concurred by denying its "approbation" to the acts, asking for repeal, and raising the possibility of "interposition."

Support of Virginia and Kentucky did not even require that much, in the view of Madison and Jefferson. Madison thought they were "leav[ing] to other States a choice of all the modes possible of concurring." Jefferson's advice, to which Madison's words responded, was that they "leave the matter in such a train as that we may not be committed absolutely to push the matter to extremities, & yet may be free to push as far as events will render prudent."[78]

Support of the Virginia and Kentucky Resolutions did not require endorsement of every part, because opposition to those resolutions has never required disagreement with every part. If it did, only one state would qualify as opposing Virginia and Kentucky, because only Massachusetts addressed most of their topics. Four opposing states did not address the unconstitutionality of the Alien and Sedition Acts or disagree with Virginia and Kentucky on that central issue, instead basing their disagreement only on the impropriety of states assessing the constitutionality of a federal law. Only one opposing state expressly addressed the important issue of interposition. And support did not require delivery of the response to Virginia and Kentucky. If it did, two of the opposing states would not be counted, because Maryland and New York's house did not transmit their responses.[79] By the standard applied to identify disagreement with Virginia and Kentucky, the Tennessee and Georgia Resolutions supported the Virginia and Kentucky Resolutions.

Tactical Deferrals and Split Legislatures

South Carolina did not receive the Virginia or Kentucky Resolutions before its annual legislative session ended in December 1798. Its governor forwarded both resolutions a week after the next session began, in late November 1799.[80] The state senate took them up at the end of its session, and passed the following resolution on December 20, 1799 (by a 14–11 vote):

> Resolved, That the Governor of the State, be required to signify to the Executive of the State of Kentucky, that the pressure of the business of the State, prevents the Legislature from taking into consideration the Resolves of the Legislature of Kentucky of the 16th day of November 1798, and to bestow on them the attention which the importance of the subject demands.

The state house concurred in that resolution that same day (without a recorded vote).[81]

Republican newspapers, including the *Aurora,* published reports that "[t]he session of the legislature of South Carolina was so short, that they had no time to take up the Kentucky Resolutions on the Alien and Sedition Laws," but in the opinion of "a very respectable member" of the legislature, "if the resolutions above alluded to had been acted on, they would certainly have been concurred in." Those articles continued by reporting that South Carolina effectively voided the Alien Act by "declaring that all foreigners migrating to that state, shall, upon complying with some slight formalities, be deemed citizens," passing the house with only one dissent and the senate with three.[82]

The *Aurora*'s prediction was probably right. Wilson Cary Nicholas, the Virginia legislator who passed both the Virginia and the Kentucky Resolutions from their secret authors to their legislative sponsors, believed that because "the legislature of South Carolina have given strong indications of republicanism, we expect they will concur in what we have done." The legislature indeed had acquired a "highly Republican cast" in the fall 1799 elections, as one member commented.[83] South Carolina electors voted for Jefferson in both the 1796 and 1800 elections. Though Federalism remained strong, it was a moderate southern variety of Federalism. The state's Federalist governor, Edward Rutledge, believed the Sedition Act to be contrary to "liberty of the press, & the freedom of speech." The state's leading Federalist politician and vice presidential candidate, Charles Cotesworth Pinckney, similarly viewed the Sedition Act as unconstitutional.[84]

Thus, South Carolina was probably sympathetic to the Virginia and Kentucky Resolutions, but its legislature did not act because of "the pressure of the business of the State." By contrast, its sister state, North Carolina, did act but its legislative chambers took opposite positions.

North Carolina's governor forwarded the Kentucky Resolutions to the legislature just before Christmas in 1798; the Virginia Resolutions did not arrive before adjournment.[85] The state house of commons passed resolutions characterizing the Alien and Sedition Acts as unconstitutional, and calling for their repeal, by a 58–21 vote:

> *Resolved,* . . . The General Assembly of North-Carolina view with pain the Alien and Sedition acts, at the last session of Congress of the United States. They conceive these acts as not only operating a violation of the principles of the Constitution, but as being altogether improper and unnecessary, therefore
>
> *Resolved,* That the Senators of this state in the Congress of the United States, be directed, and that the Representatives of the state be requested to use every endeavour in their power to cause that the above mentioned acts be repealed without delay.[86]

The house's action was on the last day of the session, perhaps delayed to make senate interference impossible before adjournment. If that was the plan, the state senate did not fall for it, but instead tabled the house resolution, which effectively killed it for that session. When some senators objected, a vote was taken and was 31–9 for tabling the house resolutions. In the next legislative term, beginning in mid-November, the Virginia Resolutions were transmitted by the governor, but the divided legislature did not act on them, probably seeing another split as unavoidable.[87]

The lopsided votes make clear that North Carolina's house had come under Republican control, despite losses in the mid-1798 elections after the XYZ Affair, while the state's senate remained under Federalist control.[88] One of those Federalist state senators, former governor Samuel Johnston, wrote that when the Kentucky Resolutions first arrived, the senate, "*with great impatience,* hearing them read, ordered them to lie on the table; and I believe, in the temper they were then in, might easily have been prevailed on to have thrown them into the fire."[89] That was the same treatment as was given to the house response. Tempers ran hot between the divided legislative chambers.

The two remaining states, like the southern states, are routinely described as opposing the Virginia and Kentucky Resolutions—New Jersey and Pennsylvania are said to have "placed themselves on record against the principles of these Resolutions."[90] Neither state did so.

New Jersey's general assembly reacted to the Virginia and Kentucky Resolutions by a resolution to dismiss them, in mid-January 1799. The legislative journal reported the final votes as 19–15 for dismissal of the Virginia Resolutions (and 20–14 for the Kentucky Resolutions). However, the actual vote tied at 17–17, and the Federalist speaker of the assembly broke the tie, so that the final vote dismissing the Virginia Resolutions was 18–17 (and for the Kentucky Resolutions 18–16). The reason for the discrepancy between the legislative journal and the actual vote, was that two legislators had *"voted in the negative, but wished their votes altered the next morning, which the house, contrary to every former practice, as is said, allowed."*[91] Federalist newspapers stated that the resolutions were *"thrown under the table,"* and that "[n]ot one solitary voice was heard in their favor; men of every d[e]scription of political opinions, united in venting their reprobation of such unconstitutional and wicked proceedings." Republican newspapers seemed to describe an entirely different scene, and expressed surprise "that the merits of the question were not touched upon at all" (the constitutionality of the Alien and Sedition Acts or the soundness of the Virginia and Kentucky Resolutions).[92] But that was by Republican design.

The Republicans, recognizing the Federalist one-vote majority in the general assembly, had intentionally avoided the main issues and had slyly argued against showing disrespect to a sister state by dismissing its resolutions; "the Republican minority simply was playing the political game to the hilt."[93] The Federalists had not pressed for a vote on the main issues because they were unsure of winning, and consequently were teased by Republican newspapers as having feared "that upon a fair and candid investigation of the Constitutionality of the Alien and Sedition Acts, they would have been declared unwarrantable by the Legislature." Tactics aside, the Republicans did not dislike the Virginia and Kentucky Resolutions; their resolution in Essex County (the day before the general assembly vote), their demonstrations in Bergen and Morris Counties, and their newspaper essays, showed their support for the resolutions.[94]

The result was that New Jersey did not oppose the Virginia and Kentucky Resolutions; one legislative chamber voted not to consider them and the other did nothing. As the historian of the state's Republican Party stated, the "tactical victory went to the Republicans."[95] If tabling by the senate and favorable action by the house in North Carolina is not support of the resolutions, then inaction by the legislative council and dismissal by the general assembly in New Jersey is not opposition to the resolutions. And the same was true of Pennsylvania.

Pennsylvania's senate voted against tabling the Kentucky Resolutions, by a 14–8 vote in January 1799, and then against tabling the Virginia Resolutions, in March. Federalist newspapers got into print first saying the resolutions were "thrown under the table," and other papers copied that description.[96] The senate did not pass counter-resolutions, nor did it approve the house resolutions.

The state house, acting first on the Kentucky Resolutions, debated and approved a moderately detailed response, which said both that judgments about constitutionality were only to be made by the federal judiciary, and that the Alien and Sedition Acts were constitutional. "The sedition and alien acts this house conceive contain nothing terrifying, but to the flagitious and designing," because the Sedition Act only prohibits "false, scandalous and malicious aspersions against the government," while the Alien Act only removes "foreigners, whose views and conduct are inimical." The separate votes on each resolution oscillated around 38–28.[97] The leading Federalist newspaper chortled that it was "probable Kentucky is yet semi-barbarian in its legislature, as in its morals, manners and literature." The response to the Virginia Resolutions was less detailed and less polemical, and it was approved by 43–24 vote.[98]

The consequence was that Pennsylvania's legislature divided, as its senate failed to concur in the house resolutions or to pass its own resolutions. The Republican minority in the state house got its licks in by approving a dissent to the legislature's florid address to John Adams, which said the minority was "not convinced of the constitutionality" of the Sedition Act, causing the Federalist majority to refuse to include it in the legislative journal. Though the Pennsylvania senate and house were Federalist controlled during most of 1799, the Republican minority in the house soon became a majority in the elections of 1799–1800.[99]

Thus, only half of the sixteen states opposed the Virginia and Kentucky Resolutions, four by merely denying that a state could judge the constitutionality of acts of Congress, three by also affirming the constitutionality of the Alien and Sedition Acts, and one by only taking the latter approach. The other half of the states did not oppose the Virginia and Kentucky Resolutions, four instead supporting a call for repeal of the Alien and Sedition Acts (besides Virginia and Kentucky, the overlooked Tennessee and Georgia Resolutions), and four by nonopposition through divided legislatures (North Carolina and Pennsylvania) and through votes not to consider the resolutions (narrowly divided New Jersey and favorably disposed South Carolina). That is very different from no state supporting and all states opposing the Virginia and Kentucky Resolutions, and from no southern state responding favorably—an old perspective that should be superseded. Support or nonopposition toward those resolutions included all southern states and almost half the middle states, while opposition came from the remaining middle states and all the northern states.

This perspective has many consequences. Virginia's and Kentucky's condemnation of the Alien and Sedition Acts as unconstitutional becomes less isolated and more widely held. Their understanding of First Amendment freedoms of press and speech as broad protections appears more widely accepted, and the narrow Blackstonian understanding of those freedoms as merely prohibitions of prior restraints appears less dominant—in fact it was endorsed only by the Massachusetts response. Their view of the Constitution's balance of federal and state powers seems less extreme and more toward a moderate position.[100] The Virginia and Kentucky Resolutions become not abject failures but positive milestones in forming an opposition party, and in establishing a strategy and an informal platform for the 1800 election. They cease to amount to fringe positions, and instead amount to a Republican groundswell in opposition to the declining Federalist consensus. The Republican interest becomes more powerful than has been assumed during the war hysteria of 1798, and the Federalist hegemony becomes more temporary. Those Republican and Federalist groupings are seen less as interests or protoparties, by late 1798, and more as developing parties. The Republicans become more capable of victory two years later, and the Federalists become weaker and more exposed to defeat, than they are commonly seen. The upcoming Republican domination for six presidential terms is less surprising, and the Federalist self-destruction and disappearance is more predictable.

A Federal Common Law of Crimes?

A prominent issue in the debates about the Virginia and Kentucky Resolutions, as well as in prosecutions under the Sedition Act, was whether there was a federal common law, separate from each state's common law. If there was, federal courts had very broad jurisdiction, especially of crimes such as seditious libel and seditious speech. If there was not, federal courts had very narrow jurisdiction of crimes, limited to the handful of offenses listed in federal statutes and other prohibitions necessary and proper to federal powers; and federal courts and prosecutors lacked jurisdiction over the seditious libel cases they brought under federal common law against Benjamin Franklin Bache, John Daly Burk and James Smith, and William Durell.

Both the Virginia and Kentucky Resolutions claimed repeatedly that the Alien and Sedition Acts exercised "power no where delegated to the federal government," and contended that the Constitution delegated "no power over the freedom of religion, freedom of speech, or freedom of the press." In response, the Virginia minority, the congressional committee, and the Massachusetts answer argued that a federal common law already criminalized seditious libel and seditious speech, and authorized deportation of aliens if dangerous or if war began. Hence, the Alien and Sedition Acts merely codified the existing common law, and were within constitutional powers of the federal government.[101] Virginia's Report provided a thoughtful and typical Republican reply.

The Existence of a Federal Common Law

There was no dispute about the existence of *state* common law. Most states during the Revolutionary War had adopted the English common law, unless repugnant to state constitutions or laws, by passing reception statutes.[102] The question whether the federal government had adopted, or inherited, a *federal* common law was another matter entirely.

The congressional committee report, Virginia minority address, and Massachusetts address briefly argued for a federal common law generally, before thoroughly arguing for a federal common law crime of seditious libel. The congressional report assumed its conclusion, saying that "the judicial power of the United States is expressly extended to all offences arising under the constitution. By the constitution, the government of the United States is established, for many important objects, as the GOVERNMENT OF THE COUNTRY; and libels against that government, therefore, are offences arising under the constitution." Virginia's minority similarly assumed most of its conclusion, in defining "cases arising under the constitution" as "cases triable by a rule which exists independent of any act of the legislature of the union," and saying that "[t]hat rule is the common or unwritten law which pervades all America." Massachusetts claimed that seditious practices "were punishable, on the principles of common law, in the courts of the United States, before the act in question was passed." Thus, none of the governmental defenses of the Alien and Sedition Acts provided much reasoning for assertions that there was a federal common law, in contrast with their greater discussion of the assertion that that common law made seditious libel a federal offense.[103]

In reply, Virginia's Report rejected the concept of a federal common law, and gave six grounds. It had never been adopted for "the whole as one society," either for the colonies, in the Confederation, or by the Constitution. Instead, the common law "was not the same in any two of the colonies" or states. A federal common law was not adopted or implied by the claimed basis, the Constitution's grant of federal judicial power over "all Cases, in Law and Equity, arising under this Constitution, the Laws of the United States, and Treaties." Such a common law would raise "difficulties and confusion" about such conundrums as whether the federal common law incorporated British statutes or left the vices of common law that those statutes corrected, or which version of common law was adopted where states differed. A federal common law would apply "the whole code with all its incongruities, barbarisms, and bloody maxims." It would "confer on the judicial department a discretion little short of a legislative power." Finally, it would have "vast consequences in extending the powers of the federal government, and in super[s]eding the authorities of the state governments," imposing on the country "a law of vast extent and complexity, and embracing almost every possible subject of legislation, both civil and criminal."[104]

Scholars have divided, some finding a historical basis for the Federalist insistence on a federal common law,[105] and others finding the historical evidence to support the Republican acceptance of only state common law and not federal common law.[106] The United States Supreme Court resolved the issue in 1812, holding that there is no federal common law, though it was light on reasoning.[107]

It appears that the Supreme Court was right, for several reasons. In the first Congress, Sen. Abraham Baldwin said that "we have not adopted the common law," and just before becoming the chief justice, John Marshall said not even "one man can be found who maintains" that England's common law was "adopted as the common law of America by the Constitution." Instead, that first Congress passed a criminal statute, which was unnecessary if the proscribed crimes were already part of federal law via a federal common law.[108] The Constitution did not expressly adopt the common law as federal law, even though it could have done so with fewer words than this sentence contains. The Constitution did expressly state the federal courts' jurisdiction without intimating a federal common law. Conferring federal court jurisdiction over a federal common law would have been a vast multiplication of that stated jurisdiction. Just in the area of criminal law, federal adoption of English common law would have created, without any express provision, over 160 capital offenses and even more noncapital felonies and misdemeanors. Thus, Jefferson's response was that the claim of a federal common law was an "audacious, barefaced and sweeping pretension to a system of law for the US. without the adoption of their legislature," which was "the most formidable" of all the Federalist doctrines to expand the federal government. The Alien and Sedition Acts were "unconsequential timid things in comparison."[109] There was no federal statute for reception of English common law. By contrast, nearly all the states had passed statutes to accept English common law as state common law, and obviously believed that a statutory or constitutional provision was necessary to do so.[110]

The first Supreme Court justices during the 1790s similarly denied the existence of a federal common law, as they sat on Circuit Court panels, until some shifted with the approach of the Alien and Sedition Act polarization. Before the federal criminal statute was enacted, Justice James Wilson listed as federal crimes only treason and crimes under specific statutes. Justice William Cushing, pressing for passage of the criminal statute, warned about the "predicament our Courts will be [in] as to carrying into Execution punishments for pyracies & felonies on the h[igh] seas & some other matters." After the criminal statute passed, Justice Wilson "enumerated . . . the crimes and offences known to the constitution and the laws of the United States" by listing the crimes in that statute and in revenue laws. He said what the legitimate role of common law was: "for the definition or description of the crimes" that were "*named,* but have not been *described* or *defined.*"[111] Justice James Iredell, who during the ratification debates said that Congress "have no power to define any other crime whatever" than under specific constitutional provisions, told a grand jury that crimes must be itemized "by fixed and general laws" and he then read the crime statute to the jurors. Justice William Paterson agreed that "the penal code of the U. States is plain and concise, and reduced, in its most important points, to written exactitude and precision," then listed some crimes in the criminal statute.[112] Before the 1798 crisis, no grand jury charge or opinion by a Supreme Court justice said that all common law crimes could be prosecuted as federal crimes. These federal grand jury charges are usually overlooked by those who argue to the contrary. The federal court decisions during the 1790s that touched on the existence of federal crimes outside the criminal statute only required or supported jurisdiction over offenses under "the Law of Nations" or under treaties, over which the Constitution gave Congress power and federal courts jurisdiction.[113] Those decisions are discussed elsewhere.[114]

Justice Samuel Chase is sometimes quoted for his lonely opinion that "the United States, as a Federal government, have no common law," but his inconsistent later opinions imply strongly that he was insincerely trying to undercut an argument being raised against the necessity of a sedition law.[115] So his opinion should have no weight on the issue.

The Existence of a Federal Common Law Crime of Seditious Libel

If there were no federal common law, there was no federal crime of seditious libel prior to the Sedition Act, and the Sedition Act could not be justified as merely restating and ameliorating the common law. On the other hand, if there was a federal common law, did it include a crime of seditious libel, a narrow Blackstonian definition of freedoms of press and speech, and a broad power of regulation of press and speech?

The congressional committee addressed these questions, more elaborately than Massachusetts or the Virginia minority. First, it claimed (following Blackstone) that "liberty of the press has always been understood in this manner, and no other," to mean "permission to publish without previous restraint" but not immunity from subsequent punishment "for any abuse" of that liberty. It offered as evidence that most state constitutions protected liberty of the press, yet those states' laws "provide for the punishment of libellous publications." Second, the committee asserted that liberty of the press never extended to "false, scandalous and malicious writings against the government," and so liberty of the press could not be violated by punishing what there was no right to do. Third, similarly, the Sedition Act "makes nothing penal that was not penal before," but instead "is merely declaratory of the common law," and in fact ameliorated the common law by reducing the potential fine and imprisonment and by allowing a defense of truth. And fourth, the First Amendment only prohibited laws "abridging" freedom of speech or press, unlike the more potent prohibition of any "law respecting" religion. Thus, Congress "may legislate respecting the press, may pass laws for its regulation, and to punish those who pervert [it] into an engine of mischief."[116]

In response, Virginia's Report said the narrow Blackstonian definition of liberty of the press seemed a "mockery," to proclaim "that no law should be passed, preventing publications from being made, but that laws might be passed for punishing them in case they should be made," as we saw earlier. The Report added that liberty of the press must extend to alleged "false, scandalous and malicious writings against the government," saying "it is manifestly impossible to punish" that "without striking at the right of freely discussing public characters and measures," which is essential to informed citizen choices in voting. And Virginia's report disagreed that the wording of the First Amendment allowed regulation of press and speech short of abridgment, saying that Congress had no delegated power to do either and that the First Amendment was an additional prohibition.[117]

Even if there were a federal common law, it did not contain the crime of seditious libel enacted in the Sedition Act, for several reasons. Such a criminal restriction on spoken or printed criticism of government and its officials would be a law "abridging the freedom of speech, or of the press" that was directly contrary to the First Amendment. Whatever the common law was before the First Amendment, that aspect was overridden by the prohibition of the First Amendment.

Further, I would suggest that English common law did not contain the narrow definition of freedoms of press and speech that the congressional committee claimed, until Blackstone misdescribed the common law to contain that in his last volume in 1769, and until Lord Chief Justice Mansfield then introduced the narrow definition into the common law in 1770. That narrow definition was not embraced by any of the first twelve justices of the United States Supreme Court until the Alien and Sedition Act crisis of 1798–1801.[118] Instead, an expansive definition was predominant in public discussion in Britain and America, from the mid-1760s through ratification of the Bill of Rights during 1789–1791 and until the crisis began in 1798.[119] Similarly, an expansive definition was predominant in Republican editors' discussion of freedoms of press and speech well before 1798, as we saw in the chapters on Bache, Burk, Matthew Lyon, and Thomas Adams, and as we will see in the chapters on William Duane, Charles Holt, Anthony Haswell, and Thomas Cooper.

The Virginia and Kentucky Resolutions, and the immediate responses, marked the end of the federal government's first campaign to enforce the Alien and Sedition Acts and to suppress the opposition. The second campaign of enforcement soon began in reaction to the Fries Rebellion in Pennsylvania.

THE SEDITION ACT SECOND CAMPAIGN (EARLY 1799)

THE REBELLION THE ARMY COULD NOT FIND

Beware, my Dear Sir, of magnifying a riot [the Fries Rebellion] into an insurrection, by employing in the first instance an inadequate force. Tis better far to err on the other side. Whenever the Government appears in arms it ought to appear like a *Hercules*. . . .

Will it be inexpedient to put under marching Orders a large force provisionally, as in eventual support of the corps to be employed—to awe the disaffected?

—Major General Alexander Hamilton to Secretary of War James McHenry (March 18, 1799)

CHAPTER EIGHT

The Fries Rebellion and Sedition

THERE WAS a second campaign of Sedition Act prosecutions and plans between the mid-1798 campaign launched by Secretary of State Timothy Pickering as the Sedition Act was being enacted and the later 1799 campaign against the opposition as the 1800 elections approached. That second campaign, which began in early 1799, has been overlooked, along with most of its prosecutions, but is a vital part of an accurate picture of the surprisingly extensive enforcement of the Alien and Sedition Acts.[1]

The second campaign included not only some prosecutions of editors and other individuals for opposition press and speech connected to the Fries Rebellion but also most prosecutions of groups of individuals for participating in that rebellion. In sheer numbers of defendants, it dwarfed the first and third campaigns to enforce the Alien and Sedition Acts. It also added a fearsome new dimension, the army and its use against domestic enemies rather than foreign enemies, in peacetime. Even as Pickering launched the second campaign in early 1799, part of the new army led the enforcement, and the effective commander of the new army, Gen. Alexander Hamilton, proposed also to use the army to suppress the opposition in Virginia and elsewhere (as the next chapter will discuss).

The Fries Rebellion in Pennsylvania, lasting from autumn 1798 through March 1799, was a tax protest. In July 1798, Congress had passed two tax statutes: a property tax and an act to value houses, lands, and enslaved

FIGURE 8.1. Sun Inn, Bethlehem, Pennsylvania, site of the Fries Rebellion rescue. Photograph by Andre Jenny. Alamy Stock Photo.

people as the basis of that tax. Rural Pennsylvanians, particularly German Lutherans and German Reformed parishioners, vehemently opposed the tax, and they obstructed assessors as they sought to measure houses and to collect the tax in Northampton, Bucks, and Montgomery Counties and in three other eastern counties.[2] When seventeen individuals were arrested for obstruction of the tax and were being taken to Philadelphia for trial, John Fries and a force of 70–200 men, mostly armed, rescued them from the makeshift jail in Bethlehem in Northampton County. The rescue occurred on March 7, 1799.

John Fries was an auctioneer (a vendue crier) living in Bucks County, Pennsylvania. He spoke fluent German, which was an asset in that German-majority area, and his surname and ancestry were German, though his father emigrated from Wales. His wife, Margaret Brunner, was also German. Fries had commanded a militia company in the Revolutionary War, and then as a captain he led a company of militia under President George Washington and Alexander Hamilton to crush the Whiskey Rebellion in 1794. Fries lived in a log cabin with his wife and seven surviving children, and by 1798 owned twelve acres.[3]

Fries was arrested, charged, and convicted of treason in April 1799 for hindering the tax assessors and leading the rescue, and after the conviction was overturned because of a biased juror, was again convicted in April 1800. Both times, he was sentenced to be hanged.[4]

The Fries Rebellion

The usual view of the Fries Rebellion,[5] then and now, was expressed by Abigail Adams as she briefed her son John Quincy Adams, an ambassador in Europe:

> [T]he stupid spirit of Insurrection which so blindly led the ignorant people of Northampton, was soon quelld, by the appearance of some troops; and [by] the energy of Government their leader Fries, was taken, and about a dozen more who opposed the Marshall in the Execution of the Laws. [T]he Jury were unanimous with respect to Fries, but his counsel have contrived to obtain a new trial for him, as they proved, that one of the Jury had exprest an opinion respecting his guilt, previous to trial. [T]he rest of the insurgents were convicted."[6]

Similarly, Pickering wrote to the president, who reported to Congress, that it was "necessary to call out a military force to repress the insurrection" in Pennsylvania and that that "has been done." Justice Samuel Chase stressed that the "insurrection" was "speedily quelled by the Vigilance and Energy of our Govt," and by the "skill of the General appointed to this duty." In Federalist public discussion and newspapers, the Fries Rebellion assumed great significance, because it provided the only armed opposition to the federal government during the crisis years of 1798–1801[7] (even though it was only momentary and its elevation to a treasonous insurrection required twisting the truth), and because it provided the only actual use and justification for the large new army in the absence of any French troops landing on the shores.

In Federalist private discussions, however, the Fries Rebellion was conceded to be a small affair. President John Adams wrote to his wife that it was "a silly Insurgence in Northampton County," and much later he wrote to Thomas Jefferson that it was merely an "outragious Riot and Rescue," and not "Treason, Rebellion as the World . . . pronounced it."[8] Secretary of Treasury Oliver Wolcott wrote to his brother that it was "a paltry insurrection here, which I am inclined to think will be subdued without difficulty," though things could get worse. The commanding general of the army, Gen. Alexander Hamilton, called it "a riot" and denied it was an insurrection, as he warned the secretary of war to beware "of magnifying a riot into an insurrection, by employing in the first instance an inadequate force." Instead, he called for force "like a *Hercules*," and proposed "to put under marching Orders a large force provisionally" in order "to awe the disaffected," supplemented by a "large corps of auxiliary cavalry" from four states. Justice James Iredell, who would soon preside over the trials of Fries Rebellion defendants, said "I don't doubt it can be easily suppressed."[9] Federalist editors have been paraphrased as complaining that "the crafty rebels, by their peacefulness, sought to evade punishment"! Republicans too downgraded the Fries Rebellion, calling it the "Hot Water Insurrection" based on what they treated as its most violent act, the occasional pouring of hot water on the heads of assessors as they measured windows.[10]

Quite a different scene has been described by the leading scholar of the Fries Rebellion, Paul Douglas Newman. "Throughout the entire affair, not a single assessor or any federal official came to harm. There was absolutely no interpersonal violence, outside of threats," and Fries himself "worked diligently to protect" the assistant assessors and to calm the bystanders. Though Fries and his armed supporters rescued those who the marshal had arrested, they did so only after repeatedly trying to have bail set to release the prisoners until their appearance in court was required, and only after the marshal adamantly refused. "Within minutes, all parties dispersed, the streets emptied, and Fries's Rebellion peacefully concluded without gunfire, fisticuffs, or bloodshed."[11] Five days later the president issued a proclamation instructing the participants to disperse and retire peacefully; and three days after that, Fries and his colleagues met, voted unanimously to comply, and ceased any resistance. That made no difference, however, because "even before the President spoke the administration had decided to send troops to the region," using the rebellion to gain authority to call up units of the newly-authorized Eventual Army.[12] The military expedition only began marching four weeks after the rescue—three weeks after the unanimous vote that ended any opposition. Throughout, "these 'rebels' never intended to make war against the governments of the state or nation"; they only sought "to expand the role of the people within the political system," particularly in opposing or criticizing governmental action. There was "no French connection"; even Judge Richard Peters said the resisters "were generally disposed against the French; he found none at all in favour of them."[13]

Despite all this, federal prosecutors chose to portray "the tax resistance as an insurrection," if not civil war, bringing treason charges and diverting attention from "the resisters' real ideological, political, and economic grievances." Those grievances included not only the new taxes, but scarcity of currency that made it difficult to pay taxes and debts, as Terry Bouton has shown. Also high among those grievances was the Sedition Act; the protesters "correctly perceived the Sedition Act and the new system of taxation . . . threatened their liberties."[14]

In the meantime, the federal army, arriving weeks after resistance vanished and after Fries and others voted to comply with the president's proclamation, wreaked havoc on the innocent citizenry. "Soldiers turned the countryside upside down, searched dozens of homes in the middle of the night, and took it upon themselves to find and destroy every liberty pole in the affected area."[15] During the campaign, one officer wrote that seven prisoners were "detained in irons . . . whose wrists are raw to the bone with the hand-cuffs," and another lamented that and also that "a number of the troops . . . live at free quarters on the people." "Bail to any amount has been offered . . . , but this would not suit the system of terror, nor would it act as a warning to those who may be disposed to vote as they think best." Another officer recounted that homes were "entered at the dead of night by a body of armed men" who "dragged [the rebels] from your wife and screaming children." He added that simply by persuasion "the magistrates could have effected everything that government could require" of the army. Another officer wrote that "this expedition was not only unnecessary, but violently absurd," because "a sergeant and six men might have performed all the service for which we have been assembled at so heavy an expence to the United States."[16]

Historians of the Alien and Sedition Acts, and of the Federalist period, have uniformly overlooked the prominent place of the Fries Rebellion in the enforcement of the Alien and Sedition Acts. The reason, as Robert Churchill notes, why historians "have overlooked their role" is "because they have not appreciated the full dimensions of the Alien and Sedition Act Crisis."[17] Also overlooked have been the brief mentions, by a few scholars of the Fries Rebellion, of the role of the Sedition Act in quelling that rebellion, which one noted is "normally not associated with the Northampton Insurrection" by historians.[18]

The second campaign of enforcing the Sedition Act included six prosecutions connected to the Fries Rebellion involving seditious press or speech, including efforts to suppress the region's two leading Republican newspapers printed in the German language. Those prosecutions were brought under Section 2 of the Sedition Act, and they will be discussed in the remainder of this chapter. The second campaign of enforcement also included eleven cases—all the nontreason cases connected to the Fries Rebellion—involving seditious opposition to the federal government. Those prosecutions were brought under Section 1 of the Sedition Act, and they will be discussed in Chapter 9.

Jacob Greenawalt Deriding the Tax Collectors

Jacob Greenawalt, Jr. (1751–1839) owned a farm and a tannery in Greenwich Township, Berks County, at the time of the Fries Rebellion. Sixty years before, his father immigrated from Switzerland as an indentured servant, and soon married a native of Germany. Buying a few hundred acres, he established a tannery and gristmill. The family's religious faith was German Reformed, and they baptized their children into that faith. The son, Jacob Jr., and his wife Maria Stambauch had four sons and five daughters.[19] During the Revolutionary War, he served briefly with Pennsylvania volunteers and then served in the militia as a captain.[20] After the war, Jacob Jr. bought 142 acres and established his own tannery. The family name was variously spelled as Grunwald, Grunnwalt, Grunewald, Grunewalt, Greenawald, and most commonly Greenawalt.

Jacob Greenawalt, Jr., livid over the new tax on houses and land, said to Jacob Bowen that if the tax assessor "John Whitman came to Greenwich Twp[.] they would tie him to the Liberty Pole, until he accounted to them for the money he received." Greenawalt believed that "John Whitman either spent the Money on Drink or on Women." Hearing that, Bowen brought Greenawalt before "Squire" Philip Kreamer, and Greenawalt added that "they would pay no more Taxes, until he had accounted to them for the Money he had received—and that the officers of Government were a Sett of Ragamuffins." Kreamer "sent him to gaol for indecent and intemperate Behaviour" on January 8, 1799. Kreamer gave a similar account, and recalled that Greenawalt said "we had nothing but mean & dirty Ragamuffins for officers in Government."[21] Whether those state charges were further prosecuted is not known.

As Judge Richard Peters left court to issue arrest warrants and to take statements in the field in early April 1799, he heard testimony from Michael Babst and recorded it in a written deposition. Babst related that "Grenwalt was put in Gaol for abusing the Government."[22] The judge had Greenawalt brought to court the next day,[23] and Greenawalt posted bond, in part by two sureties, to assure his appearance at trial later in April 1799. In court eleven days later, on April 22, he pled guilty, and was required to post bond for good behavior for a year, in the amount of $2,000 personally and $2,000 more by two friends.[24] The amount of the bond came from the maximum fine for seditious speech or press under Section 2 of the Sedition Act, which was $2,000. Though the bond was high, the court did not sentence Greenawalt to a fine or imprisonment. Consequently, Greenawalt had the lightest sentence of any defendant under the Sedition Act, and another Pennsylvanian, Langford Herring, had the next-lightest sentence (court costs only, also without any imprisonment).

Greenawalt's case showed that spoken words, as well as printed newspapers, could be treated as seditious in violation of the Sedition Act. It also showed that not much was required to violate that law. His case joined other prosecutions of speech apart from press: those of Lespenard Colie's damning the president, Matthew Lyon's speech reading a letter about the president's bullying speech, David Brown's roving speeches, Luther Baldwin's and Brown Clark's jests about a cannonball hitting the president's posterior, David Garvin's damning the president for an old fool, and as we shall see, Langford Herring's damning the president and Jacob Eyerman's "seditious counseling."

Morris Llewellyn and Friends and Their Liberty Pole

Morris Llewellyn (c. 1750–1828),[25] a weaver, also served in the Revolutionary War.[26] His father, John Llewellyn, was the grandson of a Welsh immigrant. The younger Llewellyn was on the assessment list for the unpopular tax on houses, lands, and slaves, because he had a residence and a rental cottage.[27] With six daughters and six sons, he likely found even a low tax onerous.

Llewellyn, with friends Samuel Young, George Britson, Archibald Menges, and James Jackson, raised a liberty pole on December 22, 1798. They were at the property of Henry Helmbolt, and Helmbolt told Jackson to make a liberty cap for the pole, out of pasteboard and red and black ribbon. They "nailed a Board about the middle" of the pole, which proclaimed "The Constitution sacred, No Gagg Laws[,] Liberty or Death." Three days later, Helmbolt told Jackson that a "troop was coming to cut it down," and Llewellyn advised them "not to hinder them from cutting it down." The Federalist troop did cut off the liberty pole, and many others, but a large number of "sedition poles" remained in the Pennsylvania region that hosted the Fries Rebellion.[28]

The original indictment of Morris Llewellyn and his friends,[29] approved by the grand jury in Philadelphia on April 24, 1799, charged them with violations of both the first and second sections of the Sedition Act. The group had combined and conspired to impede the operation of the Sedition Act, in violation of its first section. And the group, in violation of the second section, raised a liberty pole with a "seditious label," and

> did write, utter and publish, and knowingly & willingly did assist and aid in writing, uttering and publishing the false scandalous and malicious writing and words following, that is to say[,]
>
> The Constitution sacred[,]
> no gag law,
> liberty or death
>
> with intent to stir up sedition within the said United States and to excite unlawful combinations therein for opposing and resisting an act of the Congress of the said United States entitled an act in addition to an act [the Sedition Act].[30]

In other words, it was criminal sedition to oppose the Sedition Act. David Brown and Benjamin Fairbanks had been similarly prosecuted for raising a liberty pole whose caption condemned the Sedition Act, and Jedidiah Peck would be indicted for circulating petitions against the constitutionality of that law. And every opposition newspaper that was prosecuted had heatedly opposed the Sedition Act.

Because they pleaded not guilty, Llewellyn and his colleagues were scheduled for trial in October 1799, when the Circuit Court next met. Llewellyn and Jackson posted bonds, and the United States attorney served a subpoena requiring Helmbolt and other witnesses to come to testify. The United States attorney also revised the indictment to shorten the quotations from the placard to "No gag Law," showing even more starkly that the criminal activity was speaking or writing against the Sedition Act.[31] The grand jury's approval of that revised indictment was ineffective, however.

The reason was that all actions taken at the October 1799 court session were invalid, because the marshal, William Nichols, let his commission lapse, which meant that all his subpoenas, notices, and other "acts as marshall are void," as Justice Bushrod Washington wrote. That justice was "overwhelmed with mortification and chagrin at knowing that there is an end to our further proceedings," and Judge Richard Peters called it "the blowing up of the Court." Peters reported to Timothy Pickering that both judges "have no Doubts on the Subject" and "cannot remedy" the problem. Peters also wrote that they were concealing the problem and publicizing a pretext: "We do not say anything about the true Reason of our breaking up," and instead "assigned as a Reason that we had discovered since the last Adjournment an Error in the Proceedings, . . . & also that, from the small Number of Jurors attending, the Trials were not likely to proceed."[32] That prevarication opened a window on the campaign to prosecute Fries Rebellion defendants, and more broadly on the campaigns to prosecute sedition: they must be won even at a cost to truth or justice.

In the April 1800 court session, a new indictment was approved by the grand jury, with the wording changes from the prior October.[33] The new indictment also dropped James Jackson as a defendant in exchange for him signing the deposition that was quoted above, describing the actions of Llewellyn and colleagues in raising the liberty pole with its caption. Llewellyn and his other colleagues took advantage of the fact that their one-year bonds would expire on April 29, and they arranged not to be found by the marshal, according to notes on the unserved arrest warrants. They also escaped trial at the next court session, in October 1800, probably repeating that ploy.[34]

Langford Herring's "Seditious Words"

Langford Herring (c. 1766–1859)[35] grew up in Pittsylvania County, Virginia. He moved to Philadelphia, where he was in the militia in 1794.[36] While Herring's occupation was described as brickmaking in the *Aurora*, it might be better described as larceny. In a reported 1795 case he was charged with "fraudulently, unlawfully, and wickedly" procuring a merchant to endorse a "forged and counterfeited" promissory note for $1,470. Herring fled the state and did not appear at trial, so he was not convicted of the crime.[37] In 1796 Pennsylvania located him and tried to bring him to trial. It paid $100 to extradite Herring "from the gaol of Baltimore" to "the gaol of the city and county of Philadelphia."[38] Later, when Herring was arrested by state authorities in December 1798 for damning the president, Federalist newspapers reported that "[t]he low fellow who was lately committed to the jail of this city for seditious expressions, like most of his associates in Jacobinism, is no stranger to prison walls," and claimed that he had avoided the halter by informing "against his less artfull accomplices." In 1800 the leading Federalist paper recounted sarcastically that "[t]he noted LANKFORD HERON, has been lately sentenced in the Supreme Court of this State, to four years imprisonment, on conviction of four several Larcenies." A correspondent wrote to correct that, saying that "Langford Herring" was only found guilty for three of the four larcenies—and identified him as the same person who had been "indicted for sedition."[39] Perhaps to make his arrest difficult, Herring moved to Delaware. There, he volunteered for the militia during the War of 1812 and lived until his death.[40]

Herring's arrest by state authorities in December 1798 was "for damning the President, all that took his part and [all] that wore the Black Cockade" sported by Federalists.[41] Whatever happened in the state courts, by April 27, 1799 he was indicted by the federal grand jury.[42] That indictment was based on the same outburst on December 1, 1798, and alleged that Herring, "intending to vilify and defame the character of John Adams, President of the United States of America, did openly and publicly . . . utter and publish . . . the false scandalous malicious and seditious words following . . . damn the President . . . and all those who take his part" ("meaning thereby all those good citizens . . . who support the government"). The indictment charged him with a second offense, occurring ten days later, when he said that President John Adams was "an enemy to the government," because "the heavy weight of taxes particularly the stamp act is owing to his influence. The law . . . has been passed & put in force to the great injury of the people." That was alleged, using the language of the Sedition Act, to be with intent "to defame the said President of the United States and to bring him into contempt and disrepute[,] to render the laws of the said United States odious to the citizens thereof[,] and to excite opposition & resistance as well to the public acts and measures." The offense was summarized on the court's file jacket as "seditious expressions."[43]

The next month, Herring posted bond to assure his appearance at trial in October 1799. Shortly before that session began, he struck a deal with the prosecutor to drop the prosecution with Herring paying only court costs.[44] The court records do not disclose the reason, but it is likely that Herring agreed to provide testimony useful to the prosecutor in another case. Dismissal of Sedition Act cases was a rarity—of John Daly Burk when his newspaper was shuttered and he agreed to leave the country, and, as we will see, of Judah P. Spooner and Alden Spooner when their testimony was no longer needed, of Ann Greenleaf when one newspaper was closed permanently and the other temporarily, and of Jedidiah Peck when he gave up his petition campaign.

Rev. Jacob Eyerman's "Seditious Counseling"

Jacob Eyerman was a German Reformed minister of a Kirchenleute congregation in Northampton County in 1799.[45] The Kirchenleute (church people) were the German Lutherans and Reformed, who were typically Republicans and were predominant among Fries Rebellion participants. They contrasted with the Sektenleute of Moravians and Mennonites, allied with Quakers, who often had been tories and typically were Federalists.

Eyerman's background is described in his deposition; he had been a Calvinist Reformed Church pastor in Weisenbach in what is now southern Germany, and left because "the French had destroyed the place of his residence" during the Napoleonic wars. He arrived in Philadelphia in June 1796, and after two weeks moved to Springfield Township in Bucks County, where he stayed a year and a half, then moving to Hamilton Township in Northampton County, Pennsylvania.[46]

The new tax began with a major strike against it, since the collectors and assessors were Moravians, Quakers, and others unpopular with the Kirchenleute. The supervisor for Northampton County was a Moravian, and the supervisor for Bucks and Montgomery counties was a Quaker; both appointed equally objectionable assistants. Eyerman was a resolute opponent of the new tax and of its collectors and assessors. He brought to the dispute persuasive powers and a rough frontier style that once resolved a congregational disagreement by a tavern brawl.[47]

Eyerman was initially arrested under a warrant issued by Judge Richard Peters on February 20, 1799.[48] A newspaper article said that when he was arrested, Eyerman "was holding a Funeral Discourse." He was among the prisoners who were rescued on March 7, and upon being freed he fled to New York. Federalist reports of the capture of "the seditious Parson" were gleeful but premature.[49]

Secretary of State Timothy Pickering was eager to bring Eyerman to trial. After the clergyman fled, Pickering wrote to New York's governor to have "this miscreant" arrested and extradited to Pennsylvania:

> today I have procured depositions against & a description of the person of Mr. Eyrman, the insurgent German preacher who, when rescued from the Marshall in Northampton County, fled from Pennsylvania to New York; & by tomorrows post they will be sent to Judge Hobart, to enable him to issue a warrant against him. This Eyrman has been in America but two years & a half; & wears a clerical garb to cloak his licentiousness in morals as well as politics. I earnestly hope this miscreant may be arrested & secured.

Pickering gave instructions to Judge John Sloss Hobart in New York City to issue a warrant so Eyerman could be "prosecuted without delay," and warned that "the villain" is "as corrupt in his morals, as in politics."[50] When Eyerman was found a couple of weeks later, Pickering asked Judge Hobart to issue a warrant to transfer him to Philadelphia, which Hobart did promptly. Pickering notified John Adams of the upcoming trial of Eyerman, and agreed with the attorney general that Eyerman, as a newcomer, was "not only thus early a sower of sedition in the country where he has found an asylum, but of an infamous, immoral character."[51]

Eyerman was not indicted in the April 1799 session of the Circuit Court, because he was still at large.[52] That was remedied at the October 1799 session, when he was indicted for the one offense of escape, and three days later was reindicted for three offenses, which the jacket summarized as prison break, conspiracy, and "seditious counselling." The prosecutor, William Rawle, confirmed that the second and third counts, whose wording paraphrased the Sedition Act, were brought under that law.[53]

At his trial in mid-October 1799, witnesses testified to Eyerman's words opposing the new tax and its collection. One assessor, John Serfass, recounted how Eyerman would "rip out in a violent manner against this taxation, saying that Congress had made laws which were unjust, and the people need not take up with them." If the people complied, "they certainly would be put under great burdens." On another occasion, Eyerman told a group that "he knew the laws very well, and that Congress and the government only made such laws to rob the people, and that they were nothing but a parcel of damned rogues," so that the people "had no right to submit to it." John Sneider testified that Eyerman said he would "take arms," that he "would rather lay his black coat on a nail, and fight the whole week, and preach for them Sundays, than it should be so" that the house tax was implemented as in the old country.[54] After the prosecution finished presenting its case, Eyerman "refused to make any defence," because his "pecuniary circumstances" did not allow him to be represented by counsel.

Justice Bushrod Washington charged the jury, and among other things said that Eyerman was "the prime cause and adviser of this opposition," and that "the proof is as clear against him as any thing can possibly be." Not surprisingly, the jury deliberated only fifteen minutes, and found Eyerman guilty on all three counts. However, "the blowing up of the court" invalidated that fall 1799 trial. Since its announcement was delayed and understated, the voiding of court proceedings did not prevent most newspapers from carrying a paragraph about Eyerman's conviction.[55]

At the April 1800 session, a new indictment was approved by the grand jury, very similar to the more recent indictment. The first count was for Eyerman's prison break and escape. The second count, under the Sedition Act, was for his combining and conspiring to impede the operation of the valuation law, evidently by sermons and speeches. The third count, also under the Sedition Act, was for Eyerman's counseling and advising and unlawful assembly and combination with intent to impede the operation of the valuation law and the direct tax law.[56] Again, he faced trial without an attorney.

Eyerman was singularly unlucky. Having lost with a jury, he decided to retract his plea of not guilty and to "Submit to the Court protesting his innocence," leaving his fate to the mercy of the judges. Unfortunately, mercy was in short supply during that court session, because the panel of judges was Justice Samuel Chase along with Judge Richard Peters. Chase sentenced Eyerman to imprisonment of one year, a fine of $50, and good behavior bonds of $1,000 personally and $1,000 from two sureties.[57]

The case illustrates the breadth of the reach of the Sedition Act. It was a crime for Eyerman to speak words opposing the two tax laws and encouraging people to obstruct the tax assessors. There was no allegation that Eyerman actually took up arms, hurt or struck anyone, or incited anyone to violence. For his criminal words, he was sentenced to a year in prison.

Benjamin Mayer and Conrad Fahnestock Questioning the Fries Prosecution

After Fries Rebellion participants were processed at the April 1799 session of the Circuit Court, the federal prosecutor turned his attention to the leading two German-language newspapers. The marshal arrested the editors of the *Harrisburg Morgenröthe* in August, and Pickering gave instructions to prosecute the editor of the *Readinger Adler* the month before. They blamed newspapers and pamphlets for the Fries Rebellion, as did Secretary of the Treasury Oliver Wolcott. "The late insurrection in Pennsylvania is to be attributed to misrepresentations of the measures of government, in seditious pamphlets and newspapers, and in letters from popular characters."[58]

Benjamin Mayer (c. 1762–1824)[59] and Conrad Fahnestock (1763–1803)[60] were the editors of the first of those newspapers. Mayer, the son of Isaac and Catherine Mayer, had seven children with his wife Mary. He became "a vigorous politician, wielding considerable personal influence, as most of the outspoken Republican or Federalist editors did. Fahnestock, whose grandparents Diedrick Fahnestock and Anna Margaretta Hertz immigrated from Westphalia in 1726 seeking religious freedom, served at the end of the Revolutionary War, and a few years later married Mary Harlacher and had four children. After leaving the *Morgenröthe*, Fahnestock became a merchant in Middletown, Pennsylvania.[61]

Mayer and Fahnestock established the *Unpartheyische Harrisburg Morgenröthe Zeitung* in March 1799, as part of a large crop of Republican newspapers started during the Alien and Sedition Act years.[62] The reason their German-language newspaper was often called the "Dutch *Aurora*"[63] was because it was nearly as vocal a Republican paper as Bache's and Duane's *Aurora*.

Two months before Mayer and Fahnestock were indicted,[64] they were arrested by the marshal, William Nichols, who decided to awe the citizens of Harrisburg by being "accompanied by a troop of horsemen" who "made their entry into town up Front street" in August 1799. The editors were required to post bond to assure their appearance at trial during the upcoming Circuit Court session in October, in the amount of $2,000 each and $2,000 by two sureties. News of their arrest appeared in a large number of newspapers. Fahnestock evidently saw trouble coming, because he left the partnership as of the August 6 issue of the newspaper.[65]

Mayer and Fahnestock were indicted on October 18, 1799. The Circuit Court's minutes and the file jacket summarized the case as "Libel on the administration of justice."[66] The basis of the indictment was an article in the *Morgenröthe* that discussed the conviction of John Fries and that contended that his actions did not constitute high treason. Since the article was in German, the translation in the indictment will be used here. The article began with the Constitution's definition of treason: "only in levying War against [the United States], or in adhering to their Enemies, giving them Aid and Comfort."[67] It then asked, "what has Fries done?" Its answer was that he rescued prisoners, some of whom "would not consent that their houses should be measured" by federal assessors, and others of whom "with hot water levied war against the United States." The article next said that convicting Fries of treason on that basis was "not founded upon the law of the land," and the indictment said that meant the newspaper was arguing that the conviction must have been "the result of party motives." The article then asked "what will not the Tories [the judges and jury] finally declare to be treason"? The next topic was whether rescue, emptying "a bowl of hot water on an assessor," or hindering the assessor's "measuring or searching my house" could be treason. Fries himself "poured no hot water on the assessors" neither did he "oppose their opening his doors, searching or measuring his house"; he only rescued people charged with those acts. "Is this crime a levying of war" or "abetting their enemies?" The answer was that, under the law, the crime of rescue "cannot be greater than the crimes of those whom he rescued." The article quoted both federal law and common law establishing that point.[68] It concluded,

> And if Fries . . . is sentenced for High Treason it cannot have been according to law. His sentence . . . must rest on another foundation. Perhaps it is grounded on the word expedience, a ground which has produced the sedition and alien bills . . . and standing army in time of peace. . . . And if Congress . . . and the Judges [do this], how far may they . . . go. . . . Who will not be declared guilty by a Marshall's jury?[69]

The indictment characterized that article as seditious libel. It was "intending to vilify and defame the Government of the United States and the administration of justice therein," and "to cause it to be believed that the judicial courts . . . were actuated by unlawful motive" and not by the duty of following the Constitution. The editors' offense was to "print and publish" such things.[70]

At their arraignment that same day, Mayer and Fahnestock "submit[ted] to the Court protesting their Innocence." Because that amounted to consenting to a bench trial or to sentencing without a trial, the statement that "[t]here is no indication that the editors were tried" is mistaken.[71] They evidently were bullied into "submitting to the court," because such a large proportion of defendants did at the October 1799 and April 1800 sessions. However, everything done in their case at that October session of the court was invalidated, along with everything done in other cases, because of the problem with the marshal's commission. Mayer and Fahnestock did not appear in the court records for the April 1800 session,[72] perhaps because the marshal was overwhelmed in bringing people to trial or to sentencing in that packed session, or perhaps because Justice Chase had to leave before all cases were processed in order to seek indictments in Annapolis, and to indict and try James T. Callender in Richmond.

What the Mayer and Fahnestock prosecution involved was their newspaper printing an editorial disagreeing with a court decision and contending that Fries's actions did not constitute treason. The editors' criticism of the judges' and jury's conclusion was not treated as speech or press protected by the First Amendment but instead as seditious libel—a "Libel on the administration of justice"—that was a crime. A half year later, ironically, President John Adams reached much the same conclusion, as he wrestled with whether Fries's actions amounted to treason (with its death penalty), and he implicitly determined that they did not by granting a pardon.[73]

Jacob Schneider and the *Readinger Adler*

Jacob Schneider (c. 1763–1830)[74] was the grandson of Hans Schneider, who immigrated from Germany to Berks County in 1736. Both the grandfather and his son, Peter Schneider, were farmers. Jacob Schneider, before establishing the *Readinger Adler*, had worked as "a teacher, a silversmith, a clockmaker, a miller, a book-binder, a hotel landlord, the owner of a billiard table, a sign painter," an editor's helper, and a post rider. (Schneider responded that the source of that quotation, Gottlob Jungmann, had been unsuccessful as "a teacher, a musician, a clerk in a store, a weaver, a notorious card player and a soldier.") Schneider's work as a newspaper printer lasted from 1796 until 1804, when he became a county justice, and five years later he gained a further steady salary as county register and recorder. He was a contributor to, and presumably a member of, Trinity Lutheran Church in Reading.[75]

After an unsuccessful attempt to establish an English-language paper in Reading in 1796, Schneider founded the German-language *Unpartheyische Readinger Adler* at the beginning of 1797, in partnership with Georg Gerrish. It was one of the most influential German newspapers and was circulated in all the counties where the Fries Rebellion centered.[76] Gerrish left the paper in 1802, closely followed by debt collectors and a criminal charge for horse-stealing.[77]

The *Adler* was consistently Republican. Schneider condemned President John Adams and Federalist policies toward the French Republic. As the Alien and Sedition Acts were debated and enacted, he helped form a German Society in Reading and printed its messages. Later in 1798, Schneider published a stream of articles on petitions that denounced those laws.[78] He also directed his ire at the new excise tax, and lauded a Republican opponent of the tax for trying to thwart the "Tories" in threatening German property by imposing taxes. Schneider was even more outspoken in opposing the new house tax, describing it as the first step in a scheme to deprive hard-working Germans of their property, and more broadly as part of a Federalist conspiracy to succor British interests and to restore monarchy. In 1799, Schneider's dominant topic became the mistreatment of the Fries rebels. "A Farmer" had warned that, while Federalists "boast that they always can do with the Germans whatever they want to, that they are patient asses," they would be disproved in the 1797 election.[79] Schneider set out to disprove them again in the 1799 election.

Sedition by Supporting the Opposition Candidate

Schneider's *Adler* printed an "Address to the Germans of Cumberland County," urging them to vote against Federalist Sen. James Ross and for Republican Thomas McKean, in the hotly fought election for the Pennsylvania governorship in 1799. The address ended with "LET McKEAN BE OUR GOVERNOR," and the rest of it was no more subtle.[80] It began with denunciation of the "tories and federal aristocrats, who prefer a monarchy to our constitution," who work ceaselessly "to reduce us again to dependance," who are "the enemies of liberty" and of "republican America." The causes of their concerns were to be found in "*the administration.*" The next topic was the "sedition bill by which your mouths are gagged and speaking and printing [is] in a degree prohibited," so that "a citizen is highly punishable for saying, the President or either house of Congress had passed an unconstitutional law" or "were unworthy of any trust." Thus, "if you find fault with us [officials] or with any thing we do, you are guilty of sedition." In the Sedition Act, "Congress has not only infringed the liberty of speech, but likewise the liberty of the press." The discussion then shifted to Sen. James Ross, who "produce[d] the sedition bill" and whose endeavors "were to enslave you." Germans were "almost unanimously against Ross and the Sedition Bill, and for McKean." The final topic was the effects of the Sedition Act. The standing army soon would be "billeted in your dwellings" and would plunder your food, and "if you say, write, or print any thing against it, you will be served" under the Sedition Act. Citizens are "now robbed in the most ungraceful manner of their most precious liberty, the freedom of speech," by the Sedition Bill, and deprived of the "liberty of the press" that is the vehicle for "investigating the conduct of our government . . . and the right of reprimanding them when they deserve it." The prose became purple: "the sedition bill, and the dreadful army of 30,000 men will be put in motion—then follow—the dark cell, chains, bars and bolts, &c—Look farther—the halter, the gallows, the scaffold." The "plants of the federal nursery" included "the sedition bill," and "who was the chief gardener . . . ? Answer: James Ross!" The address called on Germans "to bring those political murderers of our liberty to the punishment they deserve."[81] In the election later in the year, they did, and Ross lost to McKean.

Secretary of State Timothy Pickering wrote to the United States attorney and instructed him to prosecute Schneider (with the usual courteous language about if the United States attorney shared his opinion that prosecution was warranted).

> I enclose a letter recd. yesterday . . . covering a newspaper printed at Reading by one Schneider in the German language, and a translation of that passage it [sic] which is entitled "An Address to the Germans, in the County of Cumberland." If any passages in the address in your opinion make the printer liable to a prosecution, I pray you to direct its being commenced.

Pickering's bias was shown when the same address was reprinted two weeks later in the Federalist *Porcupine's Gazette*, edited by William Cobbett. There was no instruction to prosecute Cobbett for seditious libel, like that to prosecute Schneider.[82]

The federal court records do not show that a prosecution of Schneider was begun. The statement is mistaken that "Rawle instituted sedition proceedings against him and the *Adler*."[83] The reason was likely that Rawle was overwhelmed with the prosecutions and sentencings of Fries resisters that were already scheduled for the October 1799 session.

Alternative Justice, Federalist Style

Though there was no indictment or trial, the standing army that Schneider dreaded had already exacted justice, Federalist style, when in April 1799 a troop of light horse dragged him out of his newspaper office in Reading and beat him in the town marketplace. Schneider had published an article poking fun at the "Herculean adventures" of the arriving army doing battle with liberty poles, as well as terrorizing civilians, violating the law, and stirring the people against the government.[84] Immediately after the beating, Schneider published his own account:

> On Saturday afternoon last, the troops who were sent to seize upon some people in Northampton, called insurgents, on their return from that expedition, arrived in town. . . . [T]hey carried their trade so far as to enter the houses and abuse peaceable and unoffending citizens in a manner the most scandalous and cowardly.
>
> As for example, a part of them came to my printing-office on Saturday last, not as men of character desirous of supporting the law and the security of the peaceable citizen, but like a banditti of robbers and assassins; they tore the clothes off my body, and forcibly dragged me from my house before their captain. . . . He ordered his troopers to take me to the public market-house and give me *twenty five* lashes on the bare back, and they proceeded to obey his orders accordingly, and certainly would have fulfilled them exactly, had not some of Capt. Leiper's troop, of Philadelphia, interfered, reproached them for their illegal and tyrannical conduct, in consequence of which only a part of the sentence of Capt. Montgomery [*six lashes*] was inflicted.[85]

The *Aurora* immediately printed what would now be called an editorial on the incident, calling it an example of the danger of a standing army to liberty, and calling "the fictitious insurrection in Northampton" an "electioneering machination." Schneider's article, and the *Aurora* commentary, were reprinted in most Republican newspapers, and in many others.[86] In the meantime, the *Aurora* published a stream of articles on Schneider's mistreatment, for example asking what the army and the administration were going to do to punish the malefactors, and asking "[w]hat is the use of passing laws against sedition" when "every friend to *order and good government* has a right" to take justice into his own hands "from the *bleeding back* of his free and independent *fellow man!!*"[87]

The effective leader of that first troop was none other than a House of Representatives sponsor of the Sedition Act, Rep. Robert Goodloe Harper, serving as aide-de-camp to Gen. William MacPherson who commanded the army's expedition against the Fries Rebellion. Harper, in responding to Schneider's article, confirmed that Schneider was forced from his office, taken involuntarily to the town square, and subjected to six lashes. The troops' mission, Harper said, was "cutting down several sedition-poles."[88] He obviously found no violation of the First Amendment in federal troops beating a person because he published opinions or facts critical of the government, in the place of charging the person with a crime and bringing him to court. The generals found no violation either, because the army charged no one with improper conduct, despite Republican demands; there was no court martial.

These six prosecutions related to the Fries Rebellion—of Jacob Greenawalt, Morris Llewellyn and friends, Langford Herring, Rev. Jacob Eyerman, and of the editors of two leading German newspapers, Benjamin Mayer, Conrad Fahnestock, and Jacob Schneider—were brought principally under the section of the Sedition Act making it a crime to write, print, utter, or publish virtually anything critical of the government, Congress, or the president. There were still more prosecutions related to the Fries Rebellion that are discussed in Chapter 9, which were brought under the other section of the Sedition Act making it a crime to combine or conspire to oppose the government or its measures.

CHAPTER NINE

The Army and the Sedition Act

ALL THE Fries Rebellion prosecutions, except the treason prosecutions, were Sedition Act cases.[1] The reason scholars have not treated the non-treason prosecutions during the Fries Rebellion cases as Sedition Act prosecutions is that all leading Fries Rebellion cases were for treason rather than sedition, and all Sedition Act cases except those connected to the Fries Rebellion involved the familiar crime under Section 2: to "write, print, utter or publish" criticism of "the government . . . or either house of Congress . . . or the President" with intent to defame them. However, a less familiar crime was prohibited under Section 1 of the Sedition Act: to "combine or conspire . . . with intent to oppose any measure" of the government, or to "counsel, advise or attempt" any riot or unlawful assembly. More precisely, what was criminalized under Section 1 was:

> That if any persons shall unlawfully combine or conspire together, with intent to oppose any measure or measures of the government of the United States, . . . or to impede the operation of any law of the United States, or to intimidate or prevent any person holding a place or office in or under the government of the United States, from undertaking, performing or executing his trust or duty; and if any person or persons, with intent as aforesaid, shall counsel, advise or attempt to procure any insurrection, riot, unlawful assembly, or combination, . . . they shall be deemed guilty of a high misdemeanor.[2]

The punishment was a fine up $5,000 and imprisonment for six months to five years.

Significantly, all of the nontreason cases in connection with the Fries Rebellion were brought under that less familiar provision, other than the cases discussed in Chapter 8 that were pursued under the more familiar provision of the Sedition Act.[3] The first of three court sessions that held Fries-related trials began with a charge to the grand jury that the Sedition Act "has specially provided . . . against combinations to defeat the execution of the laws," and the third began with the senior judge describing many of those trials as for "seditious combinations."[4] The indictments, like most at the time, did not cite any particular federal statute. However, the Sedition Act was hidden in plain view, because the indictments tracked the words of its Section 1, as will be evident in the quotation below from the first indictment of Fries rebels for conspiracy. And the Sedition Act was the only federal statute at the time criminalizing conspiracy and obstruction. The Sedition Act was the basis of the second and third counts of the Jacob Eyerman indictment, the prosecutor, William Rawle, said, and those were worded similarly to the indictments in the eleven cases discussed in this chapter.[5]

Eleven Cases with Eighty-Three Defendants

Eleven cases were brought under Section 1 of the Sedition Act for the crimes of combining, conspiring, or rescue. Each case involved groups ranging from two to thirteen defendants; the total was eighty-three defendants. For those cases, grand jury indictments, arraignments to plead guilty or not guilty, taking of appearance bonds, trials, and sentencing consumed most of the time left in the April 1799, October 1799, and April 1800 sessions of the United States Circuit Court in Pennsylvania, once the treason cases of John Fries and others were handled. Some time was also devoted to the cases discussed in Chapter 8—in the April 1799 session were indictments of Jacob Greenawalt (for saying the assessor "spent the excise money on drink or idle women"), Morris Llewellyn and friends (for a "seditious label" on a liberty pole), and Langford Herring (for "seditious words" about the president); in the October 1799 session Herring was settled, Llewellyn was reindicted, Rev. Jacob Eyerman was indicted and tried (for "seditious counseling" against the tax laws), and Benjamin Mayer and Conrad Fahnestock were indicted (for an editorial questioning the Fries prosecution); and in the April 1800 session Llewellyn and Eyerman were reindicted.

Those eleven cases charged the following eighty-three defendants with violating Section 1 of the Sedition Act—with combining and conspiring with intent to impede the tax laws and assessors:[6]

Henry Ohl, Andrew Leutzingen, Adam Laeb, Nicholas Miller, Martin Hester, Michael Best
—for combining and conspiring in Heidelberg Township, Northampton County, on December 3, 1798 and January 1, 1799, and impeding the assessor George Lintz on December 15, 1798.[7]

John Shimer, John A. Engelman, Jacob Engelman, John Mumbower, Henry Huber, George Seider, Peter Keefer
—for combining and conspiring in Upper Milford Township, Northampton County, and impeding the assessor Christian Heckewelder on January 1, 1799.[8]

Daniel Klein, Jacob Klein, Adam Breisch, George Gettman, William Gettman
—for combining and conspiring in Northampton County, by preventing enforcement of arrest warrants and appearances in court, amassing troops on March 6, 1799, and rescuing prisoners on March 7, 1799.[9]

John Eberhardt, John Huber, Christopher Sax (Sox), John Klein, Jr., John Klein, John Fox
—for combining and conspiring in Northampton County, by preventing enforcement of arrest warrants and appearances in court, amassing troops on March 6, 1799, and rescuing prisoners on March 7, 1799.[10]

George Goltner, Peter Styerwaldt, John Lechlider, John Smith, William Rex, Charles Styerwaldt, Tobias Shlosser, Jacob Fritz, Laurence Ebner, Andrew Feller, George Hetler, John Kuntz, Peter Rabenholdt
—for combining and conspiring in Penns Township, Northampton County, and impeding the assessor Peter Zehner on January 25, 1799.[11]

Abraham Samsel, Peter Hundsberg, Abraham Shantz, George Mumbower, Henry Mumbower, Peter Hager, Peter Gable, Jacob Gable, Daniel Gable, John Miller, John Marks, Henry Smith, Valentine Kuder
—for combining and conspiring in Northampton County, by amassing troops on March 6, 1799, and rescuing prisoners on March 7, 1799.[12]

Henry Jarrett, Henry Shankweiler, Herman Hartman, Adam Stephan, Daniel Kevely, Jacob Klein, George Shaefer
—for combining and conspiring in Macungie Township, Northampton County, and impeding the assessor John Romick (Romig) on January 15, 1799.[13]

Henry Shiffert, Christian Ruth, Samuel Schwartz, Henry Stahler, Daniel Schwartz, Jr., John Kayser, Daniel Dillinger, George Shaefer, Daniel Schwartz, Adam Stahlnecker
—for combining and conspiring in Northampton County on February 15, 1799, and preventing enforcement of arrest warrants and appearances in court, and rescuing prisoners on March 7, 1799.[14]

Michael Yeisley, John Smyer, Michael Smyer, Jacob Smyer, Philip Ruth, Peter Rothenberger, John Huber, Jacob Eisenhardt, George Ehrich, Frederick Hayns, John Stadtler

—for combining and conspiring in Bethlehem, Northampton County, and preventing enforcement of arrest warrants and appearances in court, and rescuing prisoners, all on March 7, 1799.[15]

Anthony Stahler, Jacob Klein, Philip Desh
—for combining and conspiring in Bethlehem, Northampton County, and preventing enforcement of arrest warrants and appearances in court, and rescuing prisoners, all on March 7, 1799.[16]

Conrad Marks, John Marks
—for combining and conspiring in Lower Milford Township, Bucks County, by amassing troops on March 6, 1799.[17]

Notably, all of the Fries rebels challenged the constitutionality of the two laws whose enforcement they impeded. All shared a cultural view that a tax on homes, like the German hearth taxes that their parents or grandparents had fled, was a tax on freedom and a threat to freedom.[18]

Secretary of State Timothy Pickering was left with a free hand to press for merciless prosecutions, and Secretary of War James McHenry, along with General Alexander Hamilton, were left with free hands to continue the military expedition "like a Hercules" against the disbanded Fries rebellion, because President John Adams left for Quincy, Massachusetts the day he signed his proclamation to disperse.[19]

The First Charges and Trials of the Fries Rebels

Justice James Iredell presided over the April 1799 session of the Circuit Court, joined for most of the session by the District Court judge, Richard Peters. Iredell, before being appointed to the United States Supreme Court by President George Washington in 1790, had been a pre-Revolution customs collector in North Carolina, then a superior court judge for a half year, the state's attorney general for two years, a member of the council of state, and more notably, a leader in his state's fight for ratification of the Constitution.[20] Before the April 1799 session, Peters, under instructions from Pickering, had been consumed with issuing arrest warrants for at least 142 people, compelling them to come to Philadelphia to post appearance bonds to assure their presence at trials.[21]

Iredell opened the session, as was usual, with a charge (instructions) to the grand jury that would then consider the United States attorney's recommendations for indictments. Almost the full charge was Iredell's "deliberate opinion as a Judge" defending the constitutionality of the Alien and Sedition Acts, and adopting Sir William Blackstone's argument that "Liberty of the Press . . . consists in laying no *previous* restraints upon publications" rather than in "freedom from censure for criminal matter when published."[22] The charge ended by addressing the "insurrection" in Pennsylvania, and claimed that it was caused by "incessant calumnies [that] have been poured against the government for supposed breaches of the constitution." Iredell prejudged the defendants, saying that "many certainly have been guilty of combinations to resist the laws of the United States," and condemned the Republican Party indirectly, asserting that "the principles of republicanism" were "the perpetual theme of their declamations" as efforts were "made to vilify and undermine the government." The grand jury made its bias clear, and its handpicking by the marshal even clearer, by its fulsome reply to Iredell's charge. That reply said that the grand jury unanimously found his "Charge, fraught with such clear and just observations on the nature and operation of the constitution and laws of the United States," at a time "when false philosophy and the most dangerous and wicked principles are spreading with rapidity, under the imposing garb of Liberty," by French conquests.[23]

During April 22–26, the grand jury approved indictments for treason of John Fries and nine other individuals; it refused to approve an eleventh indictment for treason.[24] The federal court showed its resolute plan to charge and try a large number of Fries rebels by preprinting form indictments for treason with blanks for the offender's name, and it did not waste them. It also showed its bias, besides Iredell's charge, by captioning the record "Rebellion & Insurgents."[25]

During April 26–30, the grand jury also approved indictments under Section 1 of the Sedition Act of the first nine groups of defendants—those headed by Henry Ohl, John Shimer, Daniel Klein, John Eberhardt, George Goltner, Abraham Samsel, Henry Jarrett, Henry Shiffert, and Michael Yeisley. Like the preprinted indictments for treason, the court prepared prewritten indictments in many cases with blanks for defendants' names.[26]

The Ohl indictment was typical. It tracked the language of Section 1 of the Sedition Act in charging that Ohl and his codefendants did

> unlawfully combine and conspire together with intent to impede the operation of a law of the United States entitled An Act to provide for the valuation . . . [and] An Act to lay and collect a direct tax . . . and to intimidate and prevent the assessors and other persons appointed to execute the same.

That first count was followed by four more counts that also tracked Section 1, charging that Ohl and others did "counsel advise and attempt to procure an insurrection riot and unlawful assembly," "oppose and prevent the execution of an Act of the Congress," "intimidate and prevent" the assessor from executing his duties by "menaces threats and assembling together," and "combine and conspire . . . to intimidate and prevent the assessor."[27] In each of the cases, the combination and conspiracy, counseling and advising, preventing execution of law, and intimidating and preventing the assessor, were in connection with the two unpopular tax laws—the house tax and the valuation law.

What actually happened in the Ohl case was less typical of the other cases and instead more verbally combative. At a meeting at Ohl's tavern with the assessor at the beginning of December 1798, others made threats of firing at the assessor if he proceeded with his work. Ohl, a bombastic tavern-keeper, insisted that the revenue officer for the area should perform the assessments himself, and said he would "cut him to pieces and make sausages of him," and that in fact Ohl would fire at his own father if he did the valuations. The day after, most of the men of that township gathered again at the tavern and agreed to an "Association" (mirroring prerevolutionary ones) pledging to impede assessments of their houses and land. They believed that a tax on homes, like Germany's "hearth tax," was a road to serfdom and was not constitutional.[28] That fanciful understanding of the dangers of the house tax, and more broadly of the federal government, was widely held in the rural counties involved in the Fries Rebellion. More typically, John Shimer's case arose from arranging a town meeting where he cried that "all those that are for Liberty shall swing their hats and huzza for Liberty," after which they all took oaths to impede the assessor.[29] Because these cases were similar to the other Section 1 cases, their facts, which are masterfully recounted by Paul Douglas Newman, will not be repeated. Their chronology is given in Table A.2.

Five of the eleven cases also had a count for the rescue, claiming the defendants had joined with John Fries in releasing prisoners on March 7, 1799. They were the groups headed by Daniel Klein, John Eberhardt, Henry Shiffert, Michael Yeisley, and Anthony Stahler.

Once indictments were handed down and appearance bonds were taken, May 1–9 was devoted to the treason trial of John Fries.[30] It was far from a fair trial, as a number of things showed. The judges had their minds made up beforehand, according to Pickering, who said he "before[hand] knew that the two judges were perfectly agreed as to the *treasonable* matter, and the *guilt* of the prisoner." They had also discussed the cases with Pickering, the official supervising federal prosecutions, in order for him to know the judges' views before trial. The defendant's motion to avoid an unfair jury by moving the trial to Northampton County, or by bringing jurors from there, was denied, even though it was precisely what the Judiciary Act of 1789 provided for in capital cases: that "the trial shall be had in the county where the offence was committed, or where that cannot be done without great inconvenience, twelve petit jurors at least shall be summoned from thence."[31] One of the judges testified as a government witness; Judge Peters described officials "endeavouring to bring those criminals to justice" and being intimidated from issuing subpoenas, and other magistrates "flattering the prejudices of the people, and engaging in seditious practices." He also testified "that the prisoners had been rescued, by force of arms," and that he witnessed Fries signing a confession. He said he discovered "manifest signs of terror coming from the districts" and attempts "to raise troops to oppose the army." When all testimony was finished, Judge Peters's summary to the trial jury concluded that "both facts and law . . . are too plain to admit a reasonable doubt," evidently finding his own testimony quite convincing.[32] At the time, summations like that by a judge were common, but a widespread practice did not convert such statements into a fair trial. Finally, Justice Iredell's charge to the trial jury, like that to the grand jury, laid down an aggressively broad definition of treason: "an attempt by force and violence to impede the operation of a single act, shall be treason, and under the description of levying war," and "the English authorities and definition of those terms should be much respected," at the least. When legal wrapping is removed, what Fries did was to draft an association paper while saying that "we never shall submit to the [tax] law but it shall be repealed," and to lead armed men to Bethlehem while negotiating unarmed for release of prisoners on bail and, failing that, rescuing the prisoners without firing a shot.[33]

The jury found Fries guilty of treason. But as he entered the courtroom to be sentenced to death, his attorneys filed a motion for a new trial because one of the jurors had said before trial that Fries "ought to be hung." A new trial was granted. Justice Iredell claimed to find it difficult to contemplate sentencing Fries to death, but he found it much more traumatic when he had to set aside the treason verdict that required that death penalty.[34] Pickering found it worse than traumatic to see the treason verdict voided, writing incredulously that "that juror only thought and spoke, as any other person did who was equally informed of the facts." His view was that "an *example* or *examples* of *conviction* and *punishment* of such high handed offenders were *essential,* to *ensure future obedience to the laws,* or *the exertions of our best citizens to suppress future insurrections.*"[35] The "best citizens," of course, were the upper echelon of Federalists.

Further Proceedings against the Fries Rebels

Justice Bushrod Washington presided over the October 1799 session, joined by local Judge Richard Peters. Washington, the first president's nephew, before being appointed to the United States Supreme Court by President John Adams in September 1798, had practiced law and written the first books of Virginia case reports.[36] The court session appeared to be achieving much—indicting Eyerman and Mayer and Fahnstock, indicting William Duane of the *Aurora* for claiming that there had been British influence in appointing a high American official, and processing many of the combination and conspiracy cases—until the defect in the marshal's authority invalidated all actions of the court in the session.[37] Everything that had to be redone, or that was not reached, piled up for the April 1800 session.

Justice Samuel Chase presided over the April 1800 session, joined as usual by Judge Peters. Chase did not arrive with an impartial mind; immediately upon hearing of "the Insurrection in Northampton," he wrote to Justice Iredell and stated his hope that "a body of horse and foot are ordered to seize the insurgents."[38] Opening court, Chase's grand jury charge began by proclaiming a distinctive Federalist view of the restricted role of the people to disagree with government, and of a party to oppose government. The people's role is to elect good representatives, and then "[*p*]*rivate* opinion must give way to *public* Judgement," even "[i]f Congress should pass *burthensome*, or *oppressive* Laws"; the remedy is to elect new representatives to repeal them. And "until it is repealed, it is the *Duty* of every Citizen to submit to it; and to give up his *private Sentiments* to the *public Will.*" Similarly, the people and juries may not allege that a law is unconstitutional; the judiciary is "the only proper and competent authority to decide any Law . . . is contrary to or in Violation of the *federal* Constitution."[39]

Chase then turned to opposition to a law and the Fries Rebellion. "The man who *openly* opposes, and the man who *secretly* advises opposition is *equally criminal;* and the *latter* is the most despicable and dangerous character." It is a false patriot "who *professes himself a friend to Liberty,* and yet *wilfully misrepresents* his Government, and the conduct of its Officers," and "creates distrust and suspicion" of them or "encourages *opposition* to the execution of the Laws" (all of which was sedition). This was all directed at the Fries rebels: "I have made these observations, Gentlemen, in consequence of the *former* and late insurrection" in Pennsylvania that was "speedily quelled by the Vigilance and Energy of our Govt." The grand jury had a "*bounden and indispensable duty* to present" or indict those who violated the Sedition Act, though it had "*no right* to decide on the *Justice,* or the *validity* of the *Law.*" Chase's charge ended with praise for "our illustrious patriotic and beloved President," "that wise and vigilant Statesman," and with an admonition "to support . . . the present administration."[40]

The grand jury, invigorated if not incited, approved indictments or reindictments in nine treason cases, with the help of a fresh supply of preprinted indictments. It also issued new indictments in most of the nine combination or conspiracy cases and approved indictments in a tenth and an eleventh case against various defendants for combination or conspiracy—the Anthony Stahler group and the Conrad Marks group—after they had been successful in defeating treason charges.[41] The number of defendants indicted or reindicted in the April 1800 session under Section 1 of the Sedition Act was forty-five, according to the court's total, in addition to twelve jury trials and nine treason indictments. The United States attorney greased the process with some prewritten indictments under Section 1 with blanks for the persons to be charged.[42]

The court also held the second trial of John Fries.[43] In an attempt to shorten it, Chase handed out a written opinion that foreclosed defense arguments or evidence about the definition of treason, by laying down an aggressively broad definition. In effect, Chase scuttled the defense case that was built around the argument that opposing enforcement of two laws was not treason, and was at most a rescue, or riot, or sedition. He instead ruled that opposition to any law was treason.[44] That peremptory opinion and other mistreatment of Fries became the first of eight charges in the impeachment case against Chase during 1804–1805.[45] In response to that opinion, the outraged defense attorneys walked out of the trial, leaving poor Fries without counsel. Chase assured Fries that he and Judge Peters "will be your counsel," a role in which they were not notably successful. The justice's advice drove Fries to not testify or provide any defense.[46] Multiplying his prejudicial error, Chase informed the jury that Fries had already been convicted in his first trial, and that the judges concluded that "every overt act is treasonable."[47] It is strange that these major things were not viewed as denying Fries a fair trial, while the marshal's failure to renew his commission properly was viewed as rendering everything void that was done in the preceding court session. The jury instructions endorsed the prosecutor's very broad definition of treason: "any such . . . rising to resist, or to prevent by *force* or *violence*, the execution of any statute of the United States . . . is a *levying war*," and thus treason. Not surprisingly, Fries was convicted of treason, and Chase sentenced him to hang.[48]

The court also oversaw the indictment and held the trial of Thomas Cooper, which is discussed in Chapter 13. In that trial, Chase excluded any witness who could not prove an entire defense to a charge (saying that two witnesses would not be allowed each to prove half of a defense), and reversed the presumption of innocence by requiring the defendant to prove every defense "to the marrow." At the end of the trial, Chase prowled the circuit to press the Maryland grand jury to indict the editor of "one of the most licentious presses in the United States," and to pressure the Virginia grand jury to indict James T. Callender.

Chase virtually set speed records, as he raced to end the court session, by sentencing thirty people during the last two days in combination and conspiracy cases to fines of $40–$1,000 and imprisonment of six months to two years (and until fines were paid and bonds were posted), in addition to ruling on other matters. The majority of defendants did "retract his plea of non cul. [not guilty] and submit to the court protesting his innocence," likely as the result of judicial bullying. Harsh sentences invariably followed.[49] When the combination and conspiracy cases are included, Justice Chase was the Supreme Court justice who sentenced the largest number of Sedition Act defendants—and who meted out the harshest sentences overall—and Justice James Iredell was the jurist who oversaw the largest number of indictments under the Sedition Act.

President John Adams was troubled by the concept that opposing enforcement of any single federal law was treason, a capital offense. He asked his cabinet whether the Fries rebellion was "any thing more than a riot . . . for the purpose of a rescue," and whether there was "great danger in establishing such a construction of treason, as may be applied to every sudden, ignorant, inconsiderate heat." He had already reviewed the arguments of defense counsel and others. Despite the cabinet's unanimous negative response, Adams pardoned John Fries and the other two Pennsylvanians convicted of treason.[50] Those pardons brought violent objections from High Federalists, seeming to confirm their apprehensions that Adams was cravenly subordinating principle to popularity, or worse, conspiring with Thomas Jefferson over the upcoming presidential election of 1800. Those objections culminated in condemnation by Alexander Hamilton in his pamphlet cataloguing Adams's political sins.[51]

Was what Fries and other rebels did treasonable?[52] They did not oppose all laws, just the house tax and the valuation law. In opposing those laws, they consciously emulated the patriots before the American Revolution, holding town meetings to approve petitions to the legislature, forming associations committed to not paying the tax, putting up liberty poles, and condemning the tax as hostile to liberty and to the Constitution. The rebels' only action with arms was to rescue prisoners, and their reasons were that they believed the arrests were unconstitutional because the two tax laws were unconstitutional, and that they believed the prisoners' Sixth Amendment rights would be violated by depriving them of an impartial jury of their peers by moving them from German-American counties to Philadelphia. Even before and during the rescue, Fries consistently left weapons behind when conferring with the marshal. Immediately, he and the other rebels obeyed the presidential proclamation and voted unanimously to comply with the two challenged laws. Newman puts it nicely:

> Their plan was to nonviolently obstruct the collection of the Direct Tax until the Sixth Congress responded to their petitions and until they were sure that other counties and other states were complying with the tax. Some expected to be prosecuted for their refusal to pay the rate, and perhaps for disturbing the peace, but none even remotely expected to be charged with treason and sedition and to be hunted down by a federal army.[53]

The judges' opinions in the treason trials, however, were that "rising to resist or to prevent by *force* . . . the execution of any statute . . . is a *levying war,*" and that "military weapons . . . are not necessary . . . because numbers may supply the want of military weapons," as Justice Chase ruled. That expansive definition followed English common law and recent Circuit Court decisions involving the Whiskey Rebellion's leaders.[54] But that definition was extraordinarily broad—for example, it would make treasonous the prerevolutionary effort to prevent the implementation of the Stamp Act by a number of people.

The attorneys for Fries argued in his first trial, and would have argued in the second, that only "a forcible opposition to the powers of government, with the intent to subdue and overthrow it," is levying war.[55] Further, the Constitution's narrow definition of treason clearly rejected the broad English common law definition, which treated a number of things as levying war, such as "taking arms, not only to dethrone the king, but under pretence to reform religion, or the laws, or to remove evil counsellors, or other grievances"; or "an insurrection with an avowed design to pull down *all* inclosures, *all* brothels, and the like"; as well as an amorphous group of constructive treasons.[56] Also, other federal statutes defined rescue and obstruction of process as different and lesser crimes,[57] and the Sedition Act defined combining and conspiring to impede laws and procuring a riot as different and lesser crimes. Thus, those things could not be treason. One of those, not treason, was the crime committed by Fries, his attorneys had contended.

Overall, the Sedition Act cases connected to the Fries Rebellion were a disaster for the Federalists. They drove a large portion of German-Americans—including John Fries himself—from the Federalist Party to the Republican Party. They multiplied the enforcement—and the fearsomeness—of the Sedition Act. And they used the army to hunt down domestic critics and to crush an already ended resistance. The fact that the army was used once to enforce the Sedition Act raised the concern that it could be used again to destroy dissent or the opposition party.

The Army and Virginia: Plans for Forcible Suppression or Forcible Resistance?

Enforcement of the Alien and Sedition Acts has been usually viewed in isolation. But it was not an isolated thing. As the second campaign of prosecutions began, the federal army became involved in enforcement, as part of the army was used to round up and suppress whatever it could find of the Fries Rebellion in Pennsylvania for sedition as well as treason trials. The de facto commander of the new army, Major General Alexander Hamilton, wanted to use more of the army against the Fries rebels, complaining to George Washington that "every thing continues to wear the character of feebleness, in respect to the measures for suppressing it."[58] Hamilton had done exactly that in response to another incident of internal disaffection, the Whiskey Rebellion, five years earlier. He now proposed using the army to crush the Virginia opposition to the Alien and Sedition Acts and to the Adams administration. Many Federalists supported the idea. But just as the Hamiltonian quest for war with France had been defeated by Adams's insistence on a new mission to France, their quest for military suppression of dissent was defeated by Adams's mistrust of a large army under Hamilton's command.

Hamilton's justification was that Virginia and Kentucky not only opposed several laws duly enacted by Congress, but they conspired toward and planned an insurrection that would split the country apart. Whether Virginia contemplated the use of force against the federal government is not clear-cut.

Gen. Alexander Hamilton and Threats of Forcible Suppression

The Federalist administration was already using force against critics of the Alien and Sedition Acts, by prosecuting newspaper editors and others who questioned the constitutionality of those laws or violated them, and by using part of the army against the Fries rebels. To High Federalists, it was no leap at all to advocate using force against Virginia and Kentucky, since those states' resolutions in November and December 1798 were seen as seditious, and it was not much of a leap to advocate using force against the Republican opposition itself. Indeed, "Federalists in private asserted repeatedly:

FIGURE 9.1. Alexander Hamilton. Portrait by William J. Weaver (c. 1806). Courtesy Indianapolis Museum of Art at Newfields.

the need for an army to 'save us from internal opposition,'" as Richard Kohn noted in *Eagle and Sword.*[59]

Gen. Alexander Hamilton's plans were of paramount importance, because he commanded the army (except if George Washington took active command in event of a declaration of war). Hamilton immediately concluded that "the proceedings of Virginia and Kentucke" were "evidence . . . of a regular conspiracy to overturn the government." He had long believed the "truth" that there was *"a faction . . . subversive of the principles of good government and dangerous to the union."* He believed unshakably that the "powerful faction which has for years opposed the Government is determined to go every length with France," "to *new model* our constitution under the *influence* or *coertion* of France," and in substance "to make this Country a province of France."[60]

At the beginning of February 1799, Hamilton wrote to Sen. Theodore Sedgwick, a fellow High Federalist who believed the Virginia and Kentucky Resolutions were "little short of a declaration of war,"[61] asking "Dear Sir, what are you going to do with Virginia," and answering with Hamilton's own proposals. A congressional committee should respond to the resolutions, and Hamilton listed what it should conclude: its report should "support the constitutionality and expediency" of the Alien and Sedition Acts, should find that the Virginia and Kentucky Resolutions tend "to destroy the Constitution of the UStates," and should divulge a "conspiracy to overturn the government" by Virginia and Kentucky. At the same time, the army should be used against Virginia:

> When a clever force has been collected let them be drawn towards Virginia for which there is an obvious pretext—& then let measures be taken to act upon the laws & put Virginia to the Test of resistance.[62]

Hamilton's proposal was to bait Virginia with enforcement of the Alien and Sedition Acts, hoping that the state would resist, and then to use the federal force to crush Virginia's resistance.

Hamilton continued the letter with a warning against relying on the militia instead of his army: "[w]henever the experiment shall be made to subdue a *refractory* & powerful *state* by Militia, the event will shame the advocates" because the militia would fail. Instead, he proposed strengthening the army with the Eventual Army Act, which was soon passed. That law authorized use of the army not only to repel invasion but to "suppress [domestic] insurrections."[63]

That letter was not atypical of Hamilton's thought in 1799.[64] Late in the year, Hamilton again advised federal military action and again advised portraying it as a response to Virginia's offensive activity, in a letter to the outgoing speaker of the house:

> The late attempt of Virginia & Kentucke to unite the state legislatures in a direct resistance to certain laws of the Union can be considered in no other light than as an attempt to change the Government.
>
> It is stated, in addition, that the opposition-Party in Virginia, the head Quarters of the Faction, have followed up the hostile declarations which are to be found in the resolutions of their General Assembly by an actual preparation of the means of supporting them by force.[65]

The federal response should be with force, and the army should be made "permanent." Hamilton added several other recommendations, including "subdivision of the great states" to eliminate their power to resist—which was so "indispensable" that it "ought to be a cardinal point in the Foederal policy"—as well as expansion of the Sedition Act to criminalize criticism of "any Officer whatsoever of the UStates" rather than just the president.[66] The majority of historians addressing the issue have understood Hamilton to propose "that the newly organized and invigorated federal army might be used to coerce Virginia into obedience," as James R. Sharp concluded,[67] though some have seen his plan as much less. Hamilton clearly had objectives beyond protecting the country from invasion, since he and his cabinet minions continued obsessive preparation and reauthorization of the army long after the chance of French invasion had evaporated. His horrified view of the opposition party was that "all tend[ed] to mischief—some of them to the overthrow of the Government by stripping it of its due energies[,] others of them to a Revolution after the manner of Buonaparte"[68]—either allowing or executing that overthrow.

The key members of the cabinet supported Hamilton's plan to use force against Virginia and other internal enemies. Secretary of State Timothy Pickering saw the Virginia and Kentucky Resolutions as "hostile to the General Government," "outrageous attempts to break the union," and "rebellious resolves." Secretary of the Treasury Oliver Wolcott stressed that the army "would give the first advantage to government . . . , by allowing the cause of order and law to take the upper hand" and to "decide the event against faction." He ended his letter by asking that "it may be destroyed, and the contents remain a secret."[69] Secretary of War James McHenry virtually always followed Hamilton's recommendations.

Hamilton's military plans to suppress domestic opposition appear more real when they are viewed alongside his military plans[70] (in his own words) "of taking possession of those countries [the Floridas and Louisiana] for ourselves" and "detach[ing] South America from Spain." Not only should that be done if France took those colonies from Spain, but that should be made possible by "impowering the President . . . to declare that a state of war exists" with France.[71] That summary in late January 1799, communicated to a leading congressional Federalist, was only one of many discussions by Hamilton, Adams, Pickering, and Rufus King about annexation of Florida and Louisiana and about the plan of Francisco de Miranda, a general from South America, to foment a revolution and to secure the independence of Spain's colonies.[72] A year before, Miranda had sent to President Adams his "instructions" that amounted to a program for revolution by the Spanish colonies in the Americas.[73] Around the same time, Rufus King, the American minister to Great Britain, reported in ciphered letters to Pickering about the revival of the project for "the complete Independence of South America to be effected by the co-operation of England and the U.S." Elements of the project were that if France attacked Spain "*England will immediately commence the execution of a Plan . . . for the compleat independence of Sh. America,*" and that "*an Expedition has been prepared . . . for the purpose of beginning the Revolution of So. America*" with "*the cooperation of, the United States.*" In the meantime, Pickering asked Hamilton "[w]hat ought we to do, in respect to *Louisiana?*," hoping to gain control of it.[74]

In response to Miranda's letters in the spring of 1798, Hamilton wrote that, though United States approval was necessary, "Winter however may mature the project" to bring "cooperation with the Ustates." "The plan in my opinion ought to be, a fleet of Great Britain, an army of the ustates, a Government for the liberated territorey" acceptable to both. The same day, Hamilton wrote to Rufus King about his favorable view and his anticipated command:

> With regard to the enterprise in question I wish it much to be undertaken but I should be glad that the principal agency was in the UStates—they to furnish the whole land force necessary. The command in this case would very naturally fall upon me—and I hope I should disappoint no favourable anticipation. The independence of the separated territory under a *moderate* government . . . would be the sum of the results to be accomplished.[75]

In the fall of 1798, Rufus King reported privately to Pickering that "[a]s England is ready she will furnish a fleet and military stores and we should furnish the army." By June 1799, Hamilton chided the secretary of war for the administration having "no general plan," and was of course quick to offer one. Part of his plan was "to complete and prepare the land force," not only for "security against invasion," but because "we ought certainly to look to the possession of the Floridas & Louisiana—and we ought to squint at South America."[76] The unlikelihood at that point of a declared war with France did not reduce Hamilton's interest in foreign conquests—it increased it—and he doubtless noticed that that activity would help preserve his army from being disbanded. At the same time, the prospect of preserving peace drove President Adams to delay and to avoid authorizing Hamilton's plans.

Clearly, Hamilton wanted to annex the Floridas and Louisiana and to effectuate Miranda's revolution of South America, though historians debate whether the plan was close to or far from execution.[77] If Hamilton would attack Florida, Louisiana, and South America, with or without the provocation of a French invasion, would he hesitate to attack Virginia or other domestic enemies with the provocation of the forcible resistance that he thought he saw?

Virginia and Forcible Resistance

Republican leaders behind the scenes were not organizing the state militia or planning other forcible resistance. Instead, they were actively discouraging any violent response, recognizing that Hamilton and Pickering were trying to provoke precisely that. Jefferson, the unofficial head of the Republican Party, counseled party leaders that "any thing like force would check the progress of public opinion & rally them round the errors of the government." He advised Madison that protests should be made, "but nothing [was] to be said or done which shall look or lead to force, and give any pretext for keeping up the army."[78] Gov. James Monroe of Virginia anticipated that "an attempt will be made to carry the sedition law into effect here, as an electioneering trick" to influence the election of 1800 by provoking Virginia to violent opposition. "[T]hey must be deprived of a plausible pretext" by discouraging any resistance other than a legal defense at trial, Monroe added. After the Circuit Court indicted and tried James T. Callender in Richmond, Monroe exulted that the "conduct of the people on this occasion was exemplary," showing "respect for law and order," even though "everything that could was done to provoke it [different conduct]." Madison was equally delighted that the Federalist project "of making the Camp at Warwick [an army base] an auxiliary to the Judicial department" failed, averting "so odious a perversion of military force."[79]

Republican members of Congress fought the Alien and Sedition Acts by peaceful means, in several phases. They spoke and voted against those laws when they were proposed and passed in mid-1798. Then they encouraged a petition campaign from local gatherings, and the publication of the petitions and commentary in Republican newspapers. Republicans then turned to resolutions from the state legislatures, led by the Virginia and Kentucky Resolutions in late 1798, and the appeal to other states to concur that the Alien and Sedition Acts were unconstitutional. Many Federalists agreed with Sedgwick that those resolutions were "little short of a declaration of war," but the resolutions did not threaten force and instead called for peaceful repeal of the Alien and Sedition Acts,[80] though the resolutions did not say what interposition entailed.

Many Federalists, believing Republican appeals to lawful means to be a Trojan horse, found every defensive step by Virginia and other Republican states against French threats to be preparation for attack. John Nicholas apostatized from his family's Republican faith by publishing allegations that Virginia's legislature was collecting weapons and fomenting rebellion.[81] (He was the brother of Wilson Cary Nicholas, who arranged legislative sponsors for the Virginia and Kentucky Resolutions, and who responded by demanding that his brother change his surname.) Sedgwick, again condemning the resolutions of "Virga. and its satellite Kentucky," charged that Virginia "has displayed an anxiety to render its militia as formidable as possible, and to supply its arsenals & magazines." Hamilton expressed much the same thought, damning the "hostile declarations" and identifying Virginia's "actual preparation of the means of supporting them by force": putting "their militia on a more efficient footing," "preparing considerable arsenals and magazines," and "go[ing] so far as to lay new taxes." Other Federalists repeated these claims.[82]

Virginia indeed bought arms. But so did nearly every Federalist-controlled state in 1798, because of the possibility of French invasion. Pennsylvania enlisted Pickering's help in getting delivery of "ten thousand stand of arms" that it ordered the year before. Connecticut's governor recommended the purchase "of a number of stands of good fire arms, to be lodged in public stores."[83] Massachusetts appropriated $50,000 to buy and install cannon. South Carolina had the American minister arrange for Britain to cede "a number of Iron Cannon." New York authorized the purchase of "a further supply of arms"—not "less than three thousand Muskets and Bayonets."[84] Those states' purchases of thousands of arms did not show that they planned a forcible response to unpopular legislation, and for that reason Virginia's purchase did not either. Philip G. Davidson reached the same conclusion about Virginia's legislation for the militia, arsenals, and taxes, concluding that "reorganization of the militia was a problem in 1793, the purchase of arms was taken up in 1796, and plans for the armory were made in 1797," long before the crisis of 1798–1801. He found unpersuasive the after-the-fact statements of John Randolph (1816) and William B. Giles (1825), and the speculative claims of Sedgwick and Hamilton, though he was unaware of that contemporaneous statement of John Nicholas.[85]

Although some influential historians agreed with Davidson,[86] most have concluded that Republicans secretly planned forcible resistance to the Alien and Sedition Acts and other Federalist legislation. James R. Sharp noted that "the fact that the purchase of arms, the building of an armory, and so forth had been *discussed* prior to 1798 does not eliminate any relationship between the Alien and Sedition Acts and the *passage* of those defense measures," and he concluded that "the Virginia Republican leadership were . . . preparing for any eventuality in 1798–99."[87] However, Sharp did not claim that the Alien and Sedition Acts and planned resistance provided the primary impetus for passing defense measures, in view of real concern about invasion or a slave revolt.

There was one eventuality when the Republicans stated they would have used the militia to enforce the Constitution—that was if the Federalists had refused to transfer the presidency to the victorious Republican candidate after the election of 1800. Jefferson, apparently with the concurrence of the Republican leadership, said "that the day such an act passed the middle states would arm, & that no such usurpation even for a single day should be submitted to."[88] The governor of the largest middle state, Thomas McKean, said that the state "Militia would have been warned to be ready" with "arms for upwards of twenty thousand," that "an order would have issued for the arresting & bringing to justice every member of Congress, or other person found in Pennsylvania, who should have been concerned in the treason," and a proclamation would have required "all officers civil & military" in Pennsylvania to respect the election result. The governor of the largest southern state, James Monroe, said that in response to usurpation he would convene the legislature, and in the meantime, he prepared to seize arms in the federal arsenal in Virginia.[89] The eventual resolution of the election of 1800 mooted those plans.

THE SEDITION ACT THIRD CAMPAIGN (LATE 1799–1800)

"THE REIGN OF WITCHES" AND THE ELECTION OF 1800

[A] little patience and we shall see the reign of witches pass over, their spells dissolve, and the people recovering their true sight, restore their government to it[]s true principles.

—*Thomas Jefferson to John Taylor (June 4, 1798)*

CHAPTER TEN

A New Round of Enforcement

THE ADAMS administration launched a third campaign of enforcement of the Sedition Act in the latter half of 1799, which was timed to cause defendants to be indicted and arrested during the autumn sessions of the United States Circuit Courts, and then to be brought to trial during the spring sessions of those courts—shortly before the state and federal elections in 1800. The campaign was begun by a series of nearly identical letters sent by Secretary of State Timothy Pickering to the United States attorneys in several states just before and during August 1799.[1] The third campaign's targets were almost exclusively newspaper editors—they were the most influential Republicans, other than legislators (who were more difficult to reach because of legislative immunities). The new campaign had three elements.

First, the new editors of the leading Republican newspapers in the two largest cities (Philadelphia and New York) were prosecuted, along with the editors of outspoken newspapers in smaller cities. Thus, in Philadelphia, multiple prosecutions were brought against William Duane, the editor of the foremost Republican newspaper, the *Aurora*. In New York, a prosecution under the Sedition Act was brought against Ann Greenleaf, the editor of the leading Republican newspaper in New York City, the *Argus* (after the demise of the *Time Piece*); and another case based on common law seditious libel was engineered by Alexander Hamilton against her printer, David Frothingham. Other prosecutions under the Sedition Act were initiated against Charles Holt of Connecticut's leading Republican newspaper, the New London *Bee,* and against Anthony Haswell of Vermont's leading opposition paper, the *Vermont Gazette,* as well as against Judah P. Spooner of Vermont's *Scourge of Aristocracy.* Further instructions for prosecutions were aimed in mid-1799 at Meriwether Jones, editor of Virginia's foremost Republican newspaper, the Richmond *Examiner,* and at Alexander Martin, editor of Maryland's leading opposition paper, the Baltimore *American,* in addition to Jacob Schneider of the *Readinger Adler.*[2] And prosecutions were begun in the spring of 1800, with immediate trials before elections, of Thomas Cooper of the *Sunbury and Northumberland Gazette* and James T. Callender of the Richmond *Examiner,* with attempts at indictments and similar flash trials of Alexander Martin again and of James J. Wilson of Delaware's prominent Republican newspaper, the Wilmington *Mirror of the Times.* All were Republican newspapers except Alden Spooner's. Pickering's ambitious plan amounted to legal attacks against nearly every leading Republican newspaper, as well as against many smaller ones.

Also, the surviving editors who had been subjected to two of the first three prosecutions of opposition newspapers in 1798 under the common law of seditious libel were now reindicted under the Sedition Act. John Daly Burk and Dr. James Smith, the former editors of the dormant *Time Piece* in New York, who had been charged with seditious libel before the Sedition Act was passed, were reindicted under the Sedition Act in September 1799, notwithstanding that Burk had entered a settlement agreement, and they were slated for trial at the next session in April 1800. William Durell, the editor of the *Mount Pleasant Register,* who had also been arrested and charged with common law seditious libel in mid-July 1798, before the region's United States attorney received a copy of the final version of the Sedition Act, was also reindicted under the Sedition Act in September 1799 and was also scheduled for trial in April 1800. Additionally, Matthew Lyon, owner of *The Scourge of Aristocracy* in Vermont, was again indicted in October 1799.

Finally, some other influential Republicans were indicted or were scrutinized for prosecution. Jedidiah Peck was targeted for circulating petitions to repeal the Alien and Sedition Acts. Dr. Samuel Shaw was aimed at for helping fund or publish the Barlow letter criticizing the president and Congress. Dr. Joseph Priestley was considered for prosecution as an influential radical who criticized the government.

Why was this third campaign of prosecutions so broad? Because the narrower first and second campaigns had proved insufficient to cripple the Republican opposition. Prosecuting the leading Republican newspapers in the three largest cities had left two standing and a new crop of Republican newspapers flourishing. Prosecuting a few Republican leaders had left the others as outspoken as before and had multiplied their numbers.

It was no coincidence that this new burst of prosecutions, all planned or initiated in the summer and autumn of 1799, would place the newspaper editors under high bonds that they and their sureties would lose if they were charged with additional violations of the Sedition Act in late 1799 or early 1800 before the spring court sessions—to deter their Republican commentary. And it was no coincidence that the new burst of prosecutions would come to trial in the spring of 1800—to intimidate them and potentially shut down their Republican newspapers before the elections in 1800. That was not only the year of elections for Congress, but for most state legislatures, and for presidential electors (by state legislators in two-thirds of the states, and by general tickets or districts in the other states[3]). In fact, Pickering admitted that the purpose of the campaign was to defeat Jefferson by combating the administration's "enemies" including particularly the "Jacobin Papers":

> The enemies to the present system of our government are using every possible means to introduce Mr. Jefferson as President at the next election; and as they stick at nothing, they may succeed. . . . [O]ur Jacobin Papers . . . daily teem with atrocious lies and perverse misrepresentations against the President and all the chief officers of government and leading members in Congress.

Sen. Stevens Thomson Mason of Virginia, like most other Republicans, believed what was happening was the "most vigorous and undisguised efforts" to "crush the republican presses, and stifle enquiry as it may respect the ensuing election of P & V Pt."[4]

Jefferson too had no doubt about what was occurring. He wrote to his son-in-law that "this onset on the presses is to cripple & suppress the republican efforts during the campaign which is coming on."[5]

Targeting William Duane and the *Aurora* Again and Again

William Duane (1760–1835), one of the most prominent transatlantic radicals, edited the *Aurora,* the foremost Republican newspaper of the Alien and Sedition Act period.[6] He did so from late 1798 after the death of its founding editor, Benjamin Franklin Bache, through that crisis period and for two decades beyond.[7] Duane was born to middle-class Irish parents after their arrival in St. John's, Newfoundland, according to Duane's most recent biographer, though earlier sources place his birth after their move to the Lake Champlain region of New York.[8] The accusation that he was born

FIGURE 10.1. William Duane, second editor of the Philadelphia *Aurora*. Engraving by Charles Balthazar Julien Févret de Saint-Mémin (1802). Courtesy National Portrait Gallery, Smithsonian Institution, gift of Mr. and Mrs. Paul Mellon.

in British Canada (or Ireland) rather than in the future United States dogged Duane in his adult years until he finally submitted papers for naturalized citizenship. After the death of his father, his mother moved the family briefly to Baltimore and Philadelphia, and then, in about 1774 when Duane was still a child, back to the parents' homeland of Clonmel, Ireland. In his teenage years, Duane declined his mother's advice to become a Roman Catholic priest, adopted secularist views, and soon married a Protestant, Catharine Corcoran.[9] In his adult years, he was a Deist.[10]

Duane's editorship of the *Aurora* was the fifth phase of his career. Earlier phases included work for an Irish newspaper as a teenager, and then for a London newspaper from 1782–1787. After that, in the second-largest city in the British empire, Duane edited two Calcutta newspapers in succession from 1789–1795. The first was closed because of seditious libel complaints about its criticism of a British ally (bringing the editor within nine days of deportation).[11] Duane then started and edited another Calcutta paper until it encountered a similar fate because of seditious libel proceedings arising from published criticism by malcontented officers of the East India Company and its private army (which, along with Duane's ardent support of the French Revolution, triggered his deportation to London). The arbitrary treatment of his liberties, coupled with a six-month transit to London confined onboard as a criminal, transformed Duane into an "embittered radical," as the foremost biographer of his American career, Kim Phillips, observed.[12] During ten months in London, Duane briefly edited the *Telegraph,* the newspaper that was the unofficial voice of the radical London Corresponding Society. Facing grave risks during Britain's period of intense suppression of opposition press and speech, he returned to America and arrived on Independence Day in 1796, with his wife and three children.[13]

The Foremost Opposition Editor

Duane's relationship with the *Aurora* began with its publication in late 1796 of his *Letter to George Washington* (written under the pseudonym Jasper Dwight), which castigated Washington's presidency, his Farewell Address, and most scandalously, Washington himself. Typical of Duane's attacks was claiming that Washington's presidency would be found devoid of any security for "freedom on the strong basis of education and moral equality," and that the Farewell Address was welcomed exultantly by "the avowed enemies of equal Liberty, . . . the open advocates of privileged and distinct classes."[14] The next year, Duane translated and the *Aurora* published a pamphlet written by the French minister to the United States, Joseph Fauchet, which praised the French Republic and its foreign policy sufficiently to attract Pickering's condemnation.[15] Duane gained permanent employment with the *Aurora* a month before Bache died in September 1798.

Duane was the new editor of the *Aurora* when the newspaper reopened in November 1798, and it claimed 1,300 subscribers at that time—a large number in that period. He filled that role for nearly all of the years until the autumn of 1822. Duane remained true to Bache's Republican principles, and he remained equally loyal to Bache's memory.[16] Two years after becoming the editor, Duane married Bache's widow, his own spouse having died just before Bache.

Duane was much more than just the editor of the *Aurora.* He waged relentless attacks against the Federalists, and as Jeffrey Pasley noted, helped change "the newspaper arena of political debate" from "a marketplace of disembodied ideas to a battleground for committed political warriors." Duane was the most prominent example of a Republican editor who was a political leader.[17] He organized the Irish community in the nation's most populous city, immediately joining the Hibernian Society that helped Irish immigrants and later becoming a leader, while cofounding the United Irish Society that held much more radical objectives as a secret organization. As a result, when the foremost Federalist newspaper published a list of alleged United Irishmen (the proscribed Irish organization), Duane was included and was exposed as "alias Jasper Dwight."[18] He was a champion of the working classes generally. He led efforts such as petitions opposing the Alien Act, and formation of a Republican militia to counter the Federalist volunteer units. Duane's larger role was to "defin[e] the political and cultural boundaries of Americanness so as to exclude [F]ederalism entirely," as Nigel Little, the leading biographer of Duane's British careers, observed.[19]

The *Aurora* remained the foremost Republican newspaper throughout the crisis years of the Alien and Sedition Acts—the newspaper whose columns other Republican papers copied. Its prominence came in part because it was in the nation's capital, where it could get the news first and sympathetic legislators' comments and leaks, and in part because its editor was original and courageous, able to skewer administration actions and to formulate a Republican point of view. That Republican perspective included support for Republican candidates as they sought to achieve majority status, support for a pro-French rather than pro-British foreign policy, opposition to the Alien and Sedition Acts and prosecutions, antagonism to the new federal "standing army" and the new federal taxes to fund it, disclosure of Federalist corruption and financial mismanagement, and endorsement of virtually all other Jeffersonian and Madisonian opposition beliefs.[20] The *Aurora* regularly led Republican efforts, in the period when Jefferson had to lie low because of potential prosecution under the Sedition Act. A Federalist newspaper complained that "on every important subject, the sentiments to be inculcated among the Democrats, has been first put into the Aurora." A Republican newspaper (edited by Charles Holt) agreed that the "Aurora has been a correct channel, through which vast political information has been diffused throughout every part of the United States." Perhaps the best known example was that, when Alexander Hamilton circulated his pamphlet attacking John Adams in 1800, Duane immediately published the "precious letter" and saw it reprinted throughout the Republican press.[21]

Hence, the *Aurora* was the particular target of Pickering and of other Federalist leaders. Duane was the first Republican editor to be subjected to prosecution in the enforcement campaign of mid-1799 and after, and the only Republican to be the defendant in more than one Sedition Act prosecution, except Rep. Matthew Lyon. Later, John Adams blamed his defeat on Republican editors—"Freneau, Duane, Callender, Cooper, and Lyon"—a "group of foreign liars," and again on "Callender, Duane, Cooper, and Lyon"—"the most influential men in the country, all foreigners and all degraded characters."[22] From the Republican side, Jefferson similarly credited Duane and "the energy of his press" with an "unquestioned effect in the revolution produced in the public mind, which arrested the rapid march of our government towards monarchy," in the election of 1800.[23]

The result was that Duane was subjected to four criminal prosecutions under the Sedition Act between July 1799 and October 1800—not just to the "two attempted prosecutions of Duane for seditious libel" that are generally accepted.[24] (The second and third prosecutions are the ones that do not appear in scholarly writings.[25]) The first prosecution was for an article alleging that British influence guided the administration's foreign policy, and the second was for a later article alleging that British secret service bribes infected that foreign policy. The third was for articles denouncing the administration's policy toward St. Domingue (later called Haiti), and the fourth was for unauthorized publication of the Ross bill that would have manipulated presidential election results. In addition, Duane was subjected to several common law prosecutions involving sedition charges (and frequent private suits for defamation).

Duane's First Sedition Act Prosecution

Timothy Pickering had long seethed at the columns of "the serpents of the 'Aurora'."[26] He fulminated to President John Adams about an article captioned "British Influence" in the *Aurora* on July 24, 1799:

> There is in the Aurora of this city an uninterrupted stream of slander on the American government. I inclose the paper of this morning. It is not the first time that the editor has suggested, that you had asserted the influence of the British government in affairs of our own, and insinuated that it was obtained by bribery. The general readers of the Aurora will believe both. I shall give the paper to Mr. Rawle, and, if he thinks it libellous, desire him to prosecute the editor.

The secretary of state added that he understood that Duane was not a citizen, leaving him also subject to prosecution under the Alien Act. That same day, Pickering wrote to William Rawle, the United States attorney for Pennsylvania, to ask him to examine that issue of the *Aurora* and, if "the slander on the American Government will justify a prosecution," to initiate it. The next day, he wrote again to Rawle to ask him to consider, in connection with stolen dispatches of the British minister, "whether the *publisher* ought not to be prosecuted" along with the thieves.[27]

Adams responded to the secretary of state that "[i]f Mr. Rawle does not think this paper libellous, he is not fit for his office; and if he does not prosecute it, he will not do his duty." The president, chafing that there was nothing "evil in the regions of actuality or possibility, that the Aurora has not suggested of me," authorized not only the Sedition Act prosecution but also an Alien Act prosecution against Duane.[28]

Rawle was quite determined not to appear unfit for office. He arrested Duane within the week, charging him with seditious libel "concerning the administration," and required him to post bond to assure his appearance in the United States Circuit Court during its October session. Bond was set at a much higher level than for most accused criminals—$2,000 from Duane and $2,000 from two sureties. Duane responded with bravado, that "neither persecution nor any other peril" would "make him swerve from the cause of republicanism." Pickering reported back to Adams that a "prosecution against Duane, editor of the Aurora, has been instituted, on the charge of English secret-service money distributed in the United States." He added that Rawle had been instructed "to examine his newspaper and to institute new prosecutions as often as he offends"[29]—an open-ended instruction.

In the October court session, the indictment of Duane for that article on "British Influence" in the *Aurora* was approved by the federal grand jury.[30] It charged him with violating the Sedition Act—"print[ing] and publish[ing] . . . false scandalous and malicious words"—on July 24, 1799, such as the following.

> British influence has been practising and with success in various instances among us (the people of the said United States meaning) we have evidence which would be conclusive under the most critical scrutiny of a court of justice. 1. We have it on the records of the British Privy Council in the most authentic form that Britain had formed a party devoted to her interests in the U. States (meaning the said United States). 2. We have it in the handwriting of John Adams now President of the United States that British influence has been employed and with effect in procuring the appointment of an officer of the most confidential and important trust under the government.

(The parentheses indicated the United States attorney's additions with his interpretations of the *Aurora*'s allegations.) Besides alleging British influence over the Federalist party and over a major appointment, the article claimed that "in America alone during the year 1798 Great Britain has expended secret service money to the amount of one hundred and eighty thousand pounds sterling or 800,000 dollars!"[31]

When Duane's case was called for an immediate trial, his lawyer surprised the judges and prosecutors by showing them a letter signed by John Adams that said what the *Aurora* had claimed. In it, Adams himself suspected "much British Influence in appointment" of Thomas Pinckney as the Minister Plenipotentiary to Britain, and observed "that our new Ambassador has many powerful Old Friends in England."[32] Though Federalists offered explanations, the words were too plain to explain away, and the *Aurora* reprinted the letter in full or part nine times over the next year.[33]

Duane's trial was delayed to the April 1800 session of the circuit court, based on his offer of the Adams letter as evidence and on his motion saying that his witnesses were not available for an immediate trial. Duane was required to post the same bond as before.[34] When all actions of the October 1799 session were invalidated because the marshal's commission had expired, it was necessary to reindict Duane in April 1800. Soon after, Rawle dismissed the case because, according to Duane, "I had the actual letter of Mr. Adams in my possession."[35]

Duane's Second Sedition Act Prosecution

Rawle, following Pickering's instructions to indict Duane each time the *Aurora* violated the Sedition Act, prosecuted the editor for an article a week later, in the August 3, 1799 issue, elaborating on the *Aurora*'s earlier allegation of British bribery.[36] The United States attorney was not the only Federalist incensed by the claim. George Washington immediately asked Pickering "whether the Officers of Government intended to be quiescent under the direct charge of bribery" in the *Aurora* article. He found "no bounds to his [Duane's] attempts to destroy all confidence that the People . . . have in their government." The former president prodded Secretary of War James McHenry with similar questions.[37]

In the October 1799 session, that second indictment of Duane was also approved by the federal grand jury. It too charged him with violating the Sedition Act by the *Aurora*'s claims about Britain's "distribution of about 800,000 in that one year [1798] for corrupt purposes." The indictment extensively quoted the *Aurora* article of August 3, 1799, such as the following passage:

> The affairs at St. Domingo must undoubtedly have required money. General Maitland . . . when in Philadelphia had a most fascinating style of arranging his money matters (thereby meaning and intending that the measures taken by the President of the United States for restoring the commercial intercourse with part of the island of St. Domingo proceeded from bribery and corruption that a certain General Maitland an officer in the service of the King of Great Britain had bribed and corrupted the executive officers of the government of the United States to adopt the measures which have been taken for restoring the said commercial intercourse)[.] Russia, Turkey and St. Domingo Secret Service money (meaning monies expended by the government of Great Britain for the purpose of bribery and corruption in Russia in Turkey and in the United States in respect to the said restoration of commercial intercourse with part of the island of St. Domingo) could not be so well accounted for . . . to the great scandal of the President of the said United States and the government of the said United States.[38]

The indictment was charging Duane with claiming that Adams and other executive officers were bribed.

The British bribery case remained paired with the British influence case. It too saw postponement of trial to the April 1800 session, reindictment at that session, and ultimately dismissal by a decision not to prosecute further (nolle prosequi).[39]

This second Sedition Act prosecution has been mistakenly described as a charge that Duane "violated the Sedition Law on August 3 [1799] with some offensive remarks about the conduct of federal troops."[40] Though the *Aurora* as a matter of policy never missed an opportunity to remark on misconduct of federal troops, that topic was not mentioned in the second indictment (or the first or third).

Duane's Third Sedition Act Prosecution

The month after Rawle arrested Duane for those articles violating the Sedition Act, Pickering had become impatient. The secretary of state wrote asking the United States attorney to initiate another prosecution of Duane if he found any basis in other issues of the *Aurora,* and also, again, to file a criminal case for "the breaking open of Mr. Liston's letters." Rawle did not do either until mid-April 1800, when he got two indictments. A year later, when nothing further had happened in those cases, Duane commented that the St. Domingue case had been "held back" and that the Liston letters case "it was understood . . . would not *be pushed!*"[41]

The reason why Rawle did not file more prosecutions against Duane doubtless included that his hands were full of prosecutions of the Fries Rebellion participants for treason and sedition but probably resulted mostly from the prosecutor's healthy fear of what Duane would print about him in the *Aurora.* That fear was evident in Rawle's delays and inactivity in most of the cases against Duane (in contrast to his quick indictments of other defendants), in his repeated failure to find and jail Duane (in contrast to a private suit that found Duane swiftly), and in his dismissal of the British influence case (by a nolle prosequi). Consequently, Rawle did what he was told to avoid being fired, but did nothing more than was required. Rawle was no fool. His legal education had been in England's Inns of Court, and he became an eminent attorney in Philadelphia, though he had to overcome his family's loyalist alignment during the Revolutionary War. His view of freedoms of press and speech was entirely consistent with Pickering's. Rawle's arguments while enforcing the Sedition Act were later restated in a treatise, where he wrote that "the punishment of dangerous or offensive publications, which . . . have a pernicious tendency, is necessary for the peace and order of government."[42]

The third indictment of Duane under the Sedition Act was approved by a grand jury in April 1800.[43] It began with a lengthy summary of a law passed in February 1799 that continued the suspension of commerce between the United States and France and its colonies. That law had a clause authorizing the president to resume commerce with particular colonies, in order to assist Toussaint L'Ouverture in revolting against France, and Adams soon issued a proclamation reopening commerce with the two major ports in St. Domingue.[44] The indictment had three counts against Duane for "defam[ing] the President of the United States and the government" about those St. Domingue matters. The first two counts reiterated the claims in the July 24, 1799 article about the administration "fomenting the dismemberment of Saint Domingo" under influence of the British "Secret Service money" equal to $800,000.[45] Those counts evidently were meant to replace the first Sedition Act prosecution, which was dismissed in the same month, by repeating most of its claims while carefully avoiding its claim of an Adams letter alleging British influence. The third count was based on the claims in the August 3, 1799 article about the $800,000 and that "[t]he affairs at Saint Domingo must . . . have required money." It added that the *Aurora* alleged that an American naval vessel brought $25,000 for which federal officials had not accounted, insinuating that it was bribe money.[46] That count was evidently included in case the planned reindictment failed for the second Sedition Act prosecution, which had been invalidated along with other actions of the ill-fated October 1799 session.

The day the indictment came down, an arrest warrant was issued for Duane. Ultimately the marshal wrote on its back that "Duane is not to be found."[47]

The St. Domingue case was ultimately dismissed (by a nolle prosequi) after Jefferson took office, under his principle that "whenever in the line of my functions I should be met by the Sedition law, I should treat it as a nullity." Thus, Jefferson repeatedly gave instructions that "the prosecution against Duane being under the *Sedition law*" may be "absolutely withdrawn."[48]

The Sedition Act violations overlapped in these three prosecutions. The reason was that Pickering had instructed Rawle to take action against each issue of the *Aurora* that violated the Sedition Act, and the *Aurora* articles themselves overlapped. That overlap explains why the second and third prosecutions have been overlooked—the first and second both discussed British influence and $800,000 bribe money, and all three condemned St. Domingue policy. At first glance, they seem to be the same case.

Duane's Fourth Sedition Act Prosecution

A bill sponsored by Senator James Ross, and supported by other Federalist senators, proposed to establish a committee "for deciding disputed elections of President and Vice President . . . and for determining the legality or illegality of the votes given for those officers in the different States." The committee would consist of six members of the Senate, six members from the House, and the chief justice—all of which were Federalist dominated—though the Constitution appeared to leave counting electoral votes with the president of the Senate or the speaker of the House.[49] Duane made the Ross bill public, and Republican reaction was explosive. Rep. Anthony New was typical. "This measure is unquestionably aimed at the next Presidential election, and is calculated to transfer to this committee, if not the choice, a most dangerous controul over those appointments." The Ross bill ultimately passed the Senate on a party vote,[50] the day after Duane was found in contempt of the Senate for making it public.[51]

Duane not only published the full text of the Ross bill, but added commentary that the bill was "calculated to influence and affect the approaching presidential election . . . and to frustrate in a particular manner, the wishes and interests of the people." In response, the Senate created a committee on privileges—a committee that had not existed before—and instructed it to recommend measures against Duane. The Federalist-dominated committee predictably found the *Aurora*'s articles "a daring and high-handed breach of the privileges of this House" as well as a defamation of the Senate. That finding was reached without a hearing, ten days before Duane was to appear.[52] Those privileges of the Senate, other than a few constitutional prerogatives, were seen by the Federalist majority as an unwritten trove of prerogatives copied from the British Parliament, such as the right to keep proceedings secret and unpublished, and the right not to be defamed (criticized) in any way. In stark contrast, the Republican position, as it was expressed by Sen. Charles Pinckney, was that Senate privileges were limited to the Constitution's short list, and that Senate prerogatives could not override the citizens' freedom of speech including "the duty of our citizens" to examine public measures "and if they find them departing from the Constitution, or exceeding their authority, instantly to announce it." Republicans added that it was not constitutional that a "single branch of a Legislature, should claim and exercise the authority, whenever they please, to send and seize any man . . . , and confine him in a loathsome dungeon, for six months together, merely because he has . . . criticised, as he has a right to do, on their legislative acts."[53]

The Senate ordered Duane to appear on March 24, 1800. He and his two attorneys, Alexander J. Dallas and Thomas Cooper, met beforehand to work out their strategy, knowing that the Federalist-controlled Senate was sure to resolve the matter against Duane. Their strategy was a brilliant stroke. As Cooper summarized it for Jefferson, Duane would request the right to have his attorneys argue his case to the Senate, and "if the request to be heard by Counsel should be refused (which we much wish) . . . he shall not obey the call" to appear. On the other hand, "if Counsel be allowed" but was stopped in objecting to "the Jurisdiction of the Senate," then "they shall expressly decline entering into any farther or other defence," and Duane would avoid attending and evade arrest.[54]

The plan went like clockwork. Duane formally requested that his counsel might argue his case. The Senate limited Duane and his counsel to offering "excuse or extenuation of his offense," barring them from raising any defense, as the Senate imposed a sentence for a predetermined violation.[55] Cooper wrote to him that the Senate's limitation meant it "has prejudged the most material questions," would "hear no objection to its jurisdiction" or "proof of the facts it controverts," and effectively as accuser "claimed a right to dictate the mode of defence to the person accused." Consequently, Cooper wrote that he would not "appear before the Senate with *their gag in my mouth.*" Dallas too wrote that "I cannot consent to act as counsel under so limited an authority," and noted that the Senate's restriction excluded the defenses that Cooper mentioned. Duane sent his former attorneys' responses to the Senate, saying that since he was "deprived of all professional assistance," he would decline to appear further.[56] He also printed the responses in the *Aurora*—they were designed to persuade the public rather than the senators. The Senate promptly found Duane in contempt and issued a warrant for his arrest. Duane arranged not to be found for the next month and a half, until the Senate adjourned and its warrant expired, even while taunting the sergeant-at-arms by publishing the *Aurora* daily and printing notices that essays and letters would reach Duane within forty-eight hours.[57]

Everything the Senate did failed. The Ross bill brought a public storm, and its planned committee for manipulating election results appeared even more devious when the Senate made such efforts to punish informing the public. The Senate proceedings to prosecute Duane were facially unfair, as the Senate acted as accuser, judge, jury, and appeals court. Those proceedings barred questioning how the Senate got judicial powers to try critics, or authority to hide its proceedings from the public; they barred any defense of the truth of Duane's publication and any appeal of the Senate's predetermined decision. The Senate's efforts to find and imprison Duane remained unsuccessful. The Senate's next attempt, to have Duane prosecuted in the courts, got nowhere either.

The Senate, unable to arrest or prosecute Duane itself after its session ended, asked the president to prosecute him. President John Adams promptly instructed the attorney general and federal attorney "to commence and carry on the prosecution" of Duane for "false, defamatory, scandalous, and malicious publications" in the *Aurora* "tending to defame the Senate."[58] Duane was notified that he was charged with "printing and publishing a false Scandalous & Seditious Libel" against the Senate, and was required to assure his appearance in court at the October 1800 session by posting bond. Duane provided a $2,000 bond and two sureties each provided another $1,000 bond.[59]

The indictment of Duane that the Senate requested (his fourth under the Sedition Act) was approved by the grand jury of the U.S. Circuit Court in October 1800, after the grand jurors were incited by Justice William Paterson's grand jury charge condemning the evils of sedition (apparently the same charge that had roused the Vermont grand jury to indict Matthew Lyon).[60] That indictment began with the claim that Duane libeled the Senate and its members by describing it "as actuated by factious and improper Views and Motives, as governed by Intrigue and the Influence of private, secret meetings, as unfit to be trusted," and by bringing the "Senate and many of the Members thereof into an ill opinion, hatred and contempt with all the good citizens of the said United States" (the essence of the crime of seditious libel).[61] The six counts charged instances of seditious libel by printing and publishing claims such as that the Ross bill was "calculated to influence and affect the approaching presidential election . . . and to frustrate in a particular manner, the wishes and Interests of the people" (a February 19, 1800 article); that the party of "Aristocrats" that supported the Ross bill was "hostile to our form of Government," in contrast to the party of Republicans (a May 19, 1800 article); that one branch of Aristocrats, the Hamiltonian or "Pickeronian party . . . set in motion all the Intrigues, and it may be said without exaggeration, all the downright Villainy that has been practiced for a long time," and other *Aurora* assertions.[62]

Duane immediately moved for delay of the trial, because his witnesses were unavailable. Most of those witnesses served in Congress, which had recently moved from Philadelphia to the District of Columbia. Duane and the prosecutor agreed on a commission that would use Duane's questions to take depositions of the senators and others when Congress reassembled. Their sworn responses would be used at trial instead of requiring them to appear.[63] The Republican commissioners showed up when witnesses were there, but the Federalist commissioners did not. Because of that, Duane pried another postponement out of hostile circuit judges in May 1801. But the case would be "tried peremptorily" in October.[64]

Jefferson, not wanting to provoke the Senate, instructed his attorney general to dismiss Sedition Act claims but not breach of privilege claims.[65] The new United States attorney, Alexander J. Dallas (Duane's former counsel), tried to comply by dismissing the October 1800 indictment, and substituting a new indictment, but his clerk clumsily copied the original indictment without dropping any charges. Finally, the grand jury put the case out of its misery by rejecting the new indictment as "not a true Bill" in October 1801.[66] Jefferson drafted, but was persuaded not to send, his eulogy: "the Sedition act . . . was contrary to the very letter of the constitution which declares that Congress shall make no law abridging the freedom of the press and consequently it was void."[67]

Common Law Prosecutions

Besides the four Sedition Act prosecutions, Duane was subjected to at least three common law prosecutions that had overtones of sedition, during 1798–1801. These political attacks were not slow arriving—the first occurred just three months after Duane became the *Aurora*'s editor.

Duane, Dr. James Reynolds, and two others were prosecuted for riot and assault (Francis Wharton called it "seditious riot") in connection with seeking signatures on a petition to repeal the Alien Act outside the Catholic St. Mary's Church after its Sunday service on February 9, 1799.[68] It was actually Dr. Reynolds, not Duane, who was assaulted by several parishioners, and who in self-defense pointed a pistol at one. Reynolds was knocked down and kicked repeatedly. Federalist newspapers christened it a "United Irish Riot" and stressed the role of "*Duane,* Mother Bache's Editor." The indictment indicated the purpose of the case, by listing Duane first even though nearly all the evidence was about Reynolds (though it turned out that the petition effort apparently was designed by Duane.) That indictment was issued in a Philadelphia county court on February 21, and Duane, Reynolds, and the other two were brought to trial the same day, surrounded by claims that they were Jacobins or (closer to the truth) United Irish. The jury found them not guilty.[69] The churchyard altercation and the immediate arrest of the Republican participants by the Federalist mayor were characteristic of the violent partisanship of the late 1790s.[70]

The next attack on Duane was not a lawsuit, but a physical attack, by volunteer Federalist troops seeking to punish Duane's criticisms of their "system of terror" and their "warning to those who . . . *vote as they think best*" in connection with the expedition against the Fries Rebellion, which was called "not only unnecessary but violently absurd"[71] as the troops roamed through Northampton County for three weeks after John Fries and other former rebels had been jailed in Philadelphia.[72] Nearly thirty Federalists appeared at the *Aurora* office on May 15, 1799, and when Duane would not back down from his criticisms or identify his source, they "seized the Editor by violence, struck him several times on the head, while others held his hands," "dragged him down stairs into Franklin court, there repeated their violence by reiterated blows, from above TEN different persons," beat him mercilessly until he was unconscious, and then beat him further with a whip. Courageously, Duane never apologized for his publication and never disclosed his source. While not disagreeing materially on the facts, the *Gazette of the United States*, and some other Federalist newspapers, expressly justified the savage attack on "this caitiff" and said it was "of no more consequence, than that of any other vagabond."[73] The attack on Duane followed the beating of Jacob Schneider by a month, and the beatings of Bache by a year.

Duane, in another common law case, was prosecuted with Daniel Thomas and two others for "misdemeanor in opening and publishing letters of a foreign minister," which the *Aurora* had printed on July 13 and 15, 1799. The British minister, Robert Liston, had sent the letters by Isaac Sweezy, who was arrested as a horse thief and whose trunk was opened; copies soon reached Duane.[74] Liston privately conceded that the letters would support Republican contentions that the diplomat sought "to produce a rupture between this Country and France, and to promote such an intimate union between the United States and Great Britain as must end in the total annihilation of American independence." He was particularly concerned that one letter acknowledged another Republican claim, that the American "government has given a new subject of provocation to France, encouraging . . . Toussaint" in St. Domingue to revolt against France.[75] At Liston's request, Pickering instructed Rawle to prosecute those who took the letters from Sweezy and, if he was liable, Duane who published them.[76]

Rawle took nearly nine months to act, but finally got an indictment of Duane, Thomas, and two others in April 1800. The indictment, approved in the federal Circuit Court, charged Thomas and two others with criminally opening and publicizing the diplomat's letters, and charged Duane and them with printing and publishing two letters. The day of the indictment, an arrest warrant was issued for Duane, but not surprisingly it was later marked "not found."[77] Nothing else happened in the case over the next eleven months. When Jefferson took office, he noted that the case was not a Sedition Act case but a common law case, and he accepted the attorney general's recommendation that it should be allowed to proceed to trial.[78] But the case was ultimately dropped by the prosecutors.

Duane finally was forced to spend time in jail, by a third common law case where he was sued for libel by Levi Hollingsworth, a Federalist merchant, based on an *Aurora* article in January 1800. The article reported on a threat by a friend of Levi Hollingsworth, when it should have said a friend of a related Hollingsworth. The libel suit, in United States Circuit Court, was really an effort to establish that Duane was not a citizen and so could be deported under the Alien Act. It dragged along until a May 1801 hearing, where Duane fell into the trap, questioning the federal court's jurisdiction because it could not hear a diversity suit between citizens of the same state. The judges and jury determined that the court had jurisdiction because Duane was not a citizen of Pennsylvania or of the United States. The court's reasoning was that he was born in New York or Canada, and was taken to Ireland before the Declaration of Independence, so he was never a citizen of the United States.[79]

Angered at the verdict and at taunting by Federalist articles, such as those captioned "British Subject—William Duane," the *Aurora* editor again fell into a trap and published criticism of the Federalist judges and of the handpicked jury. (He could have added that Chief Judge William Tilghman was the brother of Hollingsworth's attorney, Edward Tilghman.) That same day, Hollingsworth filed a motion for contempt of court against Duane, and the judges quickly found him in contempt and sentenced him to thirty days in prison. Jefferson was again talked out of issuing a pardon because the case was not based on the unconstitutional Sedition Act.[80]

To the Victor Belong No Spoils

With Jefferson's victory in 1800, visions of federal printing contracts danced in Duane's head. Two months after the inauguration, not having received anything substantial, Duane wrote separately to Jefferson and to Madison, asking their "favors" in directing federal offices to him for stationary and for publication of statutes. He reminded them that in "the season of danger, I laid aside personal considerations," and that "all ideas of profit from my newspaper [were] hopeless."[81] A month later, Duane wrote to the new president repeating his request and appealing for his sympathy, reiterating that "I cannot but think it hard, that I alone should still remain the victim" of pending prosecutions, and that the *Aurora*'s profits "do not enable me to disencumber myself from the debts" inherited from Bache's "struggles and sacrifices." The new administration discouraged the *Aurora* from moving to Washington, and instead enabled the *National Intelligencer,* edited by Samuel Harrison Smith, to become the Republican mouthpiece there. The reason was that, as Jefferson noted to Madison, "Duane's zeal merits tenderness and satisfaction, while his precipitancy makes him improper to be considered as speaking the sense of the government."[82] Duane also failed to receive the contracts for printing House of Representatives journals or most of the laws, despite borrowing $22,000 to open operations in Washington; however, he was awarded some Senate printing and ultimately the contract for printing Senate journals during 1803–1807. Duane never escaped the old debts, and he later became quite poor.[83]

In the meantime, Duane's party influence declined as the Republican party split, having lost the unifying force of opposing a common enemy. Duane suffered three libel suits brought by the Republican governor of Pennsylvania, Thomas McKean, and later faced accusations of misappropriation of federal money while finally enjoying a salaried appointment as adjutant general in the War of 1812.[84] After that war, Duane increasingly made the *Aurora* a host for dissenting beliefs, such as his opposition to the Bank of the United States and the Missouri Compromise, and his support for independence efforts in South America.

Jefferson, who Duane always treated with friendship and respect, gave a balanced view of the editor and his violent attacks on foes:

> I believe Duane to be a very honest man, and sincerely republican; but his passions are stronger than his prudence, and his personal as well as general antipathies, render him very intolerant. [T]hese traits lead him astray, & require his readers, even those who value him for his steady support of the republican cause, to be on their guard against his occasional aberrations.

Those aberrations included harsh newspaper attacks on opponents, blindness to atrocities of the French Revolution, and equivocations on slavery.[85] Jefferson became concerned that Duane would "apostatize[]" and oppose President Madison, ruefully noting that in that case he would have to abandon Duane. Duane ultimately did "defect[] from the republican ranks" and "transition to the Federalists," just as Jefferson predicted.[86]

Yet Duane had courageously and successfully guided the leading Republican newspaper through the dark years of the Alien and Sedition Acts, spearheading the nonpoliticians' attacks on that legislation, and providing daily material for other Republican newspapers, even while always being at risk of prosecution. John Quincy Adams (no friend to Duane) acknowledged Duane's effectiveness by complaining that Pennsylvania was for "about twenty years governed by two newspapers in succession: one, the Aurora . . . and the other, the Democratic Press, edited by John Binns."[87]

Broad Understanding of Freedoms of Press and Speech, and Concern about Seditious Libel

William Duane, like virtually all the other experienced Republican editors, had advocated an expansive meaning for freedoms of press and speech from his first identifiable writings, which were in 1795.[88] He did not merely come up with that view in response to the Sedition Act of 1798.

The London newspaper that he edited during 1795–1796, the *Telegraph*, was the semiofficial mouthpiece of the radical London Corresponding Society (the LCS). Though the LCS focused on "*Universal Suffrage and Annual Parliaments*," it also advocated a broad meaning of freedoms of press and speech.[89] Duane's most visible public action during his ten months in London combined his opposition to criminalizing seditious libel with his articulation of an expansive meaning of freedoms of press and speech, which increased his vulnerability to arrest and doubtless helped persuade him to leave Britain for America in June 1796.

"Citizen Duane" chaired the LCS public meeting to oppose the two proposed laws criminalizing seditious libel and constructive treason (models for the Sedition Act in 1798), and more broadly to oppose the Pitt administration's campaign of prosecuting radical Whigs for seditious libel and treason.[90] To denounce two of "the most barefaced arbitrary measures that ever defiled the page of history," the LCS held the meeting just outside London in a field near Copenhagen House on November 12, 1795, and claimed that it was attended by "upwards of three hundred thousand people."[91] Whether or not that estimate was accurate, the meeting was one of the largest political assemblies in British history to that time, and it so clogged the roads with multitudes of people that the meeting was delayed by an hour and a half. Duane gave a speech that, as summarized in the record, "asserted the right of public meetings and private deliberations; the necessity of private and public opinion, and free discussion on all topics." He condemned the proposed Treasonable and Seditious Practices Act and Seditious Assemblies Act as "detestable measures" that violated liberties. He read addresses to the King, House of Lords, and House of Commons, the latter of which proclaimed that "the vital energies of the British Constitution consist in the liberties of speech and of the press," and which protested the recent "attempts to . . . annihilate the sacred rights of political discussion . . . by the revival of those very measures which brought the House of Stuart into such general odium . . . and produce[d] that glorious Revolution."[92] In other words, seditious libel laws infringed "rights of political discussion." Duane's signature appeared at the end of each address. Despite such opposition, Parliament passed the two acts in

December 1795, and the LCS and other radical organizations were forced underground.

The day before the Copenhagen field meeting, the *Telegraph* advertised, under the heading "Liberty of the Press," a meeting at the LCS office to consider the effects of "the present alarming Bill"—the Treasonable and Seditious Practices Act—that "will annihilate the LIBERTY OF THE PRESS."[93]

Duane's opposition to the two acts expanding the crime of seditious libel was consistent with his recent experiences in Calcutta constricting his freedom of press by prosecuting him for seditious libel. There, a charge of seditious libel was the basis for his first arrest and close brush with deportation, and for the closing of the *Bengal Journal* that he edited. Then, a new charge of seditious libel was the basis for his arrest and actual deportation, and for the collapse of *The World* that he also edited.[94] In London, arrests for seditious libel, as well as for constructive treason, swirled around him as he edited the *Telegraph* and chaired the Copenhagen field meeting.

Duane's most extended writing before 1798 made many of the same points, particularly on freedom of speech and belief and the illegitimacy of its restraint. His *Letter to George Washington* recalled the first president's denunciation of Democratic-Republican Societies, and affirmed the right of "societies of your countrymen . . . *to assert their own opinions* in opposition *to yours*." It affirmed citizens' rights to a "free declaration of private judgment" on public measures. "Who are they that the constitution appoints to restrain private deliberation, and mark the line beyond which freedom becomes sedition?" The *Letter* also affirmed people's "right of opinion on matters which divide and have divided all mankind," and their right to have freedom of belief in religious matters.[95]

These pre-1798 writings were consistent with Duane's post-Sedition Act columns reiterating his views that freedoms of press and speech were broad, safeguarding censure of government and its leaders, and that criminal prosecution of seditious libel violated those freedoms. In this, Duane was like Bache, Burk, Lyon, and other Sedition Act defendants who addressed those issues before 1798.

Dr. Joseph Priestley

Joseph Priestley (1733–1804), a theologian and scientist, was also a radical intellectual.[96] Spending the first six decades of his life in England, he became a Unitarian minister and polemicist, and on the side a noted scientist as the discoverer of seven gases including oxygen. While still in England, his ardent support of the French Revolution and of radical Whig reforms placed him at risk of arrest and prosecution as the Pitt administration sought to quash the opposition; it also enticed a mob to burn his house to the ground, with his books and laboratory, in Birmingham in 1791. As a result, Priestley and his family moved to Northumberland County, Pennsylvania in 1794, where Thomas Cooper joined them. Their plan to establish a community of fleeing radicals and religious dissenters failed for lack of customers,[97] and Priestley's plan to escape government scrutiny failed for inability to avoid political discussion. Priestley remained in Pennsylvania through the 1798–1801 period and for the last decade of his life.

Priestley was already known to Pickering and other Federalists as a famous democrat and "émigré Jacobin," and he attracted further attention when he was charged with being a French spy by William Cobbett in a succession of articles in his *Porcupine's Gazette*. A month after the Alien and Sedition Acts were signed into law, Cobbett published "Priestley Completely Detected," reprinting letters from Hurtford Stone in Paris to Priestley, with Cobbett's caustic commentary that the letters showed that Priestley was "sent hither as a *spy*, or as an organizer of insurrection in favour of France."[98] Cobbett also wrote a pamphlet about that "traiterous correspondence" that reiterated "the suspicion of *your* being a spy or a traitor, or both." Even before Cobbett's publication of Stone's letters, Priestley was told that rumors about them "occasioned a good deal of notice of your democratic principles, which in the present season have irritated some persons." Priestley was concerned that under the Alien Act the president could "either confine me, or send me out of the country."[99]

In August 1799, Pickering forwarded to the president "a publication by Thomas Cooper, an Englishman, & a connection of Dr. Priestl[e]y," and pointed out that Priestley helped in its publication. Pickering said that each was "a warm opposition man," and that Priestley "was at the *democratic* assembly on the 4th of July" and had a "discontented and turbulent spirit." "But what is of most consequence, and demonstrates the Doctor's want of decency—being an alien— . . . is 'his industry in getting Mr. Cooper's address printed in handbills and distributed.'" Pickering would "wish them both removed from the U. States," and regretted that Cooper had become a citizen and was not subject to the Alien Act. Pickering noted that it was nearly a year since Adams authorized expulsions under that act, and urged prosecution of Priestley under it. Adams responded that Cooper's address "is a Libel against the whole Government and as such ought to be prosecuted," but that he did not "think it wise to execute the Alien Law against poor Priestley, at present."[100]

In the meantime, Pickering already had written to Charles Hall, an attorney who assisted William Rawle in prosecuting federal cases, and who had sent Cooper's address to the secretary of state with a note of Priestley's role. Pickering said that Priestley's "conduct in this affair is wholly unpardonable," and that "*ambition* influences him, like the mass of seditious, turbulent democrats." He fumed about the "*indecency* in these *strangers* thus meddling with our government," and he concluded the letter by authorizing Rawle to prosecute Priestley: "I hope besides that Mr. Rawle will prosecute both." Pickering did not mean prosecuting both under the Alien Act, because he had just said he was "sorry that Cooper like Priestl[e]y has not remained an alien."[101] Pickering, with his usual recommendatory language, was authorizing prosecution of Cooper and Priestley under the Sedition Act.

Neither prosecution was initiated then, however, as Rawle struggled with a backlog of Fries Rebellion cases that he must prosecute in the October 1799 session of the Circuit Court. The Sedition Act indictment of Cooper waited until April 1800, and prosecution of Priestley never came. Jefferson, shortly after his inauguration, congratulated Priestley on his near escape: "what an effort . . . of bigotry in Politics & Religion have we gone through. [T]he barbarians really flattered themselves they should even be able to bring back the times of Vandalism."[102]

Meriwether Jones and the Richmond *Examiner*

Meriwether Jones (1766–1806), a Richmond lawyer, was the editor of that city's *Examiner,* from when he founded it with John Dixon in December 1798 through just before its demise in January 1804. From the start, Jones adopted a stridently Republican tone, and with the *Examiner* he "became a hub of the state Republican party," much as Duane and the *Aurora* did in Pennsylvania. Jones also tried to establish a Republican *National Magazine,* with Matthew Lyon's son.[103] Jones was one of the most patrician of the intended victims of the Sedition Act, a fourth-generation Virginian, and a member of the Virginia Council of State (beginning 1796). And he was the only victim to die in a duel, in 1806, except for Burk two years later.[104]

Jones placed himself in Pickering's crosshairs by hiring James Thomson Callender, the radical English writer, a half year after Callender fled Philadelphia to avoid prosecution. The writer's vitriol made the *Examiner,* in Richard Beeman's words, "one of the most irresponsible newspapers in the history of American journalism." Ultimately, Callender was prosecuted under the Sedition Act for his political book, *The Prospect Before Us,* that the *Examiner*'s press printed. Callender was so volatile that, two years after his trial, he turned his venom on Jones—and Jefferson—and Republicans generally.[105]

Pickering, in August 1799 as part of his campaign, decried "audacious calumnies against the Government" in the *Examiner,* which amounted to "opposition to our own government," and he wanted to "arrest them by legal process." He instructed the United States attorney for Virginia to examine every new issue of the *Examiner,* "and whenever it contains any libellous matter against the government or its officers, . . . that the Editor or Editors may be prosecuted." The reference to "Editor or Editors" also encompassed Callender, who some identified as the "joint editor" and who Pickering called "the *actual* editor."[106] Soon, Pickering added another mortal sin to the *Examiner*'s list, saying that "a virulent Jacobin paper called the *Examiner,* printed in Richmond," first published letters between Talleyrand and Pinchon, which helped Adams in sending his new envoys to France. A month later, Pickering was still venting his spleen on the issue, writing to Sen. William Bingham about the publication of Talleyrand's letters in a "*Jacobin,* or if you please, *French* newspaper in Richmond in Virginia edited by a Mr. M. Jones." Continuing, Pickering said Jones sought "to become the champion . . . of the violent party in that state in . . . vilifying the federal government and probably to destroy it."[107] His sights were clearly set on Meriwether Jones, as well as on James T. Callender.

No prosecution was brought against Jones, and the prosecution was delayed against Callender. One reason was that Virginia, which had adopted the Virginia Resolutions and would soon adopt the Virginia Report opposing the Alien and Sedition Acts, would not be an easy place to bring a successful prosecution. Another reason was that James Monroe, the new governor of Virginia, reported to Jefferson that he would "endeavor to keep them [Jones and James Lyon] within suitable limits, in their publications," since he believed "an attempt will be made to carry the sedition law into effect here, as an electioneering trick." The Adams administration "must be deprived of a plausible pretext."[108]

CHAPTER ELEVEN

New York Prosecutions

THE ADAMS administration's third campaign to enforce the Alien and Sedition Acts moved forward in New York during the latter half of 1799 and the first half of 1800, at the same time it moved forward in Pennsylvania. On the same day in September 1799, indictments of five individuals were handed down by the federal grand jury empaneled by the United States Circuit Court in New York City. The first of those cases showed how political and repressive the Sedition Act was, as Secretary of State Timothy Pickering and the United States attorney treated a petition from citizens to the president as a crime and prosecuted it as a violation of the Sedition Act. In the meantime, the only Republican newspapers in New York City were Ann Greenleaf's two papers, the *Argus* and *Greenleaf's New York Journal,* once the *Time Piece* had been closed and its primary editor supposedly deported; and the administration concluded that Greenleaf's two papers must be suppressed. (Incidentally, Ann Greenleaf was the only woman prosecuted under the Sedition Act.) No Republican newspaper criticizing the administration and the Sedition Act was too small, as a common law case was converted to a Sedition Act prosecution against William Durell of the *Mt. Pleasant Register.* The remaining indictment in New York was of John Daly Burk and Dr. James Smith, also to convert their common law sedition case into a Sedition Act case. All of these had reason to be glad their cases were acted upon in the September 1799 session, because the foreman of the grand jury in the next session of the court was the brother-in-law of Alexander Hamilton, and one of the wealthiest men in America, John B. Church.[1]

Jedidiah Peck and the Crime of Petitions against the Alien and Sedition Acts

Jedidiah Peck (1748–1821) held a number of part-time jobs in the late 1790s—as state legislator, farmer, surveyor, carpenter, and preacher, and formerly as a bookkeeper and local judge. He grew up in a poor family, as one of the thirteen children of Elijah Peck and Hepzibah Pearson in Lyme, Connecticut, and was mostly self-educated from reading the Bible, which remained a mainstay in his life.[2] He enlisted in the Revolutionary War as a private and served four years. In 1790, he moved to Otsego County, New York, eighty miles west of Albany. He was rewarded with a county judgeship as a loyal follower of the area's wealthy developer, William Cooper. In 1798, Peck began a decade in New York's legislature, at first in the assembly from 1798–1804, and then in the senate from 1804–1808.[3] Later in life, Peck was credited with being the "father of the public school system" in New York, after he chaired the formative commission and wrote its report. His first name is correctly spelled Jedidiah,[4] as in the King James Version of the Bible, though it was often spelled Jedediah during his lifetime and currently.

Peck was a Federalist when he won his legislative seat; he signed and probably wrote Burlington's address to John Adams decrying the Directory's treatment of the American envoys, hoping France would reconsider, and promising otherwise "to gird on our warlike weapons as in the year '75." Concededly, Peck was an unusually democratic Federalist, who sometimes deviated from his party's positions. But he supported the Jay Treaty, opposed the "Jacobin party," and helped Federalist candidates.[5] Most prominent among those Federalist candidates who he supported was William Cooper, who dominated Otsego County politically, though they fell out by early 1799.[6] At that time, New York's secretary of state wrote to Cooper that Peck appeared "to be neither federal, antifederal or any thing else," and that "it would be best for himself and for Society in general that he was reinstated in his original obscurity," which "will be *compleatly* the case before long and I am happy to find that you are disposed to further the business." Peck finished the falling out by opposing the Alien and Sedition Acts, and Cooper quickly engineered his prosecution as well as his removal from his judgeship.[7]

Peck supported the Republicans in the state assembly in their unsuccessful efforts to condemn the Alien and Sedition Acts, and to support the Virginia and Kentucky Resolutions, in February 1799. He voted for their resolution that "the alien and sedition laws are unconstitutional, impolitic and contrary to the dearest interests of freemen," and should be immediately repealed. That resolution also rejected the Federalist claim that only the federal judiciary could express an opinion on the constitutionality of federal laws, and responded that the legislature and the people had the right to express an opinion as well. Peck also supported the Republican resolution that the Sedition Act "doth abridge the freedom of speech and of the press, and . . . is impolitic and unnecessary, and that the constitution of the United States does not vest in Congress any authority to pass the said act."[8] And he supported the companion resolution on the Alien Act, that the law that "all aliens not actually naturalized, are declared liable to be banished at the will of the President, without trial or indictment" is "contrary to the sense which this House entertain of the constitution of the United States." Peck also voted against the Federalist resolutions that only the federal judiciary could decide on the constitutionality of federal laws, and, earlier, that the assembly disclaimed any power to do what the Virginia and Kentucky Resolutions asked. And he voted against the Federalist efforts to avoid considering the resolutions at all.[9] Three weeks later, the Federalists punished Peck by removing him as a judge. He responded by becoming a Republican in his successful campaign for reelection to the legislature.[10]

Peck gathered signatures on petitions against the Alien and Sedition Acts in the spring of 1799. Cooper, the chief judge in the county, responded by publishing a startling warning in late April, as Peck stood for reelection as a newly-minted Republican:

> CAUTION!
>
> Every man who circulates two Seditious printed Papers, disseminated by Jedediah Peck, through this County, is liable to two years imprisonment and a fine of two thousand dollars, at the discretion of the Court. My neighbors will notice, that no author dare sign his name to them, nor dare any printer let it be known who hath done the wicked act.
>
> We have proof of Peck's bringing them into the County.—The whole, with his Letter, are sent to the District Judge.
>
> *William Cooper*[11]

What Judge Cooper threatened toward anyone circulating or signing the petitions was conviction under the Sedition Act—the imprisonment and fine he listed were the maximum punishments specified by the Sedition Act for anyone who would "write, print, utter or publish" criticism of "the government . . . or either house of Congress . . . or the President" with intent to defame them.

Cooper indeed confiscated Peck's petitions and sent them to the United States attorney, Richard Harison. Harison did not need much encouragement, because he soon received instructions from Secretary of State Timothy Pickering, the director of Alien and Sedition Act prosecutions, to be vigilant detecting sedition and enforcing the Sedition Act.[12]

To strengthen the case against Peck, Cooper and a fellow judge took sworn statements from three local citizens about events in mid-April.[13] David Goff acknowledged that Peck brought "certain printed papers into the County"—the petitions—and that Peck said that "the Alien and Sedition bills . . . were contrary to the Constitution." Nathan Patmer stated that Peck offered him some petitions "Reproaching the Measures of Government," saying the people's rights "were indangered of being destroyed by the Congress," and that "the People are much disturbed of late about the acts of the Government." Jonathan Brown testified that Peck handed him a petition, which he signed, and that he was "shocked" later to find that it contained "a pointed opposition to the present measures of Government" and called the Alien and Sedition Acts "unconstitutional." Each had to provide a $500 bond assuring that he would appear in court to testify.[14] Judge Cooper obviously saw such statements as criminal violations of the Sedition Act.

Peck was indicted by the grand jury when the United States Circuit Court convened in New York City in early September 1799. Justice William Paterson presided, joined by Judge John Sloss Hobart, and gave the grand jury "an elegant charge ag[ains]t riots, insurrections, & lies against the Government & its officers" (as the former district judge recounted).[15] The indictment was based on five passages in the petitions, which it alleged defamed "the Government . . . the Congress and President" in violation of the Sedition Act. First, the petition claimed the measures passed by Congress were "a Series of Evils . . .—a foreign war, a violated Constitution and a divided People." Second, it said the administration's policy toward France betrayed "a miserable Jealousy or criminal Scepticism" in treating France's "Desire to conciliate" as "only empty Professions." Next, the petition asserted that the Alien Act "is cruel, unjust, unnecessary, impolitic and unconstitutional." Fourth, it similarly claimed that the "Sedition Law" was "vicious," "attacks the many," and would "convert Freemen into Slaves." Finally, the petition said the recent expansion of the army was unnecessary and dangerous.[16]

After the indictment was handed down, Peck was arrested in late September 1799. The federal marshal took him on a five-day ride over the two hundred miles of road to New York City for arraignment and posting bond. Republican newspapers recounted that he was "'taken from his bed at midnight, manacled, and dragged from his home,'" and commented that the "'rule of George Third . . . was gracious and loving compared to such tyranny.'" A nineteenth-century historian described the effect of that federal overreach:

> A hundred missionaries in the cause of democracy, stationed between New-York and Cooperstown, could not have done so much for the republican cause

> as this journey of Judge Peck, as a prisoner, from Otsego to the capital of the state. It was nothing less than the public exhibition of a suffering martyr for the freedom of speech and the press, and the right of petitioning, to the view of the citizens of the various places through which the marshal travelled with his prisoner.[17]

Reporting about Peck's arrest provided a vivid example of the gulf between Republican and Federalist newspapers. Republican newspapers recounted the five-day journey in irons, and that Peck's crime was his "stern integrity and uncorruptible attachment to the liberties of his fellow-citizens," while most Federalist newspapers printed a single sentence: "Jedediah Peck, of Burlington, Otsego co. State of New York, an influential Jacobin has been arrested under the sedition law."[18]

It is easy to overlook how incredible this prosecution was. Peck's crime was a petition to the president. The First Amendment expressly protects the right of petition: "Congress shall make no law . . . abridging . . . the right of the people . . . to petition the Government for a redress of grievances." The Bill of Rights included that provision (expanding on the right of petition in the English Bill of Rights of 1689) in order to override common law restrictions on the right of petition. Under common law, a petitioner could be prosecuted for an "indecent" petition, or one that was seditious libel, as a crime.[19] Also, a petition in England was criminal if it was signed by more than twenty people or delivered by more than ten people, unless it had been preapproved by three justices or a grand jury. If those limits were violated, each signatory and deliverer was subject to three months' imprisonment and a substantial fine. In Peck's case, a petition that the Sedition Act was unconstitutional was prosecuted as a violation of that Sedition Act! That was precisely what Rep. Albert Gallatin had predicted when the Sedition Act was under consideration. "If an individual thinking, as he himself did, that the present bill was unconstitutional, and that it had been intended . . . solely for party purposes, should avow and publish his opinion, and if the Administration thought fit to prosecute him for that supposed individual offence, would a jury, composed of the friends of that Administration, hesitate much in declaring the opinion ungrounded, or, in other words, false and scandalous, and its publication malicious?" And in reply to the point that the Sedition Act allowed a defense of truth, "how could the truth of opinions be proven by evidence?"[20]

When the Circuit Court met next, in April 1800, Peck's case was not brought to trial, and late in the month his prosecution was suspended. The reasons were given in the United States attorney's report to Pickering. Richard Harison said Peck's case "could not be tried as the witnesses all live near two hundred miles from New York [City] and did not attend."

Nor would it make sense to compel their attendance, because "[t]he Expence of procuring them on any future Occasion will be very considerable, and . . . more Good will flow from suspending the Prosecution, than from the Pursuit of it." Peck's "consequence would be augmented by . . . his Punishment," and—acknowledging the chilling effect of prosecution on freedoms of press and speech—he would be "under greater Restraint whilst he remains in his present Situation."[21] Pickering passed the recommendation to President John Adams, who left to Harison's discretion "the conduct of the prosecution against Mr. Peck." Pickering relayed the president's response to Harison,[22] who suspended Peck's case without dismissing it. Suspending the case meant trial could be scheduled at the next Circuit Court session if Peck said, published, or petitioned for anything that the administration disliked.

Peck's fortunes had finally recovered. His parade to New York City and his case "made Peck into a Republican hero." He won reelection to the state assembly soon after his trial should have occurred. The Republicans captured New York's governorship, and soon after, Peck was given Cooper's former position as the chief judge in Otsego County. In 1804 Peck won a place in the state senate, and he was given a seat on the powerful Council of Appointment.[23]

Jedidiah Peck is representative of the droves of Americans who migrated from the Federalist Party to the Republican Party in large part because of the outrageousness of the Alien and Sedition Acts. In Peck's case, Federalist political malpractice dragged him from his 1797 view of Republicans as "Jacobins . . . made up of the libertine whigs and revengeful and avaricious tories, . . . a beast, with, to be sure, seven heads, and ten horns— . . . monsters indeed," to his 1799 embrace of the Republican Party. As Alan Taylor points out, Peck is also an example (along with nearly all of the Sedition Act defendants) of an ordinary citizen, without the elite's advantages, who fought for the rights of all at great personal cost.[24]

Ann Greenleaf and the New York *Argus* and *Greenleaf's New York Journal*

Ann Greenleaf (1767–1845)[25] became the publisher of two Republican newspapers, the New York *Argus* and *Greenleaf's New York Journal,* upon the death of her husband Thomas Greenleaf in the yellow fever epidemic in September 1798. Thomas Greenleaf (1755–1798) was the son of Joseph Greenleaf of Abington, Massachusetts, a minor colonial official and anonymous radical columnist, who changed careers just before the Revolutionary

War and bought a printing house to influence the political debate. Thomas Greenleaf moved to New York and soon bought the *New-York Journal* in early 1787.[26] He renamed the newspaper *Greenleaf's New York Journal, & Patriotic Register* at the beginning of 1794, and established *The Argus, & Greenleaf's New Daily Advertiser* in May 1795. The first remained semi-weekly as a country edition and the second was daily as a city edition, with most content of the *Journal* being reprinted from the *Argus*. Greenleaf took the papers in a sharply Republican direction that "opposed the administration, attacked the measures of the venerable Washington with a great degree of virulence," and became a leading opposition publication.[27] In 1797, Abigail Adams singled out "the grose lies daily publishd in the Aurora, Argus, & Chronicle," and John Adams listed the three as the leading opposition papers.[28] They were right about the influence of the *Argus*. When prosecution of John Daly Burk and Dr. James Smith closed the *Time Piece*, Greenleaf became "the only anti-Federalist publisher among the nine newspapers then published in New York City."[29] That was one anti-Federalist publisher too many for Adams and Pickering.

The *Argus* and the *Journal* aimed regular fire at the Sedition Act. When the sedition bill was pending, one article quoted the First Amendment and called the bill "diametrically opposed to the very letter of it," and another said an "act of WAR lies on the table!!!"[30] On the day the president signed the Sedition Act into law, Greenleaf reported disapprovingly that it had been "passed by a majority of THREE!!!," and in the next issue commented sarcastically that "the majority of three were completely right, in abridging that licentiousness, wickedly called liberty of the press." On the front page of that issue, he again quoted the First Amendment and warned that the Sedition Act was "fraught with dangers" and left "their inalienable right to freedom of speech openly attacked." Greenleaf continued with an important rationale for freedoms of press and speech: citizens "must inspect narrowly into the conduct of those they employ" in government, as in business, and yet by the Sedition Act they were "deterred from animadverting on the conduct of those employed in public affairs." He was spared prosecution under the Sedition Act by his death from yellow fever, but his wife was not so fortunate.[31]

Ann Greenleaf had married Thomas Greenleaf in 1791.[32] Growing up as Ritsana Quackenbos, she was the great-great-great-granddaughter of a Dutch immigrant of 1660, Pieter Quackenbosh; her father, Johannes Quackenbos, had been a captain in the Revolutionary War; and her mother, Catharine DeWitt, was a niece of Gov. George Clinton. Ann Greenleaf inherited the two newspapers, and though publication ceased for seven weeks after Thomas Greenleaf's death, she then announced that the "same principles which have hitherto distinguished these papers, will be invariably adhered to—the Rights of the People, and the Constitution of our Country founded upon those rights."[33] She did exactly that, including in her first issue a commendation of Matthew Lyon ("had the honour of being the first victim of a law framed directly in the teeth of the Constitution") and praise of revolutionary France (which was "determined to prevent a War" if the Adams administration allowed that). The recently retired federal district judge, Robert Troup, observed that, like Margaret Bache, Ann Greenleaf "has renewed her husband's paper with as much virulence as was manifested by her husband."[34] The consequence was her indictment under the Sedition Act.

Prosecution of Greenleaf for Articles Critical of the Sedition Act and Government

Pickering instructed the United States attorney for New York to prosecute the *Argus,* in August 1799, by a form letter that he adapted and sent to the United States attorneys for some states who had not already been expressly instructed to prosecute Republican newspapers under the Sedition Act. Pickering wrote,

> The notorious calumnies against the Government, with which many of the presses devoted to promote the views of . . . opposition to our own government have lately turned, in a more than usual degree, have suggested the necessity of efficient measures to correct them by legal process. In particular, a paper is published in New York, under the title of the "Argus," which possesses the character of extreme virulence. It is not received at my office, but from the passages, which are studiously copied from it into the Aurora, I am satisfied that that character is not improperly ascribed to it. I request you to procure it daily at the public expense, and to prosecute the publisher, for every libel upon the Government or its officers which may appear therein, either originally or by republication. In the latter case be pleased to give me notice of any prosecution you may commence, that the same step may be taken against the original libeller.
>
> My request is intended to comprehend the authors of libels as well as the publisher, where you can discover the former, without relinquishing the exemplary punishment of the latter; so that unless a special case should happen in which you will use your discretion the publisher should not be encouraged to expect forgiveness on condition of rendering up the author.[35]

The reference to prosecuting "every libel upon . . . its officers" is significant, because the Sedition Act only criminalized disparagement of "the government . . . or either house of Congress . . . or the President." Pickering was expanding its reach to himself and other officers of government, except,

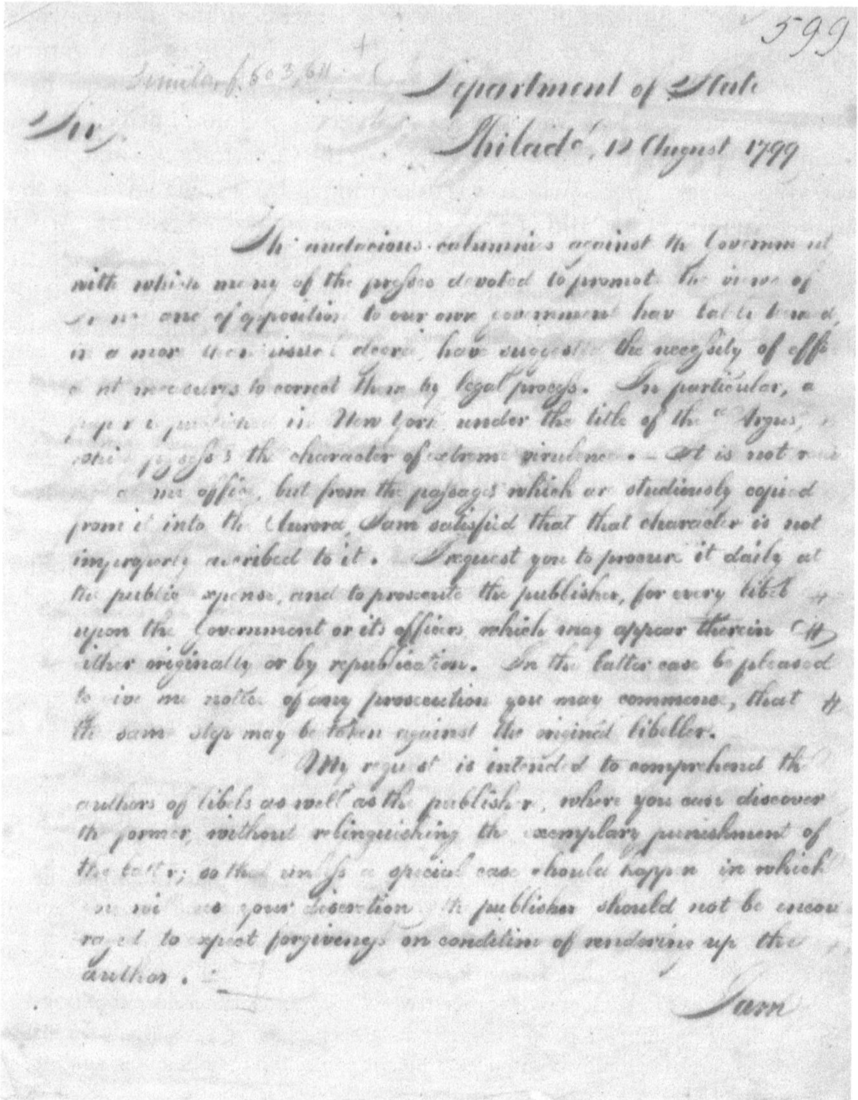

599

Department of State
Philada. 12 August 1799

Sir,

The audacious calumnies against the Government with which many of the presses devoted to promote the views of [illegible] of opposition to our own government have lately teemed, [illegible] have suggested the necessity of [illegible] measures to correct them by legal process. In particular, a paper published in New York under the title of the "Argus," [illegible] possesses the character of extreme virulence. — It is not [illegible] office, but from the passages which are studiously copied from it into the Aurora, I am satisfied that that character is not improperly ascribed to it. I request you to procure it daily at the public expense, and to prosecute the publisher, for every libel upon the Government or its officers which may appear therein [illegible] either originally or by republication. In the latter case be pleased to give me notice of any prosecution you may commence, that the same step may be taken against the original libeller.

My request is intended to comprehend the authors of libels as well as the publisher, where you can discover the former, without relinquishing the exemplary punishment of the latter; so that unless a special case should happen in which [illegible] your discretion the publisher should not be encouraged to expect forgiveness on condition of rendering up the author.

I am

FIGURE 11.1. Pickering's instructions to prosecute Ann Greenleaf. Courtesy Collection of the Massachusetts Historical Society, Timothy Pickering Papers.

apparently, the most maligned officer of government, the Republican vice president, Thomas Jefferson.

Harison got the grand jury to indict Ann Greenleaf three weeks later, in early September, for violating the Sedition Act by articles published in the *Argus* on February 9 and August 31, 1799.[36] (The same grand jury, on the same day, also indicted Jedidiah Peck, William Durell, and John Daly Burk and Dr. James Smith under the Sedition Act.) Both articles were said "to defame the Government and . . . the Congress," and "to stir up sedition," by printing, uttering, and publishing "false, scandalous and malicious" material in *Greenleaf's New Daily Advertiser* (which was the subtitle of the *Argus*).[37]

In the first article (the basis of the first count), positive language about a liberty pole, and criticism of the Alien and Sedition Acts as unconstitutional, were said to be violations of the Sedition Act. The problem language was that

> the Honest Yeomanry of that town [Flat Bush] some days before erected a Liberty Pole, what was common to be done at the commencement of the American Revolution in every Republican Town in America, . . . expressive of the high displeasure of that Town . . . at similar attempts in their opinion in the last session of Congress . . . manifested by actually passing the Tyrannical and unconstitutional alien and sedition Bills.[38]

As in Peck's case, merely calling the Sedition Act unconstitutional was treated as a violation of the Sedition Act. In the words of the indictment, "to insinuate and cause it to be believed that the said Congress had passed tyrannical and unconstitutional Laws and were inimical to the Liberties of the said People" violated the Sedition Act.

The second article (the basis of the second count) charged that government officials advanced "subversion of the National Character," that some Federalist newspapers were "in the pay of Government," and that British secret service money was spent somewhere. The language that was charged to be criminal was the following:

> To say those [British party] principles have crept into our public councils, to say that public servants advocate and forward this Gradual subversion of National Character, this insidious revolution of sentiment, would perhaps be construed into sedition. But thank God in this Country truth is not yet a libel, and I may still assert facts. . . .
>
> 1. A News Paper in Boston—Noah Websters in New-York—the Farmers Weekly Museum in New Hampshire—Fennos in Philadelphia—and Youndt and Browns paper in Baltimore, are pensioned and held in the pay of Government.
>
> 2. All those Presses continually nauseate us with Eulogiums on the British, publish nothing but the most severe Philippicks against the French. . . .
>
> 3. These papers are celebrated for venting the basest personal scurrility against every individual, particularly, Editors, that wish to keep alive that jealousy and watchfulness so essential to the preservation of civil Liberty—and endeavour to preserve the spirit and principles of our Constitution in its pristine purity.

> 4. Is it not probable that these pensioned Printers have their directions from their Masters, or that they anticipate and exercise their pleasure?
> 5. Is it not probable that . . . these venal scribblers may be British secret agents; sent here to assist in demoralizing the Political mind?
> Last year the British secret service money exceeded the amount of a whole years expenses of our Government. But who can tell thro what channel it was expended—the British . . . are seldom known to give something for nothing.[39]

The indictment called those statements an "open violation of the Laws of the United States." Here too, "to insinuate and cause it to be believed that the said Government was corrupt and inimical to the preservation of civil Liberty and to the . . . Constitution" violated the Sedition Act.[40]

Both articles were reprinted from other newspapers—a Long Island paper and the Baltimore *American*—but neither of those sources was prosecuted for printing the same language. That selective prosecution indicated that the real target was not the language but the particular newspaper.

The day after this indictment was handed down, one of Ann Greenleaf's printers testified that she was "confined to her bed" with yellow fever. The judges decided they were more afraid of her yellow fever than her sedition, and delayed the case from the September 1799 session to the April 1800 session, without requiring her to appear to enter an appearance bond.[41] This left Mrs. Greenleaf free to continue publishing her newspapers. She had not received the dose of terror that Jedidiah Peck had been dealt—a public threat, an arrest, a humiliating ride as a criminal to court, a punitively high bond. She had not yet been to court, been arrested, or been placed under bond. Something further was needed to shut down her Republican newspapers, and that was the arrest and imprisonment of her head printer.

Prosecution of Greenleaf's Head Printer, David Frothingham

David Frothingham (1765–?) was born in Charlestown, Massachusetts, to a sailor who soon died. At age nineteen, he eloped with the daughter of a wealthy New Yorker, who responded by disinheriting her. In 1791, the family moved to Sag Harbor, Long Island, where Frothingham established and published a newspaper until it failed financially in late 1798. He then accepted a job at the *Argus* as head printer.[42]

The *Argus* reprinted an article that alleged wrongdoing by Gen. Alexander Hamilton, saying that he was at the bottom of a Federalist effort to take over the Philadelphia *Aurora,* using British money or stolen public money.[43] Hamilton immediately wrote to the state attorney general, Josiah O. Hoffman, asking him to "take immediate measures towards the prosecution of the persons who conduct the inclosed paper." Hamilton self-servingly told that fellow Federalist that "public motives now compel me" to make the request, instead of continuing to ignore "the most malignant calumnies of the faction opposed to government." In justifying his request, Hamilton gave a classic formulation of the Federalist rationale for prosecuting seditious libel:

> The design of that faction [opposed to our government] to overturn our government, and with it the great pillars of social security and happiness, in this country, become every day more manifest, and have of late acquired a degree of system, which renders them formidable. One principal Engine for effecting the scheme is by audacious falsehoods to destroy the confidence of the people in all those who are in any degree conspicuous among the supporters of the Government: an Engine . . . which unless counteracted in future is likely to be attended with very fatal consequences. To counter act it is therefore a duty to the community.[44]

Hoffman did take immediate action, sending his assistant to interview Ann Greenleaf, arresting Frothingham, and bringing the case to trial two weeks after Hamilton's request.[45] That trial was in the state court system, not the federal courts.

Why did Hamilton seek to prosecute this article, and not any of the scores of others savaging him? One reason was to vindicate himself, since he wrote his letter to Hoffman for the public to read and immediately sent copies to several New York newspapers for publication.[46] But that was not the only reason, since Hamilton had written many newspaper articles and several pamphlets before to defend himself, without also initiating a prosecution. Another indication that there were other reasons was that Hamilton did not seek prosecution of the Boston newspaper that had originally published the article, or of others that had reprinted it before the *Argus* did,[47] even though his ability to influence Massachusetts Federalists (especially the Essex Junto) to prosecute was at least as strong as his ability to influence New York Federalists. The most plausible additional reason is that he hoped to take out the remaining Republican newspapers in his home city of New York, under cover of "public motives," something a prosecution of the Boston or Newark newspapers would not do, because they were not already pressed by a Sedition Act prosecution.

The day after Hamilton's letter, the assistant attorney general, in visiting Ann Greenleaf, said he wished "to avoid directing the prosecution against a woman, and a widow," and told her he would not "if she would point out the real editor or conductor of her paper." She denied being involved in managing the *Argus* and identified Frothingham as the person responsible for its content. He gallantly said he "was answerable for any publication" and "voluntarily stepped forward to shield his employer from the revenge" of Hamilton.[48] (Doubtless, Frothingham relied on the facts that no printer–journeyman had ever been held responsible for a libel in an American newspaper, and that the article was merely reprinted from another newspaper.) Hoffman's motives were not likely so gallant; he realized that the jury might sympathize with the widow, and that she already was threatened by her Sedition Act prosecution.

Greenleaf fought back in her newspapers. For example, the day before Frothingham's trial began, she published an article about Hamilton's faults—the "failure of his projects at Treason," his proposal "of a monarchical form of government," his recently admitted affair with Maria Reynolds.[49]

The indictment charged Frothingham with common law seditious libel—not libel under the Sedition Act—by designing "to injure the name and reputation of General Hamilton, and to expose him to public hatred and contempt, and to cause it to be believed that he was hostile and opposed to the Republican Government of the United States." The three passages quoted in the indictment were that Hamilton was central to efforts to buy the *Aurora* for $6,000 plus additional amounts, that he must have taken public money while in office since he recently denied having funds anything like that purchase price, and that he was buying the newspaper in cooperation with the British minister and with some British secret service money.[50]

Trial was held in mid-November 1799[51] in the local Court of Oyer and Terminer, with Judge Jacob Radcliff presiding, joined by two officials sitting as judges, Richard Varick, and Richard Harison. (Harison was both city recorder and United States attorney—the person prosecuting Ann Greenleaf—so he acted as judge in one case and as prosecutor in the other arising from the same Republican newspaper.) The Federalist judges refused to allow evidence that the newspaper claims were true (or false), and refused to allow the jury to render a general verdict.[52] In effect, the court refused to allow Frothingham the practical benefits of the *Zenger* case, where the judges had excluded evidence of truth but the defense argued it anyway, and where they had limited the jury issues but the jury acquitted the printer anyway. Under the first ruling, Frothingham's counsel was not allowed to show the jury that there indeed had been a Federalist effort to buy the *Aurora* (which a Federalist paper had reported and the *Aurora* affirmed[53]), or that other assertions in the article were accurate. Under the second ruling, the jury was limited to determining if the article was published by Frothingham, and if its references were correctly interpreted ("that the innuendoes were just"—that they meant what the indictment claimed).

Answering yes to both questions would be treated as a jury verdict of guilty on all issues.

Frothingham's attorney, left with few grounds for defending him, announced that he would make two arguments: that the wrong person was being prosecuted, and that the article was not libelous. However, the judges soon told the jury that they rejected those defenses: they were of opinion that a journeyman "was liable" for such an article, and were unanimously "of opinion that the innuendoes were just, and that the matter was libellous."[54] Frothingham's counsel tried to argue that he lacked the required intent (malice) to libel Hamilton, on the ground that the article was merely copied from another newspaper. Again, the judges ruled against the argument. The defense attorney tried to argue that Frothingham was not responsible because he was not the editor or owner of the *Argus*. The judges barred evidence on that point. Nor could the defense argue that freedom of press under the state constitution protected Frothingham's action, because New York was one of the few states without such a provision. The jury, after deliberating for two to three hours, found Frothingham guilty.[55]

The case was a political case in every regard. New York's leading Federalist insisted that it be prosecuted, and did so because of concern that Republican newspapers were destroying the people's confidence in the Federalist government, which would affect their votes. The state attorney general agreed to take the case, and rushed it to trial in ten days. The judge excluded most defenses that Frothingham's attorney could offer, and imposed a punitive sentence. And Hamilton sought to make a political point beyond destroying a pair of Republican newspapers. As Robert W. T. Martin points out, "Hamilton's theory of republicanism supported protecting the character of a public official from scandalous comments with the most restrictive understanding of seditious libel law circulating in late eighteenth-century America."[56] Contrary to the common picture of Hamilton as a voice of moderation on the Sedition Act, he was insistent on piling a seditious libel prosecution on top of a Sedition Act prosecution, and he testified zealously as a witness during the trial (over the defense's objection).

Soon after, the court held a session to sentence Frothingham. Judge Radcliff reaffirmed the various rulings in the case. Maddeningly, he reiterated that "the law would never submit the truth of the matter contained in a libel, to be adduced by way of justification of the libel"—the judges had ruled that no proof of truth or falsity of the article on Hamilton could be offered—and then the judge said that evidence of truth would have helped. "[I]f such evidence had been offered to the *Court,* it would have gone far in the mitigation of the punishment." Judge Radcliff also gave his views on challenges to "this prosecution as an attack on the liberty of the press." He responded that in "every well regulated society, there must be laws to prevent the licentiousness of the press—all well disposed people must approve the salutary restraint: or, if they should cease to approve it, he should consider it a proof of that degree of depravity, which it was to be hoped, did not yet exist in this country." He added that "this was not a question that concerned the liberties of the press, but only its *licentiousness.*"[57]

The sentence was four months in prison, a fine of $100 (more than three months' wages), which must be paid before release, and good behavior bonds of $1,000 personally and $1,000 by one or two sureties upon release.[58] The judge had rejected the printer's petition for reduced punishment based on his need to support his wife and six children, saying hardheartedly that "[i]f he had a wife and children, he ought to have thought of them before he violated the laws." After his release from prison, Frothingham was sufficiently terrorized that he left his trade as a printer.[59]

The Forced Sale of Greenleaf's Newspapers

Ann Greenleaf, faced with financial burdens and Frothingham's imprisonment for four months, was compelled to sell the *Argus* and the *Journal*, and to miss the chance to boost Republicans in New York's elections two months away. Even in distress, however, she made Pickering's worst nightmare come true, selling to an even more outspoken Republican, David Denniston, effective after the March 8, 1800 issues. He renamed the *Argus* as the *American Citizen* and the *Journal* as the *Republican Watch-Tower.*[60] Though most historians refer to this as closing the *Argus* and *Journal,* the new editor announced that the *Argus* "appears this day under a new title," and published it from the same address on Wall Street. Denniston also pledged that the newspaper would make "no deviation from that *fidelity to Republicanism*" that the Greenleafs maintained, and Ann Greenleaf assured readers that she waited to sell "to persons of republican character." That ended Ann Greenleaf's newspaper career; she advertised after that as a bookseller.[61]

Mrs. Greenleaf appeared as required at the April 1800 session of the United States Circuit Court, where Justice Bushrod Washington presided. The judges delayed her case day-by-day, instead of holding the trial, and then delayed it until the fall 1800 session. In doing so, the judges required that a surety provide a $1,000 bond for her appearance in the fall, and her younger brother John Quackenbos did so.[62]

The reason that Greenleaf's case went nowhere in the April 1800 session is that the objective of the prosecution had been accomplished—her forced sale of her newspapers had closed the prior month—and Harison was stuck with the public relations nightmare of prosecuting an articulate widow with four young children for a crime consisting of political opinions. The day after the court session ended, the United States attorney summed the situation up for Pickering: "her situation as a widow and her having discontinued her Paper, together with the Length of Time that has unavoidably elapsed since the Prosecution was commenced, render it problematical whether it should go on. . . . The Offence, which was not of a very heinous nature, has since been forgotten," and the severity of prosecution "would without Doubt be censured more extensively, if in Consequence of it she should be subjected to any Punishment which might operate as an Example." President John Adams, having received the letter from Pickering, found those reasons "quite sufficient for me to consent and indeed to direct a *nolle prosequi,*" ending prosecution. Pickering passed the instruction to Harison that "the President directs a nolle prosequi to be entered"—Pickering was careful not to say that *he* supported that lenient outcome or agreed that Greenleaf's offense was anything less than "a very heinous nature."[63]

William Durell and the *Mount Pleasant Register*

William Durell (1766–1845), the son of a potter, Jonathan Durell, and Frances Thompson, was a printer and bookseller in New York City throughout the 1790s, until his move thirty miles northward to publish the *Mt. Pleasant Register* from 1797 through its closure the next year.[64] Soon after his trial in 1800, Durell moved back to New York City and resumed his prior work, until he was appointed an inspector of customs (according to his probate papers).[65] Most of the books he published were Protestant theological works, though he also published nontheological ones such as the American edition of the important abolitionist book by Equiano. Durell married Maria Schenk in 1789 and, a year after her death, married Sarah Street in 1798.[66] Though his name is spelled Durrell in most discussions of his case and in some federal court documents, it was actually Durell as his imprints and his marriage and probate records show.[67]

Durell printed the article that would be the basis of his prosecution in his *Mt. Pleasant Register* on June 19, 1798,[68] before the sedition bill was introduced in Congress. Soon after learning of it, Timothy Pickering gave instructions to Richard Harison to prosecute him, on June 28, while the bill was pending. An arrest warrant was issued and Durell was arrested on

July 17,[69] three days after John Adams signed the Sedition Act but before a final copy reached Harison in New York City. The arrest and charge must have been under the common law of seditious libel,[70] as was the case with Benjamin Franklin Bache, John Daly Burk, and Dr. James Smith. Durell was the first newspaper publisher or editor arrested after passage of the Sedition Act, but not under the Sedition Act at that time.

Upon being arrested, Durell was taken into the United States District Court in New York City in order to provide bond for his appearance at the next Circuit Court session.[71] Then nothing happened with his case for over a year.[72] Though he was required to appear at the September 1798 session, he and most others did not because of the yellow fever epidemic, and nothing was done at the April 1799 session because no Supreme Court justice attended.[73]

Part of Pickering's third campaign to enforce the Sedition Act, in the summer and fall of 1799, was that pending common law prosecutions of seditious libel were reindicted as Sedition Act prosecutions. Durell was rearrested in July 1799 and required to provide a new recognizance bond to assure his appearance at the upcoming court session. There, Durell was indicted by the grand jury on September 4, 1799, the same day Peck and Greenleaf were indicted.[74] Durell's 1799 indictment was under the Sedition Act, because reindictment was pointless if it was again under common law, and because the new indictment was very similar to Peck's and Greenleaf's, which were indisputably under the Sedition Act. The common statements that Durell's trial was under common law instead are mistaken, as are those that "the indictment . . . ha[s] been lost, leaving no record of the objectionable remarks."[75]

Indictment for Criticizing the President

Durell's 1799 indictment, handed down by the grand jury in the Circuit Court presided over by Justice William Paterson joined by District Court Judge John Sloss Hobart, alleged that Durell published an article that was a "false, scandalous, malicious and defamatory Libel of . . . John Adams." As described in the indictment, the article said that Adams "was adverse to the Independence of the said United States and about to betray or sell the people thereof to a Foreign Power," Great Britain, and that Adams "expected to acquire an office for himself under the King." The article asked whether there was "cause of suspicion that John Adams . . . like Benedict Arnold is about to betray or sell us," and whether he "has found an asylum on Board the Vulture or some other sloop of war?"[76] The article may have been delusional, but was it criminal?

Durell appeared in court the day after his indictment and pled not guilty. The United States attorney was willing to put off the trial until the court's next session, in April 1800. To ensure his appearance there, the court required Durell to provide a recognizance bond for $2,000, and required someone else (his father) to provide one for $1,000, in each case providing that if Durell did not appear then their household and other property could be levied upon.[77]

Durell's trial was held on April 4, 1800, with Justice Bushrod Washington presiding along with Judge Hobart. At the end of the day, the jury found him guilty. As Durell appeared in court the next morning for sentencing, he saw Alexander Hamilton and Aaron Burr rise as the joint attorneys for the plaintiff in the unrelated first case of the day.[78] Later that morning, Durell gave the judges a petition for clemency, which listed a number of grounds. The first ones showed the impact of a Sedition Act prosecution on freedoms of press and speech. Durell said he should have rejected the article as containing material contrary to his belief, groveling in a way that showed the prosecution had been quite successful in intimidating him. Further, "I immediately discontinued the publication of my paper," and "since the commencement of the prosecution I have been out of business . . . nearly two years," except for completing a few children's books.

The next grounds for Durell's petition showed the disastrous impact of prosecution on a publisher's family. Because of closing the newspaper and losing most printing business for nearly two years, his earnings had dried up, and "all my property real and personal in the County of West-Chester has been sacrificed by the Sheriff in the autumn of 1799, in consequence of which I am obliged to borrow the scanty furniture with which I keep house." That sheriff's sale had taken away all his furniture and household goods. Durell added that he "has a *wife* and five *helpless children,* who have no one to provide for them but himself."

One other ground for clemency was entrapment by a conniving Federalist. Durell said that the offending article was brought to him by the very person whose affidavit about its publication caused his arrest, "with a premeditated intent of bringing me into the difficulty, which has been the result."[79]

Despite Durell's pitiable plea, Justice Washington sentenced him to imprisonment for four months, beginning immediately and without bail, a fine of $50, and before his release, a recognizance bond of $1,000 from himself and $1,000 from two sureties, to ensure his good behavior for two years.[80]

Even the federal prosecutor, Harison, thought that was too harsh, given that the big objective had been accomplished—Durell "discontinued his news-paper." In reporting back to Pickering, Harison recited the sentence and noted that Durell "appears to be very poor at present, has a large Family to maintain, and has a considerable time since discontinued his news-paper," and "pretends also that the Libel was inadvertently copied from another paper, and that it would not have been published in his, if he had been fully apprised of its nature." Worried that the harsh sentence was "scarcely an Object for Example," Harison said the judges had hinted "that it might be worthy of consideration whether a Remission" of all but the bond "might not operate beneficially." (He did not say the judges' hint was that the sentence was too harsh or might be unjust.) In response, the president authorized a pardon of all but the bond, and Pickering forwarded it to the United States attorney to implement.[81] It does not appear coincidental that the only pardons and the only dismissals that John Adams authorized of Sedition Act cases involved newspapers that had closed (Durell) or had been compelled to be sold (Greenleaf). Because of the pardon, Durell was imprisoned just under two weeks, rather than his four month sentence.

The Influence of Politics in Pardons and Dismissals

These New York prosecutions were political prosecutions of Republican enemies. That was evident in the selective prosecutions of vulnerable Republican newspapers. It was also evident in Alexander Hamilton's parallel efforts to manipulate the selection of New York's presidential electors, so they would be elected by the outgoing Federalist legislature rather than the newly elected Republican legislature.

After the Republicans swept New York's assembly in the May 1800 elections, Hamilton wrote a startling letter to Gov. John Jay.

> The moral certainty therefore is that there will be an Anti-foederal Majority in the Ensuing Legislature, and this very high probability is that this will bring *Jefferson* into the Chief Magistracy; unless it be prevented by the measure which I shall now submit to your consideration, namely the immediate calling together of the existing Legislature.
>
> I am aware that there are weighty objections to the measure; but the reasons for it appear to me to outweigh the objections. And in times like these in which we live, it will not do to be overscrupulous. . . .
>
> . . . They [scruples] ought not to hinder the taking of a *legal* and *constitutional* step, to prevent an *Atheist* in Religion and a *Fanatic* in politics from getting possession of the helm of the State.
>
> You Sir know in a great degree the Antifoederal party, but I fear that you do not know them as well as I do. Tis a composition . . . all tending to mischief—some of them to the overthrow of the Government by stripping it of its due energies[,] others of them to a Revolution after the manner of Buonaparte. . . .

> The calling of the Legislature will have for object the choosing of Electors by the people in Districts. This (as Pennsylvania will do nothing) will insure a Majority of votes in the U States for Foederal Candidates.[82]

Jay did not respond to Hamilton, and simply wrote at the bottom of his copy, "Proposing a measure for party purposes wh. I think it wd. not become me to adopt."[83] It was indeed, like the parallel sedition prosecutions in New York, "for party purposes."

CHAPTER TWELVE

New England Prosecutions

THE THIRD CAMPAIGN of enforcement of the Alien and Sedition Acts was designed to indict opposition newspaper editors at the fall 1799 sessions of the United States Circuit Courts, to place them under forfeitable bonds, and then to bring the prosecutions to trial in the spring 1800 sessions, all in order to intimidate and quiet Republican voices and to influence both state and federal elections. The timing of events was set by the existing schedules for the Circuit Courts. Thus, in Pennsylvania the prosecutions of William Duane moved forward during the session held October 11–22, 1799, while in New York the prosecutions of Jedidiah Peck, Ann Greenleaf, and William Durell began with indictments during the session held September 2–6. In Connecticut the Circuit Court session was September 17–26, and in Vermont it was October 3–11.[1]

New England, the most Federalist and least Republican part of the country in the late 1790s, had little tolerance for an opposition movement or an opposition newspaper. Even a small Republican newspaper in Connecticut, New London's *Bee,* was enough of an outrage that its editor, Charles Holt, was indicted under the Sedition Act in 1799. Another small Republican newspaper in Vermont, the *Vermont Gazette,* attracted prosecution of its editor, Anthony Haswell, by its criticism of a federal marshal in a back-page advertisement. That advertisement also provided a basis for initiating another prosecution against Rep. Matthew Lyon, one of New England's few Republicans in Congress. Prosecutions carried over from

1798 were reactivated in 1799 to force testimony against Lyon and against a new defendant, Dr. Samuel Shaw, apparently for funding or arranging for Lyon's press to publish a pamphlet critical of President John Adams. This New England portion of the third enforcement campaign under the Sedition Act kept the federal Circuit Courts busy in September and October 1799 and then in May 1800.

Charles Holt and the New London *Bee*

Charles Holt (1772–1852) started a Republican newspaper, the *Bee,* in 1797 in his hometown of New London, Connecticut.[2] Initially he stated an objective of impartiality, but quickly found that the consequence of publishing Republican submissions along with Federalist ones was a boycott and reprobation by the Federalist standing order that dominated Connecticut politics.[3] Holt shifted the *Bee* to a more Republican stance, and that brought the Sedition Act prosecution and imprisonment that this chapter describes. Shortly after his release, Holt married Mary Dobbs of New York City, the daughter of a former privateer captain; over the years they had eight children. Two years later in 1802, Holt moved the *Bee* to Hudson, New York, and sold it eight years later after starting a new newspaper, *The Columbian,* in New York City.[4]

Holt had quickly realized that "the duty of an impartial printer to communicate to the public on *both sides* freely" was not being observed by Federalist newspapers. Instead, "nine tenths of the newspapers in Connecticut are decidedly partial to *one side,* and keep the *other* totally out of sight." Consequently, four months after the Alien and Sedition Acts passed, the editor changed his editorial policy to state that "so long as my brethren in this state print on *one side only,* so long will I print on *the other.*" Still, Holt sometimes "decline[d] publishing the animadversions" submitted on "the flagrant conduct of *certain notorious individuals,*" because he did not want to give opportunity to "men determined on the ruin of our paper."[5] However, he was radicalized by his indictment and arrest under the Sedition Act, and stepped up the *Bee*'s attacks on the Alien and Sedition Acts, the Adams administration, and Federalist misrule. After his trial, Holt rapidly became, as Jeffrey Pasley said, "a nearly full-time party operative" alongside his day job as a Republican editor.[6]

Editing a Republican newspaper in Connecticut was bolder and riskier than elsewhere, because the state was the most Federalist-dominated state, and because in 1797 there was only one other among the twelve newspapers

FIGURE 12.1. Identified as Charles Holt. Miniature by Mary Way (1800). Courtesy I. E. Lieverant.

in the state. Holt's *Bee* quickly became the leading Republican newspaper in New England except for Boston's *Independent Chronicle*.[7]

Founding a Republican newspaper anywhere was an unprofitable endeavor, as Holt's venture showed, and the losses would be multiplied by any Sedition Act prosecution, imprisonment, and fine. Just after the *Bee*'s second anniversary, the state's leading Federalist newspaper derided its financial woes, saying the *Bee* "goes down hill fast." It listed "all his struggles, beggings, circular letters, &c.," and warned that all Holt's "plans will fail" because the "Jacobins are too poor, too few, and too dishonest to support you." The *Connecticut Courant*'s conclusion reflected the venom of the period's partisan newspapers: "set your household in order, and like your great ancestor, *Judas Iscariot,* hang yourself"![8] When Holt moved the newspaper to New York in 1802, his last issue described the financial mess that consistently surrounded the *Bee*. "At no time has the income of the Bee been adequate to its maintenance," and it had "a *deficit* of several hundred dollars at the end of every year." Some of the reasons were the minority position of Republicans in Connecticut, the state government "debarr[ing] all business, the federal government giving its printing to a Federalist press (even under Jefferson), merchant threats to "employ no man that takes the Bee," confinement of Holt "in gaol for debt," and adversaries' success in finally having "driven *us* out of the state." Sadly, Holt was "immured in that very Prisen for debt, from whence he had been so lately liberated from persecution."[9] Another obstacle faced by Republican editors was that most advertisements were placed in Federalist papers, because merchants and wealthier consumers tended to be Federalists. For example, in the issue immediately before the Sedition Act became law, the Federalist paper in town (the *Connecticut Gazette*) contained thirty-six advertisements, and the *Bee* only had twelve. Soon after, Holt reported to his leading backer that expenses were about double the newspaper's income, leaving him insolvent.[10]

Prosecution

The basis for the Sedition Act prosecution of Holt[11] was an article he published on May 8, 1799 that criticized the army and was deemed to discourage recruiting.[12] Since the readership was too small and the article too insignificant to drive away any recruits, there obviously was an underlying reason for the prosecution. That real reason was the totality of Republican content of the *Bee*—the reprinted articles that seventy percent of the time came from the *Aurora, Independent Chronicle,* or *Argus,* the original articles by John C. Ogden and others, and the excerpts from such lightning-rod sources as James T. Callender's *Prospect Before Us.*[13]

The army's recruiting was a sensitive subject, because it had barely begun ten months after Congress authorized it. Five days before Holt published the fateful article, Gen. Alexander Hamilton wrote to commanding Gen. George Washington that finally "the recruiting for the additional regiments has begun in *Connecticut New York New Jersey Pennsylvania* and *Delaware,*" and "might now also proceed in Maryland and Massachusetts," though not yet in Virginia. The appointment of officers was only slightly ahead; Hamilton added that "[n]ot a single field Officer has yet been appointed" in four states.[14]

Labeling the army a "standing army," instead of a provisional army, was an even more sensitive subject, because a major bête noire of Whig belief was that standing armies were dangerous and led to dictatorships like Caesar's. Republicans had adopted that Whig aversion.[15] Holt's article called the federal army a standing army in four places, such as when lamenting "our folly in not immediately petitioning for a stop to the further progress in raising a standing army." Yet Federalists had regularly done the same thing, calling the army a standing army, without raising any consideration of a Sedition Act prosecution. Secretary of State Timothy Pickering himself—the official who supervised enforcement of the Sedition Act—said that eight or twelve regiments would be added "to the Standing Army," in several official letters less than a year before Holt's reprinted essay.[16] A different standard obviously applied to Federalists.

The fall session of the United States Circuit Court was held in Hartford, Connecticut in September 1799. Chief Justice Oliver Ellsworth, while awaiting instructions to leave on the new diplomatic mission to France, presided alongside Judge Richard Law. Ellsworth, who was appointed to the Supreme Court by President George Washington in 1796, had served in Congress during the Revolutionary War and as a state court judge afterwards, and had a major role in the Constitutional Convention before becoming one of Connecticut's original senators under the new Constitution.[17] In giving the grand jury charge on September 17, 1799,[18] the chief justice referred to the Sedition Act, in saying that actions were misdemeanors if they "oppos[ed] the existence of the national government," and he adverted to seditious libel, in glowingly describing the common law as part of federal law.[19]

Later that day, the grand jury indicted Charles Holt for the essay on the army, charging that it defamed, brought into contempt, and incited hatred against the government, the president, and both houses of Congress. By criticizing the army, Holt was charged with inciting "unlawful combinations therein, for opposing and resisting the laws," and "resist[ing] oppos[ing] and defeat[ing] such laws" for establishment of an army. The indictment quoted the entire essay and selected out several passages for interpretive comments. The essay began by saying that potential recruits would never enlist because of possible problems with a "standing army." The prosecutor turned those problems around to make them calumnies of Congress and of the president: "(meaning that . . . regiments . . . had been by the President and the said Congress directed to be raised . . . for the purpose of gratifying an inordinate thirst for power and domination, and to satiate a grasping ambition existing in the president . . . and . . . Congress . . . with an intent and design to oppress the good people of these United States, and to trample upon, and destroy the liberties of the good people.)"[20] The essay referred to a future time when John Quincy Adams "is lord protector of the United States." The prosecutor again interpreted all preceding language into a claim that the army would forcibly and unconstitutionally install the president's son in that Cromwellian office: "(meaning that the said regiments had been, by the President, and . . . Congress, . . . raised for the purpose of subverting the Constitution . . . for the purpose of establishing arbitrary and despotic power in the hands of the said president . . . and in the hands of the said John Quincy Adams)." The essay ended by asking who would fight the army's battles, since "those who by rancour have excited war" were exempt as government officials. The prosecutor turned those general references into specific aspersions: "(meaning, that the said president of and. . . . Congress . . . , by their rancourous perverse and wicked Conduct, have purposefully provoked and excited hostilities, on the part of the French republic.)"[21] No Sedition Act case interpreted the meaning of statements more aggressively.

Three days later, an arrest warrant was issued to bring Holt to court, to answer the charge against him, and to post bond for his appearance at trial in the spring; he was arrested and taken to jail the next day, and bond was set at $1,000 from him and $1,000 from sureties. Holt asked for trial to be delayed, submitting an affidavit that he had been "immediately brought to Hartford, & committed to gaol," and that he was "entirely unprepared for a trial in the present term."[22] The implication is that Chief Justice Ellsworth expected a man who had been surprised by an arrest, and carried immediately to jail like a violent criminal, to go straight to trial in the remaining three days of the court session.

The spring session of the Circuit Court opened for business in New Haven, Connecticut, when Justice Bushrod Washington appeared on April 14, 1800 to join District Judge Richard Law.[23] The first president's nephew was following his circuit from New York City, where he had presided over the trial of William Durell and over the day-to-day delays of the trials of Jedidiah Peck and Ann Greenleaf. He was not wearied of Sedition Act trials yet.

Holt's trial took place that first day of the session. The trial was relocated from the State House to the Fair Haven Meeting House, because the crowd of onlookers was too large for the usual courtroom.[24] As described by a Federalist newspaper, the *Commercial Advertiser*, most of the trial consisted of argument about the constitutionality of the Sedition Act, with the judges unanimously upholding it on the grounds argued by the United States attorney. That attorney argued that because the Constitution empowered the federal government to raise armies for defense and protection, that power included the authority to punish interference with them. Further, a free government depended on the confidence of the people, and had the right "to defend its measures, from such slanderous attempts" as "malicious falsehoods." Citizens did not have the right "of uttering lies; malicious lies," so the "only liberty abridged by this law, is the liberty of *lying maliciously.*" Holt's lead attorney, David Daggett, argued that the Sedition Act was unconstitutional because the "powers of the general government" were specified and did not include creating such a crime, and because the necessary and proper clause could not be "extended by construction" to create new federal powers. Incredibly, Holt's counsel did not argue that the Sedition Act was unconstitutional because of the First Amendment, probably because Daggett was a Federalist and could not bring himself to make that argument.[25] Nor, apparently, did he argue that the question was far from being a "liberty of lying maliciously," and was instead a liberty of giving opinions and of informing the voters about governmental actions. He did argue that the essay was not libelous, because it was true or at least was a nonmalicious opinion.

Justice Bushrod Washington gave the jury charge. As described by a Federalist paper, it was "given in an unrivalled manner," and it "established the [Sedition] act to be constitutional, by a train of reasoning too powerful to be resisted." The justice resolved not only legal issues but fact issues as well. He "also proved the publication to be libellous, beyond even the possibility of doubt." Justice Washington then warned of the grave dangers posed by seditious libels: he "point[ed] out the tendency which libels on a free government have, to discredit and destroy the Government itself." And he pointed out "the heinous and aggravating circumstances which attended the publication of the libel" by Holt. The Federalist account became rhapsodic at this point: the justice "explained and pronounced the law in such a mild, clear and masterly manner, as to satisfy all parties, even the prisoner himself," and imposed the sentence "in a manner so commanding, and still so dignified, as to make the prisoner blush for his crime, and be satisfied with the punishment inflicted."[26]

Not surprisingly, the jury found Holt guilty. The judges sentenced him to three months in prison, a $200 fine, and continued imprisonment until the fine was paid. Prison was to start four days later, and just in case Holt did not appear, the judges, after sentencing him, issued a warrant.[27]

The Plasticity of the Sedition Act and of Seditious Libel

The indictment, and Holt's conviction under it, highlighted the plasticity of the Sedition Act. Negative words about the army were characterized as a seditious libel on the government since the army was part of it, on the members of Congress who voted for the bill to enlarge the army, and on the president who signed that bill. Every general comment on a danger of standing armies was inflated into a specific aspersion on the government, Congress, and the president. No protection was given for opinion, such as the opinion that the federal army amounted to a standing army (not just a provisional army) or the time-hallowed opinion that a standing army was a dangerous thing. The Sedition Act's defense of truth was not helpful, because opinions generally cannot be demonstrated to be true.

The trial and imprisonment also showed the severe chilling effect of a Sedition Act prosecution. Holt shut down his newspaper a week and a half prior to trial, and soon prison rendered him unable to publish it for three months. He wrote in his first post-prison issue of the *Bee* that he was now "instructed so well in the doctrines and consequences of libels and sedition," that "there is little danger of his again suffering for want of knowledge or discretion on these points."[28]

The case also showed how the Sedition Act could be used against political enemies. Holt's prosecution was initiated by Federalist competitors, Barzillai Hudson and George Goodwin of the *Connecticut Courant,* who sent the fatal essay in the *Bee* to the United States attorney.[29] They had long been publishing (and perhaps writing) articles that urged prosecution of Holt, such as noting a "very important partnership" of "JOHN COSENS OGDEN, now in Litchfield gaol, and CHARLES HOLT of New-London, printer of the Bee, and candidate for some other gaol, for publishing sedition." They had some help; Republican newspapers reported that two of Goodwin's brothers sat on the grand jury that indicted Holt.[30]

After his release from prison, Holt's fine was paid by Republicans, led by Sen. Stevens Thomson Mason, who the prior year had ridden to Vermont with Rep. Matthew Lyon's fine in his saddlebags. Holt's attorney was probably also paid by them. The fine was finally repaid by the federal government, after decades of effort, in 1844.[31]

The result of Holt's imprisonment was that the *Bee* was closed for nearly five months, from the April 2, 1800 issue shortly before trial, when the editor wrote that the issue "probably closes the editorial career of the printer," to the August 27 issue, when he wrote that the "Editor is extremely happy in once more commending the publication of the Bee."[32] During that period, Holt lost newspaper income and compensation as editor, and continued to face unpaid debts from earlier operation at a loss. He announced that he would publish a pamphlet account of his trial, but he was never able to afford to do so. The editor hoped for, but never received, federal printing business from the Jefferson administration.[33] The *Bee*'s financial distress required Holt to move it to another state, and Republicans in Hudson, New York collected a fund to pay for the move, in 1802. Holt's Republican newspaper was not welcome by the Federalists of Hudson, however, and their newspaper's editor, Harry Croswell, began attacking Holt even before the move, in the *Balance.* Croswell even established a special-purpose paper, the *Wasp,* to ridicule the *Bee,* commenting venomously that until Holt the river had "been tolerably free from these reptiles" (Democrats).[34] Holt also was physically attacked. Two years later, Croswell was prosecuted for seditious libel by the ascendant Republicans in New York, because of an article in the *Balance* attacking President Thomas Jefferson. Making the exchange of positions complete, Alexander Hamilton represented the newspaper editor in appealing his conviction and successfully advocated a liberalized standard for seditious libel cases.[35]

Holt sold his successor newspaper, the *Columbian,* in 1816 when he was finally able to get government employment.[36] His views of freedoms of press and speech long before the Alien and Sedition Act period are unknown, because he only established a newspaper in 1797 and was only twenty-four years old. The next victim's views, however, are visible from a much longer publishing career beginning in the 1780s.

Anthony Haswell and the *Vermont Gazette*

Anthony Haswell (1756–1816), editor of the *Vermont Gazette* in Bennington, was born in England to a shipyard carpenter, and came to Massachusetts with his father and a brother at age thirteen, after his mother's death. As a poor child in Boston, he was apprenticed to a pottery maker, and upon showing promise in composing ballads, he was released to be apprenticed to a noted patriot printer, Isaiah Thomas. Haswell came to Boston at an interesting time—he watched the Boston Massacre soon after his arrival, took part in the Sons of Liberty, and likely was part of the Tea Party. He enlisted in the Massachusetts militia during the Revolutionary War in 1776–1777,[37] and then returned to printing Whig newspapers in Worcester, Hartford, and then Springfield. He moved to Vermont and, with encouragement from a legislative committee, started a newspaper for the western half of the state, the *Vermont Gazette,* in 1783. He edited it until 1806, and then assisted his sons and others in publishing successor newspapers for the rest of his life.[38] Like other newspaper editors, Haswell also printed books and pamphlets, and his total of 201 publications included Thomas Paine's *Rights of Man,* though governmental and religious works predominated. He had ten children by his first wife, Lydia Baldwin, who died in April 1799, and seven children by his second wife, Betsey Rice.[39]

Haswell was a radical. In the early 1790s, he was a member of a Vermont Democratic–Republican Society and regularly published its resolutions in the *Vermont Gazette,* along with accounts of the societies elsewhere. He embraced egalitarian democracy with open arms.[40] His thought was outlined in an oration in August 1799. The American government "is the absolute will of the sovereign people," and officials are "amenable to them for their conduct"—and those officials are traitors if they "exceed the limits assigned to them." Haswell spurned the idea that the people's only role in government is to elect representatives, and then watch quietly. He defined liberty broadly as each person's right "to act for his own happiness without injuring others," and he praised "that immortal patriot Jefferson" and the

Declaration of Independence's assertion of a right to replace despotic government, which Haswell understood to be a continuing right. The oration ended with the aphorism "resistance to tyrants is obedience to God."[41] It was not difficult to guess which officials Haswell thought were exceeding their limits and necessitated resistance.

And Haswell stood squarely with Rep. Matthew Lyon in resisting tyrants. While Lyon was imprisoned under the Sedition Act, and had arranged a lottery to raise money to pay his fine (which Lyon called his "ransom"), Haswell printed an advertisement for the lottery that described Lyon's mistreatment by the federal marshal, Jabez Fitch. When Lyon was released and undertook his celebratory parade, Haswell composed a ballad—"Patriotic Exultation on Lyon's Release from the Federal Bastile, in Vergennes"—and led in serenading Lyon as he reached Bennington in February 1799. Its words could not have been better designed to enrage Federalist foes and particularly the federal marshal (who Lyon called a "hard-hearted savage"):

> Come let us raise the flowing strain,
> To bid our hero welcome,
> Our charter'd rights we will maintain,
> Tho' Fitch, or fiends [from] hell come.
> . . . .
> Come take the glass and drink his health,
> Who is a friend to LYON,
> First martyr under the federal law,
> The junto dared to try on.[42]

Haswell also gave Bennington's oration to Lyon, proclaiming that the representative had "suffered for admitting . . . what your enemies were pleased to call sedition, to be printed, while the panders of power have scattered that identical publication in their prostituted papers with impunity."[43]

Haswell's *Vermont Gazette* was the state's most important Republican newspaper. Throughout 1799, it published a constant drumbeat of criticism of the Federalists, denunciation of the Alien and Sedition Acts, support for Lyon and other victims, and description of Lyon's mistreatment, along with advertisements for Lyon's lottery.[44] That drumbeat did not go unnoticed.

Indictment for Sedition

Haswell was indicted at the October 1799 session of the United States Circuit Court for violating the Sedition Act.[45] Justice William Cushing presided over the court, and was joined by Judge Samuel Hitchcock, in Rutland. The indictment had two counts, one based on Haswell's publication of the strong language in the lottery advertisement for paying Matthew Lyon's fine and the other based on Haswell's reprint of a paragraph on "British Influence" from the *Aurora*.[46]

In the first count, language in the advertisement for the lottery that disparaged the marshal's post-trial treatment of Lyon was alleged to be a "seditious libel of and concerning the s[ai]d Government of the United States and the Administration thereof and of and concerning the Administration of Justice in the said Courts of Law."[47] The words that the indictment found to be criminal were the following (with the prosecutor's interpretations):

> To the Enemies of political persecution in the Western District of Vermont.
>
> Your Representative (meaning Mathew Lyon) is holden by the oppressive hand of usurped power (meaning the power and authority of the United States exercised by the Marshall of the s[ai]d District of Vermont in pursuance of a sentence of the U.S. Circuit Court . . .) in a loathsome prison (meaning the Gaol of the United State[s] at Vergennes . . .) deprived almost of the light of heaven and suffering all the indignities which can be heaped upon him by a hardhearted Savage (meaning Jabez G. Fitch Marshall . . .) who has to the disgrace of Federalism been elevated to a station . . . where he can satiate his . . . barbarity on the misery of his . . . victims.

The advertisement, continuing, said that Lyon's "ransom" (his fine and court costs) of nearly $1,100 must be paid before his release from prison, and that the lottery was being held to raise that amount for his release "after the measure of Federal vengeance is filled up."[48]

In effect, the federal government treated criticism of a federal marshal's despicable treatment of a defendant as criminal seditious libel against the entire government, administration, and court system. Those legal gymnastics were done because the Sedition Act did not criminalize disparagement of a federal marshal or of federal justice—just of the president, Congress, or government. And the case treated printing an advertisement—written by someone else and not typically reviewed by editors—as an intentional criminal act.

In the second count, a reprinted article castigating the federal government's policy of allowing former tories to hold public office, and castigating those former tories' evil deeds, was alleged to be a seditious "libel of and concerning the s[ai]d Government and the administration thereof." The article, copied from the *Aurora*, stated that

> our administration . . . publicly notified that Tories, men who had fought against our Independence . . . who had shared in the desolation of our Towns the Abuse of our wives sisters and Daughters . . . were Men worthy of the confidence of the Government.[49]

An arrest warrant was issued the day the indictment came down, and since Haswell was being held for debt in the county jail, a habeas corpus writ was signed ordering the county jailer to turn him over.[50] When two federal assistant marshals appeared, the bewildered Haswell asked them what he was charged with, and they would not answer; the warrant only stated that he had been indicted by a grand jury. He also asked whether he needed to pack clothes, with no response. Though sick, Haswell was forced to follow the marshals on horseback for fourteen hours, in the rain, with only an hour break. He was promised a good bed, but instead they "immured me in a loathsome dungeon." He was finally given the indictment "while walking from the prison to the court house" to enter his plea.[51]

Appearing in the Circuit Court, Haswell pled not guilty. When he answered honestly that he printed both articles, the United States attorney, Charles Marsh, argued that judgment should be entered immediately against the printer, since under English common law that was the only issue a jury needed to decide for the judges to rule that the accused was guilty.[52] Declining to do that, Justice Cushing continued the trial to May 1800 so that Haswell could exercise his right to prove the published statements were true. The judges required appearance bonds of $1,000 by Haswell and $1,000 by a friend in order for the editor to be released on bail between court sessions. Haswell and a friend signed the bond documents.[53] For the trial, Haswell engaged the same attorney, Israel Smith, who Lyon had tried to retain and who informally assisted the congressman, along with Joseph Fay.

Haswell's trial took place at the May 1800 session of the Circuit Court. Justice William Paterson presided over the court, joined by Judge Hitchcock, this time in Windsor in the heavily Federalist east side of Vermont.[54] Paterson probably gave the same grand jury charge as at his next court session, in New Hampshire, where the Federalist paper said "the Judge delivered a most elegant and appropriate Charge.—The *Law* was laid down in a masterly manner: *Politicks* were set in their true light, by holding up the Jacobins, as the disorganizers of our happy Country." When the case was first called, Haswell's attorneys asked for a delay of the trial because material witnesses were absent. The judges allowed a continuance of a few days to allow witnesses in route to arrive, but refused further delay to call the secretary of war or a Virginia militia general.[55]

During the trial, Haswell attempted to respond to the first count, the advertisement's criticism of the marshal's barbarity, by offering witnesses showing that the claim was true, that Fitch "usurped a power of adding to the vigour of the law, by unnecessary severity" toward Lyon. Moreover, the advertisement's censure was only of the marshal and not of "the authority of the United States." Haswell's counsel tried to respond to the second count, the appointment of old tories, by showing that it was true as well. They also argued that Haswell lacked seditious intent, because he had not written either publication, but merely reprinted them.[56]

Justice Paterson made a number of rulings that showed bias against the Sedition Act defendant. He not only refused to allow adequate time for Haswell to call Secretary of War James McHenry and Gen. William Darke as witnesses, but said their testimony and their letters (certified copies) "would not be admissible." That prevented Haswell from proving the truth of the article that was the basis of the second count, by showing that McHenry's letter to Darke acknowledged the federal policy of permitting appointment of former tories. The letter said that there were many "old Tories," and "I can see no reason why the recommendations of such characters should not also be considered" for military offices.[57] Paterson had the audacity to include in his charge to the jury that "no attempt at justification has been made" by Haswell on that second count. If Haswell's later account is accurate, Paterson's basis for excluding any defense that the former tory article was true was that the justice required proof that "the man holding the commission" was the very same "old tory" who "personally violated your females; or who personally discharged the murderous gun, that killed a citizen of America; or the proof is irrelevant."[58] Further, Paterson referred to Matthew Lyon as "a seditious libeller of your government, a convict justly suffering the penalty of a mild law," and called the advertisement "base repetitions of his crime." The justice then read the advertisement to the jury and interjected condemnations of its various statements about Lyon's treatment like the following two examples. In response to the advertisement's "oppressive hand of usurped power," Paterson said the reference was to "the constituted authorities of your country, the legislative, executive and judiciary powers," not just to the brutal marshal. In response to the "loathsome dungeon," he commented "what situation so proper to correct a turpitude darker than its deepest gloom!" Similarly, Paterson instructed the jury in a one-sided manner, saying that if they believed "that the intent was defamatory, and the publication was made, they must convict," but apparently not saying that if they did not find those things beyond a reasonable doubt, they must acquit Haswell.[59] The justice did tell the jury that, to convict, they must find Haswell's intent criminal, the publications seditious, and the published claims false. Not surprisingly, the jury did convict Haswell.

Sentencing took place four days later, and Justice Paterson sentenced Haswell to two months in prison, a $200 fine, payment of court costs, and upon release and payment, the posting of a good behavior bond. Separate orders set the court costs at $61.75.[60] Haswell's imprisonment began that same day, in a common cell "about twelve feet square, with one little grated window." Though he pled for detention in the Bennington prison, since his chronically sick son in their hometown might have his leg amputated, the judges "refused to urge my confinement in Bennington," and the marshal (whose barbarity was at issue) insisted on incarcerating Haswell in Rutland. However, Judge Noah Smith, a fellow Mason, interceded and after four days the editor was moved to Bennington's prison.[61]

From prison, Haswell wrote to President John Adams asking for remission of his fine and prison term "to avert impending ruin" and harm to his family.[62] Adams did not respond.

Even a two-month prison term—one of the shorter sentences under the Sedition Act—threatened ruin for any printer. Haswell had nine young children, had lost his wife a year earlier, and had remarried recently.[63] He had faced a year of threats "with prosecution under the sedition law; with taring and feathering, pulling down his house, &c." after he was arrested. He "operated perpetually on the verge of bankruptcy," and three months before his indictment under the Sedition Act, Haswell was confined to the jail yard for "inability to pay their debts."[64] Haswell had been jailed again for debt—or perhaps still was at the county jail—the day he was indicted. He had to close the newspaper for six weeks after his indictment, for the week of his trial, and for most of the two months of his imprisonment. Two months without income was a serious blow. Nine months later, Haswell wrote that "I have been reduced to distress, and almost to penury."[65]

Unsuccessful Second Prosecution

The judges and the United States attorney were so zealous about shutting down Haswell and his *Gazette* that they sought another indictment against him, just four days after the first, based on Haswell's publication of Ezekiel Bacon's fourth of July oration earlier in 1799.[66] The indictment charged that the speech was a seditious libel on the government, the president, and Congress, because of its claims that the federal government "obstruct[ed] the laws for the naturalization of foreigners under specious pretexts of national security," created "a multitude of new offices" in the expanded army, imposed "extravagant taxes," planned "to suppress pretended insurrections," "suppress[ed] the inestimable freedom of speech and of the press under the insidious pretences of checking licentiousness falsehood and calumny," "suppress[ed] under the name of sedition the remonstrances" from citizens, and kept up "standing armies." Curiously, the same grand jury that approved the indictment in Haswell's first case, four days earlier, refused to approve this second indictment. Perhaps they concluded that the printer was being prosecuted enough and should not be sued for each publication. The grand jury's response was "bill not found."[67]

When Haswell's imprisonment ended on July 9, 1800, "an immense concourse of people from the neighbouring county assembled to welcome him back to liberty, and to signalize their disapprobation of his imprisonment." Bennington had delayed its fourth of July festivities until his release, and now it fired a cannon in Haswell's honor while nearly 2,000 people paraded with him through the city. Justice, however, was slower arriving than the fourth of July. Haswell's fine was only refunded by the federal government to his heirs in 1844, twenty-eight years after his death.[68]

A Broad Understanding of Freedoms of Press and Speech Since 1785

In 1798, Haswell immediately condemned the Sedition Act. After printing it, he added a paragraph on "Liberty of the press, pen, and tongue" that said that liberty should "have remained inviolate" but had been violated, and he followed that with a paragraph quoting the First Amendment. Two issues later, he wrote that legislatures of "true Americans" doubtless "will readily declare the acts alluded to, unconstitutional & oppressive."[69] When Lyon was released from prison, Haswell's ballad included "The liberty of speech and press, our sacred right by charter," and he added a verse to the published version:

> The freedom of speech, to discuss and debate
> On the deeds of our servants who govern the State,
> We'll never resign to sticklers for power.[70]

Two months before his indictment, Haswell reaffirmed that seditious libel prosecutions restrain the press: "No tyrants base our laws invading, Shall gag our mouths, our press restrain, Our purses fleece, our rights profane."[71] But what was his understanding of freedoms of press and speech before the crisis of 1798–1801?

In 1785, Haswell published an essay by Lucius that discussed the scope of the Massachusetts provision that "the freedom of the press . . . ought not therefore to be restrained." Lucius said that meant no restraint at all, whether by prohibiting "licentiousness" or by a one penny tax:

> every measure then, that has the most minute tendency to prevent, suppress or restrain the publick papers, or the liberty of the press, is repugnant to the [state] constitution.[72]
>
> The press ought to be as free, and unconfined as air, and any restraint on it, is repugnant to the feelings and principles of Americans.[73]

Haswell reprinted other essays arguing that even a small stamp tax was a "shackle on the press."[74]

During the ratification debates over the Constitution, Haswell reprinted from Thomas Greenleaf's newspaper an essay by Cincinnatus (Arthur Lee). It called for a bill of rights and, in its absence, warned that liberty of the press "would be pulled down" by seditious libel prosecutions, such as those of Zenger in New York and Woodfall in England, or would be "restrained" by prosecution "for a libel." As a federal bill of rights was considered by congressional committees in 1789, the *Vermont Gazette* published one of Cato's essays under the caption "Liberty of the Press," which reasoned that "I would rather libels should escape than the liberty of the press should suffer the least infringement."[75]

In early 1795, shortly after President Washington's condemnation of Democratic–Republican Societies, Haswell published a front-page essay that affirmed people's right to censure government, by press or speech, and that rejected the rationale for the crime of seditious libel or seditious words. Brilliantly, it acknowledged "the right of the people to express their opinions . . . concerning the government," whether individually or in associations, and warned that "if a government can suppress, or stifle free strictures [criticism], on the ground of their tendency" to produce discontent with government, then all freedom of speech is at an end. "[N]o government can remain free, which has a discretionary control over the right of examining and censuring its proceedings." The claim "that the societies have censured the government, and therefore the government may justly exercise a criminal power over the societies," is "built on a wrong and vicious principle." It is not within government's legitimate authority "to inflict censures on the people," but instead it is "an original absolute right" of "the people to censure the government," in a republic established by the people.[76] That right to censure the government, under another name, was freedom of press and speech.

Haswell's selection of lengthy essays like these, as well as the heavy preponderance of his paper's shorter essays, showed a very expansive understanding of freedoms of press and speech. He did publish opposing views, though far less frequently.[77] But the *Gazette*'s content even thirteen years before 1798 was consistent with his condemnation of the Sedition Act during 1798–1801.

Beginning a Second Prosecution of Matthew Lyon

At the United States Circuit Court in Vermont in October 1799, where Justice William Cushing and Judge Samuel Hitchcock sat, the grand jury handed down two additional indictments under the Sedition Act, and the prosecutor revived two indictments from the prior year's session that had gone nowhere. Three have heretofore been treated as rumored but unconfirmed—the new indictments of Matthew Lyon and the resuscitated indictments of Judah P. Spooner and Alden Spooner,[78] and the fourth was confirmed somewhat recently but was not much noticed—of Dr. Samuel Shaw.

All four revolved around Matthew Lyon, the Republican member of Congress whose prosecution was at the beginning of the 1798 enforcement campaign. He remained a target of Federalists after his release from prison in February 1799, and everything came to a head at the October 1799 session, when he was expected to be back in Vermont from Congress.

Lyon was indicted a second time, in October 1799, for allegedly writing or publishing the language in the lottery advertisement that protested his mistreatment by the federal marshal, Jabez Fitch.[79] The single count was similar to Haswell's first count but added that Lyon himself did "write print utter and publish" the strong language in the lottery advertisement about the marshal, protesting Fitch's "barbarity" toward Lyon and calling the marshal a "hard-hearted savage." Like Haswell's indictment, Lyon's indictment (or at least the information prepared by the United States attorney, which is all that survives) charged that the challenged language about the marshal amounted to a seditious libel on the "government and the said courts of justice." The indictment ended by claiming that the advertisement was "in open contempt and violation of the good and wholesome laws of the United States."[80]

A major problem was that Matthew Lyon did not write or publish that language. The advertisement itself listed John Wood and James Lyon as the people in charge of Lyon's lottery, making them the apparent authors of the advertisement; and they were the actual authors as Haswell would testify the next May.[81] But Lyon was the big fish that the federal government was determined to catch again, and that is why he was indicted four days after Haswell, and why Judah P. Spooner, Alden Spooner, and Dr. Samuel Shaw were summoned as witnesses in his case. The Spooner brothers had been indicted in October 1798, but only to force them to testify that Lyon wrote one letter and read the other that were the major counts in his 1798 indictment. Nothing had been done to prosecute them then or since, until their testimony was again needed to implicate Lyon in October 1799.

There were other problems with Lyon's indictment, as well. Criticism of a federal marshal was not criticism of the entire government or the courts, but it had to be extrapolated in that manner to come under the Sedition Act. Also, surely citizens had the right to express disagreement with a minor official's actions, or with a court decision, but the case treated such disagreement as a crime.

A warrant for Lyon's arrest was issued a month later, but the deputy marshal reported that it could not be served, because Lyon had the good sense to stay out of Vermont. Lyon's new case was still alive at the May 1800 session, when it was listed as "continued,"[82] but the indictment was never served on him, and Pickering's firing just after that session left prosecutions without coordination.

Judah P. Spooner

Judah P. Spooner (1748–1807), Matthew Lyon's printer in the 1790s, was the son of a house builder, Thomas Spooner, and his wife, Rebecca Paddock, who though poor owned 111 acres inherited from Thomas's father. Both were descended from Mayflower passengers and other early New England immigrants. After his printing apprenticeship ended, Judah P. Spooner married Deborah Douglas, the daughter of a printer, and had seven children. At the outbreak of the Revolutionary War, Spooner joined the earliest volunteers and fought at the battle of Bunker Hill. Later in the war, he served on two privateer ships, and upon being captured, was imprisoned in a British prison hulk anchored off Brooklyn. The experience broke his health for life.[83]

Spooner was the printer for several newspapers (with periodic gaps attributable to alcoholism): *Dresden Mercury* (1779, in what became Hanover, New Hampshire), and then Vermont's first newspaper, *Vermont Gazette, or Green Mountain Post Boy* (late 1780–1781, in Westminster), followed by eleven years of absence from his family and from regular work, except for a year with the *Morning Ray* (1791–1792, in Windsor). Spooner then printed Matthew Lyon's successive newspapers: *Fairhaven Gazette* (1795), *Farmer's Library* (1795–1798), and *Scourge of Aristocracy* (1798–1799), until Lyon's imprisonment compelled the closing of his newspaper ventures.[84] On the side, Spooner continued to print books, pamphlets, and almanacs.[85]

Spooner was indicted the day after Lyon's first indictment, in October 1798. The same day a summons was issued for him to appear as a witness at Lyon's trial, making it clear why he was indicted.[86] His main role as a witness was to establish that Lyon read the Barlow letter to audiences (to his constituents, as a member of Congress), and that Lyon or his wife participated in arranging its printing as a pamphlet. (The Barlow letter charged President John Adams with making a "bullying speech" about France and deserving "a madhouse," while characterizing the Senate's response as "stupid" and "servility.") After Spooner testified,[87] nothing further happened in his case for a year, but the indictment was left hanging over him, probably to compel future testimony (if future prosecutions of Lyon and Haswell were contemplated) and to deter Republican printing.

Spooner's indictment charged him with printing the Barlow letter, which Matthew Lyon had been indicted for reading during speeches, and with aiding, abetting, and assisting its publication. Those two counts were similar to Lyon's second and third counts in 1798. In the indictment's words, Spooner did "write, print, utter, and publish . . . a certain false, feigned, scandalous and seditious libel entitled '*Copy of a letter from an American diplomatic character in France,*[']" and did "aid abet & assist" in that "seditious writing or libel," on the first of September 1798.[88] In fact, a pamphlet version of the Barlow letter was printed before Lyon's indictment and trial in October 1798, according to Lyon, and the printing was "at *Matthew Lyon's* press," according to Federalist newspapers.[89]

The day after the Circuit Court opened its October 1799 session, another arrest warrant was signed for Spooner, and he was quickly put in custody. The warrant stated that he was arrested to answer the October 1798 indictment, "and further to do and suffer as to Law and Justice appertains."[90] But not much law or justice appertained. The purpose for arresting Spooner was not to prosecute his case, because nothing happened. Instead, the purpose was again to compel his testimony as a witness. The day after his arrest came the indictment of Anthony Haswell, then three days later the indictment of Dr. Samuel Shaw, and then the next day the new indictment of Rep. Matthew Lyon. The facts in all of the cases overlapped. Spooner's testimony turned out not to be needed in 1799, because Haswell admitted printing the lottery advertisement and the old tory article, and Lyon could not be found and served in the district in order to bring him to trial, and Shaw's case was not ready for trial. After Spooner testified, and before the October 1799 session ended, Spooner's prosecution was dismissed.[91] That made it obvious that he was only indicted to pressure him to give the prosecutors helpful testimony, particularly if he was no longer needed if Dr. Shaw testified about the printing of the pamphlet.

Newspapers, which in 1798 had sporadically reported Spooner's indictment, extensively reported a new indictment in 1799. There was none; the original report probably mistook the continued appearance of Spooner's 1798 case on the 1799 court docket to be a new indictment. After the 1799 court session, a few articles related that the case was "discharged."[92]

Newspapers also reported the indictment and arrest of Lyon's son, James Lyon, who ran his father's printing shop. To the contrary, James Lyon was never a Sedition Act defendant, according to the court records, though he led a charmed life to avoid being indicted, so extensive were his activities as Lyon's editor and then as a founder of Republican newspapers elsewhere.

Alden Spooner

Alden Spooner (1757–1827), Judah P. Spooner's younger brother, worked nearly his entire career as editor of the *Vermont Journal.*[93] After serving in the Revolutionary War and working with his brother in Dresden and Westminster, Alden Spooner and a business partner established the *Vermont Journal* in Windsor in 1783, and he became the sole editor upon his partner's retirement five years later until his own retirement in 1818.[94] He and his wife, Sarah Burton, had nine children.

He was a Federalist during Adams's and Madison's presidencies, though he apparently lapsed to become a Republican during Jefferson's administration.[95] He did publish Lyon's letter that led to the first count of Lyon's and his own indictments, but he also published the scorching attack on Lyon ("Knight of the Wooden-Sword") that provoked that response. When Lyon was convicted and began his prison term, Spooner the Federalist wrote that it may prove "a noble triumph of liberty and our equal laws over that unbridled spirit of opposition to government, which is, at the present moment, the heaviest curse of America."[96] Consequently, the common assertion that under the Sedition Act "every defendant was a Republican"[97] is not quite true, since Alden Spooner and Jedidiah Peck were Federalists until the Sedition Act and prosecution under it changed their allegiances. That may explain why, though the Spooner brothers were indicted the same day in the same court, only Judah was mentioned in newspaper reports and not Alden.

Like his brother, Alden Spooner was indicted under the Sedition Act in October 1798,[98] and was required by a summons to bring the original of the Matthew Lyon letter that he published in *Spooner's Vermont Journal* and to testify in Lyon's case about receiving it from Lyon.[99]

Spooner's indictment charged him with violating the Sedition Act by printing and publishing that letter, which accused the president of subordinating the public welfare to power and pomp and of firing and rejecting qualified officials. That was alleged to be a seditious libel and "to defame the said government . . . and John Adams the President."[100]

As with his brother's prosecution, Alden Spooner's case was dismissed during the October 1799 term, doubtless for the same reasons.[101]

Dr. Samuel Shaw

Dr. Samuel Shaw (1768–1827), a Vermont physician, was a Republican activist and a Lyon supporter. Born in Dighton, Massachusetts, he moved to

Vermont in 1789, and made his home in Castleton, just five miles from Lyon's home in Fairhaven. Shaw was elected to the state legislature, serving 1800–1807, and then to the federal House of Representatives, serving 1808–1813. After that, he enlisted in the army as a surgeon, during the War of 1812.[102]

Shaw was prosecuted for an unspecified role in connection with the Barlow letter pamphlet. His indictment was issued in October 1799, as Justice William Cushing and Judge Samuel Hitchcock held court.[103]

His indictment charged him with "seditiously" causing the Barlow letter pamphlet to be "written uttered and published," and in aiding and assisting its "writing uttering and publishing." The indictment quoted the same passages that were quoted in Lyon's and Judah P. Spooner's indictments, and added several other passages such as that President Washington repeatedly terminated ministers friendly to France and replaced them with ministers antagonistic to that ally, and that President Adams was not sincerely trying to resolve differences with the Directory.[104] Four weeks after Shaw was indicted, an arrest warrant was issued to bring him into court to enter a plea and to post an appearance bond for the upcoming May 1800 session. Thus, he was not indicted merely to force his testimony, as the Spooner brothers were. It was not until February 1800 that Shaw was arrested, appeared, and was required to provide a $2,000 bond himself and two $1,000 bonds from others.[105]

Shaw's trial took place on the eighth of May 1800.[106] No information about the arguments or evidence has been located; the editor most likely to report on it, Anthony Haswell, lost his case three days earlier and had been required to begin his prison sentence immediately.

Shaw was acquitted by the jury[107]—and became the only Sedition Act defendant who won his case. That was an overwhelming result, but the press coverage was quite underwhelming. Though the acquittal was mentioned widely in the press, it was mentioned only in a single sentence that followed a paragraph on Haswell's conviction: "Doctor Shaw of Castleton, was likewise tried for sedition, and acquitted." Even someone turning the news into verse could not bring himself to exceed one sentence. "But e'er the late sedition law, Was not a match for Doctor Shaw."[108] A measure of vindication came when the court required the government to pay his costs—$19 to Shaw to reimburse his attorney fees ($5 was for the trial, and the balance was for reading the indictment and being on retainer), and additional amounts to pay the marshal and the witness fees, for an overall total of $155.20.[109]

What was Shaw's role in connection with the pamphlet? He was a zealous Republican, but that was not enough to implicate him. He did not provide the Barlow letter to Lyon, because Lyon testified that he received it from Sen. Abraham Baldwin. One clue is that Shaw was not indicted when Lyon and the two Spooners were indicted, in October 1798, but instead a year later. But his actions were at the same time as theirs, since they all did something in connection with the pamphlet that the government said was published the first of September 1798. Apparently Shaw's role was unknown to the prosecutor in October 1798, but was known by October 1799. Another clue is the dismissal of Judah P. Spooner's indictment within days of the handing down of Shaw's own indictment. That implies that Spooner implicated Shaw and agreed to testify about his role. Seditious libel law provided for the printer to be initially sued but to be dismissed when he disclosed the anonymous author or other person responsible for a seditious publication. A further clue is the summoning of Spooner, a printer, as a witness, and his actual testimony at Shaw's trial. There is no reason to think that Shaw, a physician, set type or pressed copies. His likely role, which Spooner might know, was either arranging for publication of the pamphlet or providing funds for its publication. Financial backing was needed, because Lyon at his trial testified that he could not pay a high fine or bail, and from his prison cell wrote that he could not pay his "ransom" to be released at the end of his four month sentence.[110] A final clue supports a financial role—the excessively exuberant description of Shaw by James Lyon a year and a half later. The day after visiting with Thomas Jefferson, Lyon wrote to the new president:

> I assure you that Dr. Shaw possesses an extensive knowledge of the people of Vermont,—of their interests and wishes; is a member of their Legislature, a Major in the militia and a man of handsome property (for that State) all of which he has acquired by the practice of Physic and Surgery, in which professions none there excell him! Never did a Mussleman [Muslim] visit the tomb of his Prophet at Mecca with more sincere pleasure and devotion.[111]

James Lyon was clearly grateful to Shaw for helping him in some critical way.

The 1799–1800 campaign for enforcement of the Sedition Act hit New England hard, suspending Connecticut's foremost Republican newspaper, suspending Vermont's leading Republican paper, threatening Rep. Matthew Lyon with a second prosecution should he seek reelection in Vermont, and intimidating two printers by leaving their 1798 indictments open for a year. One ray of Republican hope also escaped New England, as Dr. Samuel Shaw won his Sedition Act prosecution, becoming the only defendant acquitted anywhere.

CHAPTER THIRTEEN

Prowling the Circuit Stalking Sedition

WHEN THE CRUCIAL election year of 1800 dawned, the Adams administration's third campaign of enforcement of the Alien and Sedition Acts broke the pattern followed by the circuits in Pennsylvania, New York, Connecticut, and Vermont, which had gotten indictments in the fall 1799 sessions in order to hold trials in the spring 1800 sessions of the United States Circuit Courts. The administration instead sought both indictments and immediate trials in the spring 1800 sessions. One reason was that no time was left in order to influence the 1800 elections; fall trials would be too late. Secretary of State Timothy Pickering stressed to Justice William Paterson "the importance of bringing the criminal trials referred to, to a conclusion at this term" of court.[1] The other reason was that the person pressing for indictments during those spring 1800 sessions was Justice Samuel Chase

Chase, prowling the circuit to trample sedition wherever he sniffed it, pressed for the indictment of Thomas Cooper, nominally because of a handbill in rural Pennsylvania responding to criticism of Cooper for sending a job application to President John Adams, but more directly because of Cooper's public refusal to represent William Duane of the *Aurora* because of the Senate's "'gag." Chase held Cooper's trial during the Pennsylvania circuit session of April 11–May 2, 1800, between trials and sentencings in the Fries Rebellion cases. After leaving Pennsylvania for Virginia, Chase then pressed for the indictment of James T. Callender, who had raised calumny to an art form by his new book and his Richmond *Examiner* columns. Callender's trial was held during the Virginia session of May 22–June 4. In between, Chase virtually demanded indictment of the leading Republican editor in Maryland (May 7–16), and after Virginia, he insisted on indictment of the only Republican editor in Delaware (June 27–28). That fateful spring circuit provided the grounds for seven of the eight articles of impeachment against Chase during 1804–1805.

The Republicans were quite aware that these Sedition Act cases amounted to an election-year campaign that Pickering and Chase led, and planned to respond to political trials with political defenses. Consequently, the two central defendants acquiesced in immediate trials of their cases and emphasized Republican objections to Federalist policies. Cooper, from the "Prison of Philadelphia," published his account of his prosecution to show that it was a "political trial," and he had written his essays and handbill to show the same thing. Virginia's governor, James Monroe, cautioned Vice President Thomas Jefferson that "an attempt will be made to carry the sedition law into effect here, as an electioneering trick," and planned to discourage any protest that might provide "a plausible pretext" for Federalist gain from it.[2] Callender served as a magnet for that attempt, in the last and most important Sedition Act prosecution.

Thomas Cooper, and Prosecution for Disparaging the President's Political Mistakes

Thomas Cooper (1759–1839) was a polymath lawyer, chemist, economist, and political radical.[3] He only edited a newspaper, the rural *Sunbury and Northumberland Gazette,* for two months in 1799, but that was enough to attract a Sedition Act prosecution. Born to an affluent gentleman landowner in England, Cooper completed the course of study at University College, Oxford, though he did not receive a degree, probably because he was unwilling to subscribe to the Anglican Church's articles of faith. Afterwards, he practiced as a barrister, did limited medical studies and practice, and invested in a calico printing factory. In England, Cooper's political activities included writing a political treatise to advocate popular government, supporting the parliamentary reform movement, and visiting revolutionary France on behalf of one of the Constitutional Societies, where he spoke at the Paris Jacobin Society to the consternation of Edmund Burke.[4] Cooper's journey and his heated response to Burke's reproach placed him at risk of prosecution for sedition in England; some of his compatriots were charged with sedition in July 1793.[5] Consequently, in 1794 he emigrated to rural

FIGURE 13.1. Thomas Cooper. Engraving by Asher Brown Durand (1829). Courtesy Emory University's Rose Manuscript, Archives and Rare Book Library.

Pennsylvania with his wife Alice Greenwood and their children, and there he joined his close friend and fellow radical Dr. Joseph Priestley.

Cooper's broad interests are reflected in the books he wrote, on bankruptcy law (1801), chemistry (1812), an edition of Justinian's Institutes (1812), fabric dyeing and printing (1815), gas lights (1816), medical jurisprudence (1819), seditious libel law (1830), and the official edition of South Carolina statutes (1836–1839). He also wrote substantial pamphlets on the slave trade, political issues, chemistry, tariffs, state's rights, and economics.[6]

The "Indecency in These Strangers Thus Meddling with Our Government"

Cooper assisted the editor of the *Sunbury and Northumberland Gazette* by editing it for a little over two months in 1799 and by writing essays to fill unused space. His farewell essay was an "Address to the Readers" in late June 1799.[7] The address noted that one political party was "accused of an indiscriminate opposition to the measures of Government," while the other was accused of "indiscriminate support of every measure calculated to encrease the power of the executive." Cooper then outlined a thought experiment, asking what "system should I pursue?" if he were president and wished "to extend the influence of the governing powers" and "to encrease the authority and prerogative of the Executive."

Cooper's answer was eight steps that such a scheming president would pursue. Those included expanding federal power by claiming implied powers, and "restrict[ing] by every means in my powers the liberty of the press," particularly "the free discussion of public characters." Other steps were treating with "abhorrence the doctrines of the Rights of Man, and the Sovereignty of the people" and prohibiting immigration of foreigners who might hold those doctrines, limiting federal appointments and jobs to those of the president's party, gaining the support of the clergy, and favoring merchants over farmers. Finally, "the grand engine, the most useful instrument of despotic ambition would be a standing army" that would employ and arm partisans of the ruling party while intimidating the opposition, even if to get a standing army it was necessary "to invent, to forge, to create reasons," and adding to that an established navy which might induce foreign war if fortune smiled.[8] The resemblance of these theoretical steps to Adams administration policies was unmistakable.

Cooper's address was reprinted in the *Aurora* and in a number of Republican newspapers. It also was reprinted as a handbill through the efforts of Dr. Priestley, who fell off the wagon of political abstinence because he simply could not resist publicizing the address.[9]

A local resident, Charles Hall (who prosecuted cases for the United States attorney), saw the handbill and forwarded the "seditious address" to Pickering, in late July, adding that Dr. Priestley had the handbill printed and circulated. Pickering urged Hall to expand the observations in his letter and publish them as a handbill or pamphlet—and promised to have the government reimburse Hall for the printing cost. Pickering called Cooper's address "poison," regretted that the recently naturalized citizen had "not remained an alien," castigated the "indecency in these strangers thus meddling with our government," and hoped that "Mr. Rawle will prosecute both" Cooper and Priestley.[10] The same day, Pickering forwarded the *Aurora*'s reprint of Cooper's address to President Adams, and identified the author as "a warm opposition man," again expressing his sorrow that Cooper had become a citizen since he would "wish them both removed from the U. States." Adams responded by conjecturing that Cooper, who had written to Adams in 1797 unsuccessfully soliciting an appointment, was now "indulging his Revenge." The president said of the address that a "meaner, a more artful or a more malicious Libel has not appeared," and that he had "no doubt it is a Libel against the whole Government and as such ought to be prosecuted." A few weeks later, Abigail Adams wrote to a family member that "the whole address is one continued libel upon the Government," and "lets the cat out of the Bag for Cooper," because his failure to get a federal appointment "excited his Malovelence." The president had no more love for Cooper, viewing him as part of the newspaper "group of foreign liars."[11]

Pickering did not ask the United States attorney to begin a prosecution yet, however, because although he understood that Cooper's address was a Republican description of what President John Adams was doing, it did not unambiguously cast its stones at Adams. A jury might believe that the essay spoke only of what a hypothetical president might do.

Instead, Pickering came up with a devious plan to entrap Cooper in order to make a Sedition Act prosecution more secure, using the information that Adams had given him about Cooper's job application to lure him to respond. In late October 1799, Pickering wrote a long anonymous letter and sent it to a newspaper in Cooper's area.[12] It began by asking whether the Thomas Cooper who wrote the address "be the same *Thomas Cooper,* an Englishman," who had applied to the president for an appointment, and had misrepresented his political views as "agreeable to the PRESIDENT and government." Pickering goaded Cooper by twisting Priestley's recommendation letter to assure Adams of "the pliability of his friend Cooper's democratic principles." Pickering continued by saying that Adams "rejected *Cooper*'s application with disdain," and that Cooper wrote his address "in revenge." Pickering baited the hook with summaries of Cooper's application letter and Priestley's recommendation that implied a reliable source, and with reprinting the newspaper article as a handbill in Cooper's own county to make it difficult to ignore.[13] Cooper took the bait.

Cooper's response, at the beginning of November, was as heated as Pickering could hope. His handbill denied writing in revenge for being denied the appointment in 1797, and denied being inconsistent as a "democrat" in applying to a Federalist president because at that point Adams had only been in office five months and so was barely "in the infancy of political mistake." Then Cooper released his frustration at the anonymous newspaper attack by Pickering, and listed the "political mistake[s]" that Adams had committed in the ensuing two and a quarter years.[14] It was this response that Pickering sent to Rawle to prosecute.

Indictment and Trial

The United States Circuit Court in Philadelphia opened upon the arrival of Justice Samuel Chase. He charged the grand jury on April 12, 1800, and focused on the citizen's duty to obey such laws as the Alien and Sedition Acts, even if that citizen believed them to be unconstitutional. It "is the Duty of every Citizen to submit to it; and to give up his private Sentiments." Only the federal courts can decide if a federal law is unconstitutional; a jury "have no right to decide on the Justice, or the validity of the Law." Further, the grand jurors should "support your Federal Government, and the present administration thereof," and should support "our illustrious patriotic and beloved President, . . . that wise and vigilant Statesman."[15] Chase was quite aware that 1800 was an election year.

Cooper was indicted that same day, April 12, 1800, based on his responsive handbill of November 2, 1799.[16] The portions quoted in the indictment about Adams's political mistakes were the following:[17]

> Nor do I see any impropriety in making this request of Mr. Adams. At that time he had just entered into office; he was hardly in the infancy of political mistake; even those who doubted his capacity, thought well of his intentions. . . . Nor were we yet saddled with the expence of a permanent navy, or threatened under his auspices with the existence of a standing army. Our credit was not yet reduced so low as to borrow money at 8 per cent in time of peace, while the unnecessary violence of official expressions might justly have provoked a war. . . . Mr. Adams had not yet projected his Embassies to Prussia, Russia, and the Sublime Porte; nor had he yet interfered as President of the United States to influence the decisions of a Court of Justice. . . . This melancholy case of Jonathan Robbins. . . . which the people ought to be fully apprized before the election.[18]

These opinions about a president's "mistake[s]" were treated as crimes. The indictment tracked the Sedition Act to charge that Cooper "did write print utter and publish a false scandalous and malicious writing against the said President," with intent to defame him, bring him into contempt, and excite the people's hatred of him. Cooper pled not guilty.[19]

The week before Cooper was indicted, he was arrested in order to make him sign an appearance bond (or remain in jail until his trial began). Four days after the indictment, the court held a pretrial hearing on subpoenas, on official copies of documents, and whether the president could be compelled to testify (evidently to establish that he disclosed Cooper's application for a position, which compelled the applicant to defend himself, Cooper said).[20]

The five-month gap between the November 1799 handbill and the April 1800 indictment has drawn speculation about whether the handbill was the real cause of the indictment. The delay in indicting Cooper was unavoidable, because the next session of the Circuit Court after the November handbill was that April 1800 session.[21] However, the delay in arresting and binding him was not unavoidable, and the arrest and bond appear to have been triggered by an event in the preceding two weeks. That was Cooper's actions in Duane's proceeding in the Senate (Chapter 10), in his very public letter refusing to represent Duane because of the Senate's *"gag in my mouth,"* referring to its restrictions that effectively silenced most defense arguments. Federalists complained of that "impudent letter" to the Senate by a "notoriously infamous" "Jacobin," and correctly believed that it was carefully planned theater. Cooper's public letter followed escalating criticism in the Federalist press of the "runaway English Jacobin," who "fled his country to escape the noose of justice."[22]

Cooper's trial was held on April 19, 1800 in the Circuit Court in Philadelphia, with Chase joined by Richard Peters as the judges—and with Timothy Pickering sitting with them at the judges' bench.[23] The trial's significance was shown by the attendance of most of the cabinet and many members of Congress. The morning began with "considerable altercation between Judge Chase and the defendant with regard to the character of the evidence to be produced." The issue was Chase's opinion "that no man should hazard an assertion but upon sufficient and legal evidence"—that before making any assertion Cooper should have had the documentary proof in hand—so that he should not be allowed to subpoena government witnesses and government documents before or during trial to prove his assertions.[24] That opinion was in response to Cooper's request for subpoenas of the president, Pickering, and eight members of Congress, in order to have them testify. Chase had refused to subpoena the president, refused to follow state procedure on subpoenaing other witnesses, and denied there was any right to subpoena official copies of public records. Now Chase questioned whether Cooper's claims about Adams's mistakes would be permitted to be proved to be true by testimony from the other witnesses, and the justice said those witnesses would not be allowed unless the defendant first persuaded the judges "they are material witnesses"—what their testimony would be and what it would prove.[25] As a result of these rulings, Cooper did not call any witnesses, though several arrived. By contrast, Chase did not require the prosecutor to persuade the judges in advance that his witness was material.

The United States attorney, William Rawle, made two arguments. First, Rawle stressed that seditious libel was a very dangerous thing, repeating the rationale for the Sedition Act. It was lamentable that everyone "should think he had a right to attack and overset those authorities and officers" of government. It "was high time for the law to interfere and restrain the libellous spirit . . . against the highest and most deserving characters" in office. Otherwise, "the peace of the country would be endangered." "Error leads to discontent, discontent to a fancied idea of oppression, and that to insurrection," like the Whiskey Rebellion and the Fries Rebellion. Second, Rawle contended that Cooper committed an "aggravation of the offence" by identifying himself as author, in the early November response and in a statement to a magistrate. Unlike most writers of essays who wrote anonymously or used pseudonyms, Cooper "availed himself of those advantages" of signing his name in order to increase the response's influence by the signature of a lawyer. A person of "education has it more in his power to extend the mischief" that he propagates. "Such conduct must have arisen from the basest motives."[26]

Rawle then put on a single witness to prove a single thing: that Cooper was the author of the early November response. Rawle again followed English common law, that the only issue for the jury to decide was whether the defendant wrote or printed the detraction (unless there was also an issue of what the "innuendos" or unclear references meant in the publication). Once the jury determined that, the judges determined whether the publication was libelous, and then inferred malicious intent from it being libelous, and assumed damages from those things. Typically, the judges tricked the jury into wording its trifling determination as a general verdict, and wrapped into it the unannounced determinations of the judges about libel, intent, and damages.[27]

Next, Cooper attempted to present his case, representing himself. He began by saying that the jury must find two things in order to convict him: that the publication was false and that it was "published from malicious motives." He would show that everything published was true, and everything was disseminated from innocuous motives as shown by it all relating "to an examination of [the president's] public conduct, and no improper motives are imputed to him." Cooper noted that the country is "almost equally divided, into two grand parties" with opposing views. For example, Federalists believed "the liberties of our country endangered by the licentiousness" of the press and Republicans believed liberties were endangered "by the restrictions of the press." He said he trusted the jury to decide fairly because "you have some character to support and some character to lose."[28] Much of Cooper's defense, as Joanne Freeman points out, was a consummate example of "the logic and language of honor"—not only did he trust the jury to protect its own character, but he had assaulted only public character and not private character, and objected to the October attack on his own private character.[29] The rest of Cooper's arguments were an implicit appeal to voters in the upcoming elections, rather than an appeal to judges and jury.

Cooper raised another defense—freedom of the press. He noted the injustice that "the press is open to those who will praise" the administration, but "the threats of the law hang over those who blame the conduct of the men in power." He suggested that his published assertions "would have been better confuted by evidence and argument than by indictment." And he pointed out the tie to an informed electorate, saying he did not see "how the people can exercise on rational grounds their elective franchise, if perfect freedom of discussion of public characters be not allowed"—"if these prosecutions in *terrorem* close all the avenues of information." Moreover, it was entirely appropriate for Cooper to respond to Pickering's "cowardly slander which dragged me in the first instance before the public."[30]

Cooper then tried to address each of the president's mistakes, as listed in the November handbill, to show that his descriptions were true and nonmalicious. When he referred to the early morning altercation, Justice Chase denied that "the public documents" must be "at your service," because "[i]f you undertake to publish without having proper evidence before you to justify your assertions, you do it at your own risk." However, after a caution from Judge Peters, Chase relented and allowed Cooper to use public documents as evidence and to read from anything he wished.[31]

Rawle began his rebuttal by saying he was astounded that Cooper claimed to be "best qualified to judge whether the measures adopted by our government" are well chosen, rather than the president "to whom this country has thought proper to confide its most important interests." The United States attorney said that Cooper's malicious intention was shown by the very fact of trying to influence the public to disagree with the president ("a settled design to persuade the public that the President of the United States is not fit for the high office he bears"), and by the unmerited criticisms themselves ("suspecting him of the motives he disclaims" because Cooper's assertions "cast an unmerited reflection on the general character and conduct of the President"). Totally ignoring the presumption of innocence and the government's burden of proof, Rawle said Cooper's malicious intention was also conclusively proved by "the words of this charge in the indictment."[32] The uselessness of the defense of truth in the Sedition Act was shown by Rawle making no effort to prove the publication was (in the words of the act) "false" as well as "scandalous and malicious," as well as by Cooper being blocked from subpoenaing documents and some witnesses to show the publication to be true.

More Bias from Justice Samuel Chase

Justice Chase began his jury charge with a defense of the Sedition Act. Punishing libelous publications "is necessary to the peace and welfare of this country," because our government is "founded on the opinions and confidence of the people." Thus,

> All government which I have ever read or heard of punish libels against themselves. If a man attempts to destroy the confidence of the people in their officers, their supreme magistrate, and their legislature, he effectually saps the foundation of the government. A republican government can only be destroyed in two ways: the introduction of luxury, or the licentiousness of the press. This latter is the more slow, but most sure and certain, means of bringing about the destruction of the government. The legislature of this country, knowing this maxim, has thought proper to pass a law to check this licentiousness of the press.[33]

The bulk of Chase's charge was a stream of rulings that favored the prosecution and made conviction certain. That flow of bias belied claims that he showed "moderation" and was "fair," and better supported the claim of Republican Sen. Stevens Thomson Mason (who was there) that "Chase in his charge to the Jury . . . shewed all the zeal of a well fee'd lawyer and the rancour of a vindictive and implacable enemy."[34] Chase said the prosecution must prove that Cooper published the handbill, and that he did it with "intent to defame"—and then said both things had been proved. "The fact of writing and publishing is clearly proved," and Cooper's conduct "showed that he intended to dare and defy the government, and to provoke them." Further, "if there are doubts as to the motives of the traverser, he has removed them," by saying his "motives in this publication were to censure the conduct of the President." Chase then made explicit what he had implied, that censuring the president is criminal. "It is no apology for a man to say, . . . that he [the president] has done acts which prove him unworthy the confidence of the people, . . . and unfit for the important office to which the people have elected him."[35]

Chase refuted each assertion in Cooper's handbill, such as the president obliging the country "to borrow money at eight per cent. *in time of peace.*" He added, "I cannot suppress my feelings at this gross attack upon the President." Similarly, Chase objected to the assertion that the president helped form a "standing army." To assert "that we have a standing army in this country, betrays the most egregious ignorance, or the most wilful intentions to deceive the public." Yet the president himself, within four weeks of Cooper's trial, objected to the "exorbitant interest" rate of eight percent, in a letter to the treasury secretary, and other leading Federalists, such as former judge Robert Troup, reported that the interest rate was "complained of."[36] And even Pickering had called the army a "standing army," as we saw in the last chapter. After contradicting each assertion, such as about Jonathan Robbins, Chase then characterized it as seditious and malicious. "[T]his is a charge on the President, not only false and scandalous, but evidently made with intent to injure his character, and . . . to operate on the passions of Americans." The charge was "made with intent to bring the President into contempt and disrepute." Chase objected most vehemently to Cooper's statement that his last assertion would inform voters "before the election," and treated any effort to influence voters as a crime rather than as part of freedoms of press and speech. Cooper's perfidious design was "to arouse the people against the President so as to influence their minds against him on the next election," and that "proves, that the traverser was actuated by improper motives." "This publication is evidently intended to . . . inflame their minds against the President, and to influence their votes on the next election," something that the justice saw as clearly seditious.[37] Chase was also bothered by who Cooper wanted to influence the people to elect—"that party who are incessantly opposing and calumniating the government." The justice ended his rebuttal of Cooper's assertions with a summary: the publication "is the boldest attempt I have known to poison the minds of the people." Chase ignored Cooper's defense of freedom of press and speech—until after the jury had delivered its verdict—after which Chase, at sentencing, padded the record by acknowledging Cooper's "right to express your sentiments."[38]

Finally, Chase instructed the jury on the burden of proof, and placed it squarely on the accused rather than on the prosecution. Cooper "in his defence must prove every charge he has made to be true; he must prove it to the marrow. If he asserts three things, and proves but one, he fails; if he proves but two, he fails in his defence, for he must prove the whole of his assertions to be true." Cooper's earlier point was ignored, as well as contradicted, that the prosecutor had the burden of proving that his publication was false and that his intent was criminal. Not surprisingly, the jury found Cooper guilty. And equally unsurprisingly, Judge Peters later commented that he least liked to sit with Chase in Circuit Court, because "he was forever getting into some intemperate and unnecessary squabble."[39]

The court, four days later, gave Cooper an opportunity to provide financial information that might mitigate his sentence. Chase said he suspected that the Republican party would pay Cooper's fine, and if that were true, "I would go to the utmost extent of the power of the court" with a high fine. Judge Peters disagreed with considering party backing, and Cooper denied any such arrangement. Chase then described his own intent in Sedition Act prosecutions: "I will restrain, as far as I can, all such licentious attacks on the government of the country."[40]

Cooper was sentenced the next day, to a fine of $400, imprisonment for six months, and before release, a good behavior bond of $1,000 from himself and $500 each from two sureties. Pickering's secretary jested that, by being sent to prison, Cooper's application to Adams for a place had finally been approved![41] Soon after he took his place, Cooper, while expressing his appreciation to friends who proposed to petition to cancel his sentence, defiantly said he would not leave prison until he received "a satisfactory acknowledgment from Mr. Adams, of the impropriety of his conduct to us;" he would not be a pawn of "electioneering clemency." So Cooper was only released from prison in October. His suffering was greater than most Sedition Act defendants, because his wife died "a few days before" his imprisonment ended.[42]

Despite this, Cooper won what he called his "political trial" under the Sedition Act.[43] He sought to be prosecuted, courageously defended himself on the basis of truth and freedoms of press and speech, refused to seek to shorten his sentence or reduce his fine, continued writing Republican articles—and immediately published an account of the trial from "Prison of Philadelphia." His trial was a public relations coup for Republicans shortly before the elections of 1800, and a sobering demonstration of the repressiveness of the Alien and Sedition Acts and of the Adams administration.

Two weeks after his release, Cooper traveled to New York to demand that Alexander Hamilton be prosecuted under the Sedition Act for his newly published attack on John Adams, which was significantly harsher than Cooper's criticisms. Cooper wrote that his purpose was "instituting against you, Sir, a prosecution under the detestable . . . *'Sedition Law'*," to show "whether *Republicanism* is to be the victim of a law, which *Aristocracy* can break through with impunity."[44] As Cooper doubtless expected, no federal official showed any interest in prosecuting Hamilton, and that was precisely what Cooper sought to show. Cooper also began a lifelong campaign to have the federal government repay his fine. His posthumous success did not come until fifty years later.[45]

Cooper, like many other Sedition Act defendants, had long before advocated a broad understanding of freedoms of press and speech, a right of "publishing every opinion on subjects of importance, whatever may be its real or supposed tendency."[46]

Life after Prison

Cooper's career after his Sedition Act prosecution took some unexpected turns. He was rewarded by Pennsylvania's Republican governor with appointment as a presiding judge of a common pleas court district in 1804, though he was removed seven years later as Pennsylvania's Republican Party split.[47] The year after his judicial removal, Cooper was appointed professor of chemistry at the predecessor to Dickinson College, and then at

University of Pennsylvania four years afterwards. He was elected to serve on the faculty of University of Virginia in chemistry, natural philosophy, and temporarily law, as Thomas Jefferson sought to establish a world-class faculty, but he never served because the legislature appeared to be on course to thwart the appointment based on Cooper's religious doubts. Nevertheless, Jefferson's assessment was that "Cooper is acknowledged by every enlightened man who knows him to be the greatest man in America in the powers of mind and in acquired information."[48] Cooper was more successful with the predecessor to University of South Carolina, where he became professor of chemistry and then, in 1820, president.

Cooper entered another controversy when, forsaking his earlier condemnation of slavery, he defended it as just and unavoidable and held enslaved people.[49] He supported nullification and secession during the nullification crisis, and was "the schoolmaster of state rights" at University of South Carolina.[50] There, he survived an attempt to remove him as president because of religious heterodoxy, but resigned soon after in 1833.[51] Only one other Sedition Act defendant had more unexpected turns in his final years: James T. Callender.

James T. Callender

James T. Callender (1758–1803), a writer and immigrant radical, was the defendant in the last trial under the Sedition Act, a case that furnished the majority of the grounds for impeachment of Justice Samuel Chase. Born in Scotland to a tobacconist father, Callender's life was a series of failures—he failed to gain financial support for a literary life, was dismissed after seven years as a clerk in a government title office, and had to flee the country when a warrant was issued for his arrest for seditious libel based on his book, *The Political Progress of Britain.* Arriving in Philadelphia in May 1793, he wrote reports on congressional proceedings for a Federalist newspaper, the *Philadelphia Gazette,* until he was terminated for also writing anonymous pieces for the leading Republican newspaper, the *Aurora.*[52] When Callender made plans to work for the British minister, Robert Liston, to write pro-Federalist material, Benjamin Franklin Bache intervened and hired the writer in May or June 1798 (displacing William Duane to do so). Bache was rewarded with complaints about not allowing some of Callender's columns to be printed.[53]

When Congress passed the Sedition Act in July 1798, and soon after his wife's death, Callender fled again, to Virginia on foot, leaving his children in the care of a Philadelphia Republican leader. The leading Federalist newspaper announced his move, saying that "a little dirty toper, with a shaved head and greasy jacket, nankeen pantaloons, and woolen stockings, was arrested at a whisky distillery . . . under the vagrant act," and that he identified himself as Callender. The newspaper, making it clear Callender was not at a distillery by accident, hoped measures would be taken "to suppress this apostle of sedition," "the notorious Scotch fugitive, the calumniator of Washington, Adams, law, order, government, God."[54] After a period of hiding, Callender began writing for a Republican paper in Richmond, the *Examiner.* We will come back to his disappointments after release from prison—his fruitless demands for a federal job, his mounting threats against Jefferson and other Republicans, his editing a Federalist newspaper—the Richmond *Recorder*—and his articles attacking Republican leaders. Callender died in 1803, by suicide through drowning in the James River, though the coroner's jury pronounced it an accident connected to his alcoholism.[55]

No one, then or now, would challenge Callender for the title of the most scurrilous of the Republican writers of the 1790s. John Adams was struck by his vitriol the year after his arrival in Philadelphia, calling Callender's book that led to his British indictment the "most astonishing Concentration of Jacobitical Malevolence that ever Scottish Spite exhibited."[56] Callender's best-known publication, in July 1797, alleged that Alexander Hamilton, while secretary of treasury, engaged in "very improper transactions" with James Reynolds of New York. To defend himself, Hamilton had to admit and detail an affair with Maria Reynolds and to state that the payments in question were blackmail payments to her husband.[57]

Instructions from Pickering

Callender's columns for the Richmond *Examiner* flayed Adams and his administration. In response, Pickering fumed about the *Examiner*'s "audacious calumnies against the Government" and wished to "arrest them by legal process." In August 1799, the secretary of state sent instructions to the United States attorney for Virginia to scrutinize every issue of the *Examiner* for "any libellous matter against the government or its officers, . . . that the Editor or Editors may be prosecuted."[58] As the reference to "Editors" showed, Pickering sought prosecution of both Meriwether Jones, the owner and nominal editor, and Callender, who Pickering called "the *actual* editor" (a role Callender denied). Two months after those instructions, Pickering added to those complaints that "a virulent Jacobin paper called the *Examiner,* printed in Richmond," published letters between Talleyrand and Pinchon. (Pickering's objection was mostly that the letters were helpful to the president's new initiative to send envoys to France, which he opposed.)

Pickering was not Callender's only opponent. In July 1799, a Federalist committee was formed in Richmond for "peaceably conveying this *political impostor*, out of the limits of our city," or in a less sanitized version, to beat Callender and destroy the *Examiner* office in order to end the intrusion of his opinions on the public. Richmond authorities protected him with a volunteer militia company.[59]

Callender also wrote on the side, and in early 1800 came out with the first volume of *The Prospect Before Us*, a book dripping with invective against Adams and other Federalists, which became the basis of Callender's indictment and trial under the Sedition Act. Its preface began by stating that the "design of this book is to exhibit the multiplied corruptions of the Federal Government, and more especially the misconduct of the President, Mr. Adams." In that election year, it warned that "nothing but the dismission of Mr. Adams can save the United States, either first or last, from the calamities of a French war." From there, the book became more strident. The next page charged Secretary of the Treasury Oliver Wolcott with presiding over "scenes of plunder, which might force a blush into the beak of the most hungry cormorant, that ever took his flight from Connecticut to roost on the Federal Treasury," and prescribed for the secretary of state "the necessity of sending Timothy Pickering to a *mad house*." Quoting a Virginia Republican, the preface said the proper title of the act creating the Bank of the United States was "'an act of *perjury*,'" and that Hamilton's funding system was contrived "'to enable speculators and monied men, to *defraud* the great bulk of the community'" and to transfer wealth "'to those who *pilfered* it.'"[60]

A Richmond Federalist, John B. Walton, saw the newspaper announcement for the forthcoming book, and wrote a letter to Pickering that said "the many invectives charged against the Executive Officers of the Gen. Government should meet with a decided investigation of the Author[']s conduct, whether his charges are libelous." He lamented that Virginia's legislature and courts "are so crowded with Jacobins and French partisans that the attempt would be vain" there. Walton's letter said he enclosed a copy of *The Prospect Before Us*, but ended with a postscript that it was "not out of the press" yet. Thus, his description of the book's content as worthy of investigation for seditious libel was not based on seeing an actual copy of the as yet nonexistent book. But his description helped credential him as a loyal Federalist, and he did not delay sending the letter and did not rewrite it, because its main point was to apply for a federal appointment. Four weeks later, Walton wrote again to send the book, warning that its "abuses of Government" were "too black and degrading" to describe.[61]

Trial of Callender

In May 1800, a copy of *The Prospect Before Us* was given to Justice Samuel Chase when his circuit brought him from Cooper's trial in Philadelphia through Maryland to Callender's trial in Richmond. The donor was Luther Martin, the Federalist attorney general of Maryland, who marked passages that he deemed to violate the Sedition Act.[62] The Baltimore *American,* a Republican newspaper, reported that Chase said "if a *virtuous* jury can only be collected, he'll punish *Callender* with a vengeance." The justice publicly said that "he would teach the lawyers in Virginia the difference between the liberty and the licentiousness of the press."[63]

After Justice Chase arrived in Richmond, the United States Circuit Court convened on May 22, 1800, where he was joined by the local Judge Cyrus Griffin eight days later.[64] Chase gave the same charge to the Richmond grand jury that he gave to Cooper's grand jury, and it was equally effective in impelling a grand jury of Federalists to indict a Republican for seditious libel. The grand jury approved a short presentment that Callender's book violated the Sedition Act, on May 24, and then approved a sixteen-page indictment that was entered in court the next Monday, May 26.[65] The United States attorney, Thomas Nelson, evidently drafted the presentment without having Callender's book, and then got Chase's copy and drafted the indictment.

The indictment charged Callender with seditious libel in criticizing President John Adams in *The Prospect Before Us.* The indictment's opening quotation of a criminal passage was Callender's statement (an opinion) that

> The reign of Mr. Adams has been one continued tempest of malignant passions. As President, . . . the grand object of his administration has been to exasperate the rage of contending parties, to calumniate and destroy every man who differs from his opinions.[66]

The indictment cited many examples of the president's malignancy—he brought "a French war, an American navy, a large standing army, an additional load of taxes, and . . . despotism"; he sought to yoke "us into an alliance with the British tyrant"; his hands reeked "with the blood of the poor, friendless Connecticut sailor," Jonathan Robbins; he "completed the scene of ignominy which Mr. Washington began." Adams was "[f]oremost in whatever is detestable," a "professed aristocrat," a "hoary headed incendiary," an "object . . . of horror." Even more intolerable than those detractions, *The Prospect* sought to influence voters, who would "make your choice between innocence and guilt, between freedom and slavery," and "between Adams, war and beggary, and Jefferson, peace and competency."

The indictment listed about twenty such quotations, in two counts, the first for writing, printing, uttering, or publishing the writings, and the second for printing or publishing them.[67]

Immediately after the grand jury indicted Callender, Chase issued an arrest warrant and "dispatched the Marshall instantly in pursuit of him" to bring him into court. The court had subpoenaed ten witnesses to testify to the grand jury, and subpoenaed most of them to testify at trial.[68]

Chase showed bias at every turn. The defendant, after being found three days later, on May 27, asked that the court subpoena seven witnesses for his defense, and was required by Chase to list in an affidavit what each witness would say. Chase evidently excluded the proposed testimony of five of them, because only two were summoned. By contrast, the prosecution was not required to list its witnesses' testimony, and did not have any witnesses excluded. Callender was represented by three attorneys: Philip Norborne Nicholas (Virginia's attorney general), George Hay (the governor's son-in-law), and William Wirt (later the federal attorney general). Chase rejected their request for postponement of the trial to the November session despite their protests that defense counsel could not possibly be ready for an immediate trial and that witnesses and documents could not be obtained; the justice instead would hold the trial in just five days (which he ultimately postponed by one day further). Making one concession, he released Callender on a modest bond.[69] According to testimony in Chase's impeachment proceeding, when the first effort to find Callender failed, Chase said "I am afraid we shall not be able to get the damned rascal this court," and when the jury panel was listed, Chase asked if it "had any of those creatures or people called democrats on it," and said if so "to strike them out." In the meantime, Chase intimidated a witness and editor, Meriwether Jones of the Richmond *Examiner*, by writing to demand that Jones compel the author of an article disparaging Chase to identify himself, saying that "I will sue him" and "pledge myself to . . . prove that he is a false, scandalous, wicked, and malicious *slanderer and caluminator*."[70]

The day of Callender's trial, June 3, began with Justice Chase hearing motions from Callender's attorneys. They again requested that the trial be postponed, asking how they could show the truth of Callender's statements if their witnesses were not there. Chase again denied their motion.[71] They argued that the Sedition Act, which was violated by statements that were both false and malicious, was not violated by "erroneous deductions or opinions," and that no one should be expected to prove or disprove an opinion. The justice ruled that the Sedition Act could be contravened by opinions too—Callender could not call the president "a thief, a despot and a tyrant" and then defend it as "mere opinion." The attorneys sought to show the jury panel's bias by asking each juror if he had formed "an opinion on the book entitled, '*The Prospect Before Us*.'" Chase said that the "question is improper, and you shall not ask it," ruling instead that the attorneys could ask whether each juror had formed "an opinion upon the charges contained in the indictment," though the jurors "had never seen the indictment, nor heard it read." The attorneys then asked for the indictment to be read to the jury at that time. Chase refused.[72] One juror said that "he had formed an unequivocal opinion, that such a book as '*The Prospect Before Us*,' came within the sedition law." Chase did not strike him, saying no objection was made to him. Only after questions ended and the jurors were sworn was the indictment read to them. The clerk of court later testified that all the jurors were "opposed to him [Callender] in political sentiments."[73]

The prosecutor, Thomas Nelson, told the jury in his opening statement that if the book was "a candid and fair discussion" they should not find Callender guilty under the Sedition Act, but if the book was not "candid evidence and fair discussion . . . , and that it does not contain the truth in all parts, you must find the traverser guilty." Even though Nelson was limiting freedoms of press and speech to whatever a jury found to be "fair discussion" that "contain[ed] the truth in all parts," Chase remained silent. Further, Nelson was placing the burden of proof on the accused—Callender must show that "the facts and allegations averred in the paper are true," while the prosecutor must only show "that it does not contain the truth in all parts"; Callender "must *prove* the fact," and it "is not necessary for me [the prosecutor] to *disprove*." Chase still remained silent. The prosecution then presented its case, which consisted of a number of witnesses saying that Callender published or wrote the book, the prosecutor's argument, and the prosecutor's long commentary on each passage that the indictment quoted and charged was criminal.[74] Throughout, it does not appear that Chase made a single significant ruling against the prosecutor, but his treatment of the defense was another matter.

Samuel Chase for the Prosecution

As the defense began its case, fireworks started. When the first witness, former Sen. John Taylor of Caroline, took the stand, Chase asked "what they intended to prove by the witness," and "demanded a statement in writing of the questions intended to be put to the witness." He gave as his reason that "[j]uries are only to hear legal evidence." Callender's attorney objected that the prosecutor had not been required to submit his questions in advance, and that he did not know exactly what the witness would establish. Chase insisted on the list of questions in writing. He then excluded that first witness, ruling "Taylor's evidence to be inadmissible," for the same extraordinary reason as was given in Cooper's trial.

> No evidence, said the Judge, is admissible that does not go to justify the whole charge. The charge . . . is, that the President is a professed aristocrat, and that he has proved serviceable to the British interest. You must prove both these points, or you prove nothing. Now as you do not attempt to prove the whole of one specific charge, but only a part of it, your evidence cannot be received; . . . he who justifies, must justify an entire charge.[75]

When Callender's counsel said he would "prove one part of a specific charge by one witness, and another part by another, and thereby prove the charge," Chase ruled against "the young gentleman." The justice twisted that to say that it would mislead the jury to allow evidence to prove "a minute part of the charge by one witness, and another minute part by another witness," ignoring the defense proposal to prove half by one witness, and half by another witness.[76] Chase then criticized the defense attorneys in front of the jury: "You have all along mistaken the law, and press your mistakes on the court." A bold George Hay tried again, and though Chase recommended that Nelson "permit those questions to be put to the witness," though they were "irregular," Nelson declined. Consequently, the defense could not present the testimony of any witnesses.

Mixed in with that discussion, Chase addressed what each side must prove. To win, the government "must prove the publication, and the fallacy [falsity?] of it," while the defense "must prove a justification, and this justification must be entire and complete, as to any one specific charge; a partial justification is inadmissible." In saying that, Chase relieved the government of having to prove libelousness and criminal intent, and imposed on the defense the obligation to prove the truth of each statement beyond a reasonable doubt—not to prove merely that there was a reasonable doubt.[77]

The defense wrapped up its case with its most important point, as William Wirt attempted to argue that the Sedition Act violated the First Amendment and could not be enforced. Chase interrupted him immediately, instructing him to "[t]ake your seat, sir, if you please," and telling the jury that "it is not competent to the jury to decide on this point." Chase "read part of a long opinion, to show that the jury had not the right" to "decide on the constitutionality of a law." Chase told all that his "opinion is the result of mature deliberation," and indeed it was, because it offered a clever way to cut off any defense based on freedom of press or speech. Wirt responded that the Sedition Act expressly gave the jury the "right to determine the law and the fact" (to render a general verdict), and on that built a syllogism. "Since, then, the jury have a right to consider the law, and since the [C]onstitution is law, the conclusion is . . . that the jury have a right to consider the Constitution." Chase pronounced that a "*non sequitur,* sir." The other defense attorney, Philip Nicholas, rose to give another try at the constitutional argument, followed by Hay. Chase "again interrupted Mr. Hay, and briefly expressed his opinion of the law." When Chase bid him to proceed, Hay refused, after "fold[ing] up and put[ting] away his papers." As in the Fries case and the Duane Senate case, the defense attorneys quit because they could not present their case.[78]

Chase then read in full his lengthy opinion that the "jury have no right to decide on the constitutionality" of the Sedition Act," and that the "court will not allow the counsel for the traverser [defendant] to argue before the petit jury, that they have a right to decide on the constitutionality of the statute."[79] Of course, that was not quite what Callender's counsel had said; their point was that a jury expressly authorized "to determine the law and the fact" must consider the supreme law, the Constitution, and could treat a law contrary to it as no law at all. But then, Chase was not primarily talking about the power of juries; he was speaking of the power of state legislatures, and indirectly condemning the Virginia Resolutions of late 1798 and Virginia's Report of early 1800. And the defense attorneys were not primarily presenting Callender's case; they were theatrically attacking the Sedition Act and concluding an election vignette. The jury found Callender guilty.

Most of those rulings by Justice Chase amounted to indisputable judicial bias, as Republicans were quick to point out. Chase's comments when announcing Callender's sentence showed similar bias.[80]

The next day, Chase sentenced Callender to a $200 fine, nine months in prison, and a bond before release of $600 from the defendant and $600 total from two sureties. Chase had set the fine to equal, exactly, Callender's net worth, after asking him "the amt. of his fortune" and despite leaving his three "children without support in the interim."[81] Chase said that "his offence against the laws was great, and that it was aggravated by its having been wilfully committed," because Callender "must have known that Mr. Adams was far from deserving the character which he had given."

The justice then addressed the First Amendment, an issue that he had carefully avoided until the jury was dismissed, just as he did in Thomas Cooper's trial. Chase stated "that there was a very great difference between the liberty and the abuse or licen[t]iousness of the press"—though he again did not define the distinction—and warned ominously "that the licentiousness of the press would most certainly destroy any government." He defined liberty of the press in equally meaningless terms: "the liberty of the press consisted in the unrestrained but fair discussion of principles and conduct." He then said that the crime was aggravated by trying to help one side in the upcoming elections: "Callender avowedly for an electioneering purpose had ascribed to Mr. Adams a worse character than . . . the worse of tyrants."[82] According to Chase, freedoms of press and speech were not supremely applicable to election discussions—they were supremely inapplicable—and opponents of the Federalist administration sought to influence elections at their peril without constitutional protection.

Soon after Jefferson was inaugurated as president, he pardoned Callender and ordered his fine repaid. But it had little practical effect, since Chase had set the prison sentence to end on inauguration day, and the Federalist marshal did everything humanly possible to delay repayment of the fine. In the meantime, President John Adams was not troubled by Chase's well-publicized handling of Callender's trial, writing to his new secretary of state that "the merit of Judge Chase" was "very great in my estimation."[83]

The net effect of the Callender trial, in Madison's memorable words, was that the Federalist Party "industriously co-operat[ed] in its own destruction." The Republicans were careful not to interfere, and Gov. Monroe was active in "preventing trouble" and encouraging respect for law and order.[84] When Callender's trial was over, Republicans immediately used it as an election piece. The *Aurora* called for the impeachment of Chase for "this and other arbitrary acts," and an article in most Republican papers called "Judge Chase AN UNPRINCIPLED tyrant, totally unfit to be intrusted with any power over the lives or liberties" of citizens. A poem spoke volumes:

> Cursed of thy father, scum of all that's base,
> Thy sight is odious and thy name is _____.

Republican papers used the trial to condemn the "Gag" Law as well as Chase.[85]

Callender's Unshakable Loyalty to the Highest Bidder

In Richmond's jail, Callender finished the second volume of *The Prospect Before Us,* and incorporated newspaper essays that he also wrote. He had been a martyr for the Republican cause, but he did not plan to be a martyr any longer, believing that if anyone deserved a lucrative federal appointment he did. Callender pelted Jefferson, Madison, and other leaders with requests and then demands for appointment as the Richmond postmaster or something equally remunerative.[86] By late May 1801, he was threatening "that he was in possession of things which he could & would make use of in a certain case." In the meantime, Callender became more and more upset as repayment of his fine was delayed.[87] Soon, Callender changed sides.

He became the editor of a Federalist newspaper, Richmond's *Recorder,* in February 1801; he became a partner with the founder early the next year. The paper attacked Republicans low and high, such as Meriwether Jones, Callender's former employer.[88] Callender claimed that Jefferson had paid him to attack Adams and other Federalists, such as by disclosing Hamilton's affair with Maria Reynolds and writing *The Prospect.* When Jefferson told friends that he had used the "pretext" of paying subscription amounts for large numbers of copies "to cover a mere charity," toward which the author showed "base ingratitude," Callender printed some of their letters that showed that Jefferson paid him $50 in September 1799 and $50 in October 1800.[89] In truth, Jefferson had made not just those payments but quite a few more, taking steps to conceal their nature. By that time, Jefferson recognized that after Callender failed to get the postmaster position, Callender "began to haul over immediately to federalism, and is now an open enemy," and finally admitted that *The Prospect* was teeming with "scurrilities."[90] The most remarkable aspect of the Callender story is that Jefferson, usually politically astute, ever placed his reputation at risk with him.

Callender's most publicized articles were soon to come, as he broke the Sally Hemings story in September 1802 with an account that Jefferson "for many years past has kept, as his concubine, one of his own slaves," Sally Hemings, by whom "our president has had several children. . . . THE AFRICAN VENUS is said to officiate, as housekeeper at Monticello."[91]

His alcoholism raged worse than ever, and by July 1803 he was found drowned in Richmond's river. Jefferson kept quiet, but late in life described Callender as "a poor creature, . . . hypochondriac, drunken, penniless and unprincipled."[92]

We have seen that the other editors who were Sedition Act defendants had all advocated an expansive understanding of freedoms of press and speech well before the crisis of 1798. The same was true of Callender. For instance, in 1795 he affirmed that "one of the most sacred rights" was "the right of discussing and expressing an opinion on public men or measures,—of influencing by argument—by words . . . over to our opinions."[93] Other examples will not be given, however, since Callender's statements are devalued by his mercenary tendencies.

The Impeachment of Justice Samuel Chase

As threats of impeachment of Chase circulated, the other judge in Callender's trial, Cyrus Griffin, tried to avoid being involved and wrote to Jefferson to repaint the Callender trial's canvas. Griffin claimed not to have "exerted even my small influence" at the trial (though he did not dissent from any of Chase's rulings), misrepresented that Callender's attorneys "declined to argue the unconstitutionality of the sedition law," and trivialized the sentence as "a small fine, and a short confinement."[94]

Articles of impeachment against Chase were approved by the House of Representatives in March 1804, as the Jeffersonians sought to restrain the Federalist-dominated judiciary. Five of the eight articles arraigned Chase's rulings in Callender's case: refusing to exclude the biased juror, refusing to allow testimony supporting part of a charge, making biased determinations such as requiring the defendant's proposed questions of witnesses to be written and reviewed, not following state procedure by holding an immediate trial and by imprisoning Callender upon being indicted, and refusing to postpone the trial to the fall session. (The other articles involved Chase's actions in the Fries trial, the Delaware circuit stop after the Callender trial, and a later Maryland grand jury charge.) Ironically, Chase got the delay that he denied Callender, after arguing that "it is manifest, that for preparing such an answer as I have a right to make, . . . a considerable time must be necessary."[95] Chase also got the legal representation—the leading Federalist lawyers in the country—that he drove away for Fries and Callender. Although impeached, Chase was not convicted by the required two-thirds of the Senate, in its trial in February 1805, though a majority voted for conviction on two Callender trial counts and the Maryland count. Afterwards, Chase complained bitterly of "the cruel persecution I have suffered."[96] The result of the unsuccessful impeachment effort was to eliminate the risk of Republicans sweeping "the supreme judicial bench clean." The full story of Chase's impeachment has been well told by Peter Charles Hoffer, and will not be retold here.[97]

Threatening Republican Newspapers in Maryland and Delaware

Justice Samuel Chase, as he traveled from Philadelphia and Thomas Cooper's trial to Richmond and James T. Callender's trial, stopped in Annapolis to hold the United States Circuit Court for Maryland. After he left Richmond, he stopped in Wilmington to hold court for Delaware. In each place, he pressed hard for the grand jury to approve indictments of those responsible for each state's Republican newspapers.

Alexander Martin and Baltimore's American

Alexander Martin (c. 1777–1810), the editor of Baltimore's *American,* has attracted little attention. He was a printer for Boston's *Federal Orrery* from 1795–1796, then for the city's *Polar Star* during 1796–1797 (which John Daly Burk edited), and, moving to Baltimore, then for the *Intelligencer* from 1797 until it folded in 1799. He founded the *American* in May 1799.[98] More can be gleaned about Martin from scattered records. He was the son of Alexander Martin, Sr., a baker, and Elizabeth Robertson of Boston. His obituary says that the former editor of the Baltimore *American,* a native of Boston, died at age 33 in October 1810.[99]

The *American,* at its inception, proclaimed its Republican purpose and mocked the "hypocritical protestations of those editors" who "avow a rigid *impartiality.*" It quickly became the largest of the few Republican papers in Maryland. The newspaper became one of the many Republican papers suffering a physical attack, in its case by Federalist marines in June 1799. It survived for 129 years, ultimately being acquired by William Randolph Hearst.[100]

As Pickering launched his 1799–1800 campaign of enforcing the Sedition Act, he expressly instructed the United States attorney for Maryland, Zeb Hollingsworth, to "prosecute the publisher" of a newspaper "published at Baltimore, under the title of the 'American' which possesses the character of extreme virulence." Hollingsworth was to review each issue, and to seek indictments "for every libel upon the Government or its officers."[101] Hollingsworth singled out an article fifteen days later, but did not secure an indictment at the fall session of the Circuit Court.

At the spring session of the Circuit Court in Annapolis, during May 7–16, 1800, Justice Chase (sitting with local Judge James Winchester) tried to end the foot dragging. According to newspaper reports, Chase added to his grand jury charge that "one of the most *licentious* presses in the United States was supported in Baltimore," and pressed the grand jury to approve an indictment "which the *sentimental Zeb Hollingsworth* had prepared against the Editor of the AMERICAN. . . . One of the principal *counts* in the indictment was for a publication under the title of 'A Bone to Knaw,' published in this paper in August last!"[102] That article asserted that there was collusion between "Federal writers" and federal officials that "sets up examples of *British* jurisprudence, *British* valor, and *British* laws, as examples worthy of our imitation . . . to render us a more easy prey to *British* subjugation." The grand jury declined to find a true bill, or in other words, to approve the indictment.[103]

Chase's severe partiality was shown not just by his actions in the courtroom, but by those outside. In the middle of the Maryland court session, he wrote to James McHenry, who had just been forced to resign as secretary of war, to ask "your Idea" whether the New York vote meant "that Mr. Jefferson will be elected," and to ask "the State of the Votes as You expect it will be in each State." After the circuit ended, Republican newspapers unflatteringly described "*Chase* mounted on a stump, with a face like a full moon, vociferating in favor of the present President" against Jefferson.[104]

James J. Wilson and Wilmington's Mirror

James J. Wilson (1775–1824), the editor of the *Mirror of the Times* in Wilmington, Delaware, was a son of farmers. Upon completing a printing apprenticeship, he moved to Wilmington to be the printer and a writer for the *Mirror* soon after it started in 1799. He moved back to New Jersey to become a partner of Trenton's *True American* in mid-1801, and its significance as a major Republican paper made Wilson an influential party leader. After serving as a captain and as New Jersey's adjutant general in the War of 1812, Wilson was elected for one term in the United States Senate in 1814.[105] He also kept his Delaware paper going, continuing the *Mirror* until 1806, and then founding the *American Watchman* in Wilmington.[106]

Pickering was aware of Wilson's paper and its vocal Republican material, whether or not he pushed the United States attorney or Justice Chase to seek an indictment, as they talked at the trials of Fries and Cooper. In February 1800, Col. Allan McLane wrote to Pickering to report articles by John C. Ogden (Lyon's petition bearer) "in our little Jacobin paper" in Wilmington, leaving McLane "almost delerious at seeing our once happy Country disordered by such infamous instruments" as Ogden "plotting against his Country." McLane's delirium doubtless deepened with typical articles in the *Mirror* defending Jacobins and democrats, and castigating the Adams administration for its standing army, Alien and Sedition Acts, and Jonathan Robbins affair.[107]

The spring session of the United States Circuit Court was held in New Castle, Delaware, on June 27–28, 1800, as Justice Samuel Chase arrived to join local Judge Gunning Bedford, Jr. Chase, determined not to repeat his failure to get an indictment of the Baltimore *American,* pressed the Wilmington grand jury much harder to indict Delaware's "seditious printer." The *Mirror* published what it said was the statement of a gentleman who attended the court, which agreed with the *Aurora*'s account from a New Castle resident.[108] According to the *Mirror,* after Chase delivered his grand jury charge, the grand jury reported that it could find nothing to indict. Chase asked, "Have you found *no bill,* Gentlemen of the Jury!!—Mr. Attorney, have you nothing to prefer to the Grand Jury?" The United States attorney responded that "[n]o indictable offence has come under my notice." Chase pressed still more:

> *J.Ch.* Well, but can't you *find something?* Have you no person in this state guilty of libelling the Government of the United States? I am credibly informed, and report says you have a printer who publishes a *very seditious paper* in this state. . . . Have you not *two* printers in this state? . . .
>
> *J.Ch.* Very well; one of them is said to be a seditious printer, and *must be* taken notice of. It is part of *my* duty and it *shall* be attended to. . . . It is high time, Sir, that the *spirit of sedition* which prevails among many of our printers should be checked. Can you not obtain some of this man's papers by to-morrow, and *enquire,* and *examine,* and *search diligently,* whether he has not libelled the Government of the U. States? It is your duty, Sir, and it *must be done* . . .
>
> *J.Ch.* . . . I *am determined* to have those seditious printers prosecuted *to the extremity of the law.* The safety and prosperity of the Government depend upon it.[109]

Chase refused to excuse the grand jury, despite their protest that remaining the next day was very inconvenient, especially for farmers. The next day, the grand jury again failed to find an indictment. Chase's charge did provoke one thing—the *Aurora*'s article saying people of "republican principles" were "disgusted with the charges which are commonly given to juries by the judges of our federal courts," by which "the bench is perverted into an engine of party."[110]

These events became the seventh article of impeachment of Chase, in 1804. Though Chase's attorneys denied that Chase said any of this, the judge who had sat with him, Judge Gunning Bedford, testified that Chase had said most of what the *Mirror* quoted. Bedford added that, at the end of the session, Chase said "that it was hard he could not get a single man indicted in Delaware, while he could in every other place."[111]

When Chase was safely out of Delaware, Wilson celebrated his close escape by printing July 4 toasts in the *Mirror,* thumbing his nose at Chase. They provide a Republican valedictory after this last attempted prosecution under the Alien and Sedition Acts:

> The President of the United States—May he enjoy a long and lasting retirement. . . .
>
> The officers and soldiers of the disbanded army—May the gratuity of 3 months' undeserved pay be considered by them as full compensation for their arduous struggle with *lice* and *fleas.* . . .
>
> Liberty of Speech and Freedom of the Press—no sedition law—no perverted common law—no erection of a branch of the national legislature into a *star-chamber,* to crush a Printer [Duane] for telling the truth. . . .

> Republican Printers, who have stood vigilantly at their posts at the hazard of bankruptcy, imprisonment, and death—They have deserved well of their country.[112]

Criticism of the President by Republicans and Federalists

Cooper and Callender, like many others, were prosecuted under the Sedition Act for criticizing the president. As we saw earlier, no Federalists were prosecuted for their asperities toward the president, or for their even more violent condemnations of such Republicans as Jefferson. Yet as Callender's trial occurred, Timothy Pickering had just written (five days before) denouncing "the President's unbounded vanity, ambition, selfishness, revenge and a heart cankered with envy," and Alexander Hamilton was about to write (three days after) that Adams "is more mad than I ever thought him" and "as wicked as he is mad."[113] As Republicans regularly complained, "*Porcupine* [Cobbett] and *Fenno,* are allowed with impunity to insult the chief Magistrate," and Hamilton was not far from writing his letter on John Adams that listed his political mistakes just as Cooper and Callender, and other defendants, had done. Hamilton's letter, at first privately circulated and then printed in late October 1800, overflowed with detraction of Adams such as that "there are great and intrinsic defects in his character, which unfit him for the office of Chief Magistrate," and that Adams had "a vanity without bounds, and a jealousy capable of discoloring every object."[114]

These were not the only examples. In the year when Republicans were most prosecuted from criticism of the president, other Federalists freely deprecated the president long before the Hamilton letter. Secretary of the Treasury Oliver Wolcott said "the people believe that their President is Crazy," and gave his own opinion that "no administration of the government of President Adams could be successful," because his "prejudices are too violent, and his resentments of men of influence are too keen." Outgoing Secretary of War James McHenry agreed that at times "he would speak in such a manner . . . as to persuade one that he was actually insane," and Benjamin Goodhue joined in deploring "Mr. Adams' insufferable madness and vanity."[115] Fisher Ames found the president "vindictive," vain, suffering "want of character," and acting "most absurdly," and George Cabot deprecated the president's "caprices, ill humour, selfishness, and extreme vanity." Thomas Fitzsimmons said "we have to fear" from Adams "the destruction of our government," and Charles Cotesworth Pinckney lamented "A's abandonment of federal principles, his attempt to form a party with Jefferson, and his unfitness to be President."[116] The Sedition Act only criminalized Republican, not Federalist, criticisms of the president.

Other Possible Prosecutions under the Sedition Act and Other Laws

Several other people have been mentioned as possible defendants in Sedition Act cases, and I have discussed them in more depth elsewhere. Two were at least at serious risk of prosecution—Dr. John Vaughan and Dr. John Tyler. Another, John Courtney, was threatened by local officials without jurisdiction. Three were unrelated to the Sedition Act: Tristram Jordan, and Daniel Dodge and Aaron Pennington.[117]

John Vaughan (1775–1807), a physician,[118] wrote to Thomas Jefferson in January 1801 that he had "passed thro the whole catalogue of Federal persecutions, attempted persecutions under the, *ignoble,* Sedition law not excepted," which were "honors purchased rather dearly." How would a medical doctor experience an attempted persecution under the sedition law? Vaughan wrote his letter from Wilmington, to which he moved in 1799, where he rapidly became an influential Republican.[119] A partnership named Vaughan & Coleman began being listed as the owners of the *Delaware Gazette* in March 1799, and it announced two months later that it would be succeeded by the "Delaware Gazette and Mirror of the Times," which James J. Wilson would publish. A leading Delaware historian identified the newspaper owner, Vaughan, as the physician.[120] Thus, Vaughan's brush with the Sedition Act was being at risk of being indicted as owner of *Mirror of the Times,* when Chase tried to indict James J. Wilson as editor, and others, in June 1800. Court records support newspaper accounts that the grand jury refused to indict anyone.

John Tyler (1763–1841), a pioneer of cataract surgery,[121] was described to James Madison the month after Justice Chase attended Circuit Court in Maryland. A fellow resident of Fredericktown (as Frederick was then called) wrote that "Doctr. John Tyler" wrote a letter that "the *leading friends of Order*" published "with such comments as their *malice* suggested, and forwareded it to the Genl. Government in hopes to have the Docr prosecuted under the Sedition Law." The writer hoped "to make such use of this infamy, as will ultimately serve the Republican cause." Tyler was an active Republican, standing to be a Maryland presidential elector for Jefferson, and writing partisan articles for Republican newspapers.[122] He may have been at risk of indictment in May 1800, when Chase pressed the Annapolis grand jury to indict Alexander Martin of the Baltimore *American* and others. The court records and newspaper accounts show that no indictments were issued.

John Courtney, a printer, moved to Staunton, Virginia to help start a Republican paper, the *Political Mirror.*[123] A Federalist competitor stirred up opposition. According to another Republican paper, the Richmond *Examiner,* in early 1800 a "number of justices of the peace, and others met, and cited Mr. Dourtney [Courtney] to appear before them, under the authority of the Sedition Act." Courtney refused, saying they "had no jurisdiction under that statute." Opponents then "threatened to burn the office," though they did not do so.[124] Nothing further has been found to show any action beyond a threat under the Sedition Act, and no independent corroboration has been located.

The proceedings against Tristram Jordan did not involve the Sedition Act. Jordan, a justice of the peace in Pepperelborough, Massachusetts (now Saco, Maine), was charged with "seditious expressions."[125] The basis was his alleged exclamation "that JOHN ADAMS ought to have lost his head 4 years ago, that he was the cause of all the depredations on our commerce, that he duped President Washington to sign the cursed British treaty, and then persuaded him to resign, that he might get his place." Jordan was summoned before the legislature to show cause why he should not be removed as a justice of the peace. Jordan immediately disavowed saying those words or embracing those sentiments, and averted removal.[126] The matter did not involve federal law or federal courts.

Similarly, the prosecution of Daniel Dodge and Aaron Pennington, editors of the *Centinel of Freedom* in Newark, was not under the Sedition Act. Scholars have thought "they were victims of the Sedition Act" because of newspaper articles saying that Dodge and Pennington were summoned to appear before "an honorable Justice of the Supreme Court" so the matter may be "determined by a grand jury of the country."[127] However, it was a state court action, and the reference was to the state supreme court and a grand jury of New Jersey. Dodge and Pennington apparently faced two state court actions for seditious libel under state law, one for publishing a letter criticizing the governor (for example, his "shower of filthy, bilious, and excrementitious matter") and refusing to divulge the author,[128] and a second action for reprinting an article from the *Time Piece* assailing Federalist enmity toward France and support for Britain. The grand jury refused to indict them.[129] Others were not so forgiving. Pennington was beaten by a gang of Federalist youth in April 1799, and the city's postmaster sued both editors for libel. By October 1799, the strain of lawsuits was enough that Dodge and Pennington sold the *Centinel* and retired.[130]

Why did Sedition Act trials end with James T. Callender in June 1800? The director of enforcement, Pickering, was fired the month before. His instruction had been to bring the criminal trials to a conclusion at the spring term of court that year, so they would chill and hopefully close Republican newspapers before that year's elections. And the failure of the Sedition Act prosecutions to suppress Republican newspapers and sentiments was becoming more and more evident. As Wolcott reported to Hamilton, "we cannot now prevent the mischiefs" that Republican newspapers produced—opposition newspapers kept multiplying, and "we may as well attempt to arrest the progress of fire in a mess of gun powder as to suppress these calumnies."[131] The Republican victories in the elections of 1800 sealed the fate of Sedition Act enforcement.

THE ALIEN ACT (1798–1800)

"WORTHY OF THE 8TH. OR 9TH. CENTURY"

[T]he barbarians really flattered themselves they should even be able to bring back the times of Vandalism.

—Thomas Jefferson to Dr. Joseph Priestley (March 21, 1801)

CHAPTER FOURTEEN

French Intriguers and Hordes of Wild Irishmen

THE ALIEN FRIENDS ACT, which took effect on June 25, 1798, gave virtually unchecked power to the president to select and deport aliens, as we saw have seen. The president was given power to expel any noncitizens if either "he shall judge [them] dangerous to the peace and safety of the United States, or shall have reasonable grounds to suspect [they] are concerned in any treasonable or secret machinations against the government."[1] The crime was to worry the president, or to invite his suspicion.

The person who wielded that power, President John Adams, had little love in his heart for foreigners. His views were expressed in responses to laudatory addresses, just before and after the Alien Act took effect. The president cautioned the citizens of Baltimore that divisions were hazardous "when foreign nations interfere, and by their arts and agents excite and ferment them into parties and factions. Such interference and influence must be resisted and exterminated." He told the grand jury of Dutchess County, New York to take it as a "warning" if disaffection with government arises from "the influx of foreigners, of discontented characters," and to "beware" that under the "pretext" of "making our country an asylum . . . it is not made a receptacle of malevolence and turbulence, for the outcasts of the universe."[2] Adams reputedly made a list of individuals to be expelled.[3]

The official charged with enforcing the Alien Act, Secretary of State Timothy Pickering, had even less affection for noncitizens, and he appeared to believe that most of the outcasts of the universe spoke French. A typical comment was that the objective of the "unprincipled French rulers and their partisans in this country" was "to divide and enfeeble, that we may become an easier prey to French ambition and rapacity, in the fruits of which our own miscreants expect to share."[4] Those miscreants, of course, were the Republicans.

Many other Federalist leaders were equally eager to see the Alien Act used. Alexander Hamilton believed that "the mass [of aliens] ought to be obliged to leave the Country," and only merchants and "a few" political refugees ought to be allowed to stay. Fisher Ames, recently retired from Congress, said the health of the republic "plainly requires the power of expelling or refusing admission to aliens," particularly since "the rebel Irish, and negroes of the West Indies so much augment the danger," not to mention the Jacobins who had "sent runners everywhere to blow the trumpet of sedition."[5] The district court judge who would hear the largest number of Sedition Act cases, Richard Peters, wrote that he and the United States attorney "are uneasy under the Movements of the internal foes who are plotting Mischief," and would "not fail to take advantage of every means to get rid of a Lot of Villains who are ready to strike when they think the Crisis arrives."[6]

The noncitizens against whom those Federalists most wanted to enforce the Alien Act—the targets of the law when it was passed—were the French, along with Republican newspaper editors and radicals, and the Irish.

The French, warned Rufus King, minister to Great Britain, attempted "to plant in our chief Towns a corps of revolutionary agents"—its consuls and other agents—and to count "upon many friends and Partizans among us."[7] More and more as the 1790s progressed, Federalists excoriated Republicans as Jacobins and the Republican Party as the French Party, and leading Federalists ultimately came to the conclusion that Republicans would support invaders from France.

The "numerous refugees who had become newspaper editors and pamphleteers" were a particular target of the Alien Act, as Jeffrey Pasley noted.[8] They included "the editors of the most important newspapers in the Jeffersonian movement"—particularly Philip Freneau, John Daly Burk, Matthew Lyon, William Duane, Thomas Cooper, and James T. Callender, who we met in earlier chapters, and John Binns and Mathew Carey.[9] John Adams fumed and Abigail Adams seethed over the foreign-born editors, for instance saying of the *Aurora* that "all the writers in that paper are said to be foreigners, many of them fugitives from the Halter in their own Country, incend[i]aries who kindle Flames where ever they go."[10]

Other radicals as well as those editors were disproportionately foreign-born.[11] Most had been driven from England, Scotland, or Ireland by the British crackdown on dissent in reaction to the French Revolution.[12]

The "hordes of wild Irishmen," as Harrison Gray Otis described them, were a magnet to Federalist alarm and condemnation. Sen. Uriah Tracy of Connecticut spoke for many Federalists when, traveling through Pennsylvania, he saw "many, very many Irishmen" and warned that "with a very few exceptions, they are United Irishmen, Free Masons, and the most God-provoking Democrats on this side of Hell."[13]

The distinction between alien and citizen had not yet hardened to its current rigidity, but in 1798 it was hardening fast with the Naturalization Act, the Alien Enemies Act, and the Alien Friends Act.[14]

The constitutionality as well as the utility of the Alien Act was defended by leading Federalists.[15] It was equally denounced by leading Republicans. Thomas Jefferson called the first Senate draft "an Alien bill worthy of the 8th. or 9th. century," and he derided the final Senate draft as something that put aliens "under absolute government" and that was "so palpably in the teeth of the constitution as to shew they mean to pay no respect to it." Madison deplored that first draft as "a monster that must for ever disgrace its parents."[16]

Alarm over French Aliens

French assistance had been pivotal to American success in the Revolutionary War, and many of the French officers and soldiers settled in America afterwards, joining the Huguenots and other long-settled émigrés. The French Revolution was at first welcomed by most Americans as a successor to the American Revolution, and French citizenship and the keys to the Bastille were gratefully received by President George Washington. Then the refugees from revolutionary France, and tales of horrors, began to arrive, and the Federalists mostly shifted to hostility to the French Republic while Republicans remained Francophilic. By 1793, roughly 10,000–25,000 émigrés had reached the United States from France and from its most prosperous Caribbean colony, St. Domingue.[17] After 1793, an upsurge of "thousands upon thousands" of immigrants from France disembarked. Even controversial French refugees were given safe haven, such as Talleyrand when out of power, Edmond Genet after his removal as the French minister, and the future "Z" of the XYZ Affair, Lucien Hauteval.[18] But most Federalists were moving beyond opposition to the French Revolution to grave concern about its threats to America—the rise of a "French party" and of Democratic Societies, the political activities of Genet and his successors, the mounting French attacks on American ships and on European countries, and by 1798 the possibility of French invasion of the United States.

As the Alien Friends Act was being debated in Congress in May and June 1798, rumors circulated about massive numbers of French arriving from St. Domingue, and just after the law was signed, the rumors proved true. Gov. Thomas Mifflin of Pennsylvania reported to the president that a fleet of vessels loaded with French had arrived in Philadelphia, Charleston, and other ports, resulting from the triumph of Toussaint L'Ouverture and the British evacuation of Port-au-Prince. Mifflin enclosed reports that over 4,000 more "were preparing to come with the next fleet."[19] In fact events in St. Domingue continued to cause mass French immigration to America. The first lady complained that the president "is now embarressd with Ship loads of French west Indian Blacks & Molatoes as well as white people."[20]

The French population in the United States anxiously read Federalist statements in newspapers, such as Rep. Samuel Sitgreaves's speech on the naturalization bill, calling to "destroy the cankerworm which is corroding the heart of the country" in the form of "a great number of aliens in this country" from France and "emissaries amongst us . . . who have endeavored to create divisions amongst our own citizens." Later in 1798, Chief Justice Francis Dana of Massachusetts expressed a widespread Federalist belief to the president, asking for "something being done under the Alien Act; to rid ourselves of *every* Frenchman not naturalized." Sen. Jacob Read of South Carolina stated his belief that the French were a "Faithless Volatile Intriguing Race, Honour and Honesty are not to be found" among them.[21]

"The threatening appearance from the Alien bills have so alarmed the French who are among us that they are going off," Jefferson reported in early May 1798. "A ship chartered by themselves for this purpose will sail within about a fortnight for France with as many as she can carry." Soon, Pickering wrote, the "French refugees from St. Domingo are fast leaving us."[22] The ship that Jefferson described, the *Benjamin Franklin,* received a permit from Pickering dated June 1. After the Alien and Sedition Acts were signed into law, the pace picked up for ships carrying French citizens back to France or its Caribbean colonies. The *Liberty,* the *Lark,* and the *Harriett* were given permits dated July 14, the *William* on the 16th, the *Amiable-Adele* on the 18th, the *Commerce* on the 19th, the *Mermaid* and the *Swallow* on the 23rd, the *Ranger* on the 31st, the *General Greene* on August 1, the *Liberty* on the 3rd, the *Adrastus* on the 7th, the *Dorade* on the 8th, and the *Rambler* and the *Fame* on the 13th. Most carried away French citizens, though some vessels departed because of the suspension of commerce with France. More self-deportations occurred after these, and Pickering encouraged them by refusing permits unless ships carried French passengers away.[23]

Thus, the Alien Act caused a number of deportations, as Attorney General Charles Lee acknowledged in suggesting a triumphal paragraph for the president's speech that would open Congress in December 1798:

> The [Alien Act] I am happy to inform you has produced the most desireable and salutary effect on our internal strength. It suggested to Alien french men the necessity of departing out of our territory and a great number of them have in consequence actually departed; an event that tends to prevent an invasion of our country by the french republic, or if it shall be made the invaders will find fewer of their countrymen here ready to join their standard.[24]

While these self-deportations were not ordered under the open-ended terms of the Alien Act, they occurred because of that law and would not have occurred in its absence.[25] They were not caused by the prospect of war with France, because that loomed for months before the boatloads that left, and for months after. The self-deportations occurred at the time the Alien Act was rumored, debated, and passed.

New Light on the Three Deportation Orders against "Suspicious Characters"

President Adams signed three deportation orders under the Alien Friends Act. The first has been correctly understood to be directed at French General Victor Collot. The second has been understood to be directed at a shadowy person known only as "Mr. Schweitzer," who has not been identified. The third has been misunderstood to be directed at Pierre Samuel Dupont, but was actually directed at someone deemed so dangerous as to be referred to only as the "person mentioned in Mr. King's letter," who has not been identified.

General Victor Collot

Georges-Henri-Victor Collot (1750–1805), during the years when Adams claimed "French Spies then swarmed in our Cities and in the Country," in fact was a spy for the French Republic. He had served as an aide to General Rochambeau during the American Revolution, and more recently had been the governor of Guadeloupe, until he was forced to surrender that colony to the British.[26]

Collot led an expedition along the entire western border of the United States, for nine months in 1796, to facilitate secession and French accession of western territories and southern states. In his own sanitized words to the French minister, Pierre Auguste Adet, Collot's purposes included determining "the attitude of the people of the Southern states toward the Federal government and toward France," and "the best way to support the Southern states in case they break with those of the East," among other things. Collot assessed fortifications, drew plans of each outpost he passed, and corrected maps of the Ohio and Mississippi Rivers.[27] The Washington administration quickly learned that the expedition was authorized by the French minister and funded by the French government, and was alarmed that the expedition's purposes included encouraging westerners "to secede from the Union, and form a separate connection with a foreign power." The administration instructed the territorial governor to have Collot watched and to seize the expedition's papers, and it employed a double agent (Collot's quartermaster) for surveillance of the general's progress.[28] Secretary of State Timothy Pickering started investigating and watching Collot when he received a letter, in November 1797, reiterating that the general and other French emissaries were plotting to split the southern and western territories from the United States.[29]

The day after Sen. James Hillhouse offered his motion for developing an alien bill, Jefferson told Madison that it "is understood to be meant for Volney & Collot," though "it will not stop there." He was right on both counts. While the bill was pending, Federalist newspapers were incredulous that "that artful French incendiary, and spy, C_____, is still in America! at the very seat of government!!" When the Alien Act passed, the president's list of individuals to expel, according to one account, "was headed by Volney, General Collot," and Moreau de St. Méry.[30]

However, it took Pickering two months after the Alien Act was signed to consider using it, and another month to propose enforcement against most specific foreigners. The reasons for Pickering's delay included his preoccupation with the first prosecutions under the Sedition Act, his recognition that boatloads of French citizens were leaving and making his work simpler, and his belief that defects in the Alien Act might hinder its use. At the end of August 1798, Pickering mentioned to the president that some wrongdoers "were objects of the alien law, and ought to be sent out of the country," but immediately added that he was apprehensive that "an embarrassment will arise . . . out of the law itself, in its not authorizing the Executive to apprehend & confine, or require sureties for their going, until they can be sent off."[31] In other words, once the president ordered foreigners to be expelled, they could hide and avoid deportation, since the law did not provide for their being held or placed under punitive bonds until they left. Despite those concerns, Pickering was spurred into action by a September letter from Secretary of War James McHenry, enclosing a report from his intelligence source, Col. Francis Mentges, saying that Collot and Schweizer—"suspicious characters"—were lodging with "seven other Frenchmen" in eastern Pennsylvania, and had asked for a plan of the fortifications on Mud Island there.[32]

At the beginning of October, Pickering began his first effort at enforcing the Alien Act, against Collot and unnamed "other foreigners." He wrote to the president that "I have for some time thought that General Collot and some other foreigners ought to be ordered to depart from the U. States: I will prepare the form of an order and submit it to you in a day or two."[33] Five days later, Pickering sent to Adams "some copies of an order for requiring the departure of aliens," and asked him "to sign and return the blank orders" and, during the president's time at home in Quincy, Massachusetts, to "authorize the heads of departments to confer and decide on such alien cases."[34] Pickering was asking the president to sign deportation orders without knowing the targets, and to leave it to the cabinet to fill in the orders with aliens' names.

That raised the question of how to implement the Alien Act, which only said that the president could expel aliens, during those months when the president was away from the seat of government, Philadelphia. Pickering recognized that Adams might find his proposal inconsistent with the law, and sent a second letter that day suggesting that the president at least approve three deportations and sign three orders—for Gen. Collot, "Mr. Sweitzer," and a third person. "If it should appear to you neither lawful nor expedient to delegate to the joint deliberation of the Heads of Departments . . . the case of Aliens deemed unsafe to the U. States, I conceive there can be little doubt of the propriety of requiring the departure of General Collot, and of Mr. Sweitzer. . . . And if the person described in Mr. King's letter of August 14th . . . should arrive in the U. States, & be discovered, he ought if possible, not to be allowed even to breathe the air of the U. States." Pickering then asked Adams to designate the person who would take "the proofs permitted to be given by Aliens to establish their innocence"—to seek a license to stay—and said that Secretary of Treasury Oliver Wolcott suggested the secretary of state for that role. Finally, Pickering indicated how zealously he would fill that role. "With respect to some Aliens (such a man as Collot, for instance) the permission to offer proofs can be merely formal, in compliance with the *letter* of the law: for it is impossible for him to offer a good reason for staying here, or any facts to prove that he is not a French intriguer & bitter enemy to this country."[35]

Those "copies of an order for requiring the departure of aliens," which Pickering sent the president on October 11, were printed for mass use. The form order began as follows:

JOHN ADAMS, PRESIDENT OF THE UNITED STATES OF AMERICA. . . .

WHEREAS by an Act of Congress, intituled, "An Act concerning Aliens," . . . *it shall be lawful for the President of the United States to order all such Aliens as he shall judge dangerous to the peace and safety of the United States, or shall have reasonable grounds to suspect are concerned in any treasonable or secret machinations against the government thereof, to depart out of the territory of the United States* . . .

AND WHEREAS it appears to me, That ____________________ and an alien to the United States, is a person within the meaning and description of the aforesaid Act . . .

NOW THEREFORE, I do hereby require you to give notice to the said ________________ that he depart, and he is hereby ORDERED to depart out of the territory of the United States, within __ days. . . .

[signed] John Adams[36]

The remainder of the form could be used to seek a license to remain.

Adams signed the three orders and authorized Pickering to issue them to "General Collot, Mr. Schweitzer, and the person mentioned in Mr. King's letter." However, he said the Alien Act should be strictly followed, and so he could not delegate decisions to the cabinet. The president agreed that Pickering should be in charge of taking proofs "to establish their innocence, in order to obtain licenses."[37]

Nothing happened for a year in the cases of Collot, Schweizer, or the third person mentioned (to whom we will return). Pickering wrote to the president, in August 1799, to explain the delay as for the purpose of identifying other malefactors. "Colonel Mentges, who was engaged in getting information of Schweitzer's *names* and conduct, kept me long in suspense until at length he informed me that *General Serrurier* was in the country in disguise," and Pickering did not want to "give an alarm to him by arresting the other two." After months he learned the rumor was groundless, and then "when other business pressed, the pursuit of these aliens was overlooked." Schweizer was "about to embark for Hamburgh," so there was no need to proceed against him. However, "Collot remains, and is deemed as much as ever disposed to do all the mischief in his power." Pickering proposed that, since Collot was a paroled prisoner of war to the British, they "compel him to place himself under their jurisdiction, where he could do no harm."[38]

Adams, however, did not want to have to trust the British to control Collot, and wanted to check Collot off his deportation list. He responded that "Collot is a pernicious and malicious intriguer," and "I have been always ready and willing to execute the alien law upon him," because it is "necessary to remove such an instrument of mischief from among our

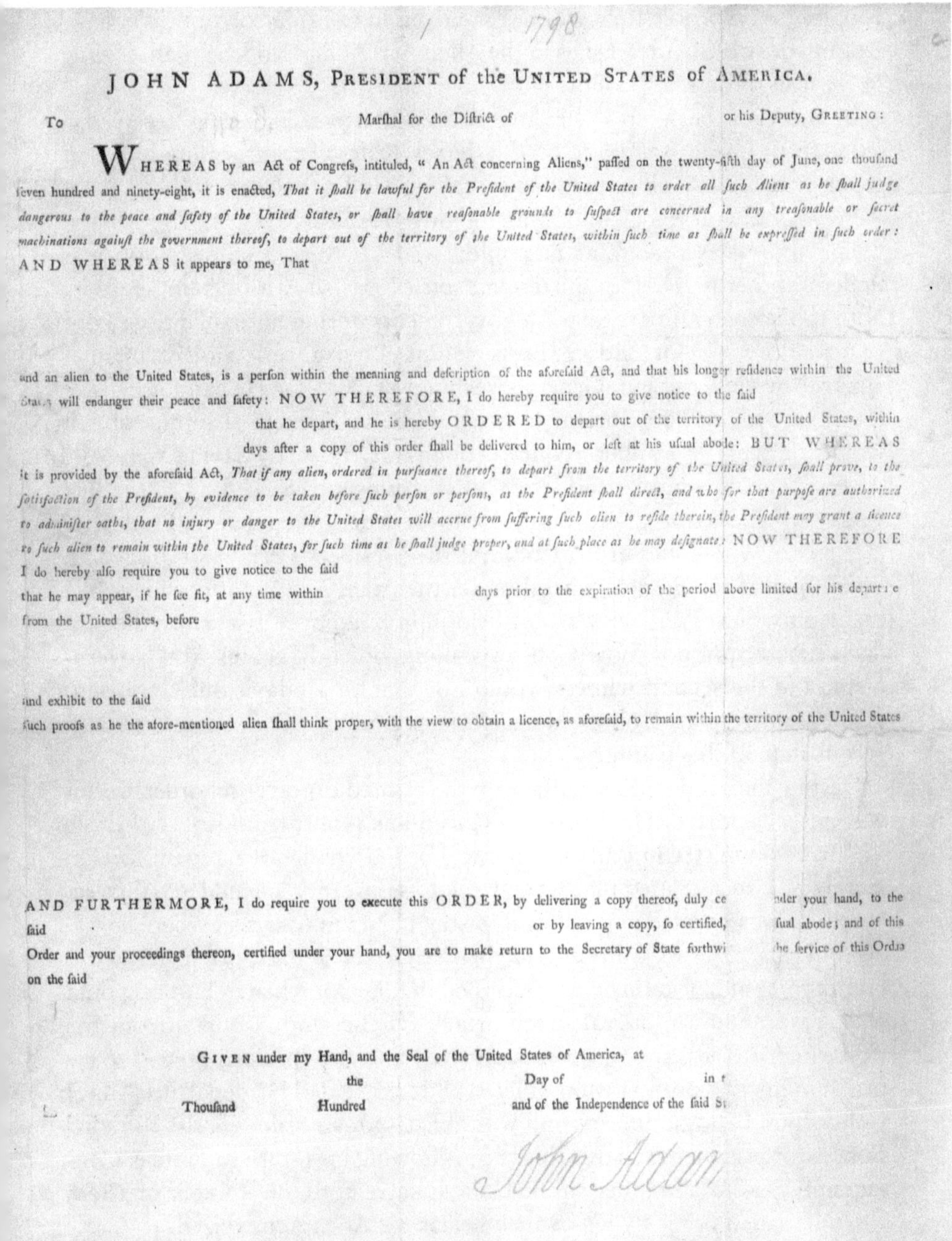

1798

JOHN ADAMS, President of the United States of America.

To Marſhal for the Diſtrict of or his Deputy, Greeting:

WHEREAS by an Act of Congreſs, intituled, "An Act concerning Aliens," paſſed on the twenty-fifth day of June, one thouſand ſeven hundred and ninety-eight, it is enacted, *That it ſhall be lawful for the Preſident of the United States to order all ſuch Aliens as he ſhall judge dangerous to the peace and ſafety of the United States, or ſhall have reaſonable grounds to ſuſpect are concerned in any treaſonable or ſecret machinations againſt the government thereof, to depart out of the territory of the United States, within ſuch time as ſhall be expreſſed in ſuch order:* AND WHEREAS it appears to me, That

and an alien to the United States, is a perſon within the meaning and deſcription of the aforeſaid Act, and that his longer reſidence within the United States will endanger their peace and ſafety: NOW THEREFORE, I do hereby require you to give notice to the ſaid that he depart, and he is hereby ORDERED to depart out of the territory of the United States, within days after a copy of this order ſhall be delivered to him, or left at his uſual abode: BUT WHEREAS it is provided by the aforeſaid Act, *That if any alien, ordered in purſuance thereof, to depart from the territory of the United States, ſhall prove, to the ſatisfaction of the Preſident, by evidence to be taken before ſuch perſon or perſons, as the Preſident ſhall direct, and who for that purpoſe are authorized to adminiſter oaths, that no injury or danger to the United States will accrue from ſuffering ſuch alien to reſide therein, the Preſident may grant a licence to ſuch alien to remain within the United States, for ſuch time as he ſhall judge proper, and at ſuch place as he may deſignate:* NOW THEREFORE I do hereby alſo require you to give notice to the ſaid that he may appear, if he ſee fit, at any time within days prior to the expiration of the period above limited for his departure from the United States, before

and exhibit to the ſaid ſuch proofs as he the afore-mentioned alien ſhall think proper, with the view to obtain a licence, as aforeſaid, to remain within the territory of the United States

AND FURTHERMORE, I do require you to execute this ORDER, by delivering a copy thereof, duly ce[rtified u]nder your hand, to the ſaid or by leaving a copy, ſo certified, [at his u]ſual abode; and of this Order and your proceedings thereon, certified under your hand, you are to make return to the Secretary of State forthwi[th after t]he ſervice of this Order on the ſaid

Given under my Hand, and the Seal of the United States of America, at the Day of in t[he year of our Lord one] Thouſand Hundred and of the Independence of the ſaid St[ates]

John Adam[s]

FIGURE 14.1. Alien Act form order for deportation (1798). Courtesy Collection of the Massachusetts Historical Society, Timothy Pickering Papers.

people, for his whole time will be employed in exciting corrupt divisions." Despite possible inadequacies in the Alien Act, Adams added, "I am willing to try it in the case of Collot."[39]

In the time between their August 1799 letters, Pickering received a letter from Elisha Boudinot, a New Jersey Federalist, informing him that reports in Philadelphia newspapers saying Collot had left the continent were wrong, and that Collot was lodging there in Newark. The general "kept himself as private as he could," and his *Aurora* subscription was under another name. His "intriguing spirit" was shown by being paid by both the French and the Spanish governments during his expedition. Four years before, Collot had "expressed himself in a very violent manner against the Government, General Washington, &c."[40] "He cannot be here for any good, and if sufficient cause could be obtained to send him off," it would be what the public requires. Boudinot ended by saying that "the *Alien bill* . . . is a mear dead letter" if it could not be used in a case like Collot's.[41] Pickering asked Boudinot if the federal marshal had a deputy in Newark who could arrest Collot, if the president's reply authorized an order against the French general under the Alien Act. Boudinot identified the deputy but otherwise was not helpful in building a case, since the affidavit he sent did not show Collot speaking violently against the Government, and the second witness would not sign an affidavit but "wishes to avoid appearing ag. Collott," being "of opinion that Collot is a very dangerous man in this Country."[42]

Despite the president's signature on the printed deportation order, Collot was never deported. The reason was given in a report from Robert Liston, the British minister in Philadelphia, to Lord Grenville, the British foreign secretary. Liston related that when Collot as governor surrendered Guadeloupe, he was paroled and allowed to stay in North America, where he undertook his 1796 expedition and then requested a passport to return to France in 1798. Pickering was concerned that Collot when in France would seek government approval of an attack on the United States from the western territories, and so asked Liston to "find any specious pretext to refuse him my passport." Liston obliged and "prevented his departure," until Collot found another means and was able to get an order via the commissioners for prisoner exchanges in 1800, allowing his return to France. Consequently, Collot remained in the United States until the summer of 1800, when he sailed home by his own choice as the Alien Act expired.[43]

In effect, an Alien Act prime target, who was more dangerous militarily to American security than any Sedition Act defendant, was left to roam America freely, while Sedition Act targets, who were only dangerous politically to Federalist success, were relentlessly prosecuted. Pickering, who

FIGURE 14.2. Johann Caspar Schweizer. Drawing by James Sharples (c. 1800). Courtesy Zentralbibliothek Zürich, FA David Hess 8a.

had solicited appointment as head of enforcing the Alien Act, was the cause of his own complaint that "the alien law remains a dead letter."[44]

Johann Caspar Schweizer

The person "known only as Schweitzer," who was the subject of the second of the three deportation orders, has not heretofore been identified.[45] All that has been discovered about him was that he was present with Gen. Collot as "suspicious characters" lodging with "seven other Frenchmen" in eastern Pennsylvania, and that he was believed to be "about to embark for Hamburgh" in early August 1798.[46] Schweitzer was Johann Caspar Schweizer. He lived in Philadelphia at that time (from 1795–1801), having moved there to facilitate his partnership's exclusive agency to handle French trading with North America from 1794–1796. That partnership, Swan & Schweizer, had subagents in Hamburg, and the other partner, James Swan, moved to Hamburg in 1798, which likely gave rise to the rumor that Schweizer also embarked for that city. Finally, Schweizer had extensive interaction with Collot around 1798.

Johann Caspar Schweizer (1754–1811), born in Switzerland, moved to Paris in 1786 to establish the banking firm Schweizer Jeanneret & Co. When the French Revolution ignited, Schweizer was sympathetic.[47] His firm bid unsuccessfully on implementing the foreign debt component of Hamilton's funding plan. It was more successful in joining forces with James Swan, when Swan was appointed France's "agent in charge of purchases" in North America, in 1794. Within weeks, Schweizer "was appointed an associate to Swan," and their partnership operated as Swan & Schweizer.[48] Schweizer sailed to Philadelphia in 1795, and remained there even after Swan & Schweizer closed in early 1796, staying until 1801. Swan left Philadelphia earlier, in 1798, sailing for Hamburg, where the partnership's correspondent bankers had been Lubbert & Dumas.[49]

James Swan was a colorful figure. He immigrated as a teenager from Scotland to Boston, where he participated in the Boston Tea Party and was wounded at Bunker Hill. He soon served in the colony's government during the American Revolution. After moving to France in 1788 to rebuild his depleted fortune, he supported the revolution the following year. He imported foodstuffs into revolutionary France, paying with bullion from melting down ecclesiastical and noble finery and with the proceeds from selling vessels captured by French ships; he also exported French luxury goods to America. After Swan landed the appointment for trade with North America in 1794, Swan & Schweizer converted that French trade into ostensible shipping by American neutrals, by using American ships and captains, listing permissible though false destinations, obtaining insurance in Denmark where no questions would be asked, and paying bribes whenever necessary.[50] Swan & Schweizer also represented France in negotiating payoff of the United States debt in 1795, and at the same time acted for the French minister in such delicate matters as buying a copy of the still secret Jay Treaty and providing it to Benjamin Franklin Bache to be publicized.[51]

Schweizer's role in purchasing shiploads of provisions for revolutionary France and its armies qualified him for scrutiny, but it was his relationship with Gen. Victor Collot that targeted the Swiss banker and merchant for the second deportation order. Schweizer knew and interacted with Collot. He borrowed 10,000 livres from the general, who pressed hard for repayment, which Swan was tardy in funding.[52] Presumably Collot would not lend scarce funds without a prior financial relationship, and that prior relationship may have been Swan & Schweizer providing the funds for the general's reconnaissance expedition. Oddly, Pickering never found Schweizer across town in Philadelphia.

Duverne de Presle

The "person mentioned in Mr. King's letter," who was the subject of the last of the three deportation orders signed by John Adams, along with Gen.

Collot and "Mr. Schweitzer," has heretofore been identified as Pierre Samuel DuPont. And DuPont was indeed discussed in Rufus King's letter of July 14, 1798.[53] However, Adams and Pickering, in referring to the mysterious person, specified that he was "the person described in Mr. King's letter of August 14th."[54] The American minister's letter of that date said "that Duverne de Praisle, who under the name of ___ betrayed the cause of the Royalists in France, has been sent to Philadelphia with his sister" and that "some commission, not friendly to the United States has been given to them." King added that the individual was an officer who had "served in de Grasse's fleet" during the American Revolution, and that he had traveled to England and to the Black Sea. Duverne de Praisle was said to use aliases, including Dunan.[55] The minister's spelling was only approximate, and the correct name is shown by histories of the French Revolution to be Duverne de Presle (or sometimes Depresle).

Thomas-Laurent-Madeleine Duverne de Presle (1763–1844) was from a poor noble family in Nièvere, central France, and used the title chevalier. He studied at a military school, and entered the Royal Navy and with it sailed as far as the Black Sea, then he served as an officer in Grasse's fleet as it aided the American Revolution. Presle moved to Switzerland, Germany, and England to evade persecution of the nobility during the French Revolution, and was placed on the list of émigrés, so his return to France in 1792 could only be under assumed names.[56] Presle became involved in the counterrevolutionary movement, and was one of three Paris agents of the Comte de Provence (the future Louis XVIII). He helped form a royalist conspiracy in 1795, and in January 1797 he left London with lavish British promises of funding for a royalist army.[57] Presle acted under many aliases including Bertrand, Mollet, Dural, Bonnecal, and particularly Dunan. He was accused and arrested at the end of January 1797 for royalist intrigues and espionage. At the end of his trial in March, the Directory sentenced him to death. However, when he gave two lengthy confessions or declarations about the royalist conspiracy, his sentence was reduced to ten years in prison. After the revolution of September 1797, he was slated to be banished and imprisoned on the penal colony of Guyana.[58] He gained his release by informing against his coconspirators.[59] He may have boarded an American vessel in March 1798, bound for the United States.

French and British newspapers, which were copied in American newspapers in November 1797, extensively described Presle's role and his declarations. At first there were brief excerpts, Louis XVIII's letter acknowledging Presle's service, and references to Presle as a royal agent.[60] Then his full declarations from March 1797 were reprinted. The first declaration described a royalist conspiracy for "the overthrow of the existing government" of revolutionary France, and for "the pure and simple re-establishment of monarchy." Presle said that for two years he had been "at the head" of that conspiracy, and that it involved both "political and military movements," funded and backed by the British. The second declaration identified a number of participants, and disclosed a number of confidential letters.[61]

Rufus King evidently had received some intelligence that Presle was on his way to the United States. There were many reasons to think that Presle's presence could do no good and much harm. He could form conspiracies to overthrow the Canadian or American government as he had for the French government, or incite the royalists in the French community, or invite demands from France for his return. Lest anyone wish to provide asylum, King added to his first letter to Pickering that Presle was accompanied by "his sister (with whom he lived in a state of prostitution)," and that "they have a child the issue of their incestuous connexion." Three weeks later, King sent another letter to Pickering, warning that Presle "drew up and delivered to the Directory a plan to revolutionize Canada with certain portions of the United States." He said there was reason to believe that "his late mission to America is connected with this plan."[62]

Pickering did not need encouragement. He was eager to exclude Presle upon arrival—it was Presle who "ought if possible, not to be allowed even to breathe the air of the U. States."[63] The president agreed, and signed the third deportation order for Presle, who was never found. The secretary of state had much grander plans than these for use of the Alien Act.

CHAPTER FIFTEEN

At the Mercy of One Man

PLANS FOR ENFORCEMENT of the Alien Act were not limited to the three deportation orders signed by the president. John Adams wanted to deport a number of other people, and Timothy Pickering's wish list was far longer, not only of French citizens but of United Irishmen, foreign-born newspaper editors, and other radicals.

Yet the remainder of the printed deportation orders remained blank and unsigned. The French remained in large numbers; the only ones who left did so voluntarily. The Irish, including even some founders of the United Irishmen who fled to America, experienced no expulsions; the sole one who agreed to deportation went only to Virginia. The foreign-born editors continued to publish as if the Alien Act did not exist, and some evaded it by obtaining citizenship. The other radicals continued to arrive.

The problem was not lack of interest by Adams and Pickering in enforcing the Alien Act. Instead, each time they contemplated deportations, they worried about failure because of defects in the act, which did not authorize the president "to apprehend & confine, or require sureties for," the people ordered to depart. That problem was exacerbated by Pickering's very active enforcement of the Sedition Act, and other duties (including protecting the army and foreign policy from the president's agenda), which left him little time for the Alien Act. Consequently, the three deportation orders and nearly all the deportation plans occurred in the latter half of 1798, during the first campaign to enforce the Sedition Act, and little enforcement or planning occurred after 1798.

Alarm over Other French Aliens

The president's reputed list for expulsions included Comte de Volney and Moreau de St. Méry, and he proposed to exclude others including philosopher Pierre DuPont, a delegation of French philosophers, and French diplomats such as consul-general Joseph Létombe and consuls Jean Rozier, Louis Arcambal, and Theodore-Charles Mozard. Pickering pressed for deportation of those and many more French citizens, such as new consul-general Victor DuPont, and kept others under surveillance, such as individuals who can be identified as François Sébastien Lambin and John Baptiste Verdier.

Comte de Volney

Constantin-François Chasseboeuf, Comte de Volney (1757–1820), was a noted French writer on subjects ranging from Egyptian and Syrian history to despotism. He supported the French Revolution and had a seat in the States General and the National Assembly. That and his travels throughout the United States, particularly the Mississippi River region, from October 1795 to June 1798, generated mistaken Federalist concerns that he was a French spy.[1] Sen. Jacob Read reflected common Federalist beliefs when he informed Pickering that "the real object of Mr. Volney's business in the US" was very different from the claimed object "to establish a *theory of the winds* for America."[2]

The Senate alien bill was rumored "to be meant for Volney & Collot" above any others, and once the Alien Act was signed the count was placed on the president's reputed list.[3] The American minister to Great Britain had recently alerted Pickering that a "French Emissary [Volney], who has lately published his Travels thro' the United States, . . . says, 'That France wants only a footing upon the Continent to regulate the Destinies of the Citizens of the United States.' With these false representations, confirmed not only by some of our own Citizens, but supported by the uniform success of the Directory in other Countries, ought we to be surprized at the opinion that they will be able to bring about a fourth of September [revolution] at Philadelphia with as little difficulty as it was effected at Paris?" Finding the danger still dire three months later, the minister forewarned Pickering that "the Reports of Volney which are in the highest degree gross and offensive in regard to our Government, represent the separation between the northern and southern States and between them and the western country, as events that nature has ordained and which France can . . . effect." Those threats were real, as Collot's activities and the Blount conspiracy showed. While the alien bill was pending, the leading Federalist newspaper, encouraging Volney to leave, said he was "undoubtedly sensible, from the proceedings of our government, that the day is just at hand when he, with other emissaries, must quit this land." The newspaper added that he should leave because he frequently spoke "of the President of the United States and its government, in the most contemptuous terms."[4]

However, action under the Alien Act was not required, because Volney left on the first ship carrying alarmed French back to their country, on June 7, 1798.[5] His reason for departing was that he "was required to . . . leave a country that I desired to consider as a second fatherland" during America's "period of *terror,*" as he wrote privately soon after Jefferson became president. His statement strongly implies that he believed he would be deported once the Alien Act became law. His belief was probably correct. Pickering was only too glad to provide Volney a passport.[6]

The DuPonts and Other French Philosophers

Victor Marie DuPont de Nemours (1767–1827) held junior positions in the French legation to the United States during 1787–1789 and 1791–1792, and was the French consul in Charleston from 1797–1798. He was named the French consul-general in early 1798, to replace Joseph Philippe Létombe. His timing for arrival in Philadelphia could not have been worse, in the midst of the XYZ Affair.[7]

President Adams frostily refused to receive him as consul general, denying DuPont an exequatur in retaliation for France's treatment of the American envoys.[8] Pickering pressed him to expel DuPont along with all French diplomats under the Alien Act, but Adams did not have to because DuPont returned to France on the ship with Volney on June 7.[9] Just before embarking, he met secretly with Jefferson and otherwise gathered political information. Back home, DuPont briefed Talleyrand in detail on the political situation and commercial problems with the United States, and he produced a report Talleyrand requested arguing that French attacks on American shipping were counterproductive.[10] A year and a half later, DuPont joined his father and returned to America.

Pierre Samuel DuPont de Nemours (1739–1817), the consul's father, was a leading French political economist and physiocrat. He served in the States General in 1789, and was president of the Constituent Assembly in 1790, but thereafter fell out of favor and was arrested several times, narrowly missing execution in the Reign of Terror and then narrowly avoiding deportation. (Another of Pierre's sons, E. I. DuPont, later established the well known explosives company.)[11]

Rufus King warned Pickering that Pierre DuPont "with a Delegation from the [French] National Institute are going to the United States of America," under passports from the Directory. Their purpose was to form "an establishment without the limits of the United States, and within the boundaries of Spain high up the Mississippi," a purpose certain to ring Federalist alarm bells. Pickering summarized the letter for Adams.[12] The president's reaction was swift and unwelcoming. "I shall not be guilty of so much affectation of regard for science, as to be very willing to grant passports to Dupont de Nemours or any other French philosophers, in the present situation of our country. We have had too many French philosophers already, and I really begin to think, or rather to suspect, that learned academies, not under the immediate inspection and control of government, have disorganized the world, and are incompatible with social order." In saying that, Adams proved the accuracy of Jefferson's protest against the Alien and Sedition Acts, that "it suffices for a man to be a philosopher . . . to mark him as an anarchist, disorganizer, atheist & enemy of the government."[13] The elder DuPont, denied American passports, did not travel at that time nor did the delegation of philosophers.

The DuPonts figured out how to avoid problems with the Alien Act, as they left France in late 1799 and arrived in America on New Year's Day 1800, knowing that the law would remain in force for another half year and might be extended. Victor DuPont responded to a paragraph in the *Aurora* that said he arrived bearing "communications to our government from the French republic," asking the Republican newspaper to publish his contrary statement that he arrived as a private citizen without any diplomatic role.[14] The family then obtained a recommendation letter from a leading Federalist (the party's future vice presidential and presidential candidate), and retained the leading Federalist lawyer. The recommendation from Charles Cotesworth Pinkney briefed Hamilton that Pierre DuPont was "a gentleman of considerable talents, extensive knowledge, & unblemished integrity," and asked Hamilton to give DuPont advice on his planned land purchases. Victor DuPont successfully retained Hamilton's services. Hamilton then wrote a letter to Pickering, which Victor DuPont hand-delivered, assuring the director of Alien Act enforcement that the family, settling in the United States, was "desirous of being favourably viewed by our Government," and that "my intervention for this purpose has been requested." Hamilton added that Pierre DuPont was "a benevolent well disposed man," and that "the family generally impress us here," and he enclosed a copy of the younger DuPont's statement sent to the *Aurora*.[15] With Pinckney and Hamilton vouching for them, the DuPonts encountered no further problems from Pickering.

Philippe Joseph Létombe

Philippe-André-Joseph Létombe was the outgoing French consul general. His relationship with the Adams administration was overshadowed by the political activities and borderland intrigues of the French ministers throughout the 1790s—Edmond C. Genet, Jean Antoine Joseph Fauchet, and Pierre Auguste Adet—including the latter's effort to bring the defeat of John Adams for president in 1796. Pickering suspected that Létombe continued those borderland intrigues.[16]

Adams revoked the exequaturs of all French diplomats in the United States, including Létombe's, in July 1798, though the order did not require their departure at that time. The first lady likely spoke for the president in saying that if a new French consul or minister arrived, as DuPont had, "he will not find America a resting place—24 hours."[17] Nothing happened until October, when new French consuls had been named and one appeared in Boston. Pickering wrote that "the persons lately named for Consuls to be sent from France to America, if they arrive, ought to be ordered away:—Perhaps the residence of the *old* French consuls should not much longer be permitted." The president does not appear to have responded, but Sen. Uriah Tracy of Connecticut did respond explosively in May 1799, in a letter to the secretary of war. "Why in God's name is not the Alien Law inforced? Why is old Letomb permitted to exercise, the functions of his defunct Consulship—in open defiance to all the shadow of Govt. we have?"[18]

A year after his first effort to expel Létombe, in August 1799, Pickering tried again. He reported to the president with obvious dismay that "M. Letombe not only exercises those services, which, on the withdrawing of his *exequatur,* he requested permission to render to his fellow-citizens in this country, but assumes and uses the title of *Consul-General of the French Republic,* just as he did formerly." Pickering reminded Adams that Létombe "paid the bribes ordered by the French Minister Adet" and is capable of doing "any thing corruptly which his government should direct." The secretary of state ended the letter by observing "that the alien law remains a dead letter," and by urging the president to authorize enforcing it against Létombe, as well as against Dr. Joseph Priestley and Thomas Cooper.[19]

Adams responded that if Pickering could prove Létombe paid bribes ordered by Adet, or anything similar, "he ought to be sent away." However, rather than ordering him out under the Alien Act, "perhaps it would be better to signify that it is expected that he go." Pickering did not have the proof, and no further action was taken against Létombe and the other French diplomats before the Alien Act expired.[20]

Moreau de St. Méry

Médéric-Louis-Elie Moreau de St. Méry (1750–1819), born to a French family in Martinique, was a historian and lawyer. He moved to France before its revolution and supported that revolution, heading the electors of Paris and receiving the keys to the Bastille upon its fall. St. Méry fled Robespierre in late 1793, barely avoiding the guillotine during the Reign of Terror. After arriving in Virginia in early 1794, he moved to Philadelphia late that year, and to sustain his family, he became a bookseller and printer. His shop became the meeting place for leading French émigrés, and he also circulated with native intellectuals as a member of the American Philosophical Society. After St. Méry and his family self-deported to France, he held positions under Bonaparte there and then in Italy, before falling out of favor in 1806.[21]

He confided to his diary that he was on the president's "list of French people to be deported." He asked why, since Adams knew him and used to come to his house and bookshop. The reply, given through a Federalist senator in mid-July, was "Nothing in particular, but he's too French."[22] St. Méry became more of a target than most French residents because of his countrymen who congregated in his bookstore, even including Talleyrand during his American sojourn.

St. Méry began planning to depart as the Alien Act was discussed, and left because of its passage. That law's menace was underscored by the French consul, who wrote to him two days later that "all those who have no love for Robespierism had better get out and get out quick!" The consul was referring to Robespierism in the United States in the form of the Alien and Sedition Acts and other punitive laws; he did not refer to conditions in France. St. Méry noted that Americans "acted as though a French invasion force might land in America at any moment. Everybody was suspicious of everybody else; everywhere one saw murderous glances."[23] Soon after, St. Méry received unrequested passports from Pickering. He and his family left America for good in late August 1798.[24]

Other targets of the Alien Act included other French diplomats and shadowy French émigrés carefully watched by the secretary of state.

Jean Rozier, Louis Arcambal, Theodore-Charles Mozard

When Adams revoked the exequaturs of France's consuls in the United States, he listed not only Létombe but three others. They were Jean-Antoine-Bernard Rozier (-1799), the vice consul in New York, Louis Arcambal, vice consul in Newport, Rhode Island, and Theodore-Charles Mozard (1755–1810), consul in Boston.[25]

These were the diplomats referred to when Pickering wrote to Adams that "[p]erhaps the residence of the *old* French consuls should not much longer be permitted," and when Pickering reiterated that he would have expelled them along with Létombe.[26] Because the president failed to respond, all three continued to reside in the United States, though under a dark cloud.

Rozier's case was doubly complicated. First, he had been rejected as consul-general, after Victor DuPont was rejected along with France's other appointments. Also, Rozier faced a separate risk of expulsion in April 1799 when onboard a ship to Gibraltar were found his "Dispatches, written in cyphers, addressed to Citoyen TALLEYRAND." Rozier's desperation to remain in the United States, instead of facing risks in France arising from the revolution, was exhibited when he contacted Alexander Hamilton to offer to provide the code, in order to show that the dispatches were not hostile to the United States, as Hamilton reported to Pickering.[27] Pickering wrote to Rozier to accept the offer, and impressed that Rozier had "the favourable opinion of General Hamilton," Pickering was satisfied when he read the decoded letters.[28]

François Sébastien Lambin and John Baptiste Verdier

Pickering, as director of enforcement of the Alien Act, had within his files discussions about watching and deporting various French citizens. Four are described here, and there may have been more. These have not been noted in prior studies of the Alien Act.

In October 1798, a letter from Pickering to a Federalist member of Congress, Rep. Dwight Foster of Massachusetts, discussed two mysterious letters from "M. Lambin." Pickering said that correspondence from Foster's brother, Federalist Sen. Theodore Foster of Rhode Island, informed him of two letters misdelivered to Dwight Foster from M. Lambin of Cape François, St. Domingue. Those letters proposed that the senator communicate with a French general, the Comte de Hédouville. The secretary of state saw foul play: "I have no doubt that he is a deceiver, or a dupe to Hadonville, & that a snare is laid for your brother, & thro' him to injure the American Government." Pickering found the situation important enough that he notified the president, in the same letter in which he recommended that "General Collot and some other foreigners ought to be ordered to depart" under the Alien Act. Adams agreed with his assessment of foul play, describing "Abby Lambin" as a spider craftily entrapping a fly.[29] Dwight Foster, apparently quite unnerved to be at the center of the secretary of state's investigation, responded that a month earlier he had received the two packets from Lambin of Cape François containing a letter in French dated August 10. Foster gave various excuses for not having turned the packets over to Pickering sooner—they had been opened and he assumed had been inspected, he had little knowledge of French, he thought they came to him by mistake, he did not open the second package, he did not know anything about Lambin. In case his excuses were insufficient, Foster groveled. He ended his letter by asking Pickering's advice about the "mystery in this Business of which I presume you have more Information than I have obtained," assuring him that his advice would be "sacredly confidential" and would "add to the Favours already conferred on your obedt. devoted and very humble servant." Dwight Foster's assumption that Pickering had more information was very correct; Pickering's files contain Lambin's letters to five other people in the United States with French surnames, which Pickering undoubtedly had intercepted.[30]

Lambin can be identified as Abbé François Sébastien Lambin, a priest in the diocese of Liege, who ministered in St. Domingue beginning in late 1787.[31] Under a contract with the Comtesse de Villefort, Lambin served as the chaplain to her plantation in Varreux west of Port-au-Prince. His agreement was to minister for ten years, but that was interrupted by the French Revolution and then the Haitian Revolution. Lambin remained in St. Domingue until well after 1798, serving as priest in Arcahaie north of the capital.[32] If the underlying purpose for his correspondence with Foster was to engineer a move from St. Domingue to the United States, he failed.

In November 1798, a letter to Pickering from Maj. J. J. Ulrich Rivardi, a Swiss native serving in the United States Army, warned of "M. Verdier" in Philadelphia and suggested close surveillance. He identified Verdier as a former officer in the French forces during the American Revolution and a member of the Order of Cincinnati, the organization of officers of the Revolution. Rivardi added that recently Verdier was "noted in the disturbances of St. Domingue for his attachment to the most execrable measures," and "waits only for an opportunity to serve the Republic by dipping his hands in blood," apparently against the United States. "A man of that kind can not be too narrowly watched."[33] He likely was watched, though he was not deported under the Alien Act.

The Verdier who served in the American Revolution and, as a lieutenant and then captain, participated in the Society of the Cincinnati was Jean Baptiste Verdier.[34] He anglicized his name to John Baptiste Verdier by the time he petitioned for his payment certificates from the Revolution. Those certificates, which Alexander Hamilton agreed were owed for Verdier's service, had been "erroneously paid to Robert Morris" and sold shortly before the latter's bankruptcy, and the Treasury Department treated them as no longer Verdier's. Consequently, Verdier petitioned to Congress for payment, and the Committee of Claims recommended that he be compensated.[35]

Verdier's petition confirmed that he had lived in St. Domingue, where he held the office of provost at Port-de-Paix until the insurrection. He then sought refuge in the United States, where he lived when his petition was filed in April 1798. The fact that the congressional committee recommended payment to Verdier in 1800 indicates that it did not agree that he was likely to dip his hands in blood against the United States. It is likely that Rivardi confused Capt. Verdier with the French general of similar name who was accused of dipping his hands in much blood in Egypt and in Calabria, Italy.[36]

M. Cosperet and M. Morgues

In September 1798, instructions from Pickering directed the federal marshal for Pennsylvania to arrest M. Cosperet, "the officer of the French privateer," who may have "broken his parole." "If you ascertain that he has fled, violating his parole, he may be advertised . . . as a means of getting him apprehended, if he has not left the country."[37] Pickering's instructions did not specify what would happen after that—deporting Cosperet under the Alien Act or imposing some other punishment.

The following March, a letter to Pickering from Chevalier de Colbert warned that M. Morgues was an agent of the French Directory. Morgues was not employed in any visible business, was "strongly attached to the French Republic," and had been sent by the Directory to observe the public reception of Dr. George Logan's peace mission to Paris. Colbert informed Pickering that Morgues was leaving New York that day, probably for Philadelphia, and said it was "worth your attention to have the Conduct of that young M. Morgues observed."[38] Morgues had been in the United States for nearly a year, because Elbridge Gerry had written to John Adams in late March 1798 that "Morgue" would "depart in a day or two for Philadelphia," and Moreau de St. Méry had mentioned in his diary the same month that "the young Mourgues" was "going to America on personal business." Morgues was sure to attract Pickering's attention, even without Colbert's letter, because Moreau had received a letter from Talleyrand asking him to assist Morgues, and Morgues received a letter from Talleyrand to give to Moreau.[39]

Listing these French individuals who faced the Alien Act can convey the misimpression that these were the only French threatened by the Alien Act. In fact, all French individuals were at risk under the Alien Act, except the few who were nobles or became naturalized American citizens. French refugees were no exception, as Pickering implicitly said in stating United States policy toward French refugees from St. Domingue in instructions to the official in New York City who admitted or denied admittance to ships: "It is intended to exclude from St. Domingo such Frenchmen who from their turbulent and meddling associations might either be obnoxious to the Government of the island or instrumental in attempts to defeat the arrangements on which is founded the recent proclamation for restoring the [commercial] intercourse."[40] Most other noncitizens were also at risk.

Alarm over Irish Aliens, Foreign Editors, and Other Radicals

"We have much to fear from the intrigues and insidious machinations of France, but we have every thing to fear from the horde of traitors within our country"—a faction "of a few profligate Americans, . . . of United Irishmen, and fugitives from Scotland; of Frenchmen and other restless foreigners." So a leading Federalist newspaper, *Porcupine's Gazette,* reacted to the resumption of the foremost Republican newspaper, the *Aurora,* after Benjamin Franklin Bache's death as William Duane began as editor. It called Duane "a wretch, who not long since emigrated to this country" from Ireland.[41]

Adams and Pickering seriously considered action against that "horde of traitors"—United Irishmen, radical newspaper editors, and other radicals.

Irish Immigrants

Throughout the 1790s, British efforts to suppress the United Irish and other political organizations, particularly after an attempted French invasion in 1796, produced a stream of more than 30,000–60,000 Irish arriving in America, many from political motivations. "By 1797 and 1798, when the repression was at its peak, the boats were crammed with political refugees," David A. Wilson observed.[42] Once in America, the politically active Irish formed the United Irish of America, the Hibernian Society, and other organizations that were decidedly Republican. Those organizations played a central role in an alarm rung by a leading Federalist editor, William Cobbett, in the form of a pamphlet in May 1798 whose title left little else to tell. Cobbett's *Detection of a Conspiracy Formed by the United Irishmen with the Evident Intention of Aiding the Tyrants of France in Subverting the Government of the United States* described revolutionary France enlisting "the emigrated UNITED IRISHMEN" to support its invasion because they were "without principles, without country and without character" and were instead "bloody-thirsty ruffians." The United States had received "ninety nine hundredths of the factious villains, which Great Britain and Ireland have vomitted from their shores," and all were "schooled in sedition."[43]

Another Irish uprising in late May 1798, and its substantial suppression by autumn, generated "a flood of radical émigrés to the United States."[44] That flood was despite the best efforts of the American minister to Britain, Rufus King, who reported to Pickering in June 1798 that he was working with the British government to block the "thousands of the fugitive Irish" that would "seek an asylum in our Country." His reasons were that their "principles and habits would be pernicious" and that such "Malcontents" would never "become useful citizens." King soon added that "from the emigrations of past time . . . our true national character has been disfigured." Pickering responded that King's "timely interference to prevent the emigration of the Irish traitors to this Country is extremely acceptable to the President." It was also extremely acceptable to such Federalists as Sen. William Bingham of Pennsylvania, who "entirely agree[d] with you in the Danger that may arise from the Emigration of so many Irish Insurgents to this Country," because they would become Republicans. They "will join the party in opposition to the Government" and "will be discontented, & therefore disorganizing Characters, whose Residence amongst us cannot be otherwise than injurious."[45]

Pickering was already interested in suppressing the United Irish in February 1798, when he requested information about the American Society of United Irishmen. Soon after the Alien Act was signed, Judge Richard Peters wrote to him saying there were "some Rascals" nearby him in Philadelphia, "both aliens and infamous Citizens, that I want to handle if I can do it legally." Pickering immediately asked the United States attorney for Pennsylvania, William Rawle, to help him take action. "Judge Peters thinks there are some dangerous aliens in the neighborhood of Philadelphia who require his and your attention. I shall be happy to do anything to aid the measures you shall think proper respecting them," and "cheerfully engage to reimburse the expenses you shall deem necessary to be incurred in detecting the villains . . . plotting mischief against our country."[46] The villains appear to have been Irish.

However, Pickering did not take action against the Irish "villains," other than to prosecute John Daly Burk, Rep. Matthew Lyon, and William Duane under the Sedition Act, while fulminating about prosecuting them under the Alien Act. The reasons for his failure to use the Alien Act included lack of authorization from the president, who only signed the specific three deportation orders and not the stack of blank preprinted orders, and concern about the successful enforcement of the Alien Act. The reason was not lack of Irish targets, because Pickering periodically received offers of information, such as one from Gov. John Jay of New York. Jay enclosing an extract of a letter saying there was now an American Society of United Irishmen, and that "proceedings from Ireland" came regularly to its New York, Philadelphia, Baltimore, and Charlestown branches. Jay offered to gather additional information. Nor was the reason lack of pressure from Federalist leaders. Editor William Cobbett ("Porcupine") reprinted an article insisting that "every United Irishman ought to be hunted from the country, as much as a wolf or a tyger.—For a more bloody and remorseless band of organized assassins never polluted the fountains of society." Massachusetts Chief Justice Francis Dana wished "to rid ourselves" not only of "*every* Frenchman" but "of certain Irishmen, who have been & still are busy in scattering among our people their pestiferous principles."[47]

Beginning the Surveillance State

The 1798 legislation required records of all noncitizens. The Alien Friends Act required masters of ships to report all aliens "immediately upon his arrival in port . . . , specifying their names, age, the place of nativity, the country from which they shall have come, the nation to which they belong and owe allegiance, their occupation and a description of their persons." The officer receiving the report (usually the collector of customs) was required to transmit copies to the office of the secretary of state.[48] The Naturalization Act required aliens to make a declaration of their intention to become a citizen at least five years before applying for citizenship, if they wished to become citizens. The clerk of court receiving the declaration was required to transmit an abstract of the declaration, and a copy of the certificate of citizenship when later obtained, to the office of secretary of state. Also, aliens had to register as aliens "within forty-eight hours after the first arrival" into the territory of the United States. The clerk or other officer was charged with keeping a book of registrations and sending monthly reports to the office of secretary of state.[49]

Pickering reminded collectors to get the reports on arriving aliens, and to identify "aliens you may affirm to be dangerous or very suspicious, specifying as particularly as you are able [where] they intend" to reside. He directed his assistant to remind clerks of court to forward the abstracts of declarations of intent to apply for citizenship and copies of the records of admittance to citizenship.[50] To comply with the suspension of trade with France, Pickering also instructed every collector, "in granting licenses to carry away French people," to verify that they were not really sailors planning to crew future captures and that their possessions were not really merchandise to be sold. And as occurred with some of Bache's and Jefferson's correspondence, the secretary of state evidently intercepted letters that might show Alien Act violations, because various letters from or to French aliens are in Pickering's files, some sent by informers.[51]

Radical Newspaper Editors

Just after leaving office, Adams still fumed as he attributed his defeat to immigrant Republican editors: "Callender, Duane, Cooper, and Lyon," who were "the most influential men in the country, all foreigners and all degraded characters." Alexander Hamilton, in proposing legislation to the former speaker of the house, now a senator, Jonathan Dayton, fulminated about radical editors too. "Renegade Aliens conduct more than one of the most incendiary presses in the UStates—and yet in open contempt and defiance of the laws they are permitted to continue their destructive labours. Why are they not sent away?"[52] A New Jersey Federalist, David Ford, bewailed an organized army of Republican newspapers, warning that "the greatest evil that pervades our Country is the Country Presses, . . . set up & supported by the Democratic party," either "raised by their Private Collections of Money" or "hired, by the party to retail scandal against the Gouvernment." Some Federalists wished the alien law would go still further and "exclude strangers from being . . . Editors of newspapers."[53]

Eleven radical editors, who produced Republican newspapers during the crisis years of 1798–1801, are listed by Michael Durey:

John Daly Burk	*Time Piece* (New York)	1798
James T. Callender	*Aurora* (Philadelphia)	1797–1798
	Examiner (Richmond)	1800–1802
James Carey	*Carey's United States' Recorder* (Philadelphia)	1798
	Constitutional Diary (Philadelphia)	1799–1800
James Cheetham	*Republican Watchtower* (New York)	1800–1801
Thomas Cooper	*Sunbury & Northumberland Gazette* (Northumb.)	1799
Denis Driscol	*Temple of Reason* (New York & Philadelphia)	1800–1801
William Duane	*Aurora* (Philadephia)	1798–
Joseph Gales	*Raleigh Register* (Raleigh)	1799–
Thomas Lloyd	*Merchants' Daily Advertiser* (Philadelphia)	1797–1798
Morgan J. Rhees	*Western Sky* (Beula, Pennsylvania)	1798
John M. Williams	*Columbian Gazette* (New York)	1799[54]

The editors of the most influential Republican newspapers—Burk, Duane, and Callender—were considered for Alien Act prosecutions in addition to being subjected to Sedition Act prosecutions.

John Daly Burk (c. 1776–1808), a recent immigrant from Ireland, was certainly one of the "Renegade Aliens" that Hamilton described as conducting one of the most incendiary presses, the most outspoken Republican newspaper in New York City, as we saw in Chapter 3. The secretary of state told the United States attorney that the *Time Piece* was "a vehicle of the most profuse and atrocious slander, of the Government, & a ready instrument of sedition," and in a July 7, 1798 letter, instructed him to prosecute its editor for sedition (even before the Sedition Act became law). Pickering also instructed the federal attorney to ascertain if Burk was an alien, and if so he would be "sent away" under the Alien Act after he was punished for seditious libel. "If Burke be an Alien, no man is a fitter object for the operation of the Alien Act."[55] Pickering showed eagerness to enforce both new laws.

While the sedition prosecution of Burk was pending, his attorney reached a settlement with Pickering, dismissing the prosecution in exchange for Burk being deported from the United States. However, what the secretary of state and the president feared about the Alien Act came true, as Burk violated his agreement and did not leave the country, instead going to Charleston and then into hiding in Virginia. He successfully hid until the Alien Act and then the Sedition Act expired.[56]

William Duane (1760–1835), likely born in British Canada and spending his childhood in Ireland, was the editor of the leading Republican newspaper in the United States, the *Aurora,* as we saw in Chapter 10. Pickering, starting his third campaign of Sedition Act enforcement in July 1799, wrote to the president that the *Aurora*'s "uninterrupted stream of slander on the American government" was so noxious that he was giving that day's copy to the United States attorney in order to bring a Sedition Act prosecution against Duane. The secretary of state then sought the president's cooperation in an Alien Act order deporting Duane. Duane "pretends that he is an *American citizen,* saying that he was born in Vermont, but was, when a child, taken back with his parents to Ireland." However, Pickering continued, the true facts were that "he went from America prior to our revolution, remained in the British dominions till after the peace, went to the British East Indies, where he committed or was charged with some crime, and returned to Great Britain, from whence, within three or four years past, he came to this country to stir up sedition." Thus, "he is really a British subject, and, as an alien, liable to be banished from the United States." Moreover, Duane "is doubtless a United Irishman," and the militia company he formed "is probably formed to oppose the authority of the government; and in case of war and invasion by the French, to join them."[57] Those far-reaching assumptions ("doubtless," "probably") were more than enough, without verification, to support a deportation order under the Alien Act.

Adams responded in full support of the Sedition Act prosecution, and authorized enforcing the Alien Act against Duane as well. "The matchless effrontery of this Duane merits the execution of the alien law. I am very willing to try its strength upon him."[58] The Sedition Act prosecution was filed, yet nothing happened under the Alien Act. Perhaps initially Pickering's thought was the same as for Burk, that the sedition prosecution should go first because otherwise deportation could cause it to be dismissed, and then a sedition conviction would help prevent a return after deportation. However, when the four Sedition Act prosecutions of Duane, after bogging down, finally moved forward in April and May 1800, Pickering was fired, his plans for an Alien Act prosecution fell by the wayside, and the alien law was a month away from expiring anyway.

Duane was neither forgotten nor forgiven by some Federalists. Levi Hollingsworth, a Philadelphia merchant, brought a private defamation suit against Duane, and federal court jurisdiction depended on Duane not being a citizen. A major object of the suit was fulfilled when the jury determined that Duane indeed was not a citizen, after being given every encouragement from the three Federalist judges on the panel. Even if Duane had been born in the future United States, he had been taken by his mother back to Ireland before the Revolution. The jury then set Duane's damages for defaming Hollingsworth at $600, and he was sentenced to imprisonment for thirty days.[59] Duane applied for naturalization after that.

Thomas Cooper (1759–1839), an immigrant from England in 1794, was an essayist but was only a newspaper editor for two months, as was discussed in Chapter 13. Pickering described Cooper to the president as "a warm opposition man" and said he was "sorry" that Cooper had obtained citizenship. Those "who are desirous of maintaining our internal tranquillity must wish [him] removed from the United States." Adams certainly would have expelled Cooper under the Alien Act if he could, because he regarded Cooper as part of the newspaper "group of foreign liars," and the first lady believed "that vile English democrat, Cooper . . . should not breath, one more sweet gale of American air . . . which he has endeavoured to poison and contaminate by his frenchified principles."[60]

As we saw earlier, James T. Callender was a writer for the *Aurora* and then the *Richmond Examiner*. Jefferson wrote to Madison that Callender was "a principal object" of the Naturalization Act or the Alien Act, but that he "eluded it by getting himself made a citizen" in June 1798, just before moving from Pennsylvania to Virginia.[61]

Much of the Federalist press joined in the cry to expel these Republican editors under the Alien Act. For example, the *Albany Centinel* called for action against "the vile incendiary publications of foreign hirelings among us," less than a month after the Alien and Sedition Acts became law. It said that any sound American "must repel with abhorrence the insidious villain who systematically labours to stir up Sedition and Insurrection"—such "abominable miscreants deserve no place on the American soil"—and noted that "remedies have been provided at the late Session of Congress."[62]

Joseph Priestley and Other Radicals

Seventy-four radicals immigrating to the United States in the 1790s were identified by Michael Durey as "active in the popular radical movements in Britain and Ireland in the 1790s." Half were Irish, a little more than a quarter English, and a little less than a quarter were Scottish. The number of radical Irish immigrants whose prior activities cannot be traced was far larger, as David A. Wilson has shown. "With each crackdown on radicalism in their own country, a new wave of United Irishmen swept across the Atlantic."[63] And the number of English and Scottish immigrants fleeing from Britain's rigorous enforcement of its own alien and sedition and treason laws was also much larger.[64] A substantial "group of British Jacobins . . . became leading figures in the Jeffersonian movement," who Richard J. Twomey has described, among many more. The total number of immigrant radicals was vast according to many Federalist politicians and newspapers.[65] That was one of the primary reasons for most Federalists to demand the Alien Friends Act.

Dr. Joseph Priestley (1733–1804), the theologian-scientist and immigrant English radical we met earlier, was typical. A month after the Alien and Sedition Acts became law, William Cobbett, the Federalist editor, accused Priestley of being a spy, and goaded John Adams to make the radical theologian the first beneficiary of the Alien Act. Cobbett wrote, "if ever the Alien-law is to be anything more than a dead letter, here is a case in which its execution is called for." Otherwise, "they will say, and justly so, that though the President is armed with power, he is afraid to make use of it." In response to those laws, Priestley attempted, with spectacular lack of success, to stifle his political discussions, while worrying that under the Alien Act the president could "either confine me, or send me out of the country."[66]

In fact, Pickering proposed exactly that, writing to Adams that Federalists wished Priestley "removed from the United States" and writing to Charles Hall, who prosecuted Pennsylvania cases with United States Attorney William Rawle, that "I hope besides that Mr. Rawle will prosecute" Priestley. According to the secretary of state, the clergyman's sins were su-

FIGURE 15.1. Dr. Joseph Priestley. Lithograph by Albert Rosenthal (c. 1925), after portrait by Gilbert Stuart. Library of Congress.

pererogatory: he was "a warm opposition man," he attended "the *democratic* assembly on the 4th of July," he had a "discontented and turbulent spirit," and most outrageous of all, he got Thomas "Cooper's address printed in handbills, and distributed."[67]

Priestley became the only proposed deportee under the Alien Act that John Adams expressly vetoed. The president knew him and had attended many of his Unitarian sermons. Adams responded to Pickering that "I do not think it wise to execute the alien law against poor Priestley at present," though his wording left open the possibility of deportation based on Priestley's future actions. Abigail Adams evidently had not been as impressed with Priestley's sermons, because she wrote four days later that "*the Philosopher* should follow after" Cooper and also "should not breath, one more sweet gale of American air."[68]

William Cobbett, the Lone Federalist Target

William Cobbett (1763–1835), the Federalist editor known by his pen name Peter Porcupine, left England to live in the United States during 1792–1800. After his American sojourn, he edited a London newspaper, was elected to the House of Commons near the end of his life, and drifted from his rigid tory views to reformist and ultimately radical views.[69]

Cobbett was the only Federalist considered for use of the Alien Act. That only happened because—and after—he shifted to virulent opposition to the Adams administration and its new mission to France in February 1799. The president wrote to his wife that Cobbett "merited . . . the Alien Bill—But I will not take Revenge." The first lady, finding revenge not such a bad thing, responded "that he deserved the Alien Bill."[70] Other Federalists, such as the editor of New York's *Mercantile Advertiser,* suggested the same thing. Cobbett later claimed that, according to "those who knew the fact, . . . the Old Man really thought of sending me off."[71]

Republican newspapers, enjoying the Federalist internal fight, published such articles as:

> EPITAPH ON SKUNK PORCUPINE
> HERE lies a hireling fiend of PITT,
> Who liv'd & throve by slanderous wit;
> The hated Chief of *British faction,*
> Who drove COLUMBIA to distraction:
> *Aristocrats,* come all and view
> The *fœtid* champion of your crew:
> She tears of iron as you pass,
> You British Lyon's now an *Ass.*[72]

Though the poem was an indignity, it was not as serious a threat as a libel suit by Dr. Benjamin Rush that Cobbett lost. The $5,000 damage award against the editor necessitated his move out of Pennsylvania and back to England in June 1800.[73] Cobbett became the rare journalist who actually left the United States during the crisis years, though not from enforcement of the Alien Act.

Albert Gallatin

Albert Gallatin, born in Geneva, came to America in 1780. His future attacks from Federalists were foreshadowed by being denied his seat in the United States Senate in 1793, for allegedly not meeting a lengthy citizenship requirement. He was elected to the House of Representatives in 1795, and became a leading opponent of the Alien and Sedition Acts and other Adams administration legislation. Beginning in 1801, he served as Jefferson's and Madison's secretary of the treasury, followed by diplomatic positions.[74]

Thomas Jefferson wrote to James Madison in late April 1798, when a congressional member of "the war-party" declared that "they would pass a citizen bill, an alien bill, & a sedition bill," that those "threats point at Gallatin, & it is believed they will endeavor to reach him by this bill." The bill for reaching Gallatin was not the naturalization bill, since he was already a naturalized citizen; it was the alien friends bill, whose legislative process had begun the day before Jefferson's letter by a resolution offered by Sen. James Hillhouse.[75] In debates in the House over authorizing convoys of American ships, a week before Jefferson's letter, Rep. John Allen of Connecticut called Gallatin a "foreign agent." After quoting Monsieur Y's claims about "the French party in America" and about France's influence there, Allen attacked Gallatin's point that armed convoys could lead to war, asking, "Is this the language of an American who loves his country? No, sir, it is the language of a foreign agent." Like other High Federalists, Allen said much more about Gallatin's disloyalty: he "had always opposed the Executive," "condemned the proclamation of neutrality," "justified the conduct of a French Minister" appealing to the country, "by preaching up the rights of man, had produced the Western insurrection," had a "Jacobinic character," and raised "Constitutional questions" on every defense measure and otherwise "encourage[d] their party."[76] Federalists disliked Galllatin so much that Connecticut and Massachusetts pursued an amendment to the Constitution to exclude foreign-born citizens from serving in Congress.

Gallatin continued to be abused by Federalist members of Congress and by Federalist editors, but was not subjected to the Alien Act when it took form and was enacted, because it did not apply to naturalized citizens.

Thomas Paine

Thomas Paine, born in England, came to America in 1774, wrote *Common Sense* in support of the American Revolution, and remained until 1787. He then moved to Europe, and published *The Rights of Man* in defense of the French Revolution in 1791 and 1792. He participated in that revolution, but he lost favor as the Girondins fell in 1793 and was imprisoned in Paris. After his release Paine returned to England, until he was forced to leave by charges of seditious libel. Though he planned to go to America in 1797, he did not make the trip until 1802, and he lived near New York City until his death.[77]

Paine was the best known radical of the 1790s in America, in large part because of his assault on traditional religion in *The Age of Reason* in 1794 and 1796, and because of his pamphlet attack on George Washington. Paine's plan to return to America was widely known, and by Federalists was widely condemned and feared.[78]

John Adams reprobated Paine. In France, Paine and James Monroe were "servile fawning base intriguing flatterers of french Jacobins," who made the ambassador's house a battery constantly firing at "the Religion the Government the Policy of this Country." Abigail Adams equally "detested" Paine and his "Poison."[79] Paine's American citizenship was questioned, as he had been born in Britain, accepted citizenship from revolutionary France, and returned to both, though Monroe argued for Paine's American citizenship to facilitate his release from French prison. Had Paine attempted to come to the United States during 1798–1801, it is likely that the president would have excluded him, under the Alien Act or otherwise, just as Adams rejected Paine's German disciples:

> The German letter proposing to introduce into this country a company of schoolmasters, painters, poets, &c., all of them disciples of Mr. Thomas Paine, will require no answer. I had rather countenance the introduction of Ariel and Caliban, with a troop of spirits the most mischievous from fairy land.[80]

The Arbitrary Power of the Alien Act

What was the answer to Federalist Sen. Uriah Tracy's question, "Why in God's name is not the Alien Law inforced?" Hamilton certainly wanted it enforced, as did Pickering as he proposed deportations. A major reason was concern about the law's enforceability. Pickering remained concerned that "an embarrassment will arise" from the law, and Adams also worried that "[t]he alien law, I fear, will upon trial be found inadequate."[81] A second reason is that Adams failed to exercise his authority to order many deportations. Ultimately, it was the president's opinion that mattered, because unlike under the Sedition Act he was given the sole authority to authorize action under the Alien Act. Although Adams signed three deportation orders, he refused to sign more in blank and to delegate their use to the cabinet. Consequently, Pickering did what he could and used the Sedition Act when both acts applied, such as the second indictment of John Daly Burk and the prosecutions of William Duane. A further reason is that the Alien Act expired in June 1800, nine months earlier than the Sedition Act. But the number of actual deportations is not the best measure of the effect of the Alien Act, nor is the number of self-deportations by boatloads of French citizens.

The impact of the Alien Act on even a leading scientist, who was spared deportation only by the president's smile, was described by Joseph Priestley: "It does not become an *alien* to say much about Politicks, especially in these dangerous times."[82] Instead,

> I find I am at the mercy of one man, who, if he pleases, may, even without giving me a hearing, or a minute[']s warning, either confine me, or send me

> out of the country. This is not a pleasant situation. . . . None of my friends of similar principles can now join me here. They would not, I presume, be allowed to land in the country.[83]

The arbitrary power given to the president was felt by all noncitizens. Just after the Alien Act passed, Marquis de Clugny, a refugee in North Carolina, pleaded that he would not be deemed a suspicious alien. Similarly, Sylvanus Bourne, in Europe, was so "much alarmed & has . . . real anxiety" about his private letter, which an American newspaper published, that he asked the minister at The Hague to write to Pickering and vouch that he was "a warm & firm friend of the govt. & the measures of it." He hoped "that any impression which his letter may have made unfavourable to him may be removed" from Pickering's mind.[84] If some of the potential Alien Act cases seem to show only a momentary thought of deportation, we must remember that all the president needed under the law was a momentary thought to cause a noncitizen to be expelled.

Jefferson sized up the Alien Act well. It "place[d] aliens . . . under absolute government," and, with the Sedition Act, was "so palpably in the teeth of the constitution as to shew [that Congress] mean to pay no respect to it."[85]

Epilogue

THIS FIRST BATTLE over the Bill of Rights—the fight over the Alien and Sedition Acts—left a number of victims across the nation. Yet despite the defendants' losses in their prosecutions for criminal dissent, the battle over the Bill of Rights ended in victory for freedoms of press and speech in two senses. It spread belief in a broad understanding of those freedoms, while vividly demonstrating the dangers from a narrow understanding that brought criminal prosecution of opposition press and speech and of the opposition party as sedition. It also spread awareness of the danger of arbitrary power, by exhibiting the hazards of unfettered presidential power to pick and expel aliens. These were not permanent victories; the same battle is being refought today, though with the benefit of the arguments framed during 1798–1801.

The Federalist Party's association with the Alien and Sedition Acts remains an indelible stain on its record, and this must be included in evaluations of its achievements. The Federalist sponsorship and enforcement of the Alien and Sedition Acts was a major factor in that party's demise, as those acts rallied and unified Republicans and contributed to the Republican Party's electoral victory in 1800 and its political dominance for a generation. Successfully passing and enforcing the Alien and Sedition Acts were costly victories for the Federalists. Unsuccessfully opposing passage and defending martyrs under those acts were priceless defeats for the Republicans.

The Enforcement of the Alien and Sedition Acts

During the presidency of John Adams, the Alien and Sedition Acts and their enforcement were the focus of the most major counterattack by the Republican leaders James Madison and Thomas Jefferson, in the form of the Virginia and Kentucky Resolutions and Virginia's Report. That was not by happenstance. It was because Madison and Jefferson saw those laws as the most outrageous actions of the Adams administration. A year and a half later, Madison observed that by passing and enforcing those laws the Federalist Party was "industriously co-operating in its own destruction."[1] Indeed, the Alien and Sedition Acts "would serve the Republicans in a dual function: as an all-encompassing menace, and as a providential opportunity" to rally Republicans and to display the administration's repressiveness, as Stanley Elkins and Eric McKitrick noted.[2] Adams, four weeks after leaving office, lamented that the Federalists had been "completely and totally routed and defeated," and he acknowledged that part of the cause was the party "wantonly destroy[ing]" itself. He referred in particular to the battle over the Alien and Sedition Acts, since his next sentence identified a major cause of the overthrow as foreign-born newspaper editors, "Philip Freneau, Duane, Callender, Cooper, and Lyon," a "group of foreign liars." However, the former president's unrepentant belief was that they had been prosecuted too little, not too much. His son John Quincy Adams saw things differently, writing the next year that "there never was a system of measures more completely and irrevocably abandoned and rejected by the popular voice" than the Alien and Sedition Acts and other Federalist legislation.[3]

The most outrageous features of the Alien and Sedition Acts were that they were designed to attack and eliminate the political opposition, and that they violated constitutional rights.

Those 1798 laws responded to the growth of opposition newspapers—as Federalist Sen. Uriah Tracy soon complained, "[t]hey are establishing Democratic presses and newspapers in almost every town and county of the country."[4] Those new newspapers were offensive to most Federalists not just because they were Republican, but because they were often published by foreign-born editors, as John Adams repeatedly emphasized. The "most influential men in the country" were "Callender, Duane, Cooper, and Lyon, . . . all foreigners and all degraded characters."[5]

The Alien and Sedition Acts also responded to the expansion of the opposition party, and were purposely aimed at suppressing the opposition. The Alien Act was designed to expel Republican-leaning immigrants—French, journalist, radical, and Irish immigrants. The Sedition Act was designed to suppress other Republicans—not just newspaper editors but politicians and other critics of the administration.

Consequently, the acts were enforced almost exclusively against the political opposition. Under the Alien Act, all contemplated prosecutions were of members of those Republican-leaning groups, except one of a High Federalist editor, William Cobbett ("Peter Porcupine"), when he began to emulate Republicans in attacking the administration. Under the Sedition Act, all prosecutions were of Republican editors, politicians, and other critics, with only two exceptions: a Federalist editor, Alden Spooner, who was prosecuted to compel his testimony against Rep. Matthew Lyon, and a state legislator, Jedidiah Peck, who was prosecuted for opposing the Alien and Sedition Acts. Most of the enforcement of the Sedition Act planned by Secretary of State Timothy Pickering was aimed at Republican newspaper editors; the remaining prosecutions were reactive to criticism of the president or the administration by various Republican citizens. Unwittingly, John Adams acknowledged the bias of the prosecutions, confiding to his wife that some "Federalists have merited the sedition Law" though no others were prosecuted. Republicans such as Sen. Henry Tazewell of Virginia immediately raised objection to the inconsistent treatment of Republicans and Federalists, complaining that "freedom of censuring their measures was silenced whilst Porcupine and Fenno were permitted to utter every species of abuse agt. those who defended the Constitution."[6] That objection was repeated after each prosecution began.

The opposition activities that generated prosecutions under the Sedition Act were expression that claimed protection by the First Amendment: newspaper editors and others exercising their freedom of press, and citizens exercising their freedom of speech. The most prosecuted actions were negative statements about the president (seventeen cases) and about the administration (twelve cases), which of course were core activities of any opposition party, along with protests against the new taxes (eleven cases—some things never change).

There were more than twice as many prosecutions under the Sedition Act as have been confirmed before, and twice as many contemplated under the Alien Act.[7] As Sen. Tazewell predicted, those laws were "executed with unrelenting fury." The fifty-one Sedition Act prosecutions that can be documented in original court records or original prosecutor records (not just the fourteen that had been previously confirmed) include thirty-nine filed in court, eleven planned cases, and one de facto prosecution (of John C. Ogden). Those prosecutions consist of forty-three individuals for press or speech critical of the president, Congress, or administration (Section 2 of the Sedition Act), and of eighty-three individuals for seditious combinations or counseling (Section 1 of the act).[8] The twenty-two Alien Act deportations that were supported by the president or Pickering (not just the eleven that had been previously confirmed) include three signed expulsion orders (two of which have not been correctly identified before), four revocations of diplomats' exequaturs, three notable self-deportations, and twelve authorized or planned deportations (which were not executed). When all self-deportations in response to the Alien Act are counted, there were many more victims of the Alien Act than of the Sedition Act because of what the attorney general called "a great number" of unidentified noncitizens who filled many vessels, in addition to the identifiable names.[9]

The significance of many more prosecutions, actual or contemplated, is that the repressiveness of the Federalist administration and of the Alien and Sedition Acts was far more extensive than has been recognized before, in terms of victims, violations of First Amendment rights and other constitutional rights, and assaults on the opposition.

Who were the people harmed by the Alien and Sedition Acts? In one sense, everyone, because even those who did not set out to criticize the Adams administration had to watch their words to avoid the risk of Sedition Act prosecution. Under the Sedition Act, people were prosecuted for opinions (most of the defendants), questioning the law's constitutionality (John Israel, Morris Llewellyn, Jedidiah Peck, and Ann Greenleaf), symbolic speech such as raising liberty poles (Benjamin Fairbanks and Morris Llewellyn), and even drunken outbursts (Luther Baldwin and Brown Clark), as well as disapproval of the president or the Federalist administration. As for the Alien Act, even friendly noncitizens had to be cautious because they could be deported on a whim. Further, any citizen, after a declaration of war, could be prosecuted if they assisted an alien.

The victims of the Sedition Act paid a high price for speaking in opposition to the Federalist administration. That price included being arrested, jailed, tried, convicted, sentenced to prison and fines, and kept in prison if fines could not be paid. In the case of the newspaper editors, prosecution meant loss of their livelihoods during imprisonment, and sometimes afterwards as well from closing the paper. A prosecution was often sufficient to shutter a newspaper, because Republican newspapers nearly all operated on a wing and prayer—the largest one was financially shaky despite Benjamin Franklin Bache's substantial inheritance from Benjamin Franklin, while William Durell testified that he never made a cent, and Charles Holt told his main backer that his newspaper expended twice its income. The price also sometimes included suffering physical attack by Federalist militia or gangs—examples were Bache, Ogden, Thomas Adams, Jacob Schneider, William Duane, Anthony Haswell, James T. Callender, and others.[10]

However, as we see in authoritarian countries today, those judicial and extrajudicial attacks on the opposition did not work. Instead, they drove many moderate Federalist leaders into that opposition and alienated many ordinary citizens. They caused the Republican newspapers to multiply, and drove most Republican editors to stronger protest and often to political leadership roles. As former Rep. Fisher Ames wrote, two weeks after Jefferson took office, "the Jacobins owe their triumph to the unceasing use of this engine," their newspapers.[11] The Federalist attacks on the opposition party and on Republican newspapers painted the Federalist self-portrait as repressive of dissent and intolerant of citizens' rights—especially First Amendment rights—not to mention noncitizens' rights.

John Adams tried to wash his hands of responsibility for the Alien and Sedition Acts and their enforcement, and as we saw in the Introduction, various historians have helped him in that effort. Many good things can be said about the Adams administration: it left the country with "the fair prospects of a peace with all the world smiling in its face, its commerce flourishing, its navy glorious," as Adams observed shortly before leaving office.[12] However, the Alien and Sedition Acts, and their enforcement, remain a serious stain on Adams and his administration. He did not veto those acts, and he did not stop with signing them. Instead, Adams pressed for four of the prominent Sedition Act prosecutions: three of the leading Republican editor, William Duane, and one of a major Republican intellectual and temporary editor, Thomas Cooper. Adams did not object to the other prosecutions about which he received reports, and he refused to pardon any defendants except two who had become harmless because their newspapers had been closed or sold. The president praised Pickering's defense of the Sedition Act as "excellent," "concinnate and consummate." Further, Adams approved the majority of Alien Act deportations (though they were not effectuated for various reasons), such as the three orders he signed (for Gen. Victor Collot, Johann Caspar Schweizer, and Duverne de Presle), the three notables who left believing that Adams was about to expel them (Comte de Volney, Victor Marie DuPont, and Moreau de St. Méry), the four diplomats whose exequaturs Adams revoked (Philippe Joseph Létombe, Jean-Antoine-Bernard Rozier, Louis Arcambal, and Theodore-Charles Mozard), two Republican editors whose deportations Adams approved (John Daly Burk and William Duane), and two people whose entry Adams blocked or would have blocked (Pierre DuPont and Thomas Paine). The hands of John Adams cannot be washed clean of those indelible blots from the Alien and Sedition Acts.

Jefferson's administration did not enact any legislation similar to the Alien and Sedition Acts, but it is far from true that "his administration would not be stained by any such persecutions." Though the new president began his administration by instructing his attorney general to have "the experiment tried of getting along without public prosecutions for libel," the Federalist fusillades required the patience of Job, and Jefferson was no Job. In 1803, a frustrated Jefferson wrote to Gov. Thomas McKean of Pennsylvania, after cautioning that "what I say must be entirely confidential," that "a few prosecutions of the most eminent offenders would have a wholsome effect in restoring the integrity of the presses." Jefferson meant a few state prosecutions rather than federal ones, and he suggested Federalist editor Joseph Dennie, Pickering's former secretary, as a good place to start.[13] McKean ordered a Pennsylvania action against Dennie, while the Republican governor of New York brought a state action against Federalist editor Harry Croswell. The United States attorney for Connecticut brought several federal prosecutions for common law libel, which Jefferson delayed in ordering dismissed and, in the case of Barzillai Hudson and George Goodwin, failed to have dismissed. And other Republicans filed criminal libel actions against editors.[14] The Republicans were not guilty of consistency with their principles about freedoms of press and speech.

The Constitutional Principles at Stake

The parties' differing views about an opposition party, freedoms of press and speech, and the Alien and Sedition Acts appeared prominently in later correspondence between Thomas Jefferson and Abigail Adams, and then between Jefferson and John Adams.

Abigail Adams wrote to Thomas Jefferson near the end of his first term to express her sorrow about the death of his daughter, and Jefferson responded with appreciation and friendliness. He mentioned that only one act by John Adams during his presidency had caused personal displeasure, the last-minute appointments from among Jefferson's political foes.[15] The former first lady shot back that one act of Jefferson during his own presidency had "severed the bonds of former Friendship," which was his pardon of James T. Callender, liberating "a wretch who was suffering the just punishment of the Law due to his crimes for writing and publishing the basest libel, the lowest and vilest Slander, which malice could invent, or calumny exhibit against the Character and reputation of your predecessor." "The remission of Callenders fine was a public approbation of his conduct," and Jefferson had given "your compliment to him as a writer and your reward of 50 dollars." The third president disagreed, saying that his "charities to Callender" were given because Callender was "a fugitive from persecution for having written" a book in England in 1792, which Jefferson "had read and approved"; for that reason Jefferson "contributed to his relief, and afterwards repeated the contribution." (That explanation could justify the earliest contributions, but not the later payments that were ostensibly for quantities of newer books and pamphlets that were not actually delivered; and Jefferson further stretched the truth by adding that "no body sooner disapproved of his writings than I did.")[16]

Jefferson then brought up the constitutionality of the Alien and Sedition Acts, in explaining his pardon of Callender and other victims. He had "discharged every person under punishment or prosecution under the Sedition law" because he considered that law "to be a nullity as absolute and as palpable as if Congress had ordered us to fall down and worship a golden image." His basis was the First Amendment. Abigail Adams was not persuaded, however. She replied that while it was not her province to determine the constitutionality of the Sedition Act, "some restraint should be laid upon the asassin, who stabs reputation" as "all civilized Nations have assented." Nowhere else "has calumny, falshood, and revileing stalked abroad more licentiously, than in this," so that "[n]o political Character has been secure from its attacks," rendering that law essential.[17] Jefferson pointed out that treating the Sedition Act as unconstitutional did not "remove all restraint from the overwhelming torrent of slander," because the "power to do that is fully possessed by the several state legislatures." "While we deny that Congress have a right to controul the freedom of the press, we have ever asserted the right of the states, and their exclusive right, to do so"—in "punishing slander." It is important to note that his words there did not affirm a right of the states to punish seditious libel, but only to punish slander. The former first lady got in the last word, giving a typical Federalist rationale for prosecuting seditious libel. "I cannot agree, in opinion, that the constitution ever meant to withhold from the National Government the power of self defence, or that it could be considered an infringment of the Liberty of the press, to punish the licentiousness of it."[18]

The two former presidents, when they began their retirement correspondence seven and a half years later, soon brought up the constitutionality of the Alien Act. Adams objected to Jefferson's statements made in a letter to Dr. Joseph Priestley, including a description of the Alien Act as a "libel on legislation" in a period when "the barbarians really flattered themselves they should even be able to bring back the times of Vandalism."[19] The second president tried to distance himself from that law, saying he was not "concerned in the formation of it" (though he signed it rather than vetoing it), and merely signed it just as Jefferson did (though the latter's signature only appeared on it and on all laws as president of the Senate to certify that it was passed by the Senate), and "never executed [it] in any Instance" (though Adams signed three deportation orders and supported other expulsions). Adams wishfully stretched the truth as much as Jefferson had.

Jefferson ignored those transparently mistaken claims in his subsequent letters, and returned to the main objections to the Alien and Sedition Acts. He protested "the terrorism of the day" when the Alien and Sedition Acts were both "felt by one party only," the Republicans. He softened the blow by saying the "real authors" of the legislation were "the Pickerings, the Wolcotts," and other High Federalists, who were his predecessor's "secret . . . enemies."[20] Adams, though agreeing that he was "plagued by P[ickering]s," Hamilton, and other High Federalists, objected sharply to Jefferson's characterization of his administration's actions as "terrorism" toward the opposition, and claimed that his administration itself faced "Terrorism" from threats of "Revolution of Government," mobs, and menaces of Republican editors ("Shall I remind you of . . . Duane? of Callender? of Tom Paine? of Greenleaf . . .").[21]

Thus, Adams did not abandon his narrow view of freedoms of press and speech. He instead tried to escape responsibility for the Alien and Sedition Acts and prosecutions and expulsions under them, while blaming his downfall on Republican editors and on "Hamilton's ambition, intrigues, and caucusses" that "ruined the cause of federalism."[22]

By contrast, Timothy Pickering, two decades after becoming secretary of state, found it to his personal advantage to convert to a broad view of those freedoms, as he became a vocal opponent of the Jefferson and Madison administrations and a leader of secession efforts for New England.[23] The "advantage of the liberty of the Press," the deviously inconsistent Pickering wrote, was "to detect & explore the misrule of public officers" (exactly what he had prosecuted under the Sedition Act). The security of "liberties depend[s] on a vigilant attention to the conduct and characters of their rulers." The "*Liberty of the Press*" is "a liberty which we claim as our birthright," which is "so essential to the preservation of our rights as men & citizens, that it is the object of a special provision in the Constitution." He sounded as if he was quoting Madison. Pickering reprobated "the tyranny of Bonaparte" that caused France, "where there are newspapers but which are forbidden to publish any thing against the Gov.t." Incredibly, Pickering complained about Republican prosecutions that hardly differed from his own prosecutions:

> Yet this essential right cannot be exercised, in examining the conduct (which involves the characters) of our rulers, without subjecting the writers to the foulest abuse from the unprincipled abettors of the administration.[24]

Oliver Wolcott, Jr. was no more guilty than Pickering of consistency with his words and actions two decades earlier as the Federalist secretary of the treasury. He became "a political apostate" who as a newly minted Republican repeatedly won Connecticut's governorship. In amazement, a prominent Federalist asked Pickering how it could be that "Wolcott has descended from the proud Eminence on which He stood" and that Connecticut could "reward his apostacy."[25]

The statements of the Sedition Act victims show their understanding of the breadth of freedoms of press and speech, and that was in every case an understanding that those freedoms were quite expansive. They do not support the view, which is the dominant scholarly view as we saw in the Introduction, that the founding generation uniformly believed the First Amendment's protections of press and speech were narrow and "substantially embodied the Blackstonian definition and left the law of seditious libel in force." Nor do they support the view that "[n]o other definition of freedom of the press by anyone anywhere in America before 1798" existed.[26] Not one defendant had embraced the narrow Blackstone definition of freedoms of press and speech, in the years before their Sedition Act prosecutions, or during or after. Instead, each defendant whose writings survive had affirmed an expansive understanding of those freedoms that protected wide-ranging criticism of government officials and their measures.

As we have seen, all the Republican editors who wrote before 1798 embraced a broad view of the meaning of freedoms of press and speech long before the crisis period—Thomas Adams in 1784, Anthony Haswell in 1785, Thomas Cooper in 1789, Benjamin Franklin Bache in and after 1793, Matthew Lyon in 1793, John Daly Burk in 1794, and William Duane in 1795.[27] Thus, the claim is not accurate, though it is the prevailing view of historians, "that the revolutionary generation did not seek to wipe out the core idea of seditious libel, that the government may be criminally assaulted by mere words; . . . that the theory of freedom of political expression remained quite narrow until 1798, except for a few aberrant statements."[28] In contrast to that claim, an almost unlimited scope of freedom of press was articulated by essays printed by Haswell in 1785: "every measure then, that has the most minute tendency to prevent, suppress or restrain the publick papers, or the liberty of the press, is repugnant to the [state] constitution" provision for "freedom of the press." Seditious libel prosecutions were condemned as contrary to freedoms of press and speech in an essay he printed in 1787: prosecutions such as of Zenger in America and of Woodfall in England would cause liberty of the press to "be pulled down" or "restrained."[29] Duane agreed, writing in 1795 that Britain's proposed sedition act "will annihilate the LIBERTY OF THE PRESS." Conversely, a provision protecting "liberty of the press" in a federal bill of rights would eliminate the crime of seditious libel, according to an essay printed by Thomas Adams in 1787: "let the *attorney-general,* of the United States, *file an information* against me for a *libel;* I will carry that declaration ['a bill of rights'] in my hand, as my shield and my constitutional defence."[30]

Similarly, the history of the Virginia and Kentucky Resolutions and of Virginia's Report shows widespread agreement with their broad understanding of freedoms of press and speech, and with their condemnation of criminalizing dissent (seditious libel). That history does not support the claim that "none of the other fourteen state legislatures" proved "willing to lend their concurrence to them" and that "[t]en emphatically rejected the Resolutions; the other four took no action at all." While the Virginia and Kentucky Resolutions were rejected by half the sixteen states, they were not rejected by the other half. That other half included the quarter of the states that supported the Resolutions—the Tennessee and Georgia Resolutions along with Virginia and Kentucky, and the quarter of the states that produced divided legislative chambers or nonopposition by tactical plan. Similarly, the half of the states that rejected the Virginia and Kentucky Resolutions divided between two responses: only a quarter of the states resolved that the Alien and Sedition Acts were constitutional, and the other quarter merely rested on the ground that states were not "competent to declare an act of the federal government unconstitutional and void." Resolutions from numerous countries similarly divided between broad views and narrow views. The expansive understanding of freedoms of press and speech had much more appeal than has been credited.

The negative public reaction to the Alien and Sedition Acts, and the Republican victory in 1800, make more sense and generate less surprise when we acknowledge the extensive public support for a broad understanding of freedoms of press and speech, and for the Virginia and Kentucky Resolutions, and for the Republicans who generally supported both. These factors add to the conventional reasons that the Republican leaders mentioned for their victory in 1800.

Jefferson and Madison were confident that the Alien and Sedition Acts ultimately would fail, and that the Republicans would be victorious in 1800.

In late 1798, Jefferson noted that the disease would pass because "the Doctor is now on his way in the guise of a taxgatherer." In early 1799, he saw the people turning in a Republican direction as they became sensible of "the Alien & Sedition acts, the vexations of the stamp act, the direct tax, the follies of the additional army & navy, money borrowed for these at the usurious interest of 8. per cent, and mr Gerry's communications showing that peace is ours unless we throw it away."[31] Most fundamentally, Jefferson and Madison unwaveringly believed that the Alien and Sedition Acts violated the First Amendment and other constitutional provisions, and that the voters would join the Republicans in following the Constitution and in upholding individual rights.

The failure of the Alien and Sedition Acts was spectacular. Republicans were startlingly successful in the "revolution of 1800." In that election year, thirty new Republican newspapers were founded and the total of the opposition papers reached eighty-five, as Jeffrey Pasley showed. By the day Jefferson was inaugurated, "every major city and . . . most of the principal smaller towns of every state" had a Republican newspaper, and many of the editors were becoming political leaders.[32] Republicans were not suppressed or even deterred effectively; their numbers were greatly increased, and they were provoked to activism. That occurred not just with newspapers but with Republican candidates and Republican voters.[33] Federalists sought to crush Republican newspapers and the Republican party, and instead they multiplied both. The Republican belief that the Constitution and its liberties were being violated by the Federalists, and particularly by the Alien and Sedition Acts, provided an effective platform and a powerful motivation. Their reasoning was brilliantly presented by Madison in Virginia's Report of 1800 and the seven Republican treatises published in 1798–1801, as well as by earlier essayists.

It is easy to understand why the Alien and Sedition Acts failed, but how could they be adopted in the first place? That was the subject of a fascinating essay by Joanne Freeman.[34] Her suggestion was that "the Sedition Act had an internal logic that can be understood only in the political and cultural context of its time." If the archaic thought of the 1790s is ignored, the Sedition Act (and the same points apply to the Alien Act) appears to be nothing but a transparent effort to cement Federalist control and to crush Republican opposition. But if the thought of the 1790s is taken as the context, the Alien and Sedition Acts were only partially that, in Freeman's view, and were mainly seen by most Federalists as necessary measures to preserve an unstable untried government.[35] She described that context with emphasis on three factors: the fragility of the new experiment in republican government, a "climate of crisis" over war with France, and the federal government deriving its authority and respect from the character and reputation of its officers and representatives.[36]

That context of Federalist thought in the 1790s was challenged by most Republicans, along with the Alien and Sedition Acts. Central to that challenge were the Republican beliefs in freedoms of press and speech and in freedom from unlimited governmental power, and their conviction that those freedoms were violated by the Alien and Sedition Acts. That gave their challenge the mantle of advocating individual rights and of defending martyrs. Every prosecution could be characterized as a Federalist assault on those freedoms, and the totality of the prosecutions could be offered as proof that the Federalists abused their power and were undeserving of trust to rule. The inspirational quality of the Republican identification with freedoms of press and speech was well stated by Jefferson:

> to preserve the freedom of the human mind then & freedom of the press, every spirit should be ready to devote itself to martyrdom; for as long as we may think as we will, & speak as we think, the condition of man will proceed in improvement. the generation which is going off the stage has deserved well of mankind for the struggles it has made, & for having arrested that course of despotism which had overwhelmed the world for thousands & thousands of years.[37]

Those words pointed to some of the reasons why freedoms of press and speech are essential and worth defending, then and now—that they are central to freedom and to protecting human rights, and that they are the most effective means for opposing despotism. Madison added another rationale for freedoms of press and speech—that they are integral to representative government and to informed voting:

> the right of electing the members of the government, constitutes more particularly the essence of a free and responsible government. The value and efficacy of this right, depends on the knowledge of the comparative merits and demerits of the candidates for public trust; and on the equal freedom, consequently, of examining and discussing these merits and demerits of the candidates respectively.[38]

Madison also pointed to another aspect of that rationale for press and speech—that there must be a level field between officeholders and challengers. Any limitation on expression about officeholders would unfairly protect them against challengers and help them cling to office.[39]

The issues raised in the first battle over the Bill of Rights are still fought over today, as the great majority of countries restrict freedoms of press and speech, and the rest hear a crescendo of questions about the importance of those freedoms. Will governments have authority to criminalize dissent—

to punish printed and spoken words critical of the administration and its officials—whether because they are false or defamatory (to government they usually are), or because they reveal state secrets or threaten the state (to authoritarian states they always do), or because they might be offensive to other people (to opponents they always will)? Or will governments only have authority to restrict words that actually incite violence? To ask the question the other way, will citizens have a right to speak and broadcast their opinions whether negative or positive about the administration and its officials, to compare incumbents and challengers before elections occur, and to receive uncensored information and diverse points of view? Those were the overarching issues during the first battle over the Bill of Rights in 1798–1801. As we still face those issues today, we can learn from the ideas expressed and the consequences resulting from that battle.

Appendix

Alien and Sedition Act Prosecutions

TABLE A.1. First Campaign: Sedition Act Prosecutions (1798)

Defendant	Court	Steps Toward Prosecution
Common Law Sedition Prosecutions (Chapter 3)		
a. Benjamin Franklin Bache (1769–1798)†, editor of Philadelphia *Aurora*	U.S. Circuit Court for District of Pennsylvania—Philadelphia, PA	Arrest (26 June 1798) Indictment (29 June 1798) Motion in Supreme Court to stay proceedings in lower court (7 Aug.1798) Death of yellow fever (10 Sept.1798) Case "abated by death of the defendant" (Feb.1799)
b. John Daly Burk (c. 1776–1808)† and James Smith (1738–1812)†, editors of New York *Time Piece* Their case was converted to a Sedition Act prosecution—see 41 below.	U.S. Circuit Court for District of New York—New York, NY	Arrest (6 July 1798) Instruction to prosecute from Pickering (7 July 1798) Nonappearance in U.S. Circuit Court (1 Sept.1798) Dismissal of Burk (nolle prosequi) (before 22 May 1799) (Continued at 41 below)
c. William Durell (1766–1845)†, editor of *Mount Pleasant Register* His case was converted to a Sedition Act prosecution—see 40 below.	Same	Instruction to prosecute from Pickering (28 June 1798) Arrest under common law (17 July 1798) Indictment under Sedition Act (4 Sept.1799) (Continued at 40 below)
Opposition Members of Congress (Chapter 4)		
1. Rep. Matthew Lyon (1749–1822)†, owner of *Scourge of Aristocracy,* Fair Haven, VT	U.S. Circuit Court for District of Vermont—Rutland, VT	Indictment (5 Oct.1798) Warrant served (5 Oct.1798) Appearance and not guilty plea (6 Oct.1798) Trial (8 Oct.1798) Sentencing and judgment (9 Oct.1798) Imprisonment (10 Oct.1798–9 Feb.1799)
2. Rev. John Cosens Ogden (1751–1800), Troy, NY Note: Prosecution was nominally for debt collection in a state court	Litchfield Court of Common Pleas—Litchfield, CT	Instruction to prosecute from Wolcott Arrest warrant in creditor suit (4 Feb.1799) Arrest (5 Feb.1799) Judgment (26 Mar.1799) Release from jail (10 June 1799)
3. Rep. John Clopton (1756–1816), New Kent County, VA		Steps to prosecute by Pickering (23 Oct.1798)

Defendant	Court	Steps Toward Prosecution
Keeping the North Safe from Sedition (Chapter 5)		
4. Thomas Adams (1757–1799)†, editor of Boston *Independent Chronicle*	U.S. Circuit Court for District of Massachusetts—Boston, MA	Indictment (20 Oct.1798) Arrest warrant and plea (23 Oct.1798) Death (10 May 1799) Dismissal after death
5. Benjamin Fairbanks (1745–1834)†, Dedham, MA	Same	Arrest (6 Nov.1798) Plea of not guilty (7 Nov.1798) Indictment (3–7 June 1799) Plea of guilty and sentence (7 June 1799)
6. David Brown (1747–1814)†, Bethlehem, CT	Same	Search for (Nov.1798) Complaint by state (21 Mar.1799) Arrest and placed in jail (22 Mar.1799) Indictment (3–5 June 1799) Plea of not guilty (6 June 1799) Plea of guilty (8 June 1799) Sentencing (10 June 1799) Pardon followed by release (12 Mar.1801)
7. Lespenard Colie (c. 1770–1827), Springfield, NJ	U.S. Circuit Court for District of New Jersey—Trenton, NJ	Indictment (3 Oct.1798) Plea of guilty (3 Oct.1798)
8. Luther Baldwin (c. 1752–1804)†, Newark, NJ	Same	Arrest (on or after 27 July 1798) Indictment (3 Oct.1798) Plea of not guilty (2 Apr.1799) Plea of guilty at trial (3 Oct.1799)
9. Brown Clark†, Newark, NJ	Same	Arrest (on or after 27 July 1798) Indictment (3 Oct.1798) Plea of not guilty (2 Apr.1799) Plea of guilty at trial (3 Oct.1799)
Failed Prosecutions under the Sedition Act (Chapter 6)		
10. Thomas Jefferson (1743–1826), vice president, Washington, DC		Investigative trip by Wolcott and interception of letters (20 June 1798)
11. Joel Barlow (1754–1812), poet and supporter of the French Revolution, Paris, France		Listing in Lyon indictment as the person aided or abetted (5 Oct.1798) Scrutiny by Pickering (c. Oct.1798) Search by Pickering for published address (Oct.1799)

(continued)

TABLE A.1. *Continued*

Defendant	Court	Steps Toward Prosecution
12. John Israel (c. 1777–1806), editor of *Herald of Liberty*, Washington, PA		Consideration of prosecution by Pickering (22 Nov.1798) Indictments attempted and rejected by grand juries (before 22 Nov.1798 letter)
13. "Aristides"—probably Dr. Samuel Brown (1769–1830), Lexington, KY		Consideration of prosecution by Pickering (21 July 1798)
14. David Garvin (c. 1773–c. 1817), St. Mary's, GA		Arrest under Sedition Act (30 Nov.1798) Case filed by Randolph (3 Dec.1798) Indictment of Randolph (7–9 Mar.1799) Verdict against Randolph (10 Oct.1799) Dismissal of Randolph's case (8 Jan.1800)
Possibly Contemplated Prosecutions		
Gov. James Garrard of Kentucky		
Dr. George Logan of Philadelphia		
Charles Webber and Benjamin Brown of Vassalborough		
Printer in Newburgh		

† Prosecutions marked with a dagger are the previously documented ones (of three individuals for common law seditious libel and of fourteen individuals under the Sedition Act).

TABLE A.2. **Second Campaign: Sedition Act Prosecutions Around the Fries Rebellion (Early 1799–1800)**

Defendant	Court	Steps Toward Prosecution
The Fries Rebellion and Sedition Act §2 (Chapter 8)		
15. Jacob Greenawalt (1751–1839), Greenwich Township, Berks County, PA	U.S. Circuit Court for District of Pennsylvania—Philadelphia, PA (except Oct. 1799 session in Norristown, PA)	Arrest (11 Apr.1799) Sentencing (22 Apr.1799)
16. Morris Llewellyn (c. 1750–1828), James Jackson, George Britson, Samuel Young, Archibald Mengis, of Montgomery County, PA	Same	Indictment (26 Apr.1799) Plea of not guilty (first three) (29 Apr.1799) New indictment (18 Oct.1789) New indictment (without Jackson) (16 Apr.1800) Capias (arrest warrant) (16 Apr.1800)
17. Langford Herring (c. 1766–1859), Philadelphia, PA	Same	Indictment (27 Apr.1799) Prosecution ended with payment of costs (7 Oct.1799)
18. Rev. Jacob Eyerman (possibly 1760–), Northampton County, PA	Same	Instruction to prosecute from Pickering (21 May 1799) Indictment for escape (12 Oct.1799) and for conspiracy and seditious counseling (15 Oct.1799) Trial (16 Oct.1799), but conviction voided New indictment for escape, conspiracy, and seditious counseling (16 Apr.1800) Submission to court (1 May 1800) Sentencing (1 May 1800)
19. Benjamin Mayer (c. 1762–1824) and Conrad Fahnestock (1763–1803), editors of *Harrisburgher Morgenröthe*	Same	Indictment (18 Oct.1799) Plea of not guilty (18 Oct.1799) Submission to court (18 Oct.1799)
20. Jacob Schneider (c. 1763–1830), editor of *Readinger Adler*, Reading, PA		Instruction to prosecute from Pickering (5 July 1799)
The Fries Rebellion and Sedition Act §1 (Chapter 9)		
21. Henry Ohl, Andrew Leutzingen, Adam Laeb, Nicholas Miller, Martin Hester, Michael Best	U.S. Circuit Court for District of Pennsylvania—Philadelphia, PA (except Oct. 1799 session in Norristown, PA)	Indictment for conspiracy (26 Apr.1799) Indictment again of Ohl (not Leutzingen, Laeb, Miller) (2 May 1800) Rejection of indictment of Hester and Best (2 May 1800)

(continued)

TABLE A.2. *Continued*

Defendant	Court	Steps Toward Prosecution
22. John Shimer, John A. Engelman, Jacob Engelman, John Mumbower, Henry Huber, George Seider, Peter Keefer	Same	Indictment for conspiracy (26 Apr. 1799) (including George Shaefer, who was indicted the next day in the Jarrett case, below) Discontinuance of prosecution of Keefer and Shaefer (17 Oct. 1799)
23. Daniel Klein, Jacob Klein, Adam Breisch, George Gettman, William Gettman	Same	Indictment for conspiracy, rescue, and obstruction (CRO) (27 Apr. 1799) Submission to court's judgment (17 Oct. 1799) New indictment for CRO (16 Apr. 1800) Submission to court's judgment (22 Apr. 1800) Sentencing (1 May 1800)
24. John Eberhardt, John Huber, Christopher Sax (Sox), John Klein, Jr., John Klein, John Fox	Same	Indictment for CRO (27 Apr. 1799) (except John Fox and 5 others who were indicted in later cases) Nonprosecution of J. Klein, Sr. (17 Oct. 1799) Submission to court's judgment (17 Oct. 1799) (except Fox) New indictment for CRO (16 Apr. 1800), and deletion of last 2 from indictment Submission to court's judgment (22 Apr. 1800) (except Fox) Sentencing (1 May 1800) (except Kleins)
25. George Goltner, Peter Styerwaldt, John Lechlider, John Smith, William Rex, Charles Styerwaldt, Tobias Shlosser, Jacob Fritz, Laurence Ebner, Andrew Feller, George Hetler, John Kuntz, Peter Rabenholdt	Same	Indictment for conspiracy (27 Apr. 1799)
26. Abraham Samsel, Peter Hundsberg, Abraham Shantz, George Mumbower, Henry Mumbower, Peter Hager, Peter Gable, Jacob Gable, Daniel Gable, John Miller, John Marks, Henry Smith, Valentine Kuder	Same	Indictment for conspiracy (27 Apr. 1799) (except Smith and Kuder) Submission to court's judgment (17 Oct. 1799) (all except last 4) New indictment for conspiracy (16 Apr. 1800) (including Smith and Kuder, dropping Miller and Marks)

Defendant	Court	Steps Toward Prosecution
		Submission to court's judgment (22 Apr. 1800) (except Miller and Marks) Sentencing of remaining defendants (1 May 1800) (except Miller and Marks)
27. Henry Jarrett, Henry Shankweiler, Herman Hartman, Adam Stephan, Daniel Kevely, Jacob Klein, George Shaefer	Same	Indictment for conspiracy (27 Apr. 1799) Conviction of Shaefer (15 May 1799) Sentencing of Shaefer (18 May 1799) Dismissal of Stephan and Kevely New indictment for conspiracy (18 Apr. 1800) (except Schaefer) Submission to court's judgment (22 Apr. 1800 and 2 May 1800) (first 3) Sentencing of Jarrett, Shankweiler, and Hartman (2 May 1800)
28. Henry Shiffert, Christian Ruth, Samuel Schwartz, Henry Stahler, Daniel Schwartz, Jr., John Kayser, Daniel Dillinger, George Shaefer, Daniel Schwartz, Adam Stahlnecker	Same	Indictment for CRO (30 Apr. 1799) Refusal to indict Stahlnecker (30 Apr. 1799) Trial (10–15 May 1799) Conviction of Shiffert, Ruth, Stahler, Shaefer, D. Schwartz Sr. (15 May 1799), and acquittal of D. Schwartz Jr. Sentencing of Shiffert, Ruth, Stahler, Shaefer, D. Schwartz (18 May 1799)
29. Michael Yeisley, John Smyer, Michael Smyer, Jacob Smyer, Philip Ruth, Peter Rothenberger, John Huber, Jacob Eisenhardt, George Ehrich, Frederick Hayns, John Stadtler	Same	Indictment for CRO (30 Apr. 1799) Refusal to indict last 4 (30 Apr. 1799) Submission to court's judgment by John Smyer, M. Smyer, Ruth (18 Oct. 1799) New indictment of all but last 4 (29 Apr. 1800) Dismissal of John Smyer (30 Apr. 1800) Submission to court's judgment by M. Smyer and Ruth (30 Apr. 1800) Sentencing of M. Smyer, Huber, and Ruth (1 May 1800)
30. Anthony Stahler, Jacob Klein, Philip Desh	Same	Indictment for CRO (2 May 1800) Submission to court's judgment (2 May 1800) Sentencing (2 May 1800)

(continued)

TABLE A.2. *Continued*

Defendant	Court	Steps Toward Prosecution
31. Conrad Marks, John Marks	Same	Indictment for conspiracy (29 Apr. 1800) Submission to court's judgment by C. Marks (1 May 1800) Sentencing of C. Marks (1 May 1800)

† Prosecutions marked with a dagger are the previously documented ones (none for numbers 21–31).

TABLE A.3. **Third Campaign: Sedition Act Prosecutions (Late 1799–1800)**

Defendant	Court	Steps Toward Prosecution
New Round of Enforcement 1799–1800 (Chapter 10)		
32. William Duane (1760–1835)†, editor of Philadelphia *Aurora* (His first Sedition Act prosecution, for *Aurora* of 24 July 1799) He had 4 Sedition Act prosecutions, in addition to common law prosecutions.	U.S. Circuit Court for District of Pennsylvania—Philadelphia, PA	British influence case (docket no.3): Instruction to prosecute from Pickering (24 July 1799) Arrest (30 July 1799) Indictment (14 Oct.1799) Postponement to next session (16 Oct.1799) Reindictment (29 Apr.1800) Dismissal (nolle prosequi) (Apr.1800)
33. William Duane (above), editor of Philadelphia *Aurora* (His second Sedition Act prosecution, for *Aurora* of 3 Aug. 1799)	Same	British bribery case (docket no.2): Instruction to prosecute from Pickering (1 Aug.1799) Indictment (14 Oct.1799) Postponement to next session (16 Oct.1799) Reindictment (29 Apr.1800)
34. William Duane (above), editor of Philadelphia *Aurora* (His third Sedition Act prosecution, for *Aurora* of 24 July 1799)	Same	St. Domingue case (docket no.19): Instruction to prosecute from Pickering (1 Aug.1799 and 20 Sept.1799) Indictment (14 Apr.1800) Capias (arrest warrant) (14 Apr.1800) Dismissal (nolle prosequi) (5 May 1801)
35. William Duane (above)†, editor of Philadelphia *Aurora* (His fourth Sedition Act prosecution, for *Aurora* of 19 Feb. 1800)	Same	Senate proceedings and case: Senate summons and contempt resolution (21 Mar.1800, 27 Mar.1800) Senate request to prosecute (14 May 1800) Instruction to prosecute from Adams (16 May 1800) Indictment (17 Oct.1800) Continuance (18 Oct.1800) Postponement of trial (12 May 1801) Dismissal (nolle prosequi) of Sedition Act charges (28 July 1801) Reindictment (rejected by grand jury) (Oct.1801) [In addition to common law seditious libel prosecutions of Duane: Indictment (seditious riot) (21 Feb.1799) Indictment (Liston letters) (14 Apr.1800)]

(*continued*)

TABLE A.3. ***Continued***

Defendant	Court	Steps Toward Prosecution
36. Dr. Joseph Priestley (1733–1804), Northumberland County, PA		Instruction to prosecute from Pickering (1 Aug. 1799)
37. Meriwether Jones (1766–1806), editor of Richmond *Examiner*	U.S. Circuit Court for District of Virginia—Richmond, VA	Instruction to prosecute from Pickering (14 Aug. 1799) Grand jury charge pressing for indictment (22 May 1800)
New York Prosecutions (Chapter 11)		
38. Jedidiah Peck (1748–1821)†, Otsego County, NY	U.S. Circuit Court for District of New York—New York, NY	Instruction to prosecute from Pickering (12 Aug. 1799) Indictment (4 Sept. 1799) Arrest (late Sept. 1799) Suspension without trial (Apr. 1800)
39. Ann Greenleaf (1767–1845)†, editor of New York *Argus* and *Greenleaf's New York Journal*	Same	Instruction to prosecute from Pickering (12 Aug. 1799) Indictment (4 Sept. 1799) Dismissal (nolle prosequi) (22 Apr. 1800) Common law action against printer David Frothingham in N.Y. Court of Oyer and Terminer: Request by Hamilton (6 Nov. 1799) Arrest (9 Nov. 1799) Trial (21 Nov. 1799)
40. William Durell (1766–1845) (above), editor of *Mount Pleasant Register* His case was converted from a common law case—see c above.	Same	Instruction to prosecute from Pickering (28 June 1798) Arrest under common law (17 July 1798) Arrest under Sedition Act (17 July 1799) Indictment under Sedition Act (4 Sept. 1799) Trial (4 Apr. 1800) Sentencing and judgment (9 Apr. 1800) Pardon (22 Apr. 1800)
41. John Daly Burk (above) and James Smith (above), editors of New York *Time Piece* Their case was converted from a common law case—see b above.	Same	Indictment under Sedition Act (4 Sept. 1799) Appearance by Smith and apparently Burk (2–6 Sept. 1799)

Defendant	Court	Steps Toward Prosecution
New England Prosecutions (Chapter 12)		
42. Charles Holt (1772–1852)†, editor of New London *Bee*	U.S. Circuit Court for District of Connecticut—New Haven, CT	Indictment (17 Sept.1799) Arrest (21 Sept.1799) Trial (14 Apr.1800)
43. Anthony Haswell (1756–1816)†, editor of *Vermont Gazette,* Bennington, VT	U.S. Circuit Court for District of Vermont—Rutland & Windsor, VT	Indictment (7 Oct.1799) Arrest (8 Oct.1799) Trial (5 May 1800) Sentencing (9 May 1800) Second indictment rejected (11 Oct.1799)
44. Rep. Matthew Lyon (1749–1822) (second indictment)	Same	Information filed (11 Oct.1799) Arrest warrant (7 Nov.1799) Trial scheduled but not held (for 1 May 1800)
45. Judah P. Spooner (1748–1807), printer of *Scourge of Aristocracy,* Fair Haven, VT	Same	Indictment (6 Oct.1798) Summons to Lyon trial (6 Oct.1798) Arrest warrant (4 Oct.1799) Dismissal by nolle prosequi (Oct.1799)
46. Alden Spooner (1757–1827), editor of *Spooner's Vermont Journal* Windsor, VT	Same	Indictment (6 Oct.1798) Summons to Lyon trial (6 Oct.1798) Dismissal by nolle prosequi (Oct.1799)
47. Dr. Samuel Shaw (1768–1827), Castleton, VT	Same	Summons to Lyon trial (6 Oct.1798) Indictment (10 Oct.1799) Arrest warrant (7 Nov.1799) Arrest (6 Feb.1800) Warrant returned (1 May 1800) Trial and acquittal (8 May 1800) Costs taxed (9 May 1800)
Prowling the Circuit Hunting Sedition from Pennsylvania to Virginia (Chapter 13)		
48. Thomas Cooper (1759–1839)†, temporary editor of *Sunbury and Northumberland Gazette,* North-umberland County, PA	U.S. Circuit Court for District of Pennsylvania—Philadelphia, PA	Instruction to prosecute from Pickering (after 2 Nov.1799) Arrest warrant (8 Apr.1800) Arrest (9 Apr.1800) Indictment (12–14 Apr.1800) Trial (19 Apr.1800) Sentencing (23–24 Apr.1800)
49. Alexander Martin (c. 1777–1810), editor of Baltimore *American*	U.S. Circuit Court for District of Maryland—Annapolis, MD	Instruction to prosecute from Pickering (12 Aug.1799) Grand jury charge pressing for indictment (7 May 1800) Indictment rejected by grand jury (7–8 May 1800)

(*continued*)

TABLE A.3. *Continued*

DEFENDANT	COURT	STEPS TOWARD PROSECUTION
50. James T. Callender (1758–1803)†, author of *The Prospect Before Us* and writer for *Examiner*, Richmond, VA	U.S. Circuit Court for District of Virginia—Richmond, PA	Instruction to prosecute from Pickering (14 Aug.1799) Presentment (24 May 1800) Arrest warrant (24 May 1800) Arrest (27 May 1800) Indictment (entered in court 26 May 1800) Trial (3 June 1800) Sentencing (4 June 1800)
51. James J. Wilson (c. 1775–1824), editor of *Mirror of the Times*, Wilmington, DE	U.S. Circuit Court for District of Delaware—New Castle, DE	Grand jury charge pressing for indictment (27 June 1800) Indictment rejected by grand jury (28 June 1800)
Possibly Contemplated Prosecutions		
Dr. John Vaughan		
Dr. John Tyler		
John Courtney		

† Prosecutions marked with a dagger are the previously documented ones (of three individuals for common law seditious libel and of fourteen individuals under the Sedition Act).

Totals of the Prosecutions

The 51 prosecutions under the Sedition Act that can be documented in original court records or original prosecutor records consist of:

- 39 actual prosecutions filed in court;
- 11 planned prosecutions instructed to be filed in court by Secretary of State Timothy Pickering (Clopton, Barlow, Israel, Aristides, Schneider, Priestley, Jones), or Justice Samuel Chase (Martin, Wilson), or otherwise pursued (Jefferson, Garvin);
- 1 de facto prosecution instructed and filed in court by Secretary of the Treasury Oliver Wolcott (Ogden).

This does not count as additional prosecutions the reindictments of Duane and of Fries Rebellion defendants after the October 1799 court session in Pennsylvania was invalidated, or the rejected second indictments such as that of Anthony Haswell that the grand jury found were not true bills.

Those 51 prosecutions were of 126 individuals:

- 43 individuals under Sedition Act §2, grouped in 40 cases (numbered 1–14 and 32–51), for seditious press or speech; and
- 83 individuals under Sedition Act §1, grouped in 11 cases (numbered 21–31), for seditious combinations or conspiracies to oppose any measure of government, or seditious counsel, advice, or attempt of any riot or unlawful assembly.

The number of prosecutions does not equal the number of individuals for these reasons:

- Sedition Act §2 cases grouped 5 individuals in one case (Llewellyn, Jackson, Britson, Young, and Mengis), 2 individuals in one case (Burk and Smith), and 2 individuals in another case (Mayer and Fahnstock), and involved 4 cases against one individual (Duane); and
- Sedition Act §1 cases grouped 83 individuals in 11 cases.

TABLE A.4. Alien Act Contemplated Prosecutions (1798–1800)

Target		Steps Toward Enforcement
Contemplated Prosecutions (Chapters 14–15)		
a. Gen. Victor Collot (1750–1805)[††] and "some other foreigners"	First deportation order	Order to deport signed by Adams (17 Oct.1798), after recommendation by Pickering (4 Oct.1798)
b. Johann Caspar Schweizer (1754–1811)	Second deportation order	Order to deport signed by Adams (17 Oct.1798), after recommendation by Pickering (11 Oct.1798)
c. Duverne de Presle (1763–1844)	Third deportation order	Same
d. Comte de Volney (1757–1820)[††]		Listing for deportation by Adams (pre-18 July 1798), and recommendation to deport from Ambassador Rufus King to Pickering (6 Apr.1798, 1 Aug.1798)
e. Victor Marie DuPont (1767–1827)[††]		Revocation of exequatur by Adams and Pickering (13 July 1798)
f. Pierre Samuel DuPont (1739–1817)[††]		Denial of passports by Adams (16 Sept.1798), after recommendation by Pickering (11 Sept.1798)
g. "Delegation from the [French]National Institute"		Same
h. Joseph Philippe Létombe[††] "and the persons lately named for Consuls"		Revocation of exequatur by Adams and Pickering (13 July 1798), and recommendation by Pickering to expel (11 Oct.1798 and 1 Aug.1799)
i. Moreau de St. Méry (1750–1819)[††]		Listing for deportation by Adams (pre-18 July 1798)
j. Jean Antoine Bernard Rozier (–1799), Louis Arcambal, and Theodore-Charles Mozard (1755–1810)		Revocation of exequaturs by Adams and Pickering (13 July 1798), and recommendation by Pickering to expel (11 Oct.1798)
k. François Sébastien Lambin		Investigation by Pickering (6 Oct. 1798 and 4 Oct.1798)
l. Jean Baptiste Verdier		Review of intelligence by Pickering (12 Oct.1798)
m. M. Cosperet		Instructions to arrest by Pickering (4 Sept.1798)
n. M. Morgues		Review of intelligence by Pickering (7 Mar.1799)
o. "Dangerous aliens" and Irish "villains" in Philadelphia		Instructions to prosecute from Pickering (28 Aug.1798)
p. John Daly Burk (c. 1776–1808)[††]		Instructions to deport from Pickering (7 July 1798)
q. William Duane (1760–1835)[††]		Instructions to deport from Adams (1 Aug.1799), after recommendation by Pickering (24 July 1799)

Target	Steps Toward Enforcement
r. James T. Callender (1758–1803)††	Rumor was "a principal object" of the Alien Act or Naturalization Act (7 June 1798)
s. Joseph Priestley (1733–1804)††	Recommendation to deport from Pickering (1 Aug.1799), though vetoed by Adams (13 Aug.1799)
t. William Cobbett (1763–1835)††	Statement by Adams that "merited . . . the Alien Bill" (22 Feb.1799), though did not order
u. Albert Gallatin (1761–1849)	Threats during congressional debates (26 Apr.1798 and 20 Apr.1798)
v. Thomas Paine (1737–1809)	Threats by Adams (3 May 1797, 11 Aug.1800, etc.)

††Prosecutions marked with two daggers are the previously documented ones.

Abbreviations

Alien and Sedition Acts Alien Act (25 June 1798), Richard Peters, ed., *Public Statutes at Large of the United States* (Boston: Little and Brown, 1848), 1:570 (sometimes called the Alien Friends Act).*
Sedition Act (14 July 1798), *Statutes at Large,* 1:596 ("An Act in Addition to the Act . . .").*

AFC L. H. Butterfield et al., eds., *Adams Family Correspondence* (Cambridge, MA: Belknap Press of Harvard University Press, 1963–).**

American Newspapers Clarence S. Brigham, ed., *History and Bibliography of American Newspapers, 1690–1820* (Worcester, MA: American Antiquarian Society, 1947).

ANB John A. Garraty et al., eds., *American National Biography* (New York: Oxford University Press, 1999).

Annals *Debates and Proceedings in the Congress of the United States . . . Annals of the Congress of the United States* (Washington: Gales and Seaton, 1834–1856).***

ASP *American State Papers. Documents, Legislative and Executive, of the Congress of the United States [Foreign Relations Series]* (Washington: Gales and Seaton, 1832).

*Also available at avalon.law.yale.edu.

**Also available at https://founders.archives.gov.

***Also available at http://memory.loc.gov/ammem/amlaw/lwac.html.

DHSC Maeva Marcus, ed., *Documentary History of the Supreme Court of the United States, 1789–1800* (New York: Columbia University Press, 1985–2007) (vol. 1 was co-edited by James R. Perry).

F. Cas. *The Federal Cases: Comprising Cases Argued and Determined in the Circuit and District Courts of the United States from the Earliest Times to the Beginning of the Federal Reporter* (St. Paul, MN: West Publishing Co., 1894–1897).

LCM Bernard C. Steiner, ed., *Life and Correspondence of James McHenry* (Cleveland, OH: Burrows Brothers, 1907).

LRK Charles R. King., ed., *Life and Correspondence of Rufus King* (New York: Putnam's Sons, 1894–1900).

ODNB H. C. G. Matthew et al., eds., *Oxford Dictionary of National Biography* (Oxford: Oxford University Press, 2004).

PAH Harold C. Syrett et al., eds., *Papers of Alexander Hamilton* (New York: Columbia University Press, 1961–1987).**

PGW W. W. Abbot et al., eds., *Papers of George Washington: Presidential Series* (Charlottesville: University Press of Virginia, 1987–).**

PGW-R Dorothy Twohig et al., eds., *Papers of George Washington: Retirement Series* (Charlottesville: University Press of Virginia, 1998–1999).**

Pickering Papers "Timothy Pickering Papers" (Massachusetts Historical Society, Boston, original manuscripts and 69 reels).

PJM William T. Hutchinson et al., eds., *Papers of James Madison* (Chicago: University of Chicago Press, 1962–1991).**

PJM-SS Robert Brugger et al., eds., *Papers of James Madison: Secretary of State Series* (Charlottesville: University Press of Virginia, 1987–).

POW George Gibbs, *Memoirs of the Administrations of Washington and John Adams, Edited from the Papers of Oliver Wolcott* (New York: Van Norden, 1846).

PTJ Julian P. Boyd et al., eds., *Papers of Thomas Jefferson* (Princeton: Princeton University Press, 1950–).**

PTJ-R J. Jefferson Looney, ed., *The Papers of Thomas Jefferson: Retirement Series* (Princeton: Princeton University Press, 2004–).**

Senate Executive Journal *Journal of the Executive Proceedings of the Senate* (Washington, D.C.: Duff Green, 1828).

Statutes Richard Peters, ed., *Public Statutes at Large of the United States* (Boston: Little and Brown, 1848).

Wharton Francis Wharton, *State Trials of the United States During the Administrations of Washington and Adams* (Philadelphia: Carey and Hart, 1849).

WFA Seth Ames, ed., *Works of Fisher Ames* (Boston: Little, Brown, 1854).

WJA Charles Francis Adams, ed., *Works of John Adams* (Boston: Little, Brown, 1850–1856).

*Also available at avalon.law.yale.edu.

**Also available at https://founders.archives.gov.

***Also available at http://memory.loc.gov/ammem/amlaw/lwac.html.

Publishers

AAS	American Antiquarian Society
AHA	American Historical Association
BPHUP	Belknap Press, Harvard University Press
BUP	Boston University Press
CAP	Carolina Academic Press
CAUP	Colorado Associated University Press
CP	Clarendon Press
CUP	Cambridge University Press
ColUP	Columbia University Press
CorUP	Cornell University Press
DUP	Duke University Press
FDUP	Fairleigh Dickinson University Press
GPC	Genealogical Publishing Co.
GPO	U.S. Government Printing Office
HCSC	Historical Commission of South Carolina
HP	Hambledon Press, London
HSP	Historical Society of Pennsylvania
HUP	Harvard University Press
IUP	Indiana University Press
JHUP	Johns Hopkins University Press
LB	Little, Brown, Boston
LF	Liberty Fund, Indianapolis
LSUP	Louisiana State University Press
MHS	Massachusetts Historical Society
MUP	Manchester University Press
NCDAH	North Carolina Dept. of Archives & History
NJHC	New Jersey Historical Commission
NJHS	New Jersey Historical Society
NYHS	New York Historical Society
NYUP	New York University Press
OhUP	Ohio University Press
OUP	Oxford University Press
PHMC	Pennsylvania Historical and Museum Cm.
PSUP	Pennsylvania State University Press
PUP	Princeton University Press
RHS	Royal Historical Society
RUP	Rutgers University Press
SCP	Saint Catherine Press
SHSW	State Historical Society of Wisconsin
SUNYP	State University of New York Press
SUP	Stanford University Press
THC	Tennessee Historical Commission
UCP	University of California Press
UChiP	University of Chicago Press

UCSB	University of California Santa Barbara
UDP	University of Delaware Press
UGP	University of Georgia Press
UIP	University of Illinois Press
UKP	University of Kentucky Press
UMP	University of Massachusetts Press
UMoP	University of Missouri Press
UNCP	University of North Carolina Press
UNDP	University of Notre Dame Press
UNP	University of Nebraska Press
UPK	University Press of Kentucky
UPKan	University Press of Kansas
UPP	University of Pennsylvania Press
UPitP	University of Pittsburgh Press
UPV	University Press of Virginia
URP	University of Rochester Press
USCP	University of South Carolina Press
UTP	University of Tennessee Press
UWP	University of Wisconsin Press
YUP	Yale University Press

Notes

Introduction

1. This refers to the Alien Friends Act along with the Sedition Act, which appear at Statutes, 1:570 (25 June 1798) and 1:596 (14 July 1798). See John C. Miller, *Crisis in Freedom: The Alien and Sedition Acts* (Boston: LB, 1952), 2. Also enacted in June and July 1798 were the Naturalization Act, lengthening the residency requirement for citizenship to fourteen years, and the Alien Enemies Act, taking effect only in wartime.
2. Throughout, quotations use the spelling, capitalization, italics, and punctuation of the original, except in citing captions for period newspaper articles. Long book titles are shortened.
3. E.g., Max M. Edling, *A Revolution in Favor of Government* (New York: OUP, 2003); Jonathan Den Hartog, *Patriotism and Piety: Federalist Policies and Religious Struggle in the New American Nation* (Charlottesville: UPV, 2014); Linda K. Kerber, *Federalists in Dissent* (Ithaca, NY: CorUP, 1970), 140, 183; David H. Fischer, *The Revolution of American Conservatism: The Federalist Party in the Era of Jeffersonian Democracy* (New York: Harper, 1965), 16, 167. Even the magnum opus on Federalism downplays the significance of the acts, saying that President Adams "had misgivings," while Federalists in Congress "did not press their efforts with the kind of concerted conviction that has most often been attributed to them." Rather than being unconstitutional, the implementation under the Sedition Act was merely clumsy and inept. The Alien Enemies Act passed with "Republican insistence," while the Alien Friends Act was watered down, strictly interpreted by Adams, and "never invoked." Stanley Elkins and Eric McKitrick, *The Age of Federalism* (New York: OUP, 1993), 590,

700, 704, 591–592. Accord William Chlumsky, "Setting Bounds to Passions: Federalist Communication Policy and the Making of the Sedition Act of 1798" (Ph.D. diss., University of Illinois–Chicago, 2015), 280–316 (not partisan, not to punish opposition, not to restrict speech).

4. Alexander Hamilton to Timothy Pickering (7 June 1798), Harold C. Syrett, ed., *The Papers of Alexander Hamilton* (New York: ColUP, 1961–1987), 21:494, 495 ("*PAH*"); Alexander Hamilton to Oliver Wolcott (29 June 1798), ibid., 21:522.
5. Alexander Hamilton to Theodore Sedgwick (2 Feb.1799), ibid., 22:452, 453; accord ibid., 22:393, 394; 22:519.
6. Alexander Hamilton to Jonathan Dayton (Oct.–Nov.1799), ibid., 23:599, 604; see Robert W. T. Martin, "Reforming Republicanism: Alexander Hamilton's Theory of Republican Citizenship and Press Liberty," *Journal of the Early Republic* 25 (2005): 21–46, at 36–45; James M. Smith, "Alexander Hamilton, the Alien Law, and Seditious Libels," *Review of Politics* 16 (1954): 305–333.
7. Alexander Hamilton to Harrison Gray Otis (26 Jan.1799), *PAH*, 22:440, 441; accord ibid., 21:349 n.5; 21:399; 22:425, 426.
8. For brief treatment, e.g., Douglas Ambrose and Robert W. T. Martin, eds., *The Many Faces of Alexander Hamilton* (New York: NYUP, 2006) (except Martin's essay). For silence, e.g., Michael P. Federici, *The Political Philosophy of Alexander Hamilton* (Baltimore: JHUP, 2012); Willard S. Randall, *Alexander Hamilton* (New York: HarperCollins, 2003); Gerald Stourzh, *Alexander Hamilton and the Idea of Republican Government* (Stanford: SUP, 1970).
9. E.g., Melvin I. Urofsky and Paul Finkelman, *A March of Liberty: A Constitutional History of the United States,* 3rd ed. (New York: OUP, 2011), 1:202, 210 (opposed Alien and Sedition Acts); Miller, *Crisis in Freedom,* 73 (passed "against the advice of Alexander Hamilton"); see Karl-Friedrich Walling, *Republican Empire: Alexander Hamilton on War and Free Government* (Lawrence: UPKan, 1999), 272 ("moderation . . . in opposing the Alien and Sedition Acts and in reacting to the *Virginia and Kentucky Resolutions*"); Lawrence S. Kaplan, *Alexander Hamilton: Ambivalent Anglophile* (Wilmington, NC: SR Books, 2002), 145–146 (position "unclear"); and the older sources cited in James M. Smith, *Freedom's Fetters* (Ithaca, NY: CorUP, 1956), 153 n.44, such as Claude G. Bowers, *Jefferson and Hamilton* (Boston: Houghton Mifflin, 1925), 377.
10. George Washington to Alexander Hamilton (26 June 1796), *PAH,* 20:237, 239; George Washington to Bushrod Washington (31 Dec.1798), Dorothy Twohig et al., eds., *The Papers of George Washington: Retirement Series* (Charlottesville, UPV, 1998–1999), 3:302; George Washington to John Marshall (30 Dec.1798), ibid., 3:297; George Washington to William Vans Murray (26 Dec.1798), ibid., 3:286.
11. George Washington to Alexander Spotswood, Jr. (22 Nov.1798), ibid., 3:216; George Washington to Timothy Pickering (4 Aug.1799), ibid., 4:221; accord Marshall Smelser, "George Washington and the Alien and Sedition Acts," *American Historical Review* 59 (1954): 322–334.
12. E.g., John H. Rhodehamel, *George Washington: The Wonder of the Age* (New Haven: YUP, 2017), 293–302; Joseph J. Ellis, *His Excellency: George Washington* (New York: Knopf, 2004); Gary L. Gregg II and Matthew Spalding, eds.,

Patriot Sage: George Washington and the American Political Tradition (Wilmington, NC: ISI Books, 1999); Richard Brookhiser, *Founding Father: Rediscovering George Washington* (New York: Free Press, 1996).

13. John Adams to Timothy Pickering (1 Aug.1799), Charles Francis Adams, ed., *The Works of John Adams* (Boston: LB, 1850–1856), 9:5 (*"WJA"*); John Adams to Charles Lee (16 May 1800), ibid., 9:56; Stephen G. Calabresi and Christopher S. Yoo, *The Unitary Executive: Presidential Power from Washington to Bush* (New Haven: YUP, 2008), 60–62. Besides Adams authorizing three prosecutions of Duane, he authorized the prosecution of Thomas Cooper. John Adams to Timothy Pickering (13 Aug.1799), *WJA,* 9:13, 13–14. On the Sedition Act's constitutionality, see John Marshall to St George Tucker (18 Nov.1800), Herbert A. Johnson et al., eds., *Papers of John Marshall* (Charlottesville: UPV, 1974–2006), 4:14, 15; John Adams to Timothy Pickering (15 Oct.1798), *WJA,* 8:605.
14. John Adams to Timothy Pickering (16 Sept.1798), *WJA,* 8:596; John Adams to Timothy Pickering (16 Oct.1798), ibid., 8:606; e.g., John Adams to Benjamin Rush (25 Dec.1811), *WJA,* 10:10.
15. E.g., Luke Mayville, *John Adams and the Fear of American Oligarchy* (Princeton: PUP, 2016); David McCullough, *John Adams* (New York: Simon and Schuster, 2001), 505 ("never invoked" Alien Act); C. Bradley Thompson, *John Adams and the Spirit of Liberty* (Lawrence: UPKan, 1998), 275; Jean S. Holder, "The John Adams Presidency" (Ph.D. diss., American University, 1983), 143, 149; Stephen G. Kurtz, *The Presidency of John Adams* (Philadelphia: UPP, 1957), 321–322, 359; and the otherwise enormously insightful biography, Joseph J. Ellis, *Passionate Sage: The Character and Legacy of John Adams* (New York: Norton, 1993); see also Miller, *Crisis in Freedom,* 225. For a friendlier view of Adams and the Alien and Sedition Acts, see Walter Brown, *John Adams and the American Press* (Jefferson, NC: McFarland, 1995), 102–103.
16. Robert Maxwell to Thomas Jefferson (15 May 1801), Julian P. Boyd et al., eds., *Papers of Thomas Jefferson* (Princeton: PUP, 1950–), 34:113 ("*PTJ*"); William Duane, "The Beauties of John Adams's Political Opinions," *Aurora* (Philadelphia), 6 Oct.1800, in ibid., 32:202; [John Daly Burk], [No Caption], *Time Piece* (New York), 30 Aug.1798, 3.
17. The exceptions were Alden Spooner, who was indicted to obtain testimony, and who was dismissed when no longer needed to prosecute Matthew Lyon; and Jedidiah Peck, who was in flux. In 1798 Peck signed a supportive address sent to John Adams, but in September 1799 he was indicted for circulating a petition opposing the Alien and Sedition Acts.
18. Thomas Jefferson to James Madison (7 June 1798), William T. Hutchinson et al., eds., *Papers of James Madison* (Chicago: UChiP, 1962–1991), 17:143.
19. Leonard Levy, *Emergence of a Free Press* (New York: OUP, 1985), xii; accord 294, 89, 136, 272, 297; ibid., 281; Leonard W. Levy, "Liberty and the First Amendment, 1790–1800," *American Historical Review* 68 (1962): 22–37, at 27.
20. Gordon S. Wood, *Empire of Liberty: A History of the Early Republic, 1789–1815* (New York: OUP, 2009), 258; Phillip I. Blumberg, *Repressive Jurisprudence in the Early American Republic: The First Amendment and the Legacy*

of English Law (New York: CUP, 2010), 6, 7–9, 52–71; Richard Labunski, *James Madison and the Struggle for the Bill of Rights* (New York: OUP, 2006), 258 and n.16; Richard D. Brown, "The Shifting Freedoms of the Press in the Eighteenth Century," in Hugh Amory and David D. Hall, eds., *The Colonial Book in the Atlantic World* (Cambridge: CUP, 2000), 366, 375; Walt Brown, *John Adams and the American Press* (Jefferson, NC: McFarland, 1995), 32–34; Elkins and McKitrick, *Age of Federalism,* 700 and n.25; Norman L. Rosenberg, "Seditious Libel," in Kermit L. Hall, ed., *Oxford Companion to the Supreme Court of the United States* (New York: OUP, 1992), 765, 766; Stanley C. Brubaker, "Original Intent and Freedom of Speech and Press," in Eugene W. Hickok, Jr., ed., *The Bill of Rights: Original Meaning and Current Understanding* (Charlottesville: UPV, 1991), 82, 83; James R. Wiggins, "Afterword: The Legacy of the Press in the American Revolution," in Bernard Bailyn and John B. Hench, eds., *The Press and the American Revolution* (Worcester, MA: AAS, 1980), 365, 368; Walter Berns, *The First Amendment and the Future of American Democracy* (New York: Basic Books, 1976), 84; Richard Buel, *Securing the Revolution: Ideology in American Politics, 1789–1815* (Ithaca, NY: CorUP, 1972), 244–245; Gordon S. Wood, *Creation of the American Republic, 1776–1787* (Chapel Hill: UNCP, 1969), 63; James P. Martin, "When Repression Is Democratic and Constitutional: The Federalist Theory of Representation and the Sedition Act of 1798," *University of Chicago Law Review* 66 (1999): 117, 125–126 nn.14–15; Andrew Lennar, "Separate Spheres: Republican Constitutionalism in the Federalist Era," *American Journal of Legal History* 41 (1997): 250, 273 and n.107; William R. Casto, "Oliver Ellsworth," *Journal of Supreme Court History* 1996 (1996): 73, 83; Norman L. Rosenberg, "Another World: Freedom of Press in the Eighteenth Century," *Reviews in American History* 16 (1988): 554, 556–558; Philip B. Kurland, "The Original Understanding of the Freedom of the Press Provision of the First Amendment," *Mississippi Law Journal* 55 (1985): 225, 233–235; Walter Berns, "Freedom of the Press and the Alien and Sedition Laws: A Reappraisal," *Supreme Court Review* 1970 (1970): 109–159, at 135–142; Joseph I. Shulim, "John Daly Burk: Irish Revolutionist and American Patriot," *Transactions of the American Philosophical Society* 54 (1964): 1, 26; Merrill Jensen, "Legacy of Suppression," *Harvard Law Review* 75 (1961): 456, 458.

21. Russell L. Weaver and Donald E. Lively, *Understanding the First Amendment,* 4th ed. (Newark: Lexis-Nexis, 2012), 7, 4; Eric Barendt, *Freedom of Speech* (New York: OUP, 2005), 163–164 and n.47; William Cohen, *The First Amendment: Constitutional Protection for Expression and Conscience* (New York: Foundation Press, 2003), 5; James Magee, *Freedom of Expression* (Westport, CT: Greenwood Press, 2002), 23–24; John P. Reid, *Constitutional History of the American Revolution: The Authority of Rights* (Madison: UWP, 1986), 1:4; Michael I. Meyerson, "The Neglected History of the Prior Restraint Doctrine," *Indiana Law Review* 34 (2001): 295, 311–313, 320 and n.178, 321–322; David Lowenthal, *No Liberty for License: The Forgotten Logic of the First Amendment* (Dallas: Spence Publishing, 1997), 12–13; Philip A. Hamburger, "Natural Rights, Natural Law, and American Constitutions," *Yale Law Journal* 102

(1993): 907, 911–912 (with restrictions); Michael T. Gibson, "The Supreme Court and Freedom of Expression from 1791 to 1917," *Fordham Law Review* 55 (1986): 263, 327, 331; Philip A. Hamburger, "Development of the Law of Seditious Libel and the Control of the Press," *Stanford Law Review* 37 (1985): 661, 745–746 n.261; Robert H. Bork, "Neutral Principles and Some First Amendment Problems," *Indiana Law Journal* 47 (1971): 1, 22; Jerome L. Merin, "Libel and the Supreme Court," *William and Mary Law Review* 11 (1969): 371, 375–78.

22. E.g., Blumberg, *Repressive Jurisprudence*, 7, 53; Terri Diane Halperin, *The Alien and Sedition Acts of 1798: Testing the Constitution* (Baltimore: JHUP, 2016), 65; Peter Charles Hoffer, *The Free Press Crisis of 1800* (Lawrence: UPKan, 2011), 52; Cohen, *The First Amendment*, 6, 5; Brown, *John Adams and the American Press*, 105; Elkins and McKitrick, *Age of Federalism*, 700–701; Martin, "When Repression," 126 n.15; Lennar, "Separate Spheres," 276 n.126; Kurland, "Original Understanding," 236–237, 247–248; Rosenberg, "Another World," 597; June Eichbaum, "The Antagonism Between Freedom of Speech and Seditious Libel," *Hastings Constitutional Law Quarterly* 5 (1978): 445, 455; Berns, "Freedom of the Press," 110; Shulim, "John Daly Burk," 26; Jensen, "Legacy of Suppression," 458; see Wood, *Empire of Liberty*, 258; Rosenberg, "Seditious Libel," 765; Meyerson, "Neglected History," 322; Paul A. Freund, "Political Libel and Freedom of the Press," *Proceedings of the American Philosophical Society* 112 (1968): 117–120, at 118.

23. *Reports of Committees in Congress to Whom Were Referred Certain Memorials and Petitions Complaining of the Acts of Congress, Concerning the Alien & Sedition Laws* (Richmond: Thomas Nicholson, 1799), 6; Sir William Blackstone, *Commentaries on the Laws of England* (Oxford: Clarendon Press, 1765–1769), 4:151. Blackstone similarly defined liberty of speech ("liberty of private sentiment") as liberty to speak without "any restraint hereby laid upon freedom of thought or enquiry," but not as liberty from punishment for "disseminating, or making public, of bad sentiments," which "is the crime which society corrects." Ibid., 4:152.

24. Wendell Bird, *Press and Speech under Assault: The Early Supreme Court Justices, the Sedition Act of 1798, and the Campaign against Dissent* (New York: OUP, 2016), 394–458.

25. "Friday, December 26," *Aurora*, 26 Dec.1794, 3; "From the New-York Daily Gazette," *Aurora*, 26 Dec.1793, 2.

26. Wendell Bird, "Liberties of Press and Speech: 'Evidence Does Not Exist To Contradict the . . . Blackstonian Sense' in Late 18th Century England?," *Oxford Journal of Legal Studies* 36 (2016): 1–25; Wendell Bird, "The Revolution in Freedoms of Press and Speech: From Blackstone to the First Amendment" (New York: OUP, forthcoming 2020).

27. James M. Smith, *Freedom's Fetters: The Alien and Sedition Laws and American Civil Liberties* (Ithaca, NY: Cornell University Press, 1956).

28. Ibid., 185. The fourteen indictments include two that have been (erroneously) treated as of two defendants each (Benjamin Fairbanks and David Brown, and Luther Baldwin and Brown Clark).

29. The original federal court records are the case files, indictments, dockets, minute books, and other documents in each case. Their location is identified at the beginning of the discussion of each arrest or trial. The printed case reports that exist for four cases are not original records, because unlike modern case reports, they consisted of reprinted newspaper accounts or, in one case, the party's own account, all assembled a half century later. Francis Wharton, *State Trials of the United States During the Administrations of Washington and Adams* (Philadelphia: Carey and Hart, 1849), 333n., 659n., 684n., 688n. (part). They were then reprinted in *Federal Cases,* after another half century, in 1894–1897.)
30. Terri Diane Halperin, *The Alien and Sedition Acts of 1798: Testing the Constitution* (Baltimore: JHUP, 2016) (pp.78–96 on prosecutions); Charles Slack, *Liberty's First Crisis: Adams, Jefferson, and the Misfits Who Saved Free Speech* (New York: Atlantic Monthly Press, 2015); John C. Miller, *Crisis in Freedom: The Alien and Sedition Acts* (Boston: LB, 1952). The same is true of nearly all books on the individuals prosecuted. E.g., Aleine Austin, *Matthew Lyon* (University Park: PSUP, 1981), 170 n.1.
31. E.g., Smith, *Freedom's Fetters,* 185; Saul Cornell, *The Other Founders: Anti-Federalism and the Dissenting Tradition in America, 1788–1828* (Chapel Hill: UNCP, 1999), 233; Carol S. Humphrey, *The Press of the Young Republic, 1783–1833* (Westport, CT: Greenwood Press, 1996), 61; James R. Sharp, *American Politics in the Early Republic* (New Haven: YUP, 1993), 218–220; Elkins and McKitrick, *Age of Federalism,* 703; Maeva Marcus, ed., *Documentary History of the Supreme Court of the United States, 1789–1800* (New York: ColUP, 1990), 3:233; Norman L. Rosenberg, *Protecting the Best Man: An Interpretive History of the Law of Libel* (Chapel Hill: UNCP, 1986), 87; Dumas Malone, *Jefferson and His Time* (Boston: LB, 1948–1981), 4:227; Julius Goebel, *History of the Supreme Court of the United States, Vol.1—Antecedents and Beginnings to 1801* (New York: Macmillan, 1971), 1:637–38 and n.107; John C. Miller, *The Federalist Era* (New York: Harper, 1960), 235; Miller, *Crisis,* 65–66, 97–130, 194–223; Frank M. Anderson, "The Enforcement of the Alien and Sedition Acts," *American Historical Review* 18 (1912): 113, 120.
32. E.g., Slack, *Liberty's First Crisis,* 233; Halperin, *Alien and Sedition Acts,* 6; Patrick Novotny, *The Press in American Politics, 1787–2012* (Santa Barbara, CA: Praeger, 2014), 17–23; Urofsky and Finkelman, *March of Liberty,* 1:203; Wood, *Empire of Liberty,* 260; Susan Dunn, *Jefferson's Second Revolution* (Boston: Houghton Mifflin, 2004), 112; Geoffrey R. Stone, *Perilous Times* (New York: Norton, 2004), 63; John E. Ferling, *Adams vs. Jefferson: The Tumultuous Election of 1800* (New York: OUP, 2004), 122; Marc Lendler, "'Equally Proper at All Times and at All Times Necessary': Civility, Bad Tendency, and the Sedition Act," *Journal of the Early Republic* 24 (2004): 419–444, at 422; Joanne B. Freeman, "Explaining the Unexplainable: The Cultural Context of the Sedition Act," in Meg Jacobs et al., eds., *The Democratic Experiment* (Princeton: PUP, 2003), 20, 32, 45 n.38; Michael Kent Curtis, *Free Speech, "The People's Darling Privilege": Struggles for Freedom of Expression* (Durham, NC: DUP, 2000), 93; Francis D. Cogliano, *Revolutionary America, 1763–1815*

(New York: Routledge, 2000), 157. Other writers discussing the canon of three plus fourteen prosecutions are listed in Wendell Bird, "New Light on the Sedition Act of 1798: The Missing Half of the Prosecutions," *Law and History Review* 34 (2016): 541–614, at 574–575.

33. Smith, *Freedom's Fetters*, 155 (first quotation); Timothy Pickering to Rufus King (4 May 1799), in Charles R. King, ed., *Life and Correspondence of Rufus King* (New York: Putnam, 1894–1900), 3:12, 13 (second quotation).
34. A Confederationist, "From the Pennsylvania Herald," *Independent Chronicle*, 15 Nov.1787, 2; accord "London Association. Liberty of the Press," *Independent Chronicle*, 9–13 Aug.1798, 1.
35. Cincinnatus [Arthur Lee], "From the New York Journal," *Vermont Gazette*, 26 Nov.1787, 1, reprinting Cincinnatus, "Number I," *New-York Journal*, 1 Nov.1787, 2.
36. E.g., Carol Berkin, *A Sovereign People: The Crises of the 1790s and the Birth of American Nationalism* (New York: Basic Books, 2017), 201–243; Robert W. T. Martin, "The Censorship of Public Opinion: James Madison, the Sedition Act Crisis and Democratic Press Liberty," in Geoff Kemp, ed., *Censorship Moments* (London: Bloomsbury Academic, 2015); Geoffrey R. Stone, *Perilous Times: Free Speech in Wartime, from the Sedition Act of 1798 to the War on Terrorism* (New York: Norton, 2004), 15–78; Jeffrey L. Pasley, *The Tyranny of Printers: Newspaper Politics in the Early American Republic* (Charlottesville: UPV, 2001), 79–104, 132–195; Curtis, *Free Speech*, 80–94.

1. Federalist and Republican Views of Government

1. Max M. Edling, *A Hercules in the Cradle: War, Money, and the American State, 1783–1867* (Chicago: UChiP, 2014), 50–107; Donald F. Swanson and Andrew P. Trout, "Alexander Hamilton, 'the Celebrated Mr. Neckar,' and Public Credit," *William and Mary Quarterly* 47 (1990): 422–430; "The First Conflict in the Cabinet," in Julian P. Boyd et al., eds., *Papers of Thomas Jefferson* (Princeton: PUP, 1950–), 18:611 ("*PTJ*"); Stanley Elkins and Eric McKitrick, *The Age of Federalism* (New York: OUP, 1993), 92–123, 133–161.
2. Peter McPhee, *Liberty or Death: The French Revolution* (New Haven: YUP, 2016); Elkins and McKitrick, *Age of Federalism*, 303–373.
3. Jerald A. Combs, *The Jay Treaty* (Berkeley: UCP, 1970), 159–188; Nathaniel C. Green, "'The Focus of the Wills of Converging Millions': Public Opposition to the Jay Treaty and the Origins of the People's Presidency," *Journal of the Early Republic* 37 (2017): 429–469, at 434–459; Todd Estes, "Shaping the Politics of Public Opinion: Federalists and the Jay Treaty Debate," *Journal of the Early Republic* 20 (2000): 393–422.
4. Robert W. T. Martin, *Government by Dissent: Protest, Resistance, and Radical Democratic Thought in the Early American Republic* (New York: NYUP, 2013), 83–113, 147–175; Matthew Schoenbachler, "Republicanism in the Age of Democratic Revolution: The Democratic-Republican Societies of the 1790s," *Journal of the Early Republic* 18 (1998): 237–261; Thomas P. Slaughter, *The*

Whiskey Rebellion (New York: OUP, 1986), 190–221; Elkins and McKitrick, *Age of Federalism*, 461–474.

5. The background events of the 1790s, including the challenges of state formation, the French Revolution, immigration, partisanship, and mutual suspicion, are superbly summarized by Terri Diane Halperin and thoroughly chronicled by Stanley Elkins and Eric McKitrick. Terri Diane Halperin, *The Alien and Sedition Acts of 1798: Testing the Constitution* (Baltimore: JHUP, 2016); Elkins and McKitrick, *Age of Federalism.*
6. A Citizen [Thomas Cooper], "On the Terms Democrat, Jacobin, Antifederalist, &c. with a Description of the Parties in This Country" (June 1799), in Thomas Cooper, *Political Essays* (Northumberland, PA: Andrew Kennedy, 1799), 26–31, at 30.
7. James R. Sharp, *American Politics in the Early Republic* (New Haven: YUP, 1993), 10, 113–116; Elkins and McKitrick, *Age of Federalism*, 123–131; on Federalist beliefs, see Andrew Lenner, "A Tale of Two Constitutions: Nationalism in the Federalist Era," *American Journal of Legal History* 40 (1996): 72–105, at 90–104.
8. John Adams, *Defence of the Constitutions of Government of the United States of America,* reprinted in Charles Francis Adams, ed., *Works of John Adams* (Boston: LB, 1850–1856), 4:271, 358 ("*WJA*"); "John Adams to Young Men of the City of New York" (2 June 1798), *WJA*, 9:197, 199.
9. A Citizen [Cooper], *Political Essays,* 30–31; accord Elkins and McKitrick, *Age of Federalism,* 257–302; Thomas Jefferson to James Madison (26 Nov. 1799), William T. Hutchinson et al., eds., *Papers of James Madison* (Chicago: UChiP, 1962–1991), 17:280 ("*PJM*"); Thomas Jefferson to Elbridge Gerry (26 Jan.1799), *PTJ*, 30:645, 646; see Andrew Lenner, "Separate Spheres: Republican Constitutionalism in the Federalist Era," *American Journal of Legal History* 41 (1997): 250–281, at 251–278.
10. George Cabot to Oliver Wolcott (16 Dec.1799), George Gibbs, *Memoirs of the Administrations of Washington and John Adams Edited from the Papers of Oliver Wolcott* (New York: Van Norden, 1846), 2:312; George Cabot to Oliver Wolcott (19 Jan.1798), ibid., 2:8, 9; Fisher Ames to Oliver Wolcott (15 Dec.1800), ibid., 2:457; Fisher Ames to Oliver Wolcott (12 Jan.1800), ibid., 2:318, 319.
11. James McHenry to John McHenry, Jr. (20 May 1800), Harold C. Syrett et al., eds., *Papers of Alexander Hamilton* (New York: ColUP, 1961–), 24:507 ("*PAH*"); Oliver Wolcott to Fisher Ames (10 Aug.1800), Gibbs, *Wolcott,* 2:400, 404; see David Hackett Fischer, *The Revolution of American Conservatism: The Federalist Party in the Era of Jeffersonian Democracy* (New York: Harper, 1965), 2–17.
12. Alan Taylor, "'The Art of Hook & Snivey': Political Culture in Upstate New York During the 1790s," *Journal of American History* 79 (1993): 1371–1396, at 1380–1386; "New-York, December 10," *Greenleaf's New York Journal,* 10 Dec.1794, 3.
13. Ronald P. Formisano, "Deferential-Participant Politics: The Early Republic's Political Culture, 1789–1840," *American Political Science Review* 68 (1974): 473–487.

14. Bernard Bailyn, *The Ideological Origins of the American Revolution,* enlarged ed. (Cambridge, MA: BPHUP, 1992), 34–45, 23–26; J. G. A. Pocock, *Virtue, Commerce, and History: Essays on Political Thought and History* (Cambridge: CUP, 1985), 253–273; Caroline Robbins, *The Eighteenth-Century Commonwealthman* (Cambridge, MA: HUP, 1959).
15. Eric Slauter, "Rights," in Jane Kamensky and Edward G. Gray, eds., *Oxford Handbook of the American Revolution* (New York: OUP, 2012), 447, 456; accord Jack P. Greene, *The Constitutional Origins of the American Revolution* (New York: CUP, 2011), 185–186.
16. Alan Taylor, "From Fathers to Friends of the People: Political Personae in the Early Republic," in Doron Ben Atar and Barbara B. Oberg, eds., *Federalists Reconsidered* (Charlottesville: UPV, 1998), 225, 226.
17. Edward Countryman, "Indians, the Colonial Order, and the Social Significance of the American Revolution," *William and Mary Quarterly* 53 (1996): 342–362, at 362, 342; accord Alfred F. Young and Gregory H. Nobles, *Whose American Revolution Was It? Historians Interpret the Founding* (New York: NYUP, 2011), 144–172, 224–255, 172–192; Gary B. Nash, *The Forgotten Fifth: African Americans in the Age of Revolution* (Cambridge, MA: HUP, 2006), 1–67.
18. Richard Hofstadter, *The Idea of a Party System: The Rise of Legitimate Opposition in the United States, 1780–1840* (Berkeley: UCP, 1969), 40–121; Brian W. Dotts, "Citizen Dissent in the New Republic: Radical Republicanism and Democratic Educational Thought During the Revolutionary Era" (Ph.D. diss., Indiana University, 2005).
19. Inaugural Speech (4 Mar.1797), *WJA,* 9:105, 108; James R. Sharp, *American Politics in the Early Republic* (New Haven: YUP, 1993); William N. Chambers, *Political Parties in a New Nation: The American Experience, 1776–1809* (New York: OUP, 1965), 17–33; e.g., Alexander Hamilton to George Washington (19 May 1798), *PAH,* 21:466, 467.
20. John Adams, "To the Mayor, Aldermen, and Citizens of the City of Philadelphia" (Apr.1798), *WJA,* 9:182; John Adams, "To the Inhabitants of the Town of Hartford" (10 May 1798), ibid., 9:192; John Adams, "To the Students of Dickinson College" (May 1798), ibid., 9:204, 205.
21. Wendell Bird, *Press and Speech under Assault: The Early Supreme Court Justices, the Sedition Act of 1798, and the Campaign against Dissent* (New York: OUP, 2016), 248–320.
22. Samuel Chase's Charge (C.C.D. Pa. 12 Apr.1800), Maeva Marcus, ed., *Documentary History of the Supreme Court of the United States, 1789–1800* (New York: ColUP, 1985–2007), 3:408, 411, 412, 413 ("*DHSC*") (v.1 was coedited by James R. Perry); James Iredell's Charge (C.C.D. Md. 8 May 1797), ibid., 3:173, 174, 176. Cooper's case is discussed in Chapter 13.
23. William Paterson to Euphemia Paterson (17 Nov.1800), ibid., 3:455; James Iredell's Charge (C.C.D. Pa. 11 Apr.1799), ibid., 3:332, 347.
24. John Adams, "To the Inhabitants of the County of Burlington" (8 May 1798), *WJA,* 9:191; Noah Webster to Oliver Wolcott (23 June 1800), Gibbs, *Wolcott,* 2:373; Fisher Ames to Oliver Wolcott (12 Jan.1800), Gibbs, *Wolcott,* 2:318, 320.

25. See discussion of Hamilton, Washington, and Adams and the Sedition Act in the Introduction; Robert W. T. Martin, "Reforming Republicanism: Alexander Hamilton's Theory of Republican Citizenship and Press Liberty," *Journal of the Early Republic* 25 (2005): 21–46.
26. Sir William Blackstone, *Commentaries on the Laws of England* (Oxford: CP, 1765–1769), 4:151, 152; see Philip Hamburger, "The Development of the Law of Seditious Libel and the Control of the Press," *Stanford Law Review* 37 (1985): 661–765.
27. Joanne B. Freeman, *Affairs of Honor: National Politics in the New Republic* (New Haven: YUP, 2001), xvi–xxiii; Joanne B. Freeman, "Explaining the Unexplainable: The Cultural Context of the Sedition Act," in Meg Jacobs et al., eds., *The Democratic Experiment* (Princeton: PUP, 2003): 20–49, at 29–36; see Marcus Daniel, *Scandal and Civility: Journalism and the Birth of American Democracy* (New York: OUP, 2009), 12–13.
28. Nonadoption of Blackstone by the twelve earliest Supreme Court justices before 1798 is shown in Bird, *Press and Speech under Assault,* 113–247. Adoption of the opposite by Republican editors well before 1798 is shown in this book's discussions of them—Bache and Burk (Chapter 3), Lyon (Chapter 4), Thomas Adams (Chapter 5), Duane (Chapter 10), Haswell (Chapter 12), and Cooper (Chapter 13). See also Wendell Bird, "Liberties of Press and Speech: 'Evidence Does Not Exist To Contradict the . . . Blackstonian Sense' in Late 18th Century England?," *Oxford Journal of Legal Studies* 36 (2016): 1–25.
29. Fischer, *Revolution of American Conservatism,* 129–149; Jeffrey L. Pasley, *The Tyranny of Printers: Newspaper Politics in the Early American Republic* (Charlottesville: UPV, 2001), 48–257, 407–409.
30. Bernard Bailyn and John B. Hench, eds., *The Press & the American Revolution* (Worcester, MA: AAS, 1980); Arthur M. Schlesinger, *Prelude to Independence: The Newspaper War on Britain 1764–1776* (New York: Knopf, 1957), 51–301; Philip Davidson, *Propaganda and the American Revolution, 1763–1783* (Chapel Hill: UNCP, 1941).
31. Charles E. Clark, "Early American Journalism: News and Opinion in the Popular Press," in Hugh Amory and David D. Hall, eds., *The Colonial Book in the Atlantic World* (New York: CUP, 2000), 1:347, 355; "Appendix 1," ibid., 1:504, 512; Lawrence H. Leder, "The Role of Newspapers in Early America 'In Defense of Their Own Liberty,'" *Huntington Library Quarterly* 30 (1966): 1–16.
32. *PAH,* 13:106, 13:142, 15:579; John Fenno, "An Address" (1 Jan.1789), in John B. Hench, ed., "Letters of John Fenno," *Proceedings of American Antiquarian Society* 89 (1980): 299, 312–313.
33. Negotiation was through Madison, James Madison to Thomas Jefferson (24 July 1791), *PTJ,* 20:667; Philip Freneau to Thomas Jefferson (4 Aug.1791), ibid., 20:754. For employment, see Thomas Jefferson to Philip Freneau (28 Feb.1791), ibid., 19:351; Thomas Jefferson to James Madison (21 July 1791), ibid., 20:657; accord "Jefferson, Freneau and the Founding of the *National Gazette,*" ibid., 20:718–753; Daniel, *Scandal and Civility,* 62–108; Lewis Leary,

That Rascal Freneau: A Study in Literary Failure (New Brunswick, NJ: RUP, 1941).

34. Alexander Hamilton to Edward Carrington (26 May 1792), *PAH,* 11:421, 430; T. L. [Alexander Hamilton], "No.1" (25 July 1792), ibid., 12:107; T. L. [Alexander Hamilton], "No.2" (28 July 1792), ibid., 12:123.
35. Thomas Jefferson to George Washington (9 Sept.1792), *PTJ,* 24:351, 354; *PAH,* 12:157, 158–59; 12:188; 12:193; 12:379, 393, 578; 12:570; 12:633.
36. John Fenno to Alexander Hamilton (9 Nov.1793), ibid., 15:393, 394; Alexander Hamilton to Rufus King (11 Nov.1793), ibid., 15:395–396; Alexander Hamilton to John Kean (29 Nov.1793), ibid., 15:418.
37. Daniel, *Scandal and Civility,* 8; e.g., David A. Wilson, ed., *William Cobbett: Peter Porcupine in America* (Ithaca, NY: CorUP, 1994), 50–257; *PTJ,* 20:749n.; George Washington to David Stuart (28 Mar. 1790), W. W. Abbot et al., eds., *Papers of George Washington: Presidential Series* (Charlottesville: UPV, 1987–), 5:286, 287 ("*PGW*")
38. Jeffery A. Smith, *Franklin and Bache: Envisioning the Enlightened Republic* (New York: OUP, 1990); James Tagg, *Benjamin Franklin Bache and the Philadelphia Aurora* (Philadelphia: UPP, 1991); Daniel, *Scandal and Civility,* 109–147, 231–274; Pasley, *Tyranny of Printers,* 407–409, 79–257.
39. Pasley, *Tyranny of Printers,* 118.
40. Thomas Jefferson to James Madison (26 Apr.1798), *PJM,* 17:120.
41. John Adams to William Cunningham (20 Mar.1809), *Correspondence Between the Hon. John Adams . . . and the Late Wm. Cunningham, Esq.* (Boston: E.M. Cunningham, 1823), 100, 107; accord James McHenry to James McHenry, Jr. (20 May 1800), *PAH,* 24:507, 508.
42. Gordon S. Wood, *Empire of Liberty: A History of the Early Republic* (New York: OUP, 2009), 273–274; Sharp, *American Politics,* 159–162.
43. Oliver Wolcott to James McHenry (18 July 1800), Gibbs, *Wolcott,* 2:381; Oliver Wolcott to Fisher Ames (29 Dec.1799), ibid., 2:313, 315; Manning J. Dauer, *The Adams Federalists* (Baltimore: JHUP, 1953), 120–265; Benjamin Goodhue to Timothy Pickering (26 Oct.1798), Henry Cabot Lodge, ed., *Life and Letters of George Cabot,* 2nd ed. (Boston: LB, 1878), 179 n.1; George Cabot to Rufus King (10 Mar.1799), Charles R. King., ed., *Life and Correspondence of Rufus King* (New York: Putnam's Sons, 1894–1900), 2:551, 552.
44. The best biography of Pickering is Gerard H. Clarfield, *Timothy Pickering and the American Republic* (Pittsburgh: UPitP, 1980), esp. 180–210; see Gerard H. Clarfield, *Timothy Pickering and American Diplomacy, 1795–1800;* John A. Garraty et al., eds., *American National Biography* (New York: OUP, 1999), 17:478 ("*ANB*"). An older less useful source is Octavius Pickering and Charles W. Upham, *The Life of Timothy Pickering* (Boston: LB, 1867–1873). For his termination by Adams, see John Adams to Timothy Pickering (12 May 1800), *WJA,* 9:55.
45. John Adams to William Cunningham (7 Nov.1808), Cunningham, ed., *Correspondence,* 42, 44, 50; Clarfield, *Timothy Pickering and the American Republic,* 173–174.

46. The best biography of Wolcott is Neil A. Hamilton, "Connecticut Order, Mercantilistic Economics: The Life of Oliver Wolcott, Jr." (Ph.D. diss., University of Tennessee, 1988); the published biography is Gibbs, *Wolcott;* see *ANB,* 23:722. For his resignation, see Oliver Wolcott to John Adams (8 Nov.1800), *WJA,* 9:88.
47. The best biography of McHenry is Karen E. Robbins, *James McHenry, Forgotten Federalist* (Athens: UGP, 2013); see *ANB,* 15:80. An older less useful source is Bernard C. Steiner, *The Life and Correspondence of James McHenry* (Cleveland, OH: Burrows, 1907). For his resignation, see James McHenry to John Adams (6 May 1800), *WJA,* 9:51.
48. Alexander Hamilton to George Washington (29 July 1798), *PAH,* 22:36, 38; Oliver Wolcott, Jr. to Alexander Hamilton (1 Apr.1799), ibid., 23:1.
49. *Journal of the Executive Proceedings of the Senate* (Washington: Duff Green, 1828), 1:275–276. The best biography of Stoddert is Michael A. Palmer, *Stoddert's War: Naval Operations During the Quasi-War with France, 1798–1801* (Columbia: USCP, 1987); see *ANB,* 20:825.
50. Elkins and McKitrick, *Age of Federalism,* 625, 630; Clarfield, *Pickering and American Republic,* 163.
51. Though Pickering's biographer denied any loyalty to Hamilton, evidence is extensive. John Ferling, *John Adams: A Life* (New York: Holt, 1996), 343–344, 352, 359. For Stoddert, see Benjamin Stoddert to John Adams (12 Oct.1809), Lodge, *Cabot,* 200.
52. E.g., James McHenry to Alexander Hamilton (6 Sept.1798), *PAH,* 22:176; James McHenry to Alexander Hamilton (12 Sept.1798), ibid., 22:179, 180; James McHenry to Alexander Hamilton (5 Oct.1798), ibid., 22:194, 195; James McHenry to Alexander Hamilton (16 Oct.1798), ibid., 22:199.
53. Alexander DeConde, *The Quasi-War: The Politics and Diplomacy of the Undeclared War with France 1797–1801* (New York: Scribner, 1966); Palmer, *Stoddert's War*; see Bradford Perkins, *The First Rapproachement: England and the United States, 1795–1805* (Berkeley: UCP, 1967).
54. Palmer, *Stoddert's War,* 6; accord Paul A. Gilje, "Commerce and Conquest in Early American Foreign Relations, 1750–1850," *Journal of the Early Republic* 37 (2017): 735–770, at 755.
55. Albert H. Bowman, *The Struggle for Neutrality: Franco-American Diplomacy During the Federalist Era* (Knoxville: UTP, 1974), 259–263.
56. Speech to Both Houses of Congress (16 May 1797), in *American State Papers. Documents, Legislative and Executive, of the Congress of the United States [Foreign Relations Series]* (Washington: Gales and Seaton, 1832), 2:111, 114, 115–117 ("*ASP*"); *Debates and Proceedings in the Congress of the United States . . . Annals of the Congress of the United States* (Washington: Gales and Seaton, 1834–1856), 7:54–59 (16 May 1797) ("*Annals*") (all quotations are for 5th Congress); see Nathan Perl-Rosenthal, "Private Letters and Public Diplomacy: The Adams Network and the Quasi-War, 1797–1798," *Journal of the Early Republic* 31 (2011): 283–311, at 303–308.
57. E.g., John Dawson to James Madison (18 May 1797), *PJM,* 17:6; "From a Correspondent," *Aurora* (Philadelphia), 18 May 1797, 3; William C. Stinchcombe, *The XYZ Affair* (Westport, CT: Greenwood Press, 1980), 20–21.

58. France (31 May 1797), *ASP,* 2:19; DeConde, *Quasi-War,* 27–29; Spain, Great Britain, and France (22 June 1797), *ASP,* 2:28.
59. William Vans Murray to James McHenry (22 June 1797), Steiner, *McHenry,* 227, 229.
60. Jeremy D. Popkin, *Revolutionary News: The Press in France, 1789–1799* (Durham, NC: DUP, 1990), 52–54, 173–175; Samuel F. Scott and Barry Rothaus, *Historical Dictionary of the French Revolution 1789–1799* (Westport, CT: Greenwood Press, 1985), 1:265–267.
61. John Adams to Oliver Wolcott, Jr. (27 Oct.1797), *WJA,* 8:558, 559; John Adams to Timothy Pickering (31 Oct.1797), ibid., 8:559, 560; Speech to Both Houses of Congress (23 Nov.1797), *WJA,* 9:121.
62. John Adams to the Heads of Department (21 Jan.1798), *WJA,* 8:561; Rufus King to Timothy Pickering (14 Jan.1798), Charles R. King., ed., *Life and Correspondence of Rufus King* (New York: Putnam's Sons, 1894–1900), 2:271, 272 ("*LRK*"); Plan of a Decree (8 Jan.1798), *ASP,* 2:151 (passed a few days later); *PJM,* 17:144 n.1.
63. John Adams to Congress (5 Mar.1798), *ASP,* 2:150; Envoys to Timothy Pickering (8 Jan. 1798), ibid.; *WJA,* 9:156; John Adams to Congress (19 Mar.1798), *ASP,* 2:152.
64. John Adams to Congress (3 Apr. 1798), *ASP,* 2:153, 157–168. They were published in newspapers and in *Message of the President of the United States, to Both Houses of Congress, April 3d, 1798, with the Despatches from the Envoys . . .* (Philadelphia: [Fenno], 1798).
65. "Despatches from the Envoys to the Secretary of State" (22 Oct.1797–21 Dec.1797), *ASP,* 2:157–168; Carol Berkin, *A Sovereign People: The Crises of the 1790s* (New York: Basic Books, 2017), 151–200; William Stinchcombe, *The XYZ Affair* (Westport, CT: Greenwood Press, 1980), 54–69; DeConde, *Quasi-War,* 48–49. "W," "X," and "Y" were European bankers, Nicholas Hubbard, Jean Conrad Hottinguer, and Pierre Bellamy; "Z" was a courier and translator, Lucien Hauteval. Stinchcombe, *XYZ Affair,* 55–57; William Stinchcombe, "The Diplomacy of the WXYZ Affair," *William and Mary Quarterly* 34 (1977): 590–617; *PAH,* 428–429 n.28.
66. Envoys to Timothy Pickering (9 Mar.1798), *ASP,* 2:186–188; Marvin R. Zahniser, *Charles Cotesworth Pinckney, Founding Father* (Chapel Hill: UNCP, 1967), 185–191; George A. Billias, *Elbridge Gerry, Founding Father and Republican Statesman* (New York: McGraw-Hill, 1976), 280–286; Timothy Pickering to Rufus King (12 June 1798), *LRK,* 2:347.
67. Dispatch (30 Oct. 1797), *ASP,* 2:163, 164.
68. John Adams, "To the Inhabitants of the Town of Wells" (28 May 1798), https://founders.archives.gov/documents/Adams/99-02-02-2512 (captioned John Adams to George Thatcher); John Adams, "To the Inhabitants of the Town of Hartford, Connecticut" (10 May 1798), *WJA,* 9:192; Alexander Hamilton to George Washington (19 May 1798), *PAH,* 21:466, 467.
69. Such as Rep. Robert Goodloe Harper, a Sedition Act sponsor, in the debate on that bill. *Annals,* 8:2164–2165 (10 July 1798); e.g., Abigail Adams to Mercy Otis Warren (25 Apr.1798), *AFC,* 526, 527.

70. Robert Troup to Rufus King (3 June 1798), *LRK,* 2:328, 329; Robert Troup to Rufus King (10 June 1798), ibid., 2:344; William Austin, ed., *A Selection of the Patriotic Addresses, to the President of the United States. Together with the President's Answers* (Boston: Folsom, 1798); Thomas M. Ray, "'Not One Cent for Tribute': The Public Addresses and American Popular Reaction to the XYZ Affair, 1798–1799," *Journal of the Early Republic* 3 (1983): 389–412.
71. "Answers to Addresses," *WJA,* 9:180–236. For moderation, John Adams, "To the Legislature of New Hampshire" (29 June 1798), ibid., 9:203; accord 9:216–217. For bellicosity, John Adams, "To the Inhabitants of Dedham and Other Towns" (14 July 1798), ibid., 9:209; accord 9:196.
72. Robert Troup to Rufus King (3 June 1798), *LRK,* 2:328, 329; accord Robert Troup to Rufus King (10 July 1798), ibid., 2:362, 363; George Cabot to Oliver Wolcott (9 June 1798), Gibbs, *Wolcott,* 2:53; accord George Cabot to Oliver Wolcott (26 Mar.1798), ibid., 2:42, 43.
73. Robert Troup to Rufus King (16 Nov.1798), *LRK,* 2:465; "New Song," *Gazette of the United States* (Philadelphia), 10 May 1798, 3; William Bingham to Rufus King (5 June 1798), *LRK,* 2:331.
74. Thomas Jefferson to James Madison (21 June 1798), *PJM,* 17:155; Thomas Jefferson to Thomas Mann Randolph (3 May 1798), *PTJ,* 30:325, 326; accord James Monroe to Thomas Jefferson (4 May 1798), ibid., 30:328, 329.
75. John Adams to the Heads of Departments (13 Mar.1798), *WJA,* 9:568; Timothy Pickering to Robert Goodloe Harper (21 Mar.1798), in DeConde, *Quasi-War,* 84. Pickering in early May did not expect a declaration of war but a continued sea war. Timothy Pickering to Rufus King (3 May 1798), *LRK,* 2:320.
76. Alexander Hamilton to Theodore Sedgwick (1–15 Mar.1798), *PAH,* 21:361, 362; Alexander Hamilton to George Washington (19 May 1798), ibid., 21:466, 467.
77. Rufus King to Timothy Pickering (6 Apr.1798), *LRK,* 2:304, 306; Fisher Ames to Christopher Gore (25 Feb. 1798), Seth Ames, ed., *Works of Fisher Ames* (Boston: LB, 1854), 1:220, 221 ("*WFA*").
78. James Madison to Thomas Jefferson (3 June 1798), *PJM,* 17:141; Timothy Pickering to Alexander Hamilton (9 June 1798), *PAH,* 21:501, 505; Rufus King to Alexander Hamilton (14 July 1798), *PAH,* 22:1, 3.
79. Thomas Pinckney to Rufus King (18 July 1798), *LRK,* 2:369; e.g., Fisher Ames to Rufus King (12 June 1799), ibid., 3:42; Theodore Sedgwick to Rufus King (1 July 1798), ibid., 2:352; Stephen Higginson to Oliver Wolcott (11 July 1798), Gibbs, *Wolcott,* 2:70.
80. E.g., James McHenry to John Adams (25 Nov. 1798), *WJA,* 8:604 n.4; George Cabot to Oliver Wolcott (25 Oct.1798), Gibbs, *Wolcott,* 2:109. For Republicans, e.g., Thomas Jefferson to Edmund Pendleton (2 Apr.1798), *PTJ,* 30:240, 242; Thomas Jefferson to John W. Eppes (11 Apr.1798), ibid., 30:263.
81. Act To Establish . . . Department of the Navy (30 Apr.1798), Richard Peters, ed., *The Public Statutes at Large of the United States* (Boston: LB, 1848), 1:553

("Statutes"); Act To Provide an Additional Armament (27 Apr.1798), ibid., 1:552; Act Supplementary to . . . Ports and Harbors (3 May 1798), ibid., 1:554; Act to Authorize . . . Gallies (4 May 1798), ibid., 1:556; Frederick C. Leiner, *Millions for Defense: The Subscription Warships of 1798* (Annapolis, MD: Naval Institute Press, 2000), 24–27; see Marshall Smelser, *The Congress Founds the Navy, 1787–1798* (Notre Dame, IN: UNDP, 1959). Titles of statutes are shortened here.

82. Act Authorizing . . . a Provisional Army (28 May 1798), Statutes, 1:558; Act Providing Arms for the Militia (6 July 1798), ibid., 1:576; Act for the Establishing . . . a Marine Corps (11 July 1798), ibid., 1:594.

83. Act To Suspend the Commercial Intercourse (13 June 1798), Statutes, 1:565; Act To Authorize the Defence of Merchant Vessels (25 June 1798), ibid., 1:572; Act To Declare the Treaties . . . No Longer Obligatory (7 July 1798), ibid., 1:578; see John Ferling, "'Father and Protector': President John Adams and Congress in the Quasi-War Crisis," in Kenneth R. Bowling and Donald R. Kennon, eds., *Neither Separate Nor Equal: Congress in the 1790s* (Athens: OhUP, 2000); Proclamation Revoking the Exequaturs of the French Consuls (13 July 1798), *WJA,* 9:170.

84. Act To Lay and Collect a Direct Tax (14 July 1798), Statutes, 1:597; Act To Provide for the Valuation of Lands and Dwelling-Houses, and . . . Slaves (9 July 1798), ibid., 1:580; Act To Enable the President . . . To Borrow Money (18 July 1798), ibid., 1:607; Act . . . To Authorize the President To Obtain a Loan (16 July 1798), ibid., 1:609.

85. The two forces that only existed on paper—the Provisional Army and Eventual Army—and the three forces that existed in actuality—the frontier Regular Army of 3,000 soldiers, the Additional Army or New Army, and volunteer corps—are well described in Richard H. Kohn, *Eagle and Sword: The Federalists and the Creation of the Military Establishment in America, 1783–1802* (New York: Free Press, 1975), 219–255; Paul D. Newman, "The Federalists' Cold War: The Fries Rebellion, National Security, and the State, 1787–1800," *Pennsylvania History* 67 (2000): 63–104, at 84–85; "Introductory Note," *PAH,* 22:383–388. See Act Authorizing . . . Provisional Army (28 May 1798), Statutes, 1:558; Act To Augment the Army (16 July 1798), ibid., 1:604.

86. Kohn, *Eagle and Sword,* 215, 217–218, 225–227.

87. Act Supplementary to . . . "Act to Establish an Uniform Rule of Naturalization" (18 June 1798), Statutes, 1:566; Act Respecting Alien Enemies (6 July 1798), ibid., 1:577; Act Concerning Aliens [Friends] (25 June 1798), ibid., 1:570; Act in Addition to the Act, Entitled "An Act for the Punishment of Certain Crimes against the United States" (14 July 1798), ibid., 1:596.

88. American Envoys to Talleyrand (17 Jan.1798), Herbert A. Johnson et al., eds., *The Papers of John Marshall* (Chapel Hill: UNCP, 1974–), 3:331–381, printed as *Message of the President of the United States, to Both Houses of Congress. May 4th, 1798* (Philadelphia: n.p., 1798).

89. John Adams to Congress (5 June 1798), *ASP,* 2:185, enclosing Envoys to Timothy Pickering (9 Mar.1798), ibid., 2:186–188; John Adams to Congress

(18 June 1798), ibid., 2:188, enclosing Talleyrand to American Envoys (18 Mar.1798), ibid., 2:188–191. Adams also provided other correspondence hand-carried by Marshall. Ibid., 2:199–200. See William Stinchcombe, "Talleyrand and the American Negotiations of 1797–1798," *Journal of American History* 62 (1975): 575–590.

90. DeConde, *Quasi-War,* 147, 161; Copy of a Decree (16 Aug.1798), *ASP,* 2:229; Extract from the Registers of the Deliberations of the Executive Directory (31 July 1798), ibid., 2:222.

91. *Journal of the Executive Proceedings of the Senate* (Washington: Duff Green, 1828), 1:284 (2–3 July 1798) ("*Senate Executive Journal*"); before asking Washington, John Adams to George Washington (7 July 1798), Dorothy Twohig et al., eds., *Papers of George Washington: Retirement Series* (Charlottesville: UPV, 1998–1999), 2:389 ("*PGW-R*").

92. *Senate Executive Journal,* 1:292 (18 July 1798); Timothy Pickering to George Washington (6 July 1798), *PGW-R,* 2:386; John Adams to James McHenry (14 Aug.1798), *WJA,* 8:580; John Adams to James McHenry (29 Aug.1798), ibid., 8:587, 588; John Adams to James McHenry (13 Sept.1798), ibid., 8:593; John Adams to George Washington (9 Oct.1798), *PGW-R,* 3:87; see "Introductory Note," *PAH,* 22:4–17.

93. James McHenry to Alexander Hamilton (21 Jan.1799), *PAH,* 22:428; Alexander Hamilton to George Washington (3 May 1799), ibid., 23:98, 99.

94. E.g., ibid., 22:429; George Washington to James McHenry (15 Oct.1798), *PGW-R,* 3:97, 99; James McHenry to Alexander Hamilton (18 Dec.1798), *PAH,* 24:560 n.34.

95. James McHenry to Alexander Hamilton (22 Apr.1799), *PAH,* 23:58; Theodore Sedgwick to Rufus King (29 Dec.1799), *LRK,* 3:162.

96. Recruiting was suspended in February 1799, and disbanding was ordered in May. Act To Suspend in Part, an Act (20 Feb.1800), Statutes, 2:7; Act Supplementary to the Act To Suspend (14 May 1800), ibid., 2:85. See Theodore Sedgwick to Rufus King (26 July 1799), *LRK,* 3:68, 69.

97. George Cabot to Christopher Gore (9 June 1799), Lodge, *Cabot,* 232, 233; John Adams, "To the Boston Marine Society" (7 Sept.1798), *WJA,* 9:220, 221; John Adams to James McHenry (22 Oct.1798), *WJA,* 8:612, 613.

98. Alexander Hamilton to James McHenry (Jan.–Feb.1798), *PAH,* 21:341, 343; see Aaron N. Coleman, "'A Second Bounaparty?' A Reexamination of Alexander Hamilton During the Franco-American Crisis, 1796–1801," *Journal of the Early Republic* 28 (2008): 183–214, at 183–189 (summary of views and defense of Hamilton).

99. Speech to Both Houses of Congress (8 Dec.1798), *WJA,* 9:128, 130–131.

100. George Washington to James McHenry (13 Dec.1798), *PAH,* 22:341, 345; Alexander Hamilton to Harrison Gray Otis (27 Dec.1798), ibid., 22:393, 394.

101. John Adams to the Senate (18 Feb.1799), *ASP,* 2:239; *WJA,* 9:161; John Adams to the Senate (25 Feb.1799), *ASP,* 2:240; *WJA,* 9:162; see DeConde, *Quasi-War,* 178–185; Stephen G. Kurtz, "The French Mission of 1799–1800," *Political Science Quarterly* 80 (1965): 543–557.

102. Talleyrand to Citizen Pichon (28 Sept.1798), *ASP*, 2:239; Minister of Exterior Relations to William Vans Murray (12 May 1799), *ASP*, 2:243.
103. Timothy Pickering to George Washington (21 Feb.1799), *PGW-R*, 3:389, 389–390; Timothy Pickering to Alexander Hamilton (25 Feb.1799), *PAH*, 22:500; Timothy Pickering to George Cabot (21 Feb.1799), Lodge, *Cabot*, 221; John Adams to Timothy Pickering (15 Jan.1799), *WJA*, 8:621.
104. Timothy Pickering to George Washington (24 Oct.1799), *PGW-R*, 4:362, 363; Timothy Pickering to William Loughton Smith (28 Oct.1799), "Timothy Pickering Papers" (Massachusetts Historical Society, Boston, manuscripts and 69 reels), 12:298, 299; Oliver Wolcott, Jr. to George Cabot (4 Nov.1799), Lodge, *Cabot*, 251, 253.
105. Convention Between the French Republic, and the United States (30 Sept.1800), Hunter Miller, ed., *Treaties and Other International Acts of the United States* (Washington: GPO, 1931), 1:457; DeConde, *Quasi-War*, 253–258. Ellsworth reported that "[m]ore could not be done." Oliver Ellsworth to Alexander Hamilton (16 Oct.1800), *PAH*, 25:160.
106. Oliver Wolcott, Jr. to Timothy Pickering (28 Dec.1800), Gibbs, *Wolcott*, 2:461; John Adams to James Lloyd (6 Feb.1815), *WJA*, 10:114, 115.
107. Timothy Pickering to Alexander Hamilton (15 May 1800), *PAH*, 24:490, 491; Oliver Wolcott, Jr. to Alexander Hamilton (3 Sept.1800), ibid., 25:104; Oliver Wolcott, Jr. to James McHenry (18 July 1800), Gibbs, *Wolcott*, 381.
108. Oliver Wolcott, Jr. to George Cabot (16 June 1800), Gibbs, *Wolcott*, 371; Oliver Wolcott, Jr. to Fisher Ames (10 Aug.1800), ibid., 400, 401, 403; Oliver Wolcott, Jr. to Timothy Pickering (28 Dec.1800), Gibbs, *Wolcott*, 461.
109. Timothy Pickering to Rufus King (28 May 1800), *LRK*, 3:248; Alexander Hamilton to James McHenry (6 June 1800), *PAH*, 24:573. After being fired, Pickering was much more censorious. E.g., Timothy Pickering to George Cabot (16 June 1800), Henry Cabot Lodge, ed., *Life and Letters of George Cabot*, 2nd ed. (Boston: LB, 1878), 275, 277.
110. Oliver Wolcott to Alexander Hamilton (3 Sept.1800), *PAH*, 25:104, 108; Oliver Wolcott to George Cabot (18 June 1800), Lodge, *Cabot*, 278, 279; James McHenry to John McHenry (20 May 1800), Gibbs, *Wolcott*, 2:346, 347.
111. James McHenry to John Adams (31 May 1800), *PAH*, 24:552, 557; John Adams to Benjamin Rush (25 Jan.1806), https://founders.archives.gov/?q=%20Author%3A%22Adams%2C%20John%22%20Recipient%3A%22Rush%2C%20Benjamin%22%20Period%3A%22Jefferson%20Presidency%22&s=1111311111&r=8&sr=rush.
112. Alexander Hamilton to Oliver Wolcott (26 Sept.1800), *PAH*, 25:122.
113. Alexander Hamilton, *Letter from Alexander Hamilton, Concerning the Public Conduct and Character of John Adams, Esq.* (New York: George F. Hopkins, 1800), 4, reprinted *PAH*, 25:186, 186 (24 Oct.1800).
114. James McHenry to Oliver Wolcott (9 Nov.1800), Gibbs, *Wolcott*, 2:445.

2. Passing Laws against Internal Enemies

1. Alexander Hamilton to Edward Carrington (26 May 1792), Harold C. Syrett et al., eds., *Papers of Alexander Hamilton* (New York: ColUP, 1961–), 11:426, 429 ("*PAH*").
2. David J. Siemers, *Ratifying the Republic: Antifederalists and Federalists in Constitutional Time* (Stanford: SUP, 2002), 135–163; James R. Sharp, *American Politics in the Early Republic* (New Haven: YUP, 1993), 53–162; Richard H. Kohn, *Eagle and Sword: The Federalists and the Creation of the Military Establishment in America, 1783–1802* (New York: Free Press, 1975), 195–206; Carey M. Roberts, "Men of Much Faith: Progress and Declension in Jeffersonian Thought, 1787–1800" (Ph.D. diss., University of South Carolina, 1999), 189–207; Matthew Q. Dawson, "From Rags to Riches: America's 'French Party' and America's Napoleon Bonaparte" (Ph.D. diss., Florida State University, 1998).
3. John Quincy Adams to John Adams (3 Apr. 1797), in Worthington C. Ford, ed., *Writings of John Quincy Adams* (New York: Macmillan, 1913–1917), 2:155.
4. [Alexander Hamilton], "A French Faction" (Apr. 1798), *PAH,* 21:452; George Washington to James McHenry (27 Mar. 1798), Dorothy Twohig et al., eds., *Papers of George Washington: Retirement Series* (Charlottesville: UPV, 1998–1999), 2:160 ("*PGW-R*"); Alexander Hamilton to George Washington (19 May 1798), *PAH,* 21:466, 467.
5. Rufus King to Timothy Pickering (1 Aug. 1798), Charles R. King., ed., *Life and Correspondence of Rufus King* (New York: Putnam's Sons, 1894–1900), 2:379, 380 ("*LRK*"); accord Marshall Smelser, "The Jacobin Phrenzy: Federalism and the Menace of Liberty, Equality, and Fraternity," *Review of Politics* 13 (1951): 457–482.
6. Jedidiah Morse, *A Sermon Delivered at the New North Church in Boston . . . May 9th, 1798* (Boston: Samuel Hall, 1798), citing John Robison, *Proofs of a Conspiracy Against All the Religions and Governments of Europe, Carried on in the Secret Meetings of Free Masons, Illuminati, and Reading Societies* (Philadelphia: T. Dobson, 1798).
7. Gen. Henry Knox to John Adams (26 June 1798), "Timothy Pickering Papers" (Massachusetts Historical Society, Boston, manuscripts and 69 reels), 8:598, 600 ("Pickering Papers"); William Cobbett to Timothy Pickering (27 June 1798), ibid., 22:241, 244.
8. [Alexander Hamilton], "For the Gazette of the United States" (13 June 1798), *PAH,* 21:506.
9. William Heth to Alexander Hamilton (14 Jan.1799), *PAH,* 22:413, 415; George Cabot to Timothy Pickering (1 Nov.1799), Pickering Papers, 25:263.
10. Fisher Ames, "Eulogy on Washington" (8 Feb.1800), Seth Ames, ed., *Works of Fisher Ames* (Boston: LB, 1854), 2:71, 82; "Jacobin Tricks," *Gazette of the United States* (Philadelphia), 6 Apr.1799, 2; "Essay II," *Gazette* (Portland), 11 Feb.1799, 3.

11. Thomas Jefferson to Philip Mazzei (24 Apr.1796), Julian P. Boyd et al., eds., *Papers of Thomas Jefferson* (Princeton: PUP, 1950–), 29:81, 82 ("*PTJ*"); James Madison to James Monroe (17 Dec.1797), William T. Hutchinson et al., eds., *Papers of James Madison* (Chicago: UChiP, 1962–1991), 17:61, 62 ("*PJM*").
12. James Madison to Thomas Jefferson (21 Jan.1798), *PJM*, 17:69; James Madison to Thomas Jefferson (20 May 1798), ibid., 17:133, 134; e.g., James Madison to Thomas Jefferson (27 May 1798), ibid., 17:137.
13. Timothy Pickering to Alexander Hamilton (9 Apr.1798), *PAH*, 21:408, 409; Fisher Ames to Timothy Pickering (10 July 1798), Ames, *Fisher Ames*, 1:232, 233.
14. George Cabot to Oliver Wolcott (25 Oct.1798), George Gibbs, ed., *Memoirs of the Administrations of Washington and John Adams Edited from the Papers of Oliver Wolcott* (New York: Norden, 1846), 2:109.
15. Charles Lee to John Adams (8 Mar.1798), https://founders.archives.gov/documents/Adams/99-02-02-2368; George Washington to William Heth (5 Aug.1798), *PGW-R*, 2:491, 491–492; "Logan," *Gazette of the United States*, 19 Nov.1798, 3.
16. Rufus King to Alexander Hamilton (2 July 1798), *PAH*, 21:524; Tristram Dalton to John Adams (26 Mar.1797), https://founders.archives.gov/documents/Adams/99-02-02-1910.
17. Alexander Hamilton to Harrison Gray Otis (27 Dec.1798), *PAH*, 22:393, 394; Alexander Hamilton to James Gunn (22 Dec.1798), ibid., 22:383, 389; Alexander Hamilton to John Jay (7 May 1800), *PAH*, 24:464, 465; accord Alexander Hamilton to Charles Carroll (7 Aug.1800), ibid., 25:60.
18. Richard H. Kohn, *Eagle and Sword: The Federalists and the Creation of the Military Establishment in America, 1783–1802* (New York: Free Press, 1975), 226.
19. Alexander Hamilton to Theodore Sedgwick (2 Feb.1799), *PAH*, 22:452, 453; "War Department, 18th Dec.1798," *Gazette of the United States*, 27 Feb.1799, 3.
20. Timothy Pickering to Rufus King (6 Feb.1799), *LRK*, 2:537; Timothy Pickering to Rufus King (4 May 1799), ibid., 3:12, 13; Theodore Sedgwick to Rufus King (20 Jan.1799), *LRK*, 2:514, 518.
21. John Adams to Thomas Jefferson (14 June 1813), Lester J. Cappon, ed., *The Adams-Jefferson Letters* (Chapel Hill: UNCP, 1959), 2:329; Noah Webster to Timothy Pickering (17 July 1798), Pickering Papers, 22:303.
22. Douglas Bradburn, *The Citizenship Revolution: Politics and the Creation of the American Union, 1774–1804* (Charlottesville: UVP, 2009), 224–227; accord Michael Durey, *Transatlantic Radicals and the Early American Republic* (Lawrence: UPKan, 1997); Samuel E. Morison, ed., *The Life and Letters of Harrison Gray Otis, 1765–1848* (Boston: Houghton Mifflin, 1969), 108.
23. Charles Lee to John Adams (8 Mar.1798), https://founders.archives.gov/documents/Adams/99-02-02-2368; George Cabot to Oliver Wolcott, Jr. (10 Oct.1798), Gibbs, *Wolcott*, 2:110, 111.
24. Theodore Sedgwick to Rufus King (20 Jan.1799), *LRK*, 2:514, 515.

25. Thomas Jefferson to James Madison (21 June 1798), *PJM,* 17:155.
26. Paul D. Newman, "The Federalists' Cold War: The Fries Rebellion, National Security, and the State, 1787–1800," *Pennsylvania History* 67 (2000): 63–104, at 85, 67; David Narrett, *Adventurism and Empire: The Struggle for Mastery in the Louisiana-Florida Borderlands* (Chapel Hill: UNCP, 2015); *Proceedings on the Impeachment of William Blount* (Philadelphia: Joseph Gales, 1799).
27. Gautham Rao, *National Duties: Custom Houses and the Making of the American State* (Chicago: UChiP, 2016); Larrie D. Ferreiro, *Brothers at Arms: American Independence and the Men of France and Spain Who Saved It* (New York: Knopf, 2016).
28. 36 Geo. 3 c.7 and c.8 (1795); Manning J. Dauer, *The Adams Federalists* (Baltimore: JHUP, 1953), 157–159; see Circular to Consuls (9 July 1798), *LRK,* 2:359.
29. *Debates and Proceedings in the Congress of the United States . . . Annals of the Congress of the United States* (Washington: Gales and Seaton, 1834–1856), 8:2016 (21 June 1798) ("*Annals*").
30. An Act Concerning Aliens [Friends] (25 June 1798), Statutes, 1:570; An Act in Addition to the Act, Entitled "An Act for the Punishment of Certain Crimes against the United States" (14 July 1798), ibid., 1:596.
31. An Act Supplementary to . . . "An Act to Establish an Uniform Rule of Naturalization" (18 June 1798), Statutes, 1:566; An Act Respecting Alien Enemies (6 July 1798), ibid., 1:577. Further detail on their congressional passage is in James M. Smith, *Freedom's Fetters: The Alien and Sedition Laws and American Civil Liberties* (Ithaca, NY: CorUP, 1956), 22–49.
32. Act To Establish a Uniform Rule of Naturalization (29 Jan.1795), ibid., 1:414; Naturalization Act §§4–5 (1798), ibid., 1:567–568; *Annals,* 8:1572 (2 May 1798).
33. E.g., William J. Novak, "The Legal Transformation of Citizenship in Nineteenth-Century America," in Meg Jacobs et al., eds., *The Democratic Experiment: New Directions in American Political History* (Princeton: PUP, 2003), 85–119; Richard D. Brown, *The Strength of a People: The Idea of an Informed Citizenry in America, 1650–1870* (Chapel Hill: UNCP, 1996), 26.
34. *Annals,* 8:1427 (17 Apr.1798), 8:1568 (2 May 1798); Stanley Elkins and Eric McKitrick, *The Age of Federalism* (New York: OUP, 1993), 695; John M. O'Keefe, "From Legal Rights to Citizens' Rights and Alien Penalties . . ." (Ph.D. diss., George Washington University, 2012), 69–71.
35. *Annals,* 8:1567–1568 (2 May 1798); William Smith Shaw to Abigail Adams (20 May 1798), L. H. Butterfield et al., eds., *Adams Family Correspondence* (Cambridge, MA: BKHUP, 1963–), 13:44 ("*AFC*").
36. *Annals,* 8:1778, 1780 (21 May 1798); ibid., 8:1776 (21 May 1798) (House 41–40), 7:577 (12 June 1798) (Senate 11–10).
37. Act To Establish a Uniform Rule of Naturalization (14 Apr.1802), Statutes, 2:153; Gerald L. Neuman, "The Lost Century of American Immigration Law (1776–1875)," *Columbia Law Review* 93 (1993): 1833–1901, at 1882.
38. The president must first issue a public proclamation of the declaration of war or invasion; the courts must be courts of criminal jurisdiction.

39. Report on Revision of the Naturalization Act (1 May 1798), in *American State Papers. Documents, Legislative and Executive, of the Congress of the United States [Foreign Relations Series]* (Washington: Gales and Seaton, 1832), 2:180 ("*ASP*"); *Annals,* 8:1453–1454 (resolution, 19 Apr.1798), 8:1566 (1 May 1798), 8:1630–1631 (8 May 1798).
40. *Annals,* 8:2049 (House, 26 June 1798), 7:598 (Senate, 3 July 1798), see 8:2088 (3 July 1798); 50 U.S. Code §§21–24.
41. Thomas Jefferson to James Madison (26 Apr.1798), *PTJ,* 30:299, 299–300.
42. *Annals,* 7:548 (25 Apr.1798), 7:549 (26 Apr. 1798).
43. Ibid., 7:554–555 (4 May 1798); "A Bill Concerning Aliens," *Gazette of the United States,* 7 May 1798, 3 (§9); "A Bill Concerning Aliens," *Aurora* (Philadelphia), 8 May 1798, 2; "The Alien Bill," *Aurora,* 9 May 1798, 3.
44. Bill §§1, 3, 5, 10–11; *Annals,* 7:575 (8 June 1798).
45. Ibid., 8:1974, 1980, 1978 (19 June 1798). Rep. Edward Livingston made a stronger attack. Ibid., 8:2005–2015. The debate appears at 8:1972 and 8:1974–2028; the *Annals* mislabel it "Alien Enemies" instead of "Alien Friends." The debate is described in detail in Smith, *Freedom's Fetters,* 63–93.
46. *Annals,* 8:2035 (25 June 1798); ibid., 8:1986–1989 (19 June 1798), 8:2016–2020 (21 June 1798).
47. Ibid., 8:1974 (19 June 1798).
48. Ibid., 8:2028–2029 (21 June 1798). The party-line vote is charted in Dauer, *Adams Federalists,* 306–309 (item 24). The Senate accepted the House changes the next day. *Annals,* 7:586 (22 June 1798).
49. An Act Concerning Aliens [Friends] §§1–2 (25 June 1798), Statutes, 1:570; see Richard D. Brown, *Self-Evident Truths: Contesting Equal Rights from the Revolution to the Civil War* (New Haven: YUP, 2017), 76; David P. Currie, *The Constitution in Congress: The Federalist Period 1789–1801* (Chicago: UChiP, 1997), 255–258.
50. Ibid., §§3, 5, 6.
51. "Tuesday, June 14," *Aurora,* 14 June 1798, 3, quoted in Smith, *Freedom's Fetters,* 56.
52. Thomas Jefferson to James Madison (7 June 1798), *PJM,* 17:143; Alexander Hamilton to Timothy Pickering (7 June 1798), *PAH,* 21:494, 495; accord Aaron N. Coleman, "'A Second Bounaparty?' A Reexamination of Alexander Hamilton During the Franco-American Crisis, 1796–1801," *Journal of the Early Republic* 28 (2008): 183–214, at 210.
53. Abigail Adams to Mary Smith Cranch (19 June 1798), *AFC,* 13:135, 136.
54. Thomas Jefferson to Thomas Mann Randolph (9 May 1798), *PTJ,* 30:341; James Madison to Thomas Jefferson (20 May 1798), *PJM,* 17:133, 133–134. They spoke of the 4 May version, which Jefferson saw in the 8 May issue of the *Aurora.*
55. Sedition Act §2, Statutes, 1:596 (14 July 1798).
56. Thomas Jefferson to James Madison (26 Apr.1798), *PTJ,* 30:299, 300; Abigail Adams to Mary Smith Cranch (26 Apr.1798), *AFC,* 12:529, 531. Some question an anti-Republican purpose. William Chlumsky, "Setting Bounds to Passions: Federalist Communication Policy and the Making of the

Sedition Act of 1798" (Ph.D. diss., University of Illinois–Chicago, 2015), 282, 313.

57. *Annals,* 8:2162 (10 July 1798); Doron Ben-Atar and Barbara B. Oberg, eds., *Federalists Reconsidered* (Charlottesville: UPV, 1998), 5; e.g., David Ford to Alexander Hamilton (11 Apr.1798), *PAH,* 21:410–411; Fisher Ames to Timothy Pickering (4 June 1798), Ames, *Fisher Ames,* 1:226, 227.
58. Summarized in Wendell Bird, *Press and Speech under Assault: The Early Supreme Court Justices, the Sedition Act of 1798, and the Campaign against Dissent* (New York: OUP, 2016), 31–40, 49–55; Philip Hamburger, "The Development of the Law of Seditious Libel and the Control of the Press," *Stanford Law Review* 37 (1985): 661–765.
59. Sir William Blackstone, *Commentaries on the Laws of England* (Oxford: CP, 1765–1769), 4:151, 152; e.g., A Gentleman of the Middle Temple [Matthew Bacon], *A New Abridgment of the Law,* 3rd ed. (London: J. Worrall, 1768), 3:490–498; Trial of John Tutchin, (1704) 14 State Trials 1095, 1128; Holt K.B. 424, 424, 90 Eng. Rep. 1133, 1133–1134 (K.B.).
60. Abigail Adams to Mercy Otis Warren (25 Apr.1798), *AFC,* 12:526, 528.
61. Blackstone, *Commentaries,* 4:151–152.
62. Wendell Bird, *The Revolution in Freedoms of Press and Speech* (New York: OUP, forthcoming 2020), Chapter 1; Wendell Bird, "Liberties of Press and Speech: 'Evidence Does Not Exist To Contradict the Blackstonian Sense' in Late 18th Century England?," *Oxford Journal of Legal Studies* 36 (2016): 1–25, 5. The decision was Case of Henry Sampson Woodfall, (1770) 20 State Trials 895, 903; Lofft 776, 781, 98 Eng. Rep. 914, 916; 5 Burr. 2686, 98 Eng. Rep. 398 (K.B.).
63. Theodore Sedgwick to Rufus King (9 Apr.1798), *LRK,* 2:310; accord Thomas Jefferson to James Madison (24 Jan.1798), *PJM,* 17:71.
64. Thomas Jefferson to James Madison (26 Apr.1798), *PTJ,* 30:299.
65. *Annals,* 8:1771 (18 May 1798); "A Bill for the Prevention and Restraint of Dangerous and Seditious Persons," *Aurora,* 6 June 1798, 2; *Annals,* 8:1868 (4 June 1798).
66. Ibid., §2.
67. *Annals,* 8:1954–1971 (16 June 1798) (mostly about alien provisions); ibid., 8:1970–1971 (16 June 1798).
68. The most convenient reprint of drafts and amendments is in Dauer, *Adams Federalists,* 343–348. Further detail on debates is in Smith, *Freedom's Fetters,* 94–155.
69. "A Bill To Define More Particularly . . . ," Dauer, *Adams Federalists,* 343–345; "A Bill To Define More Particularly . . . ," *Aurora,* 28 June 1798, 2.
70. Dauer, *Adams Federalists,* 343–344 (§§1, 3–4).
71. Alexander Hamilton to Oliver Wolcott, Jr. (29 June 1798), *PAH,* 21:522; *Annals,* 7:591 (27 June 1798).
72. Dauer, *Adams Federalists,* 345–347; see *Annals,* 7:596, 597 (2–3 July 1798); James Lloyd to George Washington (4 July 1798), *PGW-R,* 2:375.
73. *Annals,* 7:599 (4 July 1798); Henry Tazewell to Thomas Jefferson (5 July 1798), *PTJ,* 30:440.

74. *Annals,* 8:2093–2114 (5 July 1798). Harper proposed seven amendments. Ibid., 8:2115–2115 (5 July 1798). Debate continued most of the day on the 9th of July, ibid., 8:2133–2139, and then all day on the 10th, ibid., 8:2139–2171.
75. Ibid., 8:2093, 2094, 2096, 2097, 2100.
76. Ibid., 8:2094; ibid., 8:2097, 2095–2096, 2100–2101.
77. Ibid., 8:2098.
78. Ibid., 8:2097, 8:2102.
79. Ibid., 8:2112 (Samuel W. Dana—Connecticut), 2148–2149 (Otis), 2167–2168 (Harper).
80. Ibid., 8:2105, 2111; accord 8:2105 (Nathaniel Macon—North Carolina), 2106 (Joseph McDowell—North Carolina), 2151 (Macon), 2153 (Livingston). For rejecting Blackstone, ibid., 8:2160–2161 (Gallatin).
81. Ibid., 8:2133–2139 (9 July 1798), 8:2139–2171 (10 July 1798).
82. Ibid., 8:2140; accord 8:2160 (Gallatin).
83. The background of many is discussed in Robert W. T. Martin, *The Free and Open Press: The Founding of American Democratic Press Liberty, 1640–1800* (New York: NYUP, 2001), 138–154; Federalist arguments are summarized in Marc Lendler, "'Equally Proper at All Times and at All Times Necessary': Civility, Bad Tendency, and the Sedition Act," *Journal of the Early Republic* 24 (2004): 419–444, at 425–444; common law arguments are in Chapter 7 below.
84. *Annals,* 8:2141 (Harper); accord 8:2146 (Otis).
85. Ibid., 8:2141–2142 (Nicholas); accord 8:2152 (Macon), 2157 (Gallatin).
86. Ibid., 8:2167 (Harper); accord 8:2149 (Otis); ibid., 8:2140 (Nicholas).
87. Ibid., 8:2165–2167 (Harper), 8:2144 (Nicholas).
88. Ibid., 8:2146 (Otis); accord 8:2164 (Harper); ibid., 8:2152 (Macon); accord 8:2158–2159 (Gallatin).
89. Ibid., 8:2156 (Dana); accord 8:2168 (Harper); ibid., 8:2154 (Livingston); accord 8:2164 (Gallatin)
90. Ibid., 8:2171 (10 July 1798); Dauer, *Adams Federalists,* 306–309; Henry Tazewell to James Madison (12 July 1798), *PJM,* 163.
91. John Adams, "To the Soldier Citizens of New Jersey" (31 May 1798), Charles Francis Adams, ed., *Works of John Adams* (Boston: LB, 1850–1856), 9:196 ("*WJA*"); John Adams to Timothy Pickering (15 Oct.1798), ibid., 8:605–606 (speaking of Pickering reply to Prince Edward County address).
92. An Act in Addition to the Act, Entitled "An Act for the Punishment of Certain Crimes against the United States" [Sedition Act], Statutes, 1:596 (14 July 1798).
93. Sedition Act §§1, 2.
94. Ibid. §3; Blackstone, *Commentaries,* 4:150; Bird, *Press and Speech under Assault,* 41–46. The provision was added on July 9, 1798. *Annals,* 8:2134.
95. Martin, *Free and Open Press,* 133–134; Stanley N. Katz, ed., *A Brief Narrative of the Case and Trial of John Peter Zenger* (Cambridge, MA: BPHUP, 1963), 132; *Annals,* 8:2162 (Gallatin, 10 July 1798).
96. Sedition Act §3; Blackstone, *Commentaries,* 4:151; Bird, *Press and Speech under Assault,* 56–63; see Mark DeWolfe Howe, "Juries as Judges of Criminal

Law," *Harvard Law Review* 52 (1939): 582–616. It was added on July 9, 1798. *Annals,* 8:2135–2138.

97. Katz, *Brief Narrative,* 132.
98. Phillip I. Blumberg, *Repressive Jurisprudence in the Early American Republic: The First Amendment and the Legacy of English Law* (New York: CUP, 2010), 89; Leonard Levy, *Emergence of a Free Press* (New York: OUP, 1985), 297; June Eichbaum, "The Antagonism Between Freedom of Speech and Seditious Libel," *Hastings Constitutional Law Quarterly* 5 (1978): 445–461, at 454.
99. *Annals,* 8:2138 (9 July 1798), 8:2171 (10 July 1798); John F. Hoadley, *Origins of American Political Parties, 1789–1803* (Lexington: UKP, 1986), 202–209; Dauer, *Adams Federalists,* 299, 306, 312, 318, 322.
100. Ibid., 8:2134 (9 July 1798), 8:2116 (5 July 1798). The original House and Senate bills had no expiration dates. Ibid., 8:1868 (4 June 1798); "A Bill to Define More Particularly . . . ," *Aurora,* 28 June 1798, 2.
101. Ibid., 10:975, 1038; Dauer, *Adams Federalists,* 322–325.
102. The Alien Friends Act initially was to last a year and until the end of the next session of Congress, and then for two years. "A Bill Concerning Aliens," *Gazette of the United States,* 7 May 1798, 3 (§13); Smith, *Freedom's Fetters,* 54.
103. Mark DeWolfe Howe, "Freedom's Fetters," *William and Mary Quarterly* 13 (1956): 573–576, at 575, 576; Levy, *Emergence,* xi; Walter Berns, "Freedom of the Press and the Alien and Sedition Laws: A Reappraisal," *Supreme Court Review* 1970 (1970): 109–159; Leonard W. Levy, "Liberty and the First Amendment, 1790–1800," *American Historical Review* 68 (1962): 22–37, at 28; Thomas F. Carroll, "Freedom of Speech and of the Press in the Federalist Period: The Sedition Act," *Michigan Law Review* 18 (1920): 615–651, at 650.
104. George Anastaplo, *Reflections on Freedom of Speech and the First Amendment* (Lexington: UKP, 2007), 71–77; David Jenkins, "The Sedition Act of 1798 and the Incorporation of Seditious Libel into First Amendment Jurisprudence," *American Journal of Legal History* 45 (2001): 154–213, at 195; William T. Mayton, "Seditious Libel and the Lost Guarantee of a Freedom of Expression," *Columbia Law Review* 84 (1984): 91–142, at 121–130.
105. David A. Anderson, "The Origins of the Press Clause," *UCLA Law Review* 30 (1983): 455–541, at 515–521; Bird, *Press and Speech,* 395–396.
106. Bird, *Press and Speech under Assault,* 399–400 nn.24–27 (citing claims).
107. John Marshall, "To a Freeholder," *Virginia Herald* (Fredericksburg), 2 Oct.1798, 2, reprinted in Herbert A. Johnson et al., eds., *The Papers of John Marshall* (Chapel Hill: UNCP, 1974–), 3:503, 505.
108. George Cabot to Timothy Pickering (26 Oct.1798), Lodge, *Cabot,* 174, 175; Benjamin Goodhue to Timothy Pickering (26 Oct.1798), ibid., 179 n.1; Timothy Pickering to Theodore Sedgwick (6 Nov.1798), Pickering Papers, 9:570.
109. Abigail Adams to John Quincy Adams (2 Dec.1798), *AFC,* 13:293; Fisher Ames to Christopher Gore (18 Dec.1798), Ames, *Fisher Ames,* 1:245, 246; Theodore Sedgwick to Rufus King (11 May 1800), *LRK,* 3:236, 237; George Cabot to Rufus King (26 Apr.1799), ibid., 3:7, 9.
110. John Marshall to Timothy Pickering (11 Aug.1798), Johnson, *Papers of John Marshall,* 3:484, 485.

111. Bird, *Press and Speech under Assault,* 406–409; John Jay to Peter A. Jay (17 May 1798), "Papers of John Jay," https://dlc.library.columbia.edu/jay.

112. Bird, *Press and Speech under Assault,* 404; *Annals,* 8:2171 (10 July 1798); Dauer, *Adams Federalists,* 305–309; Norman K. Risjord, *Chesapeake Politics 1781–1800* (New York: ColUP, 1978), 532.

113. Ibid.; *Annals,* 9:3016–3017 (25 Feb.1799); Dauer, *Adams Federalists,* 311–314.

114. Ibid.; *Annals,* 10:423–424 (23 Jan.1800); Dauer, *Adams Federalists,* 317–320.

115. Ibid.; *Annals,* 11:975–976 (25 Jan.1801), 11:1038–1039 (19 Feb. 1801); Dauer, *Adams Federalists,* 322–325.

116. Fisher Ames to Oliver Wolcott, Jr. (12 June 1800), Gibbs, *Wolcott,* 2:367, 369; accord Philp Schuyler to Alexander Hamilton (31 Mar.1798), *PAH,* 21:387, 388.

117. Judiciary Act §33 (24 Sept.1789), Statutes, 1:73, 93; Edmund Randolph to George Washington (26 Dec.1791), *ASP (Legislative and Executive),* 1:46; Julius Goebel, *History of the Supreme Court of the United States, Vol.1—Antecedents and Beginnings to 1801* (New York: Macmillan, 1971), 1:564, 683, 726.

118. Judiciary Act §33, Statutes, 1:92–93; Goebel, *History,* 1:611–613; "Compensation to District Attorneys" (25 May 1796), *ASP (Legislative and Executive),* 1:152.

119. Goebel, *History,* 1:611; Leonard D. White, *The Federalists: A Study in Administrative History 1789–1801* (New York: Free Press, 1948), 406–408; Saikrishna Prakash, "The Chief Prosecutor," *George Washington Law Review* 73 (2005): 521–597, at 558–561.

120. Jeffrey L. Pasley, *The Tyranny of Printers: Newspaper Politics in the Early American Republic* (Charlottesville: UPV, 2001), 125; Goebel, *History,* 1:545–546, 633 n.89; Timothy Pickering to Francis Corbin (4 Apr.1799), Pickering Papers, 11:559.

121. Timothy Pickering to Zeb Hollingsworth (12 Aug.1799), Pickering Papers, 11:603; accord Timothy Pickering to Thomas Nelson (14 Aug.1799), ibid., 11:611.

122. White, *Federalists,* 408.

123. Judiciary Act §11 (1789), Statutes, 1:79; Samuel Chase's Charge to the Grand Jury (C.C.D.Pa. 12 Apr.1800), Maeva Marcus, ed., *Documentary History of the Supreme Court of the United States, 1789–1800* (New York: ColUP, 1985–2007), 3:408, 414.

124. Judiciary Act §33, Statutes, 1:91; see David Lynch, *The Role of Circuit Courts in the Formation of United States Law in the Early Republic* (Oxford: Hart Publishing, 2018).

125. Timothy Pickering, Response to "Address from the Freeholders of Prince Edward County" (29 Sept.1798), in Octavius Pickering and Charles W. Upham, *The Life of Timothy Pickering* (Boston: LB, 1867–1873), 3:471, 475–476, 473, 472; Douglas Bradburn, "A Clamor in the Public Mind: Opposition to the Alien and Sedition Acts," *William and Mary Quarterly* (3rd series) 65 (2008): 565–600, at 569 n.7.

126. [No Caption], *Gazette of the United States,* 10 Oct.1798, p.1.
127. James Madison to Thomas Jefferson (5 May 1798), *PJM,* 17:126.

3. Common Law Sedition Prosecutions

1. Thomas Jefferson to James Madison (26 Apr. 1798), Julian P. Boyd et al., eds., *Papers of Thomas Jefferson* (Princeton: PUP, 1950–), 30:299, 300 ("*PTJ*"). Quotations throughout this book follow the original, except in removing capitalization of entire words and as indicated by brackets.
2. Matthew Bacon, *A New Abridgment of the Law,* 4th ed. (London: W. Strahan and M. Woodfall, 1778), 3:490–498, at 491; accord Giles Jacob and J. Morgan, *A New Law-Dictionary,* 10th ed. (London: W. Strahan and W. Woodfall, 1782), *s.v.* Libel; Sir William Blackstone, *Commentaries on the Laws of England* (Oxford: CP, 1765–1769), 4:150–153.
3. That is shown for most Sedition Act defendants as each is discussed, and is shown for the general public in Wendell Bird, *The Revolution in Freedoms of Press and Speech* (New York: OUP, forthcoming 2020), Chapters 3–9.
4. James Iredell's Charge to the Grand Jury (C.C.D.N.Y. 6 Apr.1795), Maeva Marcus, ed., *Documentary History of the Supreme Court of the United States, 1789–1800* (New York: ColUP, 1985–2007), 3:14, 19 ("*DHSC*"). His charge listed federal crimes, and did not include any common law crimes.
5. Benjamin F. Hall et al., eds., *Official Opinions of the Attorneys General of the United States* (Washington: GPO, 1852–1919), 1:52 (17 Sept.1794); Marcus Daniel, *Scandal and Civility: Journalism and the Birth of American Democracy* (New York: OUP, 2009), 360 n.78. Greenleaf's article was in the 13 Sept.1794 issue.
6. Julius Goebel, Jr., *History of the Supreme Court of the United States* (New York: Macmillan, 1971), 1:629; Daniel, *Scandal and Civility,* 360 n.78; Daniel N. Hoffman, "Contempt of the United States: The Political Crime That Wasn't," *American Journal of Legal History* 25 (1981): 343–360, at 346–348; Oliver Ellsworth's Charge to the Grand Jury (C.C.D.N.Y. 1 Apr.1797), *DHSC,* 4:158.
7. William Rawle to Timothy Pickering (29 July 1797), "Timothy Pickering Papers" (Massachusetts Historical Society, Boston, manuscripts and 69 reels), 6:480 ("Pickering Papers"); Hall et al., *Official Opinions,* 1:71. On Cobbett generally, see Daniel, *Scandal and Civility,* 187–230, esp. 225–230; Karen K. List, "The Role of William Cobbett in Philadelphia's Party Press, 1794–1799" (Ph.D. diss., University of Wisconsin-Madison, 1980).
8. William Rawle to Timothy Pickering (12 Apr.1798), Pickering Papers, 22:123; Hall et al., *Official Opinions,* 1:71 (27 July 1797). Pennsylvania's separate prosecution of Cobbett, and actions to collect on bonds, began in August 1797 after the state's 1796 prosecution failed. Trial of William Cobbett for Libel, Wharton's State Trials 322–332 (Pa. S. Ct. Nov.1797); William Cobbet, *The Republican Judge* (London: J. Wright, 1798); see Respublica v. Cobbet, 3 U.S. (3 Dall.) 467 (1798).

9. Federal cases that are often described as for common law crimes are discussed in Chapter 7.
10. The best intellectual biography of Bache is Jeffery A. Smith, *Franklin and Bache: Envisioning the Enlightened Republic* (New York: OUP, 1990); the best general biography of Bache is James Tagg, *Benjamin Franklin Bache and the Philadelphia Aurora* (Philadelphia: UPP, 1991). Other useful biographical sources are Daniel, *Scandal and Civility,* 109–147; Jeffrey L. Pasley, *"The Tyranny of Printers": Newspaper Politics in the Early American Republic* (Charlottesville: UPV, 2001), 79–104; John A. Garraty et al., eds., *American National Biography* (New York: OUP, 1999), 1:821 ("*ANB*"). Older less useful sources are Bernard Faÿ, *The Two Franklins: Fathers of American Democracy* (Boston: LB, 1933); Bernard Faÿ, "Benjamin Franklin Bache: A Democratic Leader of the Eighteenth Century," *Proceedings of the American Antiquarian Society* 40 (Part II) (1930): 277–304.
11. Smith, *Franklin and Bache,* 86.
12. Isaiah Thomas, *The History of Printing in America,* ed. Marcus McCorison (New York: Weathervane, 1970), 371; Tagg, *Bache,* 23–80; Smith, *Franklin and Bache,* 88–90; Garraty, *ANB,* 6:934.
13. "To the Public," *General Advertiser* (Philadelphia), 1 Oct. 1790, 1; Smith, *Franklin and Bache,* 103, 111.
14. Smith, *Franklin and Bache,* 112–119; Tagg, *Bache,* 158–166, 170–197, 205–231; Daniel, *Scandal and Civility,* 116–119, 121–128; Arthur Scherr, "'A Genuine Republican': Benjamin Franklin Bache's Remarks (1797), the Federalists, and Republican Civic Humanism," *Pennsylvania History* 80 (2013): 243–298, at 245–248.
15. Thomas Jefferson to Benjamin Franklin Bache (22 Apr.1791), *PTJ,* 20:246.
16. Pasley, *Tyranny of Printers,* 83–84; Daniel, *Scandal and Civility,* 121–128; George Washington to Henry Lee (21 July 1793), W. W. Abbot et al., eds., *Papers of George Washington: Presidential Series* (Charlottesville: UPV, 1987–), 24:260, 261; John Adams to Abigail Adams (2 Jan.1793), L. H. Butterfield et al., eds., *Adams Family Correspondence* (Cambridge, MA: BPHUP, 1963–), 9:366 ("*AFC*").
17. "To the Noblesse and Courtiers of the United States," *General Advertiser,* 2 Jan.1793, 2 (part in capital letters); accord "Mirabeau," "Forerunners of Monarchy and Aristocracy in the United States," *General Advertiser,* 7 Dec.1792, 2.
18. Donald H. Stewart, *The Opposition Press of the Federalist Period* (Albany: SUNYP, 1969), 611; Kim T. Phillips, "William Duane: Revolutionary Editor" (Ph.D. diss., University of California–Berkeley, 1968), 49, 55; Pasley, *Tyranny of Printers,* 90–92, 94–97, 101.
19. Smith, *Franklin and Bache,* 109; "To the Public," *Aurora* (Philadelphia), 8 Nov.1794, 2. After its renaming, the *Aurora General Advertiser* is referred to and cited as the *Aurora.*
20. Jerald A. Combs, *The Jay Treaty* (Berkeley: UCP, 1970), 160–162; *PTJ,* 28:400; A Citizen, "For the Aurora," *Aurora,* 29 June 1795, 3; "This Day Published," *Aurora,* 1 July 1795, 3; *[Authentic.] Treaty of Amity, Commerce, and*

Navigation, between His Britannick Majesty, and the United States of America (Philadelphia: Bache, [1795]).

21. Alexander Hamilton to Oliver Wolcott (20 Sept.1795), Harold C. Syrett et al., eds., *Papers of Alexander Hamilton* (New York: ColUP, 1961–), 19:278 ("*PAH*").
22. Daniel, *Scandal and Civility*, 133–142, who the *Aurora* had been regularly attacking since 1793. Ibid., 128; Smith, *Franklin and Bache*, 142–147.
23. *PAH*, 19:350 (quoting "Calm Observer" [John Beckley], *Aurora*, 23 Oct.1795). The secretary of the treasury responded, followed by Hamilton. Oliver Wolcott, "To the Editor of the Aurora," *Aurora*, 26 Oct.1795, 2.
24. *Letters from George Washington to Several of His Friends, in June and July, 1776* (Philadelphia: The Federal Press [Bache], 1795); George Washington to Jeremiah Wadsworth (6 Mar.1797), Dorothy Twohig et al., eds., *Papers of George Washington: Retirement Series* (Charlottesville: UPV, 1998–1999), 1:17 ("*PGW-R*").
25. Thomas Jefferson to George Washington (19 June 1796), *PTJ*, 29:127; George Washington to Thomas Jefferson (6 July 1796), ibid., 29:141, 142–143.
26. Thomas Paine, *Letter to George Washington* (Philadelphia: Bache, 1796); "This Day Is Published," *Aurora*, 12 Dec.1796, 3; James Madison to Thomas Jefferson (10 Jan.1796), *PTJ*, 28:576, 577; Oliver Wolcott, Jr. to Alexander Hamilton (8 Dec.1796), *PAH*, 20:435, 436.
27. Jasper Dwight [William Duane], *A Letter to George Washington, President of the United States: Containing Strictures on His Address* (Philadelphia: For the Author [By Bache], Dec. 1796), 4, 47–48. Dwight was Duane. David A. Wilson, *United Irishmen, United States* (Ithaca, NY: CorUP, 1998), 42; Phillips, "William Duane," 50.
28. [Benjamin Franklin Bache], *Remarks Occasioned by the Late Conduct of Mr. Washington, as President of the United States* (Philadelphia: Bache, 1797); see Scherr, "Genuine Republican," 249–262, 262–277. Bache is generally viewed as the author. James D. Tagg, "Benjamin Franklin Bache's Attack on George Washington," *Pennsylvania Magazine of History and Biography* 100 (1976): 191–230, 224–225; Tagg, *Bache*, 286; *AFC*, 12:257 n.4. However, John Beckley has been alternatively offered as the author. Daniel, *Scandal and Civility*, 142.
29. [Bache], *Remarks*, iv, 2, 64.
30. Elizabeth Hewson to Thomas T. Hewson (5 June 1797), quoted in Tagg, "Attack," 226 n.118.
31. Tagg, *Bache*, 290–294, Walter Brown, "John Adams and the American Press, 1797–1801," (Ph.D. diss., University of Notre Dame, 1974), 163–165, after a brief period following the election when the *Aurora* was positive toward Adams, Brown, "John Adams," 144–160. Scherr sees the positive period as longer, Arthur Scherr, "'Vox Populi' versus the Patriot President: Benjamin Franklin Bache's Philadelphia *Aurora* and John Adams (1797)," *Pennsylvania History* 62 (1995): 503–531, at 504–514; Scherr, "Genuine Republican," 247–249, as he does for the positive period toward Washington, ibid., 245–248.

32. Abigail Adams to Mary Smith Cranch (15 Nov.1797), *AFC,* 12:287, 289; Abigail Adams to Mary Smith Cranch (12 Dec.1797), ibid., 12:322, 323; Abigail Adams to John Quincy Adams (23 Nov.1797), ibid., 12:306, 308.
33. South Front Street, "For the Aurora," *Aurora,* 24 Jan.1798, 3; Timothy Pickering, "For the Aurora," *Aurora,* 26 Jan.1798, 3. Dr. Reynolds immediately published his version of the facts, generally agreeing with the merchant, Thomas Wotherspoon, whose affidavit Pickering attached to his submission to the *Aurora.* James Reynolds, "From the Philadelphia Gazette," *Aurora,* 29 Jan.1798, 3. Some of these sources are reprinted in Octavius Pickering and Charles W. Upham, *Life of Timothy Pickering* (Boston: LB, 1867–1873), 3:307–312.
34. Timothy Pickering to George Washington (27 Jan.1798), *PGW-R,* 2:51; Timothy Pickering to Rev. John Clarke (26 Jan.1798), Pickering Papers, 37:265, 265–265A.
35. Timothy Pickering to Rev. John Clarke (26 Jan.1798), Pickering Papers, at 37:266.
36. *Society of United Irishmen of Dublin. Established November IX. MDCCXCL* (Dublin: n.p., 1794), 98; Marianne Elliot, *Partners in Revolution: The United Irishmen and France* (New Haven: YUP, 1982), 49, xiii.
37. David A. Wilson, *United Irishmen, United States* (Ithaca, NY: CorUP, 1998), 20–23 & n.28, 37, 41–44, 60; Margaret Jacob and James Jacob, *The Origins of Anglo-American Radicalism* (Boston: Allen and Unwin, 1984), 293–295. On the *Aurora,* see *AFC,* 12:204n. (quoting *Aurora,* 6 Mar.1797); Wilson, *United Irishmen,* 42 & n.17 (authorship); Tagg, *Bache,* 285 (same). Dr. Reynolds was not the same man as James Reynolds whose wife had a widely-discussed affair with Alexander Hamilton.
38. William Rawle to Timothy Pickering (27 Feb.1798), Pickering Papers, 22:48. The incomplete court records for this period do not contain pleadings for the case.
39. "For the Aurora," *Aurora,* 5 Feb. 1798, 2.
40. Smith, *Freedom's Fetters,* 201 n.27; Timothy Pickering to William Rawle (14 Dec.1800), Pickering Papers, 13:569.
41. Thomas Paine, *Letter to George Washington* (Philadelphia: Bache, 1796), pp.11–12; "Extract of a Letter from a Gentleman in Philadelphia," *Aurora,* 27 Apr.1798, 2.
42. Abigail Adams to Mary Smith Cranch (28 Apr.1798), *AFC,* 12:536, 537; Abigail Adams to Mary Smith Cranch (20 Mar.1798), ibid., 12:454, 454–455; Abigail Adams to William Smith (20 Mar.1798), ibid., 12:457, 458; Abigail Adams to Mary Smith Cranch (31 Mar.1798), ibid., 12:470, 472; Abigail Adams to Mary Smith Cranch (26 Apr.1798), ibid., 12:529, 531.
43. Abigail Adams to John Quincy Adams (14 July 1797), *AFC,* 12:203; Abigail Adams to Mary Smith Cranch (26 Apr.1798), ibid., 12:529, 531.
44. [William Cobbett], "The French Faction," *Porcupine's Gazette* (Philadelphia), 12 Mar. 1798, 2; *Debates and Proceedings in the Congress of the United States . . . Annals of the Congress of the United States* (Washington: Gales and Seaton, 1834–1856), 8:1484 (20 Apr.1798) ("*Annals*") (all quotations are for 5th Congress, 2nd session).

45. Thomas Jefferson to James Madison (3 May 1798), William T. Hutchinson et al., eds., *Papers of James Madison* (Chicago: UChiP, 1962–1991), 17:123, 124 ("*PJM*"); Thomas Jefferson to James Madison (26 Apr.1798), ibid., 17:120; *Annals,* 8:2094–2097, 2100 (5 July 1798).
46. [Benjamin Franklin Bache], *Truth Will Out!* ([Philadelphia: Bache, 1798]), i–ii; Benjamin Franklin Bache, "To the Public," *Aurora,* 6 Apr.1797, 3; "Thursday Evening, August 9," *Gazette of the United States,* 9 Aug.1798, 3; Smith, *Franklin and Bache,* 159–161.
47. Original court records for *United States v. Benjamin Franklin Bache* are listed in n.60. Useful secondary sources include Smith, *Freedom's Fetters,* 188–204, which reprints James Morton Smith, "The Aurora and the Alien and Sedition Laws," *Pennsylvania Magazine of History and Biography* 77 (1953): 3–23; and John C. Miller, *Crisis in Freedom* (Boston: LB, 1952), 65–66, 93–97.
48. "Important State Paper," *Aurora,* 16 June 1798, 2 (Talleyrand letter dated 18 Mar.1798); Timothy Pickering to John Pickering (16 June 1798), Pickering Papers, 8:576, 580.
49. *Annals,* 8:1972 (18 June 1798); Thomas Jefferson to James Madison (21 June 1798), *PJM,* 17:155.
50. "Philadelphia. Tuesday, June 19," *Aurora,* 19 June 1798, 2; "Tories in an Uproar," ibid.
51. "Monday Evening, *June* 18," *Gazette of the United States* (Philadelphia), 18 June 1798, 3.
52. Stephen Higginson to Timothy Pickering (26 June 1798), J. Franklin Jameson, ed., "Letters of Stephen Higginson, 1783–1804," in *Annual Report of the American Historical Association for the Year 1896* (Washington: GPO, 1897), 1:813, 814.
53. Note, *PTJ,* 30:186–187n.
54. An Enemy to Traitors, "For the Gazette of the United States," *Gazette of the United States,* 20 June 1798, 3.
55. "Talleyrand's Letter," *Aurora,* 21 June 1798, 3.
56. Benjamin Franklin Bache, "The Plot [U]nravelled," *Aurora,* 25 June 1798, 3.
57. *Diary of William Dunlap (1766–1839)* (New York: NYHS, 1930) (vol. 52 of *Collections of New York Historical Society*), 1:294.
58. Bache, "The Plot [U]nravelled," 3; "New-York, June 22," *Aurora,* 25 June 1798, 2.
59. Abigail Adams to Cotton Tufts (29 June 1798), *AFC,* 13:165, 166. The first lady said the arrest was "not at the Instance of the President," who learned afterwards.
60. *DHSC,* 1:309 (fine minutes), 462–465 (original minutes), 521–522 (docket), 535 (notes for docket entries). Also, Robert Troup, the U.S. District Court judge in New York, wrote that "Bache is under recognizance in Philadelphia for a similar offense" to Burk's—"libelling the President and Secretary of State." Robert Troup to Rufus King (10 July 1798), Charles R. King., ed., *Life and Correspondence of Rufus King* (New York: Putnam's Sons, 1894–1900), 2:362, 364 ("*LRK*").

61. Which was to occur on 11 Oct. 1798 in Philadelphia. *DHSC,* 3:493. The National Archives at Philadelphia confirmed the absence of lower court records of Bache's case. Patrick Connelly to author (17 June 2015). William Rawle's papers at Historical Society of Pennsylvania (Rawle Family Papers, 1682–1921, Collection 536, series 1, especially boxes 5–6) do not include his Bache prosecution, nor do Bache's papers at the American Philosophical Society Library (youthful papers for 1779–1793 and Castle Collection).
62. That extensive coverage from both sides provides a reasonable level of accuracy of information at least where they agreed or did not challenge the other side's statements.
63. "Wednesday, June 27," *Aurora,* 27 June 1798, 3. The charge was stated similarly in the report of the hearing. "Saturday, June 30," *Aurora,* 30 June 1798, 3. Both articles were published the day after the event. Federalist papers reported the arrest and charge similarly. "Wednesday Evening, June 27," *Gazette of the United States,* 27 June 1798, 3. For Chase's opinion, see United States v. Worrall, 2 U.S. (2 Dall.) 384, 394 (C.C.D. Pa. 1798); Trial of Robert Worrall, Wharton's State Trials 189, 197 (1798).
64. [Benjamin Franklin Bache], *Truth Will Out! The Foul Charges of the Tories against the Editor of the Aurora* ([Philadelphia: Bache, 1798]), i–ii (reprinting articles from 19, 21, 23, 25 June 1798); Thomas Jefferson to James Madison (26 Apr.1798), *PJM,* 17:120; Smith, *Franklin and Bache,* 159; Tagg, *Bache,* 106.
65. "Saturday, June 30," *Aurora,* 30 June 1798, 3; "Friday Evening, June 29," *Gazette of the United States,* 29 June 1798, 3.
66. Fine Minutes (8 Aug.1798), United States v. Bache, *DHSC,* 1:309; see also 1:462–63, 465 (rough minutes), 1:521–22 (docket). Bache's attorneys also asked that the motion be held until the next Supreme Court term. The Court of Appeals session was scheduled to begin 11 October 1798. *DHSC,* 3:299 n.1, 3:493.
67. Robert Troup to Rufus King (16 Aug.1798), *LRK,* 2:391; Timothy Pickering to Rufus King (15 Sept.1798), ibid., 2:414; Docket (Feb.1799 entry), *DHSC,* 1:522.
68. [No Caption], *Independent Chronicle* (Boston), 13–17 Sept.1798, 3; "Of the Aurora," *Aurora,* 1 Nov.1798, 1.
69. Clarence S. Brigham, *History and Bibliography of American Newspapers, 1690–1820* (Worcester, MA: AAS, 1947), 2:891–892; Thomas Jefferson to William Wirt (30 Mar. 1811), Paul L. Ford., ed., *Writings of Thomas Jefferson* (New York: Putnam, 1892–1899), 9:316, 316–317; "Tuesday Evening, May 29," *Gazette of the United States,* 29 May 1798, 3.
70. "In Senate Yesterday," *Aurora,* 29 June 1798, 3; accord "Federalism," *Aurora,* 19 June 1798, 2; "A Bill," *Aurora,* 28 June 1798, 2; "Remarks on the Treason and Sedition Bill," *Aurora,* 3 July 1798, 2; "Tuesday, July 3," *Aurora,* 3 July 1798, 2; Phocion, "Remarks, for the Boston Chronicle," *Aurora,* 6 July 1798, 3.
71. "To Irish Emigrants," *Aurora,* 4 July 1798, 2; accord "From a Correspondent," *Aurora,* 19 June 1798, 3; "From the Vermont Gazette," *Aurora,* 16 July 1798, 3.

72. "Monday, July 16," *Aurora,* 16 July 1798, 3; accord "Freedom of Speech and of the Press," *Aurora,* 6 July 1798, 2; e.g., "Liberty of the Press, Pen and Tongue," *Aurora,* 18 July 1798, 3 (First Amendment supposed to be inviolate, but now sacrificed); "Saturday, July 22," *Aurora,* 21 July 1798, 3 ("measures to restrain the liberty of the press and in open violation of the constitution"); "Albany, July 27," *Aurora,* 1 Aug.1798, 2 (reprinting passage from envoys' response to Talleyrand); "Liberty of the Press," *Aurora,* 1 Aug.1798, 3 (reprinting London organization's condemnation of seditious libel prosecutions and other violations).
73. Benjamin Franklin Bache, "To the Public," *General Advertiser,* 1 Oct.1790, 1; [No Caption], *General Advertiser,* 1 Aug.1791, 3; "Tax on Newspapers," *General Advertiser,* 8 Feb.1792, 3; Sidney, "To the Editor," *General Advertiser,* 23 Jan.1793, 2; Benjamin Franklin Bache, "To the Public," *Aurora,* 8 Nov.1794, 2.
74. "Liberty of the Press. (From a London Paper.)," *General Advertiser,* 12 Mar.1791, 2; [No Caption], *General Advertiser,* 2 Mar.1793, 3; "Of the Law," *General Advertiser,* 22 Feb.1793, 2 (from London paper); see also "Liberty of the Press," *General Advertiser,* 6 Mar.1793, 3 (from London paper, and accepting seditious libel law).
75. Bache's developing radicalism is described in Tagg, *Bache,* 116–149; Smith, *Franklin and Bache,* 85–133.
76. Benjamin Franklin Bache, "To the Public," *General Advertiser,* 1 Jan.1794, 3; Corrector, "Mr. Freneau," *General Advertiser,* 25 May 1792, 2 (reprinted from *National Gazette*); "Friday, December 26," *Aurora,* 26 Dec.1794, 3; "From the New-York Daily Gazette," *Aurora,* 26 Dec.1793, 2.
77. "From a Correspondent," *Aurora,* 30 Oct.1795, 3; "The Editor to the Public," *Aurora,* 27 Nov.1795, 2; "Additional *Indirect* Tax upon Newspapers," *Aurora,* 19 May 1796, 3.
78. "Text," *Aurora,* 6 June 1798, 2; "A Bill," ibid.; "For the Aurora," *Aurora,* 18 June 1798, 3.
79. "Newark, (N.J.) Feb. 20," *Aurora,* 24 Feb.1798, 2.
80. Ibid., pp.2–3; see Tagg, *Bache,* 331–332; [Bache], *Truth Will Out!,* i.
81. The best biography of Burk is Joseph I. Shulim, "John Daly Burk: Irish Revolutionist and American Patriot," *Transactions of the American Philosophical Society* 54 (1964): 1–60; and a revision, Joseph I. Shulim, *Liberty, Equality, and Fraternity: Studies on the Era of the French Revolution* (New York: Peter Lang, 1989), esp. 69–90. Other useful biographical sources include those on American playwrights, such as Jeffrey H. Richards, ed., *Oxford Handbook of American Drama* (New York: OUP, 2014), 62; Arthur H. Quinn, *A History of the American Drama,* 2nd ed. (New York: F. S. Crofts, 1943), 117–120, 408; and *ANB,* 3:946. Older less useful sources are Charles Campbell, *Some Materials To Serve for a Brief Memoir of John Daly Burk* (Albany: Joel Munsell, 1868); Edward A. Wyatt, IV, *John Daly Burk: Patriot-Playwright-Historian* (Charlottesville, VA: Historical Publishing Co., 1936) ("Southern Sketches" series no. 7).
82. John Burk, *The Trial of John Burk, Late of Trinity College* (Dublin: For the Author, 1794), 9, 9–32.

83. "From Ireland," *Greenleaf's New York Journal,* 12 Apr.1796, 3.
84. John Burk, *History of the Late War in Ireland* (Philadelphia: Francis and Robert Bailey, 1799), 44–49, 50n.
85. Smith, *Freedom's Fetters,* 205; David A. Wilson, *United Irishmen, United States: Immigrant Radicals in the Early Republic* (Ithaca, NY: CorUP, 1998), 23; Kevin Whelan, "The United Irishmen, the Enlightenment and Popular Culture," in David Dickson et al., *The United Irishmen: Republicanism, Radicalism and Rebellion* (Dublin: Lilliput Press, 1993), 285–286; Shulim, "Burk," 8–9.
86. Shulim, "Burk," 9; Abigail Adams to William Cranch (5 July 1797), *AFC,* 12:187.
87. Brigham, *American Newspapers,* 1:334; Shulim, "Burk," 12; John Burk, *Bunker-Hill; or the Death of General Warren* (New York: T. Greenleaf, 1797); John Burk, *Female Patriotism; or the Death of Joan D'Arc* (New York: Robert M. Hurtin, 1798); Shulim, "Burk," 11, 18–22; Wilson, *United Irishmen,* 103–108.
88. Shulim, "Burk," 19, 20; Wilson, *United Irishmen,* 108–110, 100.
89. There is no full-length biography of Smith. There are occasional references in articles on his father and brother, and a note in Milton H. Thomas, *Columbia University Officers and Alumni* (New York: ColUP, 1936), 84.
90. L. H. Butterfield, ed., *Diary and Autobiography of John Adams* (Cambridge, MA: BPHUP, 1961), 2:312 n.1; Thomas, *Columbia University,* 31, 84; Robert Troup to Rufus King (10 July 1798), *LRK,* 2:362, 364.
91. Their biographies are in *ANB,* 20:305, 303. The relationship was noted by John Adams, Butterfield, *Diary and Autobiography,* 4:74–75 (21 Apr.1778); and in the newspaper, [No Caption], *Time Piece,* 13 July 1798, 3; "Monday, July 23," *Time Piece,* 23 July 1798, 3. It was corroborated by the Smith family providing part or all of Dr. Smith's bond, in cash. Shulim, "Burk," 31.
92. Doctr. James Smith to John Jay (12 Sept.1780), at 3, 1–2, "Selected Papers of John Jay," https://dlc.library.columbia.edu/jay/ldpd:46164/details?initial_page=0; see Richard B. Morris, *The Peacemakers* (New York: Harper and Row, 1965), 85; Arthur I. Bernstein, "The Rise of the Democratic-Republican Party in New York City, 1789–1800" (Ph.D. diss., Columbia University, 1964), 317 n.58.
93. Butterfield, *Diary and Autobiography,* 4:75, 50, 49 (Apr.1778); [No Caption], *Time Piece,* 13 July 1798, 3; Friend to Both Countries, *America Vindicated* (London: T. Burrough, 1774); *Thoughts upon the Present Contest, Between Administration, and the British Colonies, in America* (London: J. Brown, 1775).
94. Shulim, "Burk," 22; Brigham, *American Newspapers,* 1:696. The change of editors was noted soon after, along with the plan for Burk (and Smith) to write most of its content. "Information for the Daily Gazette," *Time Piece,* 22 June 1798, 3. Immediately after Burk's and Smith's arrest, the printer added their names as the proprietors in the issue of 9 July 1798. That was probably done to reduce the chance of the printer being arrested for seditious libel.
95. Robert Troup to Rufus King (10 July 1798), *LRK,* 2:362, 364; Burk, *Bunker-Hill,* [3]; "Communication," *Commercial Advertiser* (6 July 1798), 3; John D. Burk to Thomas Jefferson (ante-19 June 1801), *PTJ,* 34:385, 388.

96. Wilson, *United Irishmen,* 49; Burk, *Trial,* 28, 32; "New York, June 20," *Time Piece,* 20 June 1798, 3; "Letter VII to the President of the United States," *Time Piece,* 15 June 1798, 1.
97. "Communications," *Time Piece,* 27 June 1798, 3.
98. Themistocles, "To the Editor of the Commercial Advertiser," *Commercial Advertiser,* 3 July 1798, 2; Themistocles, "To the Editors," *New York Gazette,* 6 July 1798, 2; "For the Argus," 7 July 1798, 2; Themistocles, "From the Commercial Advertiser," *Gazette of the United States,* 6 July 1798, 2; "Extract from the Piece Signed Themistocles," *Aurora,* 10 July 1798, 2.
99. "City of New-York," *Greenleaf's New York Journal,* 7 July 1798, 3 (printed the day after Burk's arrest); Stephen Wendover to Timothy Pickering (13 July 1798), Pickering Papers, 22:293.
100. [No Caption], *Time Piece,* 6 July 1798, 3; "Notice," *Time Piece,* 30 Aug.1798, 3.
101. "Extract from Junius' Letters," *Time Piece,* 27 June 1798, 3.
102. [No Caption], *Time Piece,* 2 July 1798, 3; [No Caption (different article)], ibid.
103. *Annals,* 8:2097 (5 July 1798).
104. Original court records for *United States v. John Daly Burk and James Smith,* and microfilm copies, are in National Archives at New York City: "Minutes, Trial Notes, and Rolls of Attorneys of the U.S. Circuit Court for the Southern District of New York" (NARA at New York City, R.G.21.34.7, microfilm M854, roll 1), pp.130–207 ("Minutes"); "Criminal Case Files of the U.S. Circuit Court for the Southern District of New York 1790–1853" (NARA at New York City, R.G.21.34.7, microfilm M885, roll 5), no page numbers ("Criminal Case Files"). Useful secondary sources include Smith, *Freedom's Fetters,* 204–219, which reprints James Morton Smith, "The Case of John Daly Burk and His New York 'Time Piece'," *Journalism Quarterly* 30 (1953): 23–36; and Miller, *Crisis in Freedom,* 97–102.
105. Minutes, pp.144, 148, 156; Affidavit of Joseph C. Cooper (5 July 1798), Criminal Case Files; Affidavit of Stephen Wendover (5 July 1798), Criminal Case Files.
106. Recognizance (6 July 1798), as copied in Edward Dunscomb to Timothy Pickering (24 May 1799), pp.2–3 (Ohio History Connection [formerly Ohio Historical Society], "Winthrop Sargent Papers, 1776–1865," MSS 11, Box 2, Folder 5, Item 46); accord Robert Troup to Rufus King (2 Oct.1798), *LRK,* 2:428, 432.
107. Ibid.; Robert Troup to Rufus King (2 Oct.1798), *LRK,* 2:428, 431–432.
108. Timothy Pickering to Richard Harison (7 July 1798), Pickering Papers, 37:315–315A.
109. Observer, "'Two of a Trade Can Never Agree,'" *Commercial Advertiser* (New York), 16 July 1798, 2.
110. "Monday, July 23," *Time Piece,* 23 July 1798, 3; "Notice," *Time Piece,* 9 July 1798, 4 (reprinted 10 Aug.1798); "Notice," *Time Piece,* 20 July 1798, 3.
111. "J. D. Burk," *Greenleaf's New York Journal,* 5 Dec.1798, 3; Shulim, "Burk," 32.

112. Minutes, pp.130–131 (1 Sept.1798). Durell's case is discussed briefly at the end of this chapter, and more fully in Chapter 11.
113. Minutes, p.136 (4 Apr.1799); Samuel Chase to William Paterson (17 Mar.1799), *DHSC,* 3:324; *DHSC,* 3:381, 494.
114. Edward Dunscomb to Timothy Pickering (24 May 1799), pp.1–2.
115. Minutes, pp.144–145 (4 Sept.1799).
116. Affidavits of Joseph C. Cooper and Stephen Wendover (5 July 1798), Criminal Case Files; Minutes, p.138 (2–3 Sept.1799, requiring appearance the next days too).
117. Minutes, pp.143–144. Names are spelled here as there. There was a fifth indictment in a felony on the high seas case. For Troup, see Robert Troup to Rufus King (2 Oct.1798), *LRK,* 2:428.
118. John D. Burk to Thomas Jefferson (ante-19 June 1801), *PTJ,* 34:385, 386; Timothy Pickering to Richard Harison (1 Jan.1799), Pickering Papers, 37:381.
119. Wilson, *United Irishmen,* 50; John D. Burk to Thomas Jefferson (ante-19 June 1801), *PTJ,* 34:385, 387.
120. Timothy Pickering to Winthrop Sargent (22 May 1799), Pickering Papers, 37:424–424A; Jacob Wagner to Edward Dunscomb (22 May 1799), Pickering Papers, 37:423.
121. John D. Burk to Thomas Jefferson (ante-9 June 1801), *PTJ,* 34:385, 387; Shulim, "Burk," 36.
122. "Communications," *Gazette of the United States,* 1 July 1799, 3; "January 22," *Georgetown Gazette* (Georgetown, SC), 10 Apr.1799, 2; "January 23," *Oracle of Dauphin* (Harrisburg), 17 Apr.1799, 2.
123. Shulim, "Burk," 37–51; Arthur Shaffer, "John Daly Burk's History of Virginia and the Development of American National History," *Virginia Magazine of History and Biography* 77 (1969): 336–346.
124. Minutes, pp.148 (5 Sept. 1799), 156 (6 Sept.1799). Smith did not appear at the April 1800 session as required. Minutes, pp.184 (1 Apr.1800), 187 (2 Apr.1800).
125. John Wood, *The Suppressed History of the Administration of John Adams* (John H. Sherburne, ed., Philadelphia: Walker and Gillis, 1846), 163 (originally published 1802); Butterfield, *Diary and Autobiography,* 4:49, 50.
126. "Declaration of Independence," *Time Piece,* 9 July 1798, 1; "Extract," *Time Piece,* 11 July 1798, 1; Lawyer, "August 12th 1791," *Time Piece,* 11 July 1798, 2.
127. "Communications," *Time Piece,* 13 July 1798, 2; "Queries," *Time Piece,* 16 July 1798, 2; "Wednesday, July 18," *Time Piece,* 18 July 1798, 3; "Congress shall make no law," *Time Piece,* 20 July 1798, 3. For *Aurora* comments, see [No Caption], *Time Piece,* 20 July 1798, 3; "To an Alien," *Time Piece,* 13 July 1798, 2; "Botany Bay," *Time Piece,* 16 July 1798, 2.
128. [No Caption], *Time Piece,* 13 July 1798, 3; "Of Libels," *Time Piece,* 25 July 1798, 2.
129. E.g., "Liberty of the Press," *Time Piece,* 13 July 1798, 1; "Toasts," *Time Piece,* 13 July 1798, 3; "Extract. Mr. Curran in Defence of the Liberty of the Press," *Time Piece,* 11 July 1798, 2 (also 13, 16, 18, 20 July).

130. Burk, *Trial*, 25, 27–28; “Continuation of Burk’s Defence,” *Polar Star: Boston Daily Advertiser*, 20 Oct.1796, 2; “Analysis of a Modern Briton,” *Polar Star: Boston Daily Advertiser*, 18 Nov.1796, 2; “Fragment of a Letter from Baron de Montesquieu,” *Polar Star: Boston Daily Advertiser*, 20 Dec.1796, 2.
131. “To the Inhabitants of the United States,” *Time Piece*, 13 June 1798, 1.
132. “New York, June 20,” *Time Piece*, 20 June 1798, 3; “Communications,” *Time Piece*, 27 June 1798, 3; [No Caption], *Time Piece*, 2 July 1798, 3.
133. [No Caption], *Time Piece*, 2 July 1798, 3; [No Caption], *Time Piece*, 4 July 1798, 3. For the drumbeat, see “Light Articles,” *Time Piece*, 13 June 1798, 1; “Information for the Daily Gazette,” *Time Piece*, 22 June 1798, 3; “Monday, July 2,” *Time Piece*, 2 July 1798, 2 (beginning a series of extracts from Curran’s defense of liberty of press); [No Caption], *Time Piece*, 4 July 1798, 3.
134. “Wednesday, July 4,” *Time Piece*, 4 July 1798, 2, quoting (with slight punctuation and spelling variations) [John Trenchard and Thomas Gordon], *Cato’s Letters* (Ronald Hamowy, ed., Indianapolis: Liberty Fund, 1995), 1:110 (Letter No. 15).
135. Timothy Pickering to Richard Harison (28 June 1798), Pickering Papers 8:604; “Mount Pleasant, (N.Y.) July 24,” *Bee*, 1 Aug.1798, 3 (arrest Tuesday before July 24); “Mount-Pleasant,” *Centinel of Freedom*, 7 Aug.1798, 3.
136. “The System of Terror,” *Carey’s United States Recorder* (Philadelphia), 4 Aug.1798, 2.

4. Targeting Opposition Members of Congress

1. Theodore Sedgwick to Rufus King (9 Apr. 1798), Charles R. King., ed., *Life and Correspondence of Rufus King* (New York: Putnam’s Sons, 1894–1900), 2:310.
2. *Debates and Proceedings in the Congress of the United States . . . Annals of the Congress of the United States* (Washington: Gales and Seaton, 1834–1856), 8:1485 (20 Apr.1798), 8:2162 (10 July 1798) (“*Annals*”).
3. Aleine Austin, *Matthew Lyon: “New Man” of the Democratic Revolution, 1749–1822* (University Park: PSUP, 1981), 1. Other useful biographical sources are George L. Montagno, “Matthew Lyon, Radical Jeffersonian, 1796–1801: A Case Study in Partisan Politics” (Ph.D. diss., University of California–Berkeley, 1954); Stanley Elkins and Eric McKitrick, *The Age of Federalism* (New York: OUP, 1993), 706–711; Michael Kent Curtis, *Free Speech, “The People’s Darling Privilege”: Struggles for Freedom of Expression in American History* (Durham: DUP, 2000), 80–84; John A. Garraty et al., eds., *American National Biography* (New York: OUP, 1999), 14:182 (“*ANB*”). Older less useful sources are J. Fairfax McLaughlin, *Matthew Lyon, the Hampden of Congress: A Biography* (New York: Wynkoop, 1900); Bernard Mayo, “The Lyon of Democracy,” *North American Review* 244 (1937–1938): 251–269.
4. Austin, *Lyon*, 7, 10, 14–18, 20–22, 31.

5. Ibid., 25–26, 30, 32–33, 35.
6. Though Brigham does not show Lyon's role, each issue listed James Lyon as the editor, and Austin and Pasley identify Matthew Lyon as the founder, initially in Rutland and then in Fairhaven. Austin, *Lyon,* 76–77; Jeffrey L. Pasley, *The Tyranny of Printers: Newspaper Politics in the Early American Republic* (Charlottesville: UPV, 2001), 110.
7. Austin, *Lyon,* 64–75; Matthew Lyon, "For the Vermont Gazette," *Vermont Gazette* (Bennington), 3 Oct.1791, 1.
8. Judah Adelson, "The Vermont Democratic-Republican Societies and the French Revolution," *Vermont History* 32 (1964): 3, 7, 8; Judah Adelson, "The Vermont Press and the French Revolution, 1789–1799" (Ph.D. diss., New York University, 1961), 317, 273; Robert E. Shalhope, *Bennington and the Green Mountain Boys: The Emergence of Liberal Democracy in Vermont, 1760–1850* (Baltimore: JHUP, 1996), 202–203.
9. "For the Vermont Gazette," *Farmers' Library* (Rutland initially), 10 June 1793, 1; Shalhope, *Bennington,* 202–203; Austin, *Lyon,* 77, 81.
10. Pasley, *Tyranny,* 109, 110.
11. "A LYON!!," *Porcupine's Gazette* (Philadelphia), 6 June 1797, 323; "The Following Articles Are Taken from the Albany Centinel," *Porcupine's Gazette,* 14 Dec.1797, 975; "Wednesday, Dec. 6, 1797," *Porcupine's Gazette,* 7 Dec.1797, 951.
12. *Annals,* 7:194 (30 May 1797), 7:234–235 (3 June 1797).
13. "Mr. Fenno," *Gazette of the United States* (Philadelphia), 31 Jan.1798, 3; Austin, *Lyon,* 17–18. Lyon's own account is Matthew Lyon, "The Following Narrative," *Gazette of the United States,* 3 Feb.1798, 3.
14. Report of the Committee of Privileges . . . Relative to the "Expulsion from this House, of Matthew Lyon["] (Philadelphia: n.p., 1798), 4; *Annals,* 7:1008–1009 (12 Feb. 1798).
15. Quoted in Austin, *Lyon,* 100. Witness accounts are in Report of the Committee of Privileges, . . . Expulsion of Roger Griswold and Matthew Lyon (Philadelphia: n.p., 1798).
16. Joanne B. Freeman, *Affairs of Honor* (New Haven: YUP, 2001), 173–175.
17. Timothy Pickering to William Vans Murray (26 Feb.1798), "Timothy Pickering Papers" (Massachusetts Historical Society, Boston, manuscripts and 69 reels), 8:163, 164 ("Pickering Papers"); Abigail Adams to Cotton Tufts (6 Feb.1798), L. H. Butterfield et al., eds., *Adams Family Correspondence* (Cambridge: BPHUP, 1963–), 12:382 ("*AFC*"); Fisher Ames to Christopher Gore (25 Feb.1798), Seth Ames, ed., *Works of Fisher Ames* (Boston: LB, 1854), 1:220.
18. E.g., "New-York, Feb. 23," *Aurora* (Philadelphia), 26 Feb. 1798, 3; see Thomas Jefferson to James Madison (15 Feb. 1798), William T. Hutchinson et al., eds., *Papers of James Madison* (Chicago: UChiP, 1962–1991), 17:79–80 ("*PJM*"); *Annals,* 8:2171 (10 July 1798).
19. "The Spitting Irish Lyon," *Porcupine's Gazette,* 13 Feb.1798, 3; Abigail Adams to Mary Smith Cranch (21 Feb.1798), *AFC,* 12:407, 408; "Of Swords," *Porcupine's Gazette,* 12 Feb.1798, 3.

20. The *Farmers' Library* had been allowed to die in April 1798. Clarence S. Brigham, ed., *History and Bibliography of American Newspapers, 1690–1820* (Worcester, MA: AAS, 1947), 2:1083. Issue 1 of the *Scourge* is partially reprinted in McLaughlin, *Lyon,* 327–336. Issues 2–4 can be found in Sabin Americana under the title *A Republican Magazine, or, Repository of Political Truths* (referred to here as *"Scourge of Aristocracy"*). Each masthead said the newspaper was "by James Lyon."
21. McLaughlin, *Lyon,* 328, 330, 334, quoting Matthew Lyon, "A Letter from Col. Matthew Lyon," *Scourge of Aristocracy,* 1 Oct.1798.
22. Maeva Marcus, ed., *Documentary History of the Supreme Court of the United States, 1789–1800* (New York: ColUP, 1985–2007), 3:292 ("*DHSC*").
23. The leading biography of Paterson is John E. O'Connor, *William Paterson, Lawyer and Statesman, 1745–1806* (New Brunswick, NJ: RUP, 1979). His First Amendment thought and Sedition Act cases are described in Wendell Bird, *Press and Speech under Assault* (New York: OUP, 2016), 211–218, 268–285.
24. William Paterson's Charge to the Grand Jury (C.C.D.Vt. 3 Oct.1798), in *DHSC,* 3:292, 293.
25. Ibid., 3:294.
26. Reply of the Grand Jury (5 Oct.1798), ibid., 3:294, 295.
27. Original court records for *United States v. Matthew Lyon,* and microfilm copies, are in National Archives at Boston (Waltham): "Case Files, 1792–1869" (U.S. Circuit Court for District of Vermont) (NARA at Boston [Waltham], R.G.21.48.2, Box 3, Case 25 [Oct. Term 1798]) ("Case Files"); "Circuit Court Law Records 1795–1803," pp.106–111, ibid. ("Records"); and the *DHSC,* vol.3. Useful secondary sources include James Morton Smith, *Freedom's Fetters: The Alien and Sedition Laws* (Ithaca, NY: CorUP, 1956), 221–246; and John C. Miller, *Crisis in Freedom* (Boston: LB, 1952), 102–111. Other secondary sources (based on two newspaper accounts rather than on a trial transcript) are Trial of Matthew Lyon, Wharton's State Trials 333–344 (C.C.D. Vt.1798) (see 333n.) ("Wharton"), which is reprinted in In re Lyon's Case, 15 F. Cas. 1183 (C.C.D.Vt. 1798) (No. 8,646).
28. Indictment (5 Oct.1798), pp.1, 3, 5, United States v. Matthew Lyon (C.C.D. Vt. 1798), in Case Files. The indictment was copied, probably at the end of the trial, into the Records pp.106–110, along with summaries of other documents. Years later, the copy in the Records was reprinted in *Annals,* 37:479–484 (4 Dec.1820), with various changes in punctuation and capitalization. For the dates, see Indictment, pp.1, 3.
29. Elkins and McKitrick, *Age of Federalism,* 70; Curtis, *Free Speech,* 81.
30. M. Lyon, "For Spooner's Vermont Journal," *Spooner's Vermont Journal* (Windsor), 31 July 1798, 1, 2. The letter was dated 20 June 1798. The quotation comes from the original *Spooner's Vermont Journal,* not from the indictment. An annotated version appears in the Indictment, pp.1–2.
31. Indictment, pp.1, 1–2.
32. The Barlow letter was printed as a pamphlet before trial, according to Lyon. "Col. Lyon's Trial," in Wharton, 340. That printing was "at *Matthew Lyon's* press," according to a Federalist broadside version. "Barlow's Letter" (Hart-

ford: *Connecticut Courant*, 1798). The pretrial version printed by Lyon's son was *Copy of a Letter from an American Diplomatic Character in France* ("Constitution-Hill": n.p., 1798). The posttrial Federalist broadside was reprinted from the Federalist newspaper's columns: "Copy of a Letter from an American Diplomatic Character in France" (1 Mar.1798), *Connecticut Courant* (Hartford), 5 Nov.1798, 1. The quotation is taken from the *Courant*, not from the indictment. An annotated version is in the Indictment, pp.4–5.

33. Ibid.; Indictment, p.3.
34. Thomas Jefferson to James Madison (3 Nov.1798), *PJM*, 17:173.
35. E.g., Smith, *Freedom's Fetters*, 230–231. The quoted language is from Indictment, p.1 (Lyon's).
36. E.g., *An Abridgment of Burn's Justice of the Peace* (Boston: Joseph Greenleaf, 1773), 258, 260; J[ames] Davis, *The Office and Authority of a Justice of the Peace* (New Bern, NC: James Davis, 1774), 240, 242. These were copied from a 1755 English formbook. In English cases, see Trial of John Miller, (1770) 20 State Trials 869, 894 (K.B.) (per Lord Chief Justice Mansfield); e.g., Trial of Mr. Richard Francklin, (1731) 17 State Trials 625, 628 (K.B.); Trial of William Owen, (1752) 18 State Trials 1203, 1205 (K.B.).
37. Warrant (5 Oct.1798), in Case Files; Minutes (6 Oct.1798), p.25.
38. Summons of Alden Spooner (6 Oct.1798), and Summons of Samuel Shaw and Judah P. Spooner (6 Oct.1798), in Case Files. The summons of Dr. Shaw and Judah P. Spooner was joint. The third count of Lyon's indictment was "for printing . . . a letter written by Joel Barlow," as former judge Robert Troup summarized it. Robert Troup to Rufus King (16 Nov.1798), King, *Rufus King*, 2:465, 467. They appeared at trial, as shown by being paid witness fees. Bill of Costs (7–10 Oct.1798), p.1, in Case Files.
39. The account of the trial and the aftermath in *Wharton's State Trials* is an amalgam of accounts in a Federalist newspaper and a Republican newspaper, pp.333–337 (some of those Vermont sources are quoted below), followed by Lyon's own account, pp.339–342 that reprints most of "Col. Lyon's Trial" (14 Oct.1798), *Scourge of Aristocracy* (Fairhaven), 15 Oct.1798, 76–94. These are referred to as Wharton and "Col. Lyon's Trial."
40. "Col. Lyon's Trial," pp.339, 340; Wharton, 335, 336n.; "Col. Lyon's Trial," p.339; *DHSC*, 3:355.
41. Wharton, 335, 336n.; "Col. Lyon's Trial," p.339; "Trial of Matthew Lyon for Sedition," *Vergennes Gazette*, 11 Oct.1798, 3; Robert D. Rachlin, "The Sedition Act of 1798 and the East-West Political Divide in Vermont," *Vermont History* 78 (2010): 123–150, 124–126.
42. Wharton, 334; "Col. Lyon's Trial," p.340.
43. Wharton, 335; "Col. Lyon's Trial," p.340.
44. Wharton, 335; "Col. Lyon's Trial," p.340.
45. Wharton, 336. Paterson apparently had charged a jury, just three days earlier, with opposite language on how a jury should respond to an unconstitutional law. *DHSC*, 3:236 n.24; Julius Goebel, Jr., *History of the Supreme Court of the United States* (New York: Macmillan, 1971), 1:591–592.
46. Wharton, 336.

47. "Col. Lyon's Trial," p.340; Justice William Paterson's Reply to the Grand Jury (c. 5 Oct.1798), *DHSC,* 3:295.
48. Wharton, 336; "Col. Lyon's Trial," p.340; "U. States v Mr Lyon Notes," in "William Paterson Papers" (New York Public Library, Manuscripts and Archives Division, Bancroft Collection, v.300), pp.715, 717.
49. "The Following Sentiments on the Trial of Col. Lyon," *Scourge of Aristocracy,* 15 Dec.1798, 190.
50. Wharton, 336–337; see "Col. Lyon's Trial," pp.340–341.
51. Mittimus (9 Oct.1798), in Case Files. The costs were listed in Bill of Costs (7–10 Oct.1798); Extract of Costs Allowed (9 Oct.1798), in Case Files. The original amount of $60.96 was reduced by $.50 to $60.46.
52. Wharton, 339–342.
53. He was delivered to the prison on October 10, 1798 by the marshal, Jabez Fitch. Mittimus (9 Oct.1798) (marshal's notation on the back); "Conduct of the General Assembly," *Scourge of Aristocracy,* 15 Oct.1798, 95, 97.
54. "Col. Lyon's Trial," p.341; accord "Observations," *Scourge of Aristocracy,* 1 Nov.1798, 131.
55. "Extract of a Letter from Col. Lyon, in Gaol" (22 Nov.1798), *Scourge of Aristocracy,* 15 Dec.1798, 161, 162–163.
56. "Capt. John Wood's Lottery, Assigned to Col. Matthew Lyon" ([Rutland: John Walker, 1799]) (handbill); "General Mason, to Colonel Lyon," *Scourge of Aristocracy,* 15 Dec.1798, 181, 184; "The Respectful Petition of the Subscribers, Freemen of the Western District of Vermont," *Aurora,* 14 Jan.1799, 3.
57. Mittimus (9 Oct.1798) (jailer's notation on the back); e.g., "Vergennes, (Ver.) Feb. 14," *Windham Herald,* 7 Mar.1799, 3.
58. "Colonel Lyon's Address to His Constituents" (10 Jan.1799) (handbill).
59. E.g., "General Mason, to Colonel Lyon," *Scourge of Aristocracy,* 15 Dec.1798, 181, 182; Smith, *Freedom's Fetters,* 221. For martyrdom, see "The Democrat—No. III," *Bee* (New London), 20 Feb.1799, 2; see "Gen. Mason to Col. Lyon," *Aurora,* 1 Dec.1798, 2.
60. Elkins and McKitrick, *Age of Federalism,* 709; Austin, *Lyon,* 85; ibid., 142–145.
61. *Annals,* 8:2934, 2954 (20 Feb.1799); Thomas Jefferson to James Madison (18 Feb.1801), *PJM,* 17:467.
62. Matthew Lyon to Thomas Jefferson (1 Mar.1801), Julian P. Boyd et al., eds., *Papers of Thomas Jefferson* (Princeton: PUP, 1950–), 33:111 ("*PTJ*"); Matthew Lyon to Thomas Jefferson (3 Mar.1801), ibid., 33:125; Matthew Lyon, *Letter from Matthew Lyon . . . to Citizen John Adams* (Baltimore: Geo. Keating, 1801), 6, 3.
63. George L. Montagno, "Matthew Lyon's Last Frontier," *Arkansas Historical Quarterly* 16 (1957): 46–53; "Case of Matthew Lyon," *Annals,* 37:478, 479 (4 Dec.1820); see also "Sedition Law," ibid., 20:120, 122–126 (27 May 1809).
64. Oliver Wolcott to Alexander Hamilton (3 Sept.1800), Harold C. Syrett et al., eds., *Papers of Alexander Hamilton* (New York: ColUP, 1961–), 25:104, 108; James McHenry to Oliver Wolcott (12 Oct.1800), George Gibbs, ed., *Memoirs*

of the Administrations (New York: Norden, 1846), 2:433. Other examples are given in Chapter 13.

65. Matthew Lyon, "Col. Lyon's Answer to the Foregoing Address," *Farmers' Library,* 13 May 1793, 2; "For the Farmers' Library," *Farmers' Library,* 17 Feb.1794, 1.
66. "Twelve Reasons Against a Free People's Employing Practitioners in the Law, as Legislators," *Farmers' Library,* 19 Aug.1794, 1; M. Lyon, "For Spooner's Vermont Journal," *Spooner's Vermont Journal,* 31 July 1798, 1, 2.
67. "The Following Are the Names," *Scourge of Aristocracy,* 15 Oct.1798, 94; "Col. Lyon's Dialogue," *Scourge of Aristocracy,* 1 Nov.1798, 118, 123; "Lexington, (Kentucky) August 8," *Scourge of Aristocracy,* 132, 133; "Mr. Livingston's Speech, on the Sedition Bill," *Scourge of Aristocracy,* 15 Dec. 1798, 153, 154; "At a Meeting of the Freeholders of Prince Edward County," ibid., 167, 170.
68. "Mr. Livingston's Speech, on the Third Reading of the Alien Bill," *Scourge of Aristocracy,* 15 Oct.1798, 49; "Kentucky. Lexington, Aug. 15," ibid., 102; "Mr. Livingston's Speech," *Scourge of Aristocracy,* 1 Nov.1798, 109; "Col. Lyon's Dialogue," ibid., 118, 122; "Lexington, (Kentucky) August 8," ibid., 132, 133.
69. "Kentucky. Lexington, Aug. 15," *Scourge of Aristocracy,* 15 Oct.1798, 102; "Lexington, (Kentucky) August 8," *Scourge of Aristocracy,* 1 Nov.1798, 132, 133.
70. "Mr. Livingston's Speech, on the Sedition Bill," *Scourge of Aristocracy,* 15 Dec.1798, 153, 156; "Extract," *Scourge of Aristocracy,* 1 Nov.1798, 142, 143; M. Lyon, "Colonel Lyon's Address to His Constituents" (10 Jan.1799) (handbill).
71. Lyon, *Letter from Matthew Lyon,* 6, 8–9, 4, 7.
72. Thomas Jefferson to John Taylor (26 Nov.1798), *PTJ,* 30:588.
73. The best biographical article on Ogden is Alan V. Briceland, "The Philadelphia Aurora, The New England Illuminati, and The Election of 1800," *Pennsylvania Magazine of History and Biography* 100 (1976): 3–36. Other useful biographical sources are James McLachlan et al., *Princetonians: A Biographical Dictionary* (Princeton: PUP, 1976–1991), 2:93; *ANB,* 16:634.
74. Edmund B. Thomas, Jr., "Politics in the Land of Steady Habits: Connecticut's First Political Party System" (Ph.D. diss., Clark University, 1972), 88; see [John C. Ogden], *An Appeal to the Candid, upon the Present State of Religion and Politics in Connecticut* (n.p., 1798); Jonathan D. Sassi, *A Republic of Righteousness: The Public Christianity of the Post-Revolutionary New England Clergy* (New York: OUP, 2001), 113–116.
75. Rev. Jedidiah Morse, *A Sermon, Preached at Charlestown, November 29, 1798* (Boston: Samuel Hall, 1798), 68, 62, 67; Rev. Timothy Dwight, *The Nature and Danger of Infidel Philosophy* (Bristol, RI: R. Edwards, 1799) (sermon on 9 Sept.1797), 89. Some of their earlier publications argued similarly. For Ogden's response, see [John C. Ogden], *A View of the New-England Illuminati* (Philadelphia: James Carey, 1799); Briceland, "Philadelphia Aurora," 20–26; *PTJ,* 31:17–18; Donald H. Stewart, *The Opposition Press of the Federalist Period* (Albany: SUNYP, 1969), 413–414.

76. John Cosens Ogden to John Adams (9 Mar.1797), https://founders.archives.gov/documents/Adams/99-02-02-1887; Dorothy Twohig et al., eds., *Papers of George Washington: Retirement Series* (Charlottesville: UPV, 1998–1999), 3:29 n.1 *("PGW-R")*; John C. Ogden to Thomas Jefferson (7 Feb.1799), *PTJ,* 31:16, 17; John C. Ogden to Thomas Jefferson (5 Mar.1799), ibid., 31:72.
77. Thomas Jefferson to James Madison (3 Jan.1799), *PTJ,* 30:610; Briceland, "Philadelphia Aurora," 6. It was not the first petition for Lyon's release; his son had sent one signed by 200 men. William Smith Shaw to Abigail Adams (30 Dec.1798), *AFC,* 13:333.
78. "The Respectful Petition of the Subscribers, Freemen of the Western District of Vermont," *Aurora,* 14 Jan.1799, 3; [John C. Ogden], "For the Bee," *Bee* (New London), 20 Mar.1799, 2; *PTJ,* 31:18n., 73–74n. The article was "almost certainly written by Ogden." Ibid., 73n.
79. Original court records of John C. Ogden's case, and microfilm copies, are at Connecticut State Archives (Hartford): "Litchfield County Court Files" (Litchfield Court of Common Pleas, file for 1799 Tallmadge-1800 Atwater). Useful secondary sources include Alan V. Briceland, "John C. Ogden: Messenger and Propagandist for Matthew Lyon, 1798–1799," *Vermont History* 43 (1975): 103–121, at 113–120; Smith, *Freedom's Fetters,* 242–243; Austin, *Lyon,* 125. The promissory note (10 July 1785) is in those "Litchfield County Court Files."
80. [John C. Ogden], "For the Bee," *Bee,* 24 Apr.1799, 2; Attachment and Arrest Warrant (4 Feb.1799).
81. John C. Ogen to George Washington (12 Feb.1799), *PGW-R,* 3:373; Order (8 Apr.1799).
82. Frederick Wolcott to Oliver Wolcott, Jr. ([torn] Mar.1799), p.1, "Oliver Wolcott, Jr. Papers" (Connecticut Historical Society (Hartford), Box 30, Folder 9); John C. Ogden to Ephraim Kirby (7 Mar.1799), p.2, "Ephraim Kirby Papers" (Duke University (Durham), Perkins Library, Special Collections. Ogden soon wrote that Wolcott "sent on money sufficient for his maintenance until October next." [John C. Ogden], "For the Aurora," *Aurora,* 9 Apr.1799, 3.
83. [John C. Ogden], "For the Bee," *Bee,* 24 Apr.1799, 2; John C. Ogden to Col. Jeremiah Wadsworth (1 May 1799), p.1, "Jeremiah Wadsworth Papers" (Connecticut Historical Society (Hartford), Box 16, Folder 8).
84. Order (8 Apr.1799) (note on backside); Frederick Wolcott to Oliver Wolcott, Jr. (20 June 1799), p.3, "Oliver Wolcott, Jr. Papers."
85. E.g., "Extract of a Letter from Connecticut," *Gazette of the United States,* 18 Feb.1799, 3. For Ogden's articles, e.g., [John C. Ogden], "To the Enemies of Political Persecution," *Aurora,* 4 Jan.1799, 2; "Saturday, January 5, 1799," *Aurora,* 5 Jan.1799, 3; *ANB,* 16:634; Briceland, "Ogden," 110, 121; Briceland, "Philadephia Aurora," 4, 6–8.
86. E.g., "New London, Connecticut," *Gazette of the United States,* 24 May 1799, 2. For Republican papers, see "For the Aurora," *Aurora,* 9 Apr.1799, 3; [John C. Ogden], "For the Bee," *Bee,* 24 Apr.1799, 2.
87. John Cosens Ogden to John Adams (9 Mar.1797), https://founders.archives.gov/documents/Adams/99-02-02-1887 (written from New Haven); Alan V.

Briceland, "Ephraim Kirby, Connecticut Jeffersonian, 1757–1804" (Ph.D. diss., Duke University, 1965), 225.

88. John Adams to James Lloyd (6 Feb.1815), https://founders.archives.gov/documents/Adams/99-02-02-6405.

89. English common law criminalized seditious petitions, as we will see in Chapter 11. A rumor Republican newspapers reported, that Ogden was carrying the money for Lyon's fines, was quickly disproved since Ogden had little money when arrested.

90. John C. Ogden to George Washington (12 Feb.1799), *PGW-R,* 3:373; C. J. Hoadly et al., eds., *Public Records of the State of Connecticut* (Hartford: Case, Lockwood, 1894–1948), 10:vii; Austin, *Lyon,* 124–125.

91. Col. Allan McLane to Timothy Pickering (8 Feb.1800), Pickering Papers, 26:26; [John C. Ogden], "For the Bee," *Bee,* 24 Apr.1799, 2.

92. A Citizen [John C. Ogden], *A Short History of Late Ecclesiastical Oppressions in New-England and Vermont* (Richmond: James Lyon, 1799); John C. Ogden to George Washington (17 June 1799), *PGW-R,* 4:129.

93. Useful biographical sources include John T. Kneebone, *Dictionary of Virginia Biography* (Richmond: Library of Virginia, 1998–), 2:494; *ANB,* 4:150.

94. "From Samuel J. Cabell" (12 Jan.1797), Noble E. Cunningham, Jr., ed., *Circular Letters of Congressmen to Their Constituents 1789–1829* (Chapel Hill: UNCP, 1978), 1:67, 69–70.

95. James Iredell's Charge to the Grand Jury (C.C.D. Md. 8 May 1797), in *DHSC,* 3:173, 174, 176; 3:173n (also given in Virginia 22 May 1797); Presentment of the Grand Jury (22 May 1797), ibid., 3:181.

96. Samuel Jordan Cabell, "Letter," *Aurora,* 31 May 1797, *DHSC,* 3:183, 184.

97. Henry Tazewell to John Page (possibly) (3 June 1797), *DHSC,* 3:189; Henry Tazewell to James Madison (4 June 1797), *PJM,* 17:15, 18; Thomas Jefferson to Peregrine Fitzhugh (4 June 1797), *PTJ,* 29:415, 417; Thomas Jefferson to James Madison (3 Aug.1797), *PJM,* 17:35, 36.

98. Scaevola, "To James Iredell," *Daily Advertiser* (Richmond), 11 June 1797, reprinted in *DHSC,* 3:192; Peregrine Fitzhugh to Thomas Jefferson (20 June 1797), *PTJ,* 29:442, 444.

99. Marius, "To Jugurtha," *Virginia Gazette, and General Advertiser* (Richmond), 24 June 1797, reprinted, *DHSC,* 3:203, 203–205.

100. William R. Davie to James Iredell (25 June 1797), *DHSC,* 3:206; accord 3:197, 205, 207, 212, 213.

101. James Iredell, "To the Public," *Virginia Gazette, and General Advertiser,* 21 June 1797, reprinted, *DHSC,* 3:201; James Iredell's Charge to the Grand Jury (C.C.D. Pa. 11 Apr.1797), *DHSC,* 3:163; James Iredell to Hannah Iredell (25 May 1797), ibid., 3:182.

102. [Thomas Jefferson], Petition to the Virginia House of Delegates (ante-3 Aug.1797), *PTJ,* 29:493, 497; [Thomas Jefferson], Petition to the Virginia House of Delegates (ante-7 Sept.1797), ibid., 29:499, 502 (7 Aug.–7 Sept.1797); Thomas Jefferson to James Monroe (7 Sept.1797), ibid., 29:526. For Virginia's house, see *PJM,* 17:34 (28 Dec.1797); *DHSC,* 3:150; Harry

Ammon, "The Republican Party in Virginia" (Ph.D. diss., University of Virginia, 1948), 172–175.

103. In the absence of a full-length biography, useful biographical sources are Kneebone, *Virginia Biography,* 3:306; *ANB,* 5:84.
104. Ibid.; *Annals,* 8:2171 (10 July 1798).
105. "From John Clopton" (24 Jan.1797), Cunningham, *Circular Letters,* 1:72; "From John Clopton" (19 June 1797), ibid, 1:94–96.
106. John Marshall to Timothy Pickering (15 Oct.1798), Herbert A. Johnson, et al., eds., *Papers of John Marshall* (Chapel Hill: UNCP, 1974–), 3:516; "Congressional Election Campaign," ibid., 3:494; *PJM,* 17:222 n.4.
107. Buckskin, "To the Freeholders of the Henrico Congressional District," *Virginia Gazette, and General Advertiser,* 9 Oct.1798, 3; Timothy Pickering to Edward Carrington (23 Oct.1798), Pickering Papers, 9:512; John Clopton, "Mr. Davis," *Virginia Gazette, and General Advertiser,* 16 Oct.1798, 2.
108. Timothy Pickering to Edward Carrington (23 Oct.1798), Pickering Papers, 9:512; Edward Carrington to Timothy Pickering (30 Oct.1798), ibid., 23:271. It is difficult to see a basis for this letter being described as discouraging Pickering from prosecution.
109. The incident is briefly mentioned in Smith, *Freedom's Fetters,* 183, to show that the Sedition Act was seen by Pickering as reaching private utterances, and in Johnson, *Papers of John Marshall,* 3:497, to show that Pickering "wanted to initiate legal action against Clopton."
110. David S. Robarge, "John Marshall and His Times" (Ph.D. diss., Columbia University, 1995), 294; John Marshall to Timothy Pickering (15 Oct.1798), Johnson, *Marshall,* 3:516; John Marshall to Timothy Pickering (22 Oct.1798), ibid., 3:519, 520–521.
111. J. Marshall, "To a Freeholder," *Virginia Herald,* 2 Oct.1798, 2, reprinted in Johnson, *Marshall,* 3:503, 505–506.

5. Keeping the North Safe from Sedition

1. Seth Cotlar, *Tom Paine's America: The Rise and Fall of Transatlantic Radicalism in the Early Republic* (Charlottesville: UVP, 2011), 20; Abram E. Brown, *Faneuil Hall and Faneuil Hall Market* (Boston: Lee and Shepard, 1900), 192–193.
2. Clarence S. Brigham, *History and Biography of American Newspapers* (Worcester, MA: AAS, 1947), 1:307.
3. The best biography of Thomas Adams is parts of John B. Hench, "The Newspaper in a Republic: Boston's 'Centinel' and 'Chronicle,' 1784–1801" (Ph.D. diss., Clark University, 1979), 48–51, 84–87, 112–116. Other useful biographical sources are Benjamin Franklin V, ed., *Boston Printers, Publishers, and Booksellers: 1640–1800* (Boston: G.K. Hall, 1980), 5–9; William Nelson, *Notes Toward a History of the American Newspaper* (New York: Heartman,

1918), 1:294–297; Linda T. Watkins, ed., *DAR Patriot Index* (Baltimore: Gateway Press, 2003), 1:17.

4. Cotlar, *Tom Paine's America,* 20; accord Hench, "Newspaper," 56; Stephen Botein, "'Meer Mechanics' and an Open Press: The Business and Political Strategies of Colonial American Printers," *Perspectives in American History* 9 (1975): 127–225, at 225.
5. Abigail Adams to John Adams (28 Dec.1793), L. H. Butterfield et al., eds., *Adams Family Correspondence* (Cambridge, MA: BPHUP, 1963–), 9:486 ("*AFC*"); "Rights of Man," *Independent Chronicle* (Boston), 21 July 1791, 1.
6. Republicanus, "Miscellaneous Remarks upon the Supposed Cruelties Which Have Attended the French Revolution," *Independent Chronicle,* 25 July 1793, 1; A Democrat, "Mr. Adams," *Independent Chronicle,* 2 May 1793, 2; "Boston," *Independent Chronicle,* 3 Sept.1795.
7. Hench, "Newspaper," 3; Franklin, *Boston Printers,* 5; Hench, "Newspaper," 34, 51–52, 205.
8. Abigail Adams to Mary Smith Cranch (3 June 1797), *AFC,* 12:139; Abigail Adams to Mary Smith Cranch (6–8 June 1797), ibid., 12:142; Abigail Adams to William Smith (20 Mar.1798), ibid., 12:457, 458; Abigail Adams to Mary Smith Cranch (26 Apr.1798), ibid., 12:529, 531.
9. Abigail Adams to Mary Smith Cranch (10 May 1798), ibid., 13:23, 24; Abigail Adams to William Smith (7 July 1798), ibid., 13:176, 177; "Boston, August 4," *Gazette of the United States,* 9 Aug.1798, 3.
10. Hench, "Newspaper," 210; accord Clyde A. Duniway, *Development of Freedom of the Press in Massachusetts* (New York: Longmans, Green, 1906), 144.
11. Original court records for *United States v. Thomas Adams,* and microfilm copies, are in National Archives at Boston (Waltham, Massachusetts): "Case Files, 1790–1911" (U.S. Circuit Court for District of Massachusetts) (NARA at Boston, R.G.21.23.2, Box 5) ("Case Files"); and in Maeva Marcus, ed., *Documentary History of the Supreme Court of the United States, 1789–1800* (New York: ColUP, 1985–2007), vol.3 ("*DHSC*"). Useful secondary sources include James Morton Smith, *Freedom's Fetters: The Alien and Sedition Laws* (Ithaca, NY: CorUP, 1956), 247–252, 255; John C. Miller, *Crisis in Freedom* (Boston: LB, 1952), 120–123; Hench, "Newspaper," 211–213.
12. "Tuesday, October 23, 1798," *Massachusetts Mercury* (Boston), 22 Oct.1798, 2; *DHSC,* 3:300.
13. Indictment (20 Oct.1798), pp.1–2, in Case Files; Smith, *Freedom's Fetters,* 252.
14. Indictment, pp.2, 3–4, quoting Sidney, "For the Independent Chronicle," *Independent Chronicle,* 20–24 Sept.1798, 2. Punctuation and capitalization follow the indictment, not the article. Indictment, p.2 incorrectly said it was quoting an article dated 20–23 Aug.1798.
15. Indictment, pp.6, 9, 7–8, quoting "The Letter Y.," *Independent Chronicle,* 20 Sept.1798, 3.
16. Indictment, pp.9, 10–12, quoting "Communication," *Independent Chronicle,* 20–23 Aug.1798, 3. Indictment, p. 9 incorrectly said it was quoting an article dated 20–24 Sept.1798.

17. Indictment, pp.2, 9.
18. Indictment, pp.1, 6, 9, 10.
19. Arrest Warrant (23 Oct.1798), in Case Files. In that June 1799 session, Justice Samuel Chase was scheduled to preside. *DHSC,* 3:493. Adams's plea is on the backing of the indictment, and the trial date is in the recognizance.
20. "Boston, Thursday, October 25, 1798," *Independent Chronicle,* 22–25 Oct.1798, 3; "Boston, Monday, October 29, 1798," *Independent Chronicle,* 25–29 Oct.1798, 3; Recognizance (29 Oct.1798), in Case Files.
21. Affidavit of Thomas Adams (Oct.1798), in Case Files; Brigham, *American Newspapers,* 1:307–308; Nelson, *Notes,* 296; "Died," *Massachusetts Mercury* (Boston), 14 May 1799, 2.
22. Jeffrey L. Pasley, *The Tyranny of Printers: Newspaper Politics in the Early American Republic* (Charlottesville: UPV, 2001), 125; accord Donald H. Stewart, *The Opposition Press of the Federalist Period* (Albany: SUNYP, 1969), 477; Hench, "Newspaper," 267 and n.42.
23. Biographical information about Abijah Adams is in Hench, "Newspaper," 51–54; and Nelson, *Notes,* 298. Useful secondary sources on the case include Hench, "Newspaper," 213–230; Duniway, *Development,* 144–146; Frank M. Anderson, "Contemporary Opinion of the Virginia and Kentucky Resolutions," *American Historical Review* 5 (1899): 45–63, at 61–63; and 225–252, at 225–228. Counsel's defense of Abijah Adams was turned into essays in the *Chronicle:* [George Blake], "Trial of Mr. Abijah Adams," *Independent Chronicle,* 11, 15, 18, 22, 29 Apr.1799, and 2 May 1799 (all p.1).
24. Answer of Massachusetts (9 Feb.1799), Jonathan Elliot, ed., *Debates in the Several State Conventions on the Adoption of the Federal Constitution* (Philadelphia: Lippincott, 1836), 4:533, 534; "Historical Facts," *Independent Chronicle,* 18 Feb.1799, 3; "Boston, Monday, February 18, 1799," *Independent Chronicle,* 14–18 Feb.1799, 3. Hench presents a persuasive case that the articles were written by James Winthrop. Hench, "Newspaper," 225–230.
25. Thomas B. Adams to John Adams (1 Mar.1799), *AFC,* 13:423; "Supreme Court," *Massachusetts Mercury* (Boston), 22 Feb.1799, 2.
26. Anderson, "Contemporary Opinion," 225; Sir William Blackstone, *Commentaries on the Laws of England* (Oxford: CP, 1765–1769), 4:151–152.
27. "Trial," 11–15 Apr.1799, 1; "Trial," 8–11 Apr.1799, 1. The state argued that the bookkeeper also sold or distributed copies to subscribers.
28. "Trial," 8–11 Apr.1799, 1; "Trial," 11–15 Apr.1799, 1; "Trial," 15–18 Apr.1799, 1. The 25 April segment said that the account added arguments not permitted at trial and filled interstices.
29. Duniway, *Development,* 145 (and it did not find him guilty of printing); Peter O. Thacher, *Reports of Criminal Cases, Tried in the Municipal Court of the City of Boston* (Boston: LB, 1845), 459–461 n.1; accord "Sketch of Chief Justice Dana's Observations," *New Hampshire Gazette* (Portsmouth), 10 Apr.1799, 1; Hench, "Newspaper," 221; Duniway, *Development,* 145.
30. "Boston, Thursday, April 25, 1799," *Independent Chronicle,* 22–25 Apr.1799, p.3; Abijah Adams to James Winthrop (26 July 1799), quoted in Hench, "Newspaper," 227.

31. "Summary," *Independent Chronicle,* 22–25 Apr.1799, 3; Abijah Adams to James Winthrop (26 July 1799), quoted in Hench, "Newspaper," 227. Dana continued to seek indictments of the editors of the *Independent Chronicle.* Francis Dana's Grand Jury Charge (Cumberland County, 2 July 1799), Stanton D. Krauss, ed., *Gentlemen of the Grand Jury: The Surviving Grand Jury Charges* (Durham, NC: CAP, 2012), 1:456; Francis Dana's Grand Jury Charge (Norfolk County, 20 Aug.1799), ibid., 1:457; Francis Dana's Grand Jury Charge (Hampshire County, 24 Sept.1799), ibid., 1:457.
32. "Remarks on the Sedition Bill," *Independent Chronicle,* 2–5 July 1798, 3; "Philadelphia, June 26," ibid., 3.
33. "Gag Bill," *Independent Chronicle,* 2–5 July 1798, 3; "New-York, July 3," ibid., 3.
34. "Boston," *Independent Chronicle,* 16–19 July 1798, 3; "Sedition Bill" and "Alien Bill," *Independent Chronicle,* 19–23 July 1798, 1; "Communication," *Independent Chronicle,* 19–23 July 1798, 3; "The Freedom of Opinion and the Liberty of the Press," 26–30 July 1798, 2. The latter was likely by Adams because it did not indicate another source and referred to "our paper."
35. "Kentucky," *Independent Chronicle,* 18–22 Oct.1798, 1; "Worcester," ibid., 2; "Boston, Monday, October 22, 1798," ibid., 3.
36. "Boston, Thursday, October 25, 1798," 22–25 Oct.1798, 3; "Lexington," ibid., 1; "Fredericksburg," ibid., 1; "Richmond," *Independent Chronicle,* 25–29 Oct.1798, 1; "Bennington," ibid., 2; "To John Marshall, Esq.," ibid., 3.
37. Thomas Adams and John Nourse, "Boston, January 1, 1784," *Independent Chronicle,* 1 Jan.1784, 1.
38. A Confederationist, "From the Pennsylvania Herald," *Independent Chronicle,* 15 Nov.1787, 2; accord "London Association. Liberty of the Press," *Independent Chronicle,* 9–13 Aug.1798, 1.
39. I discuss a number of such references in Wendell Bird, "Liberties of Press and Speech: 'Evidence Does Not Exist To Contradict the Blackstonian Sense' in Late 18th Century England?," *Oxford Journal of Legal Studies* 36 (2016): 1–25; and in Wendell Bird, *The Revolution in Freedoms of Press and Speech* (New York: OUP, forthcoming 2020).
40. "Communications," *Independent Chronicle,* 9 Dec.1793, 3; "From a Correspondent," *Aurora* (Philadelphia), 16 Sept.1795, 3, reprinted in *Independent Chronicle,* 24 Sept.1795.
41. E.g., "Mess'rs. Adams & Nourse," *Independent Chronicle,* 20 Apr.1786, 2 (stamp tax did not violate); Liberty, "Mess'rs. Adams & Nourse," *Independent Chronicle,* 20 Aug.1789, 1 (slander and private libel punishment did not violate). Impartial reports were printed on several court cases involving libel, and very partial excerpts and letters from Thomas Paine and from English, Irish, and French correspondents were reprinted advocating liberty of press.
42. Biographical information is in Lorenzo S. Fairbanks, *Genealogy of the Fairbanks Family in America, 1633–1897* (Boston: American Printing, 1897), 88–89, 860; Charles Warren, *Jacobin and Junto or Early American Politics as Viewed in the Diary of Dr. Nathaniel Ames, 1758–1822* (Cambridge, MA: HUP, 1931), 106 (quoting the diary); Robert B. Hanson, *The Diary of Dr. Nathaniel*

Ames of Dedham, Massachusetts, 1758–1822 (Rockport, MA: Picton Press, 1998) (the full diary); Watkins, *DAR Patriot Index,* 1:897. The only published biographical information is cited in this section. Fisher Ames confirmed that Fairbanks served in the Revolution. "Circuit Court Proceedings," *Independent Chronicle,* 20 June 1799, 2, 3.

43. Shira Lurie, "Liberty Poles and the Fight for Popular Politics in the Early Republic," *Journal of the Early Republic* 38 (2018): 673–697, at 676–678; Paul A. Gilje, *The Road to Mobocracy: Popular Disorder in New York City, 1763–1834* (Chapel Hill: UNCP, 1987), 52–58; Arthur M. Schlesinger, "Liberty Tree: A Genealogy," *New England Quarterly* 25 (1952): 435–458, at 442–449.

44. Richard N. Rosenfeld, *American Aurora* (New York: St. Martin's Press, 1997), 193 (Newburgh, NY), 220–221 (Mendham, NJ), 541 (Dedham, MA), 579 (Blockley, PA), 580 (Philadelphia, PA), 615–616 (Reading, PA), 658 (Bloomfield, NJ); Warren, *Jacobin,* 103 (Wallingford, VT), 104 (Vassalboro, ME), 112n. (Bridgehampton, NY); Lurie, "Liberty Poles," 679–683; "Newark, November 20," *Centinel of Freedom* (Newark, NJ), 20 Nov.1798, 3.

45. Fisher Ames to Thomas Dwight (7 Dec.1798), Seth Ames, ed., *Works of Fisher Ames* (Boston: LB, 1854), 1:243, 244 ("*WFA*"); Fisher Ames to Timothy Pickering (10 July 1798), ibid., 1:232, 235.

46. Fisher Ames to Jeremiah Smith (22 Nov.1798), ibid., 1:240; Fisher Ames to Christopher Gore (18 Dec.1798), ibid., 1:245, 247; [Fisher Ames], "Laocoon. No. 1" (Apr.1799), ibid., 2:109, 113. For town history, see Stephen Davis, "From Plowshares to Spindles: Dedham, Massachusetts, 1790–1840" (Ph.D. diss., University of Wisconsin, 1973), esp. 387–393.

47. Indictment of David Brown (3–5 June 1798), p.12, Case Files; "Arrest of Mr. Fairbanks," *Independent Chronicle,* 8–12 Nov.1798, 3; see Indictment of David Brown, p.13.

48. Fisher Ames to Timothy Pickering (22 Nov.1798), *WFA,* 1:241, 242; "Fall of the Dedham Pole," *Massachusetts Mercury* (Boston), 9 Nov.1798, 3.

49. Original court records for *United States v. Benjamin Fairbanks,* and microfilm copies, are in the same National Archives location as Thomas Adams's: "United States Circuit Court for the District of Massachusetts Final Records Volume 1," p.304 (U.S. Circuit Court for District of Massachusetts) (NARA at Boston [Waltham], R.G.21.23.2) ("Final Records"); and in *DHSC,* vol.3. There is no file on Fairbanks in the Case Files. Useful secondary sources include Smith, *Freedom's Fetters,* 261–266; Miller, *Crisis,* 119–120; Frank M. Anderson, "The Enforcement of the Alien and Sedition Acts," *Annual Report of the American Historical Association* (1914): 113–127, at 122–123.

50. Warren, *Jacobin,* 106; Fisher Ames to Timothy Pickering (22 Nov.1798), *WFA,* 1:241, 243; "Arrest of Mr. Fairbanks," *Independent Chronicle,* 8–12 Nov.1798, 3.

51. "The Jacobin Pole," *Gazette of the United States* (Philadelphia), 14 Nov.1798, 3; "Newark, November 20," *Centinel of Freedom,* 20 Nov.1798, 3.

52. *DHSC,* 3:368, 493.

53. The leading biographies of Chase are James Haw et al., *Stormy Patriot: The Life of Samuel Chase* (Baltimore: MHS, 1980); and Stephen B. Presser, *The*

Original Misunderstanding (Durham, NC: CAP, 1991). His First Amendment thought and Sedition Act cases are described in Wendell Bird, *Press and Speech under Assault* (New York: OUP, 2016), 218–232, 285–302.

54. Final Records, p.304 (1–7 June 1798). That court record incorrectly spelled his name Fairbank. For his statement, see "Circuit Court Proceedings," *Independent Chronicle,* 20 June 1799, 2; "Circuit Court," *Massachusetts Mercury,* 21 June 1799, 2.
55. Ibid. Ames similarly told Pickering that Fairbanks was "an opulent farmer." Fisher Ames to Timothy Pickering (22 Nov.1798), *WFA,* 1:241, 243.
56. Ibid.; Final Records, p.304 (7 June 1798); Warren, *Jacobin,* 108.
57. The only published biographical information on Brown is cited in this section. Charles R. Hale, ed., "Headstone Inscriptions Town of Bethlehem, Connecticut" (Hartford: Connecticut State Library manuscript, 1937), 5 ("died Jan. 8, 1812, age 67," which is contrary to estate record's death date of 7 Feb.1814). Inventory (29 Mar.1814), in "Estate of David Brown" (Woodbury Probate District, Date 1814, No.689); Pardon for David Brown (12 Mar.1801), Julian P. Boyd et al., eds., *Papers of Thomas Jefferson* (Princeton: PUP, 1950–), 33:251 ("*PTJ*").
58. "Connecticut Church Records: Abstracts of Vital Records and Membership Records as Found in Torrington . . ." (Hartford: Connecticut State Library, 1968); Deed from Samuel Peirce to David Brown (1759), "Town Records Microfilm: Torrington Land Records and Deeds" (Hartford: Connecticut State Archives, CSL Reel 4536), vol.2, p.139; "Connecticut Vital Records: Windsor Births-Marriages-Deaths 1637–1850" (Hartford: Connecticut State Library, Barbour Collection, 1929), p.40 (born 22 Mar.1747 new style); Henry R. Stiles, *History and Genealogies of Ancient Windsor, Connecticut* (Hartford, CT: Case, Lockwood, 1892), 117–119.
59. "Circuit Court," *Independent Chronicle,* 15–17 June 1799, 3; "Circuit Court," *Massachusetts Mercury,* 21 June 1799, 1; "Arrest of an Itinerant Jacobin," *Massachusetts Mercury,* 26 Mar.1799, 2; "Bethlehem Births-Marriages-Deaths 1787–1851" (Hartford: Connecticut State Library, Barbour Collection, 1926), p.1 (they married in 1768).
60. Fisher Ames to Christopher Gore (18 Dec.1798), *WFA,* 1:245, 247; "Circuit Court Proceedings," *Independent Chronicle,* 20 June 1799, 2, 3; "Circuit Court," *Massachusetts Mercury,* 21 June 1799, 2.
61. Original court records for *United States v. David Brown,* and microfilm copies, are in the same National Archives location as Thomas Adams's and Benjamin Fairbanks's: "Case Files, 1790–1911" (NARA at Boston [Waltham, Massachusetts]), R.G.21.23.2, Box 5), and "Final Records," p.303; and in *DHSC,* vol.3. Useful secondary sources include Smith, *Freedom's Fetters,* 257–270, which reprints James M. Smith, "The Federalist 'Saints' versus 'The Devil of Sedition': The Liberty Pole Cases of Dedham, Massachusetts, 1798–1799," *New England Quarterly* 28 (1955): 198–215; Miller, *Crisis,* 114–119; Warren, *Jacobin,* 103–111; Anderson, "Enforcement," 122–125. Nonuseful sources include Frederick S. Allis, "Boston and the Alien and Sedition Laws," *Proceedings of the Bostonian Society* (1951): 25–51, at 40–45 (largely based on Anderson).

62. Indictment, pp.2–5, Case Files.
63. Indictment, pp.5–7.
64. Indictment, pp.9–12
65. Robert W. T. Martin, *Government by Dissent* (New York: NYUP, 2013), 169. The manuscript was finally published in 1922 and has been republished with commentary in Michael Merrill and Sean Wilentz, eds., *The Key of Liberty: The Life and Democratic Writings of William Manning, "a Laborer," 1747–1814* (Cambridge, MA: HUP, 1993).
66. E.g., Anderson, "Enforcement," 123, 124; Smith, *Freedom's Fetters,* 259.
67. Fisher Ames to Christopher Gore (18 Dec.1798), *WFA,* 1:245, 247; Complaint in Essex County (21 Mar.1799), p.1, Case Files. Brown was arrested the next day. Ibid., p.3.
68. Complaint, p.2; "Arrest of an Itinerant Jacobin," *Massachusetts Mercury,* 26 Mar.1799, 2; Recognizance (28 Mar.1799), Case Files.
69. Indictment (3–5 June 1799), Case Files. The federal Arrest Warrant on 5 June said the federal court had indicted Brown.
70. Arrest Warrant from Circuit Court (5 June 1799); Receipt of Gaol Keeper (6 June 1799), Case Files; "Circuit Court," *Massachusetts Mercury,* 7 June 1799, 2; "Circuit Court," *Daily Advertiser* (New York), 12 June 1799, 2.
71. Indictment, pp.2, 8, 12.
72. Final Records, p.303 (and the backing of the indictment says the same); "Circuit Court," *Independent Chronicle,* 15–17 June 1799, 3; "Circuit Court," *Massachusetts Mercury,* 21 June 1799, 1–2.
73. Final Records, p.303; Petition for Habeas Corpus (2 June 1800), Case Files. Sentencing was on 10 June. "Circuit Court," *Independent Chronicle,* 13–17 June 1799, 3.
74. Summons of Nathaniel Ames (10 June 1799), Case Files; Warren, *Jacobin,* 111, excerpting Ames's diary; David Hackett Fischer, *The Revolution of American Conservatism: The Federalist Party in the Era of Jeffersonian Democracy* (New York: Harper Torchbooks, 1965), 183.
75. Petition for Habeas Corpus (2 June 1800), Case Files.
76. Pardon for David Brown (12 Mar.1801), *PTJ,* 33:251; see Thomas Jefferson to Albert Gallatin (6 Oct.1802), ibid., 38:452.
77. "Communication," *Columbian Centinel* (Boston), 3 Aug.1811, 2.
78. John M. O'Keefe, "From Legal Rights to Citizens' Rights and Alien Penalties: Migrant Influence, Naturalization, and the Growth of National Power over Foreign Migrants in the Early American Republic" (Ph.D. diss., George Washington University, 2012), 51. Presbyterian Historical Society records show his death on 7 Dec.1827. For his teenage job, see Elmer T. Hutchinson, ed., "Marginal Jottings from the Almanacs of the Scudder Family," *Proceedings of the New Jersey Historical Society* 63 (1945): 150, 164–165, 175, 219.
79. Ronald Vern Jackson, ed., *New Jersey Tax Lists 1772–1822* (Salt Lake City: Accelerated Indexing Systems, 1981), 1:624; "For Sale," *New-Jersey Journal* (Elizabethtown), 6 Feb.1798, 4; James S. Norton, *New Jersey in 1793* (Salt Lake City, UT: n.p., 1973), 125; Hannah Cushing to Abigail Adams (8 Oct.1798), *DHSC,* 3:296.

80. Hannah Cushing to Abigail Adams (8 Oct.1798), *DHSC*, 3:296; "New-York, July 3," *Aurora*, 6 July 1798, 2. The incident did not involve Baldwin or Clark, because their exclamations were on 27 July 1798.
81. Original court records for *United States v. Lespenard Colie* on microfilm are in National Archives at New York City: "Minutes of the U.S. Circuit Court" (U.S. Circuit Court for District of New Jersey) (NARA at New York City, R.G.21.32.2, microfilm T928, roll 1 [1790–1879]), pp.137–138 ("Minutes"); and in Marcus, *DHSC*, vol.3. Secondary sources that mention Colie are Mark E. Lender, *"This Honorable Court": The United States District Court for the District of New Jersey, 1789–2000* (New Brunswick, NJ: RUP, 2006), 56. Smith mentions "a person identified only as Lespenard," and Blumberg notes "a man known to history only as Lespenard." Smith, *Freedom's Fetters*, 271; Phillip I. Blumberg, *Repressive Jurisprudence in the Early American Republic* (New York: CUP, 2010), 100.
82. The leading biography of Cushing is John D. Cushing, "A Revolutionary Conservative: The Public Life of William Cushing 1732–1810" (Ph.D. diss., Clark University, 1959). His First Amendment thought and Sedition Act cases are described in Bird, *Press and Speech*, 148–162, 309–311.
83. E.g., "New-Jersey," *Political Repository* (Brookfield, MA), 23 Apr.1799, 2.
84. Minutes, pp.137–138 (2–3 Oct.1798); William Cushing's Charge to the Grand Jury (C.C.D.Va. 23 Nov.1798), in *DHSC*, 3:305, 313, 314. This was almost certainly the same charge he gave in New Jersey, since he and other justices almost always used the same charge through each circuit.
85. Baldwin's indictment is cited in the next section. For Republican newspapers, e.g., "Sedition Law!!," *Aurora*, 8 Nov.1798, 2.
86. Though Colie's case ended in Cushing's court, Baldwin's and Clark's cases continued with their pleas of not guilty in April 1799 with Justice James Iredell presiding, and their appearance for trial in October 1799 and changed pleas with Justice Bushrod Washington presiding. Iredell and Washington also emphasized the Sedition Act in their grand jury charges. *DHSC*, 3:327–328, 328–330, 332, 341, 350; Bird, *Press and Speech*, 302–305.
87. *DHSC*, 3:305–306, 308, 314.
88. Ibid., 3:314, 315; accord Bird, *Press and Speech*, 152–156, 310–311.
89. Minutes, p.138 (3 Oct.1798).
90. Smith, *Freedom's Fetters*, 270; "Luther Baldwin," *Greenleaf's New York Journal*, 19 Oct.1799, 2.
91. Brown Clark is so named in all the court papers, though he is called John Clark in some newspaper reports. Little is available on Clark, besides statements that he was from North Farms District in Essex County, New Jersey. "Newark, December 25," *Centinel of Freedom*, 25 Dec.1798, 3.
92. The only published biographical information is cited in this section. Charles C. Baldwin, *The Baldwin Genealogy* (Cleveland, OH: n.p., 1881), 20, 298–301, 306, 320. That family history incorrectly identifies Benjamin Baldwin as the Sedition Act defendant. Ibid., 522.
93. Ronald Vern Jackson, *Index to Military Men of New Jersey 1775–1815* (Bountiful, UT: Accelerated Indexing, 1977), 16; Jackson, *New Jersey Tax Lists*.

94. "Wanted," *Centinel of Freedom* (Newark), 7 Aug.1798, 4; "Wanted," *Centinel of Freedom,* 19 Nov.1799, 4; "Natural Bridges," *Centinel of Freedom,* 8 Jan.1799, 3; "Port of New York," *American and Daily Advertiser* (Baltimore), 6 Nov.1801, 5; "Lumber for Sale," *Centinel of Freedom,* 16 Aug.1803, 1; see Carl E. Prince, *New Jersey's Jeffersonian Republicans* (Chapel Hill: UNCP, 1964), 39 (operated a "garbage scow" on the river); "Died," *Centinel of Freedom,* 8 May 1804, 3; "Died," *Aurora,* 12 May 1804, 2.
95. "Poor Luther Baldwin," *Republican; or, Anti-Democrat* (Baltimore), 10 June 1803, 1; "Veracity of the Democratic Prints," *Evening Post* (New York), 30 July 1803, 2 (also quoting Republican response).
96. George Washington to William Livingston (20 Jan.1778), W. W. Abbot et al., eds., *Papers of George Washington: Revolutionary War Series* (Charlottesville: UVP, 1985–2008), 13:297; accord Lt. Col. Francis Barber to George Washington (13 July 1778), ibid., 16:61 and n.2; James J. Gigantino II, *The American Revolution in New Jersey* (New Brunswick, NJ: RUP, 2015), 32–34; John A. Nagy, *George Washington's Secret Spy War* (New York: St. Martin's Press, 2016), 138–143; *Report of the Secretary of War on Sixty Petitions. 1794* (Philadelphia: Francis Childs and John Swaine, 1794), 19 (quoting 1790 report).
97. "July 28," *Centinel of Freedom,* 31 July 1798, 2; accord "New-York, July 28," *New-Jersey Journal* (Elizabethtown), 31 July 1798, 3.
98. "Monday, November 3," *Herald of Liberty* (Washington, PA), 3 Nov.1800, 3 (reprinting); "Indictment of Luther Baldwin for Sedition," *American Citizen and General Advertiser* (New York), 26 July 1802, 2.
99. "Men May Be Conquered, but Principles Cannot," *Kline's Carlisle Weekly Gazette* (Carlisle, PA), 23 Oct.1799, 4; accord "Men May Be Conquered, but Principles Cannot," *Herald of Liberty,* 11 Nov.1799, 4; Rudolph J. Pasler and Margaret C. Pasler, *The New Jersey Federalists* (Rutherford, PA: FDUP, 1974), 83; Minutes, p.143 (2 Apr.1799).
100. E.g., "Thursday Evening, November 8," *Gazette of the United States* (Philadelphia, PA), 8 Nov. 1798, 3; "Philadelphia, November 8," *Claypoole's American Daily Advertiser* (Philadelphia, PA), 8 Nov.1798, 3. For Republican accounts, e.g., "Newark, April 23," *Centinel of Freedom,* 23 Apr.1799, 3.
101. E.g., Andy Trees, "Private Correspondence for the Public Good," *Virginia Magazine of History and Biography* 108 (2000): 217–254, at 238.
102. Original court records for *United States v. Luther Baldwin and Brown Clark* are on microfilm in the same National Archives location as for Colie: Minutes, pp.137–143, 146–147; and in Marcus, *DHSC,* vol.3. Useful secondary sources include Smith, *Freedom's Fetters,* 270–274; Miller, *Crisis,* 112–114; Lender, "*This Honorable Court,*" 56.
103. Minutes, p.138 (3 Oct.1798); ibid., p.140 (1 Apr.1799) (mentioning their recognizance bonds).
104. Minutes, pp.141, 143 (2 Apr.1799).
105. Minutes, pp.146–147 (3 Oct.1799); Bushrod Washington to James Iredell (20 Oct.1799), *DHSC,* 3:389.
106. "From the Aurora," *Constitutional Telegraph* (Boston), 6 Nov.1799, 1.

107. "Sedition Law Vindicated," *Centinel of Freedom,* 18 Dec.1798, 3; "Newark, December 25," *Centinel of Freedom,* 25 Dec.1798, 3; "Newark, April 23," *Centinel of Freedom,* 23 Apr.1799, 3.
108. "Newark, December 25," *Centinel of Freedom,* 25 Dec.1798, 3; "Sedition Law Vindicated," *Centinel of Freedom,* 18 Dec.1798, 3.

6. Failed Prosecutions

1. Timothy Pickering to Alexander Hamilton (9 Apr.1798), Harold C. Syrett et al., eds., *Papers of Alexander Hamilton* (New York: ColUP, 1961–), 21:408, 409 ("*PAH*"); George Cabot to Oliver Wolcott (25 Oct.1798), George Gibbs, ed., *Memoirs of the Administrations of Washington and John Adams Edited from the Papers of Oliver Wolcott* (New York: Norden, 1846), 2:109 ("*POW*"); Theodore Sedgwick to Rufus King (9 Apr.1798), Charles R. King., ed., *Life and Correspondence of Rufus King* (New York: Putnam's Sons, 1894–1900), 2:310, 311 ("*LRK*"); Thomas Jefferson to James Madison (5 Apr.1798), Julian P. Boyd et al., eds., *Papers of Thomas Jefferson* (Princeton: PUP, 1950–), 30:246, 247 ("*PTJ*").
2. *Debates and Proceedings in the Congress of the United States . . . Annals of the Congress of the United States* (Washington: Gales and Seaton, 1834–1856), 8:2100 (5 July 1798) ("*Annals*") (Rep. Allen); John Adams to Timothy Pickering (2 Nov.1798), Charles Francis Adams, ed., *The Works of John Adams* (Boston: LB, 1850–1856), 8:615 ("*WJA*").
3. Barbara B. Oberg, "A New Republican Order, Letter by Letter," *Journal of the Early Republic* 25 (2005): 1–20, at 5–9; William Hindman to Rufus King (8 Apr.1799), *LRK,* 2:593; John Adams to Benjamin Stoddert (31 Mar.1801), *WJA,* 9:582.
4. "Logan," *Gazette of the United States* (Philadelphia), 19 Nov.1798, 3; accord "Logan," *Impartial Herald* (Suffield, CT), 4 Dec.1798, 3; Camden, "For the Centinel," *Columbian Centinel* (Boston), 16 Mar.1799, 2; "Essay II," *Gazette* (Portland), 11 Feb.1799, 3.
5. "Jacobin Tricks," *Columbian Centinel,* 6 Apr.1799, 2; A Federal Republican, "Jacobin Cul[p]ability," *Philadelphia Gazette,* 12 Mar.1800, 3; "To the People of the United States" (No.VII), *Windham Herald,* 21 Aug.1800, 1.
6. Don Higgenbotham, "Virginia's Trinity of Immortals: Washington, Jefferson, and Henry, and the Story of Their Fractured Relationships," *Journal of the Early Republic* 23 (2003): 521–543, at 534–539; "The First Conflict in the Cabinet," *PTJ,* 18:611.
7. Thomas Jefferson to Philip Mazzei (24 Apr.1796), *PTJ,* 29:81, 82; Dumas Malone, *Jefferson and His Time* (Boston: LB, 1948–1981), 3:267–268, 302–307; A Friend to Truth, "For the Gazette of the United States," *Gazette of the United States,* 6 May 1797, 3; "Philadelphia," *Gazette of the United States,* 16 Jan.1798, 3.
8. "Wednesday Evening, April 18," *Gazette of the United States,* 18 Apr.1798, 3; Aristides, "From the United States Gazette," *Political Repository* (Brookfield,

MA), 25 Dec. 1798, 2; Rufus King to Alexander Hamilton (17 Sept.1798), *PAH*, 22:182; William Hindman to Rufus King (13 Dec.1798), *LRK*, 2:492–493. Jefferson did issue a certificate for Logan. *PTJ*, 30:386; Stanley Elkins and Eric McKitrick, *The Age of Federalism* (New York: OUP, 1993), 553–555; Malone, *Jefferson*, 3:322–323, 393.

9. Claude G. Bowers, "Jefferson and the Bill of Rights," *Virginia Law Review* 41 (1955): 709–729, at 716; Stephen Higginson to Oliver Wolcott, Jr. (29 June 1798), *POW*, 2:68; *Diary of William Dunlap (1766–1839)* (New York: NYHS, 1930), 1:294; Fulwar Skipwith to Thomas Jefferson (17 Mar.1798, intercepted 20 June 1798), *PTJ*, 30:183, 186–187n.

10. Timothy Pickering to William Vans Murray (5 Feb. 1799), "Timothy Pickering Papers" (Massachusetts Historical Society, Boston, manuscripts and 69 reels), 10:338, 340 ("Pickering Papers"); Timothy Pickering to Rufus King (6 Feb.1799), *LRK*, 2:537; Theodore Sedgwick to Rufus King (20 Mar.1799), *LRK*, 2:579, 581; George Cabot to Rufus King (16 Feb.1799), ibid., 2:542, 543.

11. Adrienne Koch and Harry Ammon, "The Virginia and Kentucky Resolutions: An Episode in Jefferson's and Madison's Defense of Civil Liberties," *William and Mary Quarterly* 5 (1948): 145–176, at 148; accord Andy Trees, "Private Correspondence for the Public Good," *Virginia Magazine of History and Biography* 108 (2000): 217–254, at 228; John Adams to Oliver Wolcott (17 May 1799), *POW*, 2:241; Thomas Jefferson to James T. Callender (6 Sept.1799), Pickering Papers, 42:195; Thomas Jefferson to James T. Callender (6 Oct.1799), ibid., 42:203.

12. Thomas Jefferson to James Madison (5 Apr.1798), William T. Hutchinson et al., eds., *Papers of James Madison* (Chicago: UChiP, 1962–1991), 17:107, 108 n.1 ("*PJM*"); "Federalism," *Aurora*, 19 June 1798, 2.

13. Between Thomas Jefferson to James Madison (21 June 1798) and Thomas Jefferson to James Madison (26 Oct.1798), *PJM*, 17:155, 169; and between Thomas Jefferson to James Madison (26 Nov.1799) and Thomas Jefferson to James Madison (4 Mar.1800), ibid., 17:280, 367 (though Madison cautiously wrote to Jefferson during the latter period); Thomas Jefferson to James Madison (22 Nov.1799), ibid., 17:277; Thomas Jefferson to James Madison (1 Feb.1801), ibid., 17:459.

14. "Baltimore, Dec. 3," *Aurora*, 7 Dec.1798, 2 (reprinting *Intelligencer*); "Newark, December 25," *Centinel of Freedom*, 25 Dec.1798, 3; Thomas Jefferson to James Monroe (26 May 1800), *PTJ*, 31:590; Constance B. Shulz, "'Of Bigotry in Politics and Religion': Jefferson's Religion, the Federalist Press, and the Syllabus," *Virginia Magazine of History and Biography* 91 (1983): 73–91; Malone, *Jefferson*, 3:480–482.

15. Richard Buel, Jr., *Joel Barlow: American Citizen in a Revolutionary World* (Baltimore: JHUP, 2011). Besides older biographies, see Milton Cantor, "The Life of Joel Barlow" (Ph.D. diss., Columbia University, 1954); John A. Garraty et al., eds., *American National Biography* (New York: OUP, 1999), 2:166 ("*ANB*").

16. Robert F. Durden, "Joel Barlow in the French Revolution," *William and Mary Quarterly* 8 (1951): 327–354; Paul M. Spurlin, "The World of the Founding

Fathers and France," *French Review* 49 (1976): 909–925, at 921; Joel Barlow, *Advice to the Privileged Orders* (New York: Childs and Swaine, 1792); Joel Barlow, *A Letter Addressed to the People of the Piedmont, on the Advantages of the French Revolution* (New York: Columbian Press, 1795); [Joel Barlow], *The Political Writings of Joel Barlow* (New York: Mott and Lyon, 1796); see Ralph A. Manogue, "James Ridgway and America," *Early American Literature* 31 (1996): 264–288, at 270.

17. Indictment (5 Oct.1798), p.5, United States v. Matthew Lyon (C.C.D. Vt. 1798), in "Case Files, 1792–1869" (U.S. Circuit Court for District of Vermont) (National Archives at Boston (Waltham, MA), R.G.21.48.2, Box 3, Case 25 (Oct. Term 1798)).

18. [Joel Barlow], *Copy of a Letter from an American Diplomatic Character in France* ("Constitution Hill" [Fairhaven, VT: James Lyon], 1798), 1–3, 7–8, 10, 14.

19. "Walpole, November 3," *Gazette of the United States,* 13 Nov.1798, 3 (reprinted from *Weekly Museum*); "For the Connecticut Courant," *Connecticut Courant* (Hartford), 12 Nov.1798, 2; Citizen of Connecticut, "From the Connecticut Courant," *Federal Gazette* (Baltimore), 14 Nov.1798, 2 (reprinted); "New-York, Dec.29," *New-York Gazette,* 29 Dec.1798, 3.

20. "From the Connecticut Courant," *Commercial Advertiser* (New York), 21 Aug.1799, 2 (reprinted); "Thursday, May 16, 1799," *Commercial Advertiser,* 16 May 1799, 2; "More About Joel Barlow," *Spectator* (New York), 18 May 1799, 3; "A Song Written for the 4th of July, by Joel Barlow," *The Balance, and Columbian Repository* (Hudson, NY), 19 Nov.1805, 373.

21. Timothy Pickering to John Adams (c. Oct.1798), Pickering Papers, 10:221 (the microfilm is very hard to read); and in Pickering's files, Joel Barlow to Sen. Abraham Baldwin (1 Mar.1798), ibid., 29:55.

22. Stephen Higginson to Timothy Pickering (26 Oct.1799), Pickering Papers, 12:290; Passages from Some Papers of George Cabot (22 Sept.1799), Henry Cabot Lodge, ed., *Life and Letters of George Cabot,* 2nd ed. (Boston: LB, 1878), 238, 240; Robert Troup to Rufus King (16 Nov.1798), *LRK,* 2:465, 467; John Cole Mountflorence to Charles Cotesworth Pinckney (12 Mar.1799), *PAH,* 23:234.

23. George Cabot to Timothy Pickering (16 Oct.1799), Lodge, *George Cabot,* 246, 247; George Cabot to Timothy Pickering (1 Nov.1799), ibid., 250; Timothy Pickering to Alexander Hamilton (29 Apr.1797), *PAH,* 21:68, 71; see Timothy Pickering to George Washington (5 Apr.1797), Dorothy Twohig et al., eds., *Papers of George Washington: Retirement Series* (Charlottesville: UPV, 1998–1999), 1:73 ("*PGW-R*"); Timothy Pickering to Joel Barlow (13 May 1797), Pickering Papers, 37:148.

24. All his letters were from Paris. E.g., Joel Barlow to Thomas Jefferson (12 Mar.1798), *PTJ,* 30:174; Joel Barlow to George Washington (2 Oct.1798), *PGW-R,* 3:68; Joel Barlow to Thomas Jefferson (15 Sept.1800), *PTJ,* 32:141; accord *ANB,* 2:166. On a new mission, see Joel Barlow to George Washington (2 Oct.1798), *PGW-R,* 3:68; George Washington to John Adams (1 Feb.1799), ibid., 3:350.

25. John Adams to George Washington (19 Feb.1799), *PGW-R*, 3:387; John Adams to Abigail Adams (4 Dec.1798), L.H. Butterfield et al., eds., *Adams Family Correspondence* (Cambridge, MA: BPHUP, 1963–), 13:297 ("*AFC*").
26. That best biographical article is Carl E. Prince, "John Israel: Printer and Politician on the Pennsylvania Frontier, 1798–1805," *Pennsylvania Magazine of History and Biography* 91 (1967): 46–55, at 47 n.1. Another excellent biographical source is Jeffrey L. Pasley, *The Tyranny of Printers: Newspaper Politics in the Early American Republic* (Charlottesville: UPV, 2001), 112–115, 170–171. On Episcopalian grandparents, see Pasley, *Tyranny*, 170. One scholar concludes that Israel was not Jewish. William Pencak, "Jews and Anti-Semitism in Early Pennsylvania," *Pennsylvania Magazine of History and Biography* 126 (2002): 365–408, at 407.
27. Pasley, *Tyranny*, 112; Clarence S. Brigham, ed., *History and Bibliography of American Newspapers, 1690–1820* (Worcester, MA: AAS, 1947), 2:979. He ended the newspaper on 1 Feb.1802.
28. Pasley, *Tyranny*, 113–115; accord Harry M. Tinkcom, *Republicans and Federalists in Pennsylvania 1790–1801* (Harrisburg: PHMC, 1950), 232; Morris U. Schappes and Solomon Simpson, "Anti-Semitism and Reaction, 1795–1800," *Publications of the American Jewish Historical Society* 38 (1948): 109–137, at 135–136; Prince, "John Israel," 50, 51–53.
29. Brigham, *American Newspapers*, 2:967–968; Prince, "John Israel," 47, 49; Hugh Henry Brackenridge to Thomas Jefferson (19 Jan.1801), *PTJ*, 32:483, 486; Pasley, *Tyranny*, 157, 170.
30. Brigham, *American Newspapers*, 2:967; Prince, "John Israel," 54–55; "Pittsburgh, Oct.14," *United States Gazette* (Philadelphia), 22 Oct.1806, 3; Prince, "John Israel," 55.
31. Pasley, *Tyranny*, 112; accord Russell J. Ferguson, *Early Western Pennsylvania Politics* (Pittsburgh: UPitP, 1938), 151, 161–162.
32. John Israel, "To the Public," *Herald of Liberty* (Washington, PA), 6 Aug.1798, 3; Uriah Tracy to Oliver Wolcott (7 Aug.1800), *POW*, 399, 400.
33. "Philadelphia, July 11," *Herald of Liberty*, 23 July 1798, 3; "For the Herald of Liberty," ibid., 3; "Freemen of America Attend!," *Herald of Liberty*, 30 July 1798, 4; "Sedition Bill," ibid.; "Remarks on the Above from a Boston Paper," ibid.
34. "To John Clopton, Esq.," *Herald of Liberty*, 10 Sept.1798, 2; "Frankfort, Sept. 18," *Herald of Liberty*, 15 Oct.1798, 2. On prosecutions, e.g., "Philadelphia, June 27th," *Herald of Liberty*, 9 July 1798, 2 (Bache); "Philadelphia, July 11," *Herald of Liberty*, 23 July 1798, 3 (Burk and Smith); "Worcester, Oct.17," *Herald of Liberty*, 5 Nov.1798, 3 (Lyon, Spooner, Haswell).
35. Alexander Addison to Timothy Pickering (22 Nov.1798), Pickering Papers, 23:322. He said that he extended the pamphlet into a charge to the grand juries. Ibid., 23:322A.
36. Ibid., 23:322A–323
37. Ibid., 23:323. His efforts included grand jury charges in May-June and September 1798. Stanton D. Krauss, ed., *Gentlemen of the Grand Jury: The Sur-*

viving Grand Jury Charges (Durham, NC: CAP, 2012), 2:993, 998–999, 1006, 1006–1017.

38. Amen, "Prayer of John Adams for the Fast Day," *Herald of Liberty*, 30 Apr.1798, 3.
39. Pickering Papers, 23:323A.
40. "To Albert Gallatin Esq.," *Herald of Liberty*, 1 Oct.1798, 2.
41. Pickering Papers, 23:323A.
42. Timothy Pickering to Alexander Addison (30 Nov.1798), Pickering Papers, 9:673; Alexander Addison, *Liberty of Speech and of the Press. A Charge to the Grand Juries* (Washington, PA: John Colerick, 1798), 7, 11, 24.
43. Addison, *Liberty*, 6–8, 9–10, 13–16.
44. Pasley, *Tyranny*, 171 (possible third); Maeva Marcus, ed., *Documentary History of the Supreme Court of the United States, 1789–1800* (New York: ColUP, 1985–2007), 3:299 ("*DHSC*").
45. *DHSC*, 3:284; "Original Minutes of the Circuit Court of the United States of America for the Middle Circuit October Session 1790 to April 1799" (U.S. Circuit Court for District of Pennsylvania) (NARA at Philadelphia, R.G.21.40.2, microfilm M932, roll 1), p.272.
46. "More of the Budget," *Herald of Liberty*, 27 Oct.1800, 3 (suit); Pasley, *Tyranny*, 171.
47. Prince, "John Israel," 49–50; "Monday, December 2," *Herald of Liberty*, 2 Dec.1798, 3; Claude M. Newlin, *The Life and Writings of Hugh Henry Brackenridge* (Princeton: PUP, 1932), 241–242.
48. William Rawle to Timothy Pickering (21 July 1798), Pickering Papers, 25:45; Parker Campbell to William Rawle (12 July 1798), Pickering Papers, 25:22.
49. Brigham, *American Newspapers*, 1:179; Donald H. Stewart, *The Opposition Press of the Federalist Period* (Albany: SUNYP, 1969), 873.
50. *AFC*, 12:293 n.4.
51. Abigail Adams to William Cranch (15 Nov.1797), *AFC*, 12:290, 291, 293 n.4; Abigail Adams to John Quincy Adams (2 Dec.1797), *AFC*, 12:316, 317.
52. Stuart S. Sprague, "Senator John Brown of Kentucky, 1757–1837: A Political Biography" (Ph.D. diss., New York University, 1972), 15; *ANB*, 3:732; *PTJ*, 29:321n. Dr. William Brown did not study in Edinburgh. James McLachlan et al., *Princetonians: A Biographical Dictionary* (Princeton: PUP, 1976–1991), 3:291, 292.
53. For biographical information on Samuel Brown see *ANB*, 3:732; *PTJ*, 29:321n.; and on his parents, Sprague, "Senator John Brown," 1–15; McLachlan, *Princetonians*, 1:15.
54. Samuel Brown to Thomas Jefferson (4 Sept.1798), *PTJ*, 30:509, 510–511, 512n.
55. He was at least twenty-one in 1794, to be listed in the tax rolls; was alive in 1814, when he was granted sixty acres in Florida; and was dead in or soon after 1817, when his heirs brought an unsuccessful claim for 500 acres in Florida, *American State Papers. Documents of the Congress of the United States [Public Lands Series]* (Washington: Gales and Seaton, 1834–1861), 5:422, 424 ("*ASP*").

56. *Journal of the House of Representatives of the State of Georgia, for the Year 1802* (Louisville, GA: Day and Hely, 1803), 40; Ruth Blair, *Some Early Tax Digests of Georgia* (Atlanta: Georgia Department of Archives and History, 1926), 5; Mary R. Bullard, *Cumberland Island: A History* (Athens: UGP, 2003), 104.
57. Rembert W. Patrick, *Florida Fiasco: Rampant Rebels on the Georgia-Florida Border, 1810–1815* (Athens: UGP, 1954), 53; James Madison to Jared Irwin (15 Dec.1808), https://founders.archives.gov/documents/Madison/99-01-02-3821; *ASP,* 8:262, 5:424.
58. Original court records, held by the Georgia Department of Archives and History, are cited below, along with the governor's description and correspondence with the secretary of the navy. The case is further discussed in Wendell Bird, *Press and Speech under Assault* (New York: OUP, 2016), 376–380.
59. "Message of His Excellency Governor Jackson, to Both Houses of the Legislature" (10 Jan.1799), *Louisville Gazette,* 5 Feb.1799, 1, 3.
60. "Standing Army," *Aurora,* 19 Mar.1799, 3.
61. The correct spelling was Garvin, and St. Mary's was then used instead of the modern St. Marys. The reply to Stoddert was Gov. James Jackson to Benjamin Stoddert (4 May 1799), in J. E. Hayes, ed., "Governor's Letter Books of James Jackson, Governor," pp.157–158 (Georgia Department of Archives and History (1940), Drawer 241, Microfilm 52).
62. Recruiting Instructions To Commanders of Gallies (11 Sept.1798), *Naval Documents Related to the Quasi-War Between the United States and France* (Washington: GPO, 1935–1938), 1:388; To John F. Randolph (Captain of Galley) (20 Mar.1799), ibid., 2:493 (commission); Savannah Galley, ibid., 7:371.
63. David Garvin, "To the Public," *Columbian Museum & Savannah Advertiser,* 1 Jan.1799, 2.
64. Ibid.; Gov. James Jackson to Sen. Abraham Baldwin (5 Feb.1799), "Governor's Letter Books," p.57.
65. John F. Randolph, "Gentlemen," *Columbian Museum & Savannah Advertiser,* 4 Jan.1799, 3; David Garvin, "To John F. Randolph," *Columbian Museum & Savannah Advertiser,* 29 Jan.1799, 2.
66. William Blackstone, *Commentaries on the Laws of England* (Oxford: CP, 1765–1769), 4:146 (riot); "Minutes of Superior Court 1797–1809" (7–9 Mar.1799, no page numbers) (Superior Court of Camden County) (Georgia Department of Archives and History, Drawer 71, Microfilm 22). The Archives lists the book as "Grand Jury Presentments."
67. Ibid. (10 Oct.1799); State v. Jn. F. Randolph (Superior Court of Camden County) (Georgia Department of Archives and History, Drawer 27, Microfilm 69) (found guilty).
68. "Doquet Inferior Court of Camden County Commencing November Term 1796" (3 Dec.1798, no page numbers) (Inferior Court of Camden County) (Georgia Department of Archives and History, Drawer 32, Microfilm 26); ibid. (8 Jan.1800).

69. "Minutes of the U.S. Circuit Court for the District of Georgia, 1790–1842," pp.9–110 (NARA at Atlanta (Morrow), R.G.21–12–7, Microfilm M1184, Roll 1), though there is an unrelated case against Randolph over a ship condemnation, p.95 (3 May 1799); *DHSC,* 3:493–494.
70. *Journal of the House of the State of Georgia* (Augusta: John E. Smith [1800]), 48, 50; *Journal of the Senate of the State of Georgia* (Augusta: John E. Smith [1800]), 35.
71. *Naval Documents Related to the Quasi-War Between the United States and France* (Washington: GPO, 1935–1938) (7 vols.); "Papers of the War Department: 1784–1800," http://wardepartmentpapers.org; John F. Randolph, "Gentlemen," *Columbian Museum & Savannah Advertiser,* 4 Jan. 1799, 3; Bird, *Press and Speech under Assault,* 377 n.288.
72. "Standing Army," *Aurora,* 19 Mar.1799, 3; "Standing Army," *Independent Chronicle* (Boston), 18–21 Mar.1799, 4; "Standing Army," *New-Jersey Journal* (Elizabethtown), 26 Mar.1799, 3; "Standing Army," *Farmers' Register* (Chambersburg, PA), 27 Mar.1799, 203; "From the Savannah Museum," *Bee* (New London, CT), 6 Feb.1799, 3.
73. Publius [Alexander Hamilton], "Federalist No.8" (20 Nov.1787), Jacob E. Cooke, ed., *The Federalist* (Middletown, CT: Wesleyan University Press, 1961), 44, 45–48; Publius [James Madison], "Federalist No.41 (19 Jan.1788), ibid., 268, 271–274; Lois G. Schwoerer, *"No Standing Armies!"* (Baltimore: JHUP, 1974).
74. Biographical entries on Garrard include *ANB,* 8:739, and Lowell H. Harrison, ed., *Kentucky's Governors* (Lexington: UPK, 2015), 7–11.
75. "Legislature of Kentucky" (7 Nov.1798), *Claypoole's American Daily Advertiser* (Philadelphia), 10 Dec.1798, 2; accord "Lexington," *Herald of Liberty* (Washington, PA), 17 Dec.1798, 2.
76. Timothy Pickering to Rufus King (14 Dec.1798), *LRK,* 2:493; William Cobbett, "Kentucky," *Porcupine's Gazette* (Philadelphia), 12 Dec.1798, 2; "Fruits of French 'Diplomatic Skill'," *Commercial Advertiser* (New York), 14 Dec.1798, 2 (reprinted from *Gazette of the United States*).
77. Biographies of Logan include Frederick B. Tolles, *George Logan of Philadelphia* (New York: OUP, 1953); and *ANB,* 13:834.
78. *Statutes at Large,* 1:613 (30 Jan.1799).
79. [No Caption], *Columbian Centinel* (Boston), 5 Dec.1798, 3; "Boston, Tuesday, December 6, 1798," *Independent Chronicle* (Boston), 3–6 Dec.1798, 3.
80. "Vassalborough, Nov. 30," *Gazette* (Portland, ME), 10 Dec.1798, 3; "Firm Support of the Laws," *Federal Gazette & Baltimore Daily Advertiser,* 19 Dec.1798, 3.
81. *PGW-R,* 4:40 n.2; *PAH,* 17:299 n.6.
82. "Vassalborough Jacobin Pole," *Impartial Herald* (Suffield, CT), 15 Jan.1799, 3.
83. "Newark, December 25," *Centinel of Freedom* (Newark), 25 Dec.1798, 3; Brigham, *American Newspapers,* 1:707; Stewart, *Opposition Press,* 882. It was not the *Rights of Man,* which was founded later in November 1799.

84. "Newburgh, July 8," *Aurora,* 18 July 1798, 2; [No Caption], *Aurora,* 25 July 1798, 2.
85. Smith, *Freedom's Fetters,* 185 n.87, citing *Independent Chronicle* (Boston), 30 July 1798, 3; "Carlisle, July 4," *Kline's Carlisle Weekly Gazette,* 4 July 1798, 3.

7. The Virginia and Kentucky Resolutions

1. Kentucky Resolutions (House 10 Nov.1798, Senate 13 Nov.1798), in Julian P. Boyd et al., eds., *Papers of Thomas Jefferson* (Princeton: PUP, 1950–), 30:550 ("*PTJ*"); which revised "Jefferson's Draft" (ante-4 Oct.1798), ibid., 30:536. The Kentucky Resolutions are reprinted from "Kentucky Legislature. In the House of Representatives, November 10th, 1798" ([Frankfort, KY: Hunter and Beaumont, 1798]) (broadside). The resolutions are summarized in William J. Watkins, Jr., *Reclaiming the American Revolution: The Kentucky and Virginia Resolutions* (New York: Palgrave Macmillan, 2004), 55–75, 78, with Watkins's strong agreement.
2. Wilson Cary Nicholas to Thomas Jefferson (4 Oct.1798), *PTJ,* 30:556; "Editorial Note," ibid., 30:529, 531–532; K. R. Constantine Gutzman, "Old Dominion, New Republic: Making Virginia Republican, 1776–1840" (Ph.D. diss., University of Virginia, 1999), 273–302.
3. Hubbard Taylor to James Madison (3 Jan.1799), William T. Hutchinson et al., eds., *Papers of James Madison* (Chicago: UChiP, 1962–1991), 17:196, 197 n.3 ("*PJM*"); see James M. Smith, "The Grass Roots Origins of the Kentucky Resolutions," *William and Mary Quarterly* (3rd Series) 27 (1970): 221–245, at 238–243.
4. Kentucky Resolutions, *PTJ,* 30:550–555.
5. "Jefferson's Draft," *PTJ,* 30:536, 540, 539; "Editorial Note," ibid., 30:533. Also dropped was Jefferson's encouragement that states block implementation of unconstitutional laws within their borders. For that final language, see Kentucky Resolutions, *PTJ,* 30:550.
6. Virginia Resolutions (House 21 Dec.1798, Senate 24 Dec.1798), *PJM,* 17:188. The Virginia Resolutions are reprinted from *Journal of the House of Delegates* (Richmond: Jones and Dixon, 1798), 31 (21 Dec.1798). For a summary, Watkins, *Reclaiming,* 55–75.
7. Adrienne Koch, *Jefferson and Madison: The Great Collaboration* (New York: Knopf, 1950), 187–209; James R. Sharp, *The Deadlocked Election of 1800* (Lawrence: UPKan, 2010), 54; Andrew Burstein and Nancy Isenberg, *Madison and Jefferson* (New York: Random House, 2010), 307–348; Thomas Jefferson to James Madison (17 Nov.1798), *PJM,* 17:175; "Editorial Note," ibid., 17:185, 186.
8. "Editorial Note," *PJM,* 17:185, 187–188.
9. Virginia Resolutions, *PJM,* 17:188–190.
10. Extracts from the Address to the People (23 Jan.1799), Jonathan Elliot, ed., *The Debates in the Several State Conventions on the Adoption of the Federal Constitution* (Philadelphia: Lippincott, 1836), 4:529. For Madison's nonin-

volvement, see "Editorial Note," *PJM,* 17:199, 199–206. Inconsistency included minimal argument based on the First Amendment, and an implication that states had authority to prosecute seditious libel, contrary to Madison's later Report.

11. Lance Banning, *The Sacred Fire of Liberty: James Madison and the Founding of the Federal Republic* (Ithaca, NY: CorUP, 1995), 387–389; Sharp, *Deadlocked Election,* 54–58; Ralph Ketcham, *James Madison* (New York: Macmillan, 1971), 397, 403; Adrienne Koch and Harry Ammon, "The Virginia and Kentucky Resolutions: An Episode in Jefferson's and Madison's Defense of Civil Liberties," *William and Mary Quarterly* (3rd series) 5 (1948): 145–176, at 161; "Editorial Note," *PJM,* 17:187; Brian D. Steele, "Thomas Jefferson and the Making of an American Nationalism" (Ph.D. diss., University of North Carolina, 2003), 186–250; Thomas Jefferson to Wilson Cary Nicholas (29 Nov.1798), *PTJ,* 30:590.
12. James Madison to James Monroe (17 Dec.1797), *PJM,* 17:61.
13. Kurt T. Lash and Alicia Harrison, "Minority Report: John Marshall and the Defense of the Alien and Sedition Acts," *Ohio State Law Journal* 68 (2007): 435–516, at 439–516; Andrew Lenner, "A Tale of Two Constitutions," *American Journal of Legal History* 40 (1996): 72–105, at 79–80 n.26; see Theodore Sedgwick to Alexander Hamilton (7 Feb.1799), Harold C. Syrett et al., eds., *Papers of Alexander Hamilton* (New York: ColUP, 1961–), 22:469, 470 ("*PAH*"). Marshall's authorship was denied by the editors of his papers. "Editorial Note," Herbert A. Johnson et al., eds., *The Papers of John Marshall* (Chapel Hill: UNCP, 1974–2006), 3:494, 498–499 and n.1; David S. Robarge, "John Marshall and His Times" (Ph.D. diss., Columbia University, 1995), 295 and n.17.
14. *Address of the Minority of the Legislature of Virginia, to Their Fellow Citizens* (Petersburg, VA: William Prentis, 1799), 6–11, 11–16 (quotations from pp.12–13) (one of several printings).
15. *The Communications of Several States, on the Resolutions of the Legislature of Virginia, Respecting the Alien and Sedition Laws* (Richmond: Jones and Dixon, 1799), 3–20; "Answers of the Several State Legislatures," Elliot, *Debates,* 4:532–539. These are supplemented by Frank M. Anderson, "Contemporary Opinion of the Virginia and Kentucky Resolutions," *American Historical Review* 5 (1899): 45–63, 225–252, at 245–252.
16. *Debates and Proceedings in the Congress of the United States . . . Annals of the Congress of the United States* (Washington: Gales and Seaton, 1834–1856), 9:3016 (25 Feb.1799) ("*Annals*"); *American State Papers: Miscellaneous* (Washington: Gales and Seaton, 1834), 1:181.
17. *Annals,* 9:2985–2993 (25 Feb.1799); *Reports of Committees in Congress to Whom Were Referred Certain Memorials and Petitions Complaining of the Acts of Congress, Concerning the Alien & Sedition Laws* (Richmond: Thomas Nicholson, 1799), 3–10.
18. Alexander Hamilton to Theodore Sedgwick (2 Feb.1799), *PAH,* 22:452, 453.
19. Timothy Pickering to Col. David Humphreys (11 Feb.1799), "Timothy Pickering Papers" (Massachusetts Historical Society, Boston, manuscripts and 69

reels), 10:376, 378 ("Pickering Papers"); Timothy Pickering to William Vans Murray (5 Feb.1799), ibid., 10:338, 340; Timothy Pickering to Rufus King (6 Feb.1799), Charles R. King., ed., *Life and Correspondence of Rufus King* (New York: Putnam's Sons, 1894–1900), 2:537 ("*LRK*"); Timothy Pickering to Rufus King (4 May 1799), ibid., 3:12, 13; Timothy Pickering to Dr. Edward Stevens (9 May 1799), Pickering Papers, 11:68, 70.

20. Theodore Sedgwick to Rufus King (20 Jan.1799), *LRK*, 2:514, 518; George Cabot to Timothy Pickering (15 Feb. 1799), Henry Cabot Lodge, ed., *Life and Letters of George Cabot*, 2nd ed. (Boston: LB, 1878), 218.
21. Thomas Jefferson to James Madison (23 Aug.1799), *PJM*, 17:257, 257–258.
22. Thomas Jefferson to Wilson Cary Nicholas (5 Sept.1799), *PTJ*, 31:178, 179; Mary K. B. Tachau, *Federal Courts in the Early Republic: Kentucky 1789–1816* (Princeton: PUP, 1978), 196–197.
23. Kentucky Resolution of 1799, Elliot, *Debates*, 4:544 (House 14 Nov.1799, Senate 22 Nov.1799), reprinting *Journal . . . at the First Session of the Eighth General Assembly, Beginning Nov. 4, 1799* (Frankfort, KY: Hunter, 1799), 33–34. For Jefferson not drafting, see Thomas Jefferson to Wilson Cary Nicholas (5 Sept.1799), *PTJ*, 31:178, 179; Koch, *Jefferson and Madison*, 201; Noble E. Cunningham, Jr., *The Jeffersonian Republicans* (Chapel Hill: UNCP, 1957), 135. Too, the editors of the *Papers of Thomas Jefferson* do not treat him as the author in volume 31.
24. Though some authors find this change more moderate and argue that the 1799 resolution "represented a partial repudiation of the resolutions of 1798." Robert H. Churchill, "Popular Nullification, Fries' Rebellion, and the Waning of Radical Republicanism, 1798–1801," *Pennsylvania History* 67 (2000): 105–140, at 131. For the nullification language, see Elliot, *Debates*, 4:544–545; *Journal*, 33–34. Elliot italicized the nullification sentence, but the Journal did not.
25. Report (Jan.1800), *PJM*, 17:307, reprinting *Report of the Committee to Whom Was Committed the Proceedings of Sundry of the Other States . . .* (Richmond: For the General Assembly, [1800]). Legislators' discussion is in *Proceedings of the Virginia Assembly, on the Answers of Sundry States to Their Resolutions* (Philadelphia: James Carey, 1800), 3–52.
26. *Journal of the House of Delegates of the Commonwealth of Virginia [2 Dec.1799]* (Richmond: Meriwether Jones, 1799 [actually 1800]), 72 (7 Jan.1800), 94 (20 Jan.1800); James Madison to Thomas Jefferson (18 Jan.1800), *PJM*, 17:357; "Editorial Note," ibid., 17:303, 306.
27. Report, *PJM*, 17:307–316, 317–345.
28. Ibid., 17:317–326.
29. Ibid., 17:326–341 (extended quotation p.336). Abridgment is further discussed at ibid., 17:347.
30. Ibid., 17:340–341, 341–345 (extended quotation pp.344–345).
31. Proclamations, (1610) 12 Coke's Reports 74, 77 Eng. Rep. 1352, 1353 (P.C.) (cannot "create any offence" by proclamation or "alter the law"); Charles M. Gray, "Bonham's Case Reviewed," *Proceedings of the American Philosophical Society* 116 (1972): 35–58; see Alan Cromartie, *The Constitutionalist Revolu-*

tion (Cambridge: CUP, 2006), 234–282; Chisholm v. Georgia (1793), Maeva Marcus, ed., *Documentary History of the Supreme Court of the United States, 1789–1800* (New York: ColUP, 1985–2007), 5:127–273 ("*DHSC*").

32. Bill of Rights (1689), 1 W. & M. s.2, c.2; Ronald J. Krotoszynski, Jr., *Reclaiming the Petition Clause* (New Haven: YUP, 2012), 81–152; Douglas Bradburn, "A Clamor in the Public Mind: Opposition to the Alien and Sedition Acts," *William and Mary Quarterly* (3rd series) 65 (2008): 565–600, at 566; accord Douglas M. Bradburn, "Revolutionary Politics, Nationhood, and the Problem of American Citizenship, 1787–1804" (Ph.D. diss., University of Chicago), 312 n.14, 325–330.
33. Larry D. Kramer, "Putting the Politics Back into the Political Safeguards of Federalism," *Columbia Law Review* 100 (2000): 215–293, at 275; K.R. Constantine Gutzman, "The Virginia and Kentucky Resolutions Reconsidered: 'An Appeal to the Real Laws of Our Country'," *Journal of Southern History* 66 (2000): 473–496, at 474–475, 488; Karl A. Andresen, "The Theory of State Interposition . . ." (Ph.D. diss., University of Minnesota, 1960).
34. Publius [Alexander Hamilton], "Federalist No. 26" (22 Dec.1787), Jacob E. Cooke, ed., *The Federalist* (Middletown: Wesleyan University Press, 1961), 164, 169.
35. Andresen, "State Interposition," 86–89; Norman K. Risjord, *Chesapeake Politics, 1781–1800* (New York: ColUP, 1978), 538.
36. John C. Calhoun, *A Disquisition on Government and a Discourse on the Constitution* (Richard K. Cralle, ed., Charleston: Walker and James, 1851); see William W. Freehling, *The Road to Disunion* (New York: OUP, 1990), 1:257–259; Christian G. Fritz, "A Constitutional Middle-Ground between Revision and Revolution," in Hendrik Hartog and William E. Nelson, eds., *Law as Culture and Culture as Law* (Madison: Madison House, 2000), 158–226, at 164–224; Donald Ratcliffe, "The Nullification Crisis, Southern Discontents, and the American Political Process," *American Nineteenth Century History* 1 (2000): 1–30.
37. James Madison to William Cabell Rives (12 Mar.1833), Jack N. Rakove, ed., *Madison: Writings* (New York: Library of America, 1999), 863. The next year, Madison wrote an essay "On Nullification."
38. Thomas Jefferson to Abigail Adams (22 July 1804), Lester J. Cappon, ed., *The Adams-Jefferson Letters* (Chapel Hill: UNCP, 1959), 1:274, 275; Thomas Jefferson to Edmund Pendleton (14 Feb.1799), *PTJ*, 31:36, 36–37.
39. James R. Sharp, *American Politics in the Early Republic: The New Nation in Crisis* (New Haven: YUP, 1993), 196–197.
40. Thomas Jefferson to James Madison (23 Aug.1799), *PJM*, 17:257, 258; Thomas Jefferson to Wilson Cary Nicholas (5 Sept.1799), *PTJ*, 31:178, 179; Report (Jan.1800), *PJM*, 17:348, 349.
41. Gordon S. Wood, *Empire of Liberty* (New York: OUP, 2009), 270; accord James M. Smith, "The Grass Roots Origins of the Kentucky Resolutions," *William and Mary Quarterly* (3rd series) 27 (1970): 221–245, at 245.
42. Bradburn, "Clamor," 599–600; Cunningham, *Jeffersonian Republicans*, 128–129. That strategy is most clearly laid out in Thomas Jefferson to James

Madison (26 Nov.1799), *PJM*, 17:280; Koch and Ammon, "Virginia and Kentucky Resolutions," 170.

43. Lance Banning, "William J. Watkins, Jr., Reclaiming the American Revolution" (book review), *American Historical Review* 111 (2006): 164–165; H. Jefferson Powell, "The Principles of '98: An Essay in Historical Retrieval," *Virginia Law Review* 80 (1994): 689–743; Kevin R. Gutzman, "A Troublesome Legacy: James Madison and 'The Principles of '98'," *Journal of the Early Republic* 15 (1995): 569–589.
44. Andrew Lenner, "Separate Spheres: Republican Constitutionalism in the Federalist Era," *American Journal of Legal History* 41 (1997): 250–281, at 276; accord Watkins, *Kentucky and Virginia Resolutions*, 59–69; Forrest McDonald, *States' Rights and the Union: Imperium in Imperio, 1776–1876* (Lawrence: UPKan, 2000), 41; David Jenkins, "The Sedition Act of 1798 and the Incorporation of Seditious Libel into First Amendment Jurisprudence," *American Journal of Legal History* 45 (2001): 154–213, at 181; accord Richard E. Ellis, *The Union at Risk: Jacksonian Democracy, States' Rights and the Nullification Crisis* (New York: OUP, 1987), 4; June Eichbaum, "The Antagonism Between Freedom of Speech and Seditious Libel," *Hastings Constitutional Law Quarterly* 5 (1978): 445–459, at 447.
45. E.g., Walter Berns, "Freedom of the Press and the Alien and Sedition Laws: A Reappraisal," *Supreme Court Review* (1970): 109–159, at 126; William L. Richter, "Federalism and Civil Liberties: A Reappraisal of the Alien and Sedition Acts" (Ph.D. diss., University of Chicago, 1963), 9–10 ("the rights which the Republicans were defending against federal encroachment were primarily state rights and powers and not individual liberties"), 25, 35, 37, 69; Edward S. Corwin, "Freedom of Speech and Press under the First Amendment," *Yale Law Journal* 30 (1920): 48–55, at 50.
46. Richard D. Brown, "The Revolution's Legacy for the History of the Book," in Robert A. Gross et al., eds., *A History of the Book in America* (Chapel Hill: UNCP, 2010), 2:58, 63–64; accord Walter Berns, *The First Amendment and the Future of American Democracy* (New York: Basic Books, 1976), 97.
47. Koch and Ammon, "Virginia and Kentucky Resolutions," 174; accord Richard Labunski, *James Madison and the Struggle for the Bill of Rights* (New York: OUP, 2006), 257; Gutzman, "Virginia and Kentucky Resolutions Reconsidered," 488; Stanley Elkins and Eric McKitrick, *The Age of Federalism* (New York: OUP, 1993), 723; Cunningham, *Jeffersonian Republicans*, 128; Koch, *Jefferson and Madison*, 209. For different reasoning to the same conclusion, see Douglas Bradburn, *The Citizenship Revolution* (Charlottesville: UVP, 2009), 187–192.
48. Report (Jan.1800), *PJM*, 17:307, 308–317 (powers), 317–326 (Alien Act and powers and rights), 326–335 (Sedition Act and common law powers), 335–345 (freedom of press and electoral rights), 345–347 (powers and freedom of press), 347–350 (appeal for concurrence).
49. "Jefferson's Draft," *PTJ*, 30:536, 537.
50. Report (Jan.1800), *PJM*, 17:307, 340–341, 342–345; Thomas Jefferson to Elbridge Gerry (26 Jan.1799), *PTJ*, 30:645, 650.

51. Leonard Levy, *Emergence of a Free Press* (New York: OUP, 1985), xii; accord 294, 89, 136, 272, 297.
52. George Nicholas, "Political Creed," *New-York Gazette and General Advertiser,* 19 Oct.1798, 2 (dated 30 July 1798); George Nicholas, *To the Citizens of Kentucky* (Lexington: n.p., 15 Oct.1798); *A Letter from George Nicholas, of Kentucky* (Lexington, KY: John Bradford, 1798); *PTJ,* 30:521; Hortensius [George Hay], *An Essay on the Liberty of the Press* (Philadelphia: Aurora, 1799); [George Blake], "Trial of Mr. Abijah Adams," *Independent Chronicle,* 11, 15, 18, 22, 29 Apr.1799, and 2 May 1799 (all page 1).
53. Thomas Cooper, *Political Essays* (Northumberland, PA: Andrew Kennedy, 1799) (reprinted 1800); [St. George Tucker], *A Letter to a Member of Congress; Respecting the Alien and Sedition Laws* (n.p., 6 June 1799) (date on p.48); Tunis Wortman, *A Treatise, Concerning Political Enquiry and the Liberty of the Press* (New York: George Forman, 1800); John Thomson, *An Enquiry Concerning the Liberty, and Licentiousness of the Press* (New York: Johnson and Stryker, 1801).
54. Excellent discussions are in Robert W. T. Martin, *Government by Dissent: Protest, Resistance, and Radical Democratic Thought in the Early American Republic* (New York: NYUP, 2013), 157–167; Michael Kent Curtis, *Free Speech, "The People's Darling Privilege"* (Durham, NC: DUP, 2000), 97–103; Norman L. Rosenberg, *Protecting the Best Man: An Interpretive History of the Law of Libel* (Chapel Hill: UNCP, 1986), 89–99.
55. Virginiensis [Charles Lee], *Defence of the Alien and Sedition Laws* (Philadelphia: Fenno, 1798); [Henry Lee], *Plain Truth: Addressed to the People of Virginia* (n.p., 1799); Alexander Addison, *Liberty of Speech, and of the Press: A Charge to the Grand Juries* (Washington, PA: John Colerick, 1798); Inhabitant of the North-Western Territory, *Observations, on a Letter from George Nicholas* (Cincinnati, OH: Edmund Freeman, 1799); see Norman L. Rosenberg, "Alexander Addison and the Pennsylvania Origins of Federalist First-Amendment Thought," *Pennsylvania Magazine of History and Biography* 108 (1984): 399–417.
56. The reception of the Virginia and Kentucky Resolutions by the other states, and forty examples of claims that they were rejected by the other states, are discussed in Wendell Bird, "Reassessing Responses to the Virginia and Kentucky Resolutions: New Evidence from the Tennessee and Georgia Resolutions and from Other States," *Journal of the Early Republic* 35 (2015): 519–551.
57. Elkins and McKitrick, *Age of Federalism,* 720; Koch and Ammon, "Virginia and Kentucky Resolutions," 145; e.g., Timothy Pickering to Rufus King (4 May 1799), *LRK,* 3:12, 13; "Anniversary of Independence," *Philadelphia Gazette,* 6 July 1799, 3; 'Philadelphia, Wednesday Evening, March 5," *Gazette of the United States* (Philadelphia), 5 Mar.1800, 3.
58. Anderson, "Contemporary Opinion," 248 (Maryland), 248–249 (New York House); Elliot, *Debates,* 4:532–539.
59. Elliot, *Debates,* 4:533–539.
60. Ibid., 4:533–537.

61. Anderson, "Contemporary Opinion," 236; many others quoted in Bird, "Reassessing Responses to the Virginia and Kentucky Resolutions," 527 n.9.
62. Gov. John Sevier to Legislature (7 Dec.1798), in "Governor John Sevier Papers" (Tennessee State Library and Archives, G.P. 2, Box 1, Folder 6); "Tennessee House Journal 1798—Second Session," pp.52 (12 Dec.1798), 57 (19 Dec.1798) (Tennessee State Library and Archives, R.G.60 manuscript volume), reprinted in *Journals of the Senate and House of the Second General Assembly of the State of Tennessee* (Kingsport, TN: Southern Publishers, 1933), 403, 406 (printed version page in parentheses hereafter).
63. "Tennessee Senate Journal 1798–1799," p.188 (355) (4 Jan.1799) (Tennessee State Library and Archives, R.G.60 manuscript volume); "Tennessee House Journal," pp.181 (468–469), 185 (471) (4 Jan.1799).
64. "Tennessee House Journal," pp.195–196 (473–474) (5 Jan.1799); "Tennessee Senate Journal," p.199 (361) (5 Jan.1799); Kristofer Ray, "Progress and Popular Democracy on the Southwestern Frontier: Middle Tennessee, 1790–1824" (Ph.D. diss., University of North Carolina, 2003), 56; accord James H. Broussard, *The Southern Federalists, 1800–1816* (Baton Rouge: LSUP, 1978), xii.
65. "Tennessee Senate Journal," p.189 (356) (4 Jan.1799); "Tennessee House Journal," p.185 (470–471) (4 Jan.1799). The legislature's printed version replaces *&* with *and*, and slightly alters punctuation.
66. "Tennessee House Journal," p.195 (473) (5 Jan.1799); "Tennessee Senate Journal," p.198 (360) (5 Jan.1799); Legislative Message (5 Jan.1799), Robert H. White, ed., *Messages of the Governors of Tennessee* (Nashville, TN: Tennessee Historical Commission, 1952–), 1:90.
67. E.g., "Norfolk, February 7," *Aurora* (Philadelphia), 16 Feb.1799, 3; "Norfolk, February 7," *Centinel of Freedom* (Newark), 19 Feb.1799, 2; "Newark, April 23," *Centinel of Freedom,* 23 Apr.1799, 3; "Boston, Monday, May 6th," *Independent Chronicle* (Boston), 2–6 May 1799, 3.
68. "Message of His Excellency Governor Jackson, to Both Houses" (10 Jan.1799), *Louisville Gazette* (Louisville, GA), 5 Feb.1799, 1, 3, which is the best source since the January 1799 legislative journal has not survived. Accord "The Governor's Message Concluded," *Columbian Museum and Savannah Advertiser,* 29 Jan.1799, 1.
69. Gov. James Jackson to Mr. President and Gentlemen (22 Jan.1799), in J. E. Hayes, ed., "Governor's Letter Books of James Jackson, Governor," pp.6–7 (Georgia Department of Archives and History (1940), Drawer 241, Microfilm 52); Gov. James Jackson to Mr. President and Gentlemen (5 Feb.1799), ibid., p.57.
70. *Journal of the Senate of the State of Georgia* (Augusta, GA: John E. Smith, 1800), 18 (22 Nov.1799); ibid., 18–19 (22 Nov.1799); *Journal of the House of Representatives of the State of Georgia* (Augusta, GA: John E. Smith, 1800), 48 (4 Dec.1799)
71. *Journal of the House,* 50 (5 Dec. 1799); *Journal of the Senate,* 35 (5 Dec.1799).
72. *Journal of the House,* 48–50 (4–5 Dec.1799); *Journal of the Senate,* 35 (5 Dec.1799). The version on p.48 contains the modifications specified on p.50.

73. *Journal of the Senate,* 18–19 (22 Nov.1799) (superseded); *Journal of the House,* 50 (5 Dec.1799) (modifications), 48 (4 Dec.1799) (final).
74. Sharp, *American Politics,* 154, 244; Cunningham, *Jeffersonian Republicans,* 239; John Ferling, *Adams vs. Jefferson: The Tumultuous Election of 1800* (New York: OUP, 2004), 163–164. On Georgia's legislature, see George R. Lamplugh, "'Oh the Colossus! The Colossus!': James Jackson and the Jeffersonian Republican Party in Georgia, 1796–1806," *Journal of the Early Republic* 9 (1989): 315–334, at 323; George R. Lamplugh, *Politics on the Periphery: Factions and Parties in Georgia, 1783–1806* (Newark: UDP, 1986), 156.
75. Gov. James Jackson to Gov. James Monroe (24 Mar.1800), H. W. Flournoy, *Calendar of Virginia State Papers* (Richmond: R.F. Walker, 1890), 9:100.
76. Koch and Ammon, "Virginia and Kentucky Resolutions," 157; Harry Ammon, "The Republican Party in Virginia 1789 to 1824" (Ph.D. diss., University of Virginia, 1948), 184.
77. Kentucky Resolutions, *PTJ,* 30:550, 555; Virginia Resolutions, *PJM,* 17:188, 190; Report, *PJM,* 17:307, 347.
78. James Madison to Thomas Jefferson (29 Dec.1798), *PJM,* 17:191; Thomas Jefferson to James Madison (17 Nov.1798), ibid., 17:175.
79. Anderson, "Contemporary Opinion," 248–249,
80. Gov. Edward Rutledge, "Mr. Speaker and Gentlemen" (28 Nov.1799), *In the House of Representatives* (Columbia, SC: Freneau and Paine, 1799).
81. Journals of the Senate, 1790–1800, p.177 (20 Dec.1799) (South Carolina Department of Archives and History, Columbia (manuscripts)); Journals of the House, 1790–1800, pp.164–165 (20 Dec.1799) (South Carolina Department of Archives and History, Columbia (manuscripts)).
82. "Richmond, Jan. 21," *Aurora,* 30 Jan.1800, 2; accord "From a Richmond Paper," *The Times; and District of Columbia Daily Advertiser* (Alexandria, VA), 25 Jan.1800, 3.
83. Wilson Cary Nicholas to James Monroe (13 Jan.1799), Daniel Preston, ed., *The Papers of James Monroe* (Santa Barbara, CA: Greenwood Press, 2003–), 4:320; Lisle A. Rose, *Prologue to Democracy: The Federalists in the South, 1789–1800* (Lexington: UKP, 1968), 229, 236; accord John Harold Wolfe, *Jeffersonian Democracy in South Carolina* (Chapel Hill: UNCP, 1940), 123.
84. Edward Rutledge to John Rutledge, Jr. (29 July 1798), "John Rutledge [Jr.] Papers" (University of North Carolina, Chapel Hill, Southern Historical Collection, Collection 948); William Vans Murray to John Quincy Adams (22 Mar.1799), Worthington C. Ford, ed., "Letters of William Vans Murray," *Annual Report of the American Historical Association* (1912): 343, 529, 530; accord Marvin R. Zahniser, "The Public Career of Charles Cotesworth Pinckney" (Ph.D. diss., University of California-Santa Barbara, 1963), 281.
85. *Journal of the Senate. State of North-Carolina* (Wilmington, NC: Allmand Hall, [1798]), 75 (22 Dec.1798).
86. *Journal of the House of Commons. State of North-Carolina* (Wilmington, NC: Allmand Hall, 1799), 78 (24 Dec.1798); *Journal of the Senate,* 77 (24 Dec.1798). The vote is analyzed in Rose, *Prologue,* 299.

87. *Journal of the Senate,* 77 (24 Dec.1798); *Journal of the House of Commons* (Raleigh, NC: Hodge and Boylan, [1800]), 19 (30 Nov.1799).
88. Henry M. Wagstaff, "Federalism in North Carolina," in *James Sprunt Historical Publications* 9 (1910): 3–36, at 30–32; Bradburn, "Clamor," 581; Risjord, *Chesapeake Politics,* 538; Delbert H. Gilpatrick, *Jeffersonian Democracy in North Carolina, 1789–1816* (New York: ColUP, 1931), 102.
89. Samuel Johnston to James Iredell (23 Dec.1798), Griffith J. McRee, ed., *Life and Correspondence of James Iredell* (New York: Appleton, 1857–1858), 2:542.
90. Ethelbert D. Warfield, *The Kentucky Resolutions of 1798,* 2nd ed. (New York: Putnam, 1894), 115. Other examples are in Bird, "Reassessing Responses to the Virginia and Kentucky Resolutions," 543 n.43.
91. *Votes and Proceedings of the Twenty-Third General Assembly of the State of New-Jersey [23 Oct.1798]* (Trenton, NJ: Sherman, Mershon and Thomas, 1799), 10–11 (18 Jan.1799). For the actual vote, see "Legislature of New-Jersey," *Centinel of Freedom,* 22 Jan.1799, 2; accord "New-Jersey Legislature," *Genius of Liberty* (Morristown, NJ), 24 Jan.1799, 2. Newspapers, both Republican and Federalist, reported that the speaker was "obliged to decide," meaning a tie. E.g., "Extract of a Letter from a Member of the New-Jersey Legislature," *New-York Gazette and General Advertiser,* 22 Jan.1799, 3; "Extract of a Letter," *Spectator* (New York), 23 Jan.1799, 3.
92. "From the Trenton Federalist," *New York Gazette and General Advertiser,* 24 Jan.1799, 2; "From the New-Jersey Gazette," *Oracle of the Day* (Portsmouth, NH), 2 Feb.1799, 2; An Observer, "For the Genius of Liberty," *Genius of Liberty,* 7 Mar.1799, 1.
93. Rudolph J. Pasler and Margaret C. Pasler, *The New Jersey Federalists* (Rutherford, NJ: FDUP, 1974), 91 n.68; Carl E. Prince, *New Jersey's Jeffersonian Republicans* (Chapel Hill: UNCP, 1964), 35.
94. "Newark, January 22," *Centinel of Freedom,* 22 Jan.1799, 3; "At a Numerous and Respectable Meeting . . . County of Essex," *Centinel of Freedom,* 22 Jan.1799, 3; "To the Honorable Congress," *Genius of Liberty,* 17 Jan.1799, 2; Pasler and Pasler, *Federalists,* 34; e.g., William Tell, "To the Freemen of Virginia," *Centinel of Freedom,* 1 Jan.1799, 1; Democritus, "The Democrat—No. 11," *Centinel of Freedom,* 29 Jan.1799, 1.
95. Prince, *New Jersey's Jeffersonian Republicans,* 35.
96. *Journal of the Senate of the Commonwealth of Pennsylvania [4 Dec.1798]* (Philadelphia: Zachariah Poulson, 1798 [1799]), 9:88 (25 Jan.1799), 200 (9 Mar.1799); "Virginia Resolutions," *Philadelphia Gazette,* 11 Mar.1799, 3; "Virginia Resolutions," *Gazette of the United States,* 12 Mar.1799, 3.
97. *Journal of the First Session of the Ninth House of Representatives of the Commonwealth of Pennsylvania [4 Dec.1798]* (Philadelphia: Hall and Sellers, 1799), 198–200 (9 Feb.1799); Anderson, "Contemporary Opinion," 5:245, 248; *Journal of the First Session,* 199, 193, 195–197.
98. Potomac, "Calm Reflections on Rash Proceedings," *Gazette of the United States,* 13 Feb.1799, 2; *Journal of the First Session,* 291–292 (11 Mar.1799).
99. *Dissent of the Minority, of the House of Repre[s]entatives of the Commonwealth of Pennsylvania, from the Address to the President* (Philadelphia: [Duane],

1799), 7; Harry M. Tinkcom, *The Republicans and Federalists in Pennsylvania, 1790–1801* (Harrisburg: PHMC, 1950), 160, 175, 206, 243; Sanford W. Higginbotham, *The Keystone in the Democratic Arch: Pennsylvania Politics, 1800–1816* (Harrisburg: PHMC, 1952), 28; Sharp, *American Politics,* 265, 269.

100. E.g., Jeffrey Schenker, "James Madison: Consistent Defender of Republican Values" (Ph.D. diss., Drew University, 2004), 127 (connecting "radical nature" with not being "accepted by other states"); Robert H. Churchill, "'The Highest and Holiest Duty of Freemen': Revolutionary Libertarianism in American History" (Ph.D. diss., Rutgers University, 2001), 101 (Virginia and Kentucky Resolutions "fall somewhere between the moderate and radical positions").

101. Virginia Resolutions, *PJM,* 17:189; Kentucky Resolutions, *PTJ,* 30:551; *Reports of Committees in Congress,* 6–7; *Address of the Minority,* 13–14; Response of Massachusetts, Elliot, *Debates,* 4:533, 536.

102. Ford W. Hall, "The Common Law: An Account of Its Reception in the United States," *Vanderbilt Law Review* 4 (1951): 791, 799–800, 806–807.

103. *Reports of Committees in Congress,* 7; *Address of the Minority,* 12–13; Response of Massachusetts, Elliot, *Debates,* 4:536. Some of the individual authors mentioned earlier—Charles Lee, Henry Lee, Alexander Addison, and others—did provide more justification.

104. Report (Jan.1800), 326–333.

105. Stewart Jay, "Origins of Federal Common Law," *University of Pennsylvania Law Review* 133 (1985): 1003–1116, 1231–1333; Stephen B. Presser, "The Supra-Constitution, the Courts, and the Federal Common Law of Crimes," *Law and History Review* 4 (1986): 325–335; Leonard W. Levy, *Emergence of a Free Press* (New York: OUP, 1985), 274–279; Morton J. Horowitz, *The Transformation of American Law, 1780–1860* (Cambridge, MA: HUP, 1977), 9.

106. Robert C. Palmer, "The Federal Common Law of Crime," *Law and History Review* 4 (1986): 267–323, at 271–309; Kathryn Preyer, "Jurisdiction To Punish: Federal Authority, Federalism and the Common Law of Crimes in the Early Republic," *Law and History Review* 4 (1986): 223–265, at 225–242; Julius Goebel, *History of the Supreme Court of the United States* (New York: Macmillan, 1971), 1:623–633; see Gary D. Rowe, "The Sound of Silence: *United States v. Hudson & Goodwin,* the Jeffersonian Ascendancy, and the Abolition of Federal Common Law Crimes," *Yale Law Journal* 101 (1992): 919–948, at 935–948.

107. United States v. Hudson & Goodwin, 11 U.S. (7 Cranch) 32, 34 (1812); accord United States v. Coolidge, 14 U.S. (1 Wheat.) 415 (1816).

108. *Annals,* 1:1108 (20 Jan.1790); John Marshall to St. George Tucker (27 Nov.1800), *Papers of John Marshall,* 6:23; An Act for the Punishment of Certain Crimes, 1 Stat. 112 (30 Apr.1790).

109. William Blackstone, *Commentaries on the Laws of England* (Oxford: CP, 1765–1769), 4:18; Thomas Jefferson to Edmund Randolph (18 Aug.1799), *PTJ,* 31:168, 169.

110. Hall, "Common Law," 799–800, 806–807.
111. James Wilson's Charge (C.C.D.Pa. 12 Apr.1790), *DHSC*, 2:33, 41–44; William Cushing to John Lowell (4 Apr.1790), ibid., 2:21, 22; James Wilson's Charge (C.C.D.Va. 23 May 1791), *DHSC*, 2:166, 181, 176; accord James Wilson's Charge (C.C.D.Pa. 21 Feb.1791), ibid., 2:142, 144–152, 147.
112. Elliot, *Debates*, 4:219 (30 July 1788); James Iredell's Charge (C.C.D.Ga. 17 Oct.1791), *DHSC*, 2:216, 219, 220–221; see James Iredell's Charge (C.C.D.Ga. 26 Apr.1792), ibid., 2:263, 264, 265; James Iredell's Charge (C.C.D.Mass. 12 Oct.1792), ibid., 2:308, 314–315; James Iredell's Charge (C.C.D.N.Y. 6 Apr.1795), ibid., 3:14, 19; William Paterson's Charge (C.C.D.Pa. 4 May 1795), ibid., 3:40, 41; accord William Paterson's Charge (C.C.D.N.J. 2 Apr.1795), ibid., 3:10, 11.
113. Constitution art.I, sec.8 ("To define and punish . . . Offenses against the Law of Nations"), art.III, sec.2 ("The judicial power shall extend to all Cases . . . arising under this Constitution and Laws . . . and Treaties").
114. Wendell Bird, *Press and Speech under Assault: The Early Supreme Court Justices, the Sedition Act of 1798, and the Campaign against Dissent* (New York: OUP, 2016), 94–95 (Henfield's Case, Ravara, Smith, Wiscart, Worrall, McGill).
115. Ibid., 95, 299; Trial of Robert Worrall, Wharton's State Trials 189, 197 (C.C.D.Pa. 1798); United States v. Worrall, 28 F.Cas.227, 779 (C.C.D.Pa. 1798).
116. *Reports of Committees in Congress*, 6–7.
117. Report (Jan.1800), 336, 344, 340–341.
118. Bird, *Press and Speech under Assault*, 31–33, 67; ibid., 113–329, esp. 199–200.
119. Wendell Bird, *The Revolution in Freedoms of Press and Speech* (New York: OUP, forthcoming 2020), Chapters 3–9.

8. The Fries Rebellion and Sedition

1. It is discussed at more length in Wendell Bird, "New Light on the Sedition Act of 1798: The Missing Half of the Prosecutions," *Law and History Review* 34 (2016): 541–614, at 560–567, 571–584. Writings on the Alien and Sedition Acts that overlook this second campaign are listed in ibid., 544–545 nn.20–24.
2. An Act To Lay and Collect a Direct Tax, 1 Stat. 597 (14 July 1798); An Act To Provide for the Valuation of Lands and Dwelling-Houses, and the Enumeration of Slaves, 1 Stat. 580 (9 July 1798); Jeffrey S. Dimmig, "Palatine Liberty: Pennsylvania German Opposition to the Direct Tax of 1798," *American Journal of Legal History* 45 (2001): 371–390, at 384–389.
3. The best history of the Fries Rebellion is Paul Douglas Newman, *Fries's Rebellion: The Enduring Struggle for the American Revolution* (Philadelphia: UPP, 2004); the biographical section is pp.114–119. Other useful biographical sources include John A. Garraty et al., eds., *American National Biography* (New York: OUP, 1999), 8:490 ("*ANB*").

4. Original court records for *United States v. John Fries,* and microfilm copies, are in National Archives at Philadelphia: "Criminal Case Files of the U.S. Circuit Court for the Eastern District of Pennsylvania 1791–1840" (U.S. Circuit Court for District of Pennsylvania) (NARA at Philadelphia, R.G.21.40.2, microfilm M986, rolls 1–2), pp.958–957, 026–043 ("Criminal Case Files"); "Original Minutes of the Circuit Court of the United States of America for the Middle Circuit October Session 1790 to April 1799" (U.S. Circuit Court for District of Pennsylvania) (NARA at Philadelphia, R.G.21.40.2, microfilm M932, roll 1), pp.290, 303–313, 316–320, 366–371, 395 ("Minutes"); "Recognizance Book," ibid.; and in Maeva Marcus, ed., *Documentary History of the Supreme Court of the United States, 1789–1800* (New York: ColUP, 1985–2007), vol.3 ("*DHSC*"). For the Criminal Case Files and Minutes, stamped page numbers are used instead of handwritten ones, because handwritten numbers restart with each file or year; and for the Criminal Case Files, pp.948–1210 (Apr. and Oct.1799) are microfilm roll 1 and pp.19–378 are microfilm roll 2 (Apr.1800). Useful secondary sources include Newman, *Fries's Rebellion;* Whitman H. Ridgway, "Fries in the Federalist Imagination: A Crisis of Republican Society," *Pennsylvania History* 67 (2000): 141–160, at 144–153; Paul D. Newman, "Fries's Rebellion and American Political Culture, 1798–1800," *Pennsylvania Magazine of History and Biography* 119 (1995): 37–73, esp. 66–69; James Morton Smith, *Freedom's Fetters: The Alien and Sedition Laws* (Ithaca, NY: CorUP, 1956), 335. Unlike most other case reports in Wharton's State Trials, the two reports on the Fries trials were transcripts taken by an experienced transcriptionist (with some rearrangement of the appendices), in Thomas Carpenter, transcriptionist, *The Two Trials of John Fries* (Philadelphia: William W. Woodward, 1800). [First] Trial of the Northampton Insurgents, Wharton's State Trials 458 (C.C.D. Pa. 1799) ("Wharton"), which is reprinted in Case of Fries, 9 F.Cas. 826 (C.C.D. Pa. 1799) (No.5,126), modified, 3 U.S. (3 Dall.) 515 (C.C.D. Pa.1799); and Second Trial of John Fries, Wharton 610 (C.C.D. Pa.1800), reprinted in In re Fries, 9 F. Cas. 924 (C.C.D. Pa.1800) (No.5,127).
5. E.g., W. W. H. Davis, *The Fries Rebellion, 1798–99* (Doylestown, PA: Doylestown Publishing, 1899), 4, 14–114; Jane S. Elsmere, "The Trials of John Fries," *Pennsylvania Magazine of History and Biography* 103 (1979): 432–445, at 435–436.
6. Abigail Adams to John Quincy Adams (30 July 1799), L. H. Butterfield et al., eds., *Adams Family Correspondence* (Cambridge, MA: BPHUP, 1963–), 13:528, 529 ("*AFC*").
7. Timothy Pickering to John Adams (20 Nov. 1799), "Timothy Pickering Papers" (Massachusetts Historical Society, Boston, manuscripts and 69 reels), 12:359, 362 ("Pickering Papers"); Samuel Chase's Charge (C.C.D.Pa. 12 Apr.1800), *DHSC*, 3:408, 414. The rebellion was described in dire terms by the district judge, the marshal, the tax assessors, Adams's proclamation, and the secretary of war's instructions. *American State Papers: Miscellaneous* (Washington: Gales and Seaton, 1834), 1:185–189.
8. John Adams to Abigail Adams (11 Mar.1799), *AFC*, 13:435; John Adams to Thomas Jefferson (30 June 1813), Lester J. Cappon, ed., *The Adams-Jefferson Letters* (Chapel Hill: UNCP, 1959), 2:346.

9. Oliver Wolcott to Frederick Wolcott (2 Apr.1799), George Gibbs, ed., *Memoirs of the Administrations . . . Papers of Oliver Wolcott* (New York: Norden, 1846), 2:230; Alexander Hamilton to James McHenry (18 Mar.1799), Harold C. Syrett et al., eds., *Papers of Alexander Hamilton* (New York: ColUP, 1961–), 22:552–553 ("*PAH*"); James Iredell to Hannah Iredell (14 Mar.1799), *DHSC*, 3:324.
10. Kim T. Phillips, "William Duane: Revolutionary Editor" (Ph.D. diss., University of California-Berkeley, 1968), 71; e.g., "Philadelphia," *Aurora*, 15 Mar.1799, 3.
11. Newman, *Fries's Rebellion*, 42, 132; accord Stanley Elkins and Eric McKitrick, *The Age of Federalism* (New York: OUP, 1993), 697–698; Newman, *Fries's Rebellion*, 139–141, 140; accord Newman, "American Political Culture," 65.
12. Proclamation (12 Mar.1799), Charles Francis Adams, ed., *Works of John Adams* (Boston: LB, 1850–1856), 9:174 ("*WJA*"); Newman, *Fries's Rebellion*, 144, 145; [First] Trial, Wharton, 550. It was authorized five days before the rescue. An Act Giving Eventual Authority to the President of the United States To Augment the Army, 1 Stat.725 (2 Mar.1799). The secretary of war told the commanding general that he was appointed as head of the Eventual Army to quash the Fries Rebellion. James McHenry to Gen. William Macpherson (11 Mar.1799), *PAH*, 22:388.
13. Timothy Pickering to John Adams (4 Apr.1799), Pickering Papers, 10:565 (march commenced that morning); Newman, *Fries's Rebellion*, x, 57; Carpenter, *Two Trials*, 114. Newman also takes issue with the view that the Fries Rebellion was the result of "confused, illiterate, and ignorant Germans," as in Peter Levine, "The Fries Rebellion: Social Violence and the Politics of the New Nation," *Pennsylvania History* 40 (1973): 240–258; see Newman, "American Political Culture," 37–38.
14. Newman, *Fries's Rebellion*, xi; Terry Bouton, "'No Wonder the Times Were Troublesome': The Origins of Fries Rebellion, 1783–1799," *Pennsylvania History* 67 (2000): 21–42, at 22–24, 26; Newman, *Fries's Rebellion*, 70, 72, 101, 109, 131, 126, 153.
15. Robert Churchill, "Popular Nullification, Fries' Rebellion, and the Waning of Radical Republicanism, 1798–1801," *Pennsylvania History* 67 (2000): 105–140, at 127; Harry M. Tinkcom, *The Republicans and Federalists in Pennsylvania 1790–1801* (Harrisburg: PHMC, 1950), 218.
16. Davis, *Fries Rebellion*, 110, 109, 102, 139; "Extract of a Report from an Officer of the Northern Army," *Aurora*, 16 Apr.1799, 3 (last quotation).
17. Churchill, "Popular Nullification," 106–107.
18. Ibid., 130 (one sentence); Ridgway, "Fries in the Federalist Imagination," 145 (one sentence), 147 (quotation); Newman, *Fries's Rebellion*, 174–175; Dwight F. Henderson, "Treason, Sedition, and Fries' Rebellion," *American Journal of Legal History* 14 (1970): 308–318, at 312 (one sentence); see also Julius Goebel, Jr., *History of the Supreme Court of the United States* (New York: Macmillan, 1971), 638 n.107 (one sentence).
19. The only published biographical information about Greenawalt is cited in this paragraph. Morton L. Montgomery, *Historical and Biographical Annals of Berks County, Pennsylvania* (Chicago: J.H. Beers, 1909), 2:1588; Charles R. Roberts et al., *History of Lehigh County, Pennsylvania* (Allentown, PA: Lehigh

Valley Publishing, 1914), 2:774; John T. Humphrey, *Pennsylvania Births: Berks County 1710–1780* (Washington: Humphrey Publications, 1997). He was not the Jacob Greenawalt of Hummelstown, Dauphin County, who owned a public house.

20. Application of Jacob Greenewald (14 Jan.1833), in Mary Owen Steinnetz, transcriber, "Pension Applications of Revolutionary Soldiers Who Served from Berks County, Pennsylvania" (Salt Lake City: Genealogical Society of Utah, 1938), 41 (also available as "Revolutionary War Pension and Bounty-Land Warrant Applications" on www.ancestry.com).
21. Deposition of Jacob Bowen (14 Feb.1799), in "Rawle Family Papers, 1682–1921" (HSP, Collection 536, series 1, boxes 5–6, folders 8–13); Deposition of Philip Kreamer (13 Feb.1799), in ibid.
22. Timothy Pickering to Judge Richard Peters (4 Apr.1799), Pickering Papers, 37:404; James Iredell to Hannah Iredell (11 Apr.1799), *DHSC*, 3:330; Deposition of Michael Babst (10 Apr.1799), in "Rawle Family Papers, 1682–1921."
23. Original court records for *United States v. Jacob Greenawalt,* and microfilm copies, are in the same National Archives files as for Fries (Criminal Case Files and Minutes). In secondary sources, Greenawalt is mentioned in Newman, *Fries's Rebellion,* 108 (two sentences), and in Churchill, "Popular Nullification," 118 (one sentence, not connecting to Sedition Act).
24. Recognizance Book (entry on 11 Apr.1799), in Criminal Case Files, p.966. The Recognizance Book said he was "to answer" as a defendant rather than "to testify" as a witness. For bond, see Minutes, p.289 (22 Apr.1799).
25. The only published biographical information about Llewellyn is cited in this paragraph. The 1800 census showed him to be above age forty-five; his will was dated 28 Oct.1828. Ellwood Roberts, *Abstract of Wills and Administrations, Montgomery County, Pennsylvania* (Norristown, PA: n.p., 1911), 317.
26. Gloria O. Becker, "Mill Creek Valley: Architecture, Industry, and Social Change" (Ph.D. diss., University of Pennsylvania, 1984), 465; *Historical Sketches: A Collection of Papers Prepared for the Historical Society of Montgomery County Pennsylvania* (Norristown, PA: Herald Printing, 1905), 3:212.
27. Roberts, *Abstract of Wills,* 411; Charles R. Barker, "Glimpses of Lower Merion History," *Bulletin of the Historical Society of Merion County Pennsylvania* 11 (1957–1959): 232, 235; Judith Meier, "Lower Merion 'Window Pane Tax' Lists," *Bulletin of the Historical Society of Montgomery County* 24 (1983): 182–213, at 188, 206.
28. Deposition of James Jackson (23 Oct.1799), in "Rawle Family Papers, 1682–1921" (box 5, folder 13). Jackson used the spelling "Menzies," and also listed Isaac Young. See Shira Lurie, "Liberty Poles and the Fight for Popular Politics in the Early Republic," *Journal of the Early Republic* 38 (2018): 673–697, at 686–693. A liberty cap was like the tricolor hats worn by some Republicans. Newman, "American Political Culture," 49. For remaining liberty poles, see Newman, *Fries's Rebellion,* 13, 16, 39, 90, 104.
29. Original court records for *United States v. Morris Llewellyn et al.,* and microfilm copies, are in the same National Archives files as for Fries (Criminal Case Files and Minutes). In secondary sources, Llewellyn is mentioned in Newman, *Fries's Rebellion,* 1, 175 (calling him Schwelein, and not describing as a

Sedition Act prosecution); Henderson, "Treason," 315 (half-sentence); Becker, "Mill Creek," 465 ("could find no court records" except indictment); James K. Helms, "The Young Family and Merion Square," *Bulletin of the Historical Society of Montgomery County* 1 (1937): 136, 138 (inaccurate).

30. Indictment (24 Apr. 1799), in Criminal Case Files, pp.1015–1020; Minutes, p.293 (24 Apr.1799).

31. Minutes, pp.300 (29 Apr.1799), 326 (18 May 1799); Subpoena to George Savage et al. (14 Oct.1799), in Criminal Case Files, p.1207; Indictment (18 Oct.1799), in Criminal Case Files, pp.1201–1202; Minutes, p.342 (18 Oct.1799).

32. Bushrod Washington to James Iredell (20 Oct.1799), *DHSC,* 3:389, 390; Richard Peters to Timothy Pickering (23 Oct.1799), ibid., 3:391; Pickering Papers, 25:259.

33. Indictment (16 Apr.1800), in Criminal Case Files, pp.278–280; Minutes, p.351 (16 Apr.1800).

34. Subpoena (16 Apr.1800); Subpoena (24 Apr.1800), Criminal Case Files, pp.281–282 ("non est inventus"). The judges issued a capias to take them into custody. Minutes, p.353 (16 Apr.1800). For the next session, see Minutes, pp.401–416; Criminal Case Files, pp.379, 382.

35. The only published biographical information about Herring is cited in this paragraph. He was 16–21 years old in the 1787 Virginia census, and so was born 1766–1771. Netti Schreiner-Yantis and Florene Speakman Love, *The 1787 Census of Virginia* (Springfield: Genealogical Books in Print, 1987), listing for Lunenburg County. He died in August 1859. "Died," *Public Ledger* (Philadelphia), 15 Aug.1859, 2.

36. Lela C. Adams and Virginia Bassett, *Abstracts of Pittsylvania County, Virginia Wills, 1767–1820* (Easley, SC: Southern Historical Press, 1986), 95 (father William Herring's will 1798); Thomas L. Montgomery, ed., *Pennsylvania Archives* (6th Series) (Harrisburg, PA: Harrisburg Publishing, 1907), 5:507.

37. "Tuesday, December 11, 1798," *Aurora* (Philadelphia), 11 Dec.1798, 3; Respublica v. Ross, 1 Yeates 1 (Pa.S.Ct. 1795).

38. "Langford Herring who stands charged with forgery in this State may be delivered up to take his trial." Governor of Pennsylvania to Governor of Maryland (12 Oct.1795), Gertrude MacKinney, ed., *Pennsylvania Archives* (9th Series) (Philadelphia: Department of Property and Supplies, 1931), 2:1026, 1171; *Report of the Register-General of the State of the Finances of Pennsylvania For the Year 1796* (Philadelphia: Zachariah Poulson, 1797), 10.

39. E.g., "Philadelphia, Dec. 31," *Commercial Advertiser* (New York), 2 Jan.1799, 3; [No Caption], *Gazette of the United States* (Philadelphia), 8 Mar.1800, 3; "Mr. Fenno," *Gazette of the United States,* 11 Mar.1800, 2.

40. Public Archives Commission, *Delaware Archives* (Wilmington: Star Publishing, 1916), 5:826, 906.

41. "Tuesday, December 11, 1798," *Aurora* (Philadelphia), 11 Dec.1798, 3.

42. Original court records for *United States v. Langford Herring,* and microfilm copies, are in the same National Archives files as for Fries (Criminal Case Files and Minutes). In secondary sources, Herring is mentioned in two sentences in Henderson, "Treason," 315 (not connecting to Sedition Act).

43. Indictment (27 Apr.1799), in Criminal Case Files, p.1099; Minutes, p.299 (27 Apr.1799); Indictment, pp.1100, 1098.
44. Minutes, p.322 (17 May 1799); Nolle Prosequi (7 Oct.1799), in Criminal Case Files, p.1096.
45. The only published biographical information about Rev. Eyerman is cited in this paragraph. Newman, *Fries's Rebellion,* 16, 24.
46. Newman, *Fries's Rebellion,* 2, 24, 18, 28; Churchill, "Popular Nullification," 117–118; "Jacob Eyerman Being Examined" (14 June 1799), in "Rawle Family Papers, 1682–1921" (series 1, box 5, folder 13). This is consistent with Carpenter, *Two Trials,* 220.
47. Steven M. Nolt, *Foreigners in Their Own Land: Pennsylvania Germans in the Early Republic* (University Park: PSUP, 2002), 37, 160; Kenneth W. Keller, "Rural Politics and the Collapse of Pennsylvania Federalism," *Transactions of the American Philosophical Society* 72 (1982): 1–73, at 26–27; Kenneth W. Keller, "Diversity and Democracy: Ethnic Politics in Southeastern Pennsylvania, 1788–1799" (Ph.D. diss., Yale University, 1971), 238; John B. Frantz, "Revivalism in the German Reformed Church in America to 1850" (Ph.D. diss., University of Pennsylvania, 1961), 28.
48. The warrant required the marshal to bring Eyerman to court to provide an appearance bond, to ensure his appearance for trial on 11 April. Indictment (15 Oct.1799), in Criminal Case Files, p.1179.
49. "Something Respecting the Parson Eyermann," translated from *Neuer Unpartheyische Eastoner Bothe* (Easton), 2 Oct.1799, in "Rawle Family Papers, 1682–1921" (series 1, box 5, folder 13). The German original was reprinted in "Psarer Eyerman," *Unpartheyische Harrisburg Morgenröthe Zeitung,* 15 Oct.1799, 2; e.g., "Monday, 8th April, 1799," *Philadelphia Gazette,* 8 Apr.1799, 3.
50. Timothy Pickering to John Jay (21 May 1799), Pickering Papers, 37:421; Timothy Pickering to John Sloss Hobart (21 May 1799), ibid., 37:422.
51. Timothy Pickering to John Sloss Hobart ([day illegible] June 1799), ibid., 11:242; Order from Judge Hobart (11 June 1799), in "Rawle Family Papers, 1682–1921" (series 1, box 6, folder 3); Postscript by Pickering (7 Sept.1799), *WJA,* 9:23, enclosed in Timothy Pickering to John Adams (9 Sept.1799), ibid., 9:21.
52. Original court records for *United States v. Jacob Eyerman,* and microfilm copies, are in the same National Archives files as for Fries (Criminal Case Files and Minutes); and in Carpenter, *Two Trials,* 220–226. In secondary sources, Eyerman is mentioned in Newman, *Fries's Rebellion,* 41, 175–176, etc.; and in several articles without connection to the Sedition Act: Bouton, "'No Wonder,'" 21–22; Churchill, "Popular Nullification," 121–122; Henderson, "Treason," 315, 316.
53. Indictment (12 Oct.1799), in Criminal Case Files, pp.1141–1143; Indictment (15 Oct.1799), in ibid., pp.1177–1183, esp. 1177; Minutes, p.334 (12 Oct.1799), p.335 (15 Oct.1799); Abstract of the Trial of Jacob Eyerman (C.C.D.Pa. 16 Oct.1799), in Carpenter, *Two Trials,* 224.
54. Carpenter, *Two Trials,* 220–226, 222, 223.

55. Ibid., 225; Minutes, p.339 (16 Oct.1799); e.g., "Philadelphia," *Gazette of the United States,* 19 Oct.1799, 3.
56. Indictment (16 Apr.1800), Criminal Case Files, pp.158–162; Minutes, p.351 (16 Apr.1800); Indictment, pp.159–161.
57. Indictment (15 Oct.1799) (note on jacket, dated 1800), in Criminal Case Files, p.1177; Minutes, p.380 (1 May 1800). His plea of not guilty is at Minutes, pp.336 (15 Oct.1799), 353 (16 Apr.1800). For the sentence, see Minutes, p.386 (1 May 1800); Sentence, in Criminal Case Files, p.164; Carpenter, *Two Trials,* 226 (1 May 1800).
58. Oliver Wolcott to John Adams (c. 15 Nov.1799), Gibbs, *Memoirs of Wolcott,* 2:299, 305.
59. The only published biographical information about Mayer and Fahnstock is cited in this paragraph. "Starb," *Reading Adler* (Reading), 1 June 1824, 2 (died 18 May 1824 "in 64th year"); Kristen Hocker, *Marriage and Death Notices from The Harrisburg Chronicle, 1820–1834* (n.p., 2011), 99 ("in the 62nd year"). "Mayer" is the correct spelling (in the newspaper and his will), though other spellings abounded (in the censuses he was Meyer in 1800, Mayer in 1810, and Moyer in 1820).
60. H. Minot Pitman, *The Fahnestock Genealogy* (Concord, NH: Rumford Press, 1945), 36.
61. John Kean, *Autobiography of Captain John Kean* (Harrisburg, PA: Harrisburg Publishing, 1888), 12; William H. Engle et al., *Commemorative Biographical Encyclopedia of Dauphin County* (Chambersburg, PA: J.M. Runk, 1896), 99–100; Montgomery, *Pennsylvania Archives,* 3:554; Pitman, *Fahnestock Genealogy,* 36.
62. Clarence S. Brigham, ed., *History and Bibliography of American Newspapers, 1690–1820* (Worcester, MA: AAS, 1947), 2:859; Luther R. Kelker, *History of Dauphin County Pennsylvania* (New York: Lewis Publishing, 1907), 1:331. The original name was much longer; the shortened name was adopted on 11 Aug.1800. For new newspapers, see Jeffrey L. Pasley, *The Tyranny of Printers* (Charlottesville: UPV, 2001), 408–409.
63. E.g., "Harrisburg, August 28," *Gazette of the United States,* 6 Sept.1799, 2; "Harrisburg, August 28," *Springer's Weekly Oracle* (New London, CT), 16 Sept.1799, 3.
64. Original court records for *United States v. Benjamin Mayer and Conrad Fahnestock,* and microfilm copies, are in the same National Archives files as for Fries (Criminal Case Files and Minutes). Case reports are United States v. Meyer, 26 F.Cas.1242 (C.C.D. Pa. 1799) (No. 15,761), and Francis Wharton, *Precedents of Indictments and Pleas* (Philadelphia: James Kay, 1849), 562. In secondary sources, Mayer and Fahnstock are mentioned in two half-sentences in Newman, *Fries's Rebellion,* 174, 175; and a half-sentence in Henderson, "Treason," 315.
65. Kelker, *History of Dauphin County,* 1:87; "Harrisburgh, August 28," *Oracle of Dauphin* (Harrisburg, PA), 28 Aug.1799, 3; *Gazette of the United States,* 6 Sept.1799, 2; Brigham, *American Newspapers,* 2:859.
66. Minutes, p.342 (18 Oct.1799); Indictment (18 Oct.1799), in Criminal Case Files, 1187–1199. In the microfilm of the indictment, the pages are out of order;

from the original file, the correct order is 1187–1191, 1197, 1196, 1195, 1194, 1192, 1193, 1199 (1198 being a duplicate).

67. "Capt. John Fries," *Harrisburg Morgenröthe,* 21 May 1799, 2 (in German); Indictment, p.1188; U.S. Constitution, art.3, sec.3; Indictment, p.1189.
68. Indictment, pp.1190–1191, 1197, 1194. The latter page cites An Act for the Punishment of Certain Crimes §23, 1 Stat. 112, 117 (30 Apr.1790); Sir William Blackstone, *Commentaries on the Laws of England* (Oxford: CP, 1765–1769), 4:131.
69. Indictment, pp.1192–1193.
70. Ibid., p.1188.
71. Minutes, p.342 (18 Oct.1799); Indictment, p.1187. It meant waiving a jury trial and submitting to what the judges ordered—a bench trial or immediate sentencing. E.g., "Communication," *Centinel of Liberty* (Georgetown, D.C.), 31 Oct.1799, 3; "Philadelphia, October 23," *Albany Gazette,* 31 Oct.1799, 3. "Submitting to the court" was typically followed by sentencing, often the same day, as in the Klein, Eberhardt, Yeisley, Stahler, and Marks cases in Chapter 9. For no trial, see Smith, *Freedom's Fetters,* 185 n.84.
72. Henderson recounts that they were not "apprehended for trial" (retrial). Henderson, "Treason," 175.
73. John Adams to Heads of Department (20 May 1800), *WJA,* 9:57; Proclamation Granting Pardon (21 May 1800), ibid., 9:178.
74. The only published biographical information about Schneider is cited in this paragraph. "Died," *Berks and Schuylkill Journal* (Reading, PA), 24 Apr.1830, 3; Patricia E. Suter et al., *The Hanging of Susanna Cox* (Mechanicsburg, PA: Stackpole Books, 2010), 126.
75. John W. Jordan, *Colonial Families of Philadelphia* (New York: Lewis Publishing, 1911), 2:1645; James O. Knauss, "Social Conditions Among the Pennsylvania Germans in the Eighteenth Century," in *The Pennsylvania-German Society* 29 (1918): 30, 27–28; Jordan, *Colonial Families,* 2:1645; Jacob Fry, *History of Trinity Lutheran Church, Reading* (Reading, PA: The Congregation, 1894), 287.
76. Friederike Baer-Wallis, "Joining the Nation: Germans in the Early American Republic" (Ph.D. diss., Brown University, 2002), 68; Newman, *Fries's Rebellion,* 80, 28. The newspaper was originally named the *Reading Adler,* and changed that to the *Readinger Adler.*
77. Brigham, *American Newspapers,* 2:970, 969; Knauss, "Social Conditions," 30. It was only a sample issue of the paper that was published in November 1796.
78. Newman, *Fries's Rebellion,* 28; Keller, "Diversity and Democracy," 225; Newman, *Fries's Rebellion,* 104.
79. Keller, "Diversity and Democracy," 227; Newman, *Fries's Rebellion,* 80–81. On mistreatment, see Keller, "Diversity and Democracy," 241; Keller, "Rural Politics," 20.
80. "A Nearly Literal Translation of an 'Address to the Germans of Cumberland County,'" *Porcupine's Gazette* (Philadelphia), 22 July 1799, 2, 3; Donald H. Stewart, *The Opposition Press of the Federalist Period* (Albany: SUNYP, 1969), 476, quoting translation in *Aurora,* 30 July 1799. The address had been written on 30 May 1799.
81. "Nearly Literal Translation," pp. 2, 3.

82. Timothy Pickering to William Rawle (5 July 1799), Pickering Papers, 11:390; "Nearly Literal Translation," 2.
83. Keller, "Diversity and Democracy," 241.
84. Churchill, "Popular Nullification," 127; Newman, *Fries's Rebellion,* 162, citing *Readinger Adler,* 9 Apr.1799; Lurie, "Liberty Poles," 688–693.
85. "Federal Light Horse," *Centinel of Freedom* (Newark), 30 Apr.1799, 3, translating Jacob Schneider, "Reading, den 22ten April, 1799," *Readinger Adler,* 23 Apr.1799, 2. Schneider later gave more detail in a sworn statement. "Reading, May 17th, 1799," *Aurora,* 24 May 1790, 2.
86. "Order and Good Government," *Aurora,* 24 Apr.1799, 3; e.g., "Translated from 'The Reading Adler'," *Maryland Herald and Elizabeth-Town Advertiser,* 9 May 1799, 3; "Order and Good Government," *Herald of Liberty* (Washington, PA), 13 May 1799, 2.
87. "General MacPherson," *Aurora,* 6 May 1799, 3; "Richmond, May 7," *Aurora,* 15 May 1799, 3. See also Pasley, *Tyranny of Printers,* 152; Stewart, *Opposition Press,* 93–94.
88. Jonathan Williams and Robert G. Harper, "To the Editor of the Aurora," *Aurora,* 13 May 1799, 2; Baer-Wallis, "Joining the Nation," 248.

9. The Army and the Sedition Act

1. Except for four historians of the Fries Rebellion, scholars have overlooked this. Dwight F. Henderson, "Treason, Sedition, and Fries' Rebellion," *American Journal of Legal History* 14 (1970): 308–318, at 312; Whitman H. Ridgway, "Fries in the Federalist Imagination: A Crisis of Republican Society," *Pennsylvania History* 67 (2000): 141–160, at 145, 147; Robert Churchill, "Popular Nullification, Fries' Rebellion, and the Waning of Radical Republicanism, 1798–1801," *Pennsylvania History* 67 (2000): 105–140, at 127; Paul Douglas Newman, *Fries's Rebellion: The Enduring Struggle for the American Revolution* (Philadelphia: UPP, 2004), 174–175. The first three scholars devoted a single sentence to the point. The point was also recently made by Terri Diane Halperin, *The Alien and Sedition Acts of 1798* (Baltimore: JHUP, 2016), 113.
2. An Act in Addition to the Act, Entitled "An Act for the Punishment of Certain Crimes against the United States" [Sedition Act] §1, 1 Stat. 596 (1798).
3. Original court records for the Fries Rebellion prosecutions, and microfilm copies, are in National Archives at Philadelphia, in the place described in Chapter 8: "Criminal Case Files," pp.948–1210, 019–378, "Minutes," pp.290–398, and "Recognizance Book." Useful secondary sources include Newman, *Fries's Rebellion;* Ridgway, "Fries in the Federalist Imagination," 144–153; Paul D. Newman, "Fries's Rebellion and American Political Culture, 1798–1800," *Pennsylvania Magazine of History and Biography* 119 (1995): 37–73. Unlike most other case reports in Wharton's State Trials, the two reports on the Fries trials were transcripts taken by an experienced transcriptionist (with some rearrangement of the appendices), in Thomas Carpenter, transcriptionist, *The Two Trials of John Fries* (Philadelphia: William W. Woodward, 1800). [First] Trial of the Northampton Insurgents, Wharton's State Trials 458 (C.C.D.

Pa. 1799) ("Wharton"), which is reprinted in Case of Fries, 9 F.Cas. 826 (C.C.D. Pa. 1799) (No.5,126), modified, 3 U.S. (3 Dall.) 515 (C.C.D. Pa.1799); and Second Trial of John Fries, Wharton 610 (C.C.D. Pa.1800), reprinted in In re Fries, 9 F.Cas. 924 (C.C.D. Pa.1800) (No.5,127).

4. These cases are discussed at more length in Wendell Bird, "New Light on the Sedition Act of 1798: The Missing Half of the Prosecutions," *Law and History Review* 34 (2016): 541–614, at 571–584. For the judge's charge and description, see James Iredell's Charge (C.C.D.Pa. 11 Apr. 1799), Maeva Marcus, ed., *Documentary History of the Supreme Court of the United States, 1789–1800* (New York: ColUP, 1985–2007), 3:332, 350 ("*DHSC*"); Second Trial, Wharton, 624n., 623n.
5. Trial of Jacob Eyerman (C.C.D.Pa. 16 Oct.1799), Carpenter, *Two Trials,* 220, 224.
6. Names are spelled as in the indictments; spelling sometimes differs in affidavits and tax lists. Descriptions in this list come from the first indictment of each group. *CRO* means conspiracy, rescue, and obstruction.
7. Indictment (26 Apr.1799), Criminal Case Files, pp.1032–1037; Minutes, p.294. Most of the eleven cases also had subsequent indictments.
8. Indictment (26 Apr.1799), ibid., pp.1044–1049; Minutes, p.294.
9. Indictment (27 Apr.1799), ibid., pp.1054–1061; Minutes, p.298.
10. Indictment (27 Apr.1799), ibid., pp.1063–1070; Minutes, p.298.
11. Indictment (27 Apr.1799), ibid., pp.1072–1077; Minutes, p.298.
12. Indictment (27 Apr.1799), ibid., pp.1079–1082; Minutes, p.298.
13. Indictment (27 Apr.1799), ibid., pp.1084–1089; Minutes, p.299.
14. Indictment (30 Apr.1799), ibid., pp.1104–1111; Minutes, p.301.
15. Indictment (30 Apr.1799), ibid., pp.1114–1126; Minutes, p.301.
16. Indictment (2 May 1800), ibid., pp.56–63; Minutes, p.390.
17. Indictment (29 Apr.1800), ibid., pp.347–350; Minutes, p.376.
18. Terry Bouton, "'No Wonder the Times Were Troublesome': The Origins of Fries Rebellion, 1783–1799," *Pennsylvania History* 67 (2000): 21–42, at 22; Jeffrey S. Dimmig, "Palatine Liberty: Pennsylvania German Opposition to the Direct Tax of 1798," *American Journal of Legal History* 45 (2001): 371–390, at 384–388; Newman, "American Political Culture," 45.
19. Stanley Elkins and Eric McKitrick, *The Age of Federalism* (New York: OUP, 1993), 697.
20. The leading biography of Iredell is Willis P. Whichard, *Justice James Iredell* (Durham, NC: CAP, 2000). His First Amendment thought and Sedition Act cases are described in Wendell Bird, *Press and Speech under Assault* (New York: OUP, 2016), 191–200, 311–317.
21. Timothy Pickering to Richard Peters (4 Apr.1799), "Timothy Pickering Papers" (Massachusetts Historical Society, Boston, manuscripts and 69 reels), 37:404 ("Pickering Papers"); Recognizance List (Apr.1799), in Criminal Case Files, pp.981–994 (half potential defendants and half witnesses); Affidavit of David Caldwell, in Criminal Case Files, pp.21–22 (118 warrants).
22. James Iredell's Charge (C.C.D.Pa. 11 Apr.1799), *DHSC,* 3:332, 334–341, 341–348; [First] Trial, Wharton, 458. Iredell's arguments about freedoms of press and speech are analyzed in Bird, *Press and Speech under Assault,* 311–314.

23. Ibid., 3;348, 349, 350; Reply of the Grand Jury (15 May 1799), *DHSC,* 3:363; [First] Trial, Wharton, 481.
24. Minutes, pp.290–298. Fries was indicted on April 22.
25. For example, of Frederick Heany, Anthony Stahler, Conrad Marks, Valentine Kuder, Henry Huber, and Henry Stahler. Criminal Case Files, pp.955–956, 970, 974, 979, 1003, 1007, 1023, 1041. For the caption, see ibid., p.1000 (Apr.1799).
26. Ibid., pp.1054–1061, 1063–1070, 1072–1077, 1079–1082, 1084–1089, 1104–1111, 1114–1122.
27. Indictment of Henry Ohl et al. (26 Apr.1799), in Criminal Case Files, pp.1032–1037; see Minutes, p.294.
28. Newman, *Fries's Rebellion,* 99.
29. Robert H. Churchill, "'The Highest and Holiest Duty of Freemen': Revolutionary Libertarianism in American History" (Ph.D. diss., Rutgers University, 2001), 77–142; Newman, "American Political Culture," 54–55.
30. [First] Trial of the Northampton Insurgents, Wharton's State Trials 458 (C.C.D. Pa. 1799). The indictment is at ibid., 489, and at Criminal Case Files, pp.954–956; Minutes, p.290, and the trial is summarized in Minutes, pp. 303–313. Useful secondary sources on the trial include Newman, *Fries's Rebellion,* 166–173; Jane S. Elsmere, "The Trials of John Fries," *Pennsylvania Magazine of History and Biography* 103 (1979): 432–445, at 437–443.
31. Timothy Pickering to John Adams (10 May 1799), Charles Francis Adams, ed., *Works of John Adams* (Boston: LB, 1850–1856), 8:643 ("*WJA*"); Pickering Papers, 37:417; [First] Trial, Wharton, 482, 488–489; Judiciary Act of 1789 §29, 1 Stat. 73, 88.
32. [First] Trial, Wharton, 532–535, 584, 587.
33. Ibid., 587–598, esp. 592, 590; accord ibid., 584; James Iredell's Charge, *DHSC,* 3:349; Newman, "American Political Culture," 55–56.
34. Minutes, pp.313 (9 May 1799); Criminal Case Files, p.954; [First] Trial, Wharton, 598. Ordering a new trial, see Minutes, pp.316–317 (15–16 May 1799), 320 (17 May 1799); Criminal Case Files, pp.957–965, esp. 960, 967; [First] Trial, Wharton, 598–609, 608; James Iredell to Hannah Iredell (11 May 1799), *DHSC,* 3:361; James Iredell to Hannah Iredell (19 May 1799), ibid., 3:366.
35. Timothy Pickering to Rufus King (22 May 1799), Charles R. King., ed., *Life and Correspondence of Rufus King* (New York: Putnam's Sons, 1894–1900), 3:17, 18; Pickering Papers, 11:138; Timothy Pickering to John Adams (10 May 1799), *WJA,* 8:643, 644.
36. The leading biography of Washington is David L. Annis, "Mr. Bushrod Washington, Supreme Court Justice on the Marshall Court" (Ph.D. diss., University of Notre Dame, 1974); an excellent article is Herbert A. Johnson, "Bushrod Washington," *Vanderbilt Law Review* 62 (2009): 447–490. His First Amendment thought and Sedition Act cases are described in Wendell Bird, *Press and Speech under Assault,* 240–245, 302–309.
37. That defect was discussed in Chapter 8.
38. Samuel Chase to James Iredell (17 Mar.1799), Griffith J. McRee, ed., *Life and Correspondence of James Iredell* (New York: Appleton, 1857–1858), 2:548, 549.

39. Samuel Chase's Charge (C.C.D.Pa. 12 Apr.1800), *DHSC,* 3:408, 410–413.
40. Ibid., 3:413–414, 416.
41. Criminal Case Files, pp.50 (5 May 1800), 342 (26–28 Apr.1800); Minutes, p.372.
42. Affidavit of David Caldwell, in Criminal Case Files, pp.21–22; Criminal Case Files, pp.1025–1031, 056–063.
43. Second Trial of John Fries, Wharton 610 (C.C.D. Pa. 1800). The indictment is at ibid., 610, and at Criminal Case Files, pp.25–27, on April 16, Minutes, p.350; and the trial is summarized in Minutes, pp.366–371. Useful secondary sources include Stephen B. Presser, *The Original Misunderstanding* (Durham, NC: CAP, 1991), 108–118, 124–125; Stephen B. Presser, "A Tale of Two Judges: Richard Peters, Samuel Chase, and the Broken Promise of Federal Jurisprudence," *Northwestern University Law Review* 73 (1978): 26–111, at 88–93.
44. Second Trial, Wharton, 615–617n., 622n., 626n., 646 (C.C.D. Pa. 1800); ibid., 647, 634.
45. Charles Evans, transcriptionist, *Report of the Trial of the Hon. Samuel Chase* (Baltimore: Butler and Keatings, 1805), Appendix 3–4.
46. Second Trial, Wharton, 612, 620n., 624n.; Richard Peters to Timothy Pickering (25 Jan.1804), Pickering Papers, 27:44. The judges advised Fries that "whatever you say to your own crimination, is evidence . . . ; but if you say anything to your justification, it is not evidence" and severely discouraged Fries from testifying or speaking. Ibid., 629.
47. Ibid., 635, 636.
48. Ibid., 633, 634; Criminal Case Files, pp.25, 34; Minutes, pp.371, 395; Second Trial, Wharton, 636, 641.
49. Minutes, pp.380–392 (1–2 May 1799). The "submission to the court" is evident in Table A.2, at the end of this book, and in a helpful chart of many sentences in Henderson, "Treason, Sedition," 318.
50. John Adams to the Heads of Department (20 May 1800), *WJA,* 9:57, 58; Harold C. Syrett et al., eds., *Papers of Alexander Hamilton* (New York: ColUP 1961–), 25:226 n.165 ("*PAH*"); Heads of Department to John Adams (20 May 1800), *WJA,* 9:59; John Adams to Charles Lee (17 May 1799), ibid., 8:648; Paul D. Newman, "The Federalists' Cold War: The Fries Rebellion, National Security, and the State, 1787–1800," *Pennsylvania History* 67 (2000): 63–104, at 94. A year earlier, Pickering had given instructions that "to the manifestly penitent, the President will assuredly be inclined to extend his mercy." Timothy Pickering to Samuel Sitgreaves (1 Apr.1799), Pickering Papers, 10:544, 545A. For the pardons, see John Adams to Charles Lee (21 May 1800), ibid., 9:60; *DHSC,* 3:435 n.3. Adams also pardoned the other convicted rebels. Proclamation Granting Pardon to the Pennsylvania Insurgents (21 May 1800), ibid., 9:178.
51. Alexander Hamilton to Timothy Pickering (14 May 1800), *PAH,* 24:487; Alexander Hamilton, "Letter from Alexander Hamilton, Concerning the Public Conduct and Character of John Adams, Esq.," *PAH,* 25:169, 225–227.
52. Treason is defined in U.S. Constitution, art.3, §3, and in Crimes Act of 1790 §1, 1 Stat.112.

53. Newman, *Fries's Rebellion,* 163.
54. Second Trial, Wharton, 626–627 n.; accord [First] Trial, Wharton, 591; *DHSC,* 3:349. For common law and recent decisions, see Sir William Blackstone, *Commentaries on the Laws of England* (Oxford: CP, 1765–1769), 4:79–80; United States v. Vigol, 2 U.S. (2 Dall.) 346 (C.C.D.Pa. 1795); United States v. Mitchell, 2 U.S. (2 Dall.) 348 (C.C.D.Pa. 1795).
55. Second Trial, Wharton, 647; see [First] Trial, Wharton, 567–571.
56. Ridgway, "Fries," 146; Bird, *Press and Speech under Assault,* 109, 145–146; see discussion of common law in Chapter 7. For constructive treason, see Blackstone, *Commentaries,* 4:79–80, 87–92; accord John Barrell, *Imagining the King's Death: Figurative Treason, Fantasies of Regicide 1793–1796* (Oxford: OUP, 2000); D. Alan Orr, *Treason and the State* (Cambridge: CUP, 2002), 11–13.
57. Crimes Act of 1790 §§23, 22, 1 Stat.112, 117.
58. Alexander Hamilton to George Washington (3 Apr.1799), *PAH,* 23:7.
59. Richard H. Kohn, *Eagle and Sword: The Federalists and the Creation of the Military Establishment in America, 1783–1802* (New York: Free Press, 1975), 226; accord John C. Miller, *The Federalist Era* (New York: Harper, 1960), 228–229, 242.
60. Alexander Hamilton to Theodore Sedgwick (2 Feb.1799), *PAH,* 22:452; Alexander Hamilton to Edward Carrington (26 May 1792), ibid., 11:426, 429; Alexander Hamilton to George Washington (19 May 1798), ibid., 21:466, 467.
61. Theodore Sedgwick to Rufus King (20 Jan.1799), Charles R. King., ed., *Life and Correspondence of Rufus King* (New York: Putnam's Sons, 1894–1900), 2:514, 518 ("*LRK*").
62. Alexander Hamilton to Theodore Sedgwick (2 Feb.1799), *PAH,* 22:452–453.
63. Ibid., 22:453, 454 n.4; An Act Giving Eventual Authority to the President of the United States To Augment the Army (2 Mar.1799), 1 Stat.725, 726.
64. E.g., Alexander Hamilton to Harrison Gray Otis (27 Dec.1798), *PAH,* 22:303, 304; Alexander Hamilton to Rufus King (6 Feb.1799), ibid., 22:465.
65. Alexander Hamilton to Jonathan Dayton (Oct.–Nov.1799), *PAH,* 23:599, 600.
66. Ibid., 23:603–604.
67. E.g., James R. Sharp, *American Politics in the Early Republic* (New Haven: YUP, 1993), 188; accord Jeffrey S. Selinger, *Embracing Dissent* (Philadelphia: UPP, 2016), 65; Jeff Broadwater, *James Madison* (Chapel Hill: UNCP, 2012), 90; James R. Sharp, *The Deadlocked Election of 1800* (Lawrence: UPKan, 2010), 62–65; John Ferling, *Adams vs. Jefferson* (New York: OUP, 2004), 119; Ron Chernow, *Alexander Hamilton* (New York: Penguin, 2004), 577–578; Ralph A. Brown, *The Presidency of John Adams* (Lawrence: UPKan, 1975), 117–119; Stephen G. Kurtz, *The Presidency of John Adams* (Philadelphia: UPP, 1957), 356; Manning J. Dauer, *The Adams Federalists* (Baltimore: JHUP, 1953), 202–204; Adrienne Koch and Harry Ammon, "The Virginia and Kentucky Resolutions," *William and Mary Quarterly* (3rd series) 5 (1948): 145–176, at 147 n.1.
68. E.g., John L. Harper, *American Machiavelli: Alexander Hamilton and the Origins of U.S. Foreign Policy* (New York: CUP, 2004), 233; Kohn, *Eagle and Sword,* 249–252; Alexander Hamilton to John Jay (7 May 1800), *PAH,* 24:464, 465.

69. Timothy Pickering to Rufus King (6 Feb.1799), *LRK,* 2:537; Timothy Pickering to Rufus King (4 May 1799), ibid., 3:12, 13; Oliver Wolcott to Fisher Ames (23 Dec.1799), George Gibbs, *Memoirs of the Administrations of Washington and John Adams, Edited from the Papers of Oliver Wolcott* (New York: Van Norden, 1846), 2:313, 317, 318 ("*POW*").
70. Those plans are discussed in Lawrence S. Kaplan, *Alexander Hamilton: Ambivalent Anglophile* (Wilmington, DE: SR Books, 2002), 151–155; Sharp, *American Politics,* 214–215; Brown, *Presidency,* 140–148.
71. Alexander Hamilton to Harrison Gray Otis (26 Jan.1799), *PAH,* 22:440, 441. Five days earlier, Rufus King sent confirmation that Britain "will cooperate in the accomplishment in So. Amer." of revolution against Spain. Rufus King to Alexander Hamilton (21 Jan.1799), ibid., 22:425, 426.
72. Hamilton wrote in February 1798 that he had "had frequent conversations" with Miranda and "expressed ideas favourable to the object," which was "liberating S Amer from the Spanish Domination." Francisco de Miranda to Alexander Hamilton (7 Feb.1798), *PAH,* 21:350 n.9 (Hamilton note); see Aaron N. Coleman, "'A Second Bounaparty?' A Reexamination of Alexander Hamilton During the Franco-American Crisis, 1796–1801," *Journal of the Early Republic* 28 (2008): 183–214, at 205–209; Miller, *Federalist Era,* 220.
73. *PAH,* 21:400 n.3. In October 1798, Adams asked Pickering his analysis of another Miranda letter. John Adams to Timothy Pickering (3 Oct.1798), *WJA,* 8:600.
74. Rufus King to Timothy Pickering (7 Feb.1798), *LRK,* 2:278, 281; Rufus King to Timothy Pickering (26 Feb.1798), ibid., 2:283, 284; Rufus King to Timothy Pickering (6 Apr.1798), ibid., 2:304, 306; Timothy Pickering to Alexander Hamilton (25 Mar.1798), *PAH,* 21:370, 374.
75. Francisco de Miranda to Alexander Hamilton (6 Apr.–7 June 1798), *PAH,* 21:399; Alexander Hamilton to Francisco de Miranda (22 Aug.1798), *PAH,* 22:155, 155–156; Alexander Hamilton to Rufus King (22 Aug.1798), *PAH,* 22:154, 154–155.
76. Rufus King to Timothy Pickering (20 Oct.1798), *LRK,* 2:453, 453–454; Alexander Hamilton to James McHenry (27 June 1799), *PAH,* 23:227. He may have first required a rupture with Spain before "attacking the two *floridas.*" See Alexander Hamilton to James Wilkinson (3 Aug.1799), ibid., 23:303.
77. E.g., Sharp, *American Politics,* 214–215; Aaron N. Coleman, "'A Second Bounaparty?' A Reexamination of Alexander Hamilton During the Franco-American Crisis, 1796–1801," *Journal of the Early Republic* 28 (2008): 183–214, at 205–208.
78. Thomas Jefferson to Edmund Pendleton (14 Feb.1799), Julian P. Boyd et al., eds., *Papers of Thomas Jefferson* (Princeton: Princeton University Press, 1950–), 31:36, 36–37 ("*PTJ*"); Thomas Jefferson to James Madison (26 Nov.1799), William T. Hutchinson et al., eds., *Papers of James Madison* (Chicago: UChiP, 1962–1991) ("*PJM*"); accord Thomas Jefferson to John Taylor (4 June 1798), *PTJ,* 30:387.
79. James Monroe to Thomas Jefferson (4 Jan.1800), *PTJ,* 31:289, 290; James Monroe to James Madison (4 June 1800), *PJM,* 17:391; James Madison to James Monroe (23 May 1800), *PJM,* 17:389, 390.

80. E.g., Churchill, "Highest and Holiest Duty," 79 n.3; Chapter 7.
81. Koch and Ammon, "Virginia and Kentucky Resolutions," 163 and n.55; Lisle A. Rose, *Prelude to Democracy: The Federalists in the South, 1789–1800* (Lexington, KY: UKP, 1968), 221.
82. Theodore Sedgwick to Rufus King (15 Nov.1799), *LRK*, 3:145, 148; Alexander Hamilton to Jonathan Dayton (Oct.–Nov.1799), *PAH*, 23:599, 600; accord Alexander Hamilton to Rufus King (5 Jan.1800), ibid., 24:167, 168. For other Federalists, e.g., William R. Davie to James Iredell (17 June 1799), McRee, *James Iredell*, 2:577; *DHSC*, 3:318, 320.
83. *Journal of the Virginia House of Delegates* [3 Dec.1798–26 Jan.1799] (Richmond: Jones and Dixon, 1798), 76; Timothy Pickering to Gov. Thomas Mifflin (17 May 1798), Pickering Papers, 8:457; Thomas Mifflin to John Adams (12 May 1797), *WJA*, 8:542; Charles J. Hoadly et al., eds., *Public Records of the State of Connecticut* (Hartford: Case Lockwood, 1894–), 9:460 (May 1798).
84. L. H. Butterfield et al., eds., *Adams Family Correspondence* (Cambridge, MA: BPHUP, 1963–), 172 n.3; Rufus King to Lord Grenville (26 Aug.1798), *LRK*, 2:401; Gov. John Jay to Rufus King (30 Sept.1798), *LRK*, 2:475.
85. Philip G. Davidson, "Virginia and the Alien and Sedition Laws," *American Historical Review* 36 (1931): 336–342, at 339–340, 342, 336–338; Koch and Ammon, "Virginia and Kentucky Resolutions," 163 and n.55.
86. Kurtz, *Presidency*, 354–355; Adrienne Koch, *Jefferson and Madison: The Great Collaboration* (New York: Knopf, 1950), 194; Koch and Ammon, "Virginia and Kentucky Resolutions," 163 and n.55; John C. Miller, *Crisis in Freedom* (Boston: LB, 1952), 174.
87. Selinger, *Embracing Dissent*, 65–66; Sharp, *Deadlocked Election*, 52–65; Gordon S. Wood, *Empire of Liberty: A History of the Early Republic* (New York: OUP, 2009), 270 n.79; Sharp, *American Politics*, 188, 203–205; Rose, *Prologue*, 221; Dauer, *Adams Federalists*, 202. See Sharp, *American Politics*, 205.
88. Thomas Jefferson to James Monroe (15 Feb.1801), *PTJ*, 32:594.
89. Thomas McKean to Thomas Jefferson (21 Mar.1801), ibid., 33:391; James Monroe to Thomas Jefferson (27 Jan.1801), ibid., 32:511.

10. A New Round of Enforcement

1. E.g., Timothy Pickering to William Rawle (24 July 1799), "Timothy Pickering Papers" (Massachusetts Historical Society, Boston, original manuscripts and 69 reels), 11:486 ("Pickering Papers"); Timothy Pickering to Richard Harison (12 Aug.1799), Pickering Papers, 11:599; Timothy Pickering to Zeb Hollingsworth (12 Aug.1799), ibid., 11:603; Timothy Pickering to Thomas Nelson (14 Aug.1799), ibid., 11:611.
2. Timothy Pickering to Zeb Hollingsworth (12 Aug.1799), ibid., 11:603 (discussed in Chapter 13).
3. "Methods of Choosing Presidential Electors in 1800," Harold C. Syrett et al., eds., *Papers of Alexander Hamilton* (New York: ColUP, 1961–), 24:445; ibid., 24:446 ("*PAH*").

4. Timothy Pickering to John Pickering (7 Mar.1800), Pickering Papers, 13:247, 249; Stevens T. Mason to James Madison (23 Apr.1800), William T. Hutchinson et al., eds., *Papers of James Madison* (Chicago: UChiP, 1962–1991), 17:381, 382 ("*PJM*").
5. Thomas Jefferson to John W. Eppes (21 Apr.1800), Julian P. Boyd et al., eds., *Papers of Thomas Jefferson* (Princeton: PUP, 1950–), 31:531 ("*PTJ*").
6. Douglas Bradburn, *The Citizenship Revolution: Politics and the Creation of the American Union 1774–1804* (Charlottesville: UVP, 2009), 208; Donald H. Stewart, *The Opposition Press of the Federalist Period* (Albany: SUNYP, 1969), 611, 612–613.
7. The best biographies of Duane are Nigel Little, *Transoceanic Radical, William Duane: National Identity and Empire 1760–1835* (London: Pickering and Chatto, 2008); and Kim T. Phillips, *William Duane, Radical Journalist in the Age of Jefferson* (New York: Garland, 1989), photographically reprinting Kim T. Phillips, "William Duane, Revolutionary Editor" (Ph.D. diss., University of California–Berkeley, 1968). Other useful biographical sources are Marcus Daniel, *Scandal and Civility: Journalism and the Birth of American Democracy* (New York: OUP, 2009), 231–274; Jeffrey L. Pasley, *The Tyranny of Printers: Newspaper Politics in the Early American Republic* (Charlottesville; UPV, 2001), 176–195; Michael Durey, *Transatlantic Radicals and the Early American Republic* (Lawrence: UPKan, 1997), 181–182, 247–257; John A. Garraty et al., eds., *American National Biography* (New York: OUP, 1999), 6:935 ("*ANB*"). Older less useful sources are William [J.] Duane, *Biographical Memoir of William J. Duane* (Philadelphia: Claxton, 1868); Allan C. Clark, "William Duane," *Records of the Columbia Historical Society* 9 (1906): 14–62.
8. Little, *Transoceanic Radical,* 18–19, 20 (citing British manuscript records); Phillips, *Duane,* 4–5; Pasley, *Tyranny of Printers,* 176; *ANB,* 6:935; *PTJ,* 31:453n.
9. Little, *Transoceanic Radical,* 20; Phillips, *Duane,* 5; ibid., 6–7; Pasley, *Tyranny of Printers,* 178; *ANB,* 6:935.
10. Bradburn, *Citizenship Revolution,* 228; Daniel, *Scandal,* 231–232, 243–244; and has been called a Protestant, David A. Wilson, *United Irishmen, United States* (Ithaca, NY: CorUP, 1998), 54.
11. Little, *Transoceanic Radical,* 23–32, 37–65, esp. 57–65; Phillips, *Duane,* 8–11, 11–21.
12. Little, *Transoceanic Radical,* 67–78, 82–94; Pasley, *Tyranny of Printers,* 21–34. For mistreatment, see Phillips, *Duane,* 37; Pasley, *Tyranny of Printers,* 180.
13. Little, *Transoceanic Radical,* 9, 105–115; Phillips, *Duane,* 35–46. For his return, see Little, *Transoceanic Radical,* 117; Phillips, *Duane,* 46–47. Arriving in New York City, they moved to Philadelphia in October 1796.
14. Jasper Dwight [William Duane], *A Letter to George Washington, President of the United States: Containing Strictures on His Address* (Philadelphia: For the Author [By Bache], Dec. 1796), 47, 4. The author was Duane. Phillips, *Duane,* 50; Daniel, *Scandal,* 246–247.
15. Jean Antoine Joseph Fauchet, *A Sketch of the Present State of Our Political Relations with the United States of North-America* (Philadelphia: Bache, 1797); Timothy Pickering to George Washington (14 Dec.1797), Dorothy Twohig

et al., eds., *The Papers of George Washington: Retirement Series* (Charlottesville: UPV, 1998–1999), 1:516 ("*PGW-R*").

16. William Duane to Tench Coxe (15 Oct.1798), in Peter J. Parker, "The Revival of the *Aurora:* A Letter to Tench Coxe," *Pennsylvania Magazine of History and Biography* 96 (1972): 521–525, at 524; Stewart, *Opposition Press,* 610–611; James Tagg, *Benjamin Franklin Bache and the Philadelphia Aurora* (Philadelphia: UPP, 1991), 400.
17. Pasley, *Tyranny of Printers,* 176, 285–319.
18. Bradburn, *Citizenship Revolution,* 224–227; see Michael Durey, "Thomas Paine's Apostles: Radical Emigrés and the Triumph of Jeffersonian Republicanism," *William and Mary Quarterly* 44 (1987): 661–688, at 664–665; "List of United Irishmen," *Gazette of the United States* (Philadelphia), 18 Dec.1798, 3.
19. Richard J. Twomey, "Jacobins and Jeffersonians: Anglo-American Radicalism in the United States 1790–1820" (Ph.D. diss., Northern Illinois University, 1974), 138–170; Wilson, *United Irishmen,* 148–151 (though he was inconsistent toward his own laborers); Little, *Transoceanic Radical,* 9.
20. E.g., Pasley, *Tyranny of Printers,* 184–186; Stewart, *Opposition Press,* 317, 104–112.
21. Burleigh, "To the People of the United States," *Connecticut Courant* (Hartford), 18 Aug.1800, 1; "New London," *Bee* (New London, CT), 26 Mar.1800, 3, quoted in Pasley, *Tyranny of Printers,* 191; Alexander Hamilton, *Letter from Alexander Hamilton, Concerning the Public Conduct and Character of John Adams, Esq.* (1800), reprinted in *PAH,* 25:169, 186–234; "Pro Bono Publico. Hamilton's Last Letter," *Aurora,* 5 Nov.1800, 3.
22. John Adams to Benjamin Stoddert (31 Mar.1801), Charles Francis Adams, ed., *Works of John Adams* (Boston: LB, 1850–1856), 9:582 ("*WJA*"); John Adams to Christopher Gadsden (16 Apr.1801), ibid., 9:584.
23. Thomas Jefferson to James Monroe (19 Oct.1823), Paul L. Ford, ed., *The Writings of Thomas Jefferson* (New York: Putnam's Sons, 1892–1899), 10:275; see Alan V. Briceland, "The Philadelphia Aurora, The New England Illuminati, and The Election of 1800," *Pennsylvania Magazine of History and Biography* 100 (1976): 3–36.
24. Original court records for the four federal prosecutions of *United States v. William Duane,* and microfilm copies, are in National Archives at Philadelphia, in the same place described in Chapter 8 for the prosecutions of John Fries, in "Criminal Case Files," pp.1:1144–1168, 2:175–206; "Minutes," pp.279, 335, 338, 347–348, 376, 409, 411; and in Maeva Marcus, ed., *Documentary History of the Supreme Court of the United States, 1789–1800* (New York: ColUP, 1985–2007), vol.3 ("*DHSC*"). Useful secondary sources include James Morton Smith, *Freedom's Fetters: The Alien and Sedition Laws* (Ithaca, NY: CorUP, 1956), 282–306; John C. Miller, *Crisis in Freedom* (Boston: LB, 1952), 194–202; James Morton Smith, "The Aurora and the Alien and Sedition Laws, Part II," *Pennsylvania Magazine of History and Biography* 77 (1953): 123–155.
25. E.g., Phillips, *Duane,* 672; Stanley Elkins and Eric McKitrick, *The Age of Federalism* (New York: OUP, 1993), 704 (British influence case and "final effort" in Senate case).

26. Timothy Pickering to George Cabot (21 Feb.1799), Henry Cabot Lodge, ed., *Life and Letters of George Cabot,* 2nd ed. (Boston: LB, 1878), 221, 222. On this case, see Smith, *Freedom's Fetters,* 282–288.
27. Timothy Pickering to John Adams (24 July 1799), *WJA,* 9:3; Timothy Pickering to William Rawle (24 July 1799), Pickering Papers, 11:486; Timothy Pickering to William Rawle (25 July 1799), ibid., 11:495.
28. John Adams to Timothy Pickering (1 Aug. 1799), *WJA,* 9:5.
29. "Wednesday, July 31, 1799," *Aurora,* reprinted in Richard N. Rosenfeld, *American Aurora* (New York: St. Martin's Press, 1997), 667; "Saturday Evening, August 3," *Gazette of the United States,* 3 Aug.1799, 3. The arrest was on 30 July, and the bonds were on 2 August 1799. For the report to Adams, see Timothy Pickering to John Adams (1 Aug.1799), ibid., 9:6, 7; see Timothy Pickering to John Adams (10 Aug. 1799).
30. Indictment (14 Oct.1799), Criminal Case Files, pp.1163–1168; Minutes, p.335 (14 Oct. 1799). In addition to that copy, this indictment was printed as "No.I" in a pamphlet: *Copy of an Indictment* ([Philadelphia: Aurora, 1799]). This case is docket item 3 for the October 1799 session.
31. Indictment (14 Oct.1798), in Criminal Case Files, pp.1163, 1164, 1165. The indictment quoted three more examples. Ibid., p.1167.
32. *PGW-R,* 4:402 n.4; John Adams to Tench Coxe (2 May 1792), *PAH,* 25:110 n.23.
33. James McHenry to Philemon Dickinson (3 Sept.1800), *PAH,* 25:115; ibid., 25:110 n.23.
34. Minutes, pp.338–339 (16 Oct.1799); "Federal Circuit Court," in Rosenfeld, *American Aurora,* 707; "Federal Circuit Court," *Herald of Liberty* (Washington, PA), 18 Nov.1799, 1.
35. Minutes, p.376 (29 Apr.1800); Worthington C. Ford, "Letters Written by William Duane," *Proceedings of the Massachusetts Historical Society* (2nd Series) 20 (1906–1907): 257–394, at 260 (17 Apr.1800).
36. Indictment (14 Oct. 1799), Criminal Case Files, pp.1146–1152; Minutes, p.335. In addition to that copy, this indictment was printed as "No.II" in a pamphlet: *Copy of an Indictment* ([Philadelphia: Aurora, 1799]). This case is docket item 2 for the October 1799 session.
37. George Washington to Timothy Pickering (4 Aug.1799), *PGW-R,* 4:221, 222; George Washington to James McHenry (11 Aug.1799), ibid., 4:238.
38. Indictment, pp.1149, 1150–1151.
39. Minutes, pp.338 (16 Oct.1799), 376 (29 Apr.1800).
40. Smith, *Freedom's Fetters,* 285; accord Phillips, *Duane,* 83 n.70; Phillip I. Blumberg, *Repressive Jurisprudence in the Early American Republic* (New York: CUP, 2010), 118.
41. Timothy Pickering to William Rawle (20 Sept.1799), Pickering Papers, 12:82, 83; "From the Aurora," *American Citizen* (New York), 2 May 1801, 3.
42. Allen Johnson et al., eds., *Dictionary of American Biography* (New York: Scribner, 1928–1936), 15:400; Frank M. Eastman, *Courts and Lawyers of Pennsylvania* (New York: American Historical Society, 1922), 4:56–57; William Rawle, *A View of the Constitution of the United States of America* (Philadelphia: Carey and Lea, 1825), 120.

43. Minutes, p.347 (14 Apr. 1800); Indictment, in Criminal Case Files, pp.176–185 (out of order in microfilm). This case is docket item 19 for the April 1800 session.
44. Pickering "suppose[d] every body understands the main object of this provision is to open the commercial intercourse with St. Domingo" and to enable Toussaint to "declare the whole island of St. Domingo independent." Timothy Pickering to Alexander Hamilton (9 Feb.1799), *PAH,* 22:473, 474. See An Act Further To Suspend the Commercial Intercourse between the United States and France, and the Dependencies Thereof (9 Feb.1799), Statutes, 1:613.
45. Indictment, p.3, Criminal Case Files, p.184; Indictment, pp. 3–6, quoting pp.4–5, Criminal Case Files, pp.184–185, 178–181, quoting pp.185, 178.
46. Indictment, pp.6–9, quoting pp.8–9, Criminal Case Files, pp.179–181, quoting pp.181, 177.
47. Capias (14 Apr.1800), Criminal Case Files, pp.194, 197; Minutes, p.348 (14 Apr.1800).
48. Indictment (jacket), Criminal Case Files, p.176; Thomas Jefferson to William Duane (23 May 1801), *PTJ,* 34:169; Thomas Jefferson to James Madison (19 July 1801), ibid., 34:597.
49. *Debates and Proceedings in the Congress of the United States . . . Annals of the Congress of the United States* (Washington: Gales and Seaton, 1834–1856), 10:29 (23 Jan.1800) ("*Annals*"); ibid., 10:28–33 (23–24 Jan. 1800), 126–146 (28 Mar. 1800); Constitution, art.2, §1; see James R. Sharp, *American Politics in the Early Republic* (New Haven: YUP, 1993), 219–220; Elkins, *Age of Federalism,* 704; Phillips, *Duane,* 84–85.
50. "From Anthony New" (8 Apr.1800), Noble E. Cunningham, Jr., ed., *Circular Letters of Congressmen to Their Constituents 1789–1829* (Chapel Hill: UNCP, 1978), 1:194, 195; *Annals,* 10:146 (28 Mar.1800).
51. The best source for the Senate prosecution of Duane is *American State Papers. Documents, Legislative and Executive, of the Congress of the United States [Miscellaneous Series]* (Washington: Gales and Seaton, 1834), 1:208–215 ("*ASP*"). The best secondary source is Smith, *Freedom's Fetters,* 288–305.
52. As quoted in Indictment (17 Oct.1800), in Criminal Case Files, pp.1153, 1154 (quoting *Aurora,* 19 Feb.1800). The article contained an error, that the Senate had passed the Ross bill. For the committee's findings, see Report of Committee on Privileges (14 Mar.1800), *ASP,* 1:208, 208–209.
53. Constitution, art.1, §§5–6; Blumberg, *Repressive Jurisprudence,* 289–301; Leonard W. Levy, *Emergence of a Free Press* (New York: OUP, 1985), 14–15, 17–19; *Annals,* 10:71, 73, 82 (5 Mar.1800).
54. Thomas Cooper to Thomas Jefferson ([23 Mar. 1800]), *PTJ,* 31:451, 451–452; see Dumas Malone, *The Public Life of Thomas Cooper 1783–1839* (New Haven: YUP, 1923), 112–116; Twomey, "Jacobins," 70.
55. William Duane to Vice President (24 Mar.1800), *ASP,* 1:210; *PTJ,* 31:453; Report of Committee on Privileges (22 Mar.1800), *ASP,* 1:209.
56. Thomas Cooper to William Duane (25 Mar.1800), *ASP,* 1:212; Alexander J. Dallas to William Duane (25 Mar.1800), ibid., 1:211–212; William Duane to President of Senate (26 Mar.1800), *ASP,* 1:211; *PTJ,* 31:466 (dated 27 Mar.1800).

57. Report of Committee on Privileges (27 Mar.1800), *ASP,* 1:212; John Dawson to James Madison (30 Mar.1800), *PJM,* 17:375, 376.
58. *Journal of the Senate of the United States of America* (Philadelphia: John Ward Fenno, 1799), 326 (14 Mar.1800); *Annals,* 10:184 (14 May 1800); John Adams to Charles Lee and Jared Ingersoll (16 May 1800), *WJA,* 9:56; see *PJM,* 17:376 n.2; Robert Brugger et al., eds., *Papers of James Madison: Secretary of State Series* (Charlottesville: UPV, 1987–), 1:423 ("*PJM-SS*").
59. Order (27 May 1800), in Criminal Case Files, p.199.
60. Minutes, p.409 (17 Oct.1800); Indictment, in Criminal Case Files, pp.1153–1163. This case is listed as docket item 19 for the October 1800 session. For the charge, see *DHSC,* 3:452; William Paterson's Charge (C.C.D.Vt. 3 Oct. 1798), ibid., 3:292. Paterson was still using that charge a year later. "Raleigh, December 3," *Constitutional Diary* (Philadelphia), 17 Dec.1799, 1. His undated charges were from earlier. *DHSC,* 3:457–468.
61. Indictment, in Criminal Case Files, p.1154.
62. Ibid., pp.1155, 1159, 1160, and pp.1160, 1161, 1162. The last quotation was from an article of 2 May 1800.
63. Affidavit of Duane for Continuance (18 Oct 1800); Minutes, p.411 (18 Oct.1800); Agreement on Commission (16 Feb.1801), Criminal Case Files, pp.186, 189; Interrogatories (16 Feb.1801), ibid., pp.187–191; Affidavit of Duane (12 May 1801), ibid., pp.192, 202–206, 193; "From the Aurora," *American Citizen* (New York), 2 May 1801, 3.
64. United States v. Duane (C.C.D.Pa. 12 May 1801), in John B. Wallace, *Reports of Cases Adjudged in the Circuit Court of the United States for the Third Circuit* (Philadelphia: Ustick, 1801), 5; William Duane to Thomas Jefferson (10 May 1801), *PTJ,* 34:71; "Mr. Wayne," *Gazette of the United States,* 18 May 1801, 3.
65. James Madison to Alexander J. Dallas (20 July 1801), *PJM-SS,* 1:442; James Madison, Memorandum to Thomas Jefferson ([17 July] 1801), ibid., 1:423; accord Thomas Jefferson to William Duane (23 May 1801), *PTJ,* 34:169; William Duane to Thomas Jefferson (10 June 1801), ibid., 34:296.
66. Indictment jacket, Criminal Case Files, p.1153 (28 July 1801); Indictment (Oct. 1801), Criminal Case Files (not on microfilm M986).
67. Draft of Message to the Senate (ante 12 Nov.1801), *PTJ,* 35:656.
68. The most useful source is Trial of Duane, Reynolds, Moore and Cuming, for Seditious Riot, Wharton's State Trials 345 (Pa. Ct. Oyer & Terminer 1799) ("Wharton"), though it is based on Duane's own account, ibid., 345n., and on an "unskillful" court reporter, ibid., 388n., 379n.; see William Duane, *A Report of the Extraordinary Transactions Which Took Place at Philadelphia in February 1799* (Philadelphia: Aurora, 1799). Useful secondary sources include Bradburn, *Citizenship Revolution,* 206–208, 228–229; Wilson, *United Irishmen,* 53–56; Smith, *Freedom's Fetters,* 278–282; George M. Dallas, *Life and Writings of Alexander James Dallas* (Philadelphia: Lippincott, 1871), 68–72; Twomey, "Jacobins," 220–221. The petition is in Duane, *Report,* appendix p.1.
69. "United Irish Riot," *Porcupine's Gazette* (Philadelphia), 12 Feb.1799, 3; Wharton, 345, 347, 359, 358, 388.

70. Douglas Bradburn, "A Clamor in the Public Mind: Opposition to the Alien and Sedition Acts," *William and Mary Quarterly* (3rd series) 65 (2008): 565–600, at 579; Bradburn, *Citizenship Revolution*, 208.
71. See generally Phillips, *Duane*, 71–76; John Nerone, *Violence against the Press* (New York: OUP, 1994), 66; e.g., "Extract of a Report from an Officer of the Northern Army," *Aurora*, 16 Apr.1799, 3; *PTJ*, 31:152–153n.
72. Paul Douglas Newman, *Fries's Rebellion* (Philadelphia: UPP, 2004), 163.
73. William Duane, "More of Good Order and Regular Government!," *Aurora*, 16 May 1799, 2; accord "Tuesday, May 21, 1799," *Aurora*, 21 May 1799, 2; "Thursday Evening, May 16," *Gazette of the United States*, 16 May 1799, 3.
74. Indictment (14 Apr.1800), in Criminal Case Files, pp.208–213, at p.208; Minutes, p.347 (14 Apr.1800); Timothy Pickering to William Rawle (25 July 1799), Pickering Papers, 11:495; *PJM-SS*, 1:129, 131–132 n.8; Thomas Jefferson to Edmund Pendleton (19 Apr.1800), *PTJ*, 31:520, 521, 522n.; Trial of Daniel Thomas, et al., Wharton 682 (C.C.D.Pa. 1800).
75. Phillips, *Duane*, 78; Robert Liston to Mr. Russel (23 May 1799), in Wharton, 682, 683.
76. Timothy Pickering to William Rawle (25 July 1799), Pickering Papers, 11:495.
77. Indictment (14 Apr.1800), in Criminal Case Files, pp.212–213; Indictment [jacket], in Criminal Case Files, p.208 (capias); Minutes, p.348 (14 Apr.1800).
78. Thomas Jefferson to James Madison (19 July 1801), *PJM-SS*, 1:442; James Madison to Thomas Jefferson ([c. 17 July 1801]), *PTJ*, 34:583, 584.
79. The case was postponed from the October 1800 to the May 1801 session. Minutes, p.411 (18 Oct.1800). For the suit, see Hollingsworth v. Duane, 4 U.S. (4 Dall.) 353, 12 F.Cas. 356 (C.C.D.Pa. 19 May 1801) (No. 6,615); Hollingsworth v. Duane, 12 F.Cas.359 (C.C.D.Pa. 22 May 1801) (No. 6,616); "The British Subject—William Duane," *Gazette of the United States*, 19 May 1801, 3.
80. *PTJ*, 34:213–214n.; Phillips, *Duane*, 127. The article and the motion for contempt were both 20 May 1801. For that motion, see "Saturday Evening, May 23," *Gazette of the United States*, 23 May 1801, 3; Thomas Jefferson to Robert R. Livingston (31 May 1801), *PTJ*, 34:213.
81. William Duane to Thomas Jefferson (4 May 1801), *PTJ*, 34:71; William Duane to James Madison (10 May 1801), *PJM-SS*, 1:152. Jefferson assured him of the stationary business, though reality differed. Thomas Jefferson to William Duane (23 May 1801), *PTJ*, 34:169. Duane assisted Jefferson with information and opinion. E.g., Harry M. Tinkcom, *The Republicans and Federalists in Pennsylvania 1790–1801* (Harrisburg: PHMC, 1950), 267.
82. William Duane to Thomas Jefferson (10 June 1801), *PTJ*, 34:296, 298–299; Thomas Jefferson to James Madison (16 Aug.1803), *PTJ*, 41:208.
83. William Duane to Albert Gallatin (13 Dec.1801), *PTJ*, 36:121n.; see Albert Gallatin to Thomas Jefferson ([15 Dec.1801]), ibid., 36:120. On his debts, see Little, *Transoceanic Radical*, 155–159, 176–177; Phillips, *Duane*, 336–342.
84. Phillips, *Duane*, 148–170; Twomey, "Jacobins," 108–124; Pasley, *Tyranny of Printers*, 289–293; Little, *Transoceanic Radical*, 160–163, 167, 168–169; Phillips, *Duane*, 223, 241, 378–389.

85. Thomas Jefferson to William Wirt (3 May 1811), J. Jefferson Looney, ed., *The Papers of Thomas Jefferson: Retirement Series* (Princeton: PUP, 2004–), 3:601, 603 ("*PTJ-R*"); Little, *Transoceanic Radical,* 183–184; Matthew Mason, *Slavery and Politics in the Early American Republic* (Chapel Hill: UNCP, 2006), 78–80, 85; Wilson, *United Irishmen,* 136–137.
86. Thomas Jefferson to William Wirt (15 Apr.1811), *PTJ-R,* 3:563; Thomas Jefferson to James Monroe (19 Oct.1823), Ford, *Writings of Thomas Jefferson,* 10:275; *PTJ,* 31:454n.; Phillips, *Duane,* 340–344, 417–422, 424.
87. Charles Francis Adams, ed., *Memoirs of John Quincy Adams* (Philadelphia: Lippincott, 1874–1877), 5:112.
88. There is no evidence except a confused family memory that the London paper he served during 1782–1787 was John Almon's *Daily Advertiser.* Little, *Transoceanic Radical,* 30–31; contra Daniel, *Scandal and Civility,* 235–236.
89. Phillips, *Duane,* 38–39; Daniel, *Scandal and Civility,* 239; *The Correspondence of the London Corresponding Society* (London: For the LCS, 1795), 42; London Corresponding Society, "Declaration of Principles," in Michael T. Davis, *The London Corresponding Society Publications, 1792–1799* (London: Pickering and Chatto, 2002), 1:301, 302; "To the Members of the London Corresponding Society" (31 Dec. 1795), ibid., 2:401–402; see Durey, *Transatlantic Radicals,* 12–49; Albert Goodwin, *The Friends of Liberty: The English Democratic Movements in the Age of the French Revolution* (Cambridge, MA: HUP, 1997). For the LCS's importance and background, see H. T. Dickinson, *The Politics of the People in Eighteenth-Century Britain* (New York: St. Martin's Press, 1994), 237–238; Edward Vallance, *A Radical History of Britain* (London: LB, 2009), 237–238, 258–272.
90. Treasonable and Seditious Practices Act (18 Dec.1795), 36 Geo.3, c.7; Seditious Assemblies Act (18 Dec.1795), 36 Geo.3, c.8; Michael Lobban, "From Seditious Libel to Unlawful Assembly: Peterloo and the Changing Face of Political Crime c. 1770–1820," *Oxford Journal of Legal Studies* 10 (1990): 307–352; Clive Emsley, "Repression, 'Terror' and the Rule of Law in England During the Decade of the French Revolution," *English Historical Review* 100 (1985): 801–825.
91. *The History of Two Acts, Entitled An Act for the Safety and Preservation of His Majesty's Person and Government against Treasonable and Seditious Practices and Attempts, and An Act . . . Preventing Seditious Meetings and Assemblies* (London: G.G. and J. Robinson, 1796), 125, 126.
92. Ibid., 126, 127, 131; accord *Account of the Proceedings of a Meeting of the People in a Field Near Copenhagen-House* (London: Printed for Citizen Lee, 1795), 5.
93. [William Duane], "Liberty of the Press," *Telegraph,* 11 Nov.1795, 1.
94. Sir John Shore to Hon. Henry Dundas (31 Dec.1794), Holden Furber, ed., *The Private Record of an Indian Governor-Generalship* (Cambridge, MA: HUP, 1933), 60, 63.; Little, *Transoceanic Radical,* 57–65, 82–91; Phillips, *Duane,* 11–21, 21–34.
95. Jasper Dwight [William Duane], *A Letter to George Washington* (Philadelphia: For the Author [By Bache], Dec. 1796), 18, 20, 32.

96. The best biography of Priestley is Robert E. Schofield, *The Enlightened Joseph Priestley: A Study of His Life and Work from 1773 to 1804* (University Park: PSUP, 2004) (and companion volume on earlier years). Other useful biographical sources are cited below, and H. C. G. Matthew et al., eds., *Oxford Dictionary of National Biography* (Oxford: OUP, 2004), 45:351 ("*ODNB*").

97. Matthew, *ODNB*, 45:351; Joseph Priestley, *Letters to the Right Honourable Edmund Burke Occasioned by His Reflections on the Revolution in France* (London: J. Johnson, 1791) (supporting French Revolution); Ira V. Brown, "The Religion of Joseph Priestley," *Pennsylvania History* 24 (1957): 85–100, at 95 (attack). For the move, see Jenny Graham, "Revolutionary in Exile: The Emigration of Joseph Priestley to America 1794–1804," *Transactions of the American Philosophical Society (New Series)* 85 (1995): 1–213; accord J. D. Bowers, *Joseph Priestley and English Unitarianism in America* (University Park: PSUP, 2007).

98. Twomey, "Jacobins and Jeffersonians," 23–24; "Priestley Completely Detected," *Porcupine's Gazette*, 20 Aug.1798, 2. Cobbett's attacks began in 1794 on other grounds. Daniel, *Scandal and Civility*, 194–198.

99. Peter Porcupine [William Cobbett], *Remarks on the Explanation, Lately Published by Dr. Priestley, Respecting the Intercepted Letters* (London: J. Wright, 1799), 18–19; Joseph Priestley to George Thatcher (26 July 1798), "Letters of Joseph Priestley," *Proceedings of the Massachusetts Historical Society* 3 (1886–1887): 11–40, at 23, 24; see generally Graham, "Revolutionary," 109–115.

100. Timothy Pickering to John Adams (1 Aug.1799), *WJA*, 9:5, 6 (quotations conformed to original in Pickering Papers, 11:524); John Adams to Timothy Pickering (13 Aug.1799), *WJA*, 9:13, 13–14 (conformed to Pickering Papers, 25:99).

101. Charles Hall to Timothy Pickering (26 July 1799), Pickering Papers, 25:58, 59; Timothy Pickering to Charles Hall (1 Aug.1799), ibid., 11:528, 529.

102. Thomas Jefferson to Joseph Priestley (21 Mar.1801), *PTJ*, 33:393.

103. Clarence S. Brigham, ed., *History and Bibliography of American Newspapers, 1690–1820* (Worcester, MA: AAS, 1947), 2:1139; Pasley, *Tyranny of Printers*, 160; Joseph McGraw, "'To Secure These Rights,'" *Virginia Magazine of History and Biography* 91 (1983): 54–72, at 66.

104. No biography of Jones appears to exist. Biographical data is in Pasley, *Tyranny of Printers*, 159–161; David A. Rawson, "'Guardians of Their Own Liberty:' A Contextual History of Print Culture in Virginia Society, 1750 to 1820" (Ph.D. diss., College of William & Mary, 1998), 322, 324–329; L. H. Jones, *Captain Roger Jones* (Albany: Munsell's Sons, 1891), 53; "Communication," *The Enquirer* (Richmond), 22 Aug. 1806, 3.

105. Pasley, *Tyranny of Printers*, 160; Richard R. Beeman, *The Old Dominion and the New Nation, 1788–1801* (Lexington; UPK, 1972), 206; James T. Callender, *The Prospect Before Us* (Richmond: "Printed for the Author, and Sold by M. Jones" etc., 1800); Harry Ammon, "The Republican Party in Virginia, 1789 to 1824" (Ph.D. diss., University of Virginia, 1948), 259–267; James T. Callender, *The Conduct of Meriwether Jones in a Series of Letters* (Richmond: H. Pace, 1802).

106. Timothy Pickering to Thomas Nelson (14 Aug.1799), Pickering Papers, 11:611; Ammon, "Republican Party," 211; Stewart, *Opposition Press,* 10; Timothy Pickering to William Vans Murray (4 Oct.1799), Pickering Papers, 12:141, 142A.
107. Timothy Pickering to William Vans Murray (4 Oct.1799), Pickering Papers, 12:141, 142A; Timothy Pickering to William Bingham (22 Sept.1799), Pickering Papers, 12:96.
108. James Monroe to Thomas Jefferson (4 Jan.1800), *PTJ,* 31:289, 290.

11. New York Prosecutions

1. "Minutes, Trial Notes, and Rolls of Attorneys of the U.S. Circuit Court for the Southern District of New York" (NARA at New York City, R.G.21.34.7, microfilm M854, roll 1), p.184. On Church, see Harold C. Syrett et al., eds., *Papers of Alexander Hamilton* (New York: Columbia University Press, 1961–), 26:434 n.1 ("*PAH*").
2. The best biographical summary for Peck is Alan Taylor, "The Plough-Jogger: Jedediah Peck and the Democratic Revolution," in *Revolutionary Founders: Rebels, Radicals, and Reformers in the Making of the Nation,* ed. Alfred F. Young, Gary B. Nash, and Ray Raphael (New York: Knopf, 2011), 375–387. Other useful biographical sources are Alfred F. Young, *The Democratic Republicans of New York* (Chapel Hill: UNCP, 1967), 509–517; Throop Wilder, "Jedidiah Peck: Statesman, Soldier, Preacher," *New York History* 22 (1941): 290–300, 291–293; Joyce Appleby, *Capitalism and a New Social Order* (New York: NYUP, 1984), 86–87. Older less useful sources are Sherman Williams, "Our History and Our Schools," *Proceedings of the New York State Historical Association* 16 (1917): 69–81, at 75; "Obituary," *Watch-Tower* (Cooperstown), 20 Aug.1821, 3.
3. Linda T. Watkins, ed., *DAR Patriot Index* (Baltimore: Gateway Press, 2003), 3:2078; Taylor, "Plough-Jogger," 377, 380, 383–384; Young, *Democratic Republicans,* 510.
4. Sherman Williams, "Jedediah Peck," *Quarterly Journal of the New York State Historical Association* 1 (1920): 219–240; S. S. Randall, *History of the Common School System of the State of New York* (New York: Ivison, Blakeman, 1871), 10, 17–23. For spelling, e.g., Plough-Jogger [Jedidiah Peck], *The Political Wars of Otsego: Or, Downfall of Jacobinism and Despotism* (Cooperstown, NY: E. Phinney, 1796), 17, 24, 26 37 etc.; Randall, *Common School,* 23; see 2 Samuel 12:25.
5. "Address to John Adams, President," *Otsego Herald* (Cooperstown, NY), 31 May 1798, 3; Plough-Jogger [Peck], *Political Wars,* 100–101, 97–98, 48.
6. Alan Taylor, *William Cooper's Town* (New York: Knopf, 1995), 241–249; Young, *Democratic Republicans,* 508–517; see L. H. Butterfield, "Cooper's Inheritance: The Otsego Country and Its Founders," *New York History* 35 (1954): 374–411.
7. Daniel Hale to William Cooper (9 Jan.1799), quoted in Taylor, *Cooper's Town,* 269–270; L. H. Butterfield, "Judge William Cooper (1754–1809),"

New York History 30 (1949): 385–408, at 400; Taylor, *Cooper's Town,* 271, 275–276.

8. *Journal of the Assembly of the State of New-York at Their Twenty-Second Session [2 Jan. 1799]* (Albany: Loring Andrews, 1799), 120–121 (16 Feb.1799). On the Republican resolution, see ibid., 121–122 (16 Feb.1799).
9. Ibid., 122 (16 Feb.1799). On the Federalist resolutions, see ibid., 122–123 (16 Feb.1799), 115–116 (15 Feb.1799); ibid., 114–118 (15 Feb.1799).
10. Council of Appointment (9 Mar.1799), in *The Correspondence Between the Hon. Ebenezer Foote and Ambrose Spencer* (Albany: Whiting and Leavenworth, 1802).
11. "Caution!," *Albany Centinel,* 23 Apr.1799, 2.
12. Jabez D. Hammond, *The History of Political Parties in the State of New-York* (Albany: Benthuysen, 1842), 1:131–132; Taylor, "Plough-Jogger," 382; Timothy Pickering to Richard Harison (12 Aug.1799), "Timothy Pickering Papers" (Massachusetts Historical Society, Boston, original manuscripts and 69 reels), 11:599 ("Pickering Papers").
13. Original court records for *United States v. Jedidiah Peck,* and microfilm copies, are in National Archives at New York City: "Criminal Case Files of the U.S. Circuit Court for the Southern District of New York 1790–1853" (NARA at New York City, R.G.21.34.7, microfilm M885, roll 4) ("Case Files"); "Minutes, Trial Notes, and Rolls of Attorneys of the U.S. Circuit Court for the Southern District of New York" (NARA at New York City, R.G.21.34.7, microfilm M854, roll 1), pp.130–207 ("Minutes"); and in Maeva Marcus, ed., *Documentary History of the Supreme Court of the United States, 1789–1800* (New York: ColUP, 1985–2007), vol.3 ("*DHSC*"). Useful secondary sources include James Morton Smith, *Freedom's Fetters: The Alien and Sedition Laws* (Ithaca, NY: CorUP, 1956), 390–398, which reprints James Morton Smith, "The Sedition Law of 1798 and the Right of Petition: The Attempted Prosecution of Jedidiah Peck," *New York History* 35 (1954): 63–72; Taylor, *Cooper's Town,* 275–278; Taylor, "Plough-Jogger," 382; Michael Kent Curtis, *Free Speech, "The People's Darling Privilege"* (Durham, NC: DUP, 2000), 93–94.
14. Affidavit of David Goff (27 June 1799), in Case Files; Affidavit of Nathan Patmer (25 June 1799); Affidavit of Jonathan Brown (27 June 1799).
15. Indictment (4 Sept.1799), in Case Files; Minutes, p.144 (4 Sept.1799); *DHSC,* 3:381; Robert Troup to Rufus King (2 Sept.1799), ibid., 3:383.
16. Indictment, pp.1–2, 3–4.
17. DeAlva S. Alexander, *A Political History of the State of New York* (New York: Holt, 1906), 1:69; Taylor, "Plough-Jogger," 382; Hammond, *Political Parties,* 132.
18. "Albany, October 1," *Bee* (New London, CT), 16 Oct.1799, 3; [No Caption], *Gazette of the United States,* 9 Oct.1799, 2.
19. Matthew Bacon, *A New Abridgment of the Law,* 1st ed. (London: W. Strahan and M. Woodfall, 1736–1740), 3:498; Sir William Blackstone, *Commentaries on the Laws of England* (Oxford: CP, 1765–1769), 4:147; e.g., Proceedings against Mr. Wraynham, (1618) 2 State Trials 1059, 1072–1074 (Star Chamber);

Ronald J. Krotoszynski, *Reclaiming the Petition Clause* (New Haven: YUP, 2012), 81–152.

20. An Act Against Tumultuous Petitioning, 13 Car.2, stat.1, c.5 (1661); *Debates and Proceedings in the Congress of the United States . . . Annals of the Congress of the United States* (Washington: Gales and Seaton, 1834–1856), 8:2162 (10 July 1798) ("*Annals*").
21. Richard Harison to Timothy Pickering (10 Apr.1800), Pickering Papers, 26:77, 77A–78.
22. John Adams to Timothy Pickering (21 Apr.1800), https://founders.archives.gov/documents/Adams/99-02-02-4273; Timothy Pickering to Richard Harison (22 Apr.1800), Pickering Papers, 13:406.
23. Taylor, "Plough-Jogger," 382, 383–384.
24. Plough-Jogger [Peck], *Political Wars,* 97; Taylor, "Plough-Jogger," 385–386; Alan Taylor, "From Fathers to Friends of the People: Political Personas in the Early Republic," *Journal of the Early Republic* 11 (1991): 465–491, at 484–491.
25. Adriana S. Quackenbush, *The Quackenbush Family in Holland and America* (Paterson, NJ: Quackenbush, 1909), 108.
26. The best biography of Thomas Greenleaf is the chapter by Jeffrey L. Pasley, "Thomas Greenleaf: Printers and the Struggle for Democratic Politics and Freedom of the Press," in Alfred F. Young, Gary B. Nash, and Ray Raphael, eds., *Revolutionary Founders: Rebels, Radicals, and Reformers in the Making of the Nation* (New York: Knopf, 2011), 355–373. Other useful biographical sources include John A. Garraty et al., eds., *American National Biography* (New York: OUP, 1999), 9:543 ("*ANB*").
27. Clarence S. Brigham, ed., *History and Bibliography of American Newspapers, 1690–1820* (Worcester, MA: AAS, 1947), 1:646–647; Isaiah Thomas, *The History of Printing in America,* ed. Marcus A. McCorison (New York: Weathervane Books, 1970), 507; Pasley, "Thomas Greenleaf," 364–365; Alfred F. Young, *The Democratic Republicans of New York* (Chapel Hill: UNCP, 1967), 207, 349–350, 418.
28. Abigail Adams to William Smith (20 Mar.1798), L. H. Butterfield et al., eds., *Adams Family Correspondence* (Cambridge, MA: BPHUP, 1963–), 12:457; John Adams to Abigail Adams (24 Apr.1797), ibid., 12:87.
29. Donald H. Stewart, *The Opposition Press of the Federalist Period* (Albany: SUNYP, 1969), 617; Pasley, "Thomas Greenleaf," 357; Arthur I. Bernstein, "The Rise of the Democratic-Republican Party in New York City, 1789–1800" (Ph.D. diss., Columbia University, 1964), 320–321; *ANB,* 9:543, 544; Smith, *Freedom's Fetters,* 398.
30. "Remarks on the Treason and Sedition Bill," *Aurora,* 3 July 1798, 2 (reprinting from *Argus*); "Postscript," *Greenleaf's New York Journal,* 7 July 1798, 3.
31. "Friday, July 13," *Greenleaf's New York Journal,* 14 July 1798, 3; "Philadelphia, July 14," *Greenleaf's New York Journal,* 18 July 1798, 2; "Communication," ibid., 1. Those saying Thomas Greenleaf was indicted under the Sedition Act are mistaken. E.g., Phillip I. Blumberg, *Repressive Jurisprudence in the Early American Republic* (New York: CUP, 2010), 203.

32. The best brief biographical sketch for Ann Greenleaf is in Leona M. Hudak, *Early American Women Printers and Publishers, 1639–1820* (Metuchen, NJ: Scarecrow Press, 1978), 576–589. Other useful biographical sources include Joyce Appleby, ed., *Encyclopedia of Women in American History* (Armonk, NY: Sharpe Reference, 2002), 114–115.
33. Quackenbush, *Quackenbush Family,* 23–24, 33–89, 108; Brigham, *American Newspapers,* 1:610, 646; "Wednesday, November 7," *Greenleaf's New York Journal,* 7 Nov.1798, 1.
34. [No Caption], *Greenleaf's New York Journal,* 7 Nov.1798, 3; [No Caption], ibid., 3; accord Hale, "Thoughts on the Judiciary of the United States," *Argus,* 25 Oct.1799, in *DHSC,* 3:394; Robert Troup to Rufus King (16 Nov.1798), Charles R. King., ed., *Life and Correspondence of Rufus King* (New York: Putnam's Sons, 1894–1900), 2:465, 467.
35. Timothy Pickering to Richard Harison (12 Aug.1799), Pickering Papers, 11:599; e.g., Timothy Pickering to Zeb Hollingsworth (12 Aug.1799), ibid., 11:603; Timothy Pickering to Thomas Nelson (14 Aug.1799), ibid., 11:611.
36. Indictment (4 Sept.1799), in Case Files; Minutes, p.143 (4 Sept.1799).
37. Original court records for *United States v. Ann Greenleaf,* and microfilm copies, are in the same National Archives files as for Peck. Useful secondary sources include Smith, *Freedom's Fetters,* 398–403, 415–417, which reprints James Morton Smith, "Alexander Hamilton, the Alien Law, and Seditious Libels," *Review of Politics* 16 (1954): 305–333, at 313–314, 317–319, 330–331; John C. Miller, *Crisis in Freedom* (Boston: LB, 1952), 223.
38. Indictment, in Case Files, pp.1–2. The article also appeared in Greenleaf's other newspaper (quotations here are as capitalized and punctuated in the indictment, not in the printed article). "Anecdote," *Greenleaf's New York Journal,* 9 Feb. 1799, 2.
39. Indictment, pp.3–4. The article also appeared as [No Caption], *Greenleaf's New York Journal,* 31 Aug.1799, 3 (and is incorrectly referenced in some sources as 13 August).
40. Ibid., pp.4, 2.
41. Minutes, p.147 (5 Sept.1799); Richard Harison to Timothy Pickering (10 Apr.1800), Pickering Papers, 26:77, 78; Minutes, p.148 (5 Sept.1799).
42. Scanty biographical information on Frothingham appears in Beatrice Diamond, *An Episode in American Journalism: A History of David Frothingham and His Long Island Herald* (Port Washington, NY: Kennikat Press, 1964), 33–49.
43. "Extract of a Letter from Philadelphia, Dated Sept. 20," *Argus,* 6 Nov.1799, reprinted in *PAH,* 24:6 n.2.
44. Alexander Hamilton to Josiah O. Hoffman (6 Nov.1799), *PAH,* 24:5, 6, 5–6.
45. Court records for Frothingham's case are in Trial of David Frothingham, Wharton's State Trials 649 (N.Y. Ct. Oyer & Terminer 1799) ("Wharton"), which was almost all taken from newspaper reports. "Interesting Sketches," *New-York Gazette,* 25 Nov.1799, 2. Greenleaf's reporting was more detailed, from notes taken in court: "Trial of David Frothingham," *Greenleaf's New York Journal,* 11 Dec.1799, 1; "Trial of David Frothingham," *Greenleaf's New York Journal,* 14 Dec.1799, 1. Useful secondary sources include *PAH,* 24:6–8 nn.1–3; Smith, *Freedom's Fetters,* 400–414; Smith, "Alexander Hamilton," 314–331; Diamond,

Frothingham, 50–67; and Hamilton biographies such as Ron Chernow, *Alexander Hamilton* (New York: Penguin, 2004), 575–576.

46. "New-York, November 6, 1799," *New-York Gazette,* 8 Nov.1799, 3; "New-York, November 6, 1799," *Daily Advertiser* (New York), 9 Nov.1799, 2.
47. "Extract of a Letter, Philadelphia, Sept. 20," *Constitutional Telegraph* (Boston), 26 Oct.1799, 3; accord [No Caption], *Centinel of Freedom* (Newark), 29 Oct.1799, 2; "Extract of a Letter," *City Gazette* (Charleston), 2 Nov.1799, 2. Greenleaf's papers did question Hamilton on this. "New-York, Nov. 6, 1799," *Greenleaf's New York Journal,* 16 Nov.1799, 3.
48. Wharton, 650; "New-York, Feb. 1," *Bee,* 12 Feb.1800, 3; Robert W. T. Martin, "Reforming Republicanism: Alexander Hamilton's Theory of Republican Citizenship and Press Liberty," *Journal of the Early Republic* 25 (2005): 21–46, at 39.
49. [No Caption], *Greenleaf's New York Journal,* 20 Nov.1799, 4.
50. Wharton, 649.
51. Its date was November 21, 1799; it was mistakenly given by Wharton as November 16. E.g., "Saturday, November 23," *Greenleaf's New York Journal,* 23 Nov.1799, 3; "Friday, November 22, 1799," *Spectator* (New York), 23 Nov.1799, 3.
52. Wharton, 650, 651.
53. Stanley N. Katz, ed., *A Brief Narrative of the Case and Trial of John Peter Zenger* (Cambridge, MA: BPHUP, 1963). The Federalist *Gazette of the United States* had reported that unnamed "friends of government" were "raising a subscription . . . to prolong the existence of the dying Aurora." "Saturday Evening, January 5," *Gazette of the United States,* 5 Jan.1799, 3. The Republican *Aurora* affirmed that $6,000 down was offered, and that there was "the strongest reason to believe that he [Hamilton] did take an active part." "Alexander Hamilton," *Aurora,* 11 Nov.1799, 2.
54. Wharton, 651.
55. "Trial of David Frothingham," *Greenleaf's New York Journal,* 11 Dec.1799, 1; Wharton, 650, 651.
56. Martin, "Reforming Republicanism," 41.
57. "New-York, December 5," *New-York Gazette,* 5 Dec.1799, 2.
58. Wharton, 651; it incorrectly lists the fine as $500.
59. "New-York, December 5," *New-York Gazette,* 5 Dec.1799, 2; accord "Trial of David Frothingham," *Greenleaf's New York Journal,* 14 Dec.1799, 1; Jeffrey L. Pasley, *The Tyranny of Printers: Newspaper Politics in the Early American Republic* (Charlottesville: UVP, 2001), 269; Brigham, *American Newspapers,* 2:1416.
60. Stewart, *Opposition Press,* 477; Smith, *Freedom's Fetters,* 414–415; Brigham, *American Newspapers,* 1:610; Stewart, *Opposition Press,* 617–618; Pasley, "Thomas Greenleaf," 371; "To the Patrons of the Late Argus," *American Citizen* (New York), 12 Mar.1800, 2.
61. The Editors, "To the Public," *American Citizen,* 10 Mar.1800, 2; "To the Patrons of the Late Argus," ibid., 2; *Longworth's American Almanac, New-York Register, and City Directory* (New York: Longworth, 1800), 215.
62. Minutes, pp.184–188 (1–3 Apr.1800), p.203 (8 Apr.1800).

63. Richard Harison to Timothy Pickering (10 Apr.1800), Pickering Papers, 26:77, 78–78A; John Adams to Timothy Pickering (21 Apr.1800), https://founders.archives.gov/documents/Adams/99-02-02-4273; Timothy Pickering to Richard Harison (22 Apr.1800), Pickering Papers, 13:406.
64. "Died," *Spectator* (New York), 4 Jan.1845, 4; "Died," *Columbian* (New York), 17 Nov.1809, 3; "Philadelphia Earthen-ware," *New-York Gazette, and Weekly Mercury,* 24 May 1773, supp. 2; "In Chancery," *American Citizen,* 22 Sept.1804, 4. Book imprints show his location; Brigham, *American Newspapers,* 1:605.
65. There is no biography of Durell.
66. Olaudah Equiano, *The Interesting Narrative of the Life of Olaudah Equiano* (New York: W. Durell, 1791); "New-York, November 7," *Pennsylvania Mercury* (Philadelphia), 17 Nov.1789, 3; "Married," *Weekly Museum* (New York), 26 May 1798, 3.
67. Including all sources cited in this paragraph. E.g., John Moore, *Edward: Various Views of Human Nature* (Mt. Pleasant, NY: W. Durell, 1798).
68. It was reprinted from the *New Windsor Gazette,* a Federalist paper. Stewart, *Opposition Press,* 882. Its Federalist leaning probably explains why its editor was not also prosecuted.
69. Timothy Pickering to Richard Harison (28 June 1798), Pickering Papers, 8:604; "Mount Pleasant, (N.Y.) July 24," *Bee,* 1 Aug.1798, 3 (arrest Tuesday before July 24); "Mount-Pleasant," *Centinel of Freedom,* 7 Aug.1798, 3.
70. Terri D. Halperin, *The Alien and Sedition Acts of 1798: Testing the Constitution* (Baltimore: JHUP, 2016), 79; Smith, *Freedom's Fetters,* 385.
71. "Mount Pleasant, (N.Y.) July 24," *Bee,* 1 Aug.1798, 3 ($2,000 himself and $2,000 from sureties).
72. Original court records for *United States v. William Durell,* and microfilm copies, are in the same National Archives files as for Peck. Useful secondary sources include Smith, *Freedom's Fetters,* 385–390, which reprints James M. Smith, "John Adams Pardons William Durrell," *New York Historical Society Quarterly* 40 (1956): 176–181; Miller, *Crisis,* 223.
73. Minutes, p.131; *DHSC,* 3:327.
74. Warrant (17 July 1799), and Recognizance Bond (19 July 1799) ($2,000 from him and $2,000 from two sureties), in Case Files; Minutes, pp.143–144 (4 Sept.1799).
75. E.g., Smith, *Freedom's Fetters,* 385; William Chlumsky, "Setting Bounds to Passions: Federalist Communication Policy and the Making of the Sedition Act of 1798" (Ph.D. diss., University of Illinois–Chicago, 2015), 297; Jude M. Pfister, "Constitutional Development in the United States Supreme Court During the 1790s" (Ph.D. diss., Drew University, 2007), 144. For loss of the indictment, see Smith, *Freedom's Fetters,* 386–387; Blumberg, *Repressive Jurisprudence,* 132, 133.
76. Indictment, pp.1–2, in Case Files. The indictment was issued on 4 Sept.1799. Minutes, p.144.
77. Minutes, pp.146, 147 (5 Sept.1799).
78. Minutes, pp.191–192 (4 Apr.1800); ibid., p.194 (5 Apr.1800).
79. Petition of William Durrell (5 Apr.1800), in Case Files; reprinted in Minutes, pp.196–197 (5 Apr.1800).

80. Minutes, pp.206–207 (9 Apr.1800).
81. Richard Harison to Timothy Pickering (10 Apr.1800), Pickering Papers, 26:77–78; John Adams to Timothy Pickering (21 Apr.1800), https://founders.archives.gov/documents/Adams/99-02-02-4273; Timothy Pickering to Richard Harison (22 Apr.1800), Pickering Papers, 13:406.
82. Alexander Hamilton to John Jay (7 May 1800), *PAH*, 24:464, 464–465.
83. Ibid., 25:467 n.4.

12. New England Prosecutions

1. Maeva Marcus, ed., *Documentary History of the Supreme Court of the United States, 1789–1800* (New York: ColUP, 1985–2007), 3:494, 496–497 ("*DHSC*") (v.1 was coedited by James R. Perry).
2. For birth and death dates, see "Death of an Old Printer and Editor," *Daily Evening Transcript* (Boston), 5 Aug.1852, 1; C. H. Dummer, "An Unpublished Letter of John Adams," *Magazine of American History* 20 (1888): 304–308.
3. The best biography of Holt is Jeffrey L. Pasley, *The Tyranny of Printers: Newspaper Politics in the Early American Republic* (Charlottesville: UVP, 2001), 132–148. Other available biographical information is cited in this paragraph. For Connecticut's standing order, see Edmund B. Thomas, Jr., "Politics in the Land of Steady Habits: Connecticut's First Political Party System, 1789–1820" (Ph.D. diss., Clark University, 1972), 88–89; Alan V. Briceland, "Ephraim Kirby, Connecticut Jeffersonian, 1757–1804: The Origins of the Jeffersonian Republican Party in Connecticut" (Ph.D. diss., Duke University, 1965), 256.
4. E. Stuart Gregg, Jr., *A Crane's Foot . . . Dobbs and Allied Families* (Hilton Head, SC: Stuart Gregg, 1975), 294, 289–290; Clarence S. Brigham, ed., *History and Bibliography of American Newspapers, 1690–1820* (Worcester, MA: AAS, 1947), 1:52, 585, 614; William Nelson, *Notes Toward a History of the American Newspaper* (New York: Heartman, 1918), 1:l–lii.
5. C. Holt, "Wednesday, November 14, 1798," *Bee*, 14 Nov.1798, 3; [Charles Holt], "To Correspondents," *Bee*, 12 June 1799, 3.
6. Pasley, *Tyranny of Printers*, 134.
7. Donald H. Stewart, *The Opposition Press of the Federalist Period* (Albany: SUNYP, 1969), 869–871; Pasley, *Tyranny of Printers*, 407–408; Stewart, *Opposition Press*, 617.
8. "Hartford, July 29," *Connecticut Courant* (Hartford), 29 July 1799, 3.
9. [Charles Holt], "The Last Number of the New-London Bee," *Bee*, 23 June 1802, 3; Charles Johnson to Thomas Jefferson (26 Apr.1802), Julian P. Boyd et al., eds., *Papers of Thomas Jefferson* (Princeton: PUP, 1950–), 37:341, 341–342 ("*PTJ*"). Nonpayment by subscribers was an additional problem, but not one unique to Republican prints.
10. *Connecticut Gazette* (New London), 11 July 1798, and *Bee*, the same day; Charles Holt to Ephraim Kirby (25 Nov.1798), quoted in Pasley, *Tyranny of Printers*, 137.
11. Original court records for *United States v. Charles Holt*, and microfilm copies, are in National Archives at Boston (Waltham): "Case Files 1790–1911" (U.S.

Circuit Court for District of Connecticut) (NARA at Boston (Waltham), R.G.21.8.2, Box 7, Case 40) ("Case Files"); "Dockett of the Circuit Court of the United States for the District of Connecticut" (ibid.) ("Docket"); "Records of the Circuit Court of the United States of America for the District of Connecticut" (ibid.—NARA calls "Final Records Books, 1790–1911"), pp.242–250 ("Records"); and in *DHSC,* vol.3. Useful secondary sources include James Morton Smith, *Freedom's Fetters: The Alien and Sedition Laws* (Ithaca, NY: CorUP, 1956), 373–394, reprinting James M. Smith, "Political Suppression of Seditious Criticism: A Connecticut Case Study," *The Historian* 18 (1955): 41–56; John C. Miller, *Crisis in Freedom* (Boston: LB, 1952), 126–130; David L. Annis, "Mr. Bushrod Washington" (Ph.D. diss., Notre Dame University, 1974), 90–91.

12. Though published in May, the article was a submitted essay dated 14 April 1799. "For the Bee," *Bee,* 8 May 1799, 2, which was copied in the indictment (with interpretations), which in turn was reprinted just after the trial. Indictment, pp.3–8, in Case Files; "District of Connecticut," *Bee,* 21 May 1800, 1.
13. Mark A. Smith, "Crisis, Unity, and Partisanship: The Road to the Sedition Act" (Ph.D. diss., University of Virginia, 1998), 351; [John Cosens Ogden], "For the Bee," *Bee,* 20 Mar.1799, 2 (see *PTJ,* 31:73n.); "Extract from 'The Prospect Before Us,'" *Bee,* 12 Feb.1800, 1.
14. Alexander Hamilton to George Washington (3 May 1799), Harold C. Syrett et al., eds., *Papers of Alexander Hamilton* (New York: ColUP, 1961–), 23:98, 99 ("*PAH*").
15. E.g., Cato, "Against Standing Armies" and "Further Reasonings against Standing Armies," in Ronald Hamowy, ed., *Cato's Letters* (Indianapolis, IN: LF, 1995), 2:669–687; Michael P. Zuckert, *Natural Rights and the New Republicanism* (Princeton: PUP, 1994), 171–173, 177, 307. For Republican belief, e.g., [James Madison], "Political Reflections," William T. Hutchinson et al., eds., *Papers of James Madison* (Chicago: UChiP, 1962–1991), 17:237, 242 ("*PJM*"); Richard H. Kohn, *Eagle and Sword: The Federalists and the Creation of the Military Establishment* (New York: Free Press, 1975), 224–225, 227.
16. Timothy Pickering to William Vans Murray (9 July 1798), "Timothy Pickering Papers" (Massachusetts Historical Society, Boston, original manuscripts and 69 reels), 9:24, 9:25 ("Pickering Papers"); accord, Timothy Pickering to David Humphreys (16 July 1798), ibid., 9:46; Timothy Pickering to Rufus King (9 July 1798), Charles R. King., ed., *Life and Correspondence of Rufus King* (New York: Putnam's Sons, 1894–1900), 2:361, 362 ("*LRK*").
17. The leading biography of Ellsworth is William R. Casto, *Oliver Ellsworth and the Creation of the Federal Republic* (New York: Second Circuit Committee on History, 1997); see also Michael C. Toth, *Founding Federalist: The Life of Oliver Ellsworth* (Wilmington, DE: Intercollegiate Studies Institute, 2011). His First Amendment thought and Sedition Act cases are described in Wendell Bird, *Press and Speech under Assault* (New York: OUP, 2016), 232–240, 317–320.
18. Docket, p.1:256; *DHSC,* 3:385.
19. He probably used the same charge he read in the spring circuit. Oliver Ellsworth's Charge (C.C.D. S.C. 7 May 1799), *DHSC,* 3:357, 358.

20. Indictment (17 Sept.1799), p.2, in Case Files; reprinted in "District of Connecticut," *Bee,* 21 May 1800, 1; paraphrased in Records, pp.242–249; Indictment, pp.2–3, 4–5.
21. Ibid., pp.5–6, 7–8.
22. Arrest Warrant (20 Sept.1799), in Case Files; Bond (Sept.1799) on jacket of Indictment; accord "New-London," *Bee,* 2 Oct.1799, 2; Affidavit of Charles Holt (24 Sept.1799).
23. Records, p.203; *DHSC,* 3:417.
24. Records, p.203 (14 Apr.1800).
25. "Wednesday, April 15, 1800," *Commercial Advertiser* (New York), 23 Apr.1800, 3.
26. "Communication," *Connecticut Journal* (New Haven), 24 Apr.1800, 3.
27. Docket, p.2:4; Records, p.250; Indictment, p.10 (jacket); Records, p.250; Arrest Warrant (dated 17 Apr.1800, issued 18 Apr.1800).
28. "Wednesday, August 27, 1800," *Bee,* 27 Aug.1800, 3.
29. "Introduction," in Charles J. Hoadly et al., eds., *Public Records of the State of Connecticut* (Hartford: Case, Lockwood, 1894–2007), 10:vii; *PTJ,* 31:522n.; Smith, *Freedom's Fetters,* 376–377.
30. Pope Joan, "Messrs. Hudson & Goodwin," *Connecticut Courant,* 27 May 1799, 2; Smith, *Freedom's Fetters,* 377, citing *Aurora,* 17 Jan.1800.
31. Stevens T. Mason to Thomas Jefferson (11 July 1800), *PTJ,* 32:48, 49; J. Jefferson Looney, ed., *The Papers of Thomas Jefferson: Retirement Series* (Princeton: PUP, 2004–), 3:185n. ("*PTJ-R*").
32. Except for a "supplement" on 21 May. "Wednesday, April 2, 1800," *Bee,* 2 Apr.1800, 3; "Wednesday, August 27, 1800," *Bee,* 27 Aug.1800, 3; Brigham, *American Newspapers,* 1:52; Thomas, "Politics," 95.
33. "An Account of the Trial of Charles Holt," *Bee,* 3 Sept.1800, 3; Charles Holt to James Madison (3 Dec.1801), Robert Brugger et al., eds., *Papers of James Madison: Secretary of State Series* (Charlottesville: UPV, 1987–), 2:292 & n.2 ("*PJM-SS*"); Pasley, *Tyranny of Printers,* 142.
34. "Preface," *Wasp* (Hudson), 7 July 1802, 2; Stephen B. Miller, *Historical Sketches of Hudson* (Hudson, NY: Bryan and Webb, 1862), 65.
35. Milton W. Hamilton, *The Country Printer: New York State, 1785–1830* (New York: ColUP, 1936), 191; People v. Croswell, 3 Johns. Cas. 337 (N.Y. 1804).
36. *PTJ-R,* 3:185n.; Pasley, *Tyranny of Printers,* 146.
37. The best biography of Haswell is in Robert E. Shalhope, *Bennington and the Green Mountain Boys: The Emergence of Liberal Democracy in Vermont, 1760–1850* (Baltimore: JHUP, 1996), 119–126, 204–221. Other useful biographical sources are John Spargo, *Anthony Haswell, Printer-Patriot-Ballader* (Rutland, VT: Tuttle, 1925); Allen Johnson et al., eds., *Dictionary of National Biography* (New York: Scribner, 1928–1936), 8:390; see Barry Levy, "Girls and Boys: Poor Children and the Labor Market in Colonial Massachusetts," *Pennsylvania History* 64 (1997): 287–307, at 304; Linda T. Watkins, ed., *DAR Patriot Index* (Baltimore: Gateway Press, 2003), 2:1237.
38. Brigham, *American Newspapers,* 1:415, 1:408, 2:1074, 2:1072.
39. Spargo, *Haswell,* 243–288, 45–47, 58; Shalhope, *Bennington,* 125.

40. Eugene P. Link, *Democratic-Republican Societies, 1790–1800* (New York: ColUP, 1942), 144; Judah Adelson, "The Vermont Democratic-Republican Societies and the French Revolution," *Vermont History* 32 (1964): 3, 8; Shalhope, *Bennington,* 124, 207–210.
41. Anthony Haswell, *An Oration Delivered at Bennington, Vermont, August 16th, 1799* (Bennington: Haswell, 1799), 8, 14, 15, 16, 26.
42. Reprinted in Spargo, *Haswell,* 233; Shalhope, *Bennington,* 208.
43. Spargo, *Haswell,* 55.
44. Ibid., 53–58; Shalhope, *Bennington,* 208; e.g., Constitutional Federalist, "Look at Federalists!," *Vermont Gazette,* 23 Nov.1798, 2; M. Lyon, "To the Printers," *Vermont Gazette,* 12 Oct.1798, 3.
45. Original court records for *United States v. Anthony Haswell,* and microfilm copies, are in National Archives at Boston (Waltham): "Case Files, 1792–1869" (U.S. Circuit Court for District of Vermont) (NARA at Boston (Waltham), R.G.21.48.2, Box 4, Case 24 (May Term 1800)) ("Case Files"); "Circuit Court Law Records 1795–1803," pp.185–189, ibid. ("Records"); "Circuit Court Docket May Session 1799 & October Session 1799," Cases 24 and 29, ibid. ("Docket 1799"); "Circuit Court Docket May Term 1800, October Term 1800 & May Term 1801," Cases 24 and 29, ibid. ("Docket 1800"); and in Marcus, *DHSC,* vol.3. Haswell's own account is [Anthony Haswell], "A Brief Recital of the Facts, Transpiring in the Federal Reign of Terror," *Green Mountain Farmer* (Bennington, VT), 31 Mar.1813, 1, from which Spargo's account is mostly paraphrased, Spargo, *Haswell,* 59–62, 67–78. Useful secondary sources include Smith, *Freedom's Fetters,* 359–373; Miller, *Crisis,* 123–125. Other secondary sources (because they are based on newspaper accounts) are Trial of Anthony Haswell, Wharton's State Trials 684 (C.C.D. Vt. 1800) (see 684n.) ("Wharton"), which is reprinted in United States v. Haswell, 26 F.Cas. 218 (C.C.D. Vt. 1800) (No.15,324). Haswell wrote that his prosecution was under common law, but the wording of the indictment and the allowance of a defense of truth show it was under the Sedition Act. Anthony Haswell to John Adams (3 June 1800), https://founders.archives.gov/documents/Adams/99-02-02-4392.
46. *DHSC,* 3:388; Records, p.185; Indictment (7 Oct.1799), in Case Files. The Records reprint the indictment and incorrectly date it as 3 October, but the indictment itself and the docket give 7 October. Records, pp.185–188; Docket 1799, Case 24. The two publications were not in the "same issue." Smith, *Freedom's Fetters,* 361.
47. Indictment, p.2.
48. Ibid., pp.2–3. Capitalization and punctuation follow the indictment, not the original article, which is "To the Enemies of Political Persecution," *Vermont Gazette,* 24 Jan.1799, 4 (reprinted in Wharton, 684).
49. Ibid., p.4. This follows the indictment, not the article, which is "British Influence," *Vermont Gazette,* 15 Aug.1799 (partially reprinted in Wharton, 684).
50. Capias (7 Oct.1799), in Case Files; Arrest Warrant (7 Oct.1799), in Docket 1799, Case 24; Habeas Corpus (7 Oct.1799).
51. According to Haswell's later account, [Haswell], "Brief Recital," p.1.

52. [Haswell], "Brief Recital," p.1. Haswell's arguments, similar to those at trial, are summarized in "Extract of a Letter," *Gazette of the United States,* 6 Nov.1799, 3.
53. Records, p.188 (9 Oct. 1799); Bond (10 Oct.1799), in Docket 1799, Case 24.
54. *DHSC,* 3:422; Records, p.189 (5 May 1800); Docket 1800, Case 24 (5 May 1800); see Robert D. Rachlin, "The Sedition Act of 1798 and the East-West Political Divide in Vermont," *Vermont History* 78 (2010):123–150.
55. "Circuit Court," *United States Oracle* (Portsmouth, NH), 24 May 1800, 3; *DHSC,* 3:436; Wharton, 685 (28 Apr.1800).
56. Wharton, 686 (5 May 1800) (Wharton gives "vigour," but it probably was "rigour"); Spargo, *Haswell,* 73.
57. Wharton, 685 (28 Apr.1800); James McHenry to William Darke (18 Dec.1798), quoted in *PTJ,* 31:493n. and *PJM,* 17:382–383 n.4. McHenry apparently arranged for the letter to be printed in a leading Federalist paper. "War Department," *Gazette of the United States,* 27 Feb. 1799, 3.
58. Wharton, 686; [Haswell], "Brief Recital," p.1.
59. [Haswell], "Brief Recital," p.1; Wharton, 686.
60. Mittimus, p.2 (9 May 1800), in Case Files; Records, p.189 (9 May 1800); Docket 1800, Case 24; ibid.; see Indictment jacket; later increased to $62.33, Docket 1800, Case 24.
61. Anthony Haswell to Thomas Jefferson (10 May 1801), *PTJ,* 34:75, 76; [Haswell], "Brief Recital," p.1; Anthony Haswell to Betsey Haswell (9 May 1800), in Spargo, *Haswell,* 79.
62. Anthony Haswell to John Adams (3 June 1800), https://founders.archives.gov/documents/Adams/99-02-02-4392.
63. Ibid.; Spargo, *Haswell,* 45, 236, 58.
64. [No Caption], *Vermont Gazette,* 8 Sept.1798, 3; "Bennington, October 12," *Vermont Gazette,* 12 Oct. 1798, 3; Shalhope, *Bennington,* 119, 208; accord Spargo, *Haswell,* 43, 46, 94.
65. Based on gaps in America's Historical Newspaper database; Anthony Haswell to James Madison (30 Mar.1801), *PJM-SS,* 1:58.
66. Indictment (11 Oct.1799), p.4, in Case Files. There are three copies of this second indictment in the Case Files—one has written at the bottom "Bill not found," and one has the date on the jacket. Two copies are called "Information," and one is "Indictment." That case was numbered Case 29 in the Dockets, while the main prosecution was Case 24. The published oration was Ezekiel Bacon, *An Oration Delivered at Williamstown, on the 4th of July, 1799* (Bennington, VT: Haswell, 1799).
67. Indictment, pp.2–4; ibid., p.4. The grand jury rejection was at the October 1799 term, because the copy with "Bill not found" at the bottom is signed "James Meed, foreman," who was foreman of the grand jury at that term. Records, p.185.
68. Wharton, 687; Shalhope, *Bennington,* 209; Wharton, 686n.
69. "Liberty of the Press," *Vermont Gazette,* 26 July 1798, 4; "Serious Information," *Vermont Gazette,* 11 Aug.1798, 3.

70. Anthony Haswell, "Patriotic Exultation on Lyon's Release" (12 Feb.1799), Spargo, *Haswell,* 233; Smith, *Freedom's Fetters,* 362.
71. Anthony Haswell, "Song Written for the Celebration of the Sixteenth of August, 1799," Spargo, *Haswell,* 209
72. Lucius, "To the Citizens," *Vermont Gazette,* 11 July 1785, 4, reprinting Lucius, "To the Citizens [Part I], *Massachusetts Centinel* (Boston), 18 May 1785, 1, 2.
73. In his next essay. Lucius, "To the Citizens [Part II], *Massachusetts Centinel* (Boston), 28 May 1785, 1.
74. E.g., "Connecticut," *Vermont Gazette,* 27 Mar.1786, 3; "Newbury-Port, Jan.25," *Vermont Gazette,* 27 Feb.1786, 2.
75. Cincinnatus [Arthur Lee], "From the New York Journal," *Vermont Gazette,* 26 Nov.1787, 1, reprinting Cincinnatus, "Number I," *New-York Journal,* 1 Nov.1787, 2; Cato, "Liberty of the Press," *Vermont Gazette,* 17 Aug.1789, 4.
76. Z, "From the Baltimore Daily Advertiser," *Vermont Gazette,* 6 Feb.1795, 1.
77. E.g., "On the Liberty of the Press," *Vermont Gazette,* 16 Apr.1790, 1; "The Poor Man. No.1," *Vermont Gazette,* 2 Nov.1798, 2.
78. E.g., Smith, *Freedom's Fetters,* 185, 229 n.22, 365 n.17; Phillip I. Blumberg, *Repressive Jurisprudence in the Early American Republic* (New York: CUP, 2010), 139–141. The fact of Lyon's second indictment is missing from nearly all writings on the Sedition Act, including Lyon's biography. Aleine Austin, *Matthew Lyon* (University Park: PSUP, 1981), 126–130.
79. Original court records for the second prosecution, *United States v. Matthew Lyon,* and microfilm copies, are in the same National Archives files as Haswell's: "Case Files" (Box 4, Case 30), and "Dockets." See Information (11 Oct.1799), in Case Files. An information was used as the indictment (as shown by the arrest warrant being noted on its back), unlike the common practice where the United States attorney read an information to the grand jury, and then recopied it as an indictment for them to approve as a true bill.
80. Information, pp.1–2.
81. "To the Enemies of Political Persecution," *Vermont Gazette,* 24 Jan.1799, 4.
82. Arrest Warrant (7 Nov.1799), in Case Files; Docket 1800 (Case 30). On the back of the warrant, the deputy marshal wrote that he made diligent search but could not find Lyon as of April 1800.
83. The only brief biographical entries for Judah Spooner are in *National Cyclopaedia of American Biography* (New York: James T. White, 1926), 19:41; Esther Littleford Woodworth-Barnes, *Spooner Saga* (Boston: Newbury Street Press, 1997), 1–12, 343; Thomas Spooner, *Records of William Spooner of Plymouth* (Cincinnati, OH: F.W. Freeman, 1883), 1:150–154. Other useful biographical sources are John J. Duffy et al., eds., *The Vermont Encyclopedia* (Hanover, NH: University Press of New England, 2003), 276; Watkins, *DAR Patriot Index,* 3:2536.
84. Brigham, *American Newspapers,* 1:461, 2:1096, 2:1083–1084 (1795–1798); Isaiah Thomas, *The History of Printing in America,* ed. Marcus McCorison (New York: Weathervane, 1970), 302 (1773), 586–587 (1781); Harold M. Ellis, "Joseph Dennie and His Circle," *Bulletin of the University of Texas,* no.40 (1915): 9–285, at 51–52 (1791–1792); J. Kevin Graffagnino, "'We Have Long

Been Wishing for a Good Printer in This Vicinity:' The State of Vermont," *Vermont History* 47 (1979): 21, 26, 33–35 (1795–1799). For closings, see Woodworth-Barnes, *Spooner Saga,* 9–10.

85. Marcus A. McCorison, *Vermont Imprints, 1778–1820* (Worcester, MA: AAS, 1963), 82–122; e.g., *Spooner's Vermont and New York Almanack* (Bennington, VT: Judah P. Spooner at "Fairhaven," [1799]).
86. Original court records for *United States v. Judah P. Spooner,* and microfilm copies, are in the same National Archives files as Haswell's: "Case Files" (Box 3, Case 26b), and "Docket 1799" (Case 26).
87. Spooner, his brother Alden Spooner, and Dr. Samuel Shaw all appeared at Lyon's trial as witnesses—they received summonses and were paid witness fees, according to a document in Lyon's court file. Bill of Costs (7–10 Oct.1798), p.1, in Lyon's Case Files.
88. Indictment (6 Oct.1798), pp.1, 3, in Case Files.
89. [Joel Barlow], *Copy of a Letter from an American Diplomatic Character in France* ("Constitution-Hill": n.p., 1798); "Col. Lyon's Trial," in Wharton, 340; "Barlow's Letter" (Hartford: Connecticut Courant, 1798); "Barlow's Letter," *Gazette of the United States,* 17 Jan.1799, 2. Vermont's bibliographer treats it as produced by James Lyon in Fairhaven (where Spooner served as his printer). Marcus A. McCorison, *Additions and Corrections to Vermont Imprints, 1778–1820* (Worcester, MA: AAS, 1968), 1:7.
90. Arrest Warrant (4 Oct.1799), in Case Files; Docket 1799, Case 26 (Oct.1799).
91. Docket 1799, Case 26 (Oct.1799); Indictment backing (Oct.1799) (by nolle prosequi).
92. E.g., "Extract of a Letter from a Gentleman in Rutland," *Gazette of the United States,* 6 Nov.1799, 3; "Wednesday, October 16," *Mercantile Advertiser* (New York), 16 Oct.1799, 3. For the case being discharged, e.g., "New-York," *Spectator* (New York), 26 Oct.1799, 2; "New London, (Bee) Oct. 1," *Times and District of Columbia Daily Advertiser* (Alexandria, VA), 13 Oct.1800, 2.
93. The only brief biographical entries for Alden Spooner are in Spooner, *Records of William Spooner,* 157–158. He should not be confused with Judah's son, Alden Spooner (1783–1848), who edited newspapers for Sag Harbor, Long Island, and New York City. Brigham, *American Newspapers,* 2:1486. Other references are in Douglas C. McMurtrie, "The Beginnings of Printing in New Hampshire," *Library* 15 (1934): 340–363.
94. Brigham, *American Newspapers,* 2:1099; Lawrence C. Wroth, *The Colonial Printer* (New York: Dover, 1965), 25–27; Thomas, *History of Printing,* 586–587; Ellis, "Joseph Dennie," 62–63.
95. Smith, *Freedom's Fetters,* 236 n.42; Spooner, *Records of William Spooner,* 157–158. His *Vermont Journal* is excluded from Pasley's list of Republican papers. Pasley, *Tyranny of Printers,* 407.
96. One of Your Constituents, "To Mathew Lyon," *Spooner's Vermont Journal,* 28 May 1798, 2; Austin, *Matthew Lyon,* 108–109; "Communication," *Spooner's Vermont Journal,* 15 Oct.1798, 3.
97. E.g., Marshall Smelser, "The Federalist Period as an Age of Passion," *American Quarterly* 10 (1958): 391–419, at 412.

98. Original court records for *United States v. Alden Spooner,* and microfilm copies, are in the same National Archives files as Judah P. Spooner's.
99. Summons (6 Oct.1798), in Case Files.
100. M. Lyon, "For Spooner's Vermont Journal," *Spooner's Vermont Journal* (Windsor), 31 July 1798, pp.1–2; Indictment (6 Oct. 1798), p.1, in Case Files.
101. Entry "no further prosecute" on jacket of Indictment, in Case Files.
102. Biographical entries for Shaw are Bruce A. Ragsdale, ed., *Biographical Directory of the United States Congress, 1774–2005* (Washington: GPO, 2005), 1897; Prentiss C. Dodge, ed., *Encyclopedia Vermont Biography* (Burlington, VT: Ullery, 1912), 66.
103. Original court records for *United States v. Samuel Shaw,* and microfilm copies, are in the same National Archives files as Haswell's: "Case Files" (Box 3, Case 26a) (May Term 1800), "Records," pp.189–193, and "Docket, Case 26." See *DHSC,* 3:388, 3:422. The case is only mentioned in secondary sources in Julius Goebel, *History of the Supreme Court of the United States* (New York: Macmillan, 1971), 1:638 n.107 (one sentence); Blumberg, *Repressive Jurisprudence,* 138–139.
104. Indictment (10 Oct.1799), p.1, in Case Files; see Docket 1799, Case 26; Indictment, pp.1–2.
105. Arrest Warrant (7 Nov.1799), in Case Files. A notation on the back says he was arrested and posted bond on 6 Feb.1800. For appearance and bond, see Recognizance (6 Feb.1800), in Case Files.
106. Records, p.192; Docket 1800, Case 26.
107. Records, p.193; Docket 1800, Case 26.
108. E.g., "Windsor," *Spooner's Vermont Journal,* 13 May 1800, 3; "Windsor," *Connecticut Courant,* 21 May 1800, 3; "Simon Spunkey's Political Pepperpot," *Farmer's Weekly Museum* (Walpole, MA), 27 Jan. 1800, 4.
109. Costs Taxed (9 May 1800), in Case Files.
110. Summons (21 Apr.1800), in Case Files; Costs Taxed, p.2 (9 May 1800), in Case Files (witness fee to Spooner). For Lyon's financial distress, see Trial of Matthew Lyon, Wharton's State Trials 333, 340–341 (C.C.D. Vt. 1798); "To the Enemies of Political Persecution," *Vermont Gazette,* 24 Jan.1799, 4.
111. James Lyon to Thomas Jefferson (21 June 1801), *PTJ,* 34:404.

13. Prowling the Circuit Stalking Sedition

1. Timothy Pickering to William Paterson (21 Apr.1800), "Timothy Pickering Papers" (MHS, Boston, original manuscripts and 69 reels), 13:405 ("Pickering Papers").
2. James Monroe to Thomas Jefferson (4 Jan.1800), Julian P. Boyd et al., eds., *Papers of Thomas Jefferson* (Princeton: PUP, 1950–), 31:289, 290 ("*PTJ*").
3. The best biography of Cooper is Dumas Malone, *The Public Life of Thomas Cooper 1783–1839* (New Haven: YUP, 1926). Other useful biographical sources are Robert W. T. Martin, *Government by Dissent: Protest, Resistance,*

and Radical Democratic Thought in the Early American Republic (New York: NYUP, 2013), 177–195; Eugene Volokh, "Thomas Cooper, Early Public Intellectual," *New York University Journal of Law & Liberty* 4 (2009): 372–381; H. C. G. Matthew et al., eds., *Oxford Dictionary of National Biography* (Oxford: OUP, 2004), 13:280 ("*ODNB*"); John A. Garraty et al., eds., *American National Biography* (New York: OUP, 1999), 5:462 ("*ANB*").

4. Malone, *Cooper*, 4–7, 27–29, 34–72; *ODNB*, 13:280; *ANB*, 5:462. Twomey called Cooper one of the "British Jacobins." Richard J. Twomey, "Jacobins and Jeffersonians: Anglo-American Radicalism in the United States 1790–1820" (Ph.D. diss., Northern Illinois University, 1974), 1.
5. Thomas Cooper, *A Reply to Mr. Burke's Invective against Mr. Cooper* (Manchester, UK: Falkner, 1792), 8–9; Joseph Barnes to Thomas Jefferson (17 Aug.1793), *PTJ*, 26:715; Michael Durey, "Thomas Paine's Apostles: Radical Emigrés and the Triumph of Jeffersonian Republicanism," *William and Mary Quarterly* 44 (1987): 661–688, at 667; Malone, *Cooper*, 54–55, 69–70.
6. As listed in Early American Imprints database and *ODNB*, 13:280; Malone, *Cooper*, 402–409.
7. He served from 20 April to 29 June 1799, and in the Address acknowledged his authorship of essays. They were published as *Political Essays*. See Jenny Graham, "Revolutionary in Exile: The Emigration of Joseph Priestley to America 1794–1804," *Transactions of the American Philosophical Society, New Series* 85 (1995): 1–213. He was prosecuted for this publication: Thomas Cooper, "Address to the Readers of the Sunbury and Northumberland Gazette" (29 June 1799), reprinted in Thomas Cooper, *Political Essays* (Northumberland, PA: Andrew Kennedy, 1799), 31–39.
8. Cooper, *Political Essays*, 32, 33–37.
9. Thomas Cooper, "Mr. Cooper's Address," *Aurora*, 12 July 1799; Donald H. Stewart, *The Opposition Press of the Federalist Period* (Albany: SUNYP, 1969), 480. For the reprint, see Thomas Cooper, "Mr. Cooper's Address to the Readers of the Sunbury and Northumberland Gazette" (29 June 1799) (handbill); Cooper, *Political Essays*, 31–39. Priestley's role is described in Pickering's letter to Adams of 1 Aug.1799.
10. Charles Hall to Timothy Pickering (26 July 1799), Pickering Papers, 25:58, 59; Timothy Pickering to Charles Hall (1 Aug.1799), ibid., 11:528, 529. Hall's essay, when complete, was published. A True American, "Thomas Cooper, Esq.," *Gazette of the United States* (Philadelphia), 23 Oct.1799, 3.
11. Timothy Pickering to John Adams (1 Aug.1799), Charles Francis Adams, ed., *Works of John Adams* (Boston: LB, 1850–1856), 9:5, 6 ("*WJA*") (also in Pickering Papers, 11:524); John Adams to Timothy Pickering (13 Aug.1799), *WJA*, 9:13, 13–14. Abigail Adams to Thomas B. Adams (4 Sept.1799), L. H. Butterfield et al., eds., *Adams Family Correspondence* (Cambridge, MA: BPHUP, 1963–), 13:549 ("*AFC*"); John Adams to Benjamin Stoddert (31 Mar.1801), *WJA*, 9:582.
12. Though Pickering did not sign the letter, he is credibly suggested as the author by Smith, Freeman, and Hoffer. James Morton Smith, *Freedom's Fetters* (Ithaca, NY: CorUP, 1956), 313n.11; Joanne B. Freeman, "Explaining the Unexplainable: The

Cultural Context of the Sedition Act," in Meg Jacobs et al., eds., *The Democratic Experiment* (Princeton: PUP, 2003), 35; Peter Charles Hoffer, *The Free Press Crisis of 1800: Thomas Cooper's Trial for Seditious Libel* (Lawrence: UPKan, 2011), 74.

13. Thomas Cooper, "To the Public" (Northumberland: George Schusler, 1799) (handbill), in Criminal Case Files, pp.219–220, reprinting "Communication," *Reading Weekly Advertiser,* 26 Oct.1799. Pickering's letter, Cooper's application, and Priestley's recommendation were also reprinted in Joseph Priestley, *Letters to the Inhabitants of Northumberland* (Northumberland: Andrew Kennedy, 1799), 44–46; and were submitted by Pickering to other Federalist newspapers, e.g., "Communications," *Columbian Centinel,* 16 Oct.1799, 2.
14. Thomas Cooper, "To the Public" (2 Nov.1799) (Northumberland, PA: George Schusler, 1799) (handbill), in Criminal Case Files, pp.219–220, reprinted in Thomas Cooper, *An Account of the Trial of Thomas Cooper, of Northumberland; on a Charge of Libel* (Philadelphia: John Bioren, 1800), 6–7.
15. Samuel Chase's Charge (C.C.D. Pa. 12 Apr.1800), Maeva Marcus, ed., *Documentary History of the Supreme Court of the United States, 1789–1800* (New York: ColUP, 1985–2007), 3:408, 413, 412, 414, 416 ("*DHSC*").
16. Original court records for Cooper's prosecution, and microfilm copies, are in National Archives at Philadelphia, in the same place as described in Chapter 8 for the prosecutions of John Fries, in "Criminal Case Files" pp.2:214–243 and "Minutes" pp.347, 359–360, 366. Cooper also prepared a pamphlet account of the trial from a court reporter's notes, Cooper, *Account,* 2, 7–52; which was adapted by Wharton, Trial of Thomas Cooper, Wharton's State Trials 659, 659n. (C.C.D. Pa. 1800) ("Wharton"); and which was reprinted in United States v. Cooper, 4 U.S. (4 Dall.) 341, 25 F.Cas. 626, 631 (C.C.D. Pa. 1800) (Nos.14,861, 14,865).
17. Useful secondary sources on the case include an outstanding book, Peter Charles Hoffer, *The Free Press Crisis of 1800: Thomas Cooper's Trial for Seditious Libel* (Lawrence: UPKan, 2011); and also Smith, *Freedom's Fetters,* 307–333, which reprints James M. Smith, "President John Adams, Thomas Cooper, and Sedition," *Mississippi Valley Historical Review* 42 (1955): 438–465; John C. Miller, *Crisis in Freedom* (Boston: LB, 1952), 201–210; Malone, *Cooper,* 111–149; Stephen B. Presser, "Tale of Two Judges: Richard Peters, Samuel Chase, and the Broken Promise of Federalist Jurisprudence," *Northwestern University Law Review* 73 (1978): 26–111, at 93–98; Stephen B. Presser, *The Original Misunderstanding* (Durham, NC: CAP, 1991), 118–124; Michael Kent Curtis, *Free Speech, "The People's Darling Privilege": Struggles for Freedom of Expression* (Durham, NC: DUP, 2000), 89–93; Forrest K. Lehman, "'Seditious Libel' on Trial, Political Dissent on the Record: 'An Account of the Trial of Thomas Cooper' as Campaign Literature," *Pennsylvania Magazine of History and Biography* 132 (2008): 117–139, at 126–139.
18. Cooper, *Account,* 6–7; Indictment (12 Apr.1800), pp.1–3, in Criminal Case Files, pp.226, 227–229 (the indictment is reprinted in Wharton, 659–662n.; Cooper, *Account,* 7–9). The indictment was approved by the grand jury on Saturday, 12 April, and entered in the court's minutes the next Monday, the 14th.

Minutes, p.347. The quotation is from the handbill, not from the annotated version in the indictment.

19. Indictment, p.1, in Criminal Case Files, p.228; Plea (15 Apr.1800), in Criminal Case Files, pp.215–216, 226.
20. Arrest Warrant (8 Apr.1800), in Criminal Case Files, p.218; Cooper, *Account,* 3 (arrest 9 Apr.), 7 (bond 12–14 Apr.); Wharton, 661–662; Cooper, *Account,* 8–12.
21. *DHSC,* 3:494.
22. "To Tom Cooper," *Philadelphia Gazette,* 27 Mar.1800, 3; Thomas Cooper to William Duane (25 Mar.1800), *American State Papers. Documents, Legislative and Executive, of the Congress of the United States [Miscellaneous Series]* (Washington: Gales and Seaton, 1834), 1:212 *("ASP");* Thomas Cooper to Thomas Jefferson (23 Mar.1800), *PTJ,* 31:451. For Federalist criticism, e.g., "Priestley's Text," *Columbian Centinel* (Boston), 7 Dec.1799, 2; "Priestley's Text," *Philadelphia Gazette,* 13 Dec.1799, 3.
23. Minutes, pp.359–360 (19 Apr.1800); Wharton, 662; Cooper, *Account,* 64; Lehman, "'Seditious Libel,'" 119; *DHSC,* 3:426.
24. "Letter," *Aurora,* 7 May 1800, reprinted in *DHSC,* 3:424, 426; Cooper, *Account,* 64; Wharton, 662, 667; see Cooper, *Account,* 12–15, 21.
25. Requests for Subpoenas (15–16 Apr.1800), in Criminal Case Files, pp.222–225, 235–236; Cooper, *Account,* 14, 8–9; Cooper, *Account,* 14.
26. Wharton, 662–663; Cooper, *Account,* 15–16.
27. Ibid., 663; Cooper, *Account,* 17; Wendell Bird, *Press and Speech under Assault* (New York: OUP, 2016), 31–70.
28. Wharton, 664; Cooper, *Account,* 17–18. It was mostly Federalist character. Smith, *Freedom's Fetters,* 332 n.53.
29. Freeman, "Explaining," 36–38; see Joanne B. Freeman, *Affairs of Honor* (New Haven: YUP, 2001).
30. Wharton, 665–666; Cooper, *Account,* 19.
31. Cooper, *Account,* 22–34; Wharton, 667; Cooper, *Account,* 21–22, 27, 28.
32. Wharton, 668–670; Cooper, *Account,* 35–42.
33. Ibid., 670–671; Cooper, *Account,* 42–43.
34. E.g., Malone, *Cooper,* 129, 130; Hoffer, *Free Press,* 120; Stevens T. Mason to James Madison (23 Apr.1800), William T. Hutchinson et al., eds., *Papers of James Madison* (Chicago: UChiP, 1962–1991), 17:381, 382 ("*PJM*"). Cooper objected to other points in Thomas Cooper to Samuel Chase (1 May 1800), in Cooper, *Account,* 58–64.
35. Wharton, 671–672; Cooper, *Account,* 43–44.
36. Wharton, 672, 675; Cooper, *Account,* 45, 48; John Adams to Oliver Wolcott (17 May 1800), *WJA,* 9:57; Robert Troup to Rufus King (23 Jan.1799), Charles R. King., ed., *Life and Correspondence of Rufus King* (New York: Putnam's, 1894–1900), 2:523, 524 ("*LRK*").
37. Wharton, 673–674, 676; Cooper, *Account,* 46, 49.
38. Ibid., 675, 577; Cooper, *Account,* 48, 50.
39. Ibid., 676, 664; Cooper, *Account,* 49, 17. The final quotation is from Charles Warren, *The Supreme Court in United States History,* rev. ed. (Boston: LB, 1947), 1:281.

40. Wharton, 677–679; Cooper, *Account,* 50–51; *DHSC,* 3:428.
41. Sentence (24 Apr.1800), in Criminal Case Files, pp.230–231, 240; Minutes, p.366; Wharton, 679. The proceeding began 23 April, and sentencing was 24 April 1800. Most studies erroneously date sentencing as 30 April and 1 May 1800. E.g., Wharton, 677; Malone, *Cooper,* 127, 129. For Pickering's secretary, see Joseph Dennie, "Prison Eclogue," *The Porcupine* (London), 1 Nov.1800, 2.
42. Thos. Cooper, "To the Editor," *Aurora,* 16 May 1800; Thos. Cooper, "To the Editor," *Centinel of Freedom* (Newark), 20 May 1800, 3; Bond (8 Oct.1800) and Release (8 Oct.1800), in Criminal Case Files, pp.234, 233; Malone, *Cooper,* 136.
43. Cooper, *Account,* 2.
44. Alexander Hamilton, *Letter from Alexander Hamilton, Concerning the Public Conduct and Character of John Adams, Esq.* (New York: George F. Hopkins, [24 Oct.] 1800), reprinted, Harold C. Syrett et al., eds., *Papers of Alexander Hamilton* (New York: ColUP, 1961–), 25:169 ("*PAH*"); Thomas Cooper, "Precious Letter, from a Very Modest Man," *Gazette of the United States,* 20 Nov.1800, 3.
45. Dumas Malone, "The Threatened Prosecution of Alexander Hamilton Under the Sedition Act," *American Historical Review* 29 (1923): 76–81; William Nelson, ed., "Letters of Dr. Thomas Cooper, 1825–1832," *American Historical Review* 6 (1901): 725–736, at 726; Malone, *Cooper,* 172–173, 374–376.
46. Thomas Cooper, *Tracts Ethical, Theological and Political* (Warrington, UK: W. Eyres, 1789), 176, 177. Cooper's pre-1798 understanding is summarized in Wendell Bird, *The Revolution in Freedoms of Press and Speech* (New York: OUP, forthcoming 2020), Chapter 9.
47. [Thomas Cooper], *Narrative of the Proceedings against Thomas Cooper, Esquire, President Judge* (Lancaster, PA: William Hamilton, 1811); Malone, *Cooper,* 174–210.
48. Dumas Malone, *Jefferson and His Time* (New York: LB, 1970), 6:376–380; Seymour S. Cohen, "Correspondence of Thomas Jefferson and Thomas Cooper: A Previously Unpublished Manuscript of Dumas Malone," *Proceedings of the American Philosophical Society* 147 (2003): 39–64, at 52–63; Thomas Jefferson to Joseph C. Cabell (1 Mar.1819), quoted in Malone, *Jefferson,* 6:368; Malone, *Cooper,* 211–215, 229–242.
49. Steven J. Macias, *Legal Science in the Early Republic: The Origins of American Legal Thought and Education* (Lanham, MD: Lexington Books, 2016), 117–133; Alfred L. Brophy, *University, Court, and Slave: Pro-Slavery Thought in Southern Colleges and the Coming of Civil War* (New York: OUP, 2016), 84; see Manisha Sinha, *The Counter-Revolution of Slavery: Politics and Ideology in Antebellum South Carolina* (Chapel Hill: UNCP, 2000), 54, 25.
50. William H. Freehling, *The Road to Disunion* (New York: OUP, 1990), 1:256–257; Dumas Malone, "Thomas Cooper and the State Rights Movement in South Carolina, 1823–1830," *North Carolina Historical Review* 3 (1926): 184–197, at 184; Malone, *Cooper,* 281–336.

51. [Thomas Cooper], *The Case of Thomas Cooper, M.D., President of the South Carolina College,* 2nd ed. (Columbia, SC: Times and Gazette, 1832); Malone, *Cooper,* 251–280.
52. The best biography of Callender is Michael Durey, *"With the Hammer of Truth": James Thomson Callender and America's Early National Heroes* (Charlottesville: UVP, 1990), 1–17. Other useful biographical sources are Kelsie Jackson, "'Such a Tornado': The Life and Times of James Thomson Callender, Scandalmonger" (Ph.D. diss., University of Houston, 2013); Charles A. Fair, "James Thomson Callender: A Political Journalist in the Beginning of National Politics" (Ph.D. diss., Ohio University, 1978); Eric Burns, *Infamous Scribblers* 375–388, 392–394 (New York: Public Affairs, 2006); *ANB,* 4:235; *ODNB,* 9:550. For his British prosecution, see Proceedings against James Thomson Callender et al., State Trials 23:79 (Scotland High Court of Judiciary 1793); Durey, *Callender,* 44–47; Twomey, "Jacobins," 42; his book was [James T. Callender], *The Political Progress of Britain* (Edinburgh: Robertson and Berry, [1792]).
53. Jeffery A. Smith, *Franklin and Bache: Envisioning the Enlightened Republic* (New York: OUP, 1990), 167; James Tagg, *Benjamin Franklin Bache and the Philadelphia Aurora* (Philadelphia: UPP, 1991), 402; James T. Callender to Thomas Jefferson (26 Oct.1798), *PTJ,* 30:564, 565–566.
54. "Envoy Callender," *Gazette of the United States,* 13 July 1798, 3; James T. Callender to Thomas Jefferson (22 Sept.1798), *PTJ,* 30:521; "Mr. Fenno," *Gazette of the United States,* 9 Aug.1798, 3.
55. Jeffrey L. Pasley, *"The Tyranny of Printers"* (Charlottesville: UVP, 2001), 260; Ammon, "Republican Party," 211; *ANB,* 4:235; *ODNB,* 9:550.
56. Stewart, *Opposition Press,* 10; Presser, *Original Understanding,* 131; John Adams to Abigail Adams (26 Nov.1794), *AFC,* 10:275.
57. James T. Callender, *The History of the United States for the Year 1796* (Philadelphia: Snowden and McCorkle, 1797), 209, 205–206, 209–224; Alexander Hamilton, *Observations on Certain Documents Contained in No. V & VI of "The History of the United States . . ."* (Philadelphia: John Bioren, 1797), reprinted, *PAH,* 21:238–285 (Aug.1797). Callender's original pamphlets may not have survived, so his later book reprinting them is cited. See Jacob K. Cogan, "The Reynolds Affair and the Politics of Character," *Journal of the Early Republic* 16 (1996): 389–417; Durey, *Callender,* 97–102.
58. Timothy Pickering to Thomas Nelson (14 Aug.1799), Pickering Papers, 11:611.
59. Timothy Pickering to William Vans Murray (4 Oct.1799), Pickering Papers, 12:141, 142A; James T. Callender to Thomas Jefferson (18 Dec.1799), *PTJ,* 31:268; "From the Examiner," *Virginia Argus,* 2 Aug.1799, 1.
60. James T. Callender, *The Prospect Before Us. Volume I* (Richmond: "Printed for the Author, and Sold by M. Jones" etc., 1800), [3], 4, 5; Harry Ammon, "The Republican Party in Virginia, 1789 to 1824" (Ph.D. diss., University of Virginia, 1948), 259–267.
61. John B. Walton to Timothy Pickering (23 Dec.1799), Pickering Papers, 25:321, 322, 321A; John B. Walton to Timothy Pickering (19 Jan.1800), Pickering Papers, 26:16.

62. Charles Evans, transcriptionist, *Report of the Trial of the Hon. Samuel Chase* (Baltimore: Butler and Keatings, 1805), 63, 43; *PTJ,* 31:589n.
63. Reprinted in "Alexandria, June 5," *Times* (Alexandria, VA), 5 June 1800, 3; Wharton, 718n.; Evans, *Report,* 64, 43.
64. Original court records for Callender's prosecution, and microfilm copies, are in Library of Virginia (U.S. Circuit Court, Virginia District, Ended Cases-Restored, 1790–1882 (Series I), Box 17 and Microfilm Roll 669) ("Ended Cases") (not at National Archives); and *DHSC,* vol.3. Newspaper reports of the case by David Robertson, "which he took down merely for his own amusement," were collected in David Robertson, *Trial of James Thompson Callender, for Sedition* (n.p., [1804]), at 2, which was reprinted in part in Evans, *Report,* 61. Gaps in Robertson's notes were filled from other newspaper accounts, Wharton, 688n., and were published as Trial of James Thompson Callender, Wharton 688 (C.C.D. Va.1800), which was reprinted in United States v. Callender, 25 F.Cas. 239 (C.C.D. Va.1800) (No. 14,709). Useful secondary sources include Smith, *Freedom's Fetters,* 334–358, reprinting James M. Smith, "Sedition in the Old Dominion: James T. Callender and The Prospect Before Us," *Journal of Southern History* 20 (1954): 157–182; Miller, *Crisis,* 210–220; Presser, *Original Misunderstanding,* 131–142; Durey, *Callender,* 129–135; Peter G. Fish, *Federal Justice in the Mid-Atlantic South: United States Courts from Maryland to the Carolinas, 1789–1835* (Durham, NC: CAP, 2015), 91–95. For the court dates, see *DHSC,* 3:435.
65. For the Federalist composition of many grand juries, see Brent Tarter and Wythe Holt, "The Apparent Political Selection of Federal Grand Juries in Virginia, 1789–1809," *American Journal of Legal History* 49 (2007): 257–283; James Monroe to James Madison (4 June 1800), *PJM,* 17:391 (see full letter at https://founders.archives.gov/documents/Madison/02-08-02-0577). For the presentment, see Presentment of the Grand Jury (24 May 1800), *DHSC,* 3:435; Evans, *Report,* 64. The indictment date is given as 26 May on a loose sheet in Ended Cases.
66. Wharton, 688 (slightly different from indictment and book); Indictment (26 May 1800), pp.1–2, in Ended Cases; quoting Callender, *Prospect,* 1:80. The indictment is printed in Evans, *Report,* appendix 48–53.
67. Wharton, 688–690; Indictment, pp.2–16, 1, 9.
68. Capias (24 May 1800), in Ended Cases; James Monroe to Thomas Jefferson (25 May 1800), *PTJ,* 31:588, 589; Summons (23–29 May 1800), in Ended Cases.
69. Affidavit of Callender (28 May 1800), in Ended Cases; Wharton, 690–691. The two were Sen. Stevens Thomson Mason and former Rep. William B. Giles; Wharton, 690–691; Evans, *Report,* 64.
70. Evans, *Report,* 44. The marshal denied the latter statement. Ibid., 68; Samuel Chase to Meriwether Jones (26 May 1800), *DHSC,* 3:437 (printed in *Aurora* the same day). Jones had been summoned two days earlier to testify to the grand jury and would be summoned two days later to testify at trial.
71. Wharton, 692, 694–695.
72. Ibid., 692–693, 695, 696, 697.

73. Ibid., 697; Evans, *Report,* 66.
74. Wharton, 698; Evans, *Report,* 85. Nelson shifted the burden repeatedly. Evans, *Report,* 83–88. For the prosecution's case, see Wharton, 698–700, 705. There was also a long argument on whether the book could be introduced in evidence. Ibid., 700–705.
75. Ibid., 706, 707.
76. Ibid., 707.
77. Ibid., 708. Additional witnesses were planned. Durey, *Callender,* 131–132.
78. Wharton, 709–710, 711–712.
79. Ibid., 717; the opinion is pp.712–718. See Kathryn Preyer, "*United States v. Callender:* Judge and Jury in a Republican Society," in Maeva Marcus, ed., *Origins of the Federal Judiciary* (New York: OUP, 1992), 173–195.
80. E.g., James Madison to James Monroe (4 June 1800), https://founders.archives.gov/documents/Madison/02-08-02-0577; "Richmond (Examiner) June 6," *Times* (Alexandria), 12 June 1800, 2. Also, when the jury gave its verdict, Chase reportedly said "it was '*pleasing to him,* because it showed that the laws of the U. States could be enforced in Virginia, the *principal object of this prosecution*'"; and that "he did not think there was so bad a man in the United States" as Callender. "Richmond (Examiner) June 6," *Times* (Alexandria), 12 June 1800, 2.
81. Sentence (4 June 1800), in Ended Cases; Wharton, 718; James Monroe to James Madison (4 June 1800), https://founders.archives.gov/documents/Madison/02-08-02-0577.
82. "Richmond, June 6," *Federal Gazette* (Baltimore), 11 June 1800, 2; accord "James Thompson Callender," *Daily Advertiser* (New York), 14 June 1800, 2.
83. Pardon for James Thomson Callender (16 Mar.1801), *PTJ,* 33:309; James Monroe to James Madison (17 May 1801), Preston, *Monroe,* 4:507; John Adams to John Marshall (7 Aug.1800), *WJA,* 9:71.
84. James Madison to James Monroe (23 May 1800), *PJM,* 17:389, 390; James Monroe to James Madison (15 May 1800), ibid., 17:388.
85. Smith, *Freedom's Fetters,* 357 (citing *Aurora,* 8 Aug.1800); "From the Aurora," *Centinel of Freedom* (Newark), 24 June 1800, 2; "A Card to Judge Chase," *Times* (Alexandria), 25 June 1800, 3; "Richmond June 6," *Herald of Liberty* (Washington, PA), 23 June 1800, 2.
86. James T. Callender to Thomas Jefferson (23 Feb.1801), *PTJ,* 33:46 (in two parts); James T. Callender to James Madison (23 Jan.1801), *PJM,* 17:457; Thomas Leiper to Thomas Jefferson (8 Mar.1801), *PTJ,* 33:215; Thomas Jefferson to James Madison (29 May 1801), *PTJ,* 34:205; James Monroe to Thomas Jefferson (1 June 1801), ibid., 34:229; accord Malone, *Jefferson,* 4:207–212.
87. Thomas Jefferson to James Monroe (29 May 1801), *PTJ,* 34:205; James T. Callender to Thomas Jefferson (12 Apr.1801), *PTJ,* 33:573; James T. Callender to James Madison (27 Apr.1801), Robert Brugger et al., eds., *Papers of James Madison: Secretary of State Series* (Charlottesville: UPV, 1987–), 1:117 ("*PJM-SS*"); James T. Callender to James Madison (7 May 1801), ibid., 1:144; James Monroe to James Madison (14 June 1801), ibid., 1:314 (paid by private donations including Jefferson).

88. Clarence S. Brigham, ed., *History and Bibliography of American Newspapers, 1690–1820* (Worcester, MA: AAS, 1947), 2:1141; *PTJ*, 38:37n. Columns reprinted as James T. Callender, *The Conduct of Meriwether Jones* (Richmond: H. Pace, 1802); Ammon, "Republican Party," 265–266; Steven H. Hochman, "On the Liberty of the Press in Virginia: From Essay to Bludgeon, 1798–1803," *Virginia Magazine of History and Biography* 84 (1976): 431–445, at 435–444; Charles A. Jellison, "That Scoundrel Callender," *Virginia Magazine of History and Biography* 67 (1959): 295–306, at 302–305.
89. James T. Callender, "Letter VII," *Recorder* (Richmond), 5 July 1802, reprinted in *PTJ*, 38:37n. Thomas Jefferson to James Monroe (15 July 1802), *PTJ*, 38:72.
90. They are listed in *PTJ*, 38:72, 73–74n.; see Worthington C. Ford, "Thomas Jefferson and James Thomson Callender," *New England Historical and Genealogical Register* 50 (1896): 321–333, 445–458; ibid., 51:19–25, 51:153–158, 51:323–328; 51:427; 51:509, reprinted as Worthington C. Ford, *Thomas Jefferson and James Thomson Callender* (Brooklyn, NY: Historical Print, 1897); Malone, *Jefferson*, 3:469–472; Thomas Jefferson to Nathaniel Macon (17 July 1802), *PTJ*, 38:89, 90.
91. James T. Callender, "The President, Again," *Recorder*, 1 Sept.1802, quoted in *PTJ*, 38:323, 323–324n., and in Durey, *Callender*, 158; Annette Gordon-Reed, *Thomas Jefferson and Sally Hemings: An American Controversy* (Charlottesville: UPV, 1997).
92. Thomas Jefferson to Robert Richardson (20 Apr.1824), quoted in Malone, *Jefferson*, 3:470.
93. "Popular Societies. From a Correspondent," *Aurora*, 2 Mar.1795, 2, quoted in Durey, *Callender*, 69.
94. Cyrus Griffin to Thomas Jefferson (15 July 1802), *PTJ*, 38:68.
95. Articles of Impeachment (12 Mar.1804), in Evans, *Report*, appendix 3–6; Adam A. Perlin, "The Impeachment of Samuel Chase," *Rutgers Law Review* 62 (2010): 725, 742–782; Evans, *Report*, 5.
96. Evans, *Report*, 266 (1 Mar.1805); Samuel Chase to Rufus King (13 Mar.1805), *LRK*, 4:444, 445.
97. John Quincy Adams to John Adams (8 Mar.1805), Worthington C. Ford, ed., *Writings of John Quincy Adams* (New York: Macmillan, 1913–1917), 3:106, 108; Peter Charles Hoffer and N. E. H. Hull, *Impeachment in America, 1635–1805* (New Haven: YUP, 1984), 228–255; see George L. Haskins and Herbert A. Johnson, *History of the Supreme Court: Foundations of Power* (New York: Macmillan, 1981), 205–245.
98. Brigham, *American Newspapers*, 1:296, 1:334, 1:223–224. Brigham is mistaken that Martin worked in North Carolina 1792–1793.
99. There is no biography of Martin. See *Boston Directory* (Boston: Manning and Loring, 1796), 72 (the younger Alexander Martin is called "jun."); "Died," *Columbian* (New York), 9 Oct.1810, 3; "Died," *American Citizen* (New York), 11 Oct.1810, 3.
100. "To the Public," *American* (Baltimore, 18 May 1799, 1; Roxanne M. Zimmer, "The Urban Daily Press: Baltimore, 1797–1816" (Ph.D. diss., University of

Iowa, 1982), 104–115; A. Rachel Minick, "A History of Printing in Maryland, 1791–1800" (Baltimore: Enoch Pratt Free Library, 1949), 64–73 (Maryland State Archives v.439); Clayton C. Hall, ed., *Baltimore: Its History and Its People* (New York: Lewis Historical, 1912), 702.

101. Timothy Pickering to Zeb Hollingsworth (12 Aug. 1799), Pickering Papers, 11:603.

102. *DHSC,* 3:424; "Alexandria, June 5," *Times* (Alexandria, VA), 5 June 1800, 3; "Baltimore, June 4," *City Gazette* (Charleston), 20 June 1800, 2.

103. "A Bone to Gnaw," *American* (Baltimore), 27 Aug.1799, summarized in *DHSC,* 3:439n.2; "Alexandria, June 5," *Times* (Alexandria, VA), 5 June 1800, 3. The original court records do not mention Martin. "Minutes of the U.S. Circuit Court for the District of Maryland, 1790–1911" (National Archives at Philadelphia, R.G.21.22.2, Microfilm M931, roll 1); "Criminal Case Files of the U.S. Circuit Court for the District of Maryland, 1795–1860" (ibid., Microfilm M1010, roll 1).

104. Samuel Chase to James McHenry (12 May 1800), Bernard C. Steiner, ed., *Life and Correspondence of James McHenry* (Cleveland, OH: Burrows, 1907), 457; *Aurora,* 9 Aug.1800, reprinted in *DHSC,* 1:895.

105. The best biography of Wilson is Pasley, *Tyranny of Printers,* 320–329. Other useful biographical sources are Carl E. Prince, "James J. Wilson: Party Leader, 1801–1824," *Proceedings of the New Jersey Historical Society* 83 (1965): 24–39; Carl E. Prince, *New Jersey's Jeffersonian Republicans* (Chapel Hill: UNCP, 1964), 90–91; *Biographical Directory of the United States Congress, 1774–2005* (Washington: GPO, 2005), 2180. Older less useful sources include *Appleton's Cyclopaedia of American Biography* (New York: Appleton, 1889), 6:553.

106. Brigham, *American Newspapers,* 1:84, 78.

107. Col. Allan McLane to Timothy Pickering (8 Feb.1800), Pickering Papers, 26:26. Ogden's articles are reprinted in Evans, *Report,* appendix 58–60. For typical articles, see Anti-Federalist, "For the Mirror," *Mirror of the Times* (Wilmington, DE), 5 Apr.1800, 3.

108. *DHSC,* 3:442. The original court records do not mention Wilson. "Criminal Dockets, 1795–1898" (National Archives at Philadelphia, R.G.21.9.2); "Judgment Index, 1790–1912 (ibid.). For Chase's pressing, see "Letter," *Aurora,* 28 June 1800, in *DHSC,* 3:442; reprinted "Extract of a Letter to the Editor, from New-Castle County, June 28th, 1800," *Herald of Liberty,* 21 July 1800, 2.

109. *Mirror of the Times,* 4 July 1800, in *DHSC,* 3:445–446; reprinted in "From the Wilmington Mirror," *Carlisle Gazette,* 23 July 1800, 3; "Remember Judge Chase," *Centinel of Freedom* (Newark), 29 July 1800, 3. Distant Federalist papers rejected the "viperous" *Mirror*'s report. *Daily Advertiser* (New York), 9 July 1800, in *DHSC,* 3:446.

110. Ibid.; *Aurora,* 17 July 1800, reprinted in *DHSC,* 3:447.

111. Evans, *Report,* 60, 100, 96–97, 98; see John A. Munroe, *Federalist Delaware, 1775–1815* (New Brunswick, NJ: RUP, 1954), 207–208.

112. "Spirit of the Times," *Mirror of the Times,* 23 July 1800, 2.

113. Timothy Pickering to Rufus King (28 May 1800), *LRK,* 3:248; Alexander Hamilton to James McHenry (6 June 1800), *PAH,* 24:573. After being fired, Pickering was much more censorious. E.g., Timothy Pickering to George Cabot (16 June 1800), Henry Cabot Lodge, ed., *Life and Letters of George Cabot,* 2nd ed. (Boston: LB, 1878), 275, 277.

114. [No Caption], *Constitutional Telegraphe* (Boston), 23 Nov.1799, 3; Stewart, *Opposition Press,* 483; Alexander Hamilton, *Letter from Alexander Hamilton, Concerning the Public Conduct and Character of John Adams, Esq.* (New York: George F. Hopkins, 1800), 4, 7, reprinted *PAH,* 25:186, 186, 190 (24 Oct.1800).

115. Oliver Wolcott to Alexander Hamilton (3 Sept.1800), *PAH,* 25:104, 108; Oliver Wolcott to George Cabot (18 June 1800), Lodge, *Cabot,* 278, 279; James McHenry to John McHenry (20 May 1800), George Gibbs, *Memoirs of the Administrations of Washington and John Adams Edited from the Papers of Oliver Wolcott* (New York: Van Norden, 1846), 2:346, 347; Benjamin Goodhue to Oliver Wolcott (10 July 1800), ibid., 2:379.

116. Fisher Ames to Oliver Wolcott (12 June 1800), ibid., 2:367, 368; George Cabot to Oliver Wolcott (14 June 1800), ibid., 2:370; Thomas Fitzsimmons to Oliver Wolcott (24 July 1800), ibid., 2:388; Charles Cotesworth Pinckney to James McHenry (10 June 1800), Steiner, *McHenry,* 459, 460.

117. For a more detailed discussion of these cases see Bird, *Press and Speech under Assault,* 372–373, 384–388; Wendell Bird, “New Light on the Sedition Act of 1798: The Missing Half of the Prosecutions,” *Law and History Review* 34 (2016): 541–614, at 590–591, 603–607.

118. *PTJ,* 32:269–270n.; *Appleton’s Cyclopaedia,* 6:268; James Delbourgo, “Electricity, Experiment and Enlightenment in Eighteenth-Century North America” (Ph.D. diss., Columbia University, 2003), 334–336.

119. Dr. John Vaughan to Thomas Jefferson (10 Jan.1801), *PTJ,* 32:441, 442; see also Dr. John Vaughan to Thomas Jefferson (10 Oct.1801), *PTJ,* 35:427; J. Thomas Scharf, *History of Delaware, 1609–1888* (Port Washington, NY: Kennikat Press, 1888), 1:493; *PTJ,* 32:269–270n.; John Dickinson to Thomas Jefferson (25 May 1801), *PTJ,* 34:179.

120. E.g., [Masthead], *Delaware Gazette* (Wilmington), 27 July 1799, 1; Brigham, *American Newspapers,* 1:81; Munroe, *Federalist Delaware,* 184.

121. *PJM,* 17:396 n.3; J. Thomas Scharf, *History of Western Maryland* (Baltimore: Regional Publishing, 1968), 487; T. C. Williams, *History of Frederick County Maryland* (Frederick, MD: Titsworth, 1910), 2:1398; Howard A. Kelly et al., eds., *Dictionary of American Medical Biography* (New York: Appleton, 1928), 1236.

122. Charles Peale Polk to James Madison (20 June 1800), *PJM,* 17:394, 395; “George-Town, June 24,” *Centinel of Liberty* (Georgetown, D.C.), 24 June 1800, 3; Scharf, *Western Maryland,* 535.

123. Brigham, *American Newspapers,* 2:1156; Pasley, *Tyranny of Printers,* 409.

124. “From the Examiner,” *Examiner* (Richmond), 8 Mar.1800, 1.

125. “Active Federalism,” *Philadelphia Gazette,* 30 Jan.1799, 3; “Thursday, January 31, 1799,” *Aurora,* 31 Jan.1799, 3.

126. "Boston," *Russell's Gazette* (Boston), 24 Jan.1799, 3 (original all italics); "Massachusetts Legislature," *Massachusetts Mercury* (Boston), 22 Feb.1799, 2.
127. Prince, *New Jersey's Jeffersonian Republicans,* 38. For the articles, e.g., "Newark, August 28," *Centinel of Freedom,* 28 Aug.1798, 3.
128. E.g., "Newark, August 21. Memorandum," *Centinel of Freedom,* 21 Aug.1798, 3; "Newark, August 21," *Centinel of Freedom,* 21 Aug.1798, 2; A Militia Man, "To Richard Howell, Governor," *Centinel of Freedom,* 14 Aug.1798, 2.
129. "Newark, August 28," *Centinel of Freedom,* 28 Aug.1798, 3 (mentions both charges); "New-York, July 20," *Centinel of Freedom,* 31 July 1798, 2; "Newark, September 25," *Centinel of Freedom,* 25 Sept.1798, 3.
130. "Newark, April 16," *Centinel of Freedom,* 16 Apr.1799, 3; "To the Public," *Centinel of Freedom,* 1 Oct.1799, 3; Brigham, *American Newspapers,* 1:509.
131. Oliver Wolcott, Jr. to Alexander Hamilton (3 Sept.1800), *PAH,* 25:104, 108.

14. French Intriguers and Hordes of Wild Irishmen

1. An Act Concerning Aliens [Friends] §1 (25 June 1798), Statutes, 1:570.
2. "To the Citizens of Baltimore" (2 May 1798), Charles Francis Adams, ed., *Works of John Adams* (Boston: LB, 1850–1856), 9:186, 186–187 ("*WJA*"); "To the Grand Jury of the County of Dutchess" (22 Sept.1798), ibid., 9:223.
3. Kenneth Roberts and Anna M. Roberts, eds. and trans., *Moreau de St. Méry's American Journey [1793–1798]* (Garden City, NY: Doubleday, 1947), 253; Julian P. Boyd et al., eds., *Papers of Thomas Jefferson* (Princeton: PUP, 1950–), 30:361n. ("*PTJ*").
4. Timothy Pickering to James Hendricks (28 Sept.1798), in Octavius Pickering and Charles W. Upham, *The Life of Timothy Pickering* (Boston: LB, 1867–1873), 3:381, 382.
5. Alexander Hamilton to Timothy Pickering (7 June 1798), Harold C. Syrett et al., eds., *Papers of Alexander Hamilton* (New York: ColUP, 1961–), 21:494, 495 ("*PAH*"); Fisher Ames to Christopher Gore (18 Dec.1798), Seth Ames, ed., *Works of Fisher Ames* (Boston: LB, 1854), 1:245, 247–248.
6. Richard Peters to Timothy Pickering (30 Aug.1798), "Timothy Pickering Papers" (Massachusetts Historical Society, Boston, manuscripts and 69 reels), 23:96 ("Pickering Papers"), quoted in Whitman H. Ridgway, "Fries in the Federalist Imagination: A Crisis of Republican Society," *Pennsylvania History* 67 (2000): 141–160, at 142.
7. Rufus King to Alexander Hamilton (2 July 1798), *PAH,* 21:524, 525; Rufus King to William Vans Murray (31 Mar.1798), Charles R. King., ed., *Life and Correspondence of Rufus King* (New York: Putnam's Sons, 1894–1900), 2:294 ("*LRK*").
8. Jeffrey L. Pasley, *The Tyranny of Printers: Newspaper Politics in the Early American Republic* (Charlottesville: UPV, 2001), 118; Jeffrey L. Pasley, "Thomas Greenleaf: Printers and the Struggle for Democratic Politics and Freedom of the Press," in Alfred F. Young, Gary B. Nash and Ray Raphael, eds.,

Revolutionary Founders: Rebels, Radicals, and Reformers in the Making of the Nation (New York: Knopf, 2011), 355–373, at 366.

9. Richard J. Twomey, "Jacobins and Jeffersonians: Anglo-American Radical Ideology, 1790–1810," in Margaret Jacob and James Jacob, eds., *The Origins of Anglo-American Radicalism* (Boston: Allen and Unwin, 1984), 284–299, at 286; Pasley, *Tyranny of Printers,* 357; see Philip M. Marsh, "Freneau and His Circle," *Pennsylvania Magazine of History and Biography* 63 (1939): 37–59.
10. Abigail Adams to John Quincy Adams (14 July 1797), L. H. Butterfield et al., eds., *Adams Family Correspondence* (Cambridge, MA: BKHUP, 1963–), 12:203 ("*AFC*").
11. Richard J. Twomey, *Jacobins and Jeffersonians: Anglo-American Radicalism in the United States 1790–1820* (New York: Garland, 1989), reprinting Richard J. Twomey, "Jacobins and Jeffersonians: Anglo-American Radicalism in the United States 1790–1820" (Ph.D. diss., Northern Illinois University, 1974); Seth Cotlar, *Tom Paine's America: The Rise and Fall of Transatlantic Radicalism in the Early Republic* (Charlottesville: UVP, 2011).
12. Clive Emsley, "Repression, 'Terror' and the Rule of Law in England During the Decade of the French Revolution," *English Historical Review* 100 (1985): 801–825; Clive Emsley, "An Aspect of 'Pitt's Terror': Prosecutions for Sedition During the 1790s," *Social History* 6 (1981): 155.
13. Samuel E. Morison, ed., *The Life and Letters of Harrison Gray Otis, 1765–1848* (Boston: Houghton Mifflin, 1969), 108. The slur, which Otis repeated in Congress, drew Republican defenses such as John D. Burk, "Citizen Burk's Letter to Harrison G. O.," *Greenleaf's New York Journal & Patriotic Register,* 9 Sept.1797, 2. Accord Edward C. Carter II, "A 'Wild Irishman' under Every Federalist's Bed: Naturalization in Philadelphia, 1789–1806," *Pennsylvania Magazine of History and Biography* 94 (1970): 331–346, at 334; Richard D. Brown, *Self-Evident Truths: Contesting Equal Rights from the Revolution to the Civil War* (New Haven: YUP, 2017), 62–104. For Tracy, see Uriah Tracy to Oliver Wolcott, Jr. (7 Aug.1800), George Gibbs, ed., *Memoirs of the Administrations of Washington and John Adams Edited from the Papers of Oliver Wolcott* (New York: Norden, 1846), 2:399; accord "For the Salem Gazette," *Salem Gazette,* 2 Mar.1798, 1.
14. Kunal M. Parker, *Making Foreigners: Immigration and Citizenship Law in America, 1600–2000* (New York: CUP, 2015); Douglas M. Bradburn, "'True Americans' and 'Hordes of Foreigners': Nationalism, Ethnicity and the Problem of Citizenship in the United States, 1789–1800," *Historical Reflections/Réflexions Historiques* 29 (2003): 19–41, at 32–33.
15. Alexander Hamilton to Theodore Sedgwick (2 Feb.1799), *PAH,* 22:452; Timothy Pickering Response to "Address from the Freeholders of Prince Edward County" (29 Sept.1798), Pickering and Upham, *Timothy Pickering,* 3:471, 475; see Marie-Jeanne Rossignol, *The Nationalist Ferment: The Origins of U.S. Foreign Policy, 1789–1812* (Columbus: OSUP, 2004), 25–44.
16. Thomas Jefferson to Thomas Mann Randolph (9 May 1798), *PTJ,* 30:341; Thomas Jefferson to James Madison (7 June 1798), William T. Hutchinson et al., eds., *Papers of James Madison* (Chicago: UChiP, 1962–1991), 17:143

("*PJM*"); James Madison to Thomas Jefferson (20 May 1798), *PJM*, 17:133, 133–134.

17. Howard M. Jones, *America and French Culture 1750–1848* (Chapel Hill: UNCP, 1927), 134, 138–146; Doina P. Harsanyi, *Lessons from America: Liberal French Nobles in Exile, 1793–1798* (University Park: PSUP, 2010); T. Wood Clarke, *Émigrés in the Wilderness* (Port Washington, NY: Friedman, 1967).
18. Frances S. Childs, *French Refugee Life in the United States, 1790–1800* (Baltimore: JHUP, 1940), 9–10, 23–61; e.g., Catherine A. Hébert, "The French Element in Pennsylvania in the 1790s: The Francophone Immigrants' Impact," *Pennsylvania Magazine of History and Biography* 108 (1984): 451–469; John L. Earl, "Talleyrand in Philadelphia, 1794–1796," *Pennsylvania Magazine of History and Biography* 91 (1967): 282–298; Childs, *French Refugee Life*, 185; *PAH*, 21:410 n.3, 21:429–431 n.28.
19. Thomas Mifflin to John Adams (27 June 1798), *American State Papers. Documents, Legislative and Executive, of the Congress of the United States [Foreign Relations Series]* (Washington: Gales and Seaton, 1832), 2:201 ("*ASP*"), enclosing David Pinkerton to Capt. William Jones (26 June 1798), ibid., 2:201; accord James A. Dun, *Dangerous Neighbors: Making the Haitian Revolution in Early America* (Philadelphia: UPP, 2016), 143–178; John Davies, "Class, Culture, and Color: Black Saint-Dominguan Refugees and African-American Communities in the Early Republic" (Ph.D. diss., University of Delaware, 2008), 44–54.
20. Laurent Dubois, *Avengers of the New World: The Story of the Haitian Revolution* (Cambridge, MA: BKHUP, 2004); David P. Geggus, *The World of the Haitian Revolution* (Bloomington: IUP, 2009); Alan Taylor, *American Revolutions: A Continental History, 1750–1804* (New York: Norton, 2016), 417–421; Abigail Adams to Cotton Tufts (29 June 1798), *AFC*, 13:165, 166.
21. *Debates and Proceedings in the Congress of the United States . . . Annals of the Congress of the United States* (Washington: Gales and Seaton, 1834–1856), 8:1577 (3 May 1798) ("*Annals*"); Francis Dana to John Adams (3 Nov.1798), https://founders.archives.gov/documents/Adams/99-02-02-3195; Jacob Read to Timothy Pickering (17 Oct.1798), Pickering Papers, 23:243.
22. Thomas Jefferson to James Madison (3 May 1798), *PJM*, 17:123, 124; Timothy Pickering to William Vans Murray (14 July 1798), Pickering Papers, 9:38.
23. Childs, *French Refugee Life*, 189, 191; Timothy Pickering to J. A. B. Rozier (16 July 1798), Pickering Papers, 9:53 (permit for *William*); Timothy Pickering to Mr. Rabainne (31 July 1798), ibid., 9:126 (for *Ranger*). For Pickering and permits, e.g., Timothy Pickering to Otway Byrd (23 July 1798), Pickering Papers, 9:81 (permits); Timothy Pickering to Robert Duvall (23 Nov.1798), ibid., 9:647.
24. Charles Lee to John Adams (1 Nov.1798), http://founders.archives.gov/documents/Adams/99-02-02-3190.
25. James M. Smith, *Freedom's Fetters: The Alien and Sedition Laws and American Civil Liberties* (Ithaca, NY: CorUP, 1956), 159 (though not citing Charles Lee), reprinting James M. Smith, "The Enforcement of the Alien Friends Act of 1798," *Mississippi Valley Historical Review* 41 (1954): 85–104.

26. Victor Collot to George Washington (8 July 1793), W. W. Abbot et al., eds., *Papers of George Washington: Presidential Series* (Charlottesville: UPV, 1987–), 13:185 and n.1; J. Balteau et al., *Dictionnaire de Biographie Francaise* (Paris: Letouzey, 1933–), 9:307.
27. Durand Echeverria, trans., "General Collot's Plan for a Reconnaissance of the Ohio and Mississippi Valleys, 1796," *William and Mary Quarterly* 9 (1952): 512–520, at 517, 520; accord George W. Kyte, "A Spy on the Western Waters: The Military Intelligence Mission of General Collot in 1796," *Mississippi Valley Historical Review* 34 (1947): 427–442. For Collot's activities, see Michael F. Conlin, "The American Mission of Citizen Pierre-Auguste Adet: Revolutionary Chemistry and Diplomacy in the Early Republic," *Pennsylvania Magazine of History and Biography* 124 (2000): 489–520, at 502–503; Victor Collot, *A Journey in North America,* trans. J. Christian Bay (Firenze: Lange, 1924). Adet informed France's Ministry of Foreign Relations about Collot's expedition. P. A. Adet to Ministre des Rélations Exterieures (21 June 1796), Frederick J. Turner, ed., "Correspondence of the French Ministers to the United States, 1791–1797," in *Annual Report of the American Historical Association for 1903* (Washington: GPO, 1904), 2:928, 929–930.
28. Oliver Wolcott, Jr. to George Washington (19 May 1796), http://founders.archives.gov/documents/Washington/99-01-02-00530; James McHenry to Arthur St. Clair (May 1796), William H. Smith, *The St. Clair Papers* (Cincinnati, OH: Robert Clarke, 1882), 395; accord Frederick J. Turner, "The Policy of France Toward the Mississippi Valley in the Period of Washington and Adams," *American Historical Review* 10 (1905): 249–279, at 272–273; John C. Miller, *The Federalist Era* (New York: Harper, 1960), 192; Richard H. Kohn, *Eagle and Sword: The Federalists and the Creation of the Military Establishment in America, 1783–1802* (New York: Free Press, 1975), 207.
29. J. J. Ulrich Rivardi to Timothy Pickering (29 Nov.1797), Pickering Papers, 21:368; accord Thomas Jefferson, Notes on a Conversation with Hugh Henry Brackenridge (27 Mar.1800), *PTJ,* 31:467, 468–469.
30. Thomas Jefferson to James Madison (26 Apr.1798), *PJM,* 17:120; Independent Yorker, "Communication," *Gazette of the United States,* 31 May 1798, 3; accord [William Cobbett], "The Traitor-Trap," *Porcupine's Gazette* (Philadelphia), 19 June 1798, 3; Roberts, *St. Méry's American Journey,* 253 (diary entry 18 July 1798).
31. Timothy Pickering to John Adams (28 Aug.1798), Pickering Papers, 37:325. It referred to a letter from Mr. Barnes, which was from the U.S. attorney for Rhode Island but involved French merchants, not Collot or other more questionable visitors. David Leonard Barnes to John Adams (11 Aug.1798), https://founders.archives.gov/documents/Adams/99-02-02-2806.
32. James McHenry to Timothy Pickering (10 Sept.1798), Pickering Papers, 23:137. McHenry added that he "had not obtained the first name of Sweizer," but "some say his name was Fatio."
33. Timothy Pickering to John Adams (4 Oct.1798), Pickering Papers, 9:426.
34. Timothy Pickering to John Adams (11 Oct.1798, first letter), *WJA,* 8:607n.

35. Timothy Pickering to John Adams (11 Oct.1798, second letter), Pickering Papers, 9:453, 454.
36. Order (c. July–Oct.1798), Pickering Papers, 54:1.
37. John Adams to Timothy Pickering (17 Oct.1798), *WJA,* 8:606–607 (misdating it 16 Oct.); Pickering Papers, 23:241.
38. Timothy Pickering to John Adams (1 Aug.1799), *WJA,* 9:5, 6; Pickering Papers, 11:524.
39. John Adams to Timothy Pickering (13 Aug.1799), *WJA,* 9:13, 14.
40. Elisha Boudinot to Timothy Pickering (7 Aug.1799), Pickering Papers, 25:84. The newspaper report was "Friday Evening, June 21," *Gazette of the United States,* 21 June 1799, 3.
41. Ibid., 25:84A.
42. Timothy Pickering to Elisha Boudinot (13 Aug.1799), Pickering Papers, 11:607; Affidavit of Joseph A. Mercier (8 Aug.1799), Pickering Papers, 25:85; Elisha Boudinot to Timothy Pickering (26 Aug.1799), ibid., 25:115.
43. Robert Liston to Lord Grenville (4 Nov. 1800), in George W. Kyte, "The Detention of General Collot: A Sidelight on Anglo-American Relations, 1798–1800," *William and Mary Quarterly* 6 (1949): 628–630, at 629–630.
44. Timothy Pickering to John Adams (1 Aug.1799), *WJA,* 9:5, 7.
45. Gerard H. Clarfield, *Timothy Pickering and the American Republic* (Pittsburgh: UPitP, 1980), 198; Smith, *Freedom's Fetters,* 166.
46. James McHenry to Timothy Pickering (10 Sept.1798), Pickering Papers, 23:137; Timothy Pickering to John Adams (1 Aug.1799), *WJA,* 9:5, 6.
47. Schweizer's primary biographies are David Hess, *Joh. Caspar Schweizer* (Berlin: William Hertz, 1884); Frédéric Barbey, *Au Service des Rois et de La Révolution* (Paris: Perrin, 1914), 213–323. Brief descriptions are in Claudia Selheim, "Die Erinnerungen des Johann Fortunat Bansi (1792–1875)," in *Jahresbericht des Historischen Vereins für die Grafschaft Ravensberg* 84 (1997): 117–152, at 122 n.19; Janet Todd, ed., *The Collected Letters of Mary Wollstonecraft* (New York: CUP, 2003), 219; Albert H. Bowman, *The Struggle for Neutrality: Franco-American Diplomacy During the Federalist Era* (Knoxville: UTennP, 1974), 192 n.38; see James Swan to William Short (12 Dec.1790), *PAH,* 7:361 (Schweizer Jeanneret & Co.). Schweizer sometimes used the French equivalent, "Jean Gaspard Schweizer."
48. Thomas Jefferson to George Washington (6 June 1793), *PTJ,* 26:179; Pierre Auguste Adet to Committee of Public Safety (4 Oct.1795), in Abraham P. Nasatir and Gary E. Monell, *French Consuls in the United States: A Calendar* (Washington: Library of Congress, 1967), 374; Howard C. Rice, "James Swan: Agent of the French Republic 1794–1796," *New England Quarterly* 10 (1937): 464–486, at 472, 474; see Bowman, *Struggle,* 192 and n.38.
49. Rice, "James Swan," 484, 483; Hess, *Schweizer,* 143, 158–159; Selheim, "Die Erinnerungen," 122 n.19; Rice, "James Swan," 484, 475; Oliver Wolcott, Jr. to Willink, Van Staphorst & Hubbard (23 June 1795), *PAH,* 18:459 n.9.
50. Rice, "James Swan," 464–477; H. W. Small, *A History of Swan's Island, Maine* (Ellsworth, ME: Hancock, 1898), 44–58; Allen Johnson et al., eds., *Dictionary*

of American Biography (New York: Scribner, 1928–1936), 18:234; Philipp Ziesche, "Cosmopolitan Patriots in the Age of Revolution: Americans in Paris, 1788–1800" (Ph.D. diss., Yale University, 2006), 122 (one of the twelve signers of Joel Barlow's 1790 address to France's National Assembly).

51. Rice, "James Swan," 478, 480; Articles of Agreement between Oliver Wolcott, Jun., Secretary of the Treasury, and James Swan (June 1795), *American State Papers. Documents, Legislative and Executive, of the Congress of the United States [Claims Series]* (Washington: Gales and Seaton, 1834), 1:270; Oliver Wolcott, Jr. to Alexander Hamilton (18 June 1795), *PAH,* 18:379, 380.
52. Hess, *Schweizer,* 143, 159, 259–260, 259.
53. E.g., Smith, *Freedom's Fetters,* 166; Rufus King to Timothy Pickering (14 July 1798), *LRK,* 2:367.
54. John Adams to Timothy Pickering ([17] Oct.1798), *WJA,* 8:606; Timothy Pickering to John Adams (11 Oct.1798), Pickering Papers, 9:453.
55. Rufus King to Timothy Pickering (14 Aug.1798), *LRK,* 2:387; accord Rufus King to Elbridge Gerry (14 Aug.1798), ibid., 2:386; "Notes," *The Nation,* 11 Apr.1895, 60:277, 279.
56. A. V. Arnault et al., eds., *Biographie Nouvelle des Contemporains, ou Dictionnaire Historique* (Paris: Librairie Historique, 1822), 6:313–314. Presle likely died c. 1827, because a government action toward his property occurred. Ministere des Finances, *États Détailles des Liquidations Faites par la Commission D'Indemnité* (Paris: L'Imprimerie Royale, 1828), 10, 12. Presle's full name is in Stephen M. Peterson, "The Politics of Discontent: The Bordelais Royalist Movement under the Directory" (Ph.D. diss., Northwestern University, 1993), 135.
57. Maurice Hutt, *Chouannerie and Counter-Revolution: Puisaye, the Princes, and the British Government in the 1790, Part 2* (New York: CUP, 1983), 2:486; Peterson, "Politics of Discontent," 135, 137; Darrell P. Morse, "Soldiers in Politics During the First French Republic, 1795–1799" (Ph.D. diss., University of California-Berkeley, 1962), 56, 246; M. A. Thiers, *The History of the French Revolution* (Philadelphia: Carey and Hart, 1842), 94, 146, 203; see Michael Durey, *William Wickham, Master Spy: The Secret War against the French Revolution* (London: Pickering and Chatto, 2009), 70; Hutt, *Chouannerie,* 2:489, 519; Peterson, "Politics of Discontent," 137.
58. Hutt, *Chouannerie,* 2:522, 526; Peterson, "Politics of Discontent," 138–139; Durey, *William Wickham,* 74; George Duruy, *Memoirs of Barras: Member of the Directorate* (New York: Harper, 1895), 2:375, 377, 406, 446; Arnault, *Biographie,* 6:314; Thiers, *History,* 4:94n., 99, 146, 160; Henri Carré, *La Noblesse de France et L'Opinion Publique au XVIIIe Siècle* (Paris: Champion, 1920), 543; G. Lefebvre, "Charles Girault, Rochecotte et la Chouannerie Mancelle," *Annales Historiques de la Révolution Française* 132 (1953): 273–275, at 274–275. Sparrow notes that Presle's declarations were given under duress. Elizabeth Sparrow, "The Swiss and Swabian Agencies, 1795–1801," *Historical Journal* 35 (1992): 861–884, at 867. For banishment to Guyana, see Miranda F. Spieler, "Empire and Underworld: Guiana in the French Legal Imagination c.1789–c.1870" (Ph.D. diss., Columbia University, 2005), 47 n.5; Morse, "Soldiers," 246; Thiers, *History,* 4:203.

59. Durey, "The British Secret Service and the Escape of Sir Sidney Smith from Paris in 1798," *History* (Historical Association) 84 (1999): 437–457, at 450; Thiers, *History*, 4:94n., 205; *Lives of Remarkable Characters Who Have Distinguished Themselves from the Commencement of the French Revolution . . .* (London: Longman, 1814), 2:38–39.
60. E.g., "Another Revolution in France," *Commercial Advertiser* (New York), 6 Nov.1797, 2; "Paris, September 12," *Claypoole's American Daily Advertiser* (Philadelphia), 9 Nov.1797, 3; "Address of the Two Councils," *Philadelphia Gazette*, 8 Nov.1797, 2.
61. "Declaration of Duverne Dupresle, or Dunant, Annexed to the Secret Register of the Directory" (11 Ventose, Year 5 [1 Mar.1797]), in *A Collection of State Papers, Relative to the War against France* (London: Debrett, 1798), 189–197, at 191, 192, 189–190, 193; accord *Declarations de Duverne Dupresle ou Dunant, Annexées au Registre Secret du Directoire Exécutif, le 11 Ventose An 5* (Melun, France: Tarbé et Lefevre, 1797); "Declaration of Duverne Dupresse," *Aurora*, 13 Nov.1797, 2. For the second declaration, see "Second Declaration of Duverne Dupresle, or Dunant, Annexed to the Secret Register of the Directory" (17 Ventose, Year 5 [7 Mar.1797]), in ibid., 197–198; accord "Declaration of Duverne Dupresse," *Philadelphia Gazette*, 11 Nov.1797, 2.
62. Rufus King to Timothy Pickering (14 Aug.1798), *LRK*, 2:387; Rufus King to Timothy Pickering (5 Sept.1798), ibid., 2:407, 408.
63. Timothy Pickering to John Adams (11 Oct.1798, second letter), Pickering Papers, 9:453.

15. At the Mercy of One Man

1. *A Brief Sketch of the Life of C. F. Volney*, 2nd ed. (London: James Watson, 1840), 7; *Biographie Universelle (Michaud) Ancienne et Moderne* (Paris: C. Desplaces, 1843–1865), 44:64; *PTJ*, 27:390–391n.; Gordon S. Wood, *Empire of Liberty: A History of the Early Republic, 1789–1815* (New York: OUP, 2009), 552. For English editions, see M. Volney, *The Ruins: or a Survey of the Revolutions of Empires* (New York: William A. Davis, 1796); M. C-F. Volney, *Travels Through Syria and Egypt*, 2nd ed. (London: Robinson, 1788).
2. Jacob Read to Timothy Pickering (17 Oct.1798), "Timothy Pickering Papers" (Massachusetts Historical Society, Boston, manuscripts and 69 reels), 23:243, 244 ("Pickering Papers").
3. Thomas Jefferson to James Madison (26 Apr.1798), William T. Hutchinson et al., eds., *Papers of James Madison* (Chicago: UChiP, 1962–1991), 17:120 ("*PJM*"); Kenneth Roberts and Anna M. Roberts, eds. and trans., *Moreau de St. Méry's American Journey [1793–1798]* (Garden City, NY: Doubleday, 1947), 253.
4. Rufus King to Timothy Pickering (6 Apr.1798), Charles R. King., ed., *Life and Correspondence of Rufus King* (New York: Putnam's Sons, 1894–1900), 2:304, 305 ("*LRK*"); Rufus King to Timothy Pickering (1 Aug.1798), ibid., 2:379, 380; Independent Yorker, "Communication," *Gazette of the United States* (Philadelphia), 31 May 1798, 3.

5. Thomas Jefferson to James Monroe (21 May 1798), *PTJ*, 30:360; Timothy Pickering to George Washington (3 Oct.1798), Dorothy Twohig et al., eds., *Papers of George Washington: Retirement Series* (Charlottesville: UPV, 1998–1999), 3:74, 75.
6. Comte de Volney to Thomas Jefferson (24 June 1801), *PTJ*, 34:437, 440; François Furstenberg, *When the United States Spoke French: Five Refugees Who Shaped a Nation* (New York: Penguin, 2014), 291; Frances S. Childs, *French Refugee Life in the United States, 1790–1800* (Baltimore: JHUP, 1940), 189.
7. Samuel E. Morison, "Du Pont, Talleyrand, and the French Spoliations," *Proceedings of the Massachusetts Historical Society* (3rd Series) 49 (1915–1916): 63–79, at 64; Childs, *French Refugee Life*, 45–46; Allen Johnson et al., eds., *Dictionary of American Biography* (New York: Scribner, 1928–1936), 5:533; Harold C. Syrett et al., eds., *Papers of Alexander Hamilton* (New York: ColUP, 1961–), 24:229 n.1, 23:236 n.8 ("*PAH*"); J. Balteau et al., *Dictionnaire de Biographie Francaise* (Paris: Letouzey, 1933–), 12:475. The son usually used "du Pont," and the father usually used "DuPont." *PTJ*, 30:503n. The latter is used here.
8. Thomas Jefferson to James Madison (31 May 1798), *PJM*, 17:138, 140; Alexander DeConde, *The Quasi-War* (New York: Scribner, 1966), 87.
9. Timothy Pickering to John Adams (1 Aug.1798), Charles Francis Adams, ed., *Works of John Adams* (Boston: LB, 1850–1856), 9:5, 6 ("*WJA*"); Timothy Pickering to John Adams (11 Oct.1798, second letter), Pickering Papers, 9:453; DeConde, *Quasi-War*, 87; *WJA*, 9:5–6; Thomas Jefferson to James Madison (7 June 1798), *PJM*, 17:143; Thomas Jefferson to Thomas Mann Randolph (7 June 1798), *PTJ*, 30:395.
10. Morison, "Du Pont," 65, 75 n.1; DeConde, *Quasi-War*, 148–150; Victor DuPont to Talleyrand (21 July 1798), Morison, "Du Pont," 66–76; Stanley Elkins and Eric McKitrick, *The Age of Federalism* (New York: OUP, 1993), 666–668.
11. Ambrose Saricks, *Pierre Samuel du Pont de Nemours* (Lawrence: UKanP, 1965); John A. Garraty et al., eds., *American National Biography* (New York: OUP, 1999), 7:115 (for Eleuthère I. du Pont) ("*ANB*"); *PAH*, 24:228–229 n.1, 23:236 n.8; Balteau, *Dictionnaire*, 12:472.
12. Rufus King to Timothy Pickering (14 July 1798), *LRK*, 2:367; Timothy Pickering to John Adams (11 Sept.1798), *WJA*, 8:596 n.1.
13. John Adams to Timothy Pickering (16 Sept.1798), *WJA*, 8:596; Thomas Jefferson to Thomas Mann Randolph (3 May 1798), *PTJ*, 30:325, 326.
14. "The Editor of the Aurora" (22 Jan.1800), Pickering Papers, 26:51.
15. Charles Cotesworth Pinckney to Alexander Hamilton (8 Feb.1800), *PAH*, 24:228; Alexander Hamilton to Timothy Pickering (15 Mar.1800), *PAH*, 24:327, 328.
16. Harry Ammon, *The Genet Mission* (New York: Norton, 1973); Frederick J. Turner, "The Origin of Genet's Projected Attack on Louisiana and the Floridas," *American Historical Review* 3 (1898): 650–671; Conlin, "American Mission of . . . Adet," 489–520; Elkins, *Age of Federalism*, 420, 509, 520–521, 647; Paul D. Newman, "The Federalists' Cold War: The Fries Rebellion, National Security, and the State, 1787–1800," *Pennsylvania History* 67 (2000):

63–104, at 72–74; Gerard H. Clarfield, *Timothy Pickering and the American Republic* (Pittsburgh: UPitP, 1980), 198.

17. Proclamation Revoking the Exequaturs of the French Consuls (13 July 1798), *WJA*, 9:170; John Adams to Timothy Pickering (7 July 1798), ibid., 8:576; *PAH*, 23:236 n.8; Abigail Adams to Mary S. Cranch (17 July 1798), L. H. Butterfield et al., eds., *Adams Family Correspondence* (Cambridge, MA: BKHUP, 1963–), 13:192, 193 ("*AFC*").
18. Timothy Pickering to John Adams (11 Oct.1798, second letter), Pickering Papers, 9:453; Uriah Tracy to James McHenry (6 May 1799), Bernard C. Steiner, *The Life and Correspondence of James McHenry* (Cleveland, OH: Burrows, 1907), 436.
19. Timothy Pickering to John Adams (1 Aug.1799), *WJA*, 9:5, 6–7.
20. John Adams to Timothy Pickering (13 Aug.1799), *WJA*, 9:13, 14.
21. Stewart L. Mims, "Introduction," to Roberts, *St. Méry's American Journey*, ix–xxi; Furstenberg, *When the United States Spoke French;* Conlin, "American Mission," 504; Johnson, *Dictionary of American Biography*, 13:156.
22. Diary (18 July 1798), Roberts, *St. Méry's American Journey*, 253.
23. Paul M. Spurlin, "The World of the Founding Fathers and France," *The French Review* 49 (1976): 909–925, at 923; Rozier to Moreau de St. Méry (27 June 1798), Roberts, *St. Méry's American Journey*, 252.
24. Diary (14 July 1798 and 3 Aug.1798), Roberts, *St. Méry's American Journey*, 253, 254; Childs, *French Refugee Life*, 189; Diary (21 Aug.1798), Roberts, *St. Méry's American Journey*, 256.
25. Proclamation Revoking the Exequaturs of the French Consuls (13 July 1798), *WJA*, 9:170, 171; Abraham P. Nasatir and Gary E. Monell, *French Consuls in the United States: A Calendar* (Washington: Library of Congress, 1967), 550, 388; Maeva Marcus, ed., *Documentary History of the Supreme Court of the United States, 1789–1800* (New York: ColUP, 1985–2007) (vol. 1 was coedited by James R. Perry), 7:545 n.3, 7:31 n.5, 7:758 n.2 ("*DHSC*"); Citation and Return of Service, MacDonnogh v. Ship Mary Ford (U.S. Dist. Mass. 22–31 Dec.1795), ibid., 7:30, 31; Arcambal v. Wiseman (U.S. Sup. Ct. 1795), ibid., 7:550–560.
26. Timothy Pickering to John Adams (11 Oct.1798, second letter), Pickering Papers, 9:453.
27. Rufus King to Alexander Hamilton (2 July 1798), *PAH*, 21:524; Alexander Hamilton to Timothy Pickering (4 Apr.1799), *PAH*, 23:12; ibid., 23:13n.
28. Timothy Pickering to Jean Antoine Bernard Rozier (12 Apr.1799), *PAH*, 23:200 n.1; Timothy Pickering to Alexander Hamilton (18 June 1799), ibid., 23:199.
29. Timothy Pickering to Dwight Foster (6 Oct.1798), Pickering Papers, 9:436; see *PAH*, 23:12–13 n.1; Timothy Pickering to John Adams (4 Oct.1798), Pickering Papers, 9:426; John Adams to Timothy Pickering (10 Oct.1798), https://founders.archives.gov/documents/Adams/99-02-02-3098.
30. Dwight Foster to Timothy Pickering (12 Oct.1798), Pickering Papers, 23:213–215; intercepted letters are ibid., 42:105, 115, 117, 119, 122.
31. *Minutes et Répertoires du Notaire Denis Trutat, 21 Novembre 1772–14 Juin 1810* (Paris: Archives Nationales [France], 2013), 271.

32. Pierre Bardin et al., "Un Chapelain pour Une Habitation de Saint-Domingue," pp.1–2, at https://www.ghcaraibe.org/articles/2013-art08.pdf; ibid., p.8.
33. J. J. Ulrich Rivardi to Timothy Pickering (1 Nov.1798), Pickering Papers, 23:277, 277A–278.
34. John Schuyler, *Institution of the Society of the Cincinnati* (New York: Society of the Cincinnati, 1886), 366; *Report of the Committee of Claims, To Whom Was Referred, on the 25th Ultimo, the Petition of John Baptiste Verdier* ([Philadelphia: William Ross, 1800]).
35. *Report,* 3; "Enclosure: Payments for the Support of the Civil List" (26 Dec.1794), *PAH,* 17:498, 538.
36. Petition of John Baptiste Verdier (Apr.1798), in *Report,* 4; Ian F. W. Beckett, *Modern Insurgencies and Counter-Insurgencies* (New York: Routledge, 2001), 27; Milton C. Finley, Jr., "The Career of Count Jean Reynier, 1792–1814" (Ph.D. diss., Florida State University, 1972), 142–143, 96–99.
37. Timothy Pickering to William Nichols (4 Sept.1798), Pickering Papers, 9:279.
38. He was Edouard-Charles Victurnien, who participated in the American Revolution in Grasse's fleet. *PAH,* 25:51 n.2. Chevalier de Colbert to Timothy Pickering (7 Mar.1799), Pickering Papers, 24:138, 138–139.
39. Elbridge Gerry to John Adams (24 Mar.1798), https://founders.archives.gov/documents/Adams/99-02-02-2389; Talleyrand to Moreau de St. Méry (28 Mar.1798), Roberts, *St. Méry's American Journey,* 251, 367.
40. Timothy Pickering to Joshua Sands (20 July 1799), Pickering Papers, 11:471.
41. An American [probably William Cobbett], "Communication," *Porcupine's Gazette* (Philadelphia), 3 Nov.1798, 2.
42. David A. Wilson, *United Irishmen, United States: Immigrant Radicals in the Early Republic* (Ithaca, NY: CorUP, 1998), 18–35, 2; Michael Durey, *Transatlantic Radicals and the Early American Republic* (Lawrence: UPKan, 1997), 80–133; Carter, "A 'Wild Irishman,'" 333 (30,000 into Philadelphia); see David Brundage, *Irish Nationalists in America: The Politics of Exile, 1798–1998* (New York: OUP, 2016).
43. Douglas Bradburn, *The Citizenship Revolution: Politics and the Creation of the American Union, 1774–1804* (Charlottesville: UVP, 2009), 225–227; Margaret H. McAleer, "In Defense of Civil Society: Irish Radicals in Philadelphia During the 1790s," *Early American Studies* 1 (2003): 176–197; Peter Porcupine [William Cobbett], *Detection . . .* (Philadelphia: Cobbett, 1798), 4, 26–27; see Marcus Daniel, *Scandal and Civility: Journalism and the Birth of American Democracy* (New York: OUP, 2009), 264–265.
44. Bradburn, *Citizenship Revolution*, 224; Joyce Appleby, *Capitalism and a New Social Order: The Republican Vision of the 1790s* (New York: NYUP, 1984), 61; Aki Kalliomäki, "'The Most God-Provoking Democrats on This Side of Hell'—The United Irishmen in the United States" (Ph.D. diss., University of California-Santa Cruz, 2005), 14–38; see R. R. Palmer, *The Age of the Democratic Revolution* (Princeton: PUP, 1959–1964), 2:491–505.
45. Rufus King to Timothy Pickering (14 June 1798), *LRK,* 2:347, 348; Rufus King to Timothy Pickering (19 July 1798), ibid., 2:370, 371; accord Rufus King to Henry Jackson (28 Aug.1799), ibid., 2:645, 646; Timothy Pickering to Rufus King (5 Feb.1799), *LRK,* 2:644; William Bingham to Rufus King (8 Dec.1798),

ibid., 2:481, 481–482; accord William Bingham to Rufus King (30 Sept.1798), ibid., 2:425, 426.

46. Timothy Pickering to William Cobbett (3 Feb.1798), Pickering Papers, 8:105; Richard Peters to Timothy Pickering (24 Aug.1798), Pickering Papers, 23:71; Timothy Pickering to William Rawle (28 Aug.1798), ibid., 37:326.
47. John Jay to Timothy Pickering (21 Dec.1798), Pickering Papers, 23:372; "United Irishmen," *Porcupine's Gazette,* 27 Nov.1798, 3; Francis Dana to John Adams (3 Nov.1798), https://founders.archives.gov/documents/Adams/99-02-02-3195.
48. Alien Friends Act §3, Statutes, 1:570, 571–572.
49. Naturalization Act §§1–4, Statutes, 1:566, 567.
50. E.g., Jacob Wagner to Clement C. Brown (13 Sept.1798), Pickering Papers, 9:322; Timothy Pickering to Morgan Brown (13 Sept.1798), ibid., 10:151; e.g., Jacob Wagner to Richard M. Stiles (25 Oct.1798), Pickering Papers, 9:516; Jacob Wagner to Richard M. Stiles (31 Oct.1798), ibid., 9:546.
51. Timothy Pickering to John Adams (5 Oct.1798), https://founders.archives.gov/documents/Adams/99-02-02-3081; e.g., P. Pinchinat to Gen. Rigaud (31 Aug.1798), Pickering Papers, 42:80; Portsmouth Lodge to Philadelphia Lodge (1798), ibid., 42:38; W. Urquhart to Timothy Pickering (10 Aug.1798), ibid., 23:30 (enclosing French letter from Esmenard).
52. John Adams to Christopher Gadsden (16 Apr.1801), *WJA,* 9:584; Alexander Hamilton to Jonathan Dayton (Oct.–Nov.1799), *PAH,* 23:599, 604.
53. David Ford to Alexander Hamilton (11 Apr.1798), *PAH,* 21:410; Henry W. De Saussure to Timothy Pickering (6 Sept.1799), Pickering Papers, 25:138, 138A–139.
54. Michael Durey, "Thomas Paine's Apostles: Radical Emigrés and the Triumph of Jeffersonian Republicanism," *William and Mary Quarterly* 44 (1987): 661–688, at 687–688; accord Richard J. Twomey, *Jacobins and Jeffersonians: Anglo-American Radicalism in the United States 1790–1820* (New York: Garland, 1989), 1, 23–34, 52–63, 73–74, reprinting Richard J. Twomey, "Jacobins and Jeffersonians: Anglo-American Radicalism in the United States 1790–1820" (Ph.D. diss., Northern Illinois University, 1974).
55. Timothy Pickering to Richard Harison (7 July 1798), Pickering Papers, 37:315–315A.
56. Timothy Pickering to Richard Harison (1 Jan.1799), Pickering Papers, 37:381; Timothy Pickering to Winthrop Sargent (22 May 1799), Pickering Papers, 37:424; John D. Burk to Thomas Jefferson (ante-9 June 1801), *PTJ,* 34:385; Joseph I. Shulim, "John Daly Burk: Irish Revolutionist and American Patriot," *Transactions of the American Philosophical Society* 54 (1964): 1–60, at 36.
57. Timothy Pickering to John Adams (24 July 1799), *WJA,* 9:3, 4; see Nigel Little, *Transoceanic Radical, William Duane: National Identity and Empire 1760–1835* (London: Pickering and Chatto, 2008), 180–181.
58. John Adams to Timothy Pickering (1 Aug.1799), *WJA,* 9:5; see Jeffrey L. Pasley, *The Tyranny of Printers: Newspaper Politics in the Early American Republic* (Charlottesville: UPV, 2001), 184; Little, *Transoceanic Radical,* 130.
59. Hollingsworth v. Duane, 4 U.S. (4 Dall.) 353 (C.C.D. Pa. 1801); Kim T. Phillips, *William Duane, Radical Journalist in the Age of Jefferson* (New York: Garland, 1989), 124–126; Pasley, *Tyranny of Printers,* 288.

60. Timothy Pickering to John Adams (1 Aug.1799), *WJA*, 9:5, 6; John Adams to Benjamin Stoddert (31 Mar.1801), *WJA*, 9:582; Abigail Adams to Thomas B. Adams (17 Aug.1799), *AFC*, 13:540, 541.
61. Thomas Jefferson to James Madison (7 June 1798), *PJM*, 17:143; accord Michael Durey, *"With the Hammer of Truth": James Thomson Callender and America's Early National Heroes* (Charlottesville: UVP, 1990), 109.
62. "New York, August 2," *Albany Centinel*, 7 Aug.1798, 3.
63. Durey, "Thomas Paine's Apostles," 666; accord Joyce Appleby, *Capitalism and a New Social Order: The Republican Vision of the 1790s* (New York: NYUP, 1984), 60–61 and n.12; David A. Wilson, *United Irishmen, United States: Immigrant Radicals in the Early Republic* (Ithaca, NY: CorUP, 1998), 2, 36–57; David Brundage, *Irish Nationalists in America: The Politics of Exile, 1798–1998* (New York: OUP, 2016).
64. Clive Emsley, "Repression, 'Terror' and the Rule of Law in England During the Decade of the French Revolution," *English Historical Review* 100 (1985): 801–825; Clive Emsley, "An Aspect of 'Pitt's Terror': Prosecutions for Sedition During the 1790s," *Social History* 6 (1981): 155; Michael Lobban, "From Seditious Libel to Unlawful Assembly: Peterloo and the Changing Face of Political Crime c1770–1820," *Oxford Journal of Legal Studies* 10 (1990): 307–352; Boyd Hilton, *A Mad, Bad, and Dangerous People? England 1783–1846* (Oxford: CP, 2006), 72–73.
65. Twomey, *Jacobins and Jeffersonians*, 21, 12–13, 23–33, 52–74; Michael Durey, *Transatlantic Radicals*, 12–79; Seth Cotlar, *Tom Paine's America: The Rise and Fall of Transatlantic Radicalism in the Early Republic* (Charlottesville: UVP, 2011); Twomey, *Jacobins and Jeffersonians*, 42–47; see Bradburn, *Citizenship Revolution*, 211.
66. P. [William Cobbett-Porcupine], "Priestley Completely Detected," *Porcupine's Gazette*, 20 Aug.1798, 2, 3; Joseph Priestley to George Thatcher (26 July 1798), "Letters of Joseph Priestley," *Proceedings of the Massachusetts Historical Society* 3 (1886–1887): 11–40, at 23, 24; see generally Jenny Graham, "Revolutionary in Exile: The Emigration of Joseph Priestley to America 1794–1804," *Transactions of the American Philosophical Society (New Series)* 85 (1995): 1–213, at 109–115.
67. Timothy Pickering to John Adams (1 Aug.1799), *WJA*, 9:5, 6; Timothy Pickering to Charles Hall (1 Aug.1799), Pickering Papers, 11:528, 529; Timothy Pickering to John Adams (1 Aug.1799), *WJA*, 9:6.
68. John Adams to Timothy Pickering (13 Aug.1799), *WJA*, 9:13, 14; Abigail Adams to Thomas B. Adams (17 Aug.1799), *AFC*, 13:540, 541.
69. The best biographies of Cobbett's American years are David A. Wilson, ed., *William Cobbett: Peter Porcupine in America* (Ithaca, NY: CorUP, 1994), 50–257; and the chapter in Daniel, *Scandal and Civility*, 187–230. Other sources include George Spater, *William Cobbett, the Poor Man's Friend* (New York: CUP, 1982); Daniel Green, *Great Cobbett: The Noblest Agitator* (Oxford: OUP, 1985); William Reitzel, ed., *The Progress of a Plough-Boy . . . William Cobbett* (London: Faber and Faber, 1933) (autobiography); H. C. G. Matthew et al., eds., *Oxford Dictionary of National Biography* (Oxford: OUP, 2004), 12:273 ("*ODNB*").

70. John Adams to Abigail Adams (22 Feb.1799), *AFC*, 13:415; *WJA*, 1:545; Abigail Adams to John Adams (3 Mar.1799), https://founders.archives.gov/documents/Adams/99-03-02-0364 (not in *AFC*).
71. "Wednesday, February 27," *Mercantile Advertiser* (New York), 27 Feb.1799, 1 (supplement); quotation and citation in *AFC*, 13:416 n.4, from William Cobbett, *Porcupine's Works* (London: n.p., 1801), 10:153.
72. "Epitaph on Skunk Porcupine," *Greenleaf's New York Journal*, 9 Feb.1799, 3.
73. Daniel, *Scandal and Civility*, 227–230; Wood, *Empire of Liberty*, 725–726.
74. The best biographies are Ray Walters, *Albert Gallatin: Jeffersonian Financier and Diplomat* (New York: Macmillan, 1957); Henry Adams, *The Life of Albert Gallatin* (Philadelphia: Lippincott, 1879); see *ANB*, 8:639.
75. Thomas Jefferson to James Madison (26 Apr.1798), *PJM*, 17:120; *Debates and Proceedings in the Congress of the United States . . . Annals of the Congress of the United States* (Washington: Gales and Seaton, 1834–1856), 7:548 (25 Apr.1798), 7:549 (26 Apr1798) ("*Annals*").
76. *Annals*, 8:1482, 1483 (20 Apr.1798). Gallatin's primary speech was the preceding day. Ibid., 8:1466–1472 (19 Apr.1798); *Annals*, 8:1473 (19 Apr.1798), 8:1476, 1482 (20 Apr.1798).
77. The best biography focused on American years is Eric Foner, *Tom Paine and Revolutionary America* (New York: OUP, 2005); see also *ANB*, 16:925. The English seditious libel prosecution is described in Proceedings against Thomas Paine, State Trials, 22:357 (Dec.1792); the prosecution of a publisher is Proceedings in the Case of Daniel Isaac Eaton, ibid., 22:753 (1793).
78. Durey, "Thomas Paine's Apostles," 661–688; Thomas Paine, *The Age of Reason. Part the Second* (Philadelphia: Booksellers [Bache], 1796); Thomas Paine, *Letter to George Washington* (Philadelphia: Bache, 1796); Thomas Paine to Thomas Jefferson (1 Apr.1797), *PTJ*, 29:340; Thomas Jefferson to James Madison (8 June 1797), *PJM*, 17:20, 21.
79. John Adams to Elbridge Gerry (3 May 1797), https://founders.archives.gov/documents/Adams/99-02-02-1957; Abigail Adams to John Quincy Adams (17 Mar.1798), *AFC*, 12:448, 449.
80. John Adams to John Marshall (11 Aug.1800), *WJA*, 9:73.
81. Uriah Tracy to James McHenry (6 May 1799), Steiner, *McHenry*, 436; Alexander Hamilton to Jonathan Dayton (Oct.–Nov.1799), *PAH*, 23:599, 604; Timothy Pickering to John Adams (28 Aug.1798), Pickering Papers, 37:325; John Adams to Timothy Pickering (13 Aug.1799), *WJA*, 9:13, 14.
82. Joseph Priestley to George Thatcher (1 May 1798), "Letters of Joseph Priestley," *Proceedings of the Massachusetts Historical Society* 3 (1886–1887): 11–40, at 20, 21.
83. Joseph Priestley to George Thatcher (26 July 1798), "Letters of Joseph Priestley," 23, 24; Joseph Priestley, *Letters to the Inhabitants of Northumberland* (Northumberland, PA: Andrew Kennedy, 1799), 1–4.
84. Marquis de Clugny to Timothy Pickering (21 July 1798), Pickering Papers, 22:311; William Vans Murray to Timothy Pickering (8 July 1798), ibid., 22:276.
85. Thomas Jefferson to James Madison (7 June 1798), *PJM*, 17:143.

Epilogue

1. James Madison to Philip Norborne Nicholas (23 May 1800), William T. Hutchinson et al., eds., *Papers of James Madison* (Chicago: UChiP, 1962–1991), 17:389, 390.
2. Stanley Elkins and Eric McKitrick, *The Age of Federalism* (New York: OUP, 1993), 722; accord Jeffrey L. Pasley, *The Tyranny of Printers: Newspaper Politics in the Early American Republic* (Charlottesville; UPV, 2001), 369.
3. John Adams to Benjamin Stoddert (31 Mar.1801), Charles Francis Adams, ed., *Works of John Adams* (Boston: LB, 1850–1856), 9:582 ("*WJA*"); John Quincy Adams to Rufus King (8 Oct.1802), Worthington C. Ford, ed., *Writings of John Quincy Adams* (New York: Macmillan, 1913–1917), 3:7, 9.
4. Uriah Tracy to Oliver Wolcott (7 Aug.1800), George Gibbs, ed., *Memoirs of the Administrations of Washington and John Adams Edited from the Papers of Oliver Wolcott* (New York: Norden, 1846), 2:399. The growth was striking. Pasley, *Tyranny of Printers,* 117–118; David Hackett Fischer, *The Revolution of American Conservatism: The Federalist Party in the Era of Jeffersonian Democracy* (New York: Harper, 1965), 131.
5. John Adams to Christopher Gadsden (16 Apr.1801), *WJA,* 9:584.
6. John Adams to Abigail Adams (22 Feb.1799), L. H. Butterfield et al., eds., *Adams Family Correspondence* (Cambridge, MA: BPHUP, 1963–), 13:415 ("*AFC*"); Henry Tazewell to Andrew Jackson (20 July 1798), Sam B. Smith and Harriet C. Owsley, eds., *The Papers of Andrew Jackson* (Knoxville: UTP, 1980–), 1:205, 207.
7. Excepting Wendell Bird, *Press and Speech under Assault: The Early Supreme Court Justices, the Sedition Act of 1798, and the Campaign against Dissent* (New York: OUP, 2016), 330–393; Wendell Bird, "New Light on the Sedition Act of 1798: The Missing Half of the Prosecutions," *Law and History Review* 34 (2016): 541–614.
8. These are listed, and the numbers of individuals and cases are reconciled in the Appendix on p. 385.
9. Charles Lee to John Adams (1 Nov.1798), http://founders.archives.gov/documents/Adams/99-02-02-3190; e.g., Frances S. Childs, *French Refugee Life in the United States, 1790–1800* (Baltimore: JHUP, 1940), 189, 191.
10. John Nerone, *Violence against the Press* (New York: OUP, 1994), 63–66; Jeffrey S. Selinger, *Embracing Dissent: Political Violence and Party Development in the United States* (Philadelphia: UPP, 2016), 57–67.
11. Pasley, *Tyranny of Printers,* 131, 106, 153–175; Fisher Ames to Theodore Dwight (19 Mar.1801), Seth Ames, ed., *Works of Fisher Ames* (Boston: LB, 1854), 1:292, 294.
12. John Adams to F. A. Vanderkemp (28 Dec.1800), *WJA,* 9:576, 577.
13. Donald H. Stewart, *The Opposition Press of the Federalist Period* (Albany: SUNYP, 1969), 486; Thomas Jefferson to Levi Lincoln (24 Mar.1802), Julian P. Boyd et al., eds., *Papers of Thomas Jefferson* (Princeton: PUP, 1950–), 37:119 ("*PTJ*"); Thomas Jefferson to Thomas McKean (19 Feb.1803), ibid., 39:552, 553.
14. Bird, *Press and Speech under Assault,* 467–469; Phillip I. Blumberg, *Repressive Jurisprudence in the Early American Republic* (New York: CUP, 2010),

148–186; Pasley, *Tyranny of Printers,* 281–282; United States v. Hudson and Goodwin, 11 U.S. (7 Cranch) 32 (1812). For an example of Jefferson's fanciful self-defense, see Thomas Jefferson to Wilson Cary Nicholas (13 June 1809), J. Jefferson Looney, ed., *The Papers of Thomas Jefferson: Retirement Series* (Princeton: PUP, 2004–), 1:276 ("*PTJ-R*").

15. Abigail Adams to Thomas Jefferson (20 May 1804), Lester J. Cappon, ed., *The Adams-Jefferson Letters* (Chapel Hill: UNCP, 1959), 1:268; Thomas Jefferson to Abigail Adams (13 June 1804), ibid., 1:269, 270.
16. Abigail Adams to Thomas Jefferson (1 July 1804), ibid., 1:271, 273; Thomas Jefferson to Abigail Adams (22 July 1804), ibid., 1:274, 274–275.
17. Thomas Jefferson to Abigail Adams (22 July 1804), ibid., 1:274, 275; Abigail Adams to Thomas Jefferson (15 Aug.1804), ibid., 1:276, 276–277.
18. Thomas Jefferson to Abigail Adams (11 Sept.1804), ibid., 1:278, 279; Abigail Adams to Thomas Jefferson (25 Oct.1804), ibid., 1:280, 281–282.
19. John Adams to Thomas Jefferson (29 May 1813), *PTJ-R,* 6:145; John Adams to Thomas Jefferson (10 June 1813), ibid., 6:180; John Adams to Thomas Jefferson (14 June 1813), ibid., 6:191; Thomas Jefferson to Joseph Priestley (21 Mar.1801), *PTJ,* 33:393, 393–394.
20. John Adams to Thomas Jefferson (14 June 1813), *PTJ-R,* 6:191; Thomas Jefferson to John Adams (15 June 1813), ibid., 6:193, 193–194.
21. John Adams to Thomas Jefferson (30 June 1813), *PTJ-R,* 6:253, 254–255; accord John Adams to Thomas Jefferson (15 July 1813), ibid., 6:296, 297.
22. John Adams to James Lloyd (6 Feb.1815), https://founders.archives.gov/documents/Adams/99-02-02-6405; John Adams to William Cunningham (27 Sept.1808), in E. M. Cunningham, ed., *Correspondence between the Hon. John Adams . . . and the Late Wm. Cunningham, Esq.* (Boston: True and Greene, 1823), 25, 28.
23. Gerard H. Clarfield, *Timothy Pickering and the American Republic* (Pittsburgh: UPitP, 1980), 219–228, 251, 255–260.
24. Timothy Pickering, Notebook, "Timothy Pickering Papers" (Massachusetts Historical Society, Boston, manuscripts and 69 reels), 54:248, 250 (post-1810) ("Pickering Papers").
25. Richard J. Purcell, *Connecticut in Transition 1775–1818* (Washington: AHA, 1918), 332, 334; Samuel Sitgreaves to Timothy Pickering (18 Apr.1810), Pickering Papers, 44:151.
26. Leonard Levy, *Emergence of a Free Press* (New York: OUP, 1985), 281; Leonard W. Levy, "Liberty and the First Amendment, 1790–1800," *American Historical Review* 68 (1962): 22–37, at 27. Other examples are given in the Introduction.
27. The same is true for British editors and other American editors. Wendell Bird, "Liberties of Press and Speech: 'Evidence Does Not Exist To Contradict the . . . Blackstonian Sense' in Late 18th Century England?," *Oxford Journal of Legal Studies* 36 (2016): 1–25; Wendell Bird, *The Revolution in Freedoms of Press and Speech* (New York: OUP, forthcoming 2020), Chapters 3–13.
28. Levy, *Emergence of a Free Press,* xii; accord 294, 89, 136, 272, 297.
29. Lucius, "To the Citizens," *Vermont Gazette,* 11 July 1785, 4, reprinting Lucius, "To the Citizens [Part I], *Massachusetts Centinel* (Boston), 18 May 1785,

1, 2; Cincinnatus [Arthur Lee], "From the New York Journal," *Vermont Gazette,* 26 Nov.1787, 1, reprinting Cincinnatus, "Number I," *New-York Journal,* 1 Nov.1787, 2.

30. [William Duane], "Liberty of the Press," *Telegraph,* 11 Nov.1795, 1; A Confederationist, "From the Pennsylvania Herald," *Independent Chronicle,* 15 Nov.1787, 2; accord "London Association. Liberty of the Press," *Independent Chronicle,* 9–13 Aug.1798, 1.
31. Thomas Jefferson to John Taylor (26 Nov.1798), *PTJ,* 30:588; Thomas Jefferson to Nicholas Lewis (30 Jan.1799), ibid., 30:663, 664; accord Pasley, *Tyranny of Printers,* 124–131.
32. Pasley, *Tyranny of Printers,* 126, 131, 407–409.
33. Andrew W. Robertson, "Jeffersonian Parties, Politics, and Participation," in Daniel Peart, ed., *Practicing Democracy: Popular Politics in the United States from the Constitution to the Civil War* (Charlottesville: UPV, 2015), 99–122, at 105; Jeffrey L. Pasley, "The Devolution of 1800," in Gareth Davies and Julien E. Zelizer, eds., *America at the Ballot Box: Elections and Political History* (Philadelphia: UPP, 2015), 13–35, at 32.
34. Joanne B. Freeman, "Explaining the Unexplainable: The Cultural Context of the Sedition Act," in Meg Jacobs et al., eds., *The Democratic Experiment: New Directions in American Political History* (Princeton: PUP, 2003), 20–49.
35. Ibid., 31, 24.
36. Ibid., 20–31; accord Terri Diane Halperin, *The Alien and Sedition Acts of 1798* (Baltimore: JHUP, 2016), 70–71; Robert W. T. Martin, "Reforming Republicanism: Alexander Hamilton's Theory of Republican Citizenship and Press Liberty," *Journal of the Early Republic* 25 (2005): 21–46. In effect, the Alien and Sedition Acts, as Terri Diane Halperin recently argued, defined the role of the citizens in politics, restrictively. Their role was to vote in elections, to restrict activity between elections to petitions, and to support officials and the administration once elected, without criticism or opposition. Halperin, *Alien and Sedition Acts,* 50.
37. Thomas Jefferson to William G. Munford (18 June 1799), *PTJ,* 31:126, 128.
38. Report (Jan.1800), *PJM,* 17:307, 344; see ibid., 17:343.
39. Ibid., 17:344.

Acknowledgments

A project like this book requires more assistance than can possibly be listed. Those included here are due particular thanks, though any errors are solely mine and expressed opinions are not necessarily theirs.

This book would not exist without the counsel of Kathleen McDermott of Harvard University Press, my editor; the encouragement of Professor Michael R. T. Macnair of University of Oxford; and the patience of Julie, my spouse. To them words cannot express my thanks.

Emory University School of Law has been most generous to enable me to carry on research as a visiting scholar, and Professor John Witte Jr. and other scholar there have provided invaluable advice. Emory University's Woodruff Library and Law Library have been invaluable resources, as have University of Oxford's Vere Harmsworth Library and other parts of the Bodleian Libraries.

Researching the original court records, prosecutor records, and relevant manuscripts of the Alien and Sedition Act prosecutions and surrounding events requires particular thanks to the helpful staffs of many manuscript collections:

The National Archives at Boston (Waltham), New York City, Philadelphia, Washington, D.C., and Atlanta (Morrow); and a number of state archives including Connecticut State Archives, Georgia Department of Archives and History, Maryland State Archives, North Carolina State Archives' Manuscript Department, South Carolina Department of Archives and History, and Tennessee State Library and Archives.

The Library of Congress Manuscript Division; New York Public Library's Manuscripts and Archives Division; and a number of university manuscript collections including Duke University's Perkins Library Special Collections, Emory University's Rose Manuscript, Archives and Rare Book Library, Harvard Law School

Library, Library of Virginia, Rutgers University's Special Collections, University of North Carolina's Southern Historical Collection Manuscripts Department, University of Vermont, Yale University Library's Manuscripts and Archives, and other collections.

The manuscript collections of historical societies including Connecticut Historical Society, Historical Society of Pennsylvania, Maryland Historical Society, Massachusetts Historical Society, New-York Historical Society Museum and Library, Ohio Historical Society (Ohio History Connection), and Virginia Historical Society.

I thank a number of sources for the opportunity to quote from original eighteenth-century records or transcriptions: the archives listed above; Columbia University Press for the documents of the early Supreme Court; the publishers listed in Abbreviations for the papers of John Adams, Alexander Hamilton, Thomas Jefferson, James Madison, George Washington, and others; the National Archives for the *Founders Online* collection of papers of those founders and of Abigail Adams; the Library of Congress for the *Annals* and the *Statutes at Large*; Newsbank and Readex for the America's Historical Newspapers collection of eighteenth-century newspapers; Readex for the Early American Imprints collection of eighteenth-century books and pamphlets; and the Massachusetts Historical Society for the Timothy Pickering Papers.

Thanks are also due to Andrew Pierce for genealogical research on Alien and Sedition Act victims.

Index

www.ingramcontent.com/pod-product-compliance
Lightning Source LLC
LaVergne TN
LVHW091517200926
848483LV00005B/440/J